ALSO BY CHARLES A. FECHER

Mencken: A Study of His Thought

The Diary of H. L. Mencken

The Diary of
H. L. MENCKEN

Edited by

Charles A. Fecher

ALFRED · A · KNOPF   NEW YORK
1989

THIS IS A BORZOI BOOK
PUBLISHED BY ALFRED A. KNOPF, INC.

Library of Congress Cataloging-in-Publication Data

Mencken, H. L. (Henry Louis), 1880–1956.
The diary of H. L. Mencken / edited by
Charles A. Fecher.
p. cm.   Includes index.
ISBN 0-394-56877-X
1. Mencken, H. L. (Henry Louis), 1880–1956—
Diaries.   2. Authors, American—20th century—
Diaries.   I. Fecher, Charles A.   II. Title.
PS3525.E43Z463   1989
818'.5203—dc19   89-2523
[B]   CIP

Manufactured in the United States of America
First Edition

List of Illustrations

Introduction

H. L. Mencken made the first entry in his diary on November 5, 1930. He was fifty years old at the time, and that is rather late in life for someone to begin the practice of keeping a more or less daily record of the events that befall him and the thoughts that occur to him. Earlier that year he had published the book which, in his own judgment, was the best thing he had ever written (*Treatise on the Gods*), and already it had gone through seven printings. In August he had gotten married (also rather late in life) and had moved from the long-familiar surroundings of 1524 Hollins Street to a handsome apartment downtown. He was deeply and romantically in love, his love was fully returned, and the future had never looked brighter.

There is an irony—which he could neither have intended nor foreseen—in the fact that he began the diary in the first year of a new decade. The one that had ended ten months before had been his in a very real sense. It was during the 1920s that he established himself as the most powerful and original force in American literary criticism, a force that might be admired or detested but could not possibly be ignored. There had simply never been anything like it before—criticism had never spoken in such tones. Utterly unafraid, he heaped ridicule on established figures who had long been revered, and eagerly hailed new writers who were bringing a fresh and more realistic voice to the novel and short story. His influence was immense—a word of praise from Mencken could give an aspiring young author the feeling that he had arrived.

In 1924 he and George Jean Nathan, after ten years of co-editing *The Smart Set*, had founded *The American Mercury*, and with its very first issue it had taken a place beside such venerable competitors as *Harper's, Scribner's, The Atlantic Monthly*, and *The Century*. Its appeal was, quite frankly, to the "civilized minority"; its purpose, set forth in an opening editorial, was "to attempt a realistic presentation of the whole gaudy, gorgeous American scene." It succeeded far beyond the expectations of its publisher and its editors. Though he had no desire whatever to be a hero to "sophomores," that was in fact the way it turned out: to be seen carrying a copy of the *Mercury* across a college campus became an instant mark of sophistication and advanced intelligence. When, a year later, Nathan withdrew, it became literally and wholly Mencken's magazine.

Between 1920 and 1930 he published five of the six volumes of his *Prejudices*, the second and third editions of *The American Language*, a translation of Nietzsche's *Der Antichrist*, and *Notes on Democracy*. He collaborated with Nathan on *The American Credo*, "a contribution toward the interpretation of the national mind," and on a farcical play, *Heliogabalus*. He edited two volumes of "Americana," gathered from the *Mercury's* vast collection of absurd news items. The decade culminated in *Treatise on the Gods*.

During all this time, too, he was writing his celebrated Monday Articles for the Baltimore *Evening Sun*, in which he set forth his unabashed and frequently outrageous opinions on Harding, Coolidge, Hoover, Socialism, Prohibition, censorship, Fundamentalism, Methodists, the South and its whole culture, the Bible Belt and all the political and social issues of the day. These articles, though written for a local paper, achieved national recognition. He became the "Sage of Baltimore."

In 1926 Walter Lippmann, reviewing *Notes on Democracy* in *The Saturday Review of Literature*, called him "the most powerful personal influence on this whole generation of educated people." For *The New York Times*, he was simply the most powerful private citizen in America. Years later Huntington Cairns, a good friend, would describe the Mencken of those days as "the closest embodiment of the Johnsonian type of literary dictatorship the United States had known."

He could not possibly have anticipated, in November of 1930, what the next decade would bring. In that year the circulation of the *Mercury* stood at a figure of some 62,000; by 1933 it would be down to less than half that and still plummeting. True, the Depression had settled down on the land—people standing in breadlines and looking hopelessly for jobs could hardly afford to lay out fifty cents for a copy of it and would have found little consolation in its pages even if they had. But the Depression was only a partial explanation for the sudden decline in his popularity, and not even the most important part. His brand of humor simply did not seem very funny anymore. His pretense that nothing had really happened was unconvincing. His gibes at those who were seeking to bring the nation back from its economic abyss appeared in downright poor taste. The comptroller of Alfred A. Knopf, Inc., noted in a statement that the *Mercury* was essentially a "one-man magazine catering to a very selective class of readers who are followers of its editor"; now, however, it seemed that more and more of them were following him no longer.

In October of 1933 he announced his resignation and in December got out his last issue, telling friends rather lamely that ten years in the job was long enough, that he was basically an author and not an editor, and that he needed time to work on his own books.

But much worse was yet to come. In 1934 he would be publicly humiliated by no less a personage than the President of the United States, Franklin D. Roosevelt. In 1935 his beloved Sara would die, after a scant five years of ideally happy marriage, and her passing left a void in his life that not all his multifarious interests and activities would ever quite succeed in filling. A few months later a writer in the Cleveland *Press* would sarcastically refer to "the late H. L. Mencken" and then, piling insult upon injury, add, "What? You say Mencken isn't dead? Extraordinary!"

And as the Thirties drew to their close he was beginning to feel more and more estranged from the *Sunpapers,* that stately institution to which he had given more than thirty years of his life and an enormous part of his illimitable energies.

He recorded many of these things in his diary, but save for the loss of his wife there is no indication anywhere in it that they upset him, or angered him, or left him in any state of doubt or depression. He had never sought popularity, so the loss of it meant little to him. He was accustomed to abuse—had he not himself assembled and published a whole volume of it? He had the assurance, after all, of knowing that *he* was right. His body of fundamental ideas—which, he liked to point out, had not changed since he was five years old—was not going to change now. It was the world that was different, not he, and he resolutely refused to go along with it.

Work was always his anodyne, and, middle-aged now, he plunged into it with a vigor surpassing, if possible, that of his earlier years. Even while Sara was still living he had embarked on the task of writing an entirely new version of *The American Language*, using materials that had been accumulating ever since the third edition of the work had come out in 1923. After her death, alone in the apartment which she had decorated for both of them, he spent fourteen or fifteen hours a day at his typewriter, grinding away at it. When the fourth edition, "corrected, enlarged and rewritten," appeared in 1936, it was greeted with a reception that no work of his had ever gotten before—critics called it "a great book," "a valuable book," "a splendid piece of scholarship," "superb reading." "Anyone who doesn't buy and read it from cover to cover," said *The New Yorker*, "will miss not only a classic, but one of the most unfailingly entertaining books ever produced."

His reputation began to come back—a different kind this time, quieter, built upon the past but distinct from it, and much more solid.

It came back, of course, precisely during those years when the shadow of Adolf Hitler was growing ever darker across Europe and even extending to the United States. All through the 1930s the threat of war increased. When it did finally come in 1939, Mencken was convinced that his archenemy, Franklin Roosevelt, was "itching" to get into the conflict and so make a place for himself in history, and he could have no patience whatever with the *Sunpapers*, which vigorously supported the Allied war effort and Roosevelt's open moves to help it. The men who took this position were his friends, and he would not repudiate their friendship, but their views seemed to him "insane." The *Sun*'s editorial policy was "absurd," "ignominious," and "dishonest"; the page on which that policy was set forth was a "disgrace to journalism." In 1941 he abruptly ceased to write for the *Sun* (though he did not, as the diary makes clear, give up playing an active role in its management). His by-line would not appear in the paper again for seven years.

Instead, he occupied himself with a new project, one as far removed from the war and its personalities and effects as it would be possible to get. It was the writing of his autobiography. This had begun slowly—almost hesitantly, for him—a few years earlier, with a pleasant reminiscence about the black people who lived in the alley behind Hollins Street in the days of his boyhood; entitled "Ordeal of a Philosopher," it appeared in *The New Yorker* in April of 1936. The following year there had been another, related to the first, which he called "Innocence in a Wicked World." The year after that there was nothing. But then in 1939 the whole plan of the work seems to have suddenly opened itself up to him, and *The New Yorker*'s pages sparkled with piece after piece in which he re-created, with a new kind of Menckenian humor, gentle and nostalgic, an era and a way of life long since forgotten. When *Happy Days* came out in 1940, critics and public alike hailed it as the most perfect picture of an American boyhood since *Huckleberry Finn*.

Its success was so great, in fact, that Alfred Knopf wanted him to go right on and do a companion volume about his adolescence. Mencken demurred at this: his teens, he pointed out, were a very serious time and could not be treated in the same light manner as his childhood. But he did begin work almost immediately on a similar series about his days as a newspaper reporter at the turn of the century, on the long-defunct Baltimore *Morning Herald*. Again they lit up *The New Yorker*, and only a year after *Happy Days* there appeared *Newspaper Days*. It was generally agreed that he had accomplished what few authors have ever been able to do: write a sequel every bit as good as the work that preceded it.

And during the same time that he was working on the pieces which made up *Newspaper Days*, he was also arranging and cataloguing some 30,000 quotations that he had been accumulating for his own use since 1918 and now proposed to publish not so much as a rival to Bartlett and Stevenson as a complementary work to them. In 1942 the 1,346-page *New Dictionary of Quotations on Historical Principles* appeared, to much acclaim.

In 1943 there came *Heathen Days*, a third volume of memoirs which began back in the same period as *Happy Days* and traversed the years all the way down to 1936. Though it was not quite as good—or as successful—as the first two volumes, it meant that for four years in succession he had brought out a book that had been well received and added to his reputation.

But meanwhile the fourth edition of *The American Language* had been out for seven years, and was already beginning to show serious signs of dating. New material had been pouring in to him from a variety of sources, and he had meticulously filed all of it away for future use. He started to prepare a fifth edition, only to discover, as he said later, "that if I tried to get all the new material into it I'd have a volume of forbidding bulk, probably running to 2,000 pages." For several years he worked away at what would become Supplement I. When it came out in 1945, he was already at work on Supplement II.

He was beginning to feel the effects of age, and again and again in the diary he complains of days when he feels rotten, when he can get nothing done. Yet even so, his fantastic energies roared on. He kept up his immense correspondence, usually answering every letter on the day that the postman delivered it at his door. When the mood was upon him he wrote a series of brief but revealing autobiographical notes. He put together a 265,000-word selection from his out-of-print writings (*A Mencken Chrestomathy*). He assembled a smaller volume of miscellaneous notes and aphorisms culled from the thousands that had accumulated in his "bin" (*Minority Report*).

But (and here we begin to get to the special significance of the present work) much of the writing that he was doing during this period was not intended for publication—or at all events, not for publication in his lifetime. In those sometimes long stretches when he was not able to make any progress on *The American Language*, he busied himself with two independent chronicles—one a memoir of his experiences as a writer and magazine editor, the other a companion work on his years in journalism. Each of them would eventually run to thousands of manuscript pages. But inevitably they dealt with many persons still living, and Mencken, always sensitive to the feelings of others, arranged that they be sealed for thirty-five years after his death. Four volumes of "My Life as Author and Editor" and three volumes of "Thirty-five Years of Newspaper Work" sit in a fireproof vault at Baltimore's Enoch Pratt Free Library, awaiting opening on January 29, 1991.

Finally, there was the diary. When he began it in 1930 he kept it pretty regularly, but for several years after Sara's death he rarely touched it, and even when he did get back to it, it was only intermittently. Then, in the early 1940s, he began to keep it again on a regular and systematic basis. On December 31, 1943, he noted that the entries for that year alone ran to more than 65,000 words, "the equivalent of a good-sized book." But of course the diary, too, dealt—often in his characteristically blunt and forthright manner—with persons still living, and here again he had no desire to hurt anyone. He directed that it be sealed for twenty-five years after his death.

II

By the terms of Mencken's will, ownership of and control over the diary passed eventually into the hands of the Pratt Library, that institution at whose Hollins Street branch, at the age of nine, he had begun "an almost daily harrying of the virgins at the delivery desk." When the diary was opened in 1981, the library, for reasons I will go into shortly, restricted access to it only to those who had already established themselves as Mencken scholars, and to a few other persons doing research in closely related areas. All those permitted to see it had to swear solemnly in writing that they would not "copy, quote, attribute, or paraphrase the contents of the Diary, or any part of [its] contents," without the permission of the library's Board of Trustees, and they soon discovered that this permission was not readily granted.

Out of the casual, knowing comments of these privileged few there arose gradually the notion that the diary represented the "dark side" of Mencken, one at an infinite remove from the public figure and the author of the published books. According to these accounts, it was the work of a man left lonely and isolated by his wife's death, resentful of the processes of aging, soured on a world that had passed him by, and incurably cynical about all the changes that had made his life so much less pleasant than it used to be. Much of it, it was said, showed the essential narrowness of his mind and the extent of his irrational prejudices.

There is some truth in this, but not, it seems to me, very much. I venture the opinion that the Mencken of the diary is perfectly consistent with all the other Menckens of fact and legend. It tells us things about him that we had not hitherto known, but it does not tell us anything different.

Obviously, it lacks the highly polished style of the books and articles—its entries, after all, were dashed off spontaneously in spare moments and then filed away, rarely if ever to be looked at again. Just as obviously it lacks the gorgeous humor which enlivens the published works—though this is not to say that it is somber or even serious in tone. There are passages in it as funny as anything else he ever wrote.

What first strikes one, indeed, on going through its pages, is the ordinariness—almost the triviality—of so much of the life that it chronicles. This, of course, is true of all diarists—of Pepys, of Boswell, of Gide, of almost any other who might be named. As far back as

1908, in *The Philosophy of Friedrich Nietzsche,* Mencken had himself written: "We are apt to forget that a great man is thus not only great, but also a man: that a philosopher, in a life time, spends less hours pondering the destiny of the race than he gives over to wondering if it will rain tomorrow, and to meditating upon the toughness of steaks, the dustiness of roads, the stuffiness of railway coaches and the brigandage of gas companies." And it will be at once apparent that Mencken gave over relatively few hours to pondering the destiny of the race.

Instead, in the spring he and his brother August plant scarlet sage, coleus, and petunias in their backyard garden, and in late fall they pull them up. During the months between he marvels—sometimes quite poetically—at the beauty of their colors. At the end of the day the brothers relax in their sitting room, Mencken having a couple of highballs and August ale. When the servants are on vacation, they prepare their own meals by opening a can of soup and making themselves some sandwiches; afterward they do the dishes. Just before the servants get back they give the house a general cleaning so that the women will not find it in a state of disorder. Mencken slips on a highly polished living room floor and comes down with a thump, bruising his back. He complains about, and finally takes legal action against, the incessant barking of the dog next door. Once a year, around Christmastime, he and August pay a visit to their aged Uncle Charlie, disabled and confined to what would now be called a nursing home.

Altogether, it is a routine and even commonplace existence. In the preface to *Heathen Days,* he speaks of his "habitual tranquility, not to say complacency," and it is a largely tranquil and complacent life that the diary portrays.

At the same time, since he is who he is, he moves regularly both in Baltimore and in New York among the great and near-great in the worlds of literature, publishing, journalism, medicine, music and politics. And this is something that cannot be said of the average person who leads a tranquil and complacent life.

The range of his friends and acquaintances was, indeed, enormous. At an after-concert party in the Manhattan apartment of Alfred and Blanche Knopf he meets George Gershwin, Dashiell Hammett, and William Faulkner (Hammett and Faulkner, of course, are drunk). He and his wife spend the better part of a week at the Vermont home of the Sinclair Lewises (during most of which time Lewis, of course, is drunk). On his frequent trips to New York he mingles with Theodore Dreiser, Edgar Lee Masters, Harold Ross of *The New Yorker*, Abel Green of *Variety*, Walter Winchell, and his old friend and colleague George Jean Nathan. He has as lunch or dinner guests at his home men like Clarence Darrow, William Lyon Phelps of Yale, Oswald Garrison Villard of *The Nation*, and Ellery Sedgwick of *The Atlantic Monthly*. He knows all the eminent physicians and surgeons of The Johns Hopkins Hospital and School of Medicine. As a working newspaperman he interviews Bishop James Cannon of the Methodist Church, Senator Robert Taft of Ohio, Senator Arthur Vandenberg of Michigan, and "the great rabble-rouser," Gerald L. K. Smith. He is on first-name terms with a justice of the U.S. Supreme Court, Felix Frankfurter. In 1946, at a dinner of the Gridiron Club, his preëminence as a journalist is recognized when the directors put him at the elevated guest table just two places away from President Truman.

His comments on these people are pithy, incisive, typically Menckenian—which is to say that they may be just or unjust. Sometimes a man or woman is limned in a single gorgeous phrase. At other times the treatment is quite extensive, and it seems safe to say that publication of the diary will add much detail to our previous knowledge of Dreiser, Lewis, Joseph Hergesheimer (especially Hergesheimer), Edgar Lee Masters, and other literary and journalistic figures of the era.

But the point I want to make is that nowhere is there any sign of that isolation or bitterness which readers of the diary claim to have found there. Obviously a man leading such a full life could hardly feel isolated—there are times, indeed, when it is plain that he is anxious to get away from it all and back to the peace and quiet of Hollins Street. And it seems to me just as obvious that he is not the least bit bitter about anything or anybody: Mencken may describe a man as "a jackass," "a fool," "a mountebank," but this does not in the least mean that his feelings about him are bitter, or even very strong one way or the other.

This much being said, it has to be admitted that the diary does pitilessly reveal his weaknesses, or—if "weaknesses" is not exactly the right word—the extent of his stubbornly held opinions and prejudices. Some of this, naturally, is the result of age, and of aging in the particular period of history when he did. A newspaperman for almost fifty years, he laments the fact that the era of the newspaper seems to be passing and that radio will take its place. Radio, for him, addressed its message to "the stupidest people of the country, and made no effort whatever to interest their betters." It catered exclusively to "morons." Looming just behind it on the horizon was television, and Mencken fought vigorously, but unsuccessfully, to dissuade the *Sunpapers* from starting a television station. When he saw its first broadcast—from Baltimore's Pimlico racetrack—he decided that he'd "not give ten cents for an hour of such entertainment, even if it showed a massacre."

These things, however, are minor. No doubt other people getting old in the 1940s felt the same way. Much more important, and infinitely less comprehensible, are his attitudes toward the war that was raging during much of this time, toward Franklin D. Roosevelt, toward black people, and most especially toward Jews.

His feelings about World War II are incredible in a man of his intelligence, knowledge, and perception. There is no mention in the diary of the German invasion of Poland which began it, or of the Japanese attack on Pearl Harbor which brought the United States into it, or of the dropping of the atomic bomb on Hiroshima which brought it to an end. There is hardly any mention of Adolf Hitler. He seems to have had no conception at all of what a German-Japanese victory would have meant to the civilized world, or to the liberties that he himself so cherished. He grumbles about the inconveniences the war has caused him, but finds satisfaction in the fact that it has impinged relatively little on the routine of his own life. The whole obscene show is simply "Roosevelt's war."

And the war was far from being the only thing for which he blamed him. His hatred of Roosevelt was, indeed, maniacal—there is no other word to use. Even earlier, when he was still writing his Monday Articles for the *Evening Sun* and editing *The American Mercury*, he had attacked him with a savagery hitherto used only on Woodrow Wilson and William Jennings Bryan. Roosevelt was a "world-saver"; his political and economic premises were "so false as to be absurd"; the conclusions he drew from those premises were "always dubious and sometimes completely idiotic." He had repudiated every promise he had ever made, deliberately and in the most cynical manner. In the whole New Deal philosophy, Mencken charged, there was only one genuinely new and original idea, and that was the proposition that "whatever A earns really belongs to B. A is any honest and industrious man or woman; B is any drone or jackass."

It might have been possible, at the time, to dismiss this sort of thing as mere sensationalism, a conscious effort to "stir up the animals." We know now that it was not, and that he meant every word he said. The boxes of brief miscellaneous notes in the Pratt Library's Mencken Room labeled *Minority Report II* and *III*, most of which appear to have been written in the mid-forties and which have never been published, are made up in large part of incredibly bitter attacks on Roosevelt and all his words and works. Now, publication of the diary certainly removes any doubts that might have lingered. In the entry for April 13, 1945, the day after the President's sudden death at Warm Springs, Georgia, had shocked the nation, he speaks of his "skullduggeries and imbecilities" and declares that "[h]e had every quality that morons esteem in their heroes." Two days later, as the passing of the funeral train through Baltimore closes the city's saloons and restaurants, he growls that it has interfered with the meeting of the Saturday Night Club and goes on to say, "He was the first American to penetrate to the real depths of vulgar stupidity. He never made the mistake of overestimating the intelligence of the American mob. He was its unparallelled professor."

It is hard to ascribe this hatred merely to a difference in ideology. Mencken could have respect, and even something like affection, for people whose views were poles apart from his own. No man could have differed from him more than Bishop Cannon, the Methodist advocate of Prohibition; yet numerous entries in the diary make clear that he liked Cannon, enjoyed talking to him, and went out of his way to oblige him. The same thing is true of Dr. Francis E. Townsend, the old-age pension supporter. Gerald L. K. Smith, the evangelist, was for Mencken "the champion boob-bumper," but they appear to have been on a first-name basis, and in one place he speaks of Smith's "very charming" wife.

Neither does the famous incident of the Gridiron Club dinner on December 8, 1934, at which Roosevelt humiliated him by reading long sections of the article "Journalism in America," seem to have been as important as had once been thought. That might have given Mencken a personal, as distinct from an ideological, reason for hating him, but the diary makes surprisingly little reference to that event.

Ideology certainly would have had something to do with it. Roosevelt's programs of social reform—the proliferation of government agencies like the NRA, the WPA, the CCC, and the NLRB to combat the Depression, the Social Security Act to provide an income for the elderly, a welfare system to help those out of work or ill—could only have been anathema to a man who believed that the best form of government was that which came closest to being no government at all, and that the only kind of man really worth "hell room" was the one who minded his own business and paid his own way in the world. But there had to be more to it than that. Roosevelt's whole personality and manner—the famous smile, the cigarette holder tilted at such a jaunty angle, the rich silvery voice that entranced huge numbers of people in the famous "fireside chats," the phrases that illuminated his talks like "We have nothing to fear but fear itself" and "I hate war!"— all these things apparently nauseated Mencken and made him retch the more violently every time he encountered them.

Finally, it may well be that he sensed Roosevelt was ushering in a new era of social history. He had castigated and ridiculed presidents before, almost as a matter of policy—Harding ("the numskull Gamaliel"), Coolidge ("a cheap and trashy fellow . . . a dreadful little cad"), Hoover ("where his character ought to be there is almost a blank"). But these men had been unimportant, and their administrations had made no difference; they came, and went, and vanished into oblivion. Roosevelt was making a very great difference, and Mencken, deeply conservative, resentful of change, looking back upon the "happy days" of a bygone time, wanted no part of the world that the New Deal promised to bring in.

His attitude toward black people was a curious mingling of total egalitarianism on the one hand and patronizing superiority on the other. He claimed to be entirely without prejudice, and in many respects this was true. He had regularly published black authors in the *Mercury* and persuaded Alfred Knopf to bring out their books. We are only now beginning to understand and appreciate the seminal role that he played in the Harlem Renaissance of the 1920s. He was on good terms, and corresponded with, such important black journalists and public figures as James Weldon Johnson, Walter White, and George S. Schuyler. The very last thing he ever wrote—the article "Equal Rights in Parks," which appeared in the *Evening Sun* on November 9, 1948, just two weeks before the stroke that put an end to his career— attacked in the most vigorous terms a local ordinance that forbade blacks to play upon certain of the city's tennis courts and golf courses. "It is high time," he declared, "that all such relics of Ku Kluxry be wiped out in Maryland."

He and August had two black domestics who cooked and cleaned for them, and he took the most generous care of them. When either of the women became ill, he paid their medical bills (and, needless to say, in those days he was under no obligation, as an employer, to provide such benefits). When Emma Ball, the maid, lost virtually her entire wardrobe on a Greyhound bus, he reimbursed her for the value of it and then filed a claim himself, knowing there was very little chance he would ever collect anything on it. In May of 1948 Hester Denby, the cook, was stabbed to death by her deranged daughter, and his diary entries on this "appalling" event, only a few of which I have included here, show how deeply he was affected by it.

But neither the achievements of the black people he respected, nor his care for those he thought of as being in some sense his responsibility, could erase a deeply ingrained conviction that black people were by their very nature inferior to white. "It is impossible," he held, "to talk anything resembling discretion or judgment into a colored woman. They are all essentially child-like, and even hard experience does not teach them anything." One might perhaps interpret this judgment as applying only to "colored women" of a certain social class, but Emma, the maid, "belongs to the Afro-American race, and shows many of its psychological stigmata." The very use of such a word, and the fact that he considers it unnecessary to go on and explain what these "stigmata" are, may surely be taken as an indication that he was not quite as unprejudiced as he claimed to be and probably thought he was.

This brings us to what is without doubt the most inexplicable and least pleasant aspect of his personality as it is revealed to us in the diary. I refer, of course, to his feelings about Jews. In my book *Mencken: A Study of His Thought* (1978) I sought to defend him from the charge of anti-Semitism—thereby precipitating, quite unintentionally, something of a minor tempest in a very small teapot. But at that time I, like everyone else, had not seen the diary. Today I would be much less ready to take such a stand. Let it be said at once, clearly and unequivocally: Mencken was an anti-Semite.

To be sure, he was not one in the sense that Hitler was, or such men as Richard Wagner or Houston Stewart Chamberlain. He would have defended the civil rights of Jews as promptly and vigorously as those of any other group. Yet the ugly strain runs through these pages almost like a leitmotif, and it would have been intellectually and editorially dishonest to try to excise it and pretend it was not there. He is upset by the fact that the house two doors from 1524 Hollins Street has been bought by "some Jews . . . with various ratty tenants." Lawrence Spivak, who was to become publisher of the *Mercury,* is a "young Harvard Jew." The wife of a distinguished Johns Hopkins professor is characterized in two words: "French Jewess." Charles Angoff, "like most of the other young Jewish intellectuals," inclines toward Communism. Samuel Eliot Morison, the great historian, is quoted as telling him that the students in his class at The Johns Hopkins are "mainly Jews." Simon Sobeloff, the city solicitor of Baltimore (and later solicitor general of the United States) is a "smart Jew." In an entry which I did not use, he speaks of two well-known Jewish businessmen, one of whom is still living, as "dreadful kikes." A Baltimore distillery which had formerly made a very fine rye whiskey has been bought out by Jews, and the natural result is that its product has deteriorated greatly. . . .

The litany could go on. I have called it "inexplicable," and I do so because if ever any man had a right to claim that "some of my best friends are . . . ," Mencken did. Alfred and Blanche Knopf, George Jean Nathan, Philip Goodman, Louis Cheslock—these were only a few of his Jewish friends. In many areas of his life—the world of book and magazine publishing in New York, the medical circles of Baltimore—he knew large numbers of Jewish people, and appears to have been on the most cordial terms with nearly all of them. When, for any reason, he is critical of one in the intimate group of his own friends, the criticism is never couched in racial or ethnic terms: for example, he may find fault with Alfred or Blanche Knopf for something that he considers a personal weakness or an error in judgment, but the fault-finding is certainly not based on their being Jewish. Only in the case of Nathan does this element enter in, and its presence there arises out of what seems to him Nathan's effort to deny, or at all events to conceal, his Jewishness.

Why, then, did he hold the beliefs that he did and express them in such offensive terms?

Anyone who knows Mencken at all knows that he liked to deal in the most sweeping generalizations—that he lumped together all Methodists, all politicians, all bishops, all Socialists, all poets. This did not prevent him in the least from championing Maryland's Governor Ritchie for the presidency, or enjoying the friendship of the Methodist Bishop Cannon or the Catholic Bishop Kelley, or stoutly defending the civil rights of the Socialist leader Eugene Debs. One accepts the inconsistency and laughs it off. In the case of his remarks about Jews, though, it is not quite so easy to laugh. There is an ugliness about them, both when they are directed at an individual and when they are applied *en bloc*, that is very disturbing.

It is possible to argue that there was a pervasive anti-Semitism in the air and culture of the time and that he imbibed it all unconsciously. This may very well be true, but it hardly constitutes a defense. Mencken rose above many—even most—of the common prejudices and stereotypes of his day, and ought to have been able to rise above this one too. When all is said and done, there probably is no defense. One cannot ask that he be forgiven, or even excused. About all one can do is ask the reader simply to accept the fact and pass on.

III

There can be little doubt that the reason Mencken ordered the diary sealed for twenty-five years after his death was that he assumed everybody mentioned in it would be dead by that time. In this, as it turned out, he was wrong. A number of persons who figure in its cast of characters were still living when it was opened on January 29, 1981, and today, more than eight years later, some still are. The Pratt Library naturally had to show the same consideration for the feelings of these people (or, in other cases, of surviving spouses and families) that Mencken had shown originally.

But there was another and even more compelling reason why the thought of publishing the diary raised very real problems.

Each of the five wooden boxes in which it was sealed bore a label reading as follows:

> This diary is to be deposited by my Executors on the understanding that it is not to be put at the disposal of readers until twenty-five years after my death, and is then to be open only to students engaged in critical or historical investigation, approved after proper inquiry by the Chief Librarian.
>
> (s) H. L. Mencken

This raised the very legitimate question: Did Mencken intend the diary to be published at all? Like everything else he ever wrote, his language here is perfectly plain and unambiguous, and on the basis of it one may convincingly argue that he did not. The provision that even after its opening access to it was restricted to "students engaged in critical or historical investigation" would certainly seem to indicate that that was as far as he was willing to let it go.

On the other hand—and the Board and administration of the Pratt Library were acutely aware of this fact—what they had in their possession was the personal diary, kept over a period of eighteen years, of one of the most important and influential figures in twentieth-century American literature. The work of a man who had published some thirty-odd books in his lifetime, most of them controversial and some of almost classic stature, it promised to have interest and value in its own right. To keep it locked away in a vault, available only to a handful of scholarly researchers who could not quote from it anyway, simply made no sense.

The Pratt Board of Trustees is an extremely active body, and then and since it has had many other things on its collective mind besides the papers of H. L. Mencken. At various times discussion of the diary came up, but it always ended in the same blind alley: Did he or did he not intend it to be published? At length, in 1985, the Board decided to seek the official legal opinion of the then attorney general of the State of Maryland, Stephen H. Sachs, and on October 4 of that year Mr. Sachs formally ruled that "the Library has a legal right to publish the diaries."*

His reasoning, put as succinctly as possible, was that the terms set forth on the labels—or, as he preferred to style them, the "memorandum"—did not have the binding force of a will. The memorandum "was not executed with the formalities required for wills." Mencken's actual last will and testament had made a number of significant bequests (of manuscripts, papers, and books) to the library over and above what he had already given it during his lifetime, but nowhere in the will was there any mention of the memorandum. Had there been, had the will incorporated the memorandum by specific reference, then the latter would have taken on the will's own legal and binding force. But it had not, and, "accordingly," Mr. Sachs stated,

> in our view, there is no ground on which it may be concluded that Mencken's memorandum is legally effective to pre-

---

* State of Maryland, Office of the Attorney General: *Opinions of the Attorney General* (Opinion No. 85-022 [October 4, 1985]). The remaining quotations in this section are also from this document.

vent publication of his diaries. Had the bequest to the library stated, for example, that the papers were given "pursuant to the terms of the memorandum regarding their use," we might well have a different case. But that kind of incorporation by reference is not stated in the will, and it may not be inferred.

"In summary," he concluded,

it is our opinion that neither Mencken's memorandum to his executors nor the Enoch Pratt Free Library's receipt for the papers delivered to it constitutes a legally enforceable prohibition against publication of Mencken's diaries. Mencken, a self-styled "congenital disbeliever in laws," once dismissed all lawyers as "obscurantists." But in this case at least, the law is clear and permits no other conclusion.

The matter was thus settled legally. But for the library there was still some question as to whether it was settled morally—in other words, regardless of the legal ruling, it might still be possible that Mencken had not wanted the diary to be published, and in that case his wishes should be respected. The trustees continued to debate the matter for a time. But at length, on September 18, 1986, a story appeared in the Baltimore *Sun* headlined: "Pratt sets plans to publish diary of H. L. Mencken."

IV

The diary runs to about 2,100 pages of (mostly) double-spaced typing, which I would estimate at somewhere between 500,000 and 600,000 words. It goes without saying that publication of the entire work would have resulted in a volume of, to use Mencken's own term, "formidable bulk," or even in two or three volumes. The happiest alternative seemed to be a selection that would be representative of the whole and—just as important—of interest to today's reader. My task, for which I was given an absolutely free hand, was to make such a selection.

What the reader has before him, then, constitutes about one-third of the total diary, and it seems in order to say something about the principles that guided me in making my choices.

First of all, like any diary kept over a long period of years, it is repetitive. Often Mencken will make an entry forgetting that he had said almost precisely the same thing in another entry made two or three weeks before. In such a case I had to make a judgment as to which of two—or sometimes even three—such entries was the more interesting and revealing. (I have kept the entries for July 11 and August 22, 1941, as an example of this kind of duplication.)

Second, he was one of the world's great hypochondriacs, and in the diary he gravely recorded every sore throat, upset stomach, chest pain, and other malaise that afflicted him. A little bit of this goes a long way. I have given what I think is a fair sampling of such entries, but the reader may be assured that for every one included there are two or three others that could have been used.

Third, during most of the years covered by the diary he was a member of the board of directors of the A. S. Abell Company, publishers of the Baltimore *Sunpapers,* and a director, too, of Alfred A. Knopf, Inc., the New York publishing firm which brought out his own books. He took his fiduciary responsibilities with exceptional seriousness. There must have been secretaries of these boards who took minutes for the official record, but their accounts could not possibly have been as complete and detailed as those that Mencken set down in his diary. One entry that deals with his representing the *Sun* management in a hearing over a labor dispute runs to forty pages of single-spaced typing and consists almost entirely of a verbatim transcript of the testimony taken down in shorthand by his secretary, Mrs. Rosalind C. Lohrfinck. Obviously this sort of thing is of no interest whatever to today's reader, nearly half a century after the unimportant event and when all the parties involved are long since dead. Such entries eliminated themselves almost automatically.

Lastly, and for pretty much the same reason, I have omitted a number of entries which treat of his and the *Sun's* relations with the Associated Press and their involvement in its operations.

What remains after all this, I would like to think, is a full and rounded portrait of an enormously complex person. The diary catches him in all of his many-sided activities, and I have made an effort to retain some of each of them—the author at his typewriter, the journalist in the midst of his fellow-journalists, the family man with his wife, brother, sister, uncles, and niece, the neighbor who looks with a jaundiced eye at the "lintheads" moving in during the war years, the friend who meets other authors in New York and plays music and drinks beer every Saturday night with "oxidizing" colleagues in Baltimore. Precisely like the rest of us, he looks back nostalgically upon the past and frets about the future. Though the most total of skeptics, he wants to add or delete something from one of his books because the proofs run to 313 pages and 13 is an unlucky number.

He must not have been an easy person to get along with. One has a mental picture of Paul Patterson, the dignified president of the *Sun-papers*, diving under his desk when he hears Mencken coming down the hall so he won't have to listen to another tirade about the "imbecility" of the editorial page. One imagines the company's august directors sitting around the boardroom table, eyes closed and heads in hands, while for the tenth or hundredth time he rails against the idea of starting a radio or—later—a television station. One visualizes the two grouchy and eccentric old brothers, one a widower and the other a bachelor, scandalized by the "bobby-soxer" girls in the square across the street from their front door. The story goes that he once read his own obituary in the *Sun* files, approved it, and directed that a single sentence be added at the end: "As he got older, he got worse." This was undoubtedly true.

The contradictions in his character may be more apparent than real, but nonetheless they are there to fascinate us endlessly. He derides scholars, and devotes years of his life to producing a work of the most exacting scholarship. He writes books that are masterpieces of humor and wit, yet broods over the fact that he has done so little with his gifts. He regards the *Sun*'s policies as insane, but the company pays him to be an "editorial consultant" so—although he is under no obligation whatever to do so—he goes faithfully to the office every day to earn his money. He has no use for people who borrow, yet lends generously to those in need. The business world seems to him sordid and money-grubbing, but he owns stock in fifty-eight corporations.

He had not a vestige of belief in an afterlife, but wrote, catalogued, and left behind him an enormous quantity of records so that those who came after him in this life would have an accurate picture of him. Of those records, the diary is surely the most significant. With its publication, more than a quarter-century after his passing, we are able to see him, if not wholly as he was, then at least as he saw himself.

V

The editing of the diary, besides being a labor of love and a task of never-ending fascination, has deepened old friendships, created some new ones, and brought me experiences that I would not have missed for the world. Such a work as this is essentially a collaborative one, and the person whose name appears on the title page as author or editor must almost always rely on the friendly interest and generous help of a large number of persons, some of them with expertise in fields rather remote from the subject-matter of the book itself.

It is, of course, to the staff of the Enoch Pratt Free Library of Baltimore that I am chiefly indebted, and more than once in the course of my work I have offered a silent prayer of thanks to the God whom H. L. Mencken did not believe in for having inspired him to deposit most of the vast bulk of his papers with it. My first thanks must go to Mrs. Averil Kadis, director of the library's department of public relations and its representative for all Mencken matters (a virtual department in itself). It is owing to her good offices, I rather suspect, that I was chosen for the job in the first place, and she has at all times been gracious, interested, helpful, and infinitely patient. Neil Jordahl, head of the Humanities Department, provided much assistance and encouragement, as did his associates, Wilbur McGill and Thomas Himmel. Wesley Wilson, head of the Maryland Department, and Ralph Clayton of the Microform Center placed the vast resources of their respective departments fully at my disposal and provided much help in showing me how to make use of them.

Others to whom I am indebted in various ways are Gwinn Owens, whose father, Hamilton Owens, is an important member of the diary's *dramatis personae*; Dr. Alessandro Pezzoti of the University of Pennsylvania for his help in clearing up an elusive detail; Sister Barbara Wheeley, R.S.M., for her help in clearing up another; Philip A. Wagner, an old colleague of Mencken's on the *Sun*; and Harold A. Williams, whose *The Baltimore Sun 1837–1987* was an indispensable mine of information and who graciously provided me with other assistance when I called upon him.

Marion Rodgers, whose *Mencken and Sara* must stand as a model for all editors of HLM's works, was interested from the very beginning and offered encouragement throughout. And finally there is the debt I owe to Vincent Fitzpatrick, assistant curator of the Pratt's Mencken

Room, who knows more about its contents than any other person on earth. With him I could discuss any problem that arose or any doubt in my mind and be sure of a caring, sympathetic and helpful listener. He read the first draft of this introduction, disagreed vigorously with some of the things in it, and made innumerable valuable suggestions. Of Vince it may be said that if he does not know the answer to any question about H. L. Mencken, he at least knows right where to go to get it.

CHARLES A. FECHER

BALTIMORE, MD.
January 13, 1989

Notes on the Text

1. The diary is typed on standard 8½ × 11 paper, usually white but occasionally of one or another colored stock. Save for a few entries in the early years, it is double-spaced throughout. Where an entry, or the end of one, takes up only a few lines on a page, Mencken has clipped away the unused portion of the sheet, no doubt for thrifty use elsewhere.

2. About half of the diary is in Mencken's own typing; the remainder is the work of his secretary, Mrs. Rosalind C. Lohrfinck. It is very easy to distinguish between them. Mrs. Lohrfinck's typing is neat, clean, and almost entirely without errors; Mencken, despite the fact that over a period of half a century he banged out thirty-odd books and an uncountable number of magazine articles and newspaper columns, never really learned to type.

3. Where either of them has misspelled a word or a proper name, or made some other obvious mistake, I have usually corrected it without notice. In two or three instances, however, I have let the error stand and called attention to it in a note. Wherever it has been necessary to insert a word to make sense, the word is enclosed within brackets [ ].

4. Mencken's stylistic usages differ in a number of respects from those in common practice today. For example, in giving the titles of books, his own or those of others, he uses roman type between quotation marks, whereas today we give them in italics. He regularly capitalizes many terms—honorifics like *senator* or *ambassador*, the points of the compass, the names of the seasons—which have since been relegated to lower case. In general, his own usage has been reproduced

in the text, but in the notes I have followed today's practices. (It should be added that he himself is not wholly consistent in these matters.)

5. Occasionally (December 31, 1930, is an example) there are two entries bearing the same date. It is possible in these instances that one is misdated; but what seems more likely is that Mencken wished to record two different things on the same day and that, since they were unrelated, he simply made two separate entries.

6. In the matter of footnotes, I have tried to steer a sensible middle course between the one extreme of providing too much annotation and the other of not providing enough. Every effort has been made to supply adequate background information on the enormous number of people mentioned in the diary, but it has not seemed necessary to explain to the reader of this volume who Robert Frost was, for example, or T. S. Eliot, or William Faulkner, or George Gershwin. Nor, for the most part, have I provided additional information on persons whom Mencken sufficiently identifies in his own entries.

7. In not more than half a dozen places, points of ellipsis have been used to indicate the deletion of a proper name or of a passage involving a proper name. This is out of consideration for persons still living. They are the only instances of such editing in the entire text.

The Diary of H. L. Mencken

1930

As the diary begins, Mencken is living in an apartment at 704 Cathedral Street in downtown Baltimore with his bride of three months, Sara. He is still editor of The American Mercury, *and this obliges him to travel to New York at least once a month, and sometimes oftener, to get out an issue of the magazine. The Depression is now a year old, but save for the declining circulation of the* Mercury *it has had little effect on him or his way of life.*

NOVEMBER 5, 1930.

Sara and I went to West Chester on Monday afternoon, the 3rd, to visit the Hergesheimers. Joe,[1] with Alice Logan, met us at Wilmington and we motored out to West Chester. Dinner Monday evening with some Palm Beach swells from Philadelphia—dull people. The house full of Philadelphia newspaper men and photographers Tuesday morning—election day. The photographers took Joe and me with John M. Hemphill, Dorothy Hergesheimer's cousin and the Democratic candidate for Governor of Pennsylvania.

Joe was full of confidence that John would be elected, but it seemed impossible to me. A telegraph wire was run into the house and we had

1 Joseph Hergesheimer (1880–1954), American writer, author of *The Three Black Pennys, Java Head,* and *Linda Condon,* among other books. Hergesheimer's work was widely known and admired throughout roughly the 1920s but has today fallen into almost total oblivion. Mencken maintained a lifelong friendship with him and his wife Dorothy, and they appear often in the diary.

returns in the evening. Once or twice it seemed possible that John might pull through, but by 11 P.M. it was plain that he was beaten. I estimated Pinchot's[1] majority against him at 125,000, as did Dick Beamish,[2] of the Philadelphia *Record*, whom I called up during the evening. I also called up the *Sun* at home.

Late in the evening a gang of local politicians came in. They drank whiskey and ate turkey sandwiches in the pantry. Joe very sore. Ann, John's wife, spent the whole evening playing backgammon with Ned and Mary Rogers. She seemed to be glad that she would not be a Governor's wife. John, if he had won, might have become a candidate for the Democratic presidential nomination in 1932. As it is, I hope to put him behind Ritchie.[3] He tells me he will try to control the Pennsylvania delegation, despite Joe Guffey.[4] He has lately got a big fee in a will case, and hopes to continue in politics. He took his defeat very gracefully, and is a pleasant fellow.

Sara and I motored to West Philadelphia today with Maude Child,[5] wife of the former ambassador to Italy. She came in from the South yesterday afternoon. In the automobile she talked of writing for the *Saturday Evening Post*, and defended it on the ground that she liked luxury more than fame. She proceeded to Bryn Mawr to visit Gertrude Carver, who is paralyzed. I came to New York and Sara went back to Baltimore.

1 Gifford Pinchot (1865–1946) was Hemphill's opponent in the Pennsylvania gubernatorial election. He had served a term as governor from 1922 to 1926 but, being barred by state law from succeeding himself in a second term, had been out of office for four years. On this occasion he successfully returned to the governor's mansion.

2 In the preface to *Heathen Days* (p. x), Mencken acknowledges indebtedness to Richard J. Beamish, "now a member of the Public Utility Commission of Pennsylvania, but formerly a reporter as I was, and a much better one." Beamish figures in an amusing episode in chapter seventeen of that book, "Inquisition" (pp. 218–22), wherein Mencken recounts his experiences while covering the Scopes Monkey Trial at Dayton, Tennessee, in 1925.

3 Albert C. Ritchie (1876–1936), governor of Maryland from 1920 to 1935 and a candidate for the Democratic nomination to the presidency in the national conventions of 1924 and 1932. Ritchie was one of the very few politicians whom Mencken genuinely admired, chiefly because of his outspoken stand against Prohibition.

4 Joseph F. Guffey (1870–1959), Democratic senator from Pennsylvania from 1934 to 1946 and powerful party boss.

5 Mrs. Child, the former Maude Parker, was the wife of Richard Washburn Child (1881–1935), diplomat and author, who served as ambassador to Italy from 1921 to 1924.

NOVEMBER 6, 1930.

When I got to New York yesterday afternoon from West Chester, Pa., I found a message from a Swedish news agency, saying that Sinclair Lewis[1] had been given the Nobel Prize. It was splendid news to me, for it was very bad news for all the professors. The Swedes rubbed it in by saying that, after "Babbitt," they were chiefly impressed by "Elmer Gantry." This book, which is dedicated to me, aroused all the pedagogues and patriots at home, and got very few good notices.

In the evening I was at the Philip Goodmans',[2] and they discovered that Lewis and his wife, Dorothy Thompson,[3] were in town. We called upon them at their hotel in 50th street at 11 p.m. Lewis, when we got to the hotel, was in his dressing-gown. There was a bottle of whiskey on the table, but he was fairly sober. When the Associated Press called him up with the news he thought it was a joke. Convinced at last, and asked what he had to say, he said, "Another great wet Democratic victory!" The A.P. did not send this out. He and his wife are going to Stockholm in a few weeks. After that they plan to go to Russia.

Lewis, of course, made a great mistake in not refusing the Nobel Prize, as he some time ago refused (at my suggestion) the Pulitzer Prize. If I had got to him in time I'd have tried to induce him to do so. But by the time Goodman and I arrived it was all over. Dorothy was all aglow. She would have fought my proposal, and no doubt beaten me. She married a novelist somewhat in decay, and far gone in liquor—and now finds herself the wife of a Nobel prizeman, with a triumphal tour to Sweden ahead of her.

Nathan told me today that Ralph Barton,[4] the comic artist, lately

---

1 Sinclair Lewis (1885–1951) was the first American to receive the Nobel Prize for literature. In 1926 he had been awarded the Pulitzer Prize for his novel *Arrowsmith* but, at Mencken's urging, had declined it.

2 Philip Goodman (1885–1940) and Mencken were good friends for many years. Goodman set up his own publishing business and brought out two of Mencken's books: *Damn! A Book of Calumny* and *In Defense of Women* (both 1918). His venture failed, however, and the books were taken over by Knopf. The two men exchanged hundreds of letters, some sheer buffoonery, some nostalgic recollections of their respective boyhoods, and out of these there eventually came two books: a volume of reminiscences of Philadelphia by Goodman entitled *Franklin Street* (New York: Alfred A. Knopf, 1942) and Mencken's *Happy Days*.

3 Dorothy Thompson (1894–1961), American newspaperwoman and author. She was Lewis's second wife; they were married in 1928 and divorced in 1942.

4 Ralph Barton (1891–1931), artist and caricaturist for *Cosmopolitan*, *Vanity Fair*,

attempted suicide by poison. He has been in a low state for months, and has done very little work. Nathan says he moans for his third wife, now married to Eugene O'Neill, and has proposed to her that she leave O'Neill and return to him. She naturally refuses. O'Neill is now rich and has a country place in France.

NOVEMBER 7, 1930.

I am sitting to a Negro portrait painter, O. Richard Reid,[1] in Harlem. Whether he is good or bad I don't know. He tells me he began life as a bellboy in Jacksonville, and got his first lessons in drawing from a German who was a guest at the hotel—and later left between days after robbing the other guests. Reid was 21 years old before he got to Philadelphia and saw his first decent picture. He is now 32, and somewhat cocky. I sit in the apartment of another Negro named Grumby, who has a large collection of Negro books and seems to deal in them. What will become of this portrait I don't know. Nor do I know what has become of the one made by Nikol Schattenstein two or three years ago: probably he still has it.

NOVEMBER 17, 1930.

Clarence Darrow,[2] with his wife and manager, George Whitehead, here for lunch. Darrow is to debate religion at the Lyric tonight with a Catholic, a Protestant and a Jew.[3] A Baltimore *News* photographer came in and took a picture of Darrow and me standing before the lithograph of the Pabst Brewery in the dining-room. Darrow has little to say. We had a prime beef stew for lunch, with red wine. Darrow is a finicky eater. When he was last here, he came to lunch in Hollins

Harper's Bazaar, and other magazines. He had been married to the actress Carlotta Monterey, who subsequently became the third wife of Eugene O'Neill. He did commit suicide some six months later; see the entry for December 5, 1934 (p.74).

1 Oliver Richard Reid (1898–1961), black American painter. He had had several one-man shows in New York before painting the portrait of Mencken. Its present whereabouts—if indeed it survives at all—are unknown. The one by Nikol Schattenstein now hangs in the Mencken Room of Baltimore's Enoch Pratt Free Library.

2 Clarence Darrow (1857–1938), American trial lawyer and defender of radical causes. He headed the defense counsel at the Scopes trial in 1925.

3 Darrow carried on his debate with the Reverend Dr. Peter Ainslie and Rabbi Edward L. Israel, both of Baltimore, and a Catholic layman from Chicago named Quin O'Brien.

street, and there was chicken. He refused to eat it, so ham and eggs had to be prepared for him. This time his wife sent Sara a list of the things he eats. He begins to look old. He had little that was interesting to say. He roves the country engaging in debates on religion, and is said to make a lot of money.

DECEMBER 31, 1930.

Edgar Lee Masters[1] and his wife were here to lunch on December 14, passing through on their way to Washington. Masters was once the law partner of Clarence Darrow in Chicago, and apparently has small love for him. He said that they made a great deal of money at their practice and that both planned to retire from the law and devote themselves to writing. But Darrow got involved in various big criminal cases, chiefly as the defender of radicals, and was away from the office for months and even years at a time. Thus Masters had to do all the work—all, that is, that brought in any substantial profit. One day he moved out, and that was the end of the partnership. Soon afterward he duly retired from the law—and the first fruit of his career as a writer was "The Spoon River Anthology."

We fell to talking of pleasant and unpleasant things. Masters said that he got most genuine joy out of taking a chew of tobacco on arising in the morning and stepping under a shower-bath. This is also my own favorite vice.

When Sara asked Carrie Foote, the colored cook, what she wanted at Christmas she said "The Spoon River Anthology." I got a copy for her, and Masters has now sent an elegant autograph for it.

DECEMBER 31, 1930.

Dinner at Hugh H. Young's[2] house last night. Present: Governor Ritchie, Senator Tydings, President Ames of the Johns Hopkins, Ber-

---

1 Edgar Lee Masters (1868–1950), American poet and novelist. Mencken and Masters were good friends for many years, during which they exchanged hundreds of letters. Mencken had a very great admiration for *Spoon River Anthology* but took a somewhat dimmer view of Masters's fiction; see "Four Makers of Tales," *Prejudices: Fifth Series*, pp. 56–63.

2 Dr. Hugh H. Young (1870–1945), internationally famous urologist and member of the faculty of the John Hopkins Medical School from 1894 to his retirement in 1942.

nard Baruch, Herbert Bayard Swope, Dr. Dean Lewis, Frank R. Kent, Omer Hershey, and various others—twenty in all.[1] The talk was all about Ritchie's presidential candidacy, but there was little point to it. What is needed is money. It will cost a lot to round up delegates. But Baruch, though he was polite, was also evasive. Every guest made a speech. They were all short, and some of them were very fair. But telling Ritchie that he is a good fellow will not get him the nomination.

I sat between Baruch and Ames. Toward the end of the dinner Baruch went through the back of a very expensive looking antique chair. Oysters, soup, terrapin and duck—all good. Good sherry. Sauterne. Champagne. Liqueurs. It lasted until nearly 1 a.m.

Ames told me that Robert A. Millikan[2] was a great faker, and very vain. He seemed to be strongly opposed to Millikan's flirtation with the theologians. I asked him if Einstein was a faker too, but he said no.

I came into town with Ritchie, and then walked from the Belvedere to Mt. Royal Station with Baruch and Swope. Swope told me that he'd like to buy the New York *World*, but that it seemed impracticable, for Joseph Pulitzer's will made it almost impossible for his heirs to alienate either the title of the paper or the plant. Thus if the *World* were bought, the title would go to the *Evening World*, which is not for sale, and the purchaser would have to find a plant. Also, a new name.

1 Millard E. Tydings (1890–1961), U.S. senator from Maryland 1927–1951; Dr. Joseph S. Ames (1864–1943), president of the Johns Hopkins University 1929–1935; Bernard Baruch (1870–1965), financier and "adviser to presidents" from Woodrow Wilson to John F. Kennedy; Herbert Bayard Swope (1882–1945), journalist and for many years executive editor of the New York *World*—Mencken served as best man at Swope's wedding in 1912; Dean Lewis (1874–1941), professor of surgery at the Johns Hopkins Medical School and at one time president of the American Medical Association; Frank R. Kent (1877–1958), newspaperman and political commentator, author of *The Great Game of Politics* (1923); Omer F. Hershey (1867–1959), Baltimore attorney and member of various state legislative and judicial commissions.

2 Robert A. Millikan (1868–1953), American physicist, winner of the 1923 Nobel Prize for physics.

1931

I presided last night at a meeting in honor of the 75th birthday of Lizette Woodworth Reese,[1] holden in the parish hall of Emmanuel Church. The affair was arranged by the Poetry Society of Maryland, and there was a full house. I opened with a few words, and then Miss Reese read from her prose autobiography, and from some of her books of poems. She ended with a reading of "Tears." She turns out to be a most ineffective reader, and even has a small lisp. Probably three-fourths of the people present knew "Tears" by heart, and so supplied mentally what she lacked oratorically. In the course of the reading she said something that seemed curious—to wit, "I don't like to read sonnets. They are too long." This is an interesting ratification of Poe's theory.

I had never met the old lady before, and she somewhat surprised me. I had expected a rather bulky person, very schoolteacherish in manner. She turned out to be a small, brisk body, with little shyness and no apparent conventionality. She introduced me to her sister, her brother-in-law and her nephew. The brother-in-law is a huge German named Dietrich. Miss Reese told me that she was half German herself, and that she was delighted that her German relatives never ceased to be Lutherans. I had always assumed that she, herself, was a Quaker, but she told me that she was not. What her faith is she didn't say. I am inclined to believe that she is anything but pious. After the meeting

---

1 Lizette Woodworth Reese (1856–1935), Baltimore schoolteacher, poet, and essayist. Mencken had a very great admiration for her sonnet "Tears"; see "The Poet and His Art," *Prejudices: Third Series*, pp. 159–60; *Chrestomathy*, pp. 454–55.

we went to a woman's club in Hamilton Street and sat around for an hour or two. I drank some near-beer. It turned out to be less revolting than I expected.

Robert Frost, the poet, was in the audience. His daughter, who is a nurse at Union Memorial Hospital, is ill there with tuberculosis, and he has come here to take her to Colorado. Today his wife came to lunch. He, himself, had to return to New York last night. He'll come back on Friday, and then proceed Westward with his daughter. I wanted to introduce him to the audience, but he protested on the ground that it was Miss Reese's show and he didn't care to grab any of it from her.

Several young women sang settings of Miss Reese's lyrics. The music was only so-so.

JANUARY 14, 1931.

Dr. Joseph C. Bloodgood[1] told me today that Dr. William S. Halsted,[2] the celebrated Johns Hopkins surgeon, suffered greatly from tachycardia, due to excessive smoking. Bloodgood says that when he was resident surgeon at the Johns Hopkins Hospital he had to do a great deal of Halsted's work. Halsted would begin an operation and then have to abandon it because of the thumping of his heart. Said Bloodgood: "This gave me an extraordinary amount of experience, and did me a lot of good. So long as Halsted smoked, whoever was surgical resident at the Johns Hopkins had his hands full. When he stopped smoking he began to do all of his own work. The residents then got less experience, and hence amounted to less when they left."

Bloodgood told me that he visited Halsted's home very often, but that Mrs. Halsted was never present at meals. She was a curiously anti-social woman, and seldom saw any one. However, Bloodgood believes that she had a powerful effect upon Halsted's career. Many of the Halsted improvements in technique, in fact, were due to her sugges-

1 Dr. Joseph C. Bloodgood (1867–1935), surgeon at the Johns Hopkins Hospital and internationally known for his researches on cancer.
2 Dr. William S. Halsted (1852–1922) was one of the Hopkins Big Four. The others were Dr. (later Sir) William Osler (1849–1919), Dr. Howard A. Kelly (1858–1943), and Dr. William H. Welch (1850–1934). Halsted was married in 1890 to Caroline Hampton of South Carolina, who, as Mencken notes, had been head nurse in the Hopkins operating room.

tions—for she had been chief surgical nurse at the Johns Hopkins before their marriage, and was a very intelligent woman.

JANUARY 16, 1931.

After Nathan . . . left yesterday Sara and I went to the Johns Hopkins Hospital to see Mrs. Max Brödel,[1] who has had a serious operation. She is now recovering. I took her the new life of Cosima Wagner in two volumes, by some German baron whose name I forget.[2]

Nathan was so enthusiastic about a German talkie, "Zwei Herzen im drei-viertel Takt," that Sara and I went to see it last night at the Little Theatre. It seemed very dull to me. There is not much music, and most of the dialogue is stupid. No more talkies! They are even worse than movies.[3]

JANUARY 18, 1931.

Tonight I wrote the first words of "Advice to Young Men."[4] Beginning a new book is always a dreadful business. I had hoped to start January 1, but a sinus infection, set up by ten days of high wind, floored me, and for two weeks I was useless. A great deal of reading is still to be done for the book, but it is my experience that this is best done after the MS. is begun. Otherwise, there is too formidable a collection of notes.

Sara and I had dinner in Hollins street today. Before dinner August

1 Max Brödel (1870–1941), noted anatomical artist at the Johns Hopkins School of Medicine and for many years a member of the Saturday Night Club, the group of amateur (and some professional) musicians with whom Mencken played weekly from 1904 to 1948. Mrs. Brödel, the former Ruth M. Huntington of Sandusky, Ohio, came successfully through the surgery mentioned here and, indeed, lived until 1959.

2 The book was *Cosima Wagner* by Richard Count du Moulin Eckart. The two-volume English translation, done by Catherine A. Phillips, had recently been published by Knopf.

3 The film, produced in Berlin by the Deutsche-Lichtspiel Gesellschaft and directed by Geza von Bolvary, starred Walter Janssen, Oskar Karlweiss, Willy Forst, and Gretl Theimer. Mencken's judgment differed not only from Nathan's but from that of Mordaunt Hall in *The New York Times*, who called it "a delightful screen operetta, with charming melodies and a capital story."

4 For years Mencken planned to write a book called "Advice to Young Men," and in a letter of July 29, 1942, to Julian P. Boyd, librarian at Princeton, he said that he had accumulated "30 lbs. of notes" for it. But other things kept getting in the way, and the project was eventually abandoned.

and I bottled five gallons of Italian wine, apparently made in Baltimore. It filled 24 bottles.

Sara tells me tonight that Gertrude is tired of keeping house in Hollins street, and proposes to take a flat with August, probably in the suburbs.[1] It is a shock to hear of the old home being closed. Soon or late, of course, it must come, but it is still a shock. My inclination is to take over the house, lock it up, and keep it substantially as it is. I couldn't bear to think of strangers living in it. The neighborhood is fast declining. Well, it has lasted the normal time for a city neighborhood—fifty years. There is no sign of a Negro invasion, but the neighbors grow progressively poorer and so can't keep up their houses. At 1528 some Jews have the old Schlens house, with various ratty tenants. Last night a woman tenant got drunk and had hysterics in front of 1524. Union Square, because of the drought, is a sad sight. There is a movement to make it a public playground. I have protested to Kelly, secretary to the Park Board. He says the board does not favor the scheme, but that the Playground League is bringing pressure to bear on it.

FEBRUARY 1, 1931.

In Washington last night to Frank J. Hogan's annual dinner to politicians and newspaper men. Present: Longworth, Senators Bingham, Pat Harrison and McNary, Tilson (leader of the House), etc.[2] From the *Sun:* Patterson, Kent and Essary. Other newspaper men: Oulahan, Jim Wright, Harry West, Major Stofer, Walker Buell, Char-

1 Gertrude Mencken (1886–1980), Mencken's younger sister; August Mencken (1889–1967), his youngest brother. Some time after this entry was made, Gertrude (though not August) did move from the house on Hollins Street to an apartment in another section of the city. Subsequently she acquired a small farm, called Choice Parcel, near the little town of Frizzellburg in central Maryland, and lived there for the rest of her long life. She also maintained an apartment in Westminster, the county seat, where she spent the winter months. In later years Mencken and August would often visit her at the farm, where, according to one account, Mencken would devote much time to bird-watching.

2 Frank J. Hogan (1877–1944), Washington attorney and bibliophile; Nicholas Longworth (1869–1931), speaker of the House of Representatives, 1921–1935, who died just a little over two months after this entry was made; Hiram Bingham (1875–1956), U.S. senator from Connecticut, 1925–1933; Byron Patton Harrison (1881–1941), congressman and senator from Mississippi from 1910 until his death; Charles L. McNary (1874–1944), U.S. senator from Oregon from 1917 until his death; John Q. Tilson (1866–1958), at that time majority leader of the House of Representatives.

lie Ross, Holmes of the Hearst outfit, etc. A long and somewhat tiresome dinner. The first food came on at 8.15 and the last at 11.20. I sat
between Finis Garrett and McNary. Terrapin (?) cooked in a strange
and terrible style. Sourish champagne. McNary called for Scotch highballs and we drank together. He also went scouting for cigars. George B.
Christian, Harding's secretary, told me that he planned to do a
book about Harding, and said he wanted to tell me about it. I invited
him to come to Baltimore. I think it might sell. The Nan Britton and
Gaston B. Means books have kept interest in Harding alive. Moreover, there is probably a reaction in his favor. When Patterson and I
left, at 1 p.m.,[1] Longworth was at the piano, and various men were
singing.

At the *Sun* office this afternoon. Howard W. Jackson[2] was there by
invitation. He wants to be Mayor of Baltimore again, and Patterson
desired to listen to him and look him over. Present: Murphy, Patterson, the two Owenses, Harry C. Black and I.[3] Jackson made a good
impression on all of us. He seemed to be well-informed about the city's
business and very intelligent. The matter of his boozing during his first
term came up. He said, smilingly, that he was wetter than ever in
principle, but far dryer in practise.

Samuel Knopf[4] called me up from New York this morning. He has
just had a cable from his son Alfred, who is in London. Sinclair Lewis

1 Presumably he meant to say 1:00 a.m.
2 Howard W. Jackson (1877–1960) served four terms as mayor of Baltimore, from
   1923 to 1927 and again from 1931 to 1943.
3 J. Edwin Murphy (1876–1943), managing editor of the *Evening Sun* from 1920 to
   1939; Paul Patterson (1878–1952), president of the A. S. Abell Company, publishers
   of the *Sunpapers*, from 1919 to his retirement in 1951; Hamilton Owens (1888–1967),
   editor of the *Evening Sun* 1922–1938, editor of the *Sun* (morning) 1938–1943, editor-
   in-chief of all the *Sunpapers* 1943–1956; John W. Owens (1884–1968), editor of the
   Sun 1927–1938, first editor-in-chief of the *Sunpapers* 1938–1943 (the two Owenses
   were only distantly related); Harry C. Black (1887–1956), chairman of the board of
   the A. S. Abell Company from 1930 until his death.
4 Samuel Knopf (1862–1932) was the father of Alfred A. Knopf, Mencken's publisher
   and good friend. He served as business manager for his son's company and acted in

is also there and the two have been in conference. Lewis says that he has decided definitely to quit his publisher, Alfred Harcourt, and that he is ready to make arrangements with some other. He proposes that Knopf pay him $30,000 in instalments extending over two years, and promises to deliver a new novel by the end of that time. I advised S.K. to cable Alfred, objecting to the plan. Lewis has lately got the Nobel Prize money; in addition, he was been writing short stories for the *Cosmopolitan* at $3,000 or more apiece. Meanwhile, he has been drinking heavily, and has had to abandon his proposed novel about labor. I believe that advancing him $30,000 would be very risky. I'd certainly not want to bet so much on his delivering *any* novel, considering his boozing, and its demoralizing effect upon him. Moreover, his next one will probably be feeble, for his failure to put through the labor novel shows that he is by no means equal to another "Babbitt" or "Elmer Gantry." Yet more, winning the Nobel Prize will probably make him cautious, and so hobble him. He has a very active inferiority complex, and will be sure to remember his responsibilities as a Nobel prizeman. Altogether, I believe that in such hazardous times as these it would be foolish for Knopf to stake him so lavishly. I am opposed in principle to heavy advances, and am always suspicious of established authors who propose to change publishers.

NEW YORK, MARCH 10, 1931.

Dinner with Philip Goodman at the Three Stars in 47th street. Good beer. To his house in 10th street later. Present: his wife and daughter, Sinclair Lewis and wife, Franklin P. Adams[1] and wife, and Rose Wilder Lane.[2] Lewis full of interesting stuff about the Nobel Prize. The actual prize comes in the form of a check on a Stockholm bank. The prizeman has to go to the bank to get it. He is also given a gold medal and an elaborate bound certificate. Lewis said he thought of presenting the medal and certificate to some museum. I told him I thought he had better put them in his safe-deposit box.

He said that he was told he had been nominated for the prize by a Swede: he didn't know the man's name. He said that nominations

---

the same capacity for *The American Mercury* during most of the years when Mencken was editing the magazine.

1 Franklin Pierce Adams (1881–1960), better known simply as "F.P.A.," newspaper columnist, humorist, and radio personality.

2 Rose Wilder Lane (1887–1968), novelist, short story writer, and editor.

could be made only by former prizemen and by the Swedish, French and Spanish Academies. For some unknown reason the American, British and German Academies were not recognized. At one time the British Academy was on the list, but it was removed. He said the members of the Swedish Academy, or at all events the members of the prize committee, had to read all the books of any man nominated, and that they sweated under the labor. On his return from Sweden he stopped off in England, and found a good deal of resentment of the fact that Thomas Hardy had never got the prize. The friends of H. G. Wells and Arnold Bennett were also discontented. This discontent went so far that Lewis was given the cold shoulder. Thus he is now bitterly anti-English. In Germany, he says, he was received with great honor. In Sweden prizemen are public idols, and when they enter a street-car the other passengers arise.

Lewis has left his publisher, Harcourt, and is now shopping around. He approached Knopf in London, but Knopf decided against taking him on. Now he is saying, according to Goodman, that Knopf pursued him frantically, and that he said no, not liking K.'s personality. Goodman says he is negotiating with Doubleday and the Hearst outfit, but that he'll probably go to the Viking Press. Knopf asked Brace of the Harcourt firm why Lewis had left it. Brace said that he had been making the usual complaints—that his books were not advertised enough, etc. Lewis told me that Harcourt hinted to him that he (Harcourt) had had something to do with getting him the Nobel Prize. Lewis seemed to resent this, but it seems probable to me. Harcourt is a clever Dutchman, and no doubt pulled wires in Sweden. I avoided discussing this matter with Lewis, on account of Knopf. In fact, I put in most of the evening talking to Frank Adams, and left before anyone else. When authors quarrel with their publishers I usually sympathize with the publishers, for they are nearly always in the right. Harcourt has done a lot for Lewis. He suggested "Main Street," and has been very useful otherwise.

Having given up the project of a novel about a labor leader Lewis is now somewhat lost and uncertain. He seems to be avoiding heavy drinking, but he apparently has no plan for his next book. My fear is that the Nobel Prize will stand before him as he writes it, and that he will be over cautious. It is highly unlikely that he'll ever produce anything as good as "Babbitt" or "Main Street," or even "Elmer Gantry." His situation, in truth, is very difficult. The public will expect a masterpiece from him, and his new publisher will count on a best-seller.

My view is that he should have declined the Prize, as he declined the Pulitzer Prize. It would have made him stand out above all the other prize-winners. The fact would have been dug up annually, as other winners were announced. He could have afforded to lose the money. He was getting large pay from the *Cosmopolitan* for easy stuff: the $47,000, or whatever it was, represented less than his income for one year. I think losing it would have been an excellent investment. As it is, everyone remembers that he refused the Pulitzer Prize, and it is generally believed that he did so simply because the amount, $1,000, was small. He told me at Goodman's that Harry Hansen[1] had thrown this up to him. "If you refused the Pulitzer Prize," said Hansen, "because you resented the fact that better men did not get it, then why did you forget that Ibsen, Tolstoy, Hardy and Joseph Conrad never got the Nobel Prize?" "To that," said Lewis, "I could think of no answer. Hansen simply silenced me."

MARCH 12, 1931.

Hergesheimer here to lunch. He has come up to Washington from Palm Beach to look up material for his Life of Sheridan.[2] He has written 60,000 words since December 31, and now hears that some valuable letters, hitherto not available, are on deposit in the Library of Congress. He has applied to Dr. Jameson, chief of the MS. Division, for permission to see them, but Jameson replies that they are trivial. H. doubts it, and plans to see Herbert Putnam,[3] the chief librarian. He says that the Sheridan heirs are disposed to guard old Phil's fame very jealously. They deny that he was born in an immigrant ship at sea, and was thus ineligible to the Presidency. But H. says that he has the authority of the Catholic authorities for it. He went to the small town in Ohio where Sheridan was born, and examined the local records. He was the guest there of the local newspaper editor. One morn-

---

1 Harry Hansen (1884–1977), author, critic, book reviewer for the Chicago *Daily News* and later for the New York *World*.
2 Hergesheimer's biography of American army commander Philip Sheridan, *Sheridan: A Military Narrative* (Boston: Houghton Mifflin), appeared later that year. It is generally considered to add nothing to his own reputation and even less to the literature on Sheridan.
3 (George) Herbert Putnam (1861–1955) served as Librarian of Congress from 1899 to 1939.

ing he was offered a can of peas for breakfast. He says the house was extraordinarily dirty.

It amused me to hear H. deride Nathan for social pushing. For weeks past Nathan has been sending me clippings from the *New York Times*, showing H.'s social activity at Palm Beach—dinners, luncheons, backgammon parties, etc. But now H. says that N. is badly damaged by associating with Herman Oelrichs[1] and company. My opinion is that this folly has cost each of them something. Nathan wastes a great deal of time hobnobbing with rich idiots, and so does Hergesheimer. H. says that the younger element at Palm Beach is almost feeble-minded, especially the men. He says he has been associating mainly with the elders. He says that there is a great deal of drinking, but that getting drunk is frowned upon.

I took H. to the Union Memorial Hospital to see Sara.[2] She was in excellent spirits, and talked of coming home. Dan Henry[3] called up from Easton to say that he was coming to Baltimore with a mess of terrapin. I asked H. to stay for dinner, but he was giving a party at the Carleton Hotel in Washington and had to leave at 4 p.m. We ate the terrapin here. Present: Henry, Woollcott,[4] Hamilton Owens, Buchholz,[5] and I. We sat until midnight. Henry got a bit tight; the others were all sober. We drank cocktails, madeira, sherry, Beaune, Niersteiner, liqueurs, and beer. Henry brought some Maryland beaten biscuit for Sara.

1 Herman Oelrichs (1891?–1948), New York society figure, with homes on Fifth Avenue and at Newport, Rhode Island.

2 Sara Haardt Mencken (1898–1935), the wife of HLM, had always been in poor health and was frequently hospitalized both before and after their marriage. On the day that she died—May 31, 1935—Mencken told Hamilton Owens, "When I married Sara the doctors said she could not live more than three years. Actually she lived five, so that I had two more years of happiness than I had any right to expect."

3 Daniel M. Henry (1882–1953) was a lawyer in Easton, on the Eastern Shore of Maryland, a region of which Mencken seldom spoke well. Nevertheless, the two men were good friends for many years, and Mencken considered Henry "the outstanding authority on terrapin."

4 William Warren Woollcott (1877–1949), a member of the Saturday Night Club. He was the author of the club's own anthem, "I am a 100% American—Goddamn!," and it was on the grounds of his home in Catonsville, near Baltimore, that the club made its famous (if not wholly successful) attempt to play the first eight symphonies of Beethoven seriatim; see *Heathen Days*, pp. 92–95.

5 Heinrich E. Buchholz (1879–1955), president of the Baltimore publishing firm of Warwick & York and a long-time member of the Saturday Night Club. Although he did not play any instrument, he served as the club's librarian and took care of the physical arrangements for its meetings.

MARCH 14, 1931.

Raymond Pearl[1] came to me the other day with what purported to be an invitation from the governors of the University Club to join the club. I told him that I was clearly not eligible, but he replied that the governors have authority by the by-laws to invite five non-university men a year. I can see nothing in this suggestion for me. The club is full of fourth rate pedagogues and drunken lawyers. I marvel that Pearl wastes so much of his time on such people. He has put in a year of labor as a trustee of St. Johns College at Annapolis, and is full of a project to raise ten million dollars for it. Even if the money were raised, the college would still be second rate. I can't work up any interest in the education of such young men as patronize it. But Pearl is always vacillating between being a free spirit, and being an academic big-wig. Many of his difficulties are due to that fact. I think he'd be far better off if he avoided all clubs and coteries, and devoted himself undividedly to his work.

His study in longevity will occupy him for at least two years, even if he gives all his time to it. When it is completed it will be a valuable work, and his reputation will benefit. But every time he goes to a trustees' meeting at Annapolis, or wastes an evening at the University Club or the Maryland Club, he does himself an injury.

I told him that I'd consider the invitation, but it needs, of course, no consideration. I'd be as unhappy in such a gang as I'd be in the Elks.

MARCH 24, 1931.

Sinclair Lewis called up from Washington yesterday: he said he was lecturing there tonight. He said he wanted to come to Baltimore, and I asked him to come at 9.30 last night. He arrived at 9.15 along with an Englishman whose name I forget—one of the directors of the Heinemann publishing firm in London. Shortly afterward Paul Patterson and Dick Crocker, the paper man, came in. I put out Scotch, rye and gin. We sat until 12.15, at which time Lewis was somewhat

1 Raymond Pearl (1879–1940), professor of biology at the Johns Hopkins School of Medicine and a member of the Saturday Night Club.

tight. He and the Englishman had come from Washington by motor, and returned the same way.

Lewis arrived with a badly bunged nose, and with blood dripping down the front of his overcoat. He said he had tripped and fallen in Washington, but was vague about it. I tried to sponge the blood off his coat with a wet towel, but made a mess of it. He insisted upon seeing Sara, who, because of her late illness, was going to bed. She had him autograph two of his books.

He told me that he was drunk at Ray Long's[1] dinner in New York the other night, when he and Dreiser got into a quarrel and Dreiser slapped his face. He said that he had openly accused D. of plagiarizing his (Lewis's) wife's book on Russia, and called him a son of a bitch. This word, on Lewis's lips, has no meaning; he uses it constantly. But D. took offense, and so slapped him. I don't believe D. plagiarized the book. He and Mrs. Lewis simply used the same sources. D. has the sort of mind that, when it picks up a fact, also picks up the investing phrase. His book on Russia was feeble and foolish stuff, and so was Mrs. Lewis's. Both apparently succumbed to the Bolshevik press bureau.

Lewis said that he had a new novel planned. It will recount the history of three generations of an American family. The *Stammvater* will be Peter Cartwright, the Methodist evangelist, the son will be Eugene Debs, and the grandson will be Stuart Chase. Lewis said the Hearst outfit had offered him $1,500 a week for three articles or stories a week, but that he couldn't do them without shelving his novel, and so declined the offer. He said that his wife (Dorothy Thompson) had just sold her first article to the *Saturday Evening Post*—a piece about present conditions in Germany. He himself is to do some stories for the *Cosmopolitan*.

I asked him why he had left Harcourt, his publisher. He said that H. had handled his earlier books admirably, but not "the last two or three." No specifications. He told me he was negotiating with Doubleday, Cape, the Viking Press, and other publishers. Inasmuch as Heinemann and Doubleday are in close alliance, I assume that the Englishman is nursing him for Doubleday. The Englishman said that

1 Ray Long (1878–1935), for many years editor-in-chief of various Hearst magazines, including *Cosmopolitan* and *Good Housekeeping*. See also the entry for October 19, 1932 (p. 48).

Heinemann would be glad to take over my books in England, but I answered that Knopf had the matter in charge.

Lewis's lecture tour seems to me to be a folly. He is delivering three lectures—Toledo, Washington and a third place—and wasting a week about it. The bout with Dreiser has been all over the first pages. Now that he has a bunged nose everyone will laugh.

APRIL 16, 1931.

To Louis P. Hamburger's[1] house in Eutaw place last night with Sara: a supper-party following the opera. Present: the Austrian ambassador, Senator Tydings, Dr. Finney,[2] Dr. Dean Lewis, Dr. Lewellys F. Barker,[3] and many others: perhaps 50 in all. An excellent supper and a pleasant evening. Barker told me that, as a result of persistent religious training in his youth—he had to go to church three times every Sunday—he finds himself turning to prayer even today. He says he is a complete free-thinker, but that in dire emergencies he instinctively looks for supernatural aid. A new proof of my old theory that it takes three generations to make a real agnostic.

Mrs. Van-Lear Black,[4] a next-door neighbor to the Hamburgers, was present. She approached me late in the evening, and said that she knew I didn't like her. I told her she was badly misinformed. A somewhat bossy, but still handsome and impressive woman. Hamburger had some beer for me. Mrs. Black said it was brewed in her house. She said her younger children and their friends tended to drink too much gin, and she had the beer made as a substitute. She said the plan worked very well. It was anything but bad beer.

Barker is now 63. His hair is quite white, and he begins to look old, but his figure is still slim and erect.

---

1 Dr. Louis P. Hamburger (1873–1960), noted Baltimore physician, was the first student to enroll in the Johns Hopkins University School of Medicine when it opened its doors in 1893.

2 Dr. J. M. T. Finney (1863–1942) was professor of surgery at the Johns Hopkins School of Medicine, the founder of a whole dynasty of Baltimore doctors, and the author of *A Surgeon's Life* (1940).

3 Dr. Lewellys F. Barker (1867–1943) was professor of medicine at the Johns Hopkins University and an international authority on eugenics and heredity.

4 Mrs. Black was the widow of Van-Lear Black, chairman of the board of the A. S. Abell Company, who had died the year before.

APRIL 18, 1931.

It is now five years and four months since I last had any communication with Theodore Dreiser. For twenty years, from 1905 or thereabout to 1925, we were very intimate, and I seldom went to New York without seeing him. The first rift came some time toward the end of 1924 or maybe early in 1925, when he was finishing "An American Tragedy." He was in some doubt about his death-house scenes and wanted to visit the death-house at Sing-Sing. Unfortunately, he found that such visits were rigidly limited by statute, and he could not get permission. So he asked me to try to get him help from the New York *World*, with which I was then in very friendly relations. I did so, and a permit was obtained from a Supreme Court justice. But in order to get it, the *World* had to pretend that Dreiser was a member of its staff—apparently the learned judge had never heard of him—and that it had a tip that a man in the death-house was ready to confess. The idea was that Dreiser was to see this man, and write a story about him for the *World*.

There was, of course, no confession, and so there was no story in the *World*. The judge, inquiring into this, became somewhat unpleasant, and began to hint that the *World* had deceived him. So the city editor called up Dreiser and asked that he write something—in fact, anything—in order to placate the judge. He demanded $500. The *World* thereupon complained to me, and I became somewhat indignant, for it seemed to me that Dreiser was very ungrateful for the *World*'s effort to aid him; moreover, $500 was more than he could have got in the open market, at that time, for a newspaper story. So I sent him a hot telegram, and he replied with equal heat, saying that I had insulted him by accusing him of blackmail.[1] However, the matter was adjusted, he wrote a story for the *World*—what he got for it I don't know, but it was certainly not $500—and at the end of the year he visited me in Baltimore.

He came in unexpectedly on December 12, just after I had taken my mother to hospital, where she died the next day. I knew she was very ill, and was thus greatly upset. It was a cold Winter day and

1 The letters and telegram to which Mencken refers here are reproduced in *Dreiser-Mencken Letters: The Correspondence of Theodore Dreiser & H. L. Mencken*, ed. Thomas P. Riggio (Philadelphia: University of Pennsylvania Press, 1986), vol. 2, pp. 544–47.

Dreiser appeared at 1524 Hollins street toward the end of the afternoon, alone and unannounced. He said that he was motoring to the
South, and asked for a bottle of Scotch to take along. I got a bottle
for him, and also gave him a drink. At once he proposed to pay for
the bottle. This nettled me, but there was no quarrel. We sat before
the fire and talked. I asked him how he was traveling South and he
said by automobile. I asked him where his car was and he said it was
parked on Hollins street hill, a block away. I asked him if he was
alone, and he said no: his girl, Helen Richardson, was with him.

I at once went out, hatless and coatless, and fetched her into the
house, and the three of us sat for perhaps half an hour. My sister
Gertrude came in once or twice, and I think my brother August. We
were all greatly concerned about our mother's illness, and I told Dreiser that I feared she might die. But though he knew her and had been
her guest in the house he seemed uninterested, and offered no word of
hope that she would recover. Presently he left, still trying to press
money on me for the whiskey. At the door he still said nothing about
my mother. His girl, apparently noticing it, stepped back and said a
few conventional words. They departed in the dark, and I have never
seen or heard from him since. My mother died the next day, but he
sent me no message of sympathy.[1]

This episode caused me to set him down an incurable lout. There
had been other evidences to the same end during our long acquaintance, but none so gross and disgusting. Since then various persons
have approached me with suggestions of a reconciliation—whether
with Dreiser's knowledge or not I don't know—but I still feel that I
don't want to see him again.

BOSTON, APRIL 25, 1931.

Alfred Knopf and I arrived in Boston night before last and, after a
placid sleep at the Ritz-Carlton, went out to Cambridge yesterday

---

1 On January 14, 1926, Dreiser wrote a letter to Mencken that began, "Greeting. How
is your mother?" On January 20 Mencken wrote from *The American Mercury* office
in New York, "My poor mother died the day after you were in Baltimore. I suppose
that you noticed I was rather disturbed when we met. At that time, however, I still
believed that she might get well, but the next day she died, very peacefully and
painlessly." In a letter dated February 2, Dreiser informed Mencken that he had
only learned of the death of his mother that morning and offered "understanding."
Mencken acknowledged this on February 5. See Riggio, *Dreiser-Mencken Letters*,
vol. 2, pp. 550–52.

morning to see various bigwigs. Our first call was upon Sidney B. Fay,[1] the historian. He turned out to be a very pleasant fellow in the fifties, and we spent a charming hour with him. He expressed a great deal of interest in my scheme to print a psychological history of the American share in the World War, and asked me to look through my material and communicate with him. Most of it is in the stable loft in Hollins Street, and sorting it out will be a laborious and filthy job. However, I may tackle it during the summer. Fay has a pleasant and somewhat expensive house on the main street of Cambridge. It was paid for, I am told, by the proceeds from his history of the origins of the war.

We had lunch with Harlow Shapley,[2] the astronomer, at the Faculty Club. He turned out to be an inconspicuous and somewhat rustic looking man, apparently in the late forties. But the more he talked, the more his rusticity vanished. He said that the new 200-inch reflector, now being made, will be of very small value to astronomers save as an advertisement to their profession. He said that practically everything it may be expected to accomplish could be accomplished by the existing telescopes. The latter have already revealed millions of stars, and studying them will occupy astronomers for the better part of a century. Shapley said that the Harvard Observatory needed no more than two or three really competent astronomers. The rest of the work is done satisfactorily by persons with relatively meager equipment. Some of them are girls from the women's colleges. Shapley said that he was opposed to training astronomers in any number. He said that the number of places open for really competent men is small, and that it would be very easy to over-crowd the profession. He expressed strong disapproval of Robert A. Millikan, and especially of Millikan's efforts to reconcile science and religion. I gathered from his talk that he himself is a thorough-going skeptic. He told us of a devastating saying, at Millikan's expense, by Sir Ernest Rutherford, the English astronomer. Rutherford said that publicity grabbing has become one of the learned sciences and a great force in modern life, and that it has become necessary to set up a unit to measure it. This unit, he said, is the *kan*. It is, however, so large that it has become necessary to resort to a workable fraction of it. This fraction is the *millikan*.

1 Sidney B. Fay (1876–1967) was a professor of history at Harvard from 1929 to 1946. His two-volume *Origins of the World War*, to which Mencken refers here, was published in 1928, and a revised edition appeared in 1930.
2 Harlow Shapley (1885–1972), one of the most important astronomers of his time, made significant contributions to the knowledge of galaxies and nebulae.

Today we had lunch at the Tavern Club with Philip Hale,[1] the music critic, whose programme notes for the Boston Symphony Orchestra have made him famous. Hale is now 77 years old, and begins to look it. He still wears the florid Windsor tie of the Bohemians of fifty years ago, and his talk is mainly of old times. Knopf has been trying to induce him to do a book, but it is plain that he has no hope of ever getting to it. Despite his age, he is very hospitable to the newer music and, in general, shows a considerable resilience of mind. While we were at lunch various ancient members of the club were lunching at a round table in the same room. They yelled at each other horribly, and made other noises. After lunch they proceeded to play billiards in a boisterous and childish manner. One of them kept coming to our table to protest to Hale against Koussevitzky's recent programmes of modern music. This oldster, according to Hale, denies that any decent music has been written since Schumann.

Last night Arthur M. Schlesinger,[2] the historian, and his wife came to the hotel for dinner. We had a very pleasant evening, and they stayed until nearly one o'clock.

BOSTON, APRIL 26, 1931.

Alfred Knopf and I went to a concert of the Boston Symphony Orchestra last night and later on Koussevitzky,[3] the leader, and his wife took us to their home in Jamaica Plain for supper. No one else was present save Koussevitzky's nephew and niece, who apparently live in the house.

Koussevitzky talked steadily for an hour and a half. His English is greatly improved, though he still searches, now and then, for a word, or resorts to German to help out. He mentioned the common report in Boston that he is unable to read an orchestral score. He said that this notion originated in a misunderstanding of his method of preparing for conducting. First, he said, he studies a score carefully. Then he has someone play it at the piano, and stands up to work out a way of conducting it. Obviously, someone who saw this performance con-

1 Philip Hale (1854–1934) for many years wrote the program notes for the Boston Symphony Orchestra.
2 Arthur M. Schlesinger (1888–1965), professor of history at Harvard from 1924 to 1954 and author of many works on history and the social sciences.
3 Serge Koussevitzky (1874–1951), conductor of the Boston Symphony Orchestra from 1924 to 1949.

cluded that he was being taught the music, à la Caruso. It seems incredible that such nonsense should be believed. Koussevitzky has been a musician since the age of 5, and a conductor since the age of 12. He had a large orchestra in Russia before the war, and later on conducted both symphony concerts and opera in Paris. Yet it is seriously believed by many persons that he is unable to read a score.

BETHLEHEM, PA.
MAY 16, 1931.

Alfred Knopf and I are here for the Bach festival. All day yesterday—the first day—we tried in vain to get some beer. This morning, having given up all hope of getting any help from the hotel staff, I tackled a taxi driver and he took us to a low dollar-a-day hotel in the region behind the railroad station. When we rapped at the door the bartender stuck his nose through a crack and regarded us suspiciously. He said, "What do you want?" I answered, "Some beer." He then asked, "Who are you?" I said, "Two poor musicians." Then he asked, "Where are you from?" I said, "New York." He still seemed dubious, and so I held up a score of the B Minor Mass. Apparently he recognized it, for he at once opened the door and brought us in. His beer turned out to be excellent, and we got five glasses of it and a ham sandwich for 65 cents. One of the local politicians was sitting in the bar, and we presently fell into conversation with him. When he learned that we were friends of John M. Hemphill, he became extremely affable, and even confidential, and told us a long tale about the politics of the county.

I am sorry that we discovered this excellent place so late. If we had known of it last night we might have put in a couple of pleasant hours drinking the beer. As it was, we sat in our hotel room drinking Scotch highballs. Scotch does not suit Bach. His music demands malt liquor.[1]

NEW YORK, MAY 20, 1931.

Philip Goodman, Raymond Pearl and I had dinner last night at the Three Stars in 47th Street. The food was excellent, and the beer was really superb. Pearl and his wife are sailing for Europe tomorrow.

---

1 There is an amusing account of this incident in chapter seventeen of *Heathen Days*, "The Noble Experiment," pp. 204–07—though there he dates it 1924.

After dinner he and Goodman came to my quarters in the Algonquin. Goodman soon left, but Pearl stayed until after 12 o'clock. He told me some curious stuff about the last days of Noguchi,[1] the Japanese bacteriologist. He died of yellow fever in Africa a year or so ago. The new life of Noguchi depicts his finish as very placid. Pearl says that, as a matter of fact, he went crazy two or three weeks before his death, and made some dreadful scenes. He locked himself in the laboratory that had been set up in Africa, broke up all the microscopes, threw all of the pathological specimens about, and then attacked a corpse that had been brought in for autopsy. Presently he came down with yellow fever himself, and soon died.

Pearl believes that his insanity was at least partly induced by his discovery that much of his work in yellow fever had been futile. In South America a year or two before he had announced the isolation of the yellow fever organism. Simon Flexner,[2] head of the Rockefeller Institute, sent him to West Africa, where yellow fever is endemic, to confirm this work. Unfortunately, Noguchi discovered that he had probably been in error. Japanese-like, he went into a state of dreadful depression, and later there were signs of positive insanity.

JULY 12, 1931.

On July 3 Sara and I went to Vermont to visit Sinclair Lewis and his wife. Philip Goodman and his wife were with us. The four of us left New York early in the morning, and after a very dusty ride on the train reached Windsor, Vt., in mid-afternoon. There Lewis's wife, Dorothy Thompson, met us with a Lincoln car and hauled us to their place at Barnard, 23 miles away. The motor trip was very charming. The road follows the mountain streams and is thus not steep, but it winds in and out of the woods and is varied and interesting. The woods showed the full lushness of mid-Summer. There were many large banks of ferns.

1 Hideyo Noguchi (1876–1928), Japanese scientist, made important contributions to the sciences of bacteriology and immunology. In 1927 he went to Africa to study yellow fever, but contracted the disease himself and died at Accra. The "new life" referred to is *Noguchi* by Gustav Eckstein, published that year by Harper & Brothers.
2 Simon Flexner (1863–1946) helped to found the Rockefeller Institute for Medical Research and served as its director from 1924 to 1935.

The Lewises have a rather large place two miles beyond Barnard, with two separate houses, probably 1,000 feet apart. Both are well turned out, with electric lights, baths, hot water, fly-screens, etc. The Goodmans stayed with the Lewises in the larger of the two houses, which is on an eminence and has a good view of the mountains. The region is sparsely settled, and at night no lights are visible. This main house has a large studio attached, once a carriage-house. It is probably 30 feet long by 20 feet wide, and it has a large fire-place. At one end of it, in front of a huge window giving over the mountains, the dinner table is set up. There is a double terrace outdoors—a pleasant place for sitting in the evening. One evening there was a high wind, and we were driven indoors.

The smaller house is on somewhat lower ground and faces a hill. There is thus no view from it. The Lewis baby, Michael, now a year old, is quartered there, along with his nurse. Over the adjacent garage live the cook and his wife, who are Germans, and the Irish gardener, a bachelor. There is also a white maid, a native of the region. Various other functionaries, all local talent, help the gardener. Sara had a comfortable room on the second floor of the house, with a bath. I had a room and bath on the ground floor. The baby and its nurse were on the second floor. With them was Pamela, *aet.* 4, the daughter of Dorothy's sister Peggy. Lewis paid $10,000 for the place, which has 300 or 400 acres. But both houses were dilapidated, and he says that he has spent a great deal of money improving them and laying out the grounds. His total investment to date, he says, is nearly $75,000. He is still spending money freely—drilling an artesian well, building a maple-sugar house in the upper woods, and a house for farm machinery in the valley. He keeps two cows, and has four automobiles and a Ford truck. He had to bring the electric light wires two miles. His springs yield an uncertain water supply; hence the artesian well. So far the drillers have not struck water. The trained nurse is paid $200 a month, the German couple $175 and the gardener $150. It is an expensive establishment, and can be used only six months in the year. In Winter it is too cold and remote for habitation, and the Lewises have to rent a house nearer New York. Last Winter they rented Franklin P. Adams's place at Westport, Conn.

Goodman was afraid that Lewis would go on a drunk when we arrived, but for two days he kept sober. They were Saturday the 4th and Sunday the 5th. On Monday the 6th he proposed to take me down to Woodstock, nine miles away, to see various local worthies, including a garage-keeper who is a reader of the *American Mercury*. We did some shopping in the town, and then he proposed that we visit one of the doctors and get a prescription for some whiskey. The first doctor was out and he tried another. This one was also out, so he tried a third. Then he returned to the first, who was still *non est*. While we were waiting for him the garage-keeper aforesaid drove up, and offered to lend Lewis two bottles of liquor—one of Canadian rye and one of rum. Lewis thereupon arranged with the doctor's wife that when the doctor returned he should reimburse the garage man with two prescriptions. When we got into the car to drive home Lewis proposed that we try the rye, but I protested and it was not touched until we got back to the house. Then Lewis took a big drink from the bottle and handed it to me. I wetted my lips, and he took another slug. Then he hid the rye in the drawer of a desk in the studio. Dorothy was out of the house. He wanted to hide the whiskey from her. Presently he went to his room, taking the rum with him.

After lunch I told Goodman about the rye in the desk and he proposed that we seize it to prevent Lewis drinking it. But when we looked for it, it was gone. Lewis disappeared during the afternoon. When he appeared at dinner he was visibly tight. In the evening, while we were sitting on the terrace, Goodman went into the house to get me a highball. In returning he slipped on the house-step and came down heavily, spraining his ankle. On the day before, Sunday, we had discussed the length of our visit, and finally decided to return to New York on Friday, July 10th. But seeing Lewis drunk, Goodman now used his sprained ankle as an excuse for returning earlier. I proposed that we leave on Wednesday morning, the 8th, two days earlier than we had planned. Lewis and his wife objected, and we argued inconclusively. At 4 a.m. the next morning Lewis appeared at the small house and woke up Sara and me. He was in his dressing gown and palpably drunk. He wanted us to promise to stay until Friday, but we got rid of him without doing so.

The next day, Tuesday, Lewis was pretty groggy. He went to bed immediately after lunch and stayed there all afternoon. In the evening he denounced Goodman violently for proposing to go home on Wednesday. It was really not Goodman's proposal at all, but mine. Goodman's ankle had swollen and he was very uncomfortable. His wife and Dorothy went to Woodstock to get tape to bind it. By this time we had fully decided to leave on Wednesday, despite Lewis's protests. He was in bad humor all evening and sat on the terrace in silence, his head in his hands. A most unpleasant evening. All day he had been demanding drinks from Dorothy, who keeps the house supply hidden. At dinner he had a quart of Canadian ale, a mug of milk and a rye highball before him, and drank from them alternately. We had had cocktails every day before dinner, and ale with the meal. In the evenings we had high-balls or gin rickeys. But it was the two bottles got in Woodstock that really set Lewis off.

On Saturday the 4th Lewis and Dorothy took Sara, the Goodmans and me to their sugar camp up the mountains. We drove up the mountain road in two cars. Lewis and Goodman were ahead. The road, in one place, sloped sideways at an angle of probably 30 degrees, and was covered with dry and slippery leaves. We came so near turning over and plunging down the mountainside that the Goodmans and Sara and I refused to come down in the cars. Lewis ran his into a ditch at the sugar-camp—apparently deliberately, to escape the job of driving it down. But Dorothy bravely drove the other. It was less hazardous without passengers, but it was still hazardous enough. It turned out that neither had ever driven a car up the road; they had always visited the camp on foot.

We left on Wednesday morning in a heavy rainstorm, and I got soaked strapping the baggage to the back of the Lincoln. Goodman was too lame to help, and Lewis was still somewhat drunk. In Woodstock, in making a turn, Dorothy, who was driving, drove the car into the concrete base of a traffic signal. Fortunately, she was going slowly, and Goodman, who was on the front seat, yanked the emergency brake. Even so, the front of the car was badly smashed, and we had to abandon it. We hired another, and so proceeded to Windsor and the train. No one was hurt. I had a knuckle skinned and my right shoulder wrenched, but there was no real damage. The wind-shield did not break. We left Dorothy with the wrecked car. The accident occurred in front of a garage, and the garage men took charge of the car and got her home. When we reached New York Sara called her up. She said she was not hurt, and hinted that Lewis was sobering up.

He seemed to me to be in no condition to do any serious work. He showed me the MSS. of two stories written for the *Saturday Evening Post*, both very bad. One is a grotesque burlesque about an English novelist who visits the United States. The man is not real for an instant, and the episodes are all incredible. The thing shows a great deal of ill humor. Lewis dislikes the English because they treated him cavalierly after he got the Nobel Prize. I am afraid he gives away his animus too plainly, and that the story will seem idiotic, even to *S.E.P.* readers. The other story, which is somewhat better, deals with a Vermonter who goes to New York and makes great sacrifices to educate his son as a dentist. But the son prefers the mountains, and finally returns to them.

Lewis has done nothing on his next novel. He told me he hopes to begin it before the end of the year. But his present scale of expenditures makes him a slave of the *S.E.P.* He is so constituted that he can't carry on two enterprises at once. If he ever really starts the new novel he must abandon the short stories. But he will need the money they bring in. A novel done as badly as they are done would ruin him. Altogether, his future looks pretty dubious to me. I can't imagine him doing anything as good as "Babbitt," or even "Dodsworth," within the next two or three years. Dorothy labors heroically to keep his drinking within bounds, but without much success. She plainly took him to the mountains to keep him out of temptation, but he still manages to get whiskey, and she has to give him a good deal herself to keep him from running amok.

When we returned to Baltimore I sent her an outfit for making beer, with materials and directions. But 3.8% beer will not be strong enough for Lewis. He craves whiskey, and when he gets the chance he drinks it straight, drink after drink. It seems to be quite impossible for him to drink moderately. He is in a sad mess, and his poor wife is a tragic figure.

NEW YORK, JULY 29, 1931.

James M. Cain[1] came to the Algonquin to lunch. We had a meagre meal in the heat, with a couple of bottles of beer. Cain had a job as editorial writer on the New York *World*, at $200 a week, when the paper suspended. By great good luck he stepped into the managing editorship of the *New Yorker* at the same salary. That was six months

1 James M. Cain (1892–1977), novelist whose best-known books are *The Postman Always Rings Twice* and *Mildred Pierce*. Cain began his writing career on the staff of the Baltimore *Sun*.

ago. He seems to be unhappy, mainly because the *New Yorker* prints nothing that interests him. He told me that the office is a madhouse, with a staff three times as large as it ought to be, and all sorts of intrigues. Ross,[1] who runs the paper, is a noisy fellow and also very suspicious—a somewhat curious combination. Cain said that the editorial budget is $7,500 a week, a gigantic amount, considering how little matter goes into an issue. The artists are paid from $40 up for pictures. Usually they have to be supplied with ideas. For these ideas Ross pays $10 apiece to volunteers. Peter Arno[2] receives $300 a week on contract. Two of the assistant editors, both minor poets, are paid $120 and $190. There are three rewrite men and two reporters. But most of the stuff comes from non-members of the staff.

Cain proposed a crazy scheme for turning the *American Mercury* into a weekly, apparently with himself as managing editor. He said he had learned the weekly business. He argued that, if I had a weekly, I could write and print editorials on topics of the day. I told him I had no desire to discuss them.

Cain pays alimony to his first wife, a lady professor. His second wife, a Finn, has two children in their teens. She spends about half her time in Europe, visiting them. Now she proposes to bring them to America. Cain's fixed expenses are large, and he is always hard up. He has a great deal of talent, but manages himself badly.

NEW YORK, JULY 30, 1931.

Phil Goodman told me that Ernest Boyd[3] is miffed because I have seen little of him during the past year. My reason for avoiding him is that he has been devoting far more of his energies to drink than to work. In consequence, he is constantly in money difficulties. Some time ago he tried to borrow $1,000 from Harry C. Black, though he already owed Black $1,000 and had owed it for years. I detest men who borrow, and especially men who borrow as a result of their own

1 Harold Ross (1892–1951), founder and editor of *The New Yorker*.
2 Peter Arno (1904–1968), cartoonist for *The New Yorker*.
3 Ernest Boyd (1887–1946) came to the United States in 1913 as a member of the British consular service and subsequently made his home here. He was the author of numerous works on Irish and American literature and published one of the earliest studies devoted to Mencken (*H. L. Mencken*, New York: Robert M. McBride, 1925).

indolence. Boyd has some talent, but he is forever taking advances on work that he then puts off, and otherwise misconducting himself professionally. At the moment he is at Nantucket as the guest of Tom Beer.¹ He went there to spend three weeks, but as Goodman predicts, he will probably remain until Labor Day. It is a pity to see a good man get into such ways, but while he follows them he is unpleasant. I can't afford to lend him any money, and I dislike listening to his troubles. How he lives, God knows. He had jobs on *Time* and on the *New Freeman*, but now he has left *Time*, and the *New Freeman* has suspended. I lent his wife² $250 three or four years ago, at a time when she came to Baltimore for some surgery. I'll never get it back. What she is doing I don't know. The last time I heard from her she was running a literary agency, but it was making heavy weather. She and Boyd have been separated for two years. Both tell me their grievances when I meet them.

It is perhaps a fact that I am over-quick to drop friends who annoy me. The list is a long one—Dreiser, Wright,³ Nathan, Harry Barnes,⁴ and so on, not to mention other older friends. But I see no way to avoid it. Life is too short for anyone to be burdened with friends who demand too much.

Boyd spends a great deal of time, when he is in New York, drinking with Herman Oelrichs. No doubt Oelrichs gives him money.

AUGUST 15, 1931.

Sara tells me that she hears from William Cobb, who is on the staff of the Houghton Mifflin Company, that his associates all believe that I was responsible for Willa Cather⁵ leaving the Houghton office for Knopf, after "My Antonía." This is not true. I can't recall ever dis-

---

1 Thomas Beer (1889–1940), novelist, short story writer, and critic.
2 Madeline Boyd (1889–1972), the wife of Ernest, was, among other things, the literary agent for Thomas Wolfe and submitted the manuscript of *Look Homeward, Angel* to Maxwell Perkins of Scribner's.
3 Willard Huntington Wright (1888–1939) was associated with Mencken and Nathan on *The Smart Set* and served as editor of the magazine in 1913. Later, under the pen name S. S. Van Dine, he became famous as the author of the Philo Vance detective stories.
4 Harry Elmer Barnes (1889–1968), author of many works on history and sociology.
5 Willa Cather (1873–1947), novelist, author of many books, including *The Song of the Lark, My Antonía, A Lost Lady,* and *Death Comes for the Archbishop*.

cussing the matter with her. In those days, largely because of my active advocacy of "My Antonía," Cather used to write to me pretty often, and I always asked her to lunch when she had a book under way and discussed it with her. But since "Death Comes for the Archbishop" I have seen her very seldom, and never alone. She was upset by my review of it in the *American Mercury*, which I printed along with a review of Harvey Fergusson's "Wolf Song," in many ways a better book. She complained to Knopf that I should not have bracketed her with Fergusson.[1] I told him that I was not prepared to consider her wishes in such matters—that if she tried to influence me through him I'd bar her from the magazine altogether. This I have done ever since.

Cather is a 100% American, as "One of Ours" shows, and does not like the *American Mercury*. I gather from Knopf that she thinks she ought to have been consulted when it was established. I did not ask her for a contribution at the start because she was then getting high prices for her short stories—far higher than I could pay—and I didn't want to put myself under obligations to her, or seem to cash in on my whooping for "My Antonía." She never offered me any MS, either then or later. Her recent writing, of course, would not fit into the magazine. She has succumbed to Catholicism, and both "Death Comes for the Archbishop" and "Shadows on the Rock" have been widely read and praised by Catholics. Stanley Remington, the Baltimore bookseller, told me that he sold 125 copies of "Shadows on the Rock" in one day last week—a huge sale for Baltimore, and obviously due largely to Catholic demand. Knopf printed 110,000 before publication.

Cather handles herself very skillfully, and has made a good deal of money. She lives simply and is thus rich. Knopf gets on with her amicably and thus likes her, but she bothers him with all sorts of business and is something of a nuisance. When she visits him at his office she expects him to drop all other work and give her undivided attention. Some time ago she called up his father, Samuel Knopf, and asked him to get her a bottle of gin and another of brandy. She was giving a party and didn't know any bootlegger. The old man sent her two bottles out of his own stock.

My relations with women novelists have been somewhat unhappy.

---

1 Harvey Fergusson (1890–1971), novelist, author of *Wolf Song, In Those Days, Capitol Hill;* see "Essay in Pedagogy," *Prejudices: Fifth Series*, pp. 222–26.

For example, Julia Peterkin.[1] I brought her out in the old *Smart Set*, and induced Knopf to print her first book, "Green Thursday," in 1924. It naturally had hard sledding, and Knopf lost money on it. He knew in advance that this would be the case, but published it in the hope of recouping later on. But Peterkin took her next book to Bobbs-Merrill without consulting either Knopf or me, and on her third, "Scarlet Sister Mary," they made a lot of money. For this I have barred her from the *American Mercury*.

Ruth Suckow[2] has acted almost as badly. I brought her out in the *Smart Set* and induced Knopf to do her first book, "Country People," in 1924. He gave a good deal of attention to building her up, and after "The Odyssey of a Nice Girl," in 1925, her books began to sell—only moderately, to be sure, but still enough to make her a good property. About six months ago he read in a newspaper that she had signed a contract with the Hearst outfit—the Cosmopolitan Book Corporation. When he called her to task and reminded her of his own contract with her, whereby he was to get two more books from her, she burst into tears and said that she had never read the contract. Knopf was disposed to let her go, but I advised him strongly to hold her to the letter of the contract. This he seems to be doing, for he has just published her "Children and Older People." I have not seen or heard of her since this unpleasantness. The Hearst people plainly fetched her by offering her some fantastic advance. They have been going about New York rounding up all sorts of authors by that means, among them, Louis Bromfield.[3] It is curious to recall that the Stokes publishing firm refused to advertise in the *American Mercury* for six or seven years because it believed I was sworn to put down Bromfield—a sheer delusion, for he interests me too little for me to make war on him. Now he repays this devotion by jumping to Hearst!

Suckow married Ferner Nuhn, a young man from her native Iowa, in 1929. She was then 37 and he was about 25. Some time before this

1 Julia Peterkin (1880–1961), South Carolina novelist. In addition to the books mentioned by Mencken, she also wrote *Black April* and *Bright Skin*. *Scarlet Sister Mary* was awarded the Pulitzer Prize in 1929.
2 Ruth Suckow (1892–1960), Iowa novelist. She also wrote, among other things, the novels *The Bonney Family*, *Cora*, and *The Kramer Girls* and a collection of stories, *Iowa Interiors*.
3 Louis Bromfield (1896–1956), novelist. Among his many books are *The Green Bay Tree*, *Early Autumn* (which won the 1927 Pulitzer Prize), *The Strange Case of Miss Annie Spragg*, and *The Rains Came*.

I printed two short stories by him in the *American Mercury*, both very well done. I have always suspected that Suckow herself wrote them, or, at all events, carefully edited them. Of late Nuhn seems to have printed nothing save a critical essay in "The American Caravan"— somewhat vealy stuff. I suspect that he had a hand in inducing her to listen to the Hearst sirens. He could probably use more money than she has been making. I have not heard from her for a long time.

SEPTEMBER 3, 1931.

Ritchie came in last night to talk about his presidential campaign. He sat until 1.30—not late for him: he is usually good for 3 a.m., for he doesn't get up until nearly noon. He said that he had visited the headquarters of the Democratic National Committee at Washington, and found a great deal of opposition to Franklin D. Roosevelt. Most of the professionals, he said, are in favor of Owen D. Young,[1] but they have begun to lose hope that Young will run. Thus the way is open for a second choice, and Ritchie believes he may divert some of their support his way. I told him that I thought he should send emissaries into the different States, to see the local bosses. Many of the latter never come to Washington, and what they are thinking and doing is not adequately reported. I suggested Howard Bruce[2] as a suitable agent. He is Democratic national committeeman from Maryland, and thus has valuable contacts. Moreover, he is rich, and can afford the time and expense of a trip around the country. I suggested that he begin with the New England States. Ritchie professed to like this scheme, and said that he would see Bruce at lunch today and propose it to him. He invited me to the lunch, but I declined on the ground of my hay-fever.

Obviously, one man could not cover the whole country. I suggested E. Brooke Lee[3] for No. 2, and proposed that he be sent into the Far West. Ritchie said that Lee could be trusted, but that it was doubtful that he had time for the trip: he is actively engaged in business. No

1 Owen D. Young (1874–1962), attorney and corporation officer, served on many government commissions.
2 Howard Bruce (1879–1961), Maryland banker and industrialist who was also very active in the Democratic party in the state. He ran unsuccessfully for the U.S. Senate in 1940.
3 E. Brooke Lee (1893?–1934), powerful Democratic leader in Maryland.

suitable third man was discussed. I could think of none, and neither could Ritchie. He asked me to get into communication with John Hemphill, to find out what is going on in Pennsylvania. I promised to do it. Ritchie said he was receiving many friendly letters, some of them from the Pacific Coast. He said he could do little for himself, for the only feasible way was by making speeches, and he had run out of ideas for them. He said he was on good terms with a number of State bosses, but hesitated to approach them personally. He said George Creel[1] had been in Baltimore lately to interview him at length for *Collier's*. And that he had written articles himself for the *Forum* and the *North American Review*.

He seemed somewhat bewildered. He believes that the Roosevelt boom can be stopped before the convention, but he plainly fears that Raskob[2] and company, if they fail with Young, will try to put over some other candidate, as yet unknown. He has seen Raskob lately and found him friendly, but he plainly does not put much confidence in this friendly attitude. He said that he gathered from Raskob that the New York leaders were against Roosevelt, and would ditch him if they could. Whether they hope to renominate Al Smith he doesn't know, but he doubts it.

SEPTEMBER 4, 1931.

Paul Patterson and John W. Owens came in last night for a gabble and a few drinks. We discussed various *Sun* matters—the post of London correspondent, the proposed investigation of the Baltimore schools, the question of a new city editor for the *Sun*, and so on. Patterson has just returned from Europe. A fellow-passenger was Dean Roscoe Pound,[3] of the Harvard Law School, lately remarried at 61. Patterson says that Pound put in the whole voyage dancing with his new wife. The lady is no longer young, but her appetite for dancing seemed to be insatiable. Every night after dinner she and Pound launched upon the dance floor, and kept it up until the music stopped. Neither ever

1 George Creel (1876–1953), journalist and author. From 1917 to 1919 he served as chairman of the government's Committee on Public Information.
2 John J. Raskob (1879–1950), New York financier and business figure, was at that time chairman of the Democratic National Committee.
3 Roscoe Pound (1870–1964), dean of the Harvard Law School from 1916 to 1936 and author of many works on jurisprudence.

danced with anyone else. Patterson was in hopes of getting a chance for a quiet palaver with Pound, but it never offered: he was too busy with his connubial duties.

"Treatise on Right and Wrong"[1] is going very slowly. I finished the first section last week, but then hay-fever came down upon me, and I have been unfit for work ever since. I had hoped to get the book into Knopf's hands by the end of the year, but now it seems likely that it will hold me until the Spring. It is difficult stuff. I must consult authorities at every step, and there is a great deal of rewriting. The first draft of Section 1 is a mass of corrections.

How many other books I'll be able to write remains to be seen. As soon as "Treatise on Right and Wrong" is off my hands I hope to tackle the English version of Johann Burkhard Mencken's "De charlataneria eruditorum."[2] I had it translated five or six years ago, but have never finished the preface and the editing of the text. Such a book, of course, cannot sell. My plan is to print it in a limited edition at $10. Knopf has offered to stand the risk, but I'll probably offer to bear at least part of it. The book should be done in the grand manner, with reproductions of old plates, and ample notes.

After that I plan to rewrite "The American Language." A great deal of new matter has accumulated, and the new edition will probably run to two volumes. I have thought of putting all of the notes and documents into Vol. II, so that Vol. I may be sold separately.[3] When this dreadful labor is done I must also rewrite "In Defense of

1 *Treatise on Right and Wrong*, the companion volume to *Treatise on the Gods*, was not completed until 1934. Mencken himself was somewhat dissatisfied with it, and the reviews were no more than tepid.

2 Johann Burkhard Mencken (1674–1732) was a collateral ancestor of HLM's and a professor of history at the University of Leipzig. On February 9, 1713, and again on February 14, 1715, he delivered (in Latin) two lectures which, in their deadly assault on frauds and quacks in all fields, astonishingly prefigured Mencken's own work. The two lectures were subsequently published in book form and translated into many European languages. Mencken had an English version of it made by Dr. Francis E. Litz, of the Catholic University of America, in 1927, but did not get around to bringing it out for another ten years. It was published in 1937 by Knopf as *The Charlatanry of the Learned*.

3 The fourth edition of *The American Language* was published (in one volume) in 1936.

Women."¹ It has sold better than any other of my books, and it is still selling, but parts of it are out of date, and the whole needs reworking. There is some good stuff on women scattered through the six volumes of my "Prejudices." This should be worked into "In Defense of Women." My plan is to let the "Prejudices" books go out of print. Large parts of them begin to date. What is still good I shall rewrite and republish, probably in two volumes instead of six. Knopf wants me to do a volume of reprints from the *American Mercury*, the *Evening Sun* and other periodicals after "Treatise on Right and Wrong" is off my hands. If there is time I may do it. Such a book requires no more than six weeks of work. I have not printed a volume of reprints since "Prejudices VI."

I also hope to do a small book to be called "Advice to Young Men"— a frank discussion of moral problems. At one time I thought of making it the last section of "Treatise on Right and Wrong," but it seemed better to make the latter uniform with "Treatise on the Gods." The two may then be sold together, and one will help the other. I hope to induce Knopf to give "Treatise on the Gods" a new title page, and to reset the front matter. As it stands, it is rather arty. Such books, I believe, should be printed very soberly.

If I am alive two or three years hence I shall tackle "Homo Sapiens," a large treatise on the human race, setting forth all my ideas on the subject.² My plan is to document it heavily. Perhaps I'll put all of the documentation into a second volume, so that the first may be sold separately, like the first volume of the new edition of "The American Language."

After that, what? I scarcely know. I'd like to do a psychological autobiography, describing the origin and growth of my ideas, but it would probably be very difficult. I'd also like to do a book on government, larger and better than "Notes on Democracy." It would also be pleasant to do a book on music, but I'll probably never get to it. The years begin to close in. I can still work as hard as ever, but a break may come at any moment. Hay fever has disabled me this year more than ever before. Next year, if I have the money and she is able to travel, I'll take Sara abroad. But first I must cover the two national conventions for the *Evening Sun*.

---

1 No new edition of *In Defense of Women* ever appeared.
2 "Homo Sapiens" was also a book that Mencken had in mind for many years but never got around to writing. See the entry for January 25, 1948 (p. 442).

BALTIMORE, OCTOBER 9, 1931.

I went to Washington last night to see Bishop Cannon.[1] The meeting was arranged by Franklyn Waltman, Jr., of the *Sun*'s Washington bureau. His Grace received me very politely, and we put in two and a half hours of conversation and debate. Parts of what he said I am embalming in an interview to be published in the *Evening Sun*, October 12th.[2] One of the things he told me that I can't print had to do with Hoover's repudiation of the Wickersham report.[3] At about the time the report was due the Bishop was laid up in hospital in Washington. He was thus unable to see Hoover, but he sent a message to the White House through his colleague, Bishop McDowell. The burden of this message was that he, Cannon, believed that Hoover had equivocated on Prohibition long enough, that his failure to take a positive line had greatly damaged the whole cause, and that it was absolutely necessary for him to come out strongly on the dry side. A few days later Hoover wrote his celebrated message to Congress, declaring against repeal or modification, and his office undertook its celebrated and successful effort to deceive the country regarding the contents of the report. Cannon refused to let me print anything about this episode, but he was obviously greatly pleased with his own potency at the White House. He told me two or three times that he didn't claim the whole credit for Hoover's declaration, but every time he said so it was only the more evident that he believed he deserved that credit.

Cannon's office turned out to be a dreadful hole. While we sat and talked I saw at least ten large cockroaches. The windows were not screened, and I was bitten by an enormous mosquito. The place is

1 James Cannon (1864–1944) was a bishop of the Methodist Episcopal Church and the driving power behind the Anti-Saloon League of America and its efforts to bring about, and then later to enforce, Prohibition. He and Mencken were thus poles apart ideologically, but even so Mencken had a genuine affection and respect for him.
2 The Monday Article for October 12 was entitled "The Bishop Loquitur."
3 The Wickersham Commission, so named from its chairman, George W. Wickersham (1858–1936), was established by President Hoover in 1929 with the broad purpose of investigating "the entire federal system of jurisprudence and the administration of laws," but its chief task, really, was to determine "methods of enforcement of the Eighteenth Amendment." The commission's findings and recommendations were issued in fourteen separate and lengthy reports in 1931, but the one on Prohibition naturally received the greatest attention. Unhappily, it was very inconclusive, admitting that the Prohibition laws could not be enforced and yet calling for their retention. It was attacked by wets and drys alike and criticized by the President.

very small, and the furnishings are so meagre as to be mean. Cannon apparently sleeps in a small room adjoining. A bed was visible from the half open door. To the other side is a small bathroom, which he also uses as a kitchen. His wife has been in hospital for nearly a year, and so he leads a bachelor life. It would be hard to find a meaner habitation. Worse, it is on the third floor of an office building in which the elevator doesn't run at night. I was fortunate enough, when I arrived, to encounter the janitor in the lower lobby. Otherwise, I'd have spent half an hour finding Cannon's quarters, for he has no sign on the door.

NOVEMBER 21, 1931.

Pearl tells me that he was at a party the other night at which Dr. William H. Welch was also present. Welch entertained a miscellaneous company with the news that the *American Mercury* was in serious difficulties and for sale. He said he had been told by W. W. Norton, the publisher of scientific books. This is my reward for many favors done Norton, especially when he first set up business. Pearl says that Welch evidently took delight in the news. By that I am not surprised. Welch is a very shifty old fellow. He grossly deceived Pearl at the time of the Harvard episode. And during the war, though he owed his start to Germans, he joined the professional patriots in denouncing them. I warned Pearl against him long ago.

NEW YORK, NOVEMBER 27, 1931.

Last night the Knopfs gave a box party at Carnegie Hall to hear the Boston Symphony Orchestra, and a supper later at their city apartment, 400 east 57th street, in honor of the conductor, Koussevitzky, and his wife. In the box were Willa Cather, Federal Judge John M. Woolsey[1] and his wife, an old man named Seligman and his wife, a man whose name I didn't catch, Alfred Knopf, and I. Blanche Knopf[2]

---

1 John M. Woolsey (1877–1945), judge for the U.S. District Court of Southern New York from 1929 to 1943. It was Judge Woolsey who, in 1933, handed down the famous decision permitting James Joyce's *Ulysses* to be admitted into the United States.

2 Blanche Wolf Knopf (1894–1966) was the wife of Alfred Knopf, Mencken's publisher. She was very active in the operation of the business and, like her husband, a good friend of Mencken's.

was in the adjoining box with Mme. Koussevitzky. The programme embraced Mahler's Ninth Symphony, two pieces by Debussy, and a piece by Ravel. The Mahler seemed to me to be a very interesting work, though the coda of the last movement was far too long drawn out. Alfred Knopf, who followed the score, told me that Koussevitzky had made some big cuts. Willa Cather surprised me by saying that the symphony was too much for her, but that she liked the Ravel. The latter was a very cheap piece of trash. I had always thought of La Cather as a musician, but she told me that she really knew very little about music, and thus preferred Ravel's obvious banalities to Mahler's very fine writing.

After the concert I picked up Sara at the Algonquin and we went to [the] Knopf apartment. Sara was plainly a great success. Cather, Fanny Hurst[1] and various others made much of her. She looked splendid. Judge Woolsey invited me to bring her to his house in Massachusetts next summer. Others present: George Gershwin, Fania Marinoff,[2] a movie gal named Taschmann, Jim Rosenberg[3] and his wife. A lot of miscellaneous introducing. I got but one drink—a small straight Scotch. Dashiell Hammett,[4] the writer of detective stories, came in drunk, and became something of a nuisance. After we left, so Blanche told me today, she had to get rid of him. William Faulkner, the Mississippian, who came in late, also got drunk. At 4 a.m. Blanche and Eddie Wasserman[5] decided to take him to a speakeasy to dispose of him. Unfortunately, all the speakeasies in the neighborhood were closed, so they had to haul him to his hotel. He still talked rationally, but his legs had given out, and he couldn't stand up.

NEW YORK, DECEMBER 16, 1931.

William Faulkner, the Southern author who has been visiting New York for six or eight weeks past, has gone home at last, leaving a powerful odor of alcohol behind him. Judging from stories I hear on all sides, he was drunk every night he was here.

---

1 Fannie Hurst (1889–1968), novelist, playwright, radio and television personality.
2 Fania Marinoff (1887–1971), actress. She was the wife of the writer-photographer Carl Van Vechten.
3 James N. Rosenberg (1874–1970), lawyer and painter.
4 Dashiell Hammett (1894–1961), Maryland-born author of such popular detective stories as *The Maltese Falcon* and *The Thin Man*.
5 Edward Wasserman (d. 1960) was a well-to-do friend of Blanche Knopf (he later changed his name to Waterman). He spent the latter part of his life in Paris.

Among those who entertained him was Alfred Knopf. The other night Knopf was invited to a dinner somewhere else, with Faulkner as the guest of honor. Knopf took along a couple of copies of Faulkner's books and asked him to autograph them. Faulkner replied about as follows: "I am sorry, but I don't think I can do it. Too many people are asking me for autographs. Yesterday a bell-boy at my hotel wanted one. I believe that it is a mistake for an author to make his signature too common. However, inasmuch as it is you, I think I might very well autograph one of the books." This extraordinary boorishness to a man who had been hospitable to him struck the whole assemblage dumb. Knopf himself made no reply, and did not mention the books again.

Faulkner's publisher, Harrison Smith, wrote to me a week ago saying that Faulkner would stop off in Baltimore on his way South. Fortunately, he did not do so. The town is full of tales about his incessant boozing. He had a roaring time while he was here, and will go back to Prohibition Mississippi with enough alcohol in his veins to last him a year.

1932

Ellery Sedgwick,[1] editor of the *Atlantic Monthly*, was here for dinner last night. Later in the evening Paul Patterson, Hamilton Owens, and John W. Owens dropped in. When Sedgwick left, along about midnight, Patterson and John Owens remained, and I finally got to bed a little after two o'clock.

Sedgwick was full of curious anecdotes. He told about being at a dinner party with the late Moorfield Storey.[2] The name of Hearst came up, and Storey said: "Hearst married a prostitute, and then gradually dragged her down to his own level."

Sedgwick told me that the *Atlantic Monthly* article on the Sacco and Vanzetti case,[3] written by Felix Frankfurter,[4] was really inspired by the Lord Chancellor of England. Sedgwick was at a dinner in London, and happened to be put beside the Lord Chancellor. As a good Bostonian, he had always assumed that Sacco and Vanzetti were clearly guilty, but the Lord Chancellor told him that he had doubts

1 Ellery Sedgwick (1872–1960), editor of the *Atlantic Monthly* from 1908 to 1938.
2 Moorfield Storey (1845–1929), American lawyer and publicist who campaigned strongly against political corruption.
3 The Sacco-Vanzetti trial was a cause célèbre throughout much of the 1920s. Two Italian "anarchists," Nicola Sacco and Bartolomeo Vanzetti, were arrested on May 5, 1920, and charged with a payroll holdup and murder in South Braintree, Massachusetts. Their trial, which lasted from May 31 to July 14, 1921, ended in their conviction, and they were sentenced to death. The case attracted worldwide attention. The two men were executed August 23, 1927, more than seven years after their original arrest.
4 Felix Frankfurter (1882–1965) was on the faculty of the Harvard Law School from 1914 to 1939, when he was named to the Supreme Court by President Franklin D. Roosevelt. He served there until his retirement in 1962.

about it, and so when Sedgwick got back to Boston he began looking into the matter. He was informed that Frankfurter knew more about the case than anyone else, and so put him to work on the article. Frankfurter came in with a manuscript sufficient for a whole book.[1] It was boiled down for the *Atlantic Monthly*. It made a gigantic sensation in Boston, and some of the local bigwigs put Sedgwick into Coventry. He told me that the celebrated Lowell report was really the work of Stratton.[2] Stratton pretends to be a ballistics expert, and he believes that he has evidence that Sacco actually fired the shot which killed the paymaster. His conviction communicated itself to Lowell and Grant, and so they were prejudiced from the beginning of their investigation. Sedgwick told me that he believes himself that there is sound reason for suspecting Sacco of firing the shot, but that he has been unable to find any plausible evidence against Vanzetti.

At the time the Frankfurter article came out in the *Atlantic Monthly*, Harvard was carrying on a campaign to raise money for its Law School, in which Frankfurter is a professor. The rich Babbitts immediately served notice that they would give nothing, and poor Lowell was in a quandary. At this juncture, Mrs. John D. Rockefeller, Jr. sent him a check for $150,000, and so the Law School had its money. Later on, the Babbitts got over their terror, and contributed more.

APRIL 27, 1932.

F. Scott Fitzgerald and his wife were here to lunch yesterday. Mrs. Fitzgerald is a patient at the Phipps Clinic. The poor girl went insane in Paris a year or so ago, and is still plainly more or less off her base. She managed to get through lunch quietly enough, but there was a wild look in her eye, and now and then she showed plain signs of her mental distress. Fitzgerald is staying at the Rennert Hotel, looking after her. Her illness has brought him an enormous expense, and he

---

1 Frankfurter's article, entitled "The Case of Sacco and Vanzetti," ran to twenty-four pages in the March 1927 issue of *The Atlantic Monthly*. While not deciding the guilt or innocence of the two accused men, it excoriated the conduct of the trial judge and called for a new trial.

2 Governor Alvan T. Fuller of Massachusetts appointed an Advisory Committee of three men to review the case and make recommendations to him: Samuel W. Stratton, president of the Massachusetts Institute of Technology; Robert Grant, Boston jurist and author; and Abbott Lawrence Lowell, president of Harvard. The committee supported the original jury verdict.

has been forced to plug away at stories for *The Saturday Evening Post* in order to get through. He told me that Lorimer[1] had reduced him from $4,000 to $3,500 a story. He has not published a novel for six years. During that time he has been at work on one, but so far it is not finished.

He told me that he had dropped out deliberately, on the ground that he needed time to think things out anew. He began to write at 22, and had quickly exhausted all his store of experience. In the later twenties he found that his books were beginning to run thin, and so he decided to stop writing serious novels for a while and try to accumulate new experience. To that end he went to Paris, and has since done a good deal of traveling. Unfortunately, Fitzgerald is a heavy drinker, and most of his experience has been got in bars. The illness of his wife has been a great burden to him, for he seems to be devoted to her. They have one child, a girl now ten years old.

Fitzgerald is related to various old Maryland families, including that of Francis Scott Key. During his stay in Baltimore he has gone into southern Maryland to visit the tombs of his ancestors. He is a charming fellow, and when sober makes an excellent companion. Unfortunately, liquor sets him wild and he is apt, when drunk, to knock over a dinner table, or run his automobile into a bank building.

BALTIMORE, MAY 6, 1932.

Several letters come in from Philip Goodman, who lately went abroad with Sinclair Lewis. Goodman had no idea that Lewis would be going with him. One night he went to Lewis's house to say goodbye, and Lewis decided, of a sudden, to go along. They sailed on the North German Lloyd *Dresden*, and Lewis gave out an interview at the dock saying that I had gone on the water-wagon, and that marriage had ruined me. He was drunk at the time and picked up the stuff from Nathan, who had gone down to see him off, and to grab some publicity thereby.

Goodman now reports by letter that Lewis made a dreadful ass of himself on the voyage. He says: "If Red continues day after day to be

---

1 George Horace Lorimer (1867–1937) became editor of *The Saturday Evening Post* in 1899 and continued to be associated with the Curtis Publishing Company in one capacity or another until his death.

muzzy I will quit him. He is loud, endlessly narratory, and insultingly familiar. I surely let myself in for something." In another letter he speaks of Lewis's new book as follows: "If you like the Elsie Dinsmore books you'll like 'Ann Vickers,' Red's latest, though the Elsie books are better written, better planned, and their integrity, however innocent, is better preserved. That Ann, from beginning to end, is dull and commonplace is not the point of my quarrel, but that Red doesn't for a moment interest me in her dullness and commonplaceness. In a word, he, himself, is not aware of it. He certainly has hit a new low—ay, a shameful new low. You will find it filled with Red's characteristic table-chatter, parenthetically introduced, to say nothing of the most flagrantly ignorant out-of-character dialogue. But these words, remember, are for *your* eyes alone."

He also says: "There's a young honeymoon couple aboard. Red has taken a fancy to the wife. He woke me up this morning to tell me that he thinks there's 'hope' for him before the voyage is over. Leave it to him, in such matters, to know when to strike the iron when it's cold. The poor blind idiot!"

NEW YORK, SEPTEMBER 22, 1932.

Phil Goodman and his daughter and son-in-law[1] came in last night for dinner, and we spent the evening together. They were full of talk of the Sinclair Lewises. Ruth, the daughter, and her husband spent ten days at the Lewis place in Vermont during August. Lewis was on two big drunks during that time, and in the intervals stocked up heavily on Canadian beer and sherry.

He has got rid of his first wife, Gracie, by paying her $38,000 cash. In their alimony arrangement he was to pay her $10,000 a year. Gracie concluded, in view of his incessant drinking, that he hadn't much longer to live, and so she was eager to settle with him for a substantial sum in cash, for, in the event of his death, her alimony would cease altogether. She demanded $50,000, but he beat her down to $38,000. He hadn't even that much money, but his present wife, Dorothy, gave him $10,000 out of her own earnings. According to the Goodmans, Dorothy herself is convinced that Lewis can't last much longer. In fact, she is continuing her newspaper and magazine work on the the-

1 Ruth Goodman Goetz, the daughter of Philip Goodman, and her husband, Augustus Goetz (1900–1957), collaborated on many plays, and are best known for *The Heiress*, a stage and (later) screen version of Henry James' *Washington Square*.

ory that he will die soon and that she'll then have herself and her child to support.

Lewis has accumulated very little money. During the past ten or twelve years his earnings have probably run beyond $600,000, but all he has to show for them is his place in Vermont, which would probably not bring $15,000. The $30,000 advance that he drew on "Ann Vickers," now running serially in the *Red Book,* is gone. He is trying to sell the movie rights to "Ann Vickers," but so far without success. The Jews have offered him $30,000, but he is holding out for $50,000. In order to earn the $30,000 advance received from Doubleday, Doran, the book will have to sell 60,000 copies. He is receiving a straight twenty per cent., and the price is $2.50.

Goodman told me in detail of Lewis's behavior when the two of them went abroad together last Spring. They were seated at the captain's table, with Lewis on the captain's right. He began by ordering champagne for all the other guests at the table. They refused to drink with him, and he flew into a rage. At the second meal he came near getting into a fight with one of the German passengers. During the voyage he made such uproars that the head steward talked seriously of putting some restraint on him.

NEW YORK, OCTOBER 18, 1932.

Alfred Knopf and I went to Garden City today to have lunch with the executives of Doubleday, Doran and Company. The trip was a sheer horror. From the time the train emerges from the tunnel until the time it reaches Garden City it runs through an endless series of railroad yards and dilapidated suburbs. Nothing more depressing could be imagined. Today it was even worse than usual because a fine rain was falling.

At Garden City we met Nelson Doubleday, Harry E. Maule, DeGraff, Reginald Townsend,[1] editor of *Country Life,* and another man, whose name I forget. The talk was almost wholly about the horrible state of the publishing business. Standing on the floor of one

---

1 Nelson Doubleday (1889–1949), American book publisher. Harry E. Maule (1886–1971) was at that time an editor at Doubleday, Doran and later at Random House. Robert F. DeGraff (1895–1981) was a director of Doubleday, Doran. Somewhat later, as president of Pocket Books, Inc., he did much to introduce the paperback book to American culture. Reginald Townsend (1890–1977) served as editor of *Country Life* from 1920 to 1935. He was also active in a number of other businesses, including an advertising agency.

of the rooms, along one of the walls, was a series of bronze busts of authors. It included busts of Arnold Bennett, Frank Swinnerton, Edgar Wallace and Christopher Morley. They were made by Jo Davidson, and the report is that they cost Doubleday, Doran and Company $5,000 a piece. They were ordered by Doran, and his imprudence, so I hear, was one of the main reasons for his expulsion from the firm. The rest of the executives obviously look upon them with an unfriendly eye, for they were not even decently displayed.

NEW YORK, OCTOBER 19, 1932.

William Lengel,[1] of the *Cosmopolitan* magazine, came in this afternoon, and we sat for a couple of hours drinking Scotch. Lengel served on *Cosmopolitan* during the administration of Ray Long. He tells me that Long began to show a certain mental aberration two or three years ago. He became excessively jealous of the business manager of the magazine, and devoted a large part of his time to intrigues against him. Simultaneously, he developed a vast desire to shine as a literary connoisseur, and so filled the magazine with stuff that was far over the heads of its customers. In the end the business manager prevailed against him at the Hearst headquarters, and he lost his job.

Lengel hints that he received a salary of about $60,000. In addition, he had a practically unlimited expense account, and made heavy use of it. Long is now in the South Seas with a woman. She is not a movie gal, as the New York report has it, but a girl who was formerly employed by the *Cosmopolitan*. Her name is Temple. When Long departed for Tahiti with her he sent his wife $6,500, along with a letter instructing her to throw up the lease of their apartment and sell its contents, including his own clothes. He added, however, that his dress suits were to be excepted. Altogether, his fantastic trip to the South Seas suggests a romantic idiot more than a sensible man.

Lengel says that most of the money Long brought away from his *Cosmopolitan* job is now gone. He has practically withdrawn from his book publishing business, and it is headed for the rocks. Altogether, the collapse of this man seems to me to make an extraordinary story.

1 William C. Lengel (d. 1965) served in various capacities in the Hearst magazine structure from 1920 to 1933. He was also the author, usually under pseudonyms, of a number of novels, plays, and short stories.

BALTIMORE, OCTOBER 20, 1932.

Ellen Glasgow[1] was here to lunch last Sunday. She was motoring back to Richmond from New York. The old girl is deaf and carries a loud speaker, but she uses it adroitly, and is pretty good company. She drank two stiff sherrys before lunch, got her full share of a bottle of claret, and then topped off with a big drink of brandy. These stimulants made her garrulous. I had to leave at 2.30 to go to New York, but she remained on, talking to Sara. She had little to say, save gossip.

She pretended to loathe the literary teas and other such parties to which she has been going in New York, but it is well known in publishing circles that she really enjoys such things vastly, and is keenly alive to their advertising value to her books.

BALTIMORE, OCTOBER 30, 1932.

Jim Tully[2] came down from New York yesterday afternoon, and after dinner went to Pearl's house with me for the meeting of the club. Today he returned here for lunch, remaining until after four o'clock. Sometime ago he paid a visit to William Randolph Hearst at San Simeon, California, and at lunch today he was full of the story.

He says that the Hearst palace is of enormous extent, and that Hearst employs a woman architect by the year to build additions to it. Week in and week out it is filled with guests, some of them politicians and other such public characters, but most of them movie people from Hollywood. The chatelaine is Hearst's girl, Marion Davies. She now lives in the place, and presides at all meals. When a Hollywooder receives an invitation it is accompanied by a note saying that his railroad ticket is waiting for him at the station. On taking it up he finds that it entitles him to a compartment. The train reaches San Luis Obispo, the nearest railroad point, at about four o'clock in the morning. The visitors are then hauled thirty-five miles by automobile to the

1 Ellen Glasgow (1874–1945), prolific author of such Southern novels as *Barren Ground, The Romantic Comedians, They Stooped to Folly, Vein of Iron*, and *In This Our Life*, for which she won a Pulitzer Prize in 1942.
2 Jim Tully (1891–1947), "hobo" author of *Beggars of Life, Circus Parade, Shanty Irish, Laughter in Hell*. He and Mencken were good friends, and there is an extensive correspondence between them. When Sara Haardt, Mencken's future wife, went out to Hollywood in 1927 to write movie scripts, he asked Tully to take care of her.

Hearst ranch-house, which stands on the mountainside, from which the distant ocean may be seen.

Hearst does not show up for breakfast, and usually he is also invisible at lunch, but he is always present at dinner. The guests are informed that they are expected to be prompt at dinner, but sometimes Hearst keeps them waiting for an hour. They stand around somewhat uneasily, for most of them are afraid of him, especially the movie people. Tully says that the legend is that all of the servants are detectives, and that most of the rooms are fitted with dictaphones. The whole atmosphere of the place is sinister and unpleasant, and Tully says that he got out after four days with a great feeling of relief.

It is not uncommon for the guests to fight. When this happens they are summoned to their rooms, their bags are packed, and they are informed by the servant that they will be headed back to San Luis Obispo at once. Tully, who is a very innocent fellow, was in great fear that he might do something that would induce Hearst to kick him out in this manner. It is considered disgraceful in Hollywood to suffer that experience. Sometime ago Hearst heaved out an actor on the ground that the actor had brought with him a woman to whom he was not married. Despite the fact that Marion Davies was in the house, this episode did not seem humorous to the movie people. Tully says that a short while before his visit there had been an enormous fight one evening among drunken actors. As a result, Hearst forbade the circulation of jugs after dinner. This bore harshly on Tully. He was relieved by Marion Davies, who produced a couple of bottles of Scotch. They were drunk in Tully's room by Davies, Tully himself, Constance Talmadge[1] and Hearst's son, George. Champagne is served at dinner, but nothing else. It is common for forty guests to be present and Hearst, at a pinch, could entertain two hundred.

Tully says that the house is hideous, but that some of the rooms are beautifully turned out. The library, in particular, is a lovely room. Tully says that he went into it half a dozen times, but never met any other guests there. The more valuable books are all under lock and key, for it would be folly to trust them to some of the movie guests.

Tully is apparently still more or less in love with his wife, Marna, from whom he was divorced a year or two ago. Marna has since re-

---

1 Constance Talmadge (1900–1973), motion picture actress in the days of the silent screen. She retired in 1929, with the advent of the talking picture.

married. Tully is abandoning his house in Hollywood, where the two lived together, and is building a new house on a lake four or five miles away. The situation of the place, as he describes it, seems very lovely, but I suspect that he'll be lonely living in the house alone. He seems to be in mortal terror that some other girl will fetch him. My belief is that this uneasiness is well justified. He'll probably fall for a movie girl next time, and she will make off with what remains of his money. Apparently, Marna got less than report gave her at the time.

Tully has a son nineteen years old by a first marriage. The boy is apparently not much. Sometime ago Tully had to get him out of jail. He is now studying the art and mystery of a filling station manager at a school maintained by the Standard Oil Company in Los Angeles. When he graduates he will be given charge of a filling station.

Tully's daughter, who has the name of Trilby, is now fourteen years old. He says that she is very beautiful, and also intelligent. He seems to be very proud of her. She has artistic tastes, and hopes to be a designer. Tully did not say just what she proposes to design. He said that he had promised to give her a couple of years in Paris if she made good progress at home.

BALTIMORE, NOVEMBER 3, 1932.

Today the Germania Club gave a luncheon at the Southern Hotel in honor of Henry Sigerist,[1] the new Professor of the History of Medicine at the Johns Hopkins. Twenty-eight members were present, and there were four or five speeches.

I sat beside Dr. William H. Welch, who is now eighty-two or three, and begins to look it. His face is whitening, and the large yellow freckles which sprinkle it begin to stand out in an almost startling manner. The old man is a walking refutation of the doctrines of some of his colleagues. He has been a hearty eater and drinker all his life, and has been much overweight for many years. Yet he continues in reasonably good health in his eighties. Theoretically, a man of his round belly and thick neck should have died in the forties.[2]

Welch is full of interesting anecdotes about his early days in Ger-

1 Dr. Henry E. Sigerist (1891–1957) succeeded Dr. William H. Welch as director of the Institute of the History of Medicine in 1932.
2 See Mencken's article "Moral Tale," *Chrestomathy*, pp. 372–74.

many. He told me that when he notified Carl Ludwig[1] at Leipzig that he proposed to proceed to Berlin and enter Rudolf Virchow's[2] laboratory, Ludwig denounced Virchow bitterly. Welch protested that Virchow certainly deserved some respect, for he was the founder of the cellular pathology. Ludwig answered: "Well, what of it? Wasn't the cellular pathology obvious? Once it had been discovered that the normal body was made up of cells, it certainly followed inevitably that diseased tissue was of the same composition." Ludwig was so hot against Virchow that he persuaded Welch to go to Cohnheim[3] instead. This change of plans undoubtedly had a considerable effect upon the subsequent course of Welch's life and, by corollary, upon the history of pathology in America.

BALTIMORE, NOVEMBER 5, 1932.

Fred Essary[4] was at the office telling about Hoover's adventures on the stump. As everyone knows, Hoover was disinclined to make any active campaign. His original plan was to sit in Washington and maintain a magnificent silence. But when it became apparent that things were going against him, he had to take to the road. Essary says that he was in mortal terror of assassination. During his first two trips he refused absolutely to take part in any street parades.

At Cleveland the town was thick with police and militia, and guards were actually posted in the sewers under the streets that Hoover had to traverse. He was booed everywhere he went. At Detroit the police threatened to beat up any one who booed him, so the crowd compromised by thumbing its noses at him as he passed. Essary said the spectacle of thousands of people with their thumbs to their noses was really most astonishing.

As the campaign progressed and no bombs were set off Hoover began to recover his courage, and toward the end he consented to appear in parades of some length.

1 Carl Ludwig (1816–1895), German scientist who pioneered modern studies in physiology.
2 Rudolf Virchow (1821–1902), German scientist and political leader internationally known for his contributions to pathology, social medicine, and public health.
3 Julius Friedrich Cohnheim (1839–1884), German pathologist noted especially for studies of inflammation and pus formation.
4 J. Fred Essary (1881–1942) headed the *Sun*'s Washington bureau for many years.

1933

Joe Hergesheimer called up from West Chester to say that he had resigned from the National Institute of Arts and Letters. He said that he had instructed his secretary, some time ago, to go over his list of clubs, and to send in his resignation to those in which his dues were paid up. The National Institute happened to be one of them. I gathered from his talk that, if he had noticed the fact, he'd have instructed the secretary to except it. Nevertheless, he professed to be greatly pleased that he was out of it. His attitude in this matter is beyond me. It seems to me that he stooped a good deal when he allowed the National Institute to elect him in the first place. He knew very well what cads were in it, but he couldn't resist the flattery. That was eight or nine years ago. On various occasions since he told me that he was about to resign. But he actually waited until his secretary resigned for him by a sort of error.

Alfred Knopf was here over the week-end. He came in Friday night, had lunch and dinner here on Saturday, went to the Saturday Night Club with me in the evening, dropped in with Sidney Nyburg[1] Sunday afternoon, and was here for lunch on Monday. There was plenty of time for talk.

I told him that I thought it was time for me to begin thinking of

1 Sydney Nyburg (1880–1957), Baltimore attorney and bibliophile, who wrote novels and stories as an avocation.

retiring from the editorship of the *American Mercury*. At the end of
1933 I'll have had ten years of it. The job takes up a great deal of my
time. I not only edit the magazine almost single-handed, for Angoff[1]
is fit only for routine, but also write from 6,000 to 12,000 words for it
every month. I told Knopf that I thought it was unwise to identify me
with the magazine so thoroughly—that as the sales of my books fall
off it must suffer correspondingly. Soon or late I must retire, and it is
best to think of the business now, before it is forced on us. I suggested
that Henry Hazlitt, now of the *Nation*, might make a good successor.[2]
I shall see him in New York shortly, and sound him out. I told Knopf
that I'd be willing to go on contributing to the magazine—either a
regular department or occasional articles. Those articles could be so
written that they would fit into books. My present editorials are useless
for that purpose.

Knopf and I discussed the history of the magazine at great length.
He seems to be coming over to my view that it was mismanaged by
his father, who fought for a large circulation and heavy general advertising, and so forced various changes in policy on me. I told Alfred
that I thought it should be far more literary than it has been, and far
less political—that we should not try to match *Harper's*, *Scribner's* and
the *Atlantic* in their appeal to persons interested in public questions.[3]
He said that he believed that he had made an error at the start by not
putting up a definite capital for the magazine. Instead, he simply made
advances from Alfred A. Knopf, Inc. At the moment those advances
amount to about $30,000. But they are being slowly reduced, and were
never much more.

1 Charles Angoff (1902–1979) became Mencken's assistant on *The American Mercury*
   in 1925 and continued to work for him until Mencken's own retirement at the end
   of 1933. He served for a time as editor of the magazine in 1934 and 1935. Angoff's
   book *H. L. Mencken: A Portrait from Memory* (New York: Thomas Yoseloff, 1956)
   is a bitter and vitriolic attack on his former employer. He also wrote many novels
   and volumes of literary history and criticism.
2 Mencken did resign the editorship of *The American Mercury* at the end of 1933 and
   was succeeded by Henry Hazlitt (b. 1894). The arrangement proved unsatisfactory,
   however, and after only four months Knopf secured Hazlitt's resignation. See M. K.
   Singleton, *H. L. Mencken and the American Mercury Adventure* (Durham, N.C.:
   Duke University Press, 1962), pp. 238–41; also the entry for December 3, 1934
   (pp. 70–72).
3 Coming from Mencken, this remark has a certain irony in it, since it was he—
   against the wishes of both Knopf and Nathan—who from the very first issue of the
   Mercury made it a vehicle for political and social commentary, with literature and
   the other arts occupying only a minor place.

BALTIMORE, FEBRUARY 2, 1933.

T. S. Eliot has been here all week, lecturing on poetry at the Johns Hopkins. He is being entertained by George Boas,[1] associate professor of philosophy at the Hopkins and a contributor to the *Atlantic Monthly*—a brisk, clever Jew. Yesterday Boas's wife called up and said that Eliot wanted to see me. She invited Sara and me to dinner for last night. Sara is ill in bed. I asked her to tell Mrs. Boas that I couldn't come to dinner, but that I'd drop in during the evening. I got to the Boases' house at 9.45 and found the Boases, Eliot and an unknown woman named Smith sitting about the fire. Mrs. Boas was already yawning. She is a French Jewess. Though she is polite, she finds it hard to conceal her distrust of me as a German.

Eliot turned out to be a tall, somewhat ungainly fellow, looking more like an Oxford man than any Englishman. He said that he was having a quiet but tolerable time at Harvard. He lectures once a week, has a weekly tea-party open to undergraduates, and also gives a course in modern English literature—that is, since 1890. He told me that he found the last somewhat difficult, for he seldom reads modern literature, and in the main dislikes it. He said that one of the undergraduates brought a pretty girl to tea one day, and almost broke up the party. Eliot served notice that he'd prefer to have no female guests. His job leaves him time to accept lecture engagements.

An amiable fellow, but with little to say. He told me that his father was a brick manufacturer in Missouri. No talk of religion. We discussed magazine prices. He charges 7/6 a copy for the *Criterion*. He believes that J. C. Squire's effort to increase the circulation of the *London Mercury* by reducing its price from 2/6 to 1s. a copy has been a failure. I drank a quart of home-brew beer, and Eliot got down two Scotches. A dull evening. I left at 11.45, and had to take the Smith girl home. Fortunately, it turned out that she lived at Cathedral and Monument streets, only half a block from 704 Cathedral.

---

1 George Boas (1891–1980), professor of philosophy at the Johns Hopkins University. His wife, the former Simone Brangier, was a native of France and achieved a considerable reputation in this country as a sculptor.

BALTIMORE, MARCH 18, 1933.

Last night Sara and I dined with F. Scott Fitzgerald and his wife, Zelda. It was a somewhat weird evening. The Fitzgeralds live in an old-fashioned house in the woods near Towson, almost half a mile off the high-road. Its spookiness is not diminished by the fact that Zelda is palpably only half sane. She and her husband moved to Baltimore, indeed, in order that she might be near the Phipps Clinic, and three young doctors from it were the other dinner guests, along with the Fitzgeralds' ten-year-old daughter, Scotty.

The fact that Zelda is somewhat abnormal is instantly evident. She occupies herself largely in painting, and her paintings are full of grotesque exaggerations and fantastic ideas. Scott himself also begins to show signs of a disordered mind. Sometime ago he had what he now calls a nervous breakdown, and was in the hands of the psychiatrists for a couple of months. Considering his life during the past few years it is no wonder that he has begun to break up. Save when Zelda happened to be in a sanitarium, he has been in close contact with her day and night, and at various times her vagaries have been of a very disturbing and even shocking character. In addition, Scott is a heavy drinker. He has been trying for six years to write a new novel, but it remains unfinished. He told me that he had done 35,000 words on it during the past Winter, but apparently he is still rather far from the end.

Meanwhile, he has sought to raise money by writing dreadful drivel for the *Saturday Evening Post.* This work formerly brought him a large income, but of late the *Post* has greatly reduced its expenditures, and so the poor fellow is rather hard up. In fact, he told Sara that at the time of the bank moratorium two weeks ago he had only $300. in bank. Zelda's illness has probably been extremely expensive, for the psychiatrists demand extravagant fees, and the sanitariums they operate are run like Palm Beach hotels. Altogether, Scott's situation is very distressing.

Apparently Zelda takes no interest whatever in household affairs. She had not even planned the seating of her guests, and the dinner had apparently been arranged by the cook. After dinner Sara and Zelda sat on a sofa together to talk of their early days in Montgomery. Sara told me that Zelda gritted her teeth during the whole conversation.

The little girl, Scotty, is very bright, but shows a dreadful nervousness. At dinner she was constantly handling the candlesticks on the table.

Just why we were invited to dinner I don't know. Scott called up early in the week and said that he had to see me on business, but he mentioned no business while we were in the house. The evening broke in one of the busiest weeks I have ever encountered, and so I was reluctant to go.

NEW YORK, JUNE 13, 1933.

Tom Beer dropped in this afternoon with a manuscript. It turned out on reading to be very feeble stuff, and concocting an excuse for not printing it presented some difficulties. However, I managed to do so. It embodies some reminiscences of Beer's grandfather, who was a judge out in Ohio, and the central incident is a snake story in which a so-called milk snake steals milk from a nursing mother. This gave me a way out, for I could plead that the incident would offend most readers.

Beer talked at some length of George Horace Lorimer, editor of the *Saturday Evening Post*, with whom he is on close terms. He said that Lorimer for the past few years has been greatly harassed by Cyrus H. K. Curtis,[1] who died last week. Curtis believed that he was himself an editor, and so favored Lorimer with frequent advice. Since the beginning of the depression it had been to the general effect that the *Saturday Evening Post* ought to be gay in tone. Lorimer protested that filling it with trivial stuff changed its character, and probably alienated many readers, but Curtis insisted. The result was a great mass of stuff by Wodehouse,[2] and other such fluffy writers. Now that Curtis is dead, Lorimer will go back to a more serious tone. Unluckily, he'll still be harassed by advice from the front office, for Curtis' daughter and step-daughter are ladies with large opinions of their own wisdom. Lorimer is now 65, and growing somewhat weary. Unfortunately, he has brought up no likely successor to himself. His

1 Cyrus H. K. Curtis (1850–1933) was the founder of the *Ladies' Home Journal* and head of the Curtis Publishing Company, which published the *Journal* and *The Saturday Evening Post*.
2 P. G. Wodehouse (1881–1975), prolific English author of humorous novels and stories, creator of Jeeves, Bertie Wooster, Mr. Mulliner.

chief aide is Costain,[1] who is a Canadian newspaper man of some ability. But he confines himself entirely to articles, and is not interested in fiction.

Col. Amos W. W. Woodcock[2] came to lunch today. He is an Eastern Shoreman who became U.S. district attorney at Baltimore in 1922, and was made the chief investigator for the Wickersham Commission on its organization. When it made its report he became director of the Bureau of Prohibition at Washington. He went out of office with Hoover, and now proposes to write a book on his experiences. He came to see me for advice. I was not acquainted with him, but he had a letter of introduction from Raymond S. Tompkins.[3]

Woodcock said that his work for the Wickersham Commission convinced him that Prohibition was doomed. He now believes that the repeal resolution will be approved by every State—that there will be no dry States. He told me that he seldom saw Hoover, and I judge that he did not like him. He says that when he told Hoover that the 18th Amendment would have to be modified Hoover rejected the idea, saying that modification would imperil the amendment itself and that he was in favor of maintaining it. Woodcock says he does not know why Hoover issued his famous false summary of the contents of the Wickersham report. He says that the Commission had nothing to do with it.

He says that it was unusual, in his days as a prosecutor, to find bootleg beer running beyond 3.4% of alcohol by weight, which is but 2 points above the present legal beer. He says that home-brew made by small bootleggers was sometimes stronger, but that beer made in breweries was not.

1 Thomas B. Costain (1885–1965) was born in Canada but became an American citizen in 1920. He served as chief associate editor of *The Saturday Evening Post* from that year until 1934. Later he achieved fame as the author of many works, both fiction and nonfiction, on medieval English history.
2 Colonel Amos W. W. Woodcock (1883–1964) served on the Wickersham Commission and in 1930 was named director of Prohibition enforcement by President Hoover. The projected book mentioned in the same paragraph was apparently never written.
3 Raymond S. Tompkins (1890–1949) worked for the *Sun* from 1915 to 1924 but left the paper to become an officer of the Baltimore Transit Company.

W. is a small, neat, smooth-shaven, baldheaded fellow. He says that he was not greatly interested in Prohibition when he became district attorney, though he is a Methodist and a teetotaler.

BALTIMORE, AUGUST 2, 1933.

Paul Patterson has come home from Europe. He went to the Economic Conference in London, and then spent a couple of weeks loafing in France. He told me that he had a private session one night with Cordell Hull,[1] head of the American delegation. Hull complained bitterly about his associates, and discussed them frankly. Pittman,[2] he said, was simply a sales agent for the silver miners, and knew nothing else. Couzens[3] was a hollow demagogue, and cynical of the whole show. The Texas banker, whose name I forget, was only a Texas banker. Cox[4] was no more than an Ohio politician.

Paul says that when Moley[5] arrived in London accompanied by Herbert Swope the English, who believed that he was really Roosevelt's special and confidential agent, fell upon him at once, and gave him their social third degree. For four or five days and nights they played the hose on him, while Swope kept calling up the *Sun's* headquarters in the Savoy Hotel to announce that great events were impending. Finally, Moley came to Hull with the news that he had hornswoggled the English into a favorable agreement—that is, favorable to the United States. But when he described it, it turned out to be simply what they had been trying to put over on Hull. Moley, crestfallen, then vanished, and during the rest of his stay in London he was invisible.

Paul told Hull that he thought Roosevelt's cablegram blowing up the conference was an invasion of Hull's *amour propre*, and that Roo-

1 Cordell Hull (1871–1955), secretary of state in the administration of Franklin D. Roosevelt.
2 Key Pittman (1872–1940), U.S. senator from Nevada from 1913 until his death.
3 James Couzens (1872–1936), starting as an executive in the Ford Motor Company, became mayor of Detroit and subsequently U.S. senator from Michigan from 1922 until a few months before his death.
4 James M. Cox (1870–1957) served two terms as governor of Ohio. He was the Democratic candidate for president in 1920 but was defeated by Warren G. Harding.
5 Raymond Moley (1886–1975), journalist, editor, author, and political economist. In 1933 he became assistant secretary of state under President Roosevelt but later strongly criticized the administration.

sevelt ought to do or say something to make up for it. Hull replied: "I am a dumb fellow, but despite my dumbness the same idea has oc-cured to me." But he is still in office, and apparently on good terms with Roosevelt. Meanwhile, Moley seems to have dropped out of favor, for he has been reduced from *haute politique* to chasing kid-napers.

BALTIMORE, OCTOBER 19, 1933.

Hergesheimer was here last night talking about living authors. He told me that he'd rather have written Ring Lardner's "You Know Me, Al" than Cabell's "Jurgen."[1] So would I, but it seemed rather odd for Hergie to say so.

BALTIMORE, OCTOBER 23, 1933.

In the current issue of the *Atlantic Monthly* the two leading book reviews are of Atlantic Monthly Press books. In addition, Sedgwick prints an extremely favorable review, written by himself and signed by his initials, of "This Changing World," by Samuel Fels, the Cin-cinnati soap manufacturer and uplifter. Also, in this same issue, there is a full page advertisement of Fels's soap. Obviously, the New En-gland Puritans have begun to stretch the rigid moral principles of their forefathers.

1 Ring Lardner (1885–1933), humorist and short story writer. His first collection of stories, *You Know Me, Al* (1916), probably remains his best-known work. James Branch Cabell (1879–1958), Virginia-born novelist, author of *The Cream of the Jest, Jurgen, Beyond Life*. Mencken had a very great admiration for Cabell's work and wrote favorable reviews of almost all of his books; he actively defended *Jurgen* when an attempt was made to suppress it on grounds of obscenity.

1934

Raymond Pearl tells me that he hears from W. G. MacCallum, head of the department of pathology at the Johns Hopkins, that the records of the hospital show only two autopsies by William H. Welch during the whole of his career there. This news is surely not surprising. Welch was one of the laziest men ever heard of, and even in his earliest days at the Hopkins he spent most of his time trying to dodge work. After his appointment he was sent abroad by Daniel Gilman[1] to pick up the latest ideas in Germany. He overstayed his leave by at least six months, and even after he got home he did very little work. His so-called scientific achievements were of the most meagre. He discovered two bacilli, but in those days any one with a microscope could discover one at will. He was not even a good pedagogue: he was simply a medical politician.

His great fame in the world was probably due mainly to his extraordinary talent for getting publicity. He always managed to make himself the center of situations, and he greatly enjoyed the adulation which bathed him in his later years. At one of the last lunch parties he attended I happened to sit beside him. The usual extravagant compliments were hurled at him, and I asked him politely if they did not bore him. He confessed frankly that he liked them. In those later years he went out to dinner almost every night, and usually managed to attend a lunch party by day and at least one medical meeting.

It was generally believed at the Johns Hopkins that Welch, who

---

1 Daniel Coit Gilman (1831–1908) in 1875 became the first president of the Johns Hopkins University.

was a bachelor, was worth at least a million, and that all of his money would be left to the medical school. He actually left three-fourths of it to his niece and two nephews, all of whom were already rich. The fourth share he left, not to the medical school in general, but to the Welch Memorial Library and the School of Hygiene, the first of which was his monument and the second of which was his pet. He left a few bequests of $100 each to the poor old girls who slaved for him in the Welch Memorial Library. How much his estate amounts to I don't know, but it is probably less valuable than rumor made it.

Welch was one of the most selfish men ever heard of. From end to end of his life his operations were planned with a view to his own advantage. He was not above walking out on friends in difficulty, as he did notably in the case of Raymond Pearl. I think that most competent men would say that he was the least talented of the four original medical school professors. Halsted stood clearly at the head of the list, with Osler a good distance below him. Probably on a level with Osler stood Kelly; then there was another drop to Welch.

His family connections and his social talents gave him access to men of money, and he worked them to a fare-you-well. His great influence at the Hopkins was due mainly to this fact. He brought in more money than all of the other members of the faculty put together, with the Board of Trustees added—in fact, he brought in at least five times as much. He always took good care to see that this money increased the celebrity of William H. Welch.

His doings during the war were of an almost shameful character. He owed everything that he knew to Germany, but when the United States went into the war he began making speeches denying that Germany had ever made any serious contribution to medicine. It seems incredible that a man in his position should have said anything so absurd, but Dr. Chr. Deetjen[1] told me only the other day that he had heard it with his own ears. He broke out into a uniform during the war, and was always on hand when publicity was on tap.

BALTIMORE, JUNE 12, 1934.

The case of F. Scott Fitzgerald becomes distressing. He is boozing in a wild manner, and has become a nuisance. His wife, Zelda, who

1 Dr. Christian Deetjen (1863–1940), a pioneer in X-ray research and treatment, was a long-time member of the Saturday Night Club.

has been insane for years, is now confined at the Sheppard-Pratt Hospital, and he is living in Park Avenue with his little daughter, Scotty, aged 12. Some time ago he appeared at the apartment of the Duffys[1] with Scotty, and horrified Anne Duffy by his performance. What he did she refuses to say, but obviously it was very shocking. Several years ago, visiting Joe Hergesheimer at West Chester, Pa., he caused a town sensation by arising at the dinner table and taking down his pantaloons, exposing his gospel pipe. Joe has refused to have anything to do with him since. He was lately laid up at the Johns Hopkins, suffering with a liver complaint. The young doctors of Baltimore avoid him as much as possible, for he has a playful habit of calling up those he knows at 3 a.m. and demanding treatment, *i.e.*, something to drink. How he manages to get any work done I can't imagine. His liver trouble is reported to be cirrhosis. He calls up the house now and then, usually proposing that Sara and I go automobiling with him, but he is always plainly tight, and Sara always puts him off. His automobile driving is fearful and wonderful.

BALTIMORE, JUNE 16, 1934.

Bishop James Cannon, Jr., and his wife were here to lunch. We had no other guests. Mrs. Cannon is a large and somewhat stout woman, obviously much younger than the bishop, and showing traces of earlier good looks. She seemed very amiable and even jolly, and the bishop himself was in good humor. They arrived at 12.30 and stayed until nearly 4.

The bishop told me that in 1914 or thereabout he went to William Jennings Bryan,[2] then Secretary of State, and asked him to support the Eighteenth Amendment, which had recently gone before Congress. Bryan refused, saying that he was against national Prohibition and believed in local option. He further objected to taking a hand on the ground that the United States had too many other problems to solve, some of them more important. A bit later, when the Amendment polled a majority vote in Congress (it needed, of course, two-thirds)

1 Edmund Duffy (1899–1962), cartoonist for the *Sunpapers*. His work won him Pulitzer Prizes in 1931, 1934, and 1940. His wife, Anne, was a friend of Sara Mencken's.
2 William Jennings Bryan (1860–1925) was three times a candidate for the presidency of the United States and served as secretary of state in the administration of Woodrow Wilson. He ran neck and neck with Wilson and Franklin D. Roosevelt as the politician whom Mencken most thoroughly loathed.

Bryan made a sudden flop, and became one of its loudest advocates. Presently he approached Cannon, proposing to go on the stump for the Amendment in Virginia at $250 a speech. Cannon refused the offer. He told me that he was always suspicious of Bryan thereafter, and avoided him as much as possible.

Cannon is now fathering a new amendment, giving Congress "power to enact uniform laws restricting or prohibiting the traffic in alcoholic beverages in the United States and in all territory subject to its jurisdiction." This plainly marks a considerable abandonment of ground. I told Cannon that his amendment, if passed, would be useless—that it will simply keep booze in politics, with Prohibition winning now and then but always losing two years later. He professed to believe that, once it had been restored, it would stick, but it was plain to see that he was not too sure.

JULY 2, 1934.

Harry C. Black came in last night, bringing his nephew-in-law, Lieut. Alfred J. Bolton, U.S.N., and three of Bolton's shipmates, Admiral H. E. Lackey, Lieut.-Commander Carlson and Lieut. Melgaard. Admiral Lackey is commander of Cruiser Division No. 4, and is in port with his flagship, the *Northampton*. Bolton is his flag lieutenant. The others are officers of the ship. My brother August also dropped in. We had a quiet sitting, sticking to beer until midnight, when Bolton, Melgaard and I had a round of gin rickeys. It was hot in the house, but I had a big fan going, and we managed to be comfortable. Down where the *Northampton* is lying, at the B. & O. Locust Point pier, is one of the hottest spots north of the Caribbean, but I heard no complaint. Sailors take life as it comes.

These were very agreeable fellows, and it was pleasant to see the easy and yet never Kiwanish relations between the admiral and the youngsters. They plainly have a high respect for him and also a great affection. Bolton is a fine young officer, and so are the others. Both Carlson and Melgaard, I take it, are Scandinavians—blond, well set-up, and with a touch of Northern stiffness. The Naval Academy irons them all out, but it doesn't have to do much ironing of such natural sailors.

Some time ago I got myself denounced for printing a piece arguing that the officers of the Navy, taking one with another, are much su-

perior to those of the Army. I believe it the more every time I meet
men of either one service or the other. The advantage of the Navy lies
in the fact that practically all of its officers have been through Annapolis, whereas only about half of the Army men have been through West
Point. The rest come from private military academies—most of them
houses of correction for young fellows too lively for the regular colleges—, from the ranks, and from civil life. As a result there is a
considerable conflict in backgrounds and traditions, and it is not unusual to meet an Army officer who is a gentleman only by a sort of
legal fiction. The Navy shows a far greater uniformity, and a higher
average. No congenital bounder can survive the four years at Annapolis. There are too many ways to get rid of him, and too many eyes
are on the lookout.

Moreover, an officer of the Navy leads a much more civilized life
than an Army man. He travels widely, he meets his colleagues of other
Navies, and for a large part of his time he is free from the demoralizing
influence of the *Frauenzimmer*. The Army officer, at least in days of
peace, lives in a much narrower world. His post is apt to be far in the
interior, miles from anyone worth knowing, and even when he is stationed near some big coastal city he commonly lives in a cheerless fort
down the harbor, and has few contacts save with morons. Worse, his
wife follows him about, and so he is constantly involved in the petty
feuds natural to a closed society, and is forced to be content with its
imbecile amusements. At least once in his career he is likely to be given
a spell of pedagogy, teaching elementary military science to militia-
men or college students. That sort of thing is bound to leave marks
upon the best of men, as the case of General Pershing shows. The
opening of his autobiography (which, by the way, he doesn't mention
in "Who's Who in America," though he is careful to note that he is a
33° Mason) might have been written by any freshwater college professor, or even by a college president.

Thus the Army men would probably show some inferiority to the
Navy men, even if they were all West Pointers, which they are not.
They see less of the world, they are more securely hobbled by irrational conventions, and the work they do is much less interesting. Those
who have been through West Point are naturally superior to the rest,
for West Point is better than any of the American lay universities save
a few. In my editorial days I was constantly astonished by the good
writing done by West Pointers. Not a great many MSS., of course,

came from them, but practically all those that I saw showed a clear, clean English style. The graduates of none of the universities made so good a showing. Even Harvard, probably the best of them, was apparently unable to teach all of its customers how to write their native tongue decently. The cause of this I do not undertake to determine. But it may lie in the fact that the boys at West Point (as at Annapolis) are under a far stricter discipline than ordinary college boys, and are turned out with great dispatch when they show any deficiency, even if it be only in syntax—or table manners.

The *Northampton* is open to visitors, and about 7,500 went aboard yesterday. Entertaining such crowds usually costs Uncle Sam some money, for there are souvenir-hunters among them, and they pick up all sorts of loose gear. While the *Northampton* was in the North river off New York week before last a number of bayonets disappeared. But the greatest loss on record occurred some years ago, when a naval band went to West Point to help the Army celebrate something or other. On its return it appeared that the bass-drummer had lost his bass-drum! Whether it was made off with by actual thieves or by West Pointers eager to score one on the Navy is unknown to this day.

BALTIMORE, JULY 21, 1934.

Paul Patterson, John W. Owens and I went to Washington by motor on Monday, July 16, to lunch with Bishop John M. McNamara, auxiliary of the Baltimore archdiocese. This meeting was arranged by Father Edwin Leonard. The priests present besides the Bishop were Monsignor Ireton and Monsignor Quinn, both of Baltimore, and Father Sweeney of Washington. Sweeney turned out to be an extraordinarily handsome and amiable young fellow. When he went into the Church a first-rate movie star was spoiled. The meeting was very amicable, and the Bishop showed a fair and conciliatory spirit. I began the discussion by arguing that it would be impossible for the *Sun* to draw up a statement which would present its own case fairly and yet be in such terms that any priest of the archdiocese could formally approve it in advance of publication. From the *Sun*'s point of view it would have to embody some criticism of the Archbishop, and no priest could afford to associate himself with that. The Bishop agreed that this was a serious difficulty, and that the best way out would be for the

Sun to make the most conciliatory statement it could and then let the clergy take it or leave it.[1]

There was a general discussion lasting an hour and a half, and then we had an excellent lunch. Afterward we palavered for a little while longer, and the Bishop showed us his church, of which he seems to be proud, and with good reason. No agreement was reached, but we parted on the best of terms.

On Monday night, July 16, Patterson and I met at his house to discuss the *Sun*'s statement. It was hot, we were tired, and we reached no conclusion. On Tuesday he called me up to say that he had put aside all of the statements hitherto prepared and made up one of his own. He sent me a copy of it, and it seemed to me to be very effective. Unfortunately, it was made up in large part of scraps from other statements, and so it read rather roughly. I offered to rewrite it in an effort to make it more smooth and plausible, and this I did on Wednesday morning. Patterson then suggested that he put his statement and my rewriting of it before two or three men who could bring fresh minds to the problem, and this was done. The men consulted were Bill Moore and Schmick.[2] They substituted various paragraphs from my rewriting, and so finally agreed on a text. This was printed in the *Sun* for Thursday morning. Rather to the astonishment of everybody in the office, the Catholic clergy accepted the statement and declared the war off. In the *Catholic Review*, which came out on Friday, it was printed in full on the first page. Alongside it was an answer to it by Monsignor Smith, moderate in tone. Smith made some good points against the weaker parts of the *Sun*'s position, but showed no heat and ended by saying that so far as the *Catholic Review* was concerned the discussion was over.

1 S. Miles Bouton, a *Sun* foreign correspondent who had recently been expelled from Germany for writing unfavorably of the Nazi regime, published in the June 18, 1934, edition an article in which he compared Hitler to St. Ignatius Loyola. Baltimore's Archbishop Michael J. Curley was greatly incensed and demanded an apology. When one was not immediately forthcoming, he called on the Catholics of the archdiocese to boycott the *Sun*. Then he departed on a trip to Ireland, leaving the handling of the matter in the hands of his auxiliary, Bishop John M. McNamara. See my article "Mencken and the Archbishop," *Menckeniana* 93, Spring 1985, pp. 2–6.
2 William E. Moore (1878–1941) was managing editor of the *Sun*. William F. Schmick, Sr. (1883–1963), was the business manager for all the papers; he succeeded Paul Patterson as president of the A. S. Abell Company upon the latter's retirement in 1951 and continued in that capacity until 1960, when he was replaced by his son, William F. Schmick, Jr.

As I write, on Saturday July 21, I hear that the priests will tell their people tomorrow morning that the boycott of the *Sun* is off. It may be that one or two enthusiasts will deliver a parting wallop, but there will not be many of them. The higher clergy of the archdiocese have been eager from the start to make peace. All of the overtures have come from them, and their spokesmen have shown a very amiable and conciliatory spirit—in fact, Father Leonard leaned so far in the *Sun's* direction that he was kept out of the final discussion on the ground that he was a *Sun* man. I have been told that Monsignor Ireton has been hostile to the *Sun*, but if so he did not show it when we met him in the Bishop's house.

Paul Patterson dropped in on Father Wiesel, head of Loyola College, Thursday morning after the *Sun's* statement had come out. They are neighbors, and there have been some friendly exchanges by Wiesel and Mrs. Patterson. Patterson himself had not met him. The meeting was very amicable, and Wiesel said that he had been satisfied by the *Sun's* original disposition of the matter. He said that he had not replied to Patterson's letter to him simply because he regarded the dispute as ended. Patterson reported that Wiesel is a youngish man and a very pleasant fellow. Unfortunately, he is to be removed from his present position on August 1, and the report is that Father Ferdinand Wheeler of St. Ignatius is to succeed him. Wheeler has always been hostile to the *Sun*. It remains to be seen what will happen when Curley returns to Baltimore. Meanwhile, I am to keep on organizing the material that has been gathered against him, and to be prepared for any further hostilities.

The general opinion among the priests of the archdiocese seems to be that Curley sadly mismanaged the business. He allowed a fit of temper and a hot day to carry him beyond reason. He attempted to bluff the *Sun*, and when his bluff was called he found himself in serious difficulties. The boycott, as a matter of fact, was a failure. At no stage of it did the *Sun* show a loss of more than 4,000. It had hardly been put into effect before Catholics began to come back. The loss to the Sunday edition threatened to be more serious, but there was no sign that it would go far enough to cause any really heavy loss.

The position that John J. Nelligan[1] took in the business was very

---

1 John J. Nelligan (1865–1935) was a member of the Baltimore financial community and served on the board of directors of the A. S. Abell Company. His son, later Monsignor Joseph M. Nelligan, was secretary to Archbishop Curley.

creditable to him. Though he is a leading Catholic layman and the father of a priest who is actually the Archbishop's secretary, he stood by the paper from first to last, and when Patterson, Owens and I visited him last week told us that we'd naturally have to protect ourselves, and that he thought we had a right to do it by any means that seemed useful. We showed him a copy of the statement that Father Leonard had approved. He made no objection to it save to argue that in one passage we yielded too much. He told us that if the higher clergy refused to accept this statement he thought we should draw up a statement of our own, stating the facts as we saw them, and invite the clergy to take it or leave it. This was done.

BALTIMORE, OCTOBER 12, 1934.

Bishop Cannon, who is in town for Methodist orgies of some sort or other, called up this afternoon and said that he'd like to see me. He told me that he was lame and thus couldn't negotiate our high stairway, so I went down to the Lord Baltimore Hotel to wait upon him. I found him in his usual meagre room, surrounded by his usual pyramids of papers. He has been transferred to California, and apparently doesn't like it. Nevertheless, it represents victory for him, for an influential faction in his church tried to get rid of him altogether at the last general Conference. He made a tremendous battle, and the two sides compromised by sending him to California.

He told me that he was convinced that it would be impossible, at least for many years, to restore the 18th Amendment to the Constitution. He is now advocating a much milder amendment. It simply gives Congress the power to pass legislation dealing with the liquor traffic. I asked him why, after its colossal defeat in the late referendum, the Methodist church kept on howling for prohibition. He said that the reason was that if it abandoned the cause there would be no advocates of it left. There is in the whole country, he pointed out, no other agency pledged to war on the abuse of alcohol. This is true enough, but the fact remains nevertheless that the Methodists go beyond temperance to prohibition, and that the country is plainly against it, and will remain so for a good many years.

The Bishop told me a great deal of interesting stuff about the government of his church. He said that union between the North and South branches was blocked by the fact that the Northern branch had many colored members, and also a colored bishop. The Southerners, he said, would not object to a colored bishop presiding over their Conference—in fact, they have often invited colored clergymen to address them—, but if a colored bishop were assigned to a Southern Conference his power to make appointments to charges would probably get him into difficulties. In this field, under the Methodist polity, a bishop has tremendous powers. He can send a pastor anywhere he pleases within the limits of his Conference. Naturally enough, he is under constant pressure from pastors who want good charges, and from congregations which desire the best available preachers. If a colored bishop were put in this position racial animosities would constantly show themselves, and the church would face ruin. The Northern Methodists get around the difficulty by setting up a sort of diocese of colored churches and putting a colored bishop in charge of it. But this, it appears, would be difficult in the South. Nevertheless, the Bishop told me that he was hopeful that a solution would be found. He is himself very eager for church union.

I asked him what happened to a Methodist preacher who was transferred suddenly from a charge paying, say, $5,000 to one paying, say, $1,000. He replied that in the Southern Methodist Church there were actually very few charges paying as much as $5,000. He said that $3,500 a year and a house would be considered a great prize. In case a bishop decided that a clergyman with such a charge should be sent to a poorer charge the clergyman had no alternative save to obey. If he did so willingly, and without making too much of his sacrifice, he would be marked for preferment later on. The Bishop told me that he had himself lately transferred a pastor from a $2,500 charge with a good house, to one paying $900. He said that the man had made no protest whatever and had, in fact, not mentioned his discomforts. These discomforts would be very real to a man with children to educate.

NEW YORK, DECEMBER 3, 1934.

I came here today for a special meeting of the Directors of the Alfred A. Knopf company. Lawrence E. Spivak,[1] who has been busi-

---

1 Lawrence E. Spivak (b. 1900) became business manager of *The American Mercury* in 1933 and in 1939 bought the magazine from Paul Palmer. From 1944 to 1950 he was both its editor and publisher. In later years he achieved renown as the founder

ness manager of the *American Mercury* since I cleared out, has proposed to take over the magazine from the Knopf company, and the meeting was called to consider his offer. He agrees to pay $37,500 to cover the Knopf company's advances to the *American Mercury* for working capital, and also to pay $15,000 additional. These sums are to come out of his earnings, and if he gets into difficulties the magazine may be recaptured. It seems to me that the offer is a good one, and so I have voted for it.

Spivak is a young Harvard Jew, who took over the management of *Antiques* after leaving college and made a considerable success of it. Apparently he has no money, but he is energetic and intelligent. Since he became business manager of the *American Mercury* he has increased the advertising revenue, and shown his capacity in other directions. I believe that he could increase that revenue much more if the magazine were cut loose from the Alfred A. Knopf company. As things stand, it is involved in all the jealousies and animosities that afflict the publishing business. Many book publishers refuse to advertise in it simply because they have had some sort of quarrel with the Knopf company. Spivak could get rid of all this nuisance.

His editorial difficulties will be more serious. When Hazlitt blew up, Angoff, my old assistant, was put in charge of the magazine. He has done an excellent job in hunting up manuscripts, but his own contributions have probably been extremely damaging. Like most of the other young Jewish intellectuals (but unlike Spivak), Angoff inclines to Communism, and he has printed a number of ranting book reviews and other pieces whooping it up. Obviously, a magazine selling for 50¢ is no place for such vealy stuff. Angoff is an excellent managing editor, but his writings remain unimpressive, and his politics are mainly silly. Spivak hopes to restore him to his proper functions, and to prevent him writing anything for the magazine. Both Knopf and Spivak were in doubt that Angoff would consent to this. They feared that his six or eight months as editor had inflated him somewhat, and that he'd resent being put back to his old job. I doubt myself that he will rebel. He is apt to be contentious toward Knopf simply because he doesn't trust Knopf's judgment, but I think that he'll work in harmony with Spivak, whom he apparently respects. If he doesn't,

---

and producer of the popular radio—and subsequently television—show "Meet the Press."

Spivak will have to get another editor. It would simply be suicide to go on operating a Communist propaganda organ at 50¢. There has been a substantial fall in circulation, and it will go on if there is not a change.

The magazine will show a loss of $8,500 for 1934, but $4,000 of this is accounted for by the costs of getting Hazlitt in and out. Spivak tells me that he hopes to reduce expenses sufficiently to take up the probable deficit in 1935. He will save a good deal of money by moving out of the present office. The Alfred A. Knopf company charges the magazine $275 a month for rent, and in addition collects a fee of $75 a month for so-called administrative services. Spivak is moving into a small office, at much less rent.

He has made a bargain with the printers whereby he'll be allowed $1,500 a month credit for three months running. This will give him a working capital of $4,500, and should see him through. He is a modest fellow, and draws only $75 a week himself.

Getting Alfred Knopf's name off the cover as publisher will be a good thing for the Alfred A. Knopf company. Knopf is far too nervous to be a successful magazine publisher. Every time anything goes wrong he becomes alarmed. Moreover, his ideas as to what should go into a magazine are bad ones nine times out of ten. I can't recall him ever making a really good suggestion in my time. He made many, but all of them were bad. Even his father was better in this department.

The fact that Angoff has printed Communistic stuff in the magazine since my retirement has been of some benefit to me. It has at least convinced every one that I have nothing to do with it whatsoever. I'd like to make that impression a reality by severing the bond between the *American Mercury* company and the Alfred A. Knopf company, for I continue as a stockholder in the latter. I am resigning as a director of the *American Mercury* company, and turning in my one share of director's stock. All of my actual stock was exchanged for stock in the Alfred A. Knopf company four or five years ago. This exchange was an excellent piece of business. The Alfred A. Knopf company lost money in 1933, and will make very little in 1934, but it should do much better hereafter, especially if Spivak actually takes the *American Mercury* off its hands. Its credit is good with the banks, and Alfred told me today that it was getting all the working capital it needed from the Irving Trust Company at a very low rate of interest. As I recall it, he said he paid only 3%.

BALTIMORE, DECEMBER 5, 1934.

I had dinner with Dreiser in New York last night, following our correspondence about the Burton Rascoe preface to the *Smart Set Anthology*.¹ He invited me to dine with him, and it was impossible to say no. We had very little discussion of the Rascoe business. I told Dreiser that neither Knopf nor I suspected him for an instant of having anything to do with Rascoe's libels, and that I'd prefer not to waste my time discussing so transparent an ass.

Dreiser talked at some length about the recent trial of Robert Edwards at Wilkes-Barre, Pa. Edwards killed one girl in order to be free to marry another, thus imitating the hero of Dreiser's book, "An American Tragedy." Dreiser went to Wilkes-Barre to write about the trial for the New York *Evening Post*, and for other papers. He told me that his total takings for the job would run to $3,300. David Stern, publisher of the *Evening Post*, told me some time ago that some of the stuff Dreiser sent down from Wilkes-Barre was too vague and silly to be printed. The one article that I read myself was certainly bad enough.

Dreiser looks little changed from the last time I saw him, which was in December, 1925. His hair is whiter and he is somewhat thinner, but otherwise he looks the same. I observe that he still prefers rocking chairs, and that when he is in motion in one his hands are busy folding up his handkerchief. I did not see his wife. If she was in the house she made no sign. We sat in his apartment, which is at the Ansonia Hotel, for a couple of hours and then went to dinner at a bad restaurant across the street.

While we were at the Ansonia the editor of *Esquire*, whose name

1 Burton Rascoe (1892–1957), author, editor, and critic. Rascoe started out as an enthusiastic admirer of Mencken's, and his review of *A Book of Prefaces* was reprinted as a pamphlet entitled "Fanfare" (1920) by Knopf for publicity purposes. Subsequently, when he was editing *The Smart Set Anthology*, he asked Mencken's permission to include some of the things he had written for the magazine, and when Mencken refused he attacked him in the preface to the book. He stated, among other things, that "Mencken broke with Dreiser, because Dreiser would not contribute to a fund to defend the *American Mercury*." Dreiser wrote to both Mencken and Knopf indignantly denying the allegation. In a letter dated November 21, 1934, Mencken wrote: "My dear Dreiser: It goes without saying that I never suspected you for an instant of saying anything of the sort." This marked the resumption of the relationship between the two men after a break of nine years.

I don't know, dropped in.[1] He was on his way to Miami by air, and had a great deal to say about his air flights. He seemed a very shallow fellow. The next day Knopf told me that this editor had sent him a manuscript of a novel. *Esquire* is reported to be losing at least $10,000 a month. It has a large circulation, but it uses so many color plates that the cost of production is far above its revenue. It is operated by a company which owns an immensely profitable trade journal devoted to men's wear. Obviously, it was started in the hope that the advertisements of clothiers, shirt manufacturers, collar-makers, and so on could be diverted to a general magazine.

Dreiser showed me some of the Russian translations of his books. They are wretchedly printed, but they seem to be selling pretty well, for he said that his cash revenues from Russia amounted so far to $5,000. The Russians treat him with unusual politeness. Ordinarily an American author is paid in rubles and must go to Russia to receive and spend them. There is no way for him to get them out of the country. But Dreiser said that the Russians send him his own money in international funds.

He talked at length of various old friends, including Ralph Barton. He seemed to be much incensed against one of Ralph's former wives, Carlotta, who is now the wife of Eugene O'Neill. He said that after marrying O'Neill Carlotta continued to see Barton, and that it was because of her that Barton finally committed suicide. Whether or not this is true I don't know. The common report at the time was that Barton killed himself because of a young girl named Kresge, a daughter of the chain store magnate, who had deserted him for another man.

Dreiser handed me an enormous document embodying his observations and reflections on the Edwards case. It runs to 166 pages of typewriting. I am to read it and report on it. It looks very formidable.[2]

BALTIMORE, MD.
DECEMBER 6, 1934.

Colonel Patrick H. Callahan, the Catholic Dry, sends me a curious letter from a friend of his named Hickey, for years past one of the high

---

1 The editor of *Esquire* at that time was Arnold Gingrich (1903–1976).
2 Mencken's letter of December 8, 1934, embodying his reflections on Dreiser's manuscript, can be found in Riggio, *Dreiser-Mencken Letters*, pp. 568–69.

officials of the Gillette Razor Company. Hickey tells about a visit to Europe to consult with branch managers of the company. All of them had stock in it, and all of them were intensely eager to hear about its progress. Thus the company's business was talked of at every dinner party, and in the end Mrs. Hickey was moved to protest.

Finally, she and Hickey went to Rome, and being Catholics, sought an audience with the Pope. Mrs. Hickey approached His Holiness with great reverence, and was almost shocked out of her wits by what the Pope said. Speaking in English, he began:

"I am glad to welcome you both to Rome, first because we are all children of the same Holy Mother, but also because I understand, Mr. Hickey, that you are the General Manager of the Gillette Razor Company, and, you know, I have used a Gillette razor for many, many years and I think it is a wonderful invention. But tell me, what *is* the matter with the blades?"

BALTIMORE, DECEMBER 9, 1934.

On the invitation of James L. Wright, correspondent in Washington for the *Buffalo News* and President of the Gridiron Club, I went to Washington last night and made a speech at the Gridiron Club dinner. There is but one speech at each dinner—that is, aside from that of the President of the United States, who is almost always present. Usually some notorious opponent of the Administration is put up and his harangue is part of the razzing program of the Club, which is carried out further by various skits and stunts, many of them with music. These dinners, which are given twice a year, have been features of Washington life since 1885. They are now held in the large ballroom of the Willard Hotel, which seats 490 men, and they are always crowded. Several members of the Cabinet are always present, along with one or two Justices of the Supreme Court, the Vice-President, a dozen or two Senators, forty or fifty Congressmen, half a dozen foreign Ambassadors, and various other bigwigs. Invitations seem to be greatly in demand, and guests come long distances.

The tables are arranged in the form of a large gridiron. The guest tables run along three sides and are somewhat elevated, and the other tables are set in lines between them. The President of the Club sits in the center of the middle guest table, with the President of the United States on his right and the Vice-President on his left. I sat somewhat to the left of the center, with Governor Ritchie on my right and George D. Crofts, of the University of Buffalo, on my left. Next to Crofts sat Henry P. Fletcher, Chairman of the Republican National Committee; then came Harry Nice, Governor-elect of Maryland; and then Senator David A. Reed of Pennsylvania. I had never met Reed before, but Fletcher is an old acquaintance. His brother, David W. Fletcher, worked on the old *Morning Herald* with me back in 1899.

The dinner moves very slowly, and so there is a great deal of visiting among adjacent diners. The proceedings begin at 7.20 and it is usually 11.30 before the President of the United States rises to speak. The interval between the courses runs to as much as an hour, and altogether it is a rather dull show. Some of the skits are funny enough, but they must be incomprehensible to a great many of the guests.

Before dinner there are cocktail parties in the hotel. I went to one given by Bob Barry, former correspondent of the Curtis papers in Washington, who now seems to have a job in Wall Street. I also dropped in at one given by a guest of Essary's, whose name I forget. Cocktails, highballs and other such things are on tap at these parties, and the notables move in and out. At about 7 o'clock everyone proceeds to the large anteroom to the banquet hall and there is a great deal of introducing and back-slapping. In this crowd I met Chief Justice Hughes, Donald Richberg,[1] Saito, the Japanese Ambassador, Harry Hopkins,[2] and many others.

When we got into the banquet hall I went up to the antechamber on the other side, used by the members of the Club as a dressing room, and there encountered Roosevelt. I did not approach him, but he called to me and we had a pleasant meeting. He was extremely cordial, bathed me in his Christian Science smile and insisted on calling me by my first name.[3]

---

1 Donald R. Richberg (1881–1960) was a prominent member of the New Deal circle surrounding FDR and was referred to in the press as "assistant President."

2 Harry Hopkins (1890–1946) was also a principal figure in the New Deal and during World War II was virtually the president's alter ego, carrying on direct negotiations with Churchill, Stalin, and de Gaulle.

3 This entry breaks off very abruptly and leaves most of the story untold. It ends at the bottom of a page, and one cannot help wondering if Mencken was interrupted at that point and never got back to it, or if some pages have been lost. (The typing is that of his secretary, Mrs. Rosalind Lohrfinck, so the interruption hypothesis does not really hold up.) What happened was this: Mencken, as the principal speaker of the evening, got up and delivered a critical but essentially humorous and good-natured talk about Roosevelt's New Deal. A little later, when it came the president's

BALTIMORE, DECEMBER 11, 1934.

I have a letter from T. C. Wallen, Washington correspondent of the *Herald Tribune,* asking me for a copy of my Gridiron speech to send to his office in New York. Gridiron speeches, of course, can't be published, but Wallen wants it for the confidential reading of his associates. A similar request has come from T. J. White, general manager of the Hearst papers, through Paul Patterson. White is going to San Francisco, and wants to show the speech to Hearst. There have also been other requests.

I am replying to all that I have no authority to give out copies. Jim Wright has one, and if he wants to circulate it he is free to do so. I have asked him to try to get for me a copy of the memorandum from which Roosevelt read, but so far I haven't received it.

Last night Edwin C. Hill, who was present at the dinner, referred to the bout with Roosevelt in his radio talk. I missed it, but he apparently gave the impression that the affair was much more serious than it was in fact.

BALTIMORE, DECEMBER 11, 1934.

Hamlin Garland's[1] "Afternoon Neighbors," published by Macmillan, has just come in. The following appears on page 247:

"During my period of lameness I read several of Henry Mencken's books and was not greatly impressed by these essays.

"They all have the newspaper tone. Mencken sets down many true sayings but spoils his case by overemphasis. When

---

turn to speak, after a few introductory pleasantries and an acknowledgment to "my old friend, Henry Mencken," he launched into a diatribe against journalism and newspapermen so scathing that it sent cold chills up and down the spines of his listeners. It soon turned out, however, that what he was doing was quoting a long excerpt from "Journalism in America," which Mencken had published as an editorial in the October 1924 issue of *The American Mercury* and subsequently included in *Prejudices: Sixth Series* (pp. 9–37). All eyes in the room focused on Mencken, who felt publicly humiliated and swore that he would "get even." Of all this the entry says nothing. (See, however, the one for December 11 immediately following.)

1 Hamlin Garland (1860–1940), writer and social critic whose tales centered about Midwestern farm life. His best-known work is probably the autobiographical *A Son of the Middle Border* (1917). He won the 1921 Pulitzer Prize for *A Daughter of the Middle Border.* In a note in *Chrestomathy* (p. 498), Mencken said that "[H]is actual talents were very meagre, and he was shabby and devious as a man."

any critic calls *all* the other writers of his time fanatics or morons, he leaves a poor impression on his readers. Whatever his
private opinion of Wilson, George, Roosevelt or Shaw, he writes
of them as demagogues, idiots, or mountebanks. There is a bla-
tant folly in all this. I finished this book with a sense of being
entertained as by a 'cut-up' at a dinner table. It is like being
thumped on the head with a boy's wind-blown bladder filled
with dried peas. This comes ultimately to be a bore. The fact
is, Mencken in private life is a quiet and peaceable citizen. This
lessens the ferocity of his pose. He decries every other writer to
advance his own position.

"(Such was my candid reaction to his 'Prejudices' ten years
ago. He is now in retirement and married!)."

Garland's third sentence is typically idiotic, and I should add typically disingenuous. He was writing in 1925, and at that time four of
my "Prejudices" books had come out. They were full of pieces praising
such writers as Joseph Conrad, Theodore Dreiser, Edgar Lee Masters,
Willa Cather, Carl Sandburg, Vachel Lindsay, Joe Hergesheimer,
James Branch Cabell, and Sinclair Lewis. Nowhere in them was the
slightest indication that I regarded myself as superior to any of these
writers. Garland's animosity to me goes back to the time of the raid
on Dreiser's "The Genius" in 1915. At that time I was in charge of the
protest of American authors against the effort to suppress the book.
Garland not only refused to sign the protest, but was restrained only
with difficulty from breaking out in a violent denunciation of the book.
Inasmuch as some of his own earlier books had been attacked by the
Comstocks,[1] this seemed an hypocrisy, and I let my view of it be
known. He has been sore ever since.

1 Anthony Comstock (1844–1915) was secretary of the Society for the Suppression of
  Vice and carried on a ceaseless warfare against all books which, in his judgment,
  were obscene or might bring a blush of shame to the cheeks of a pure young maiden.

1935

On January 3rd I received the following letter from Dr. H. S. Canby,[1] editor of the *Saturday Review:*

January 2, 1935.

Personal and Confidential

Mr. H. L. Mencken,
704 Cathedral Street,
Baltimore, Maryland.

My dear Mencken:

The nominating committee of the National Institute of Arts and Letters of which I am chairman unanimously recommended your name for nomination, and it has received much more than the necessary two-thirds vote of the literary section. We are prepared to back you as enthusiastically in the election as in the nomination. Before doing so, however, with a person of your importance, I want to know whether you will accept an election. Please let me know within two or three days so that the matter can either be dropped quietly or carried through enthusiastically. I am very hopeful that you will join. The various people whose absence from the Institute may have irritated you in the past are all going to be brought up in the same fashion and I think you will find congenial company. Furthermore,

---

1 Henry Seidel Canby (1878–1961) founded *The Saturday Review of Literature* and was its editor from 1924 to 1936.

I think it is your duty to join. You have taken a leading part in criticism in the last ten or fifteen years. The Institute should represent the intellectual life of the country, not a point of view, and especially not an obscurantist point of view. It will, in my opinion, be a triumph for independent thinking if you come in to us. Please write and tell me to go ahead.

Sincerely yours,
(Signed) H. S. Canby.

That Canby should be stupid enough to think that I'd join the National Institute rather surprised me. But he had to have, of course, a polite answer, and so I sent him the following on January 4th:

January 4, 1935.

My dear Canby:

Thanks very much for your letter. I wish I could ask you to publish the bans, but the plain fact is that I have been on my own so long that I simply couldn't change my course now. I have always kept out of organizations, even when I was in full accord with their objects, and have also tried, at least as much as possible, to avoid sitting on committees. In the special case of the Institute I have dissented so often from some of its apparent aims and clashed so often with some of its salient figures that it would be striking a palpably false note for me to come in. Thus I fear I had better not. But I am very grateful for your thought of me, and offer my best thanks again. Please give my thanks, too, to the other brethren who join you in the invitation. I suppose I know most of them, and I am sorry that I can't write to them directly.

We meet far too seldom. The next time I am in New York I shall give myself the pleasure of waiting on you.

Sincerely yours,

On January 3rd I also received the following letter[1] from Dreiser:

---

1 The exchange of letters between Dreiser and Mencken on this matter can be found in Riggio, *Dreiser-Mencken Letters*, pp. 570–71.

Hotel Ansonia,
New York City
Jan. 3, 1935.

Mr. H. L. Mencken,
704 Cathedral St.,
Baltimore, Md.

Dear Mencken:

You are more familiar with this Association than I am. I wish you would tell me what you think of this request and whether my rejection of it will do more harm than good. I ask that because in some instances where I felt fully justified in ignoring a request of this kind I have aroused a fairly lasting bitterness that shows itself in the public as well as the personal reactions of some when I encounter them.

Has the Institute of Arts and Letters any respectable value, and what, if any, representative American writers and artists are members of it?

I certainly wish you the best for the coming year.

(signed) Dreiser.

With it he sent the following enclosure:

COPY
THE SATURDAY REVIEW
25 West 45th St.,
N.Y.C.

January 2, 1935.

Personal and confidential

Mr. Theodore Dreiser
Hotel Ansonia
73rd St. & Broadway,
New York City.

My dear Mr. Dreiser:

For some time (relatively) younger members of the National Institute of Arts and Letters have felt that our organization, if

it were to fulfill its purposes, must be more representative of
the literary ability of the country. It has a splendid plan and is
on a sound financial basis and is guaranteed permanency. The
nominating committee, this year, of which I am chairman,
unanimously recommended your name as among the few of major importance to be considered and you have received more
than two-thirds vote of all the literary section necessary to put
a name upon the final ballot. I am writing to say to you that
the committee of six is prepared to back you as strongly in the
election as in the nomination. With a writer of your importance, however, we do not wish to put your name upon the
final ballot unless we know that you are willing to accept an
election. I hope, and we all hope, that you will do so. I think
it is your duty as the leading American novelist, and I hope you
will see the matter in the same light. Won't you let me know
in two or three days so that we can either quietly drop the
suggestion or, as I trust, go through with it enthusiastically.
I am

> Sincerely yours,
> (signed) Henry S. Canby
> Editor

This was marked copy, and Dreiser had ringed the words *Personal
and confidential* and written beside them: "Regardless of this I feel at
liberty to consult you." I sent him the following reply:

January 4, 1935.

My dear Dreiser:
This letter offers you a great honor, and if you were a man
properly appreciative you'd bust into tears. The National Institute of Arts and Letters includes all of the greatest authors of
the country. Prominent among its members are: Louis Bromfield, Stephen Vincent Benét, Struthers Burt, Owen Davis, Edna
Ferber, Hermann Hagedorn, Don Marquis, Ernest Poole and
Agnes Repplier. One of the most eminent members is Hamlin
Garland, whose efforts to put down "The Genius" you will recall. These great men and women now propose to lift you up
to their own level, and I think you should be full of gratitude.

Seriously, I can't imagine any sensible man joining any such organization. When Red Lewis was elected five or six years ago he refused instantly. Masters, so far as I know, has never been a member, and neither has Anderson nor Cabell. The chief hero of the club ten years ago was Stuart Pratt Sherman.

There is a superior branch of the Institute, known as the American Academy of Arts and Letters. You must yet go a long way, of course, before you are eligible to it. Its leading light is Robert Underwood Johnson, and among its other luminaries are John H. Finley of the *New York Times*, the aforesaid Garland, Judge Robert Grant of Boston, Owen Wister and Paul Elmer More.

Here's hoping that you are lucky in 1935. Christmas in my house was a horror. My wife's mother died on December 23rd and was buried down in Alabama on Christmas morning.

Yours,

BALTIMORE, JANUARY 10, 1935.

Louis Untermeyer,[1] who is on a lecture tour, came in to dinner yesterday at 6:45. We had a pleasant dose of steamed turkey with oyster sauce, and washed it down with a bottle of Niersteiner and another of Spanish red wine. Louis was in good humor, and we spent a pleasant evening. Sara apparently liked him very much. In the course of the conversation he described Alexander Woollcott[2] as "a butterfly in heat," which seemed to me to be very neat and amusing.

Louis spends three or four months of every Winter lecturing. I gather from his talk that he averages about $100 a lecture. Sometimes he gets $125, but probably more often he has to take $75. He makes about $3,000 a year. While he is so engaged his new wife lives in Toledo, Ohio, where she is a police magistrate. They spend their Summers at Louis's place in the Adirondacks. They have no children of their own, but are bringing up two small boys, one of whom, I believe, is Louis's by one of his previous wives. This marriage is his fourth. He

1 Louis Untermeyer (1885–1977), poet and anthologist. His best-known collection, *Modern American and British Poetry*, appeared in numerous successive editions over the years.
2 Alexander Woollcott (1887–1943), author, critic, actor, and wit. He was the brother of Mencken's friend and Saturday Night Club colleague, William Warren Woollcott.

divorced his first wife, married a second, divorced the second and re-married the first. This second marriage to the first also blew up, and a bit later on he married the lady magistrate.

BALTIMORE, JANUARY 17, 1935.

H. H. Schaff,[1] of J. W. Luce and Company, my first publishers, was here last night for dinner. Schaff is a lawyer, and has been engaged in some legal business or other in Washington. He has been interested for many years in copyright law, and has a hand in the effort to make the United States a party to the international copyright convention. He tells me that he now hopes to do it by inducing the Secretary of State to sign a treaty which will bind the United States, and by then trying to sneak it through the Senate. Schaff told me that he had a meeting lately with Thorval Solberg, the former registrar of copyrights, who is now a man in the 80's. They discussed the possibility of organizing a delegation of authors to go to Washington to impress the Senate, but had to give it up because they could not think of any authors sufficiently eminent to be influential with politicians. In the old days it was easy. Whenever any such delegation was needed Mark Twain was appointed chairman, and such men as William Dean Howells and Richard Watson Gilder were members. But today there is no one of comparable eminence, at least in the view of politicoes. Schaff said that he and Solberg were almost reduced to making Ellery Sedgwick, editor of the *Atlantic Monthly*, their spokesman.

BALTIMORE, JANUARY 18, 1935.

Frank R. Kent told me the following, which he received from Alice Roosevelt (Mrs. Nicholas Longworth):[2]

When Father Coughlin,[3] the Detroit radio priest, appeared before

1 Harrison Hale Schaff (1869–1960) had long been a member of the Boston publishing firm of John W. Luce & Company, which brought out Mencken's first two (prose) books: *George Bernard Shaw: His Plays* (1905) and *The Philosophy of Friedrich Nietzsche* (1908).
2 Alice Roosevelt Longworth (1884–1980), the daughter of President Theodore Roosevelt, was a prominent figure on the Washington political and social scene throughout most of her long life.
3 Father Charles E. Coughlin (1891–1979), pastor of the Shrine of the Little Flower in Royal Oak, Michigan, became a national figure during the 1930s with his weekly Sunday afternoon radio broadcasts in which he assailed American financial interests

one of the committees of Congress Mrs. Longworth met him at the Capitol. She invited him to drop in to see her some day, and told him that she served cocktails almost every afternoon. Coughlin showed up the very next afternoon, accompanied by three other priests. He seemed somewhat stiff and suspicious, and drank only one cocktail. A few weeks later he appeared in Washington again, called up Mrs. Longworth, and told her he'd like to make her another visit. This time he appeared with two priests and drank two cocktails. A little while later he came the third time. Now he had only one priest—and drank three cocktails. Mrs. Longworth told Kent that she expected him to appear alone the next time and to drink at least a dozen cocktails.

Fulton Oursler,[1] editor of the Macfadden publications, was here to lunch yesterday with his wife. They were on their way to Washington to attend a White House reception. Oursler told me of a conversation at a recent dinner at which Coughlin was present. Oursler was not present himself, but he got the report from a friend who was. Coughlin, after a few drinks, began speculating about his own future. It soon appeared that he toyed with the vision of becoming dictator of the United States. He apparently believed that his league of radio morons would make him formidable enough for him to seize power. He said: "If I am dictator for five days, even though I be killed afterward, I'll live in history."

BALTIMORE, JANUARY 21, 1935.

Dr. Marjorie Nicolson,[2] dean of Smith College, was here for lunch yesterday. She is one of Sara's old Goucher friends. She has been in Washington attending a meeting of the Smith Alumnae Association.

---

and called for social justice. In 1936 he co-founded a new political party, the Union party, but it was resoundingly defeated in the presidential election of that year. During World War II his strident anti-Semitism and sympathy for the Nazis caused his magazine, *Social Justice*, to be barred from the mails. The Cardinal-Archbishop of Detroit thereupon ordered him to cease his broadcasts; Coughlin obeyed and soon faded into obscurity.

1 Charles Fulton Oursler (1893–1952) was, like Mencken, a Baltimorean, and began his career as a reporter for the Baltimore *American*. He served as editor-in-chief of the Macfadden group of magazines from 1922 to 1942. In 1943 he was converted to Catholicism and as a result of that experience wrote *The Greatest Story Ever Told* (1949), an immensely popular and best-selling life of Christ.

2 Marjorie Hope Nicolson (1894–1981) had taught at Goucher from 1923 to 1926, about the same period that Sara Haardt was there, and the two became good friends. She taught at Smith College from 1926 to 1941.

With her there was young Constance Morrow, sister to Mrs. Lindbergh. Constance is a student at Smith. Dr. Nicolson says that the newspaper reporters harassed Miss Morrow dreadfully in Washington, but that she gave them nothing.

Dr. William A. Neilson,[1] president of Smith, was at Flemington, New Jersey, at the time of the opening of the Hauptmann trial[2] and saw a great deal of the Lindberghs. He told Dr. Nicolson that Mrs. Lindbergh laughed at the newspaper accounts of her heroic bearing on the stand. She said that the kidnapping was now an old story to the Morrow family, and that they had begun to look at it objectively—in fact, they had reached such a point that they made limericks on the names of the witnesses at the trial. All of the shock and sorrow were endured and survived long ago.

Lindbergh, according to Dr. Neilson, goes to the trial as to a show, and is delighted that he has so good a seat. Like his wife, he has absolutely no heat against Hauptmann. The thing, he feels, is now out of his hands, and what interests him mainly is the sheer drama of it.

NEW YORK, JANUARY 25, 1935.

I had dinner last night with Theodore Dreiser. I called for him at the Ansonia Hotel, and after a drink there we started out in the snow to find a restaurant. Dreiser had in mind an Italian place in 45th street, but when we got there it couldn't be found. A taxi driver then directed us to 48th street, and after heavy struggles in the snow we finally got there. Once I lost my footing, fell into Dreiser and knocked him down. A minute later he came down on his own, and with a very heavy thump. He was, however, not injured.

The dinner was the usual Italian thing, and we drank a quart and a half of bad Chianti. We sat until after 12 o'clock. During the last hour or two we were the only customers in the restaurant.

Dreiser is full of a plan to go back to California, and then to make a motor trip to Alaska. It appears that a motor road clear to Sitka has been opened. He is taking his girl Helen along, and he proposed that

---

1 William Allan Neilson (1869–1946), president of Smith College from 1917 to 1939, was also the author or editor of many works on literature and literary criticism.
2 The reference is to the trial of Bruno Richard Hauptmann, charged with having kidnapped and murdered the eighteen-month-old son of Charles and Anne Lindbergh in 1932. Hauptmann was found guilty, and executed on April 3, 1936.

I join the party and bring Sara. Whether or not he is married to Helen I don't know. He has been living with her for at least twelve years. I have never heard of a divorce from his original wife, Sara, but maybe there is one. Sara is a couple of years older than Dreiser. She is a small woman, whose hair was red in her early days. Many years ago she turned Christian Scientist. Life with her must have been dreadful, and I always sympathized with Dreiser's determination to get rid of her. For some time she devoted herself to complaining to his friends about his treatment of her, but in late years no one seems to have heard from her. It is possible that she is dead.[1]

Dreiser and Helen spent three years in California about ten years ago. Dreiser told me that he couldn't write a line while there. I asked him why he stayed, and he said it was because of Helen. He was greatly enamored of her at that time, and she was trying to break into the movies. He told me that she was offered a lead in an important picture, but only on condition that she would desert him and go to live with the manager. This she refused to do, so they hung on for three years, with Dreiser moping around Los Angeles and accomplishing precisely nothing.

He told me that he had finished the third volume[2] of the Titan-Financier trilogy, and would soon turn it in to Simon and Schuster, his new publishers.

He broke out into an anti-Semitic tirade, somewhat to my surprise. I asked him why, if his sentiments ran that way, he had chosen a Jewish publisher. He answered simply that he had no other choice. An agent made efforts to interest Harcourt and other Christian publishers, but without success. Dreiser was left flat, of course, by the collapse of the Liveright house. When Liveright withdrew the firm came into control of a Jew named Pell, who by Dreiser's account is a fearful swine. He thereupon determined to clear out, and in order to do so he had to buy back the rights of a number of his books from Pell. The rights to the rest he already owned. He has quarreled with publishers all his life, and is completely convinced that they keep two sets of

---

1 Sara White, Dreiser's first wife, was still living at this time; she died in 1942. On June 13, 1944, he married Helen Richardson, who had lived with him for a dozen or more years. She survived him, dying on September 22, 1955.

2 *The Financier*, the first volume of Dreiser's "Trilogy of Desire," was published in 1912 and the second, *The Titan*, in 1914, but the third and concluding volume, *The Stoic*, appeared only posthumously, in 1947.

books and otherwise rook him. Years ago he approached Knopf, but I advised Knopf to avoid him. To be sure, there is some kudos in publishing him, but he demands large royalties and heavy advances, and is otherwise unprofitable to a publisher.

Dreiser told me that he received $100,000 from Jesse Lasky for the movie rights to "An American Tragedy." Of this he had to pay Liveright $10,000 but all the rest he kept for himself. After Lasky had bought the rights Elder Hays[1] made objection to his doing the book as a movie, and it was laid on the shelf. When the talkies came in Lasky got it down and finally induced Hays to give him permission to produce it. But when Dreiser heard of this he demanded an additional fee of $60,000. His contention was that he had sold the movie rights, not the talkie rights. He told me that Lasky protested bitterly, but finally paid the money. Thus Dreiser's total Hollywood revenues from the book ran to $150,000.

I asked him what truth there was in the common report that he had applied for membership in the Communist party in New York and been refused. He said that the facts were the other way 'round. The Communists had approached him, but he had refused to join. He is sympathetic with Communism, but apparently dislikes many of the American Communists. He gave me a long account of his Russian trip four or five years ago. He covered a large area, and visited such remote places as Baku, Samarkand and Odessa. He told me that the Russian government paid all of his expenses, and that he had the privilege of stopping wherever he pleased. Sometimes, he said, he would insist on stopping off at a village that happened to interest him. He would question the people at length, but inasmuch as he knew no Russian and had to use an interpreter, it is doubtful that he got all of their replies accurately.

He told me that John Chamberlain, the literary reviewer of the *New York Times*, had told him lately that all of the reviewers on the *Times* had to be very careful in their notices of heavily advertised books. When such a book turned out to be bad they would bear down on it only very gently. He said that Chamberlain's assistant, a young man named Vanderveer or something of the sort, had confirmed this.

---

1 Will H. Hays (1879–1954), attorney and Republican party official, was the first "czar" of the motion picture industry, with enormous powers of censorship over what films could show and say.

Dreiser fell to talking of Red Lewis, Hergesheimer, Cather and other novelists. Lewis's acceptance of membership in the National Institute of Arts and Letters had given him a great shock. He told me that he always thought Lewis, despite his eccentricities, was too honest a fellow to succumb. Dreiser resented the fact that the offer of membership made to him (Dreiser) by Henry S. Canby had been marked "personal and confidential." He argued that Canby had no right to send him confidential letters and put him under pledges, whether tacit or overt. He told me that he considered that he was perfectly at liberty to print the whole correspondence. As in my own case, Canby tackled him again after his first refusal. He showed me Canby's second letter, and also his own reply. It was very short and curt.

Dreiser told me that he thought that "Babbitt" was the best of all the Lewis books. He professed some admiration for Cather, but said that he could never read Hergesheimer.

We fell into talk about the disposition of his property after his death. He told me that he would leave all his money to Helen, but that he had never been able to make up his mind what to do with his papers. I suggested that he deposit them with the Library of Congress, and he seemed surprised to hear that he could do so with the provision that they should not be opened without his consent during his lifetime. He showed great interest in this, and asked me to approach Herbert Putnam, the librarian of Congress. I'll do so at the first chance. Some years ago I went to the Library to discuss the disposition of my own papers. I didn't see Putnam but fell into the hands of an old fellow named Jameson, who is head of the manuscript division. When I told Jameson that I was the owner of the original manuscript of Dreiser's "Sister Carrie" and had thought of leaving it to the Library at my death, he showed very little interest. He said that the manuscript division was mainly devoted to political documents. He added, however, that some time ago it accepted the books of an old New York firm on the theory that, while they were not really historical documents, they might throw some light on American history. He suggested calmly that the manuscript of "Sister Carrie" might do the same. It was obvious that he had heard of the book only vaguely. He hadn't the slightest idea as to what it was about. I didn't tell this to Dreiser. The next time I go to Washington I shall avoid Jameson and see Putnam.

BALTIMORE, JANUARY 29, 1935.

Paul Palmer,[1] the new editor of the *American Mercury*, came in to lunch and we spent a couple of hours discussing the magazine. Palmer is a Harvard man 34 years old. When he left college he came to see me at the old *Smart Set* office, and I gave him a note to Stanley M. Reynolds, then managing editor of the Baltimore *Sun*. Reynolds gave him a job, and he remained on the *Sun* for about six months. He then went to New York and joined the staff of the *World*, finally becoming Sunday editor.

His first wife was a newspaper woman, who now uses the name of Greta Palmer. After their divorce he married the daughter of one of the rich Lewisohns. His father-in-law, it appears, gave him $25,000 to buy a half interest in the *American Mercury* from Lawrence E. Spivak. We had sold the magazine to Spivak a couple of months ago. Under the arrangement with him, he is to pay $53,000 for the property, but he is given time enough to get it out of his profits—that is, if he makes a profit. In case he fails, the Alfred A. Knopf company recovers the magazine. After this arrangement had been made with Spivak, Palmer popped up, and Spivak sold him a half interest.

The $25,000 will be of immense value to Spivak. He has been handicapped by lack of working capital. The chances are, of course, that if it is necessary the Lewisohns will fork up more.

Charles Angoff made a considerable uproar when news of this transaction reached him. He argued that he should have been notified before, and denounced Spivak and Knopf for being discourteous to him. My belief is that Spivak should have treated him a bit more frankly. It remains, however, a fact that the transaction was not actually completed until a very short time before Angoff was told of it.

I tried to induce him to go along with Palmer as managing editor, but he refused on the ground that he was at odds with Palmer's program and couldn't serve him conscientiously. I pointed out that he had served me for nine years, though our politics differed radically, but he professed to see some difference between the two situations.

When I retired from the *American Mercury* as of January 1, 1934,

---

1 Paul Palmer bought *The American Mercury* from Knopf in 1935 and succeeded to some extent in building up its declining circulation. In 1939, however, he sold it and took a position on the staff of *The Reader's Digest*. See Singleton, *H. L. Mencken and the American Mercury Adventure*, pp. 239–40.

Angoff continued as managing editor under my successor, Henry Hazlitt. Meanwhile, Spivak had become business manager. When Hazlitt cleared out Spivak and Alfred Knopf permitted Angoff to edit the magazine. He at once converted it into a very radical organ, and insisted on printing violent book reviews denouncing every author not conspicuously Red. He also printed an article belaboring Albert Jay Nock.[1] This was a gross piece of bad taste, for he was well aware that Nock was a friend of mine and had been a faithful contributor to the magazine in its earlier days. Altogether, Angoff carried on in a most imprudent manner, and both Spivak and Knopf became seriously alarmed. They had to watch every line that he printed, and when they made suggestions he resisted them violently.

At the request of Palmer, I undertook the effort to induce Angoff to stay on. But after five minutes talk with him it was plain that he and Palmer could not work together amicably, and so I desisted. What Angoff is to do I don't know. For a year past he has done no work on the quotation book that we had had under way together. I suggested to him in New York last week that he sell me his rights for cash. He objected on the ground that he didn't want me to lay out any actual money on the book. I then suggested that he take a limited interest in return for his contributions, say, one-third of the royalties for the first year only. This proposal he is now considering. He is to communicate with me within a week.[2]

Angoff spoiled what will probably be his best chance in this life. If he had carried on the magazine with reasonable skill and discretion Knopf and Spivak would have left him in the editorship, but his rather childish radicalism so alarmed them that even if Palmer had not come in Angoff would have been fired. He tells me that he is at work on a book dealing with the history of magazine literature since 1900. This

---

1 Albert Jay Nock (1870–1945), editor and author, remembered chiefly for his autobiography, *Memoirs of a Superfluous Man* (1943).

2 In the preface to *A New Dictionary of Quotations*, which did not appear until 1942, Mencken wrote: "In March, 1933, I suggested to Charles Angoff, then my assistant on the *American Mercury*, that he join me in this enterprise, and for a couple of years thereafter the two of us proceeded with it. But in 1935 Mr. Angoff found himself unable to give it the time it needed, and so withdrew. Thereafter I continued it on my own, and have since dealt with it unaided. Mr. Angoff's researches were very valuable to the work, and without his diligent collaboration it would have come to nothing, but he is not responsible for its present contents, which represent my own undivided choice."

is a dreadful job, and he will probably make a mess of it. The truth is that he is not a writer, and has almost no critical faculty. As a managing editor under some other man he is excellent. During his nine years with me he was extraordinarily diligent and faithful, and I never had the slightest reason to doubt his loyalty. But nine months of editing on his own have filled him with a rather absurd sense of his importance, and I fear that he is headed for difficulties.

BALTIMORE, MARCH 6, 1935.

Ritchie came in last night, and we had a long talk. He looks better physically than he has looked for several years past, but he seemed to me to be somewhat lethargic in mind. He told me that he was taking his law practice very lightly. If he is up late at night he sleeps late in the morning, and often he doesn't get to his office until nearly noon. He told me that he proposes to confine himself to a few cases, and especially to those in which the fee is above $1,000. He doesn't need much extra money to sustain himself, and he is disinclined to do any unnecessary work.

Ritchie told me that the worst curse of his life as Governor was not the necessity of going to banquets and listening to idiotic speeches, but the fact that he had to sit all day seeing political plugs and being polite to them. He told me that the effort to avoid heaving them out was sometimes very fatiguing. He said that he had to do business with them in order to maintain himself in office, but that he had never been able to accustom himself to their physical presence. He said that it was now a great relief to spend his days with relatively decent and presentable people.

He said that if he had his way he would not increase the City delegation at Annapolis, but actually decrease it. He said that many of the county people, though stupid, were at least really honest, but that it was most unusual for a man of any honesty to be sent to the Legislature from the city. There were, of course, occasionally brilliant exceptions, but they were not many.

He told me that the present Legislature was engaged in blackmail on a large scale. He said that it was trying to squeeze money out of the race track owners in return for a reduction in the taxes on race tracks, and that another one of its victims is the company promoting the Chesapeake Bay bridge.

Sara Haardt Mencken died on May 31, 1935, but there is no mention of the fact in the diary at that time. With her passing, however, Mencken virtually ceased to keep it; there is only one remaining entry for this year—the one for September 14 immediately following—and only a handful for 1936. It was not until 1937 that he resumed it on anything like a regular basis. And it was not until the fifth anniversary of Sara's death, in his entry for May 31, 1940, that he dwelt on the subject at length— the circumstances of her final illness, and his feelings for her and about their life together (see p. 139).

BALTIMORE, MD., SEPTEMBER 14, 1935.

I came down from New York yesterday, Friday the 13th, leaving on the 11.30 train, Eastern Standard Time. There is another 13 in 11.30. The Pullman agent gave me seat No. 13 in car 231. Another 13 in 231, this time reversed. I fully expected the train to roll off the track. Along about Trenton I encountered Rob Hanes of Winston Salem, and we sat down for a gabble. This took my mind off the dangers confronting me, and so I got to Baltimore in good spirits, and without any material loss of weight. The rest of the day passed calmly and, indeed, rather comfortably. I begin to take an atheistic view of my private theology.

1936

On May 18th, one week after the publication of the fourth edition of "The American Language," Knopf told me that he had shipped 2,535 copies in America and 365 to England. In addition, he had placed about 350 copies on consignment in various book shops in this country, and there were 304 unfilled orders on file. Thus the first printing of 5,000 copies was pretty well exhausted. I had hoped to perfect the text before reprinting the book, but there is not time for it, so another edition from type will have to be run off. It will probably run to 3,000 copies. While it is being sold I'll correct all the errors in the present text and the book will then be plated. Hundreds of minor corrections are pouring in from readers. Some of them, of course, are merely pedantic. But a great many rectify very real errors.

BALTIMORE, MD. AUGUST 20, 1936.

A month or two ago I received a telephone call from William M. Baskervill, the head Hearst man here in Baltimore. I met him at Schellhase's[1] and he told me that Arthur Brisbane,[2] the Hearst columnist, was seriously and apparently mortally ill in Europe, and that the Hearst organization was counting on him to die within six months.

1 Schellhase's was the popular Baltimore restaurant, specializing in German dishes and Maryland seafood, where the Saturday Night Club held its meetings from the end of World War I until the club's final dissolution in 1950. The place no longer exists.
2 Arthur Brisbane (1864–1936), widely known editor and syndicated columnist. He died on December 25 of that year.

Baskervill said that he had been instructed by Hearst to ask me if I would consent to take over Brisbane's column on his death. He said that Hearst was prepared to pay $1,000 a week, and that he would probably be willing to raise the ante later on. The first contract would be for five years. I'd be expected to supply a column a day, and maybe an editorial now and again for Sundays. I told Baskervill that I was not eager to take on any such job and that, moreover, I believed I'd be happier on the *Sun*.

The interview ended pleasantly enough. Baskervill told me that Hearst had been searching the whole country for a suitable successor to Brisbane, and that he had found the available supply very small. He didn't mention any names. I pointed out to him that any column that I wrote would differ enormously from Brisbane's, and he replied that Hearst didn't care. He wasn't eager to have any particular point of view maintained. All he wanted was a column that would attract some attention. Baskervill said he realized that I dissented sharply from some of Hearst's ideas, but that Hearst was willing to give me a reasonably free hand.

It would be lunacy for me to take any such job at my age. Brisbane writes at least a column and a half every day, and seldom takes a holiday. Even when he is traveling he dictates his stuff. At this moment, though he is very ill in Europe, it comes by cable every day. He is suffering from some form of heart disease, and according to Baskervill has to stay in bed virtually all of the time. The other day Hearst left for Europe to visit him.

BALTIMORE, DECEMBER 10, 1936.

On September 22, 1920 J. H. Adams[1] and Paul Patterson were in London. They called on George Bernard Shaw, and had a long talk with him. Adams's diary, which is preserved at The *Sun* office, contains the following:

"Shaw said that he knew of Henry Mencken and had read much of his stuff. 'It makes delightful reading,' he said. 'I even recall that he once wrote a book about me.' "[2]

---

1 John Haslup Adams (1871–1927) was editor of the *Sun* from 1912 until his death.
2 Mencken's first book, aside from the youthful *Ventures into Verse*, was *George Bernard Shaw: His Plays* (1905).

1937

Some time ago I suggested at the *Sun* office that it might be well to add a typographical expert to the staff, and suggested further that such an expert might be found in the composing room. Louis Fries, the mechanical superintendent, was instructed to find him, but came back in a week or two reporting no success. Patterson and I then got hold of Wilner, the foreman of the morning *Sun* composing room. He said he knew of but two men who really had any sound acquaintance with type. One, he said, was a printer of 60 who had quarreled with the Union, left the *Sun* office and gone to work in a job plant. He allowed that this man might be recruited, but that the Union would probably refuse to re-admit him. The other, said Wilner, was an apprentice boy of 19, now working in the *Sun* office. This boy, of course, has had little experience, but Wilner says that he shows a better understanding of typography than any of the journeymen he works with. A bit later on we may give him a trial.

Certainly the *Sun* needs a typographical expert, and what is more, one constantly in the office. New heads and captions are being written almost every day, and nine times out of ten the composing room makes dreadful botches of them. Some time ago, when plans were under way for setting up a page of opinion opposite the editorial page, the composing room was asked to submit dummies. All of the heads that it sent down were crude and hideous. I spent two hours trying to devise better ones. The result was certainly not ideal, but it was at least an immense improvement upon what the printers themselves had produced.

In theory, every apprentice of the craft passes an examination in design and make-up. Actually, very few of the printers of today know anything about type. There are 200 of them in the *Sun* office, and it is surely significant that the only one who shows any genuine understanding and love of his craft is an apprentice boy. The rest are simply Union men. Their one and only object in life is to get through their day's work as quickly as possible. They have no more interest in printing as an art than they have in astrophysics.

BALTIMORE, MD.
MARCH 23, 1937.

Alfred Knopf told me in New York yesterday that the sales of "The American Language" to date run to 12,825 copies. In addition, the Book of the Month Club is printing 103,000 copies for presentation as a sort of bonus to its subscribers. I am not sure about the effects of this heavy distribution, though Knopf appears to be convinced that it will not damage the regular sale.

BALTIMORE, MD.
JUNE 10, 1937.

Manuel L. Quezon, the President of the new Philippine Republic, was at the *Sun* office for lunch today. He had been in Baltimore for three days without any one knowing it. He came here to visit a friend, who is a patient at the Johns Hopkins. He put up at the Lord Baltimore Hotel and complained bitterly of his accommodations. When he was asked why he didn't remove to some other hotel he replied that he didn't know there was any better one in Baltimore.

Quezon is a small, dark and fiery-eyed fellow of stupendous energy. He made a really excellent impression on all the brethren at the lunch. He speaks English with a curious accent, but uses words correctly and even idiomatically. He described at some length some of his political battles in the Philippines. He is at this moment the absolute boss of the country. He told us that what the Filipinos objected to principally was not political subservience to the United States, but the bad manners of the Americans sent out to govern them. These Americans, with few exceptions, treated them as if they were an inferior people, and so greatly outraged them.

Quezon described his plans for the defense of the Islands. He has introduced universal military service. Every boy on reaching the age of 18 will enter the army for six months' training. He will then go home for six months, at the expiration of which he will return to the army. This will go on for four years. By this time he will have had two years of training. In addition to the military exercises, he will be instructed in some useful art or craft. In case he is illiterate he will be taught to read and write.

Quezon says that he believes he can put together an army formidable enough to discourage any great power from undertaking to conquer the Philippines. His eye, of course, is on Japan. He says that the Corregidor fortress is now so formidable that it could not be taken by any means at present known. Thus if the Japs ever tackle it he hopes to stop them, and to inflict enough damage on them to make them think it over.

NEW YORK, JUNE 18, 1937.

There was a meeting of the Board of Alfred A. Knopf, Inc. this afternoon. Samuel Knox, Knopf's cousin, showed up rather unexpectedly. The two have been on bad terms, and Knox absented himself from the last meeting. He seemed in good humor today, and was very friendly.

Old Samuel Raymond, who had been a member of the Board for years, also appeared—for the first time in several years. He has a bad heart, is along in years, and looked dreadful.

Knopf is doing a business of about half a million dollars a year, but making very little profit—that is, above salaries. What he needs is a couple of best sellers. Unfortunately, finding them is a sheer matter of luck. His new office at 501 Madison avenue looks to me to be much more roomy than the old one, though the floor space is actually less. It has been charmingly decorated by a firm of female decorators. This afternoon they gave a cocktail party in the place to show it off to their friends. Blanche Knopf dragged me into this party, but I escaped after a few minutes, and without drinking any of the cocktails.

I rode downtown with Sam Knox. He told me that he thought Knopf's firm needed a man of business to look after its financial affairs, thus relieving Alfred A. Knopf for purely editorial duties. Sam protested that he did not have his own eye on the job, but it is obvious that he believes he should have it. He argued that Alfred has been dreadfully overworked ever since the death of his father, five years ago. This is true enough, but I doubt that the entrance of Sam Knox into the office would give him much relief. The two are naturally antagonistic, and they'd probably spend four-fifths of their time quarreling.

NEW YORK, JUNE 19, 1937.

Gerald L. K. Smith,[1] who was Huey Long's[2] chief of staff, has opened headquarters of his own in New York, under the name of the Committee of 100,000. He lives at the Murray Hill Hotel, but his headquarters are at the Hotel Pennsylvania.

I dropped in to see him this morning, and found him with his wife, a very charming woman. Gerald told me that his experience with Huey Long and Dr. Townsend[3] convinced him that it was useless to attempt to start a national movement anywhere save in New York. He accordingly moved on Manhattan and proceeded to look about him. He told me that at the start he had only three men interested, but that now he has 100,000 members on his rolls. He headed directly for the rich, and was soon invited to present the issues of the hour to the profound thinkers of the Union League Club. One of them was so impressed that he invited Gerald to repeat his speech at the Piping Rock Club. He has been in funds ever since, and tonight begins a series of thirteen radio harangues over Station WINS, which is owned by the New York *American*.

At his invitation I went with him to the station in 48th street to see and hear him perform. He had a manuscript, and it apparently cramped him during the first part of his half hour. Toward the end he discarded it and began to cut loose with his old stuff. He took his coat off and indulged himself in violent gestures, just as if he had been before an audience. The latter part of his speech, it seemed to me, was very effective as rabble-rousing. Its argument was to the general

1 Gerald L. K. Smith (1898–1976), evangelist and fiery preacher. His Committee of One Million (not 100,000, as Mencken has it in his entry) was launched as a "nationalist front against Communism," and he founded the America First Committee. In *Heathen Days* (p. 298), Mencken called him "the greatest rabble-rouser since Peter the Hermit."

2 Huey P. Long (1893–1935), U.S. senator, governor (and virtual dictator) of Louisiana, who obtained his following by a promise to "share the wealth." He was assassinated September 8, 1935, in the rotunda of the state capitol.

3 Dr. Francis E. Townsend (1867–1960) achieved fame relatively late in life with his proposal for an Old-Age Revolving Pensions plan, whereby every person sixty or over would receive $200 per month from the federal government but be required to spend it in the United States during the month following. The entry for June 2, 1943 (pp. 252–254), discusses him further.

effect that Communism and its associated heresies have begun to offer serious menace to the old flag and the old religion.

Gerald took a crack at John L. Lewis,[1] and offered various other palatable tidbits to the Economic Royalists he apparently has his eye on. One of them, name unknown, sat in the control room with me while the speech was going on. Outside was a small, homely woman, introduced as Mrs. Havemeyer. Gerald told me that he was making a play for the American Legion, and that he also had begun to develop a considerable trade among Polish Catholics. He is apparently trying to get together all the opponents of Bolshevism.

A clipping came in today denouncing him for a speech he lately made at the Hempstead High School on Long Island. It reached me because the release sent out by his publicity bureau quoted an article on him that I once wrote for the Baltimore *Evening Sun*. The quotation included the following:

> "Mr. Smith is for the Constitution until the last galoot's ashore. He loathes and abominates all the enemies of the Republic from boll weevils to Bolsheviks. He is against droughts, revolutions, atheism, Karl Marx and the dope traffic, and in favor of justice, charity, xenophobia, lawful wedlock, the care and nurture of children, going to church on Sunday, a strong navy, and the home in all its phases, however humble."[2]

Obviously, Gerald and his press agent have a sense of humor, and are not too greatly impressed by the intelligence of the persons they are trying to reach.

Gerald told me of a neat trick he played on the porch-climbers who swarmed about Townsend at the Cleveland convention last Summer. He told me he wanted to get rid of them one evening for some purpose, and so took them aside one by one and asked each: "What, above all things, would you like to have in this world?" One answered: "A radio station in California," and others made similar grandiose answers. Gerald then said to each one: "Be in room so and so at 9 o'clock tonight and stay there until you receive a visitor." He thus

---

1 John L. Lewis (1880–1969), labor leader, president of the United Mine Workers from 1920 to 1960, a co-founder and first president of the Congress of Industrial Organizations (CIO).

2 The passage is from the Monday Article for September 7, 1936, entitled "Why Not Gerald?"

planted each of the porch-climbers in a separate room, and kept them immobilized until he had finished his dirty work—whatever it was.

The Garden City complaint against him accused him of anti-Semitism. I asked him this morning if he were inclining that way and he denied it. His wife expressed horror of the thought. Nevertheless, I am convinced that Gerald is preparing to get aboard the great anti-Semitic movement now rolling up in New York.

NEW YORK, JUNE 20, 1937.

I took Alfred and Marcella du Pont[1] and Margaret Case Harriman[2] to dinner at Lüchow's. We went downtown a little after 6 and stopped in Union Square to listen to the soap-boxers. The du Ponts were very eager to hear some of the Communist brethren, but the best speeches were being made by anti-Communists. One of them, an elderly man who described himself as a machinist, made a really good harangue. It was so good, in fact, that he impressed some of the Communists, and their heckling was very mild.

We also dropped over to S. Klein's place,[3] but found it closed. The door, however, was open, and the man and woman on guard permitted us to come in. Neither Marcella du Pont nor Margaret Harriman had ever been there. They were immensely impressed by the selling system. If business had been going on both of them would have bought clothes.

The du Ponts are planning to sail on the *Kungsholm* in a couple of weeks. Alfred has just been awarded the contract to design a new hospital at Wilmington. This hospital is controlled by the anti-du Pont faction in the town, and so he is especially delighted by the award.

After dinner we went to Margaret Harriman's apartment and sat around for an hour or so. She put on a record of King Edward's abdication speech. I still maintain that it is a magnificent piece of ora-

1 Alfred and Marcella du Pont were very close friends of Mencken's for many years. They met on a Caribbean cruise which he and Sara took in the winter of 1932, and the two couples continued to see each other regularly thereafter. Following Sara's death Mencken visited them often at their home in Wilmington, Delaware, and brought Joe and Dorothy Hergesheimer into their circle. The du Ponts' marriage eventually broke up, but Mencken's friendship with Marcella lasted for the rest of his life and there is an extensive correspondence between them.
2 Margaret Case Harriman, journalist, was the daughter of Frank Case, owner of the Algonquin Hotel where Mencken always stayed on his trips to New York.
3 A New York store specializing in low-priced women's apparel.

tory. La Harriman said that she had been told that it was written for Edward by John Masefield. This I rather doubt, for Masefield's prose is not particularly good. I rather suspect some of the brethren of the London press.[1]

BALTIMORE, JUNE 20, 1937.

Three days in New York almost knocked me out. I had to eat three heavy dinners, and to drink more than was good for me. I was certainly not tight, but nevertheless I developed a most uncomfortable gastritis. Today I have subsisted on four eggs, two glasses of milk and an ice cream soda. The ice cream soda was the first that I had drunk for at least thirty years.

BALTIMORE, JUNE 21, 1937.

I had lunch in New York a couple of days ago with Paul Palmer, editor of the *American Mercury*. He told me that his circulation is now 70,000, and that the magazine is showing a profit. Unfortunately, he doesn't like the hard work that editing it involves. He has a rich wife, and lives in great luxury at Ridgefield, Conn. He says he'd prefer to run a literary magazine, but that he realizes he must print a lot of politics. This political stuff doesn't interest him greatly, and as a result he is somewhat fretful. He even talked of selling the magazine, and seems to have formulated a project to make Albert Jay Nock its new editor—apparently with some new angel. Nock, it seems to me, is too old for the job.

Palmer's success with the magazine shows its inherent vigor. If the Knopfs had operated it more economically and let me alone, we'd have all made a great deal of money out of it. Its opportunity was never better than now. The growing reaction against the New Deal sets up a situation not unlike that following the war. There is an immense audience ready for attacks on the Rooseveltian hooey, and most of the other magazines seem to be afraid to print them.

The other day, going to New York, I bought both the *Atlantic Monthly* and *Harper's*. They are almost inconceivably feeble. The writing in the *Atlantic* used to be at least respectable, but I encoun-

1 In later years the Duke of Windsor claimed to have written the abdication speech himself, with some assistance from Winston Churchill. See also the entry for July 23, opposite.

tered one article that was a downright botch. Both *Harper's* and the *Atlantic Monthly* flirted with the New Deal for four years, and are now finding it difficult to get from under it.

BALTIMORE, MD.

JUNE 24, 1937.

Edmund and Anne Duffy, who have been visiting Hervey Allen[1] at his place on the Eastern Shore of Maryland, are full of strange stories about the way he runs it. He is an enormously orderly fellow, and keeps the most elaborate accounts. The performance of his five automobiles is entered daily on a card. The card shows the amount of gasoline and oil consumed, the mileage run, and all mishaps that may have occurred. The lighting plant in Allen's house is in duplicate, so that there can be no break in the service. Every key in use on the place has its hook in a large key rack, and the key rack itself is locked.

The Duffys say that Allen spends at least half his time attending to such pedantic details of life. He made over a million dollars out of "Anthony Adverse," and is under no necessity to work. But he has just completed another novel almost as long.

BALTIMORE, MD.

JULY 23, 1937.

George Gunther, the former brewer, called me up yesterday and asked me to come to the Rennert Hotel today on important business. He lives there since his retirement, and spends most of his time lolling in the lobby. When I got to the hotel I found that the business in hand was to meet the Rev. R. Anderson Jardine, late vicar of Darlington. He turned out to be a complete jackass—indeed, he seemed even stupider than his client Davy.[2] He had his wife with him—a skinny, horse-faced woman, who looked curiously like Dr. Townsend, the Old-Age Pension fanatic.

1 Hervey Allen (1889–1949) is best known for his huge and highly popular novel *Anthony Adverse* (1933) and for his authoritative biography of Edgar Allan Poe, *Israfel* (1926).
2 "Davy" refers to the Duke of Windsor, the former King Edward VIII, who in 1936 abdicated the English throne in order to marry the former Wallis Warfield Simpson of Baltimore, "the woman I love."

The vicar is in the United States on a lecture tour, and seems to be making heavy weather of it. The heat of the Summer, of course, is a poor time for lectures. Moreover, there is very little remaining interest in the marriage of Davy and Wally Warfield. I spent ten minutes listening to the vicar and couldn't go any more.

With him were two lecture agents, and a newspaper woman from Dayton, Ohio. She was a large, motherly woman, running to bosom, and she allowed that she desired to see me at greater length a bit later on. What she is doing in Baltimore I don't know.

Today there came a letter from Stanton Leeds,[1] asking me for a copy of my *Evening Sun* article on the Windsor-Warfield marriage. He told me that Wally had told him in France that she considered it very unfriendly. God knows she had plenty of ground. It was probably the most unfriendly article on the marriage printed in all the United States.[2] I have no copy of it save one that is mounted in a book, and so I couldn't send one to Leeds. Nor could I send him a copy of my Associated Press article on the same subject.

BALTIMORE, MD.
JULY 28, 1937.

Today the last of my twenty articles on the Johns Hopkins Hospital was printed in the *Sun*. They have been running for more than three weeks, and I began collecting materials for them at least six weeks ago. I was, of course, more or less familiar with what may be called the gross anatomy of the John Hopkins, but I had never gone through it in detail. When I finished my investigation I probably knew more about the place than any single man in it. Most of the members of the staff, of course, confine their attention to their own clinics, and some of them know very little about what is going on across the hall.

The series brought me very few letters, and apparently attracted relatively little attention in Baltimore. The idea of doing it occurred to me about three years ago. Sara was then a patient at the hospital

---

1 Stanton B. Leeds (1886?–1964), author and newspaperman, at one time foreign correspondent for the Hearst papers.
2 Mencken's Monday Article for December 21, 1936, entitled "The Exile of Enzesfeld," had relatively little to say about Mrs. Simpson, or even about the marriage, but was rather a scathing indictment of the former King both as private man and as public figure.

and one day Winford Smith,[1] the director, came in to see her while I was there. We fell into talk about the needs of the Hopkins, and I told him that I'd be glad to do a series of articles for the *Sun* showing the people of Baltimore how it was carrying on its work, and under what difficulties. Sara's death at the Johns Hopkins put the matter out of my mind, and it was not until I became a patient there myself last December that it revived. Smith and I then discussed it again, and eventually I tackled the job.

One of my curious discoveries (not mentioned in the articles for the *Sun*) was that the only sex instruction offered to Johns Hopkins medical students is provided by the Phipps Clinic,[2] which is to say, by the department of lunacy. This perhaps explains the noticeable fact that medical men as a class are often singularly naïve on the subject. They are supposed to advise their patients about it, but it is my experience that their own knowledge is usually very meagre. They know, of course, what may be called the anatomy and physiology of sex, but beyond that they don't go. Even their advice about contraceptive devices is usually extremely unsound. The public, of course, assumes that they know all about the subject, and is always willing to follow them blindly.

Adolf Meyer, the head of the Phipps Institute, spoke of the sex books in his library with great contempt. He had them shelved along with books on the Freudian and other such quackeries. I am inclined to believe that this judgment is sound. Certainly I have never read one that showed any real sense.

BALTIMORE, MD.

AUGUST 9, 1937.

Sister Miriam[3] and Sister Patricia came in for lunch yesterday. Sister Miriam is professor of English at Misericordia College at Dallas,

---

1 Winford H. Smith (1877–1961) was director of the Johns Hopkins Hospital from 1911 to 1946.

2 The Henry Phipps Psychiatric Clinic was the unit of Hopkins devoted to the study and treatment of psychiatric disorders. Dr. Adolf Meyer (1866–1950) headed it from 1910 to 1941.

3 Sister Miriam Gallagher (1886–1966) was a member of the Order of Sisters of Mercy of the Union, which she entered in 1903. Her proposed dissertation on James Huneker was never completed, but she continued to correspond with Mencken for several years. He suspected—probably quite rightly—that she was subtly trying to convert him to Catholicism, but he always replied politely to her letters.

Pa. I came into contact with her seven or eight years ago, when she sent me one of the annual Year Books brought out by her pupils. It was full of extraordinarily good verse, and I wrote to her complimenting her on it. She is herself a competent minor poet, and frequently contributes to the Catholic papers.

She turned out to be a tall, bespectacled and somewhat deaf lady of middle age. Sister Patricia, who belongs to the Baltimore house of her order, came along as a sort of chaperon.

Sister Miriam is now working for her Ph.D. at the Catholic University, and her professor has assigned her James Huneker[1] as the subject for her thesis. The Catholic interest in poor old Jim is due to the report that he returned to the church on his death-bed. I have some doubt that this actually happened. Certainly while he was in the full possession of his faculties he was anything but one of the faithful. It is, however, possible that his wife, Josephine, who I believe is a Jewess, brought in a priest at the last moment, and then had him buried in consecrated ground.

Sister Miriam wanted to see my Huneker material, and talk to me about the old boy. I warned her that his letters were extremely racy, and that she had better confine herself to his doings as a critic. His chief interest was in music and, unfortunately, she appears to know nothing about the subject. When I mentioned the name of Massenet she actually asked me to spell it. Thus I fear that she is in for a hard job, especially in view of the fact that her professor seems to be a somewhat skittish fellow. I offered to lend her any of the Huneker books in my possession. One of his letters to me is pasted in the front part of each of them. Some of these letters are certainly not suitable Sunday reading for nunneries.

The two ladies came in at 11 o'clock. When lunch time approached I invited them to stay. Sister Miriam was hot for it, but Sister Patricia raised objections. She said that she had not obtained permission from her superior to stay out for the meal, and that she feared some un-

---

1 James Gibbons Huneker (1860–1921), American critic and novelist. Huneker was primarily a music critic, covering performances of the New York Philharmonic and the Metropolitan Opera for various papers and magazines, but his interest extended also to literature and painting, and he did much to encourage new developments in all three fields. His novel *Painted Veils* (1920) was considered pornographic in its time. He had a very great influence on the young Mencken, and the two men later became friends.

pleasantness if she did so. I suggested that she call up the convent, but after thinking it over she decided to take the chance.

We had a good lunch with a dash of Rhine wine. The two nuns stayed until after 2 o'clock. As I bowed them into their taxicab I noticed that various members of the Stricker family next door were at their windows. They are pious Catholics, and the son of the house is actually a priest.

My brother August sat in at lunch, but there were no other women present save the servants.

BALTIMORE, MD.

AUGUST 30, 1937.

In the Spring of 1917, after the United States had entered the war and the spy hunt had begun, I suggested to J. H. Adams, then editor of the *Sun*, that some of the things we were printing threw an unwarranted suspicion on perfectly peaceful German-Americans. I told him that many of them were quite innocent of political activity, and that the uproars going on exposed them to serious injury. Adams was a somewhat violent liberal, and I naturally supposed that he would want to print something in the *Sun* diverting the mob from these persons. To my considerable surprise, he refused to do anything of the sort. On the contrary, he told me that he believed that all German-Americans, however innocent, deserved to be harassed. This doctrine so vastly astonished me that I never opened the subject with him again.

The *Sun*, in point of fact, was less violent than most American newspapers, but nevertheless it was guilty of some outrageous inflammatory articles. Among other things, it undoubtedly had a share in the dismissal of Dr. Schumacher from the faculty of St. John's College at Annapolis. Schumacher was a perfectly harmless man and had never taken the slightest hand in the discussion that went on before the United States entered the war. In the spring of 1917 the *Sun* printed various articles calling attention to him, and as a result he was thrown out of St. John's in an extremely brutal manner. His salary had been small, and he was presently in very serious difficulties. What became of him eventually I don't know.

BALTIMORE, MD.

SEPTEMBER 6, 1937.

On Friday, September 3rd, I went to West Chester, Pa., and there had dinner with Joe Hergesheimer in the evening. It was a stag affair, with only six at table. They were: Judge Biggs, of the United States Circuit Court; Judge Windel, chief of the Chester county bench; Archie du Pont; John Hemphill; Joe and me.

We had an excellent dinner, beginning with mint juleps, and probably drank one or two drinks too many. When we got up Saturday morning both Joe and I were somewhat woozy. Nevertheless, we carried out a long contemplated plan to visit the Pennsylvania-Dutch region in Lancaster and Berks counties, Pa. Joe is himself a Pennsylvania-Dutchman, and I have lived within a hundred miles of the area all my life, yet neither of us had ever seen it.

We drove to Lancaster in the morning, and were there met by Dr. Herbert J. Beck, professor of chemistry at Franklin and Marshall College. He very kindly offered to squire us around. It turned out in a little while that he was a great deal more interested in history than we were. What we had come to see was the country people, not the historical monuments. But Beck was amiable, and quickly fell in with our plans.

We went to Lititz for lunch, and then proceeded to the northern part of the county. We stopped at several farms and had palavers with the countrymen. The most interesting we met were two enormously fat sisters near Lebanon. They are old maids and operate their rather large farm with the help of one hired man. They also take Summer boarders. Some time ago a man, whose name I forget, stayed with them for several months, and then went back to New York and wrote a book on the Pennsylvania-Dutch. The sisters greatly resented some of the things he had put into it, and especially the hint that they themselves spoke broken English. As a matter of fact, their English was excellent, and they seemed very enlightened women. Certainly their farm was beautifully kept. As we got in one of them was helping the hired man to kill chickens for Sunday. The sight of blood almost made poor Hergie sick.

We proceeded into the northern part of Lancaster county and passed through towns of such astonishing names as Blue Ball, Bird-in-Hand, and Intercourse. How Intercourse got its name no one knows. The place attracts a great many automobile tourists, who stop off to send out postcards.

We landed finally in Schaefferstown, at the head of the county—a really old-fashioned Pennsylvania-Dutch community. In the town bar the town drunk tackled us in the dialect, and we heard the saloon-keeper's wife gabbling in it with a Coca Cola delivery man.

The lunch at Lititz included fried apples, dumplings and Dutch pickles. We stopped at Lancaster in the evening. Mrs. Beck gave a reception for us, and we met most of the town notables. Some of them turned out to be very amusing people, and altogether the evening was anything but unpleasant. Beck provided a 6% beer made in Lancaster. It was certainly not bad, though one had to be careful in drinking it.

Sunday morning Hergesheimer and I started out alone for Berks county. We covered a great deal of the territory we had visited on Saturday, and in addition saw some new towns, including Ephrata, the Jerusalem of the Pennsylvania-Dutch. We stopped off long enough to see the horrible old stone house in which the pious sisters of 200 years ago used to live and work. The countryside was lovely, and the farms looked magnificent. But even the largest barns commonly have huge eyes painted on them to keep off witches. This is the domain of Pennsylvania-Dutch Hexerei, and two-thirds of the farmers undoubtedly believe in it.

We got to Reading toward the end of the morning, and then proceeded to Allentown and Bethlehem. We had lunch at Bethlehem, and then came down the beautiful valley to Norristown. By this time we were out of the Pennsylvania-Dutch territory, but it was a beautiful country nevertheless. Some of the houses in the villages were really superb. Most of them were built of red brick with white trim. Others were of white clapboard with green trim. Their complete simplicity was perfectly charming.

We arrived at West Chester late in the afternoon, and Hergesheimer's chauffeur drove me to Wilmington. I was back home in time for dinner.

The farmers throughout Lancaster were engaged in getting in their tobacco. How often as a boy I had heard of this tobacco. My grandfather used to go to Lancaster county every Summer and buy it in the field and my father followed him later on. In those days a great deal of it was worked up into cheap cigars by the farmers themselves. During the dull days of Winter they would roll two-fers.[1] All that trade is now abandoned. The tobacco goes to Lancaster and there it is made into cigars by machines.

It was a pleasant adventure, and I enjoyed every minute of it. The

1 "Two-fer" was a term referring to cheap cigars, sold usually "two for" a nickel.

weather was terribly hot on Saturday, but on Sunday morning it turned cold, with a stiff Northeast wind.

Hergesheimer doesn't look too well. His blood sugar is still above normal, and he is forbidden to eat any form of starch or drink anything alcoholic save Scotch whiskey. Inasmuch as he doesn't like Scotch, he ordinarily abstains altogether. He leads a lonely life in West Chester. His wife Dorothy is on the Jersey coast, and he lives in the house alone with his servants. He is comfortable enough physically, but the endless evenings must be rather hard to bear. He tells me that he is coming to Baltimore in a few weeks to spend the Winter. He proposes to take an apartment and bring along his cook. He has a plan in hand to write his autobiography, and he wants to do it here.

BALTIMORE, MD.

OCTOBER 3, 1937.

Dr. Francis E. Litz, translator of "De charlataneria eruditorum," has discovered a really astonishing error in the book. It is described on the title page as translated from the German. It was actually translated, of course, from the Latin. Litz says that he did not see the proof of the title page, but I suspect that he really did. It was reset several times while the book was under way, and that fact probably explains the error. It not only passed me; it also passed the proof-room of the Plimpton Press and several people on the staff of Alfred A. Knopf, Inc. It is now too late to make a correction. The book was printed in a limited edition of about 1,400 copies, and there is very little chance that there will be a reprint.

The worst errors in books often appear on title pages. No one seems to read proofs of them with any care. Years ago, when Philip Goodman brought out the first edition of my "In Defense of Women," his own name was misspelled on the title page, appearing as Phpip.[2] Goodman was a stickler for typographical niceties, and I know that he gave a great deal of hard work to the book. Nevertheless, a glaring error on the most conspicuous page completely eluded him.

---

1 Mencken has here managed to misspell the misspelling. Goodman's first name appeared on the title page of *In Defense of Women* as "Ppilip."

1938

John W. Owens, editor of the *Sun*, went to Washington the other day to see Thomas Corcoran,[1] one of Roosevelt's chief advisers. He made the trip at Corcoran's request. Corcoran told him that Roosevelt was much concerned about the vacancy on the Supreme Court caused by the death of Cardozo.[2] Roosevelt is being beset by Middle Western and Western politicians. They argue that the Court is now composed predominantly of Easterners, and that the vacancy ought to go to a Westerner. Unfortunately, they have failed so far to suggest any candidates suitable for the job. Corcoran told Owens that the Western courts seldom, if ever, produce really first-rate judges. There are forty times as many good men in New York City alone as are to be found in the whole territory west of the Mississippi.

Corcoran is strongly in favor of disregarding sectional lines in appointments to the Supreme Court, and he says that Roosevelt leans the same way. He asked Owens to write an editorial to that effect. He said that if the *Sun* took a strong line it would probably be followed by other newspapers, and that Roosevelt would thus have the body of public opinion behind him and be able to meet the onslaught of the Western politicians.

Corcoran indicated to Owens that Roosevelt begins to realize that he had better handle the Supreme Court gingerly. Corcoran says that

1 Thomas G. Corcoran (1900–1981) held various government posts during the Roosevelt New Deal years.
2 Benjamin N. Cardozo (1870–1938), named to the Supreme Court by President Herbert Hoover in 1932.

he (Corcoran) was opposed to the Court packing scheme, but went along in loyalty after it had been announced by Roosevelt.

Corcoran told Owens that he has some confidence in Hugo Black.[1] He believes that he may eventually become a competent judge. At the moment, he remains a comic character. He senses the fact that his fellow judges distrust him, and so he is full of truculence and his personal relations with them are very bad—in fact, he leads an extremely lonely life. He is especially jealous of the new judge, Reed.[2] Reed's appointment was praised almost universally. Black has told friends that this indicates to him that Reed must be a trimmer, else he would not be favored by all parties.

Black has been unable to come to terms with Chief Justice Hughes.[3] Hughes's contempt for him is not concealed, and Black resents it bitterly. His whole performance, indeed, is that of the Southern cracker that he is. He is consumed by an inferiority complex, and it manifests itself by a hostile and provocative spirit. He announces his dissents in a loud voice, and is otherwise extremely objectionable to the older judges. Black is especially hostile to Justice Stone.[4] He believes that Stone provided the materials for an article on him lately published in the *Saturday Evening Post* by Marquis W. Childs.[5] His suspicion is well-founded. Childs's material actually came from Stone, whose dislike for Black is unconcealed.

Owens says that Corcoran apparently favors Felix Frankfurter for Cardozo's place. The Roosevelt kitchen cabinet would like to see Brandeis[6] retire, for he has become quite senile. He is willing himself,

1 Hugo Black (1886–1971) was named to the Supreme Court by President Franklin D. Roosevelt in 1937. His appointment aroused considerable controversy, especially when it was discovered after his confirmation that he had once been a member of the Ku Klux Klan. See Mencken's Monday Article for October 11, 1937, entitled "Last Words on Hugo."

2 Stanley F. Reed (1884–1980) was named to the Supreme Court by President Roosevelt in 1938 and served until his retirement in 1957.

3 Charles Evans Hughes (1862–1948) was named to the Supreme Court in 1910 by President William Howard Taft but resigned in 1916 to run against Woodrow Wilson in the presidential election of that year. In 1930 President Hoover named him Chief Justice, and he served until his retirement in 1941.

4 Harlan Fiske Stone (1872–1946) was named to the Supreme Court in 1925 by President Calvin Coolidge and succeeded Charles Evans Hughes as Chief Justice upon Hughes's retirement.

5 Marquis W. Childs (b. 1903), Iowa-born journalist and political commentator.

6 Louis D. Brandeis (1856–1941) was named to the Supreme Court by President Wilson in 1916.

but his wife objects. His senility takes the form of forgetfulness. He can scarcely remember anything of recent date, though he remembers clearly things that happened years ago.

Owens, of course, heard Corcoran with a good many mental reservations. He is certainly not willing to let the New Deal theologians employ the *Sun* as a sounding board. But inasmuch as he was planning on his own motion to print an editorial arguing that sectional considerations ought to be forgotten in filling Cardozo's place, he has decided to go ahead.

BALTIMORE, MD.

OCTOBER 12, 1938.

Dean Lewis, professor of surgery at the Johns Hopkins, is laid up in the hospital in a serious state. I hear that he has aphasia. Lewis is a hard worker, and for years past has been pushing himself mercilessly. He not only does a great deal of operating; he also devotes a lot of time to teaching and, in addition, he has been busy during the past few years in fighting off the socialists who are hopeful of ruining the American Medical Association.

Some time ago, at a private gathering, Lewis expressed the opinion that Roosevelt was a paranoiac. Some one present took the news to Washington, and a little while afterward Lewis was visited by an income tax inspector. He was put through a dreadful investigation, greatly to his ire. In the end it turned out that his income tax returns were perfectly in order. The inspector, in fact, apologized for putting him to so much trouble. It seems to me quite plain that this onslaught followed directly out of Lewis's denunciation of Roosevelt.

BALTIMORE, MD.

OCTOBER 22, 1938.

A letter from Perry Molstad, a telephone official in New York who is interested in books, contains some interesting stuff about the late Thomas C. Wolfe.[1] He says, among other things, that when Wolfe's first book, "Look Homeward, Angel," was printed, and he sent a copy

1 Thomas Wolfe (1900–1938) had died at the Johns Hopkins Hospital in Baltimore just a few weeks earlier.

to his family in Asheville, N.C., he received a telegram from his mother and sister reading, "Christ had His Judas—we have you."

BALTIMORE, MD.

NOVEMBER 11, 1938.

H. R. Knickerbocker,[1] foreign correspondent for Hearst, was in Baltimore last night delivering a lecture. I met him later, and for the first time. His appearance rather astonished me. He was born in Texas and is the son of a Protestant preacher, but he looks decidedly Jewish. He has the reddish hair of a blond Jew, along with the faint freckles and pinkish eyes.

He told me that he was well acquainted with Hitler, and used to see him relatively frequently in the days before Hitler came to power. At that time there were rumors that Hitler's iron cross was bogus, and Knickerbocker one day ventured to ask him about it. Hitler said that he had got it in the following manner:

During the war he was a dispatch rider, and one day he was sent across a part of the front that was a kind of No Man's Land. The Germans assumed that there were no Frenchmen in it, but when he had got half way across Hitler heard French voices and on investigation found that there were a number of Frenchmen in a dugout. Hitler approached the only entrance and barked several loud orders, hoping to convince the men within that a considerable German party was above. The trick worked, and in a few minutes Hitler had the Frenchmen coming out one by one, their hands in the air. He was armed only with a pistol, but inasmuch as they came out wholly unarmed, he was able to line them up and march them back to the German lines. It was for this exploit that he received the iron cross.

Knickerbocker said that the story was told to him in the presence of an English correspondent. When it was finished Hitler said politely: "If these Frenchmen had been either Englishmen or Americans the chances are that I'd not be here."

Knickerbocker said that Hitler in his private relations is a very amiable fellow, and has a considerable sense of humor. But whenever he gets on public matters he begins to orate. Knickerbocker said that

---

1 Hubert R. Knickerbocker (1898–1949), journalist, war correspondent, and author.

he'll start in an ordinary tone of voice and that in a few minutes he'll be howling like a stump speaker, with his arms sawing the air.

Knickerbocker is also acquainted with Mussolini. He told me that Mussolini hates Hitler violently, and will undoubtedly walk out on him at the first chance.

BALTIMORE, MD.

NOVEMBER 25, 1938.

At the dinner to Thomas S. Cullen[1] on November 19th, I sat at a table with, among others, J. Albert Chatard.[2] Chatard is of French origin, and his people came to Baltimore from Haiti at the time of the revolution there. He is the fifth of his name to practise medicine, and his son is even now an intern at the Johns Hopkins. He was himself a student there in the days when Gertrude Stein was also a student. She graduated from Radcliffe in 1897, and spent the years from 1897 to 1902 in the Johns Hopkins Medical School. She never got her degree. Dr. J. Whitridge Williams, head of the department of obstetrics, plucked her in that subject. He detested women doctors and, in addition, had a violent prejudice against all women who were fat. La Stein, even in those days, weighed nearly 200 pounds.

Chatard told me that she was known to the other students as the Battle-ax. Women medical students were then something of a novelty and the men held aloof from them. The girls accordingly decided to give some parties. At the first attended by Chatard, Stein showed up smoking a pipe. This was a dreadful shock in those innocent days. If it had been done by a woman of normal attractiveness all the male students present would have invited her to bed at once. But inasmuch as the revolutionist was Stein, no such suggestion was made.

After the same dinner I happened to leave the banquet room directly behind Dr. J. M. T. Finney. He was talking with a visiting medico and I couldn't help overhearing what he said. The visitor inquired about Dean Lewis, professor of surgery at the Hopkins.

1 Thomas Stephen Cullen (1868–1953), long an illustrious figure on the Baltimore medical scene, succeeded Dr. Howard A. Kelly as professor of gynecology at the Johns Hopkins.
2 Joseph Albert Chatard (1879–1956) was an instructor at the Johns Hopkins for many years but was primarily what was then known as a "family doctor." On the occasion of his death the *Sun* called him "a physician in the prespecialist sense of the word."

"Lewis," said Finney, "has been pretty ill. He had a little cerebral accident." This euphemism for stroke of apoplexy struck me as very nifty. I have since been told that it is in common use among medical men.

Lewis has been out of service for six weeks. His stroke left him disabled on one side, and with his speech impaired. In all probability, he'll never be able to return to work. He is a very agreeable fellow, and has always been an immensely energetic worker. The students in the Hopkins Medical School rather dislike him, but that is only because he is a harsh examiner. He never lets them get away with bluffs. Either they know the matter under discussion or he orders them to go back to their books. His phrase, "You had better look that up," is a byword at the Medical School.

1939

When Edgar Lee Masters was here the other day he told me that Dreiser, who is now living at Glendale, California, is broke. Six or eight years ago, following several sales to the movies, Dreiser was rolling in money. Unfortunately, he put most of it into a grotesque house at Mount Kisco, New York. He invited me to spend a week-end with him there, but I always evaded the visit. People who saw the house reported that it was almost fabulous. It had been designed in large part by Dreiser himself, and he was also responsible for its painting, which was predominantly blue. Keeping up the place was too much for his resources, and he made various efforts to sell it. In the end, he probably had to part with it for a small fraction of its cost.

Two or three years ago he got into a controversy with a Jew named Pell, the heir and assign of the old Liveright publishing house. They sued each other, and Dreiser lost on all counts. He took the case to the New York Court of Appeals, but it sustained the verdicts awarded below. Altogether, according to Masters, this litigation cost him nearly $20,000.

Masters says that Dreiser went to Glendale in company with a gal whose name he forgets. He says that she is young and very saucy, and that he commonly calls her and thinks of her as "The Cricket." When she and Dreiser arrived in Glendale, Dreiser's old girl, Helen Richardson, who had been in Seattle, heard of it and descended upon them. After a sharp, short battle the Cricket was thrown out and Helen is once more mistress of the mansion. She comes from the South—I think, from Charleston—and is a good-looking and superior woman. She has stuck to Dreiser through many years, and for a long while passed under the name of Mrs. Dreiser. Dreiser's actual wife, Sara, is probably still alive. She is a small woman from the wilds of the Middle West, with red hair and a firm belief in Christian Science. She is a year or two older than Dreiser, which makes her about 70. For many years Dreiser tried to induce her to give him a divorce, but she always refused. She spent a large part of her time visiting his friends in New York and telling them what a villain he was. She had, in the days when I knew her, a job in a publishing house. What has become of her, if she is still alive, I don't know.

Dreiser is supposed to be writing a new book at Glendale. Masters believes that he'll never finish it. I am rather more optimistic. He has in his lockers the manuscripts of at least four or five unfinished books, and it would be an easy job for him to push one or another of them to completion.

Unfortunately, his publishing arrangements are not very good. After a lifetime of accusing publishers of keeping two sets of books and engaging in other such infamies, he is now in the hands of Simon and Schuster. I hear that they are not bound by their contract with him to keep his early books in print. He owns the rights to all of them, recovered from his various publishers, but Simon and Schuster simply agreed to bring out those for which there is an appreciable demand. That means, I suspect, very few of them.

Dreiser told me the last time I saw him that he had come to believe that California was the true dwelling place for an elderly literary man. He said that he could work there, and greatly preferred the climate to that of New York. He told me that Glendale was a retired spot, and that he had no contact whatever with the movie people. This last I doubt. If there are any likely-looking young gals still in the movies the old boy will certainly crawl out of his bastile to have a look at them. He has been a set-up for women all his life. I can't recall the time when he was not engaged in affairs with at least three. All the women he has lived with—a somewhat longish list in itself—have spent half their time beating off interlopers.

BALTIMORE, MD.

JANUARY 17, 1939.

At Schellhase's last night I encountered Hulbert Footner,[1] the novelist. He has a place on the Patuxent River in Southern Maryland, and usually spends the Winter in Baltimore. He has lived in Maryland for many years, and is full of amusing anecdotes about the yokels of Calvert county, the most remote and backward county in the State.

Not long ago, a farmer named Gantt was murdered down there, and within the past few weeks a young fellow and two girls were sent to prison for dispatching him. Footner knew Gantt, and often employed him at odd jobs. Some time ago, he said, he set him to work painting a room. It was to be done in two colors of blue, and Gantt labored at it for weeks. He would first paint the light blue part and then proceed to the dark blue part. Every time he made this switch some of the dark blue paint got splashed on the light blue part and the light blue part had to be done over again. When this was undertaken, some of the light blue paint splashed on the dark blue part, and so there was need for another coat. Footner says that Gantt finally got seven coats on the room. Footner then fired him, and Gantt left muttering.

He operated a small farm, and also had a concession at one of the primeval amusement parks on the Patuxent River. He always carried all his money in his pocket, and was fond of exhibiting it when drunk. This habit cost him his life. His murderers, learning that he had $900 in hand, were upset by the smell of so much wealth. They visited him at his own farm, and after a preliminary debauch dispatched him. Footner says that common opinion was to the effect that his death was good riddance.

BALTIMORE, MD.

APRIL 15, 1939.

In going through some old bills I found the other day that the house I was born in was No. 380 W. Lexington street in 1880. I wrote to the

---

1 Hulbert Footner (1879–1944), Canadian-born novelist, playwright, and historian. He served for a time on the staff of the *Sunpapers*, where he and Mencken met and became friends. His best-known book (at least to Marylanders) was *Maryland Main and the Eastern Shore* (1942), a county-by-county description of the entire state.

Appeal Tax Court asking the present number and was informed that it is now 811.[1] This morning I went down to Lexington street to have a look. I found a pleasant little three-story house, directly opposite a slum area that is being cleared off under the Federal housing scheme. The door of the place was open, and inside I found a colored man on a stepladder and a white man on another. The colored man told me that he was the new owner of the place. He had been living in his own house in the slum area, but the government had now condemned it. He told me that the price he got for it was considerably less than his investment. He had used the money to buy No. 811 and was now engaged in rehabilitating it. He was scraping the accumulated wallpaper off the parlor walls, and the white man, a plasterer, was patching the holes that this work revealed. The colored man seemed to be a very intelligent and decent fellow. He told me that he hoped some day to put in a central heating plant, and I was tempted to offer him the price. I'll probably go back to see him at some time in the near future.

Fifteen or twenty years ago my mother pointed out the house to me, but after her death I could no longer identify it. It is a three-story building in a sad state of disrepair. When I was born in it West Lexington street was almost suburban. There were trees all along both curbs, and the roadway was hardly more than a country road. The whole neighborhood has been given over to Negroes for many years, and has steadily and rapidly deteriorated. As I have said, the block opposite has been condemned as one of the worst slums in Baltimore, and is to be pulled down and rebuilt. This condemnation apparently took no account of the fact that the colored man now renovating No. 811 owned his own house and made diligent efforts to keep it in repair. In even the worst slum areas there are plenty of such men. All the older streets of Baltimore show their thrift and industry. Unfortunately, their neighbors have deteriorated so vastly that their houses become almost uninhabitable. This poor man not only got an insufficient price for his own house; he was also compelled to pay an exaggerated price for his new one, for the rebuilding operations across the street will augment its value. He is one of the forgotten men who always suffer when schemes of uplift are afoot.

1 The system of numbering Baltimore's streets and houses had been a rather haphazard one from the very beginning, and in 1880, by a city ordinance, they were all renumbered according as to whether they went north or south from Baltimore Street and east or west from Charles Street. The system has remained in effect ever since.

BALTIMORE, MD.
APRIL 21, 1939.

I went to Washington yesterday to deliver a brief speech to the Society of American Newspaper Editors. The meeting was held at the National Press Club, and was in charge of Grove Patterson, editor of the Toledo *Blade*. The chairman was William Allen White.[1] He began by delivering a speech that was too long, and the meeting itself was too long. There were no less than five scheduled speeches. I made the last of them. I had prepared a brief discussion of the probable situation of newspapers in case there is another general war. I recalled their difficulties during the last war, and predicted that Ickes,[2] who is their bitter enemy, might be put in charge of them in the next war.

As I came into the hall I saw Josephus Daniels[3] sitting in the front row. Daniels was a member of the Cabinet during the last war, and is an Ambassador under the present administration. In order to avoid embarrassing him, I toned down my speech in a few details. After the meeting I had a palaver with him, and he surprised me by saying that during the World War he had protested bitterly to Albert S. Burleson,[4] Postmaster General, against Burleson's almost insane efforts to censor the press. We did not discuss Ickes directly, but I gathered from what Daniels said that he shared my fears. Altogether, the old boy rather surprised me. He is, to be sure, a hypocrite, but I believe that he was more or less sincere. I asked him if he was drinking any tequila in Mexico, where he is American Ambassador. He confessed that he had tasted it. He is, of course, a lifelong prohibitionist.

One of the other speakers was Harry Haskell, editor of the Kansas City *Star*. The democratic boss of Kansas City, one Pendergast,[5] has

---

1 William Allen White (1868–1944) spent virtually his entire life as publisher and editor of the Emporia (Kansas) *Gazette*, from which unlikely spot he radiated an enormous influence on both journalism and politics. He was also the author of several novels and volumes of short stories.

2 Harold L. Ickes (1874–1952), controversial and curmudgeonly secretary of the interior in the administration of Franklin D. Roosevelt.

3 Josephus Daniels (1862–1948), newspaper editor and diplomat. He was secretary of the navy in the administration of Woodrow Wilson.

4 Albert S. Burleson (1863–1937) served as postmaster general in the Wilson administration.

5 Thomas J. Pendergast (1872–1945) wielded enormous political power in Kansas City. The corruption charges of which Mencken speaks here led to his conviction and

just been indicted for corruption, and Haskell indulged himself in a lot of crowing over the fact. I was tempted to ask him why, if Pendergast was really so corrupt, the *Star* had not exposed and wrecked him long ago. As a matter of fact, the *Star* is a very timorous paper, and I doubt that it had anything to do with Pendergast's final scotching. The war was carried on by other and more courageous heroes.

After the meeting, which lasted three hours and was a considerable bore, I went to the Army and Navy Country Club as the guest of Commander Leland P. Lovette,[1] head of the Navy press bureau, and an old friend. Lovette and his wife were giving a large cocktail party, and I met a great many Naval people, including a large number of Navy wives. I was greatly impressed by their uneasiness. The younger ones all asked me if I thought a war was likely. I told them that I didn't think so. That was only partially accurate, but it seemed decent to try to reassure them.

Among the older officers that I met was Captain Henry Williams, a son of T. J. C. Williams,[2] for long an editorial writer on the Baltimore *Sun*, and later judge of the juvenile court. Lovette told me that Williams is the man who actually designs battleships. He is second in rank in the bureau of construction, and a very important man. He and his wife motored me back to the station and I got home at 8 o'clock. It was a tiresome day, but interesting. I met a great many newspaper men whom I see only seldom, and it was pleasant to palaver with them.

BALTIMORE, MD.

MAY 1, 1939.

I got in this morning by sleeper from Durham, N.C., where I spent two days with Fred M. Hanes[3] and his wife. Hanes is professor of

---

imprisonment. Earlier (1934) he had been instrumental in having Harry S. Truman elected to the U.S. Senate and thus, ultimately, to the presidency.

1 Leland P. Lovette (1897–1967) advanced to the rank of vice admiral in the U.S. Navy and served as its director of public relations from 1937 to 1940 and again from 1942 to 1944. He and Mencken were good friends for many years.

2 Thomas J. C. Williams (1851–1929) served on the staff of the *Sunpapers* from 1891 to 1912 before becoming a judge of the city's juvenile court system. His son Henry (1877–1973) rose through the navy to the rank of rear admiral and, at the time of this entry, was assistant chief of the Bureau of Construction and Repair.

3 Dr. Frederick M. Hanes (1883–1946) and his wife, Betty, a Johns Hopkins nurse,

medicine at Duke University, and an old friend. I always enjoy visiting him. He is very well off, and has a really charming house at Durham. His wife is one of the most accomplished hostesses of my acquaintance. She always manages to make her guests feel perfectly at home.

On Saturday morning Hanes took me to the weekly conference of clinicians and pathologists at the Duke Medical School. The plan is for members of the staff to submit protocols of difficult cases to the professors. The professors thereupon strive to arrive at diagnoses, and after they have said their say the pathologists speak up with the autopsy findings. The first professor was Fred himself. The residents handed him a protocol describing the last days of a patient with numerous and alarming symptoms. The man, in fact, had been ill for years, and all of his vital organs seemed to be affected. There had been considerable and persistent swelling of his abdomen. He had suffered severe pains on his right side, and toward the end of his life he had had several gastric hemorrhages of clear blood. Fred arrived at the conclusion that the man had been suffering from some gall bladder disease. When he finished speaking the pathologist solemnly lifted the cloth over what remained of the patient's viscera and began holding them up one by one. They all turned out to be perfectly normal. There was, to be sure, a small lesion in the heart, but hardly sufficient to have caused the man's death. This astonishing conflict between the clinical picture and the autopsy findings caused a long discussion, but the brethren present could arrive at no conclusion. Finally, someone suggested that it might be a good idea to ask for a suggestion from the only layman present, which was myself. I replied that the man had really not died at all, and proposed that his viscera be thrown back into his abdominal cavity and he be sent home.

On Sunday Betty Hanes invited Dr. Joseph Banks Rhine[1] and his

---

were very good friends of Mencken's for a long time. Dr. Hanes had been professor of medicine at Duke University since 1933.

1 Dr. Joseph B. Rhine (1895–1980), professor of psychology at Duke. His *New Frontiers of the Mind*, which virtually introduced the term "extrasensory perception" to the language, caused enormous controversy when it was published in 1937, and the echoes of it have not entirely died down to this day. In the Monday Article for December 6, 1937, entitled "Every Man His Own Radio," Mencken described Rhine's experiments at some length and then went on: "Well, what is in it? Is it really a discovery, or is it only hooey? I am sorry to have to report, after giving Professor Rhine's exposition hard and prayerful study, that I can find nothing but the latter. The whole thing seems to me to be on all fours, intellectually speaking, with spiritualism, osteopathy, and the theology of the Holy Rollers."

wife to lunch. Rhine is one of the professors of psychology at Duke, and the author of a book, "New Frontiers of the Mind," that has aroused a great deal of interest among the credulous. It purports to present evidence of thought transference. I read the book when it came out in 1937, and came to the conclusion that Rhine's statistics were highly unreliable. After two hours of talk with him, I was more than ever convinced. He is a rustic looking fellow, with deep-set, coal black eyes, very slow-spoken and apparently somewhat slow in mind. The more I listened to his exposition the less I was impressed. Hanes, who hardly knew him, came to the same conclusion.

Rhine is the problem child of Duke. He gets more publicity than any other professor in the academic department, but most of the scientificoes regard it as excessively bad advertising for the university. This is especially true in the medical school, where no one has the slightest belief in mental telepathy. Unfortunately, it seems to be impossible to get rid of Rhine. No other university wants him, and he is very comfortable at Duke. He has managed to get together a considerable amount of money for his so-called investigations, and is still reaching out for more. They are so worthless that they have been hailed as masterly by Upton Sinclair.[1] Rhine apparently has a good deal of respect for Sinclair. When I told him that Sinclair was the worst jackass I had ever met on this earth he was plainly not pleased.

His wife seemed to be much more intelligent than he. She is a native of Ohio, and apparently of German origin, as Rhine seems to be himself. I noticed that while he was expounding his ideas she sat regarding him in silence, and with a quizzical smile. My guess is that she knows the answers, but is too discreet to utter them. I have often noticed the same look among the wives of quacks and enthusiasts. Women in general seem to me to be appreciably more intelligent than men. A great many of them suffer in silence from the imbecilities of their husbands. I daresay that poor Sara occasionally shouldered her share of this burden.

Last night the Haneses' colored chauffeur drove me from Durham to Greensboro in order that I might pick up my train. The distance is about 55 miles, and I seized the chance to set the chauffeur to talking.

1 Upton Sinclair (1878–1968), Baltimore-born novelist and social critic. His best-known book is *The Jungle* (1906), a realistic account of life in the Chicago stockyards. For many years he and Mencken carried on a correspondence which, on Mencken's side at least, was humorously critical of everything Sinclair believed in and stood for.

He turned out to be an uneducated but extremely sharp-witted colored man, and he told me a great deal of interesting stuff. The Greensboro-Durham region is the upper tip of the cotton belt—in fact, it is marginal land. With cotton down to five cents, the farmers are in a dreadful state. William, the chauffeur, apparently saw clearly that what they needed was a change in crops. He told me that he had been advocating it, but that it was impeded by the lack of competent middlemen. There was no way, in other words, to sell the new crops quickly and profitably. He told me that he was thinking of buying a couple of trucks himself and setting up as a middleman, hauling garden truck, eggs, and so on to Richmond and Washington. It has apparently never occurred to the New Deal economists that middlemen really serve a useful purpose.

William told me that the raising of hogs, which otherwise should be very profitable in such a country, was a losing venture simply because there were no buyers. The meat eaten in all those North Carolina towns comes from Chicago. If a local butcher set up business, or one of the Chicago packers opened a branch abattoir, there would be immediate prosperity for the farmers. The corn they now try to raise is almost useless to them. They can neither sell it as grain nor feed it to hogs.

NEW YORK

MAY 23, 1939.

I had lunch today with George Jean Nathan—our first meal together in several years. He looked very fit, though somewhat gray, and told me that he had given up cigars. He used to smoke eight or ten a day. He says he now confines himself to cigarettes and consumes five packages a day. He said that his old neuralgia, which used to drive him half frantic, had returned during the Winter, but that it was not as severe as formerly.

I gathered from his conversation that he has given up his social pushing, and is devoting himself mainly to literary and stage society. He said that the Depression had wiped out a large percentage of his investments. Some of them represented his own earnings and the rest came to him from his mother, who was a sister of Sam Nixon, the Philadelphia theatrical magnate. He told me that as his bonds were called he let the money lie in cash, and that he now had more than

$75,000 on deposit in various banks, with no income from it. He said that he proposed to leave most of his estate to set up a fund designed to encourage playwriting. I gathered that it is to be something on the order of the Pulitzer fund, with annual prizes for meritorious American plays.

BALTIMORE, JUNE 10, 1939.

In Washington the other day, at the convention of the Workers' Alliance of WPA workers, I heard Mrs. Roosevelt address the delegates. It was interesting indeed to observe her. There was a palpable touch of patronage in her friendliness. She spoke, not as one who has endured the miseries of her hearers, but simply as one who has observed them politely from afar. She was excessively amiable, but there was something fixed and artificial about her smile. I don't think she made much impression on the poor fish before her. They cheered when she came in and they applauded politely when she finished, but it was plain that she left them as hopeless as they were before she spoke to them. They had been listening for three or four days to a long succession of palpable quacks, beginning with General Jacob S. Coxey[1] and running down to Congressman John M. Coffee, of the State of Washington. Compared to these transparent mountebanks, Mrs. Roosevelt at least looked sincere, but her sympathy for the poor shovel-leaners was plainly that of a kindly doctor, not that of a suffering fellow patient.

AUGUST 11, 1939.

Raymond Moley called me up yesterday from New York and asked me to give him some help with his book. It has been running serially in the *Saturday Evening Post*, and will come out in volume form October 1st.[2] It is an account of Moley's adventures at the economic conference at London, and it includes a great deal of matter that is more

1 Jacob S. Coxey (1854–1951) led the famous Coxey's Army march of unemployed men upon Washington in 1894 and again in 1914. He was not a general at all, but had the title bestowed upon him at the time of the march and clung to it for the rest of his long life.
2 Moley's book, entitled *After Seven Years*, was published later that year by Harper & Brothers.

or less discreditable to Roosevelt, Hull and the other great wizards of the New Deal. Moley told me that he had heard from Washington that the New Deal brethren were making great efforts to inspire bad notices of the book. This enterprise should not be difficult, for most of the newspaper and magazine reviewers currently in practice are already ardent New Dealers, and not a few of them are downright Communists. I told Moley that I saw no way to break up this conspiracy, and argued with him that bad notices by pinks would do his book more good than harm. He apparently came over to this notion.

He wanted me to write a blurb for the book, but I refused on my usual grounds. I told him, however, that when it came out I would probably refer to it in an article in the *Sunday Sun*.

Moley is a somewhat naïve fellow, and is apparently upset by the bitter hostility of the surviving New Dealers. His book, judging by the specimens printed in the *Saturday Evening Post*, is not apt to make a very profound impression. His writing is somewhat confused, and he never sufficiently explains to the layman the financial matters that he is dealing with. In particular, he fails to explain the intricacies of foreign exchange. That subject, I suspect, will be forever unintelligible to most men. Certainly Moley does not make it clear. Nevertheless, his book throws some amusing lights on such fatheads as Hull. One cannot read the narrative without recalling Oxenstjerna's saying to his son: "My son, as you grow older you will be astonished to discover what imbeciles run the world."[1]

Hull figures in the Moley narrative not only as a complete ignoramus, but also as a vain and petty fellow. I believe that this is an accurate judgment on him.

SEPTEMBER 18, 1939.

Tonight I finished the twentieth and last chapter of "Happy Days," and so completed the manuscript. Two of the chapters were written

[1] In *A New Dictionary of Quotations*, under the rubric "Government," Mencken gives this saying as "You do not know, my son, with how little wisdom the world is governed (*An nescis, mi fili, quantilla prudentia mundus regatur*)," and then adds: "Commonly ascribed to BISHOP AXEL OXENSTJERNA, Chancellor of Sweden (1583–1654), but Büchman says in *Geflügelte Worte* that it probably originated with Pope Julius III, who said to a Portuguese monk: 'If you knew with how little expenditure of sense the world is governed, you would wonder.' "

as articles for the *New Yorker* in 1936, but I then abandoned the book and only resumed it last Winter. I finished a third chapter on February 23rd and a fourth on March 28th. Thereafter I settled down to complete the book, but unfortunately my illness during the summer greatly delayed it, and for some time I was in doubt that I'd be able to get to the end by the deadline, October 1st. This, fortunately, has now been accomplished. Doing the book has been a genuine pleasure, for it is always agreeable to ponder upon the adventures of childhood.

My physical state at the moment is not too good, for in addition to the illness that floored me in July, I am suffering from a severe hay fever. The vaccines gave me relief for five years, but last year (an extraordinarily severe season) broke down their guard, and this year things have been even worse. Dr. Vander Veer told me in New York two weeks ago that it was his belief that the vaccines always work badly in the face of a constitutional disturbance. He added that his partner, Dr. Cooke, dissented. Dr. Baker here in Baltimore tells me that hay fever has been so bad this year that virtually all the patients taking vaccines have been in difficulties.

I am undecided about my next *Arbeit.* I am tempted to complete the dictionary of quotations, and then tackle "Advice to Young Men." If the war goes on and the United States gets into it, these plans, of course, will have to be revised. Soon or late I hope to do a supplemental volume to "The American Language," and to undertake a revision of "In Defense of Women," which is now hopelessly out of date.

BALTIMORE, OCTOBER 5, 1939.

I received a letter this morning from Bishop James Cannon, Jr., of Richmond, Va., saying that he was coming to Baltimore at noon to attend a Methodist conference, and asking me to meet him at the station. I did so, and then took him to the Belvedere for lunch. He is suffering from a severe arthritis, and I have been trying to arrange for a consultation with Dr. Benjamin M. Baker, Jr. Unfortunately, the Bishop has been unable to spare the necessary four or five days for a thorough examination. He told me that he hoped to come to Baltimore to submit to it after he had finished some pending ecclesiastical business. He is now seventy-five years old and has been retired for two years, but he still visits conferences and apparently concerns himself with other church business. He told me that he has written more than

100,000 words of his autobiography, and asked me to read the manuscript.

He was full of interesting reminiscences. He said that Roosevelt was nominated for the Vice-Presidency at San Francisco in 1920 for two reasons, and two reasons only. The first was that his name was Roosevelt, and the second was that he was a dry. Cannon said that the Anti-Saloon League sent questionnaires to all the candidates, and that Roosevelt's replies were the most satisfactory. He told me that Roosevelt in those days was enormously friendly to the Prohibitionists, and that they trusted him. His subsequent betrayal greatly enraged them, and after his nomination for the Presidency in 1932 Cannon tried to organize a Methodist *bloc* against him. It failed to accomplish anything mainly because the country was set upon getting rid of Hoover.

Cannon told me at some length about his long feud with Senator Carter Glass[1] of Virginia. He said that Glass was chiefly responsible for his (Cannon's) trial before the church court in Washington after his second marriage. The allegations brought forward in this trial were highly scandalous, and the brethren of the court had a hard time reaching a verdict that would not wreck the church. They finally acquitted Cannon on all counts, but with a sort of warning to sin no more.[2] Cannon said that Glass was chiefly responsible for this proceeding, and that he (Cannon) later bought from some man in New York copies of letters from Glass that proved it. At the time Glass denied publicly that he had any interest in the case. His enmity to Cannon was due to the fact that Cannon helped to prevent his election as Governor of Virginia in the days following the World War. He was appointed United States Senator as a solatium, and has remained in the Senate ever since. But he itched to be Governor, and has never forgotten his defeat.

Cannon told me that he believed Glass lost mainly because he carried on a campaign that was too vituperative. His speeches against Claude Swanson,[3] his opponent, accused Swanson of every crime on

1 Carter Glass (1858–1946) was named secretary of the treasury in 1918 but resigned the post to fill a vacancy in the U.S. Senate two years later. He remained in the Senate until his death.

2 In 1929 Bishop Cannon had been accused of stock-market gambling, misuse of campaign funds, hoarding flour during World War I, and—after his marriage to his former secretary—of adultery. It took five years of congressional hearings, church investigations, and legal battles to clear him of all charges.

3 Claude A. Swanson (1862–1939) was governor of Virginia from 1906 to 1910, when

the calendar. Most of these accusations were true, but nevertheless the Virginia electors thought that they were laid on too violently.

Cannon told me that in his active days he traveled about 60,000 miles a year. He said that he had crossed the ocean thirty-three times on the *Berengaria* alone. His last assignment was in California. His second wife urged him on his retirement to continue living there, for she liked the climate, but he refused on the ground that all of his roots were in Virginia and Washington, and he couldn't be happy so far away. He looks to be in excellent shape for a man of seventy-five years, but his arthritis has begun to cripple his hands and some of his old fire has gone out of him.

We fell into a long discussion of theological matters, and he told me that when he was a student at the Princeton Theological Seminary he was once tried for heresy. Princeton was operated by the Presbyterians and he, of course, was a Methodist. The charge against him was that he ascribed to Methodist Arminianism. He said that he was clearly guilty and made little effort to defend himself, but that the majority of the court decided that it would be unwise to expel him and so found him not guilty. He said that the president of the court, an old-time Presbyterian theologian, delivered a speech after the verdict denouncing it vigorously.

Cannon turned out to be familiar with all the intricacies of recent American theology, not only in his own church, but also in other churches. He talked very well about the row among the Presbyterians, and professed high admiration for the late Gresham Machen, who resigned a professorship in the Princeton Theological Seminary as a protest against the growth of modernism there. He told me that he agreed with Machen theologically, but believed that he had maintained his case with too much heat. This protest against an excess of vehemence coming from Cannon naturally amused me greatly.

BALTIMORE, MD.

OCTOBER 6, 1939.

My session with Patterson was on Friday evening, September 29th. He really amazed me by saying that the course of the *Sun* regarding

---

he was appointed to the U.S. Senate to fill the vacancy created by the death of Senator John W. Daniel. He remained there for the next twenty-three years. In 1933, at the age of seventy, he was named secretary of the navy by Franklin D. Roosevelt.

the war as laid out by John W. Owens had his full approval. I still doubt that this is true. The long-standing feud between Owens and William E. Moore, the managing editor, has got Patterson into a difficult and dangerous situation. Moreover, he is well aware that a more realistic attitude toward the war would bring him trouble from various other quarters. His chief concern, of course, is to maintain the prosperity of the property. My own is quite different. I believe, and told him, that the imbecile arguments concocted and printed by Owens were doing the paper enormous damage. To be sure, they are popular at the moment, but in the long run rational readers must see their hollowness. There will follow a considerable diminution in public confidence. I am thoroughly convinced that it never pays any newspaper to compromise with the plain facts. Roosevelt is a fraud from snout to tail. Every one in Washington is well aware that he is itching to get the United States into the war. For the *Sun* to ignore or attempt to conceal that fact involves an abandonment of integrity that seems to me to be highly dangerous.

NOVEMBER 29, 1939.

Al Capone, the eminent Chicago racketeer, is a patient at the moment at the Union Memorial Hospital. He is suffering from paresis, the end result of a syphilitic infection. He is being looked after by Dr. Joseph E. Moore, head of the syphilis clinic at the Johns Hopkins. Capone says that he was infected very early in life, and assumed for years that he had been cured. He was married at 16, and is the father of a perfectly healthy son. His wife has apparently escaped infection.

The symptoms of paresis began to show themselves in Capone during the early part of his imprisonment. He was then locked up at Atlanta. The medical officers there wanted to make a lumbar puncture to ascertain his condition accurately, but Capone refused. In 1937, after he had been transferred to Alcatraz, he suddenly developed convulsions. They are often the first sign of paresis. He was there put on the malaria treatment, but after nine chills the convulsions returned and became so alarming that the treatment was abandoned. By that time Capone, who is not unintelligent, had been convinced that his condition was serious, and so he made arrangements for intensive treatment after his release. Dr. Moore was recommended, and hence Capone came to Baltimore. Dr. Moore planned to enter him at the Johns Hopkins Hospital. Dr. Winford Smith, the superintendent, consented, but the lay board of trustees interposed objections, and so Capone was sent to the Union Memorial Hospital instead. Almost the same thing happened there. The medical board was in favor of receiving him, if only on the ground that a first class hospital should take in every sick man and waste no time upon inquiring into his morals. This was the position of Dr. John M. T. Finney, head of the medical board. After Capone got to the hospital the women of the lay board began setting up a row, led by Mrs. William A. Cochran, whose husband is a famous prohibitionist and wowser. As I write this row is still going on, but Capone remains at the hospital. The lady objectors argue that his presence is keeping other patients out of the place. The medical board answers that that is unfortunate but unavoidable. It argues that a hospital, as a matter of ethics, cannot refuse any sick man who applies for treatment.

Moore has put Capone on the malaria cure, and at the moment it seems to be working very well. Capone has already developed a temperature as high as 106 degrees. I am told that he bears the accompanying discomforts very philosophically and is, in fact, an extraordinarily docile patient. His mental disturbance takes the form of delusions of grandeur. He believes that he is the owner of a factory somewhere in Florida employing 25,000 men, and he predicts freely that he'll soon be employing 75,000. This factory is, of course, purely imaginary. Otherwise, Capone's aberrations are not serious. He is able to talk rationally about his own condition and about events of the day.

He is occupying two rooms and a bath at a cost of $30 a day. He sleeps in one room himself, and the other is a sort of meeting place for his old mother, his three brothers, and his wife. The brothers spend all day playing checkers, with occasional visits to the patient. They made an effort lately to rent a house in Guilford, but were refused when their identity became known. The mother is an ancient Italian woman of the peasant type, and can barely speak English. The brothers, all of them born in this country, are relatively intelligent fellows. The wife, who is ignorant but apparently not unintelligent, moves a cot into Capone's room every night and sleeps there. He has two night nurses and one day nurse. He is naturally very popular with the hospital staff, and especially with the orderlies, for he is not only a good patient, he is also likely to leave large tips. His chills come on every second day, and Moore plans to keep him in bed here until he has had fifteen of them. He will then be transferred to Miami. The Federal

Bureau of Investigation has notified Moore that so far as it knows there is no project on foot to kill Capone. Thus no guard upon him is maintained, and any visitor to the hospital is free to barge into his room.

NOVEMBER 29, 1939.

Reading what is printed about myself, I am made to realize constantly how little a man makes himself understood by his writings. People are always assuming that I am moved by motives that are completely foreign to me. In the first days of the *American Mercury*, for example, it was generally assumed that I had some aspiration to lead the so-called opinion of college students. Nothing could have been further from my thoughts. I have, in fact, almost no interest in the ideas of college students. They seem to me to be simply immature men. They are always following fresh messiahs. That I served for a short while as one of those messiahs was not only surprising to me, but extremely offensive. I received hundreds of invitations to address college audiences, but refused all of them until it came to be generally understood that the boys were following other leaders; then I accepted a few.

It has also been assumed on frequent occasions that I have some deep-lying reformatory purpose in me. That is completely nonsensical. It always distresses me to hear of a man changing his opinions, so I never seek conversions. My belief is that every really rational man preserves his major opinions unchanged from his youth onward. When he vacillates it is simply a sign that he is stupid. My one purpose in writing I have explained over and over again: it is simply to provide a kind of katharsis for my own thoughts. They worry me until they are set forth in words. This may be a kind of insanity, but at all events it is free of moral purpose. I am never much interested in the effects of what I write. It may seem incredible in an old book reviewer, but it is a fact that I seldom read with any attention the reviews of my own books. Two times out of three I know something about the reviewer, and in very few cases have I any respect for his judgments. Thus his praise, if he praises me, is subtly embarrassing, and his denunciation, if he denounces, leaves me unmoved. I can't recall any review that ever influenced me in the slightest. I live in a sort of vacuum, and I suspect that most other writers do, too. It is hard to imagine one of the great ones paying any serious attention to contemporary opinion. Certainly there is no sign that Shakespeare did. He may have heeded now and then the practical needs of the London stage of his day, but in the realm of ideas he steered his own course, regardless of what the morons who supported him believed or thought they believed.

DECEMBER 10, 1939.

I went to Washington yesterday for the Gridiron Club dinner last night. It was the usual magnificent bore. The proceedings actually lasted from 7.20 until 11.30. The dessert did not come on the table until after 11 o'clock. The show seemed to me to be predominantly dull. There were one or two amusing skits, but the rest were labored and failed to come off. Three Ambassadors were present, and as usual they were introduced, each with a spotlight on him. The Dane got a perfunctory round of applause. The British Ambassador, Lord Lothian, got a little more, but not much more. But when the Finn arose there was a really dramatic ovation.[1] The whole audience got to its feet and the applause lasted half a minute at least. The Finn was apparently much affected. He stood as stiff as a ramrod, but tears rolled down his cheeks. He sat four or five places from Roosevelt, who called him over and shook hands with him. Roosevelt, of course, could not rise himself on account of his disablement. This was the one really dramatic feature of an extremely dull dinner. The speeches were made by the new Governor of Minnesota, whose name I forget,[2] and by Paul V. McNutt.[3] The Governor made a pretty good speech, but it was rather too long—in fact, he dislocated the whole programme, which is run strictly on schedule. McNutt made a speech that was not bad, but I gathered that he left a poor general impression. Most of the guests I spoke to afterwards seemed to think that there was a certain hollowness in his remarks, and that he failed utterly to make any really favorable impression.

1 The Soviet Union had invaded Finland on November 30, and the Finns were putting up a heroic and astonishing resistance.
2 The governor was Harold E. Stassen (b. 1907), who was governor of Minnesota from 1939 to 1943, was an unsuccessful candidate for the Republican presidential nomination three times, and served in the Eisenhower administration.
3 Paul V. McNutt (1891–1955) was governor of Indiana from 1933 to 1937 and held various government posts during World War II. He had very great ambitions to seek the presidency, but nothing ever came of them.

Thomas E. Dewey,[1] Vandenberg[2] and other candidates were present, but none of them spoke. I saw Dewey later and arranged to meet him in New York at some time in the near future to cross-examine him on his ideas.

After the dinner I went to two or three booze parties in the hotel, and then to a party given by Lyle Wilson, of the United Press, at his home in Massachusetts avenue. This last party was a pleasant one, and I stayed until 5 a.m. I got up at 11 and returned to Baltimore on the 12 o'clock train.

I met Stanley Walker[3] in the station and we gabbled during the short run from Washington to Baltimore. He told me that he was having troubles in Philadelphia, where he is editor of the *Public Ledger*. The supply of good newspapermen in the town is small, and there is little public appetite for the better sort of journalism. I gathered that Walker is by no means enamored of his job, and that he would not hold it long. He said that the coldness of Philadelphia really daunted him. He was received stiffly, and no one tried to make him feel comfortable. My own experience there in 1904 was similar.[4] I spent five weeks getting out a newspaper under great difficulties, but not a single Philadelphia newspaper man paid any attention to me whatsoever, or to my associates. We lived like sailors cast on a desert island, and were enormously glad to get home.

1 Thomas E. Dewey (1902–1971), governor of New York from 1942 to 1955, Republican nominee for the presidency in the elections of 1944 and 1948.

2 Arthur H. Vandenberg (1884–1951), U.S. senator from Michigan from 1928 until his death. He was extremely active in matters of foreign policy during the Roosevelt and Truman administrations.

3 Stanley Walker (1898–1962), newspaperman and author. He served as editor of the *Public Ledger* for only about a year, leaving in January of 1940.

4 Mencken's experiences in Philadelphia while getting out the *Herald* there after Baltimore's Great Fire of 1904 are recounted in chapter nineteen of *Newspaper Days*, "Fire Alarm," pp. 296–98.

1940

James Thurber of the *New Yorker* is in Baltimore this week, revising a play.[1] It is being performed at the Maryland theatre, and apparently needs a considerable rewriting. Paul Patterson entertained Thurber at the *Sun* office yesterday, and I had a chance to talk with him. He was full of curious stuff about Ross, editor of the *New Yorker*. He said that Ross never reads anything except *New Yorker* manuscripts. His library consists of three books. One is Mark Twain's "Life on the Mississippi"; the second is a book by a man named Spencer, falsely assumed by Ross to be Herbert Spencer, and the third is a treatise on the migration of eels. Despite this avoidance of reading, Ross is a really first-rate editor. More than once, standing out against the advice of all of his staff, he has proved ultimately that he was right. Thurber said that he is a philistine in all the other arts. He regards painting as a kind of lunacy, and music as almost immoral.

I went to Washington this morning to see Senator Robert A. Taft, one of the Republican candidates for the Presidential nomination. His secretary had fixed the hour of 9 a.m. for our meeting, and so I had to get up before seven o'clock to make it. Taft himself was ten minutes late. He turned out to be a pleasant enough fellow, and his discussion of the current issues was quite frank, but he certainly left upon me no

1 James G. Thurber (1894–1961), humorous writer and cartoonist for *The New Yorker*. The play was *The Male Animal*, written in collaboration with Elliott Nugent.

impression of real force. My guess is that his administration, if elected, would be as dull and futile as his father's. He realizes that the problem of liquidating the New Deal is full of difficulties, and that some of them verge upon the insoluble. He told me that he believed it would take two years at least, and probably three, to work any appreciable reduction in the Roosevelt spending programme. Taft is a fellow of very agreeable manners and gabbling with him was pleasant enough, but he certainly failed to inflame me with any conviction that he was a man of destiny. I know a hundred other men who are quite as able as he is, and quite as well informed. If he were not the son of a President the suggestion that he be made President himself would sound fantastic.

After sitting with Taft for an hour I went to the National Labor Relations Board building to hear my old friend, former Senator James A. Reed[1] of Missouri, argue the case brought against his wife's company, the Donnelly Garment Company of Kansas City. Reed and his wife and her secretary came in promptly, and I met Mrs. Reed for the first time. She is an extraordinary Irish woman—certainly not beautiful, but nevertheless extremely interesting and attractive. I sat beside her throughout the hearing. She started the garment factory in Kansas City twenty-five years ago with two operatives and she now employs 1,000. The National Labor Relations Board accuses her of setting up a company union and of refusing to deal with the International Ladies Garment Workers' Union. Her objection to the latter, it quickly appeared, is largely due to the fact that it is operated by New York Jews. She told me that in her own shop in Kansas City there were few if any Jews. Her operatives were mainly recruited from rural Missouri, and were almost unanimously of native American stock. She told me that nearly all of them retired soon or late to be married.

I hadn't seen Reed for some years. He looked well enough, but it was obvious that he had aged considerably. As the result of an accident he was lame, and during the hearing he had to ask for permission to sit down. He made an excellent argument, but he told me that he was convinced that it would make no impression on the Board. The new member, Leiserson, was not present.

---

1 James A. Reed (1861–1944), U.S. senator from Missouri, 1911–1929. Mencken had a very great admiration and affection for him, owing, no doubt, to Reed's bitter opposition to Woodrow Wilson and, later, to Prohibition.

During the recess J. Warren Madden, chairman of the Board, approached me amiably and I introduced him to Mrs. Reed. She immediately fell on him with considerable vehemence, denouncing the operations of his agents. He took her denunciation in good humor, and got away as fast as he could.

During the recess the two Reeds, Mrs. Reed's secretary and I had lunch in the drug store in the building housing the Board. This was my first set meal in a drug store in a long time, and I certainly did not enjoy it. The food was vile, and we were jostled all the while we ate. Unhappily, the recess was for only half an hour, and so we couldn't go to a restaurant.

BALTIMORE, MD.

MARCH 29, 1940.

In December, 1918 I printed in the *Smart Set* a review of George Moore's[1] book, "A Story Teller's Holiday," and in it called attention to the adept way in which he had differentiated between different styles in the narrative. A little while later T. R. Smith, who was the editorial chief of Moore's American publisher's office, received a letter from Moore including the following:

"I received the cutting from the *Smart Set*, and was struck by the superiority of American to English criticism. There is no critic in England, I am convinced, who possesses a sufficient insight to see that the book was written in three different styles, each appropriate to the circumstances and the characters. Give the writer my thanks if you should meet him."

BALTIMORE, MD.

MAY 11, 1940.

The enormous proliferation of government agencies has laid so heavy a burden on journalism that it has simply broken down. It is quite impossible for any newspaper, however large, to report the endless proceedings that go on every day. The National Labor Relations

---

1 George Moore (1852–1933), Irish novelist, dramatist, and poet. Mencken's review is in an article entitled "The Late Mr. Wells." (It was Mencken's practice to review a dozen or more books in a single 5,000-word article in *The Smart Set*, and very often the title that he gave to the article was based on the first book covered.)

Board alone is sometimes carrying on fifty or sixty at one time—not all of them, of course, in Washington, but scattered through the country. The newspapers, at the beginning of this riot, tried to cover the principal cases, but they soon found it impossible, and today they only attempt to cover a salient few. It is the same in many other directions. The Washington correspondents now find it completely impossible to cover the departments—indeed, they find it almost impossible to cover Congress, what with its endless committees of investigation. When one committee is on the front page, the others are forgotten, though meanwhile they may be carrying on very important work. In brief, the public can no longer find out what is going on. Measures of the first importance are undertaken without any preliminary discussion, and executed without any rational criticism. Thus the power of the bureaucracy increases constantly, and no scheme to check it seems to be workable. What the end is to be God knows. At the moment, it is certainly plain that government has got out of hand, and that all the old devices for regulating it are hopeless.

BALTIMORE, MD.

MAY 11, 1940.

I'll probably never execute my old plan to do a model funeral service for agnostics, admittedly damned. I am now too near my own need for it to give it the proper lightness of touch. Some day somebody else will do one. It is really amazing that none has ever been drawn up. An agnostic's funeral, as things stand, consists mainly of idiotic speeches—that is, when there is any ceremony at all.[1]

BALTIMORE, MAY 31, 1940.

Sara is dead five years today—a longer time than the time of our marriage, which lasted but four years and nine months. It is amazing what a deep mark she left upon my life—and yet, after all, it is not amazing at all, for a happy marriage throws out numerous and powerful tentacles. They may loosen with years and habit, but when a marriage ends at the height of its success they endure. It is a literal

1 Mencken's appeal for a suitable burial service for the "admittedly damned" may be found in "Clarion Call to Poets," *Prejudices: Sixth Series,* pp. 103–12.

fact that I still think of Sara every day of my life, and almost every hour of the day. Whenever I see anything that she would have liked I find myself saying that I'll buy it and take it to her, and I am always thinking of things to tell her. There was a tremendous variety in her, and yet she was always steadfast. I can recall no single moment during our years together when I ever had the slightest doubt of our marriage, or wished that it had never been. I believe that she was equally content. We had our troubles, especially her illnesses, but they never set up any difference between us: they always drew us closer and closer together. Indeed, it was only the last year or so that was darkened by them, for before that she always recovered quickly, and seemed to be making a steady gain in health. I knew all the while that her chances of life were not too good, but nevertheless the overt situation was usually reassuring, and so I put fears out of my mind. What I wrote of her courage in the preface to "Southern Album" was all true. It was seldom that she ever showed any sign of discouragement. I remember once—when she developed an eye infection, and Alan C. Woods, always forthright, told her that it was probably tuberculous. She came home from his office in a state close to collapse, and I had a hard time quieting her. But in a couple of days she had recovered her fortitude, and soon afterward the infection cleared up. She had a dreadful vulnerability to tuberculosis, and yet a compensatory capacity for throwing it off. Her two spells of pleurisy were both severe, and yet she recovered quickly.

Perhaps our happiest time together was in the Mediterranean, during the early months of 1934.[1] It was a long trip and full of fatigues, and some of them were rather too much for her. She could not go with me on my somewhat rough trip through Palestine, and I recall that she was full of unaccustomed terror when we came out from Tripoli to the *Columbus* in an open life-boat towed by one of the ship's launches, and a heavy sea made it toss wildly and ship water. She had an almost romantic confidence in the skill of the young German ship's officers, and yet she was afraid. I did not know it at the time, but her final illness had already begun. When we got to Egypt she was too weak to make the journey up the Nile, and when we got back to the

[1] There is an account of this trip in chapters eighteen and nineteen of *Heathen Days*, "Vanishing Act" and "Pilgrimage," pp. 239–77, but Sara is not mentioned in it. There is not only no indication that she accompanied him, there is no hint that he was or ever had been married.

Columbus, after four or five quiet days in Cairo, she began to show a temperature, and was put to bed by the ship's doctor, Dr. Fischer. She had met him before on a voyage to the West Indies, and had a high opinion of him. He was obviously puzzled by her fever, and ascribed it somewhat vaguely to the bad climate of Egypt, but when we got home her own doctor, Benjamin M. Baker, Jr., soon found what was wrong. There was a pocket of the old tuberculous infection somewhere, and it was making one of its recurrent flare-ups. During the Summer following she went to Montgomery to visit her mother, who was ill and was to die before the end of the year, and I went to Roaring Gap, N.C., where she was to join me on her return. When I met her at the junction—I think it was Greensboro—it was plain as she stepped from the train that she was ill. She looked pale and almost transparent. Our host and hostess, Dr. and Mrs. Fred M. Hanes—the former professor of medicine at Duke and the latter a Johns Hopkins nurse—saw at once that something serious was wrong, but there was nothing to do about it save encourage her to rest. When we got back to Baltimore Baker put her to bed, and she remained there from September to Christmas. I got her a hospital bed, and she endured her imprisonment with great courage. Toward the end she tried to work, but it was very difficult. After her mother's death she began to show unfavorable symptoms, and Baker sent her to the Johns Hopkins. She returned soon, but in May she was there again, and that time was the last.

Her final illness was mercifully short, but it was very painful. Baker and his chief, Louis Hamman, were hopeful for a few days that what had attacked her was not really tubercular meningitis, for some of the usual signs were lacking, but when the spinal fluid was examined it became apparent that she was doomed. It was on Sunday night, May 26, that alarming symptoms developed. Her mind became cloudy at once, though there were plenty of rational interludes. I saw her for the last time on Wednesday, May 29, along with my sister Gertrude. She was, for a few minutes, quite bright and cheerful, and asked my sister about the sheep that had been put to pasture on my sister's farm in Carroll county. But the disease was advancing fast, and she complained that her sight had grown dim. I had to tell her that the doctors had given her some belladonna. This seemed to account for her eye symptoms, and reassured her for the moment. But after that afternoon she went downhill rapidly, and Baker advised me not to see her. I never did again, and I never saw her in death. She is not forgotten. I was immensely lucky in my marriage, as I have been lucky in nearly all things. She had a sharp intelligence, and yet she was always thoroughly feminine and Southern, and there was not the slightest trace of the bluestocking in her. Marriage is largely talk, and I still recall clearly the long palavers that we used to have. Both of us liked to work after dinner in the evening, but both of us always stopped at 10 p.m. If there were no visitors, which was usually the case, we sat in the drawing-room that she was so proud of, and had a few drinks before turning in. On Sunday nights, with the servants out, she often made supper in the kitchen, and we ate it there. We had plenty to talk of. I talked out my projects with her, and she talked out hers with me. I don't think we ever bored each other. I know that, for my part, the last days of that gabbling were as stimulating as the first. I never heard her say a downright foolish thing. She had violent prejudices, but so did I have them, and we seldom disagreed. It seemed to me that she always maintained hers with great plausibility. I have never known a more rational woman, nor another half so charming. She was far too reserved to be described as a popular favorite, but she always made a good impression on people of sense, and it delighted me to see how all my old friends liked her.

Whether I made a good or bad husband is beyond human reckoning, now that the only competent witness is gone. As I have said, I think she was content with me, and not bored. Marriage gave her a kind of security that she had not known for years. Ever since her grandmother's death, when she was still in college, she had been on her own, and more than once illness had threatened her with disaster. While we were married she at least had no cares about money: my income was more than enough for both of us, and she had the leisure to do the sort of work she liked, which is always the most profitable work. Magazine editors liked her stories, and got on well with their author, and she made some good friends among them, notably Arthur H. Samuels, of *Harper's Bazaar*. We usually saw Samuels and his charming wife when we went to New York, and they visited us more than once in Baltimore. Now he is dead too. If I was busy with writing, and put in 14 hours a day in my cubby-hole of an office, she never played the neglected wife. On many a day I did not see her until lunchtime, and then left her all afternoon, and worked all evening. She was busy herself, and knew the burdens of writing. When she was ill in bed in the house, and I could spare all too little time to entertain her, she often suggested that I go out when my day's work was done, saying that I needed change and the talk of men. In those days her old teacher and friend, Dr. Ola E. Winslow,[1] of Goucher College, always came in for dinner on Saturday night. Dr. Winslow and I would dine together, and then she would sit with Sara all evening, so that I could go to the Saturday Night Club. Alone in bed for long hours, Sara always managed to entertain herself. She read, she wrote, and she listened to the radio. Not once did she ever complain of the confinement. She was the perfect patient, and cheered her doctors when there was little that they could do to cheer her.

We had often talked of death, for she was well aware that her own chances of life were less than the average. She insisted that she would die first, but it always seemed to me to be improbable, for I was her senior by 18 years, and had been badgered by all sorts of illnesses for years. A complete skeptic, she made me promise, in case she died first, to have her body cremated. When she died on that lovely May day I was uneasy about this, for I feared that her sisters might object. But when they got to Baltimore it turned out that she had told them her wish, and that they approved. I did not go to the crematory. What was left of her was taken there by my two brothers and her brother John. Her ashes are buried at the foot of the grave of my mother, and beside her there is room for mine. Thinking of her, I can well understand the great human yearning that makes for a belief in immortality, but I do not believe in it, and neither did she. We have parted forever, though my ashes will soon be mingling with hers. I'll have her in mind until thought and memory adjourn, but that is all. Whether or not it is better so I do not know, but there is the fact as I see it. We were happy together, but all beautiful things must end. *Entbehren sollst; du sollst entbehren.*[2]

---

1 Dr. Ola E. Winslow (1885?–1977) had taught Sara at Goucher, and they later became good friends—a friendship which Mencken would carry on after his wife's death. Dr. Winslow subsequently taught at Wellesley and Radcliffe and was the author of a number of important works on early American religious and cultural history. Her life of Jonathan Edwards received the Pulitzer Prize for biography in 1941.

2 The line is from Part One of Goethe's *Faust*. Mencken has slightly misquoted it; it should read "*Entbehren sollst Du! sollst entbehren!*" and may be translated "Deny yourself! you must deny yourself!"

BALTIMORE, MD.
JUNE 3, 1940.

My guess is that in the long run the newspapers will lose their more moronic customers to the radio. Thus their future lies with the relative intelligent minority. That minority holds nearly all of the money of the country. The newspapers, however, neglect it progressively. The Baltimore *Sun* has gradually lopped off every feature that appeals to intelligence, and supplanted it with something aimed directly at idiots. The whole magazine section has disappeared completely, and in place of it there is now a series of comic sections almost as large as the whole remainder of the paper. Meanwhile, the editorial policy has steadily deteriorated. There was a time following the last war when a serious effort was made to lift it to an enlightened level, but now it has got down to a point where it actually marches ahead of the boobs themselves in maudlin imbecility. One hears better talk in smoking cars and barber shops than one can get from the editorial page of what is, in theory, supposed to be a rich, intelligent and honest newspaper. My guess is that this is bad medicine. Nothing is going to be accomplished by trying to out-demagogue the radio crooners. The function of a newspaper in a democracy is to stand as a sort of chronic opposition to the reigning quacks. The minute it begins to try to out-whoop them it forfeits its character and becomes ridiculous. I believe that many people already notice this deterioration, and that it is responsible to some extent for the movement toward the radio.

BALTIMORE, JUNE 9, 1940.

I approach my sixtieth birthday in impaired health, physically, though I can notice no deterioration mentally, and still feel like work. One day last Summer, it must have been in August, I was walking down Baltimore street east of the *Sun* office when I noticed a sort of numbness in my neck, on the left side. When it failed to pass off by the next morning I saw my doctor, Benjamin M. Baker, Jr., and he sent me to the Johns Hopkins Hospital for investigation. His diagnosis, concurred in by Dr. Louis Hamman, was a "spastic cerebral episode"—in other words, a spasm of the blood vessels in the cortex. The symptoms were so light that the two doctors concluded there had not been any hemorrhage. I noticed a mild tingling on the right side of the face, and also in the right hand, but there was no disturbance of sensation or function. They kept me in bed a week or so, but after four or five days I was allowed to sit up for meals and take my own baths. They told me that if I were twenty years younger the business would be insignificant, but that at sixty it had to be taken seriously. Apparently there was nothing to be done about it, for they gave me no treatment, and offered no advice save to avoid violent exercise. The numbness still continues, though it is very faint. It is most noticeable when water touches my hands in the morning. Baker examined me at length, and found that my blood pressure was rising, though still not dangerously so. The last time it was taken it was 152. Up to last year it had never gone beyond 135. Baker also found some heart symptoms—imperceptible to ordinary examination, but detected by the electrocardiograph. Just what they were he didn't tell me, but I assume that they revealed sclerosis in the coronary artery. This is an incurable condition, and I can only look forward to its gradual worsening. Thus my life-long feeling that I would probably not live much beyond sixty appears to have been well grounded.[1]

Of late I have been very uncomfortable, with occasional pains in the right arm and foot. Four or five weeks ago I slipped on my bedroom stairway and came down heavily on my left side. There was a large bruise on my left hip for a couple of weeks, and my left elbow was lame. But no bones appeared to be damaged, and so I did not see Baker. Now I notice a small lump on my left elbow, probably bursitis, and my left shoulder joint is sore, so that lying on it at night is painful. The elbow is painless, and the shoulder does not hurt save under pressure. But I have been considerably discomforted by pains in the lower back. At first, I took them to be lumbago caused by sitting at my desk with an open window at my back, but they have persisted, and today they were pretty bad. I shall see Baker, if they don't go away, when I get back from New York. After my taxicab accident in Algiers in 1934 I went to Dr. George E. Bennett, the orthopedist, for an examination. He made x-ray pictures. He told me that my bones showed no damage from the accident, but that there were signs in my lower vertebrae of the small spines of concretions which sometimes form in the later years, causing a great deal of discomfort. He told me that nothing

---

1 He was sixty-eight when he had his incapacitating stroke and seventy-five when he died.

could be done about them, and that if they were ever painful I'd simply have to bear it.

My heart seems to be acting reasonably, sclerosis or no sclerosis. It takes really violent exertion to make me pant, and the panting then is not excessive. My pulse continues strong and regular, with no increase in rate. One night in New York, a month or two ago, it got up to 95, but that was after a long evening with too much to drink. My ordinary doses of alcohol do not seem to affect it. Of an evening, sitting with August, I usually drink either three bottles of beer or two Scotch high-balls. This is enough to make me sleep well, but I never notice any signs of Katzenjammer in the morning. I commonly get out of bed, however, feeling at my worst for the day. I feel better as the day goes on, and am usually in pretty good shape by the evening. But I tire much more readily than I used to, and unless I get a brief nap before dinner I am usually unfit for writing at night. Even so, I get through a fairly good week's work, and am full of projects. If I had another life to live I'd write a great many more books. I have definite plans for at least a dozen, but if I finish my quotation book and the supple-mental volume to "The American Language" I'll be lucky. I only hope my finish is quick. I can imagine nothing more dreadful than being disabled for a long while, unable to work, bored stiff, and gradually wasting all my savings. My uncle, William C. Abhau, has been help-less for more than four years, and has had a long series of cerebral hemorrhages. He simply sits in a chair smiling. He understands what is said to him, but his mind is so far deteriorated that he apparently never gives a thought to his situation, or that of his poor wife. He never even asks where the money is coming from that feeds and houses him. If I ever get into any such state I hope that there will be at least one interval lucid enough to enable me to make off.

Two years ago I began to be beset by distressing sensations in the region of the heart. Baker discovered that the cause was a spastic py-lorus, which inflates the stomach and causes pressure on the heart. He concluded at the time that the heart itself was not in trouble. He put me on belladonna, and after six or eight months I became comfortable. These distresses sometimes appear again, but only briefly. A few days of belladonna, and they are gone. As I have said, my heart appears to be acting more or less normally at the moment. But soon or late, of course, it will begin to show damage.

I have told very few persons about the cerebral episode of last

Summer, and have thus escaped a great deal of well-meant but annoying condolence and advice. The best plan, obviously, is to go on as long as possible as if nothing had happened. It is silly for a man of my age to be too much upset by such a situation. After all, my family has been generally short-lived, and I have already gone on beyond my reasonable expectation. I can look back upon life with little regret. Taking one day with another, the world has treated me well, and considering my limited equipment I have been very successful. In any event, I have been able to make a good living doing precisely what I wanted to do, and whenever a given job began to bore me I was able to quit it. If I had ten or fifteen more years to live I'd probably do some better books than any I have printed so far, but that is what every man says, and it is not at all a certainty. I believe that part of my content has been due to a capacity, apparently inherited from my mother, to draw a line and say "Enough." I thus gave up the *Smart Set* before it had made a slave of me, and the *American Mercury* following. I quit active newspaper work—that is, the daily grind— when I was but 35, and since then I have never sat at a newspaper desk save for three months in 1938, when I took over the editorial page of the *Evening Sun* in an effort to redesign and improve it. As with jobs, so with friends. When they begin to bore me I get rid of them. This has made me some enemies—for example, George Jean Nathan— but on the whole it has worked well. Dr. Johnson was right: friendships need occasional revision. It is foolish to go on with people who have ceased to be interesting, and become nuisances. My life, in brief, has been regulated by purely selfish motives, but I believe I have carried out my actual obligations with reasonable diligence and good humor. I have given hard service to the *Sun*, and have tried my best to make it an honest and rational newspaper. If I have failed it has been due to the incapacity of other men, not to my own neglect. First in J. H. Adams and later in John W. Owens I had to deal with editors who were, at bottom, highly conventional and unimaginative men, and hence incapable of reaching really high marks. The paper, as it stands, shows their limitations. Owens, since the current war scare began, has gone completely to pieces, intellectually speaking. Instead of trying, in a day of demagogic buncombe and mob hysteria, to maintain a rational point of view and avoid emotion, he has marched with the procession, and even ahead of it. It is a pity, but apparently nothing can be done about it. Sometimes I wonder whether any daily news-

paper, at least in America, can be really intelligent. It is possible theoretically, but in practice it never happens. In general, the better the
paper, the less prosperous it is. Paul Patterson is naturally proud of
his achievement in dragging the *Sun* out of bankruptcy and making it
rich, and I certainly do not begrudge him his pride. But his very success has made him somewhat cautious, and so he hesitates to put pressure on his subordinates when they fall short. This is now true once
more in the case of Owens. At the start, Patterson tried to dispose of
an unpleasant situation by persuading himself that he and Owens were
in accord, but he knows better now, and is very uncomfortable. It is
not only caution that stays him; there is also his amiability. He dislikes
making anyone unhappy. Thus the paper sometimes gets out of hand,
as when Hamilton Owens, as editor of the *Evening Sun*, turned it into
a New Deal organ. It was not until the Summer of 1936 that Patterson
clamped down on this imbecility, and by that time a lot of damage
had been done. Among other things, a number of third-rate editorial
writers had been convinced that it was possible and safe to resist the
policy of the paper. Some of them still believe that. They will learn
better if Patterson ever comes to a real break with John Owens.

In 1934, just after my retirement as editor of the *American Mercury*, Patterson proposed to me that I become vice-president of the
A. S. Abell Company in charge of all editorial matters, as William F.
Schmick is vice-president in charge of all business matters. I refused
for two reasons. The first was my disinclination to take on a new
routine job—and one calling for a great deal of hard work, and much
unpleasantness. The second was my feeling that Patterson, after all,
was primarily an editorial man himself, and that setting me up would
establish a sort of dual control, and make for difficulties. We think
alike about many things, but certainly not about all, and there would
have been constant differences. I told him that running the *Sunpapers*
was his responsibility and that he would have to face and endure it. I
was willing to advise him whenever asked, but I had no desire to
become an editor who, in the last analysis, would be only half an
editor. I think he saw my point, for he never brought up the matter
again. We have been on good terms ever since, and never differed on
a major point of policy until the war began to loom up, and he permitted John Owens to run amuck. I objected to this back in 1938,
when the *Sun* began printing editorials whooping up the Spanish Reds,
and articles predicting that they would win. . . . The thing came to a

head with the invasion of Poland, and for a while Patterson and I agreed tacitly in avoiding the subject, if only to get rid of vain debates. But he told me the other day that he had come over, at least to some extent, to my point of view, and that he was against the paper supporting Roosevelt in the coming campaign. Meanwhile, Owens has somewhat ameliorated his enthusiasm, and it is possible that a row may be avoided. But the general editorial situation is a bad one, and needs radical treatment. There is not a really first-rate editorial writer on the staff, and the worst are not worth hell-room. I suspect that Patterson is now too old to undertake a wholesale cleaning-out—in fact, he says as much himself—, and that it will thus be left to his successor. By that time I'll be gone myself, so I do not greatly care.

NOVEMBER 13, 1940.

The present editorial position of the *Sun* is both amusing and depressing. It represents the complete negation of the program formulated with such elaborate care in 1920. The fundamental aim of that program was to get rid of the platitudinous blather that had marked the paper's editorial course during the first World War. Specifically, it was hoped that foreign news could be purged of its propaganda and presented in a frank and realistic manner. To that end a bureau was set up in London, the Manchester *Guardian* dispatches were taken on, and efforts were made to find competent correspondents in all the other principal countries of the world. All this is now out of the window. The foreign editorials that have been printed since the beginning of the present war have been pitifully idiotic. Their obvious aim has not been to unearth and tell the truth, but simply to offer consolation to Anglomaniacs. It would be amusing to reprint some of them six months afterward. They have all predicted English triumphs, both military and diplomatic, that have never come off.

When the London bureau of the *Sun* was established, it was made a rule that no man could serve in it more than two years. The idea was that after that time he undoubtedly became an Englishman. Unhappily, the two-year period turned out to be too long. Virtually all of the men who have served as London correspondents are now conscientious Anglomaniacs. Inasmuch as they write nearly all the editorials of the paper, it is no wonder that its position is feeble and, indeed, even idiotic. I have made various attempts to persuade Patterson that another reform is necessary, but he seems to be completely under the spell of the English, and I have abandoned any effort to influence him.

John Owens is even worse. He has reduced the whole war to a simple proposition in Sunday-school morals, and it is quite impossible to talk to him rationally. A few weeks after the present war broke out, I dropped in on him and told him that I recognized moral indignation when I saw it, and was not disposed to waste time arguing with it. Since then I have never discussed the situation with him. We are on good terms and speak pleasantly when we meet, but we never sit down to consider the situation of the *Sun*. Owens turns out, as he grows older, to be an almost exact duplicate of J. H. Adams, the editor of the *Sun* in the last war. If anything, he is rather more naïve and prejudiced. He is an excellent editorial writer in certain fields, but unhappily he is rather indolent, and seldom lets himself go.

The editorial writing on the *Sun* in general is certainly quite as good as that on any other major American paper. The principal editorial writers know how to write sound English, and some of them even have some grace of style. Unfortunately, they are men of conventional mind, and several of them are notably stupid. Gerald W. Johnson is an example. The content of his mind is what one would expect to find in that of any other second-rate Southerner. He knows how to put it into graceful English, but there is never anything in it at bottom.[1] Frederic Nelson writes even better than Johnson but is, if anything, a shade less intelligent. He is a charming fellow and an earnest one, but what he believes is simply what any conventional New Englander believes. He was formerly a college professor, and his processes of thought still show the patterns of the campus.

In view of all of these facts, I believe it would be useless at this time to attempt any reformation of the paper's policies. If I am still alive after the war is over I'll certainly take advantage of the ensuing Katzenjammer, but at the moment I believe it would be quite hopeless to try to influence either Patterson or Owens. Patterson, of course, is the better of the two men, but for reasons that I can't go into here he

1 Gerald W. Johnson (1890–1980) was on the editorial staff of the *Sunpapers* from 1926 to 1943. Subsequently he was the author of many significant books on American history and biographies of such American political figures as Andrew Jackson and John Paul Jones. Mencken's unflattering reference to him here is all the more surprising because it was really he who persuaded Johnson to leave his native North Carolina and come to Baltimore to work for the *Sun*.

is afraid to oppose Owens on any major matter. I believe I could persuade him if that fear did not stand in the way. As it is, I can do nothing.

I don't care very much, for my old belief in the possibilities of the *Sun* has wasted away. Its great material success has weakened it as an editorial force, and its old influence is obviously declining. This is due in part to its own blunders, but in larger part it is due to the general tendency. Nowhere in the United States is there a newspaper as genuinely influential as the old *Sun* used to be. The movement is away from organs of opinion and in the direction of simply commercial sheets like the Washington *Star* and the Philadelphia *Bulletin*.

1941

BALTIMORE, MD.

FEBRUARY 10, 1941.

Last week, for the first time, I read Herman Melville's "Moby Dick." It really amazed me by its badness. In recent years it has been eloquently whooped up by many men who should know better, and so my expectations were high. I found an extremely overblown and windy piece of writing. The melodrama at the end simply fails to come off, and the revenge motive more than once comes perilously close to the comic. One of the things all of the brethren seem to have over-looked is Melville's heavy debt to Carlyle. His writing, whenever he really spits on his hands, becomes pure Carlylese, and usually it is bad Carlylese. Walt Whitman fell under the same influence. His early newspaper writing was in the straightforward, shabby, undistin-guished English that marked the journalist of his time, but after he became acquainted with Carlyle he concocted a Carlylese of his own, and it is to be found in all of his later prose. On the whole, it seems to me that this Carlylese was better than the journalese of Whitman's early days. But it always remained something of an affectation, and its lack of honesty was frequently visible.

The same thing is true of Melville's writing. Even when he imitates Carlyle most successfully, it remains an imitation.

Some weeks ago I read, also for the first time, two books by George Borrow—"Lavengro" and "The Bible in Spain." I need not say that they disappointed me. Borrow had a sharp eye for low life, and some of his character sketches are unquestionably skillful, but he was at bottom a superficial and shabby man, and the fact shows itself con-stantly. What he had to say of his people was seldom worth hearing.

He wrote, on the whole, better than Melville, but nevertheless there was little of the genuine stylist in him. I suspect that that fact may have been due to his linguistic abilities. The man who knows many languages seldom writes any one of them well. There have been exceptions, of course—for example, Joseph Conrad—, but they are not many. Borrow spoke ten or twelve languages fluently, and had more or less acquaintance with at least a dozen more. The fact is constantly apparent in his writing. Over and over again he seems to be thinking in one language and writing in another. His theological observations in "The Bible in Spain" are completely idiotic. He wrote precisely like a Methodist parson preaching on the Whore of Babylon. It is difficult to take seriously the ideas and opinions of so palpably silly a man.

BALTIMORE, MARCH 22, [1940.][1]

My roots in Baltimore begin to strike deep. Not only was I born here, but I have spent my whole life here. During my twenty years as a magazine editor in New York I always refused to move there. So long ago as the year 1900 Ellery Sedgwick offered me the assistant editorship of *Frank Leslie's Popular Monthly*, of which he was then editor. I refused because I didn't want to leave Baltimore. During my magazine days I commuted constantly and it was somewhat unhandy, but nevertheless it was better than living in New York. My father and mother died here and are buried here, and alongside their bodies lie the ashes of my wife. All four of my grandparents are buried here, and three of my great-grandparents.

BALTIMORE, MD.

JUNE 17, 1941.

The annual meeting of the Knopf stockholders was held today, followed by a directors' meeting. The report of Alfred A. Knopf as president showed a net profit for 1940 of $33,550. This is the best showing for some years past. It has reduced the capital deficit as of April 30 to $36,815. Unhappily, there is an accumulation of $167,000 of unpaid dividends on the preferred stock. No dividends on this stock

---

1 Mencken (or Mrs. Lohrfinck—it is her typing) has dated this entry 1940, but its position in the sheets would seem to indicate that 1941 is the correct year.

can be paid until the capital impediment is wiped out. Two more good years, of course, would dispose of it, but it is hardly likely that 1941 will be as good as 1940. The publishing business, in fact, is in a sad state at the moment, with sales greatly diminished. Knopf and I have been trying for some years past to work out a scheme whereby the accumulation of preferred stock dividends could be disposed of. Unhappily, all our proposals have been blocked by Knopf's cousin, Samuel Knox, who is a stockholder and a director. He was not present at either the stockholders' or the directors' meeting. At the former, the only outside stockholder was Samuel Kaplan. Kaplan professes to be in favor of any plausible scheme to wipe out the preferred accumulation, but both Knopf and I have some doubts that he is really serious.

Knox lives in hope that the firm will one day turn up a "Gone with the Wind," and so be able to pay him in full. I have some doubt that this will ever happen—indeed, if a new "Gone with the Wind" showed up tomorrow it would probably not yield enough profit to cover the deficit, for sudden profits are now devoured by taxes. Knox is a foolish fellow, and there is a great deal of personal feeling mixed with his hunkerousness. He expected when Samuel Knopf died to be offered the post of business manager in the organization. When no such offer reached him he went off the reservation and has been in the bad lands ever since.

The general state of the corporation is not too good, despite the fact that it is showing an operating profit. The preferred accumulations go on increasing at the rate of more than $20,000 a year, and in a few more years they will become completely impossible.

BALTIMORE, MD.

JUNE 27, 1941.

On May 5, 1941, William Griffin, editor of the *New York Enquirer*,[1] called me up from New York and offered me $250 a piece for weekly articles similar to those that I used to write for the editorial page of the *Sunday Sun*. In my *Sun* days Griffin usually reprinted my *Sun* stuff in the *Enquirer*. It was never syndicated, and so he paid nothing for it. When the series was suspended in January he called me

1 The newspaper was bought in 1952 by Generoso Pope, Jr., who changed its name in the early sixties to the *National Enquirer*.

up and offered to pay any reasonable amount for its continuance. I told him that I was not interested. A little while later he called up again. His call on May 5th was his third. I told him definitely that I would not consider his proposal. Who his backers are I haven't any idea. His paper always seemed to me to be somewhat dubious, but I made no objection to his reprinting of my articles. In general, I always gave permission to any paper that asked for it.

BALTIMORE, MD.

JULY 11, 1941.

When I came to the end of the page proofs of "Newspaper Days" I discovered to my consternation that the last page was 313, which reads 13 both ways. My long-standing suspicion about 13 suggested that I either cut the book to 312 pages or expand it to 314. In the midst of my cogitation on the subject, I took a look at "Happy Days" to see how many pages it had made. They ran to 313 precisely! I therefore decided to let "Newspaper Days" stand. Making it run precisely the same length as "Happy Days" was really an extraordinary feat of copy-reading. I shall boast of it when my real autobiography comes to be written.

BALTIMORE, MD.

JULY 17, 1941.

In New York last night I said good-bye to Paul Patterson, who is sailing for Lisbon on the Clipper leaving this morning. He hopes to proceed to London from Portugal, and to put in a couple of weeks looking over the English scene. When he first told me of this project several weeks ago I was really indignant, and denounced him rather violently. It seemed to me that his pretense that he wanted to find out the truth about the English situation was only a pretense, and I told him that I believed that even if he found unfavorable facts he would not dare print them in the *Sun*. Moreover, I predicted formally that the English propagandists would easily fetch him. He seemed to be greatly upset, and insisted that he was making the trip to endeavor to get the actual facts. On reflection, it occurred to me that I was a bit rough with him. What ails him really is a rather hopeless feeling about the *Sun*. He has got it as far as he can go, and he realizes that the days of fine projects are over. Though I have denounced his support of the Roosevelt war, I am convinced that it was virtually necessary. Any really headlong attack on the warmongers would have got the paper into serious difficulties.

Paul and I had dinner together alone in New York, and discussed the whole situation frankly. I told him that I believed his trip to London was simply an attempt to get some life and color into an existence that had become dull and unsatisfying. He admitted instantly that that was the cause. He said that the old days of adventure seemed to be closing, and he was eager to have one more fling. There is, of course, some danger in the trip, but probably not a great deal. He told me that he hopes to get back by the end of August.

After dinner he took me to the Stork Club, which I had never visited. We sat there only a little while, and then returned to No. Twenty-One. There we found a considerable party of acquaintances, and in a little while a large table was gathering. Among those present were John R. North, head of the Ringling Brothers circus, and his French wife, Harold Ross, editor of the *New Yorker*, and his new wife, and Will Durant,[1] formerly the *New York Times*' correspondent in Moscow. Various other people joined us, and we kept going until after two o'clock. I got back to the hotel with rather an overdose, and felt somewhat wobbly this morning. I made no effort to see Paul off at the airport, for I had learned in New York that it was impossible for visitors to get within a block of the departing ship. The whole place swarms with spy-hunters, and my presence might have been embarrassing to Paul himself.

BALTIMORE, JULY 27, 1941.

Working this morning in the back garden, with August. We trimmed and tied up the vines, pulled some weeds, and put fertilizer around many of the plants. I have just set the hose to spraying the fern bed under the old pear-tree. The pear-tree has been flourishing

1 One supposes that this refers to Will Durant (1885–1981), the popular historian and philosopher. Durant and his wife traveled in Russia in 1932, but their *Dual Autobiography* (1977) gives no indication that he was ever a correspondent for the *New York Times*. Walter Duranty (1884–1957), however, was, and he was also the author of numerous books on the Soviet Union. It seems virtually certain that Mencken meant to say "Walter Duranty."

since 1883, and is still in vigorous health and at least 18 inches in diameter at the base. Its pears never ripen on the branch, but some years there are thousands of them and their weight makes it necessary to prop the limbs with poles. Of late the old tree has got so thick it cuts off sunshine from the petunia bed at the kitchen door, and I have engaged a forester to thin it. I often wonder what the garden will look like five years hence, or ten, or fifteen, or twenty. The Hollins street neighborhood is slowly going downhill, and in the course of time it is bound to be a slum. Filthy poor whites from Appalachia and the Southern tidewater are already living in the 1600 and 1700 blocks, and their foul children and dogs swarm in Union Square. When I was a boy the square was very well kept, and no child thought of trampling the lawns, but now the brats of the Okeys dig them up and pull the shrubs to pieces. When the last Mencken clears out of 1524 the house will have to be sold, and in a little while all the fittings that we have put in during the past thirty years will be ruined—the mahogany doors, the parquette floors, the tiled baths, and so on. It would be impossible to overestimate the value that the family has got out of the backyard garden in 58 years—first my mother, then my sister, and now August and I. It is nearly 100 feet long, and during its long life it has grown millions of flowers. To replace the house and yard, at present prices, would cost at least $20,000 and maybe $25,000, though the whole place, fresh from the builder's hands, cost but $2,900 in 1883. If our present neighbors to east and west were to die or clear out tomorrow, their probable successors might make the house uninhabitable at once.

BALTIMORE, MD.

AUGUST 22, 1941.

The first copies of "Newspaper Days" came in yesterday. Dwiggins,[1] as always, has made a handsome book. It roughly resembles "Happy Days" in format, but there are still a number of small and ingenious differences. Knopf is planning to offer the two books in a box for the Christmas trade. This may conceivably work off some of the stock of "Happy Days" now in hand.

1 William A. Dwiggins (1880–1956), typographer and book designer. He designed many books for Knopf, including nearly all of Mencken's works.

·

When I came to the end of the page proofs of "Newspaper Days" I discovered to my consternation that the last page was number 313. I immediately began to search about for ways of either reducing the text to 312 pages or expanding it to 314. But before I actually tackled the job it occurred to me that I should find out how many pages "Happy Days" ran to. I discovered at once that the number was 313. I therefore allowed "Newspaper Days" to remain at the same number, full of confidence that the double 13 would hardly be more potent for harm than the single one.

BALTIMORE, MD.
AUGUST 28, 1941.

My old friend, Monsignor J. B. Dudek, Chancellor of the Catholic diocese of Oklahoma City and Tulsa, dropped into Baltimore day before yesterday. He is on a little holiday and has thrown off his Roman collar and purple rabat and taken to ordinary street clothes. I have been seeing him at lunch and dinner, and having a pleasant time with him. He is full of interesting stuff about the inner workings of a Catholic diocese. His chief, Archbishop Francis C. Kelley,[1] is a great traveler, and so a lot of the routine work of the diocese falls on Dudek. As Chancellor, however, he is not competent to perform such offices as Confirmation. They are handed over to the Vicar General.

Dudek reports that he and the Bishop live in a very luxurious house in Oklahoma City. The Bishop bought it at a bargain from the estate of a deceased oil magnate. It is lavishly decorated and furnished, and contains among other things a pipe organ that cost $50,000. Dudek says that the cost of living in the house runs to $800 a month. He and the Bishop are looked after by four nuns of a local order. They live on the top floor and do the cooking and all other housework, save the heavy sweeping. They receive $80 a month, board and lodging for their services. Dudek says that there are always guests in the house, chiefly traveling clergymen. Now and then a sandalled monk shows up, stays a couple of weeks, and pollutes the whole place with his

1 Bishop Francis C. Kelley (1870–1948) is the unnamed bishop who appears in chapter eighteen of *Heathen Days*, "Vanishing Act," pp. 239–55. Mencken's reference to him here as "Archbishop" is in error.

heavy aroma. Dudek says that some time ago there appeared an Irish monk who was still wearing the trousers he had brought to America twenty-six years before. These brethren are supposed to bathe as seldom as possible, and most of them interpret that to mean never.

I haven't seen Bishop Kelley for several years. He was on the S.S. *Columbus* when Sara and I made our tour of the Mediterranean, and we spent a great deal of time with him. He is a charming Irishman from Prince Edward Island, and has had a brilliant career in the Church. Unhappily, his present assignment is a sort of exile. He came to the front in the diocese of Chicago, and the late Cardinal Mundelein apparently decided to get rid of him. At first it was proposed to make him Vicar Apostolic of Hawaii. He demurred at this, so Mundelein had him appointed Bishop of Oklahoma. When poor Kelley got to his diocese he found himself in strange and depressing surroundings. A large part of his career had been spent in the diplomatic service of the Church, so he was used to the life of big cities. In Oklahoma City he found himself virtually on the frontier. The town was comfortable enough physically, though rather hot in Summer, but there was absolutely no society. These meagre surroundings are largely responsible, I suspect, for the Bishop's constant traveling. He has a hand in all the national movements of the Catholic Church, and seems to be present at all of their meetings. He comes to Washington twice a year to attend the semiannual session of the hierarchy.

Dudek is a very learned man, and is the author of an unpublished treatise on the Czech language in America that shows extremely acute observation and clear reasoning. I have made various efforts to find a publisher for it, but always in vain. I printed a few extracts from it in the *American Mercury* in my time, and several others have been printed in *American Speech*, but the bulk of the book remains unpublished, and hence unheard of. Dudek is also a stamp collector. He told me that he has nearly a million different stamps. He does not confine himself to any of the specialties that now engage philatelists, but collects stamps in general. His only condition is that they shall be uncancelled. He tells me that he has them arranged in large volumes, with an elaborate card index. He estimates the value of the collection at forty or fifty thousand dollars, though he says that he has spent much less on it.

BALTIMORE, MD.
SEPTEMBER 18, 1941.

To the *Sun* office for lunch with Paul Patterson, who returned from England yesterday. Present: Frank Kent, James C. Fenhagen,[1] and John E. Semmes.[2] Patterson was full of interesting reports of his observations in London and Manchester. He had the suite at the Savoy that the *Sun* staff occupied at the time of the Naval Conference of 1930. He said that it cost him an enormous rental, and that he was still undecided whether to pay it himself or charge it to the *Sun*. I told him that I thought it should be charged to the *Sun*. If his trip to London had any sense at all the paper ought to pay for it.

It was plain enough that the English had taken Paul without any difficulty. Through Beaverbrook, whom he had met before, he was introduced to all the principal men of the government, though Churchill was not included. These gentlemen, it appeared, were in the habit of dining at the Savoy and of continuing at table until the bar closed at 11.30. Then they would go upstairs to Paul's quarters and he would entertain them half the night. This entertaining, even aside from the cost of the suite, was extremely expensive. He said that the hotel charged 30s. a bottle for Scotch. Outside, very ordinary Scotch could be bought for 17s.6d, but whenever it was brought in the hotel charged 5s. a bottle cartage on it. The Cutty Sark that we drink here is sold by Berry Brothers in London at 21s. a bottle. Moreover, the supply is so short that it is seldom possible to get more than two or three bottles at a time. The English have shipped all their Scotch to America in order to accumulate exchange, and the domestic supply is thus very scanty. In the bars no one is permitted to have more than one Scotch at a time, and it must be a simple one, not a double. Boozers who need more have to go out and walk around the block before getting a second dose. Now that the American taxpayer has begun to pay all the English bills, it is possible that the need for exchange will not be so pressing, and that the English themselves will get more of their own whiskey. Patterson said that the beer on tap in London is completely undrinkable. Most of the upper class English

---

1 James C. Fenhagen (1875–1955), banker and member of the board of directors of the A. S. Abell Company.
2 John E. Semmes (1881–1967), member of the Baltimore law firm of Semmes, Bowen & Semmes, at that time legal counsel to the A. S. Abell Company.

drink German wines. There was an enormous supply in hand in London, and it is being sold relatively cheaply.

In theory, the amount of food every person may have is limited, but in actuality any one wealthy enough to patronize a good restaurant can get all he wants. The meals in restaurants, to be sure, are limited, but there is nothing to prevent a man eating eight or ten of them a day. Patterson said that the greatest difficulty lay in acquiring enough food to give a party in a private house. The usual way out is for the host and hostess to eat in restaurants for a week or so, and thus accumulate enough food credits to feed their guests. Buying new clothes is almost impossible. Every one has a card allowing him a certain number of credits a year. It takes nearly all of these credits to buy a suit of clothes, and it takes more than half of them to buy half a dozen shirts.

Patterson said that the work of clearing up the wreckage in London was proceeding apace—that is, everywhere save in the City. In the City the streets are almost impassable, but in the West End the bomb craters are being filled and the streets are being re-paved. Very little rebuilding, however, is going on. The Carleton Hotel is still simply four walls. The Ritz has been hit several times, but the damage was slight. So with the Savoy. Both have been repaired. There were no bombs while Patterson was in London.

It was plain from his talk that he had succumbed to the English without much resistance. They all took to addressing him as Paul on short acquaintance. He said that this custom had grown up under the stress of war. His observations were confined almost exclusively to the upper classes. He made one trip into the subways, which serve as bomb shelters, but apparently rushed through as fast as he could. He said that they have been cleaned up and no longer smell, as they once did. There are now toilets and wash-rooms. He said that the authorities require every person who has a pitch in a subway to occupy it at least three nights a week on penalty of losing it. The aim here is to keep the people in the habit of using the shelters. It is feared that if they once stayed away it would be difficult to get them back in case of new attacks.

Patterson said that the English are now convinced that Hitler will never attempt a landing in England, but they believe he will resume his bombings as soon as the Winter sets in. He said that all the newspapers of London are still being published in Fleet Street. The editorial and business offices have simply moved to the bomb-proof press rooms. Most of the papers run to but four pages a day, though the *Daily Telegraph* has six and the *Times* eight. The Manchester *Guardian*, which had been losing money for years and was supported by its evening edition, the Manchester *News*, is now in the black, chiefly because of the enormous reduction in production costs.

BALTIMORE, MD.

OCTOBER 16, 1941.

I spent a couple of hours at Schellhase's last night with Sinclair Lewis. He is in Baltimore to put on a play called "Good Neighbor," by Jack Levin, a 26-year-old Baltimore advertising agent. I dropped in at Ford's to pick him up, and found him back stage in the midst of a group of actors who seemed to be mainly Yiddish. He introduced me to several of them, but I didn't catch their names.

Lewis is on the water-wagon, and during our sitting drank nothing but iced coffee. Toward the end of the evening he asked for a plate of chocolate ice cream. After we had been at Schellhase's for an hour or more his girl showed up. She is a young Jewess rejoicing in the name of Marcella Powers, and has a part in "Good Neighbor." She turned out to be a completely hollow creature—somewhat good-looking, but apparently quite without intelligence. Lewis told me in her presence that he had been hanging up with her for more than a year.[1]

Before she came in he said that he had left Dorothy Thompson finally a year or so ago. He said that life with her had become completely impossible. She is a born fanatic and spends all of her days in howling and ranting against the wickedness of the world. Lewis told me that this oratory finally wore him down to such a point that he had to flee.

He looks almost ghastly. His face is the dead white of a scar, and he is thin and wizened. He told me that he had a new novel under way, but said that he was in some doubt that he'd ever finish it. Its principal character is a large scale do-gooder—a former college president who sits on innumerable committees and is active in every good

---

1 An extensive treatment of Lewis's relationship with the young actress Marcella Powers can be found in Mark Schorer's *Sinclair Lewis: An American Life* (New York: McGraw-Hill, 1961).

cause. Such an idiot, in his palmy days, would have been nuts for him, but I begin to doubt, as he apparently doubts himself, that he will be able to swing the job now. Obviously, he is in a state of mental collapse, not to mention physical decay. Long-continued drink and two wives of the utmost obnoxiousness have pretty well finished him. He seemed to be immensely delighted when I told him that both Cabell and Hergesheimer had told me at different times that they regard "Babbitt" as the best novel ever written in America.

BALTIMORE, MD.

OCTOBER 18, 1941.

Going to New York two days ago, I met J. Harry Covington on the train. It was so long since I had last seen him that I didn't recognize him when he spoke to me. Covington was Congressman from the Eastern Shore of Maryland from 1909 to 1914. In the latter year he resigned to become Chief Justice of the Supreme Court of the District of Columbia. He left the bench in 1918 and has been practising law in Washington ever since.

I asked him how he liked the life of a judge. He said that he found it extremely irksome, and toward the end almost unendurable. He said that there were only two kinds of lawyers who were happy on the bench. First, the lazy fellows who enjoy hearing other lawyers battle and are quite willing to let them do all the hard work, and second, the eager pushers with a frenzy to run things. He said that Felix Frankfurter is a perfect example of the second class. The present Supreme Court he described as a gang of semi-maniacs, only a few of whom know any law whatsoever. He said that it has become completely impossible for a lawyer to advise his clients. No one can say what a starry-eyed Supreme Court would do in a given case.

Covington got off at Wilmington, and so I suppose that the du Ponts are among his clients. In the course of our conversation he dropped the news that he is in the higher income brackets. He is now 71 years old, but looks as vigorous as a man of 50. He belongs to the more civilized moiety of the Eastern Shoremen, and told me that he has been greatly distressed by the rise of such imbeciles as T. Alan Goldsborough.[1]

1 T. Alan Goldsborough (1877–1951) was for eighteen years a Democratic congressman

On Sunday morning, October 12th, as August and I were working in the backyard, I received a telephone message from Anna Hildebrandt that my uncle William C. Abhau's house in Garrison avenue was afire. August and I rushed to the place as fast as we could, and found the firemen just completing their work. The whole top floor, a sort of garret, had burned off and streams of water were pouring down through the rest of the house. My sister Gertrude has an apartment on the second floor, so August and I got into it as soon as possible to see what damage had been done. We found that the damage was really next to nothing. All the wallpaper was sagging from the walls and there was water on the floors, but the salvage corps men had pulled up the rugs, taken down the pictures, and piled both on the furniture, after first grouping the latter in the middle of each room. They then covered the whole with heavy tarpaulin, and the tarpaulin took care of the water. My sister tells me now that she has found next to no damage to her goods. The insurance company has agreed to send out a furniture man to go over her furniture and make whatever slight repairs are necessary. The main damage was from the thumbs of the salvage corps men. They left some prints, but a few hours of polishing will restore the furniture. The only damage that August and I could find was the breaking of a Fensterbild.[1] In getting into one of the windows the firemen had knocked it down.

On the ground floor lived my uncle Will, who has been an invalid for seven years. He has suffered five or six cerebral hemorrhages and is virtually only a vegetable. The neighbors hauled him out, and when August and I found him he was sitting calmly in his brother-in-law's house a few steps down the street, smiling amiably. The whole thing seemed a good show to him. His house, of course, was considerably damaged. The whole garret floor was burned off, the wallpaper everywhere was ruined, the floors were soaked by water and are now curling, and some of the plastering was ruined. The insurance

---

from Maryland and in 1939 was named to the U.S. District Court for the District of Columbia.

1 *Fensterbild* means, literally, "window picture." The reference may be to the type of painted screen which was—and in many neighborhoods still is—typical of Baltimore homes.

companies have offered to pay $3,400 for the damage, which seems reasonable.

BALTIMORE, OCTOBER 29, 1941.

Max Brödel's funeral this afternoon—another reminder that my own time is fleeting. We had been sitting together at the Saturday Night Club's piano since 1911—thirty years. Max had an extraordinarily fluent and vigorous technic, and was the quickest and surest sight-reader I ever encountered, but his touch, like mine, was on the heavy side. Thus we made a great deal of noise when we played together, and the brethren called us the Busy Berthas. If there was any difference between us (save, of course, Max's enormously superior technic) it was that I banged the poor piano a shade less vociferously than he did. How many thousands of times I have grunted: "Not so loud, Max. The mark is *pp.*" The idea, as I used to tell him, was to make it sound like the flutter of angels' wings—or the sweet tinkle of angels' piss. He would take it in good part, bide his time, catch me playing a *pianissimo* passage *forte,* and then howl. We got on very well together, and I can recall only a few trivial disagreements. They usually flowed out of arguments at the *Biertisch,* after the music.

I met him for the first time in 1910, shortly after the organization of the Florestan Club,[1] of which I was a charter member. He joined early and came to the clubhouse in Charles street one night to show a colored photograph of Max Klinger's polychrome statue of Beethoven in Leipzig, and to lecture on it. His lecture, which was too long, bored me excessively, but we somehow became friends on the spot, and a little later he joined the Saturday Night Club, which then met in Al Hildebrandt's violin shop. He had a large library of piano duets, and gradually turned over most of it to the club. Thus we acquired nearly all the classical symphonies, from Haydn to Brahms. The orchestra parts I bought myself. Sometimes the club reimbursed me, but usually not. Its library today includes nearly everything worth playing—that is, everything that it can play.

Like nearly all music-lovers, Max had his blind spots. His really solid delight was in Haydn, Mozart, Beethoven, Schubert, Schumann

---

1 A brief account of the Florestan Club appears in the entry for February 5, 1942 (p. 192).

and Brahms, and he enjoyed them most when they were using the minor keys. For French music he had little liking, though he made an exception in favor of César Franck's D minor symphony. The lighter stuff appealed to him very little, though here again he excepted the Strauss waltzes. It has been the custom of the club since the beginning to end every evening of music with a waltz, and usually it has been one of Strauss's, though the library also contains many by Waldteufel, Gungl, Komzák and Ziehrer. Max always welcomed this postlude. "I begin to feel beerish," he would say—and the moment the piano lid banged down we'd be off to the beer-table. No member of the club ate and drank more heartily. He was, in fact, a really gargantuan eater, and he kept up his heavy suppers until the beginning of his last illness.

For years he had been badgered by emphysema, but it was not serious and he bore it without complaint. He got relief every Summer by going to his place in Upper Canada, but during World War I he was warned by Canadian friends that, as a German, he had better stay away, and this happened again when World War II started in 1939. Thus he was uncomfortable all through 1940, for the emphysema annoyed him in Winter, and in Summer he was discommoded by the Baltimore heat, which he never bore very well. But his general health seemed to be excellent until the Spring of 1941. He then began to complain of various malaises, and after the Summer heat came down he seldom appeared at the club. Toward the end of September, 1941, I heard (not from him) that he had been sent to the Johns Hopkins Hospital for investigation by Dr. Louis P. Hamburger, and along about October 5 I dropped in on him there. I found him in consultation with the hospital dietitian, for his blood showed some sugar. He was complaining loudly that he'd have to stop eating bread and drinking beer, but otherwise he seemed in excellent spirits. In the corridor I encountered Dr. Hamburger. He said that Max's glycosuria was too marked to be dismissed lightly, but that it seemed likely to yield to insulin, and he would be going home the next day. A week or so later I heard that he was back in hospital, and very ill. I went there at once, but did not see him: his nurse told me that he was in extreme discomfort. On October 22 his wife called me up with the staggering news that the glycosuria had turned out to be only a symptom of something much worse, to wit, cancer of the pancreas. There had been an exploratory operation that afternoon, and it revealed a hopeless situation. Max was doomed to die, and he knew it. He died during the night of October 25–26, a little after midnight.

His funeral this afternoon was at the pro-Cathedral near his house in Guilford. The house itself was too small to hold the crowd of Johns Hopkins men that were certain to show up, so his wife accepted the invitation of Canon H. N. Arrowsmith to use the pro-Cathedral. The body was brought direct to the church from the funeral-parlor in Eutaw place, where it had been lying since the autopsy. It seemed almost comic for so sturdy an agnostic to be buried from a Christian church, but there seemed no other way out. The canon conducted the Protestant Episcopal burial service, and it was mercifully short. There was an impressive group of honorary pallbearers, including nearly all the principal Johns Hopkins Medical School men. Old Dr. Howard A. Kelly sat with the family, squired by Dr. Thomas S. Cullen. He looked shrunken and pathetic, and it was obvious that his 83 years were closing in on him. The burial was in Loudon Park Cemetery. Save for the family, only a few persons went to the grave. Dr. Cullen invited me to join him in his car, along with Dr. Guy L. Hunner.[1] The two were Max's chief intimates among the Hopkins men. Cullen had been present at the autopsy. He said that it showed a really astounding spread of carcinoma. Beginning, apparently, in the pancreas, it had jumped to every organ of the abdomen. There were nodules everywhere. How long this had been going on he did not know, but apparently not very long. Max had first begun to complain of abdominal discomfort, as I recall it, in July. When he got back to hospital for the second time he was in great pain, but this passed off after the exploratory operation. His end, helped by morphine, was very easy: he simply fell into a coma, and then passed out. Always a realistic fellow, he had discussed his funeral with his poor wife. He was in fear that the Rev. F. O. Evers, pastor of Zion Church, who buries most of the German atheists of Baltimore, might be called in for the service. He disliked Evers as a theatrical fellow, given to long and maudlin oratory over the dead. He would have preferred, of course, no service at all, but realized that his death would attract some attention, and that his wife and two daughters would naturally shrink from putting him away without any ceremony at all. So he went into the grave to the tune of mumbled

1 Dr. Guy L. Hunner (1868–1957) was a member of the first class of the Johns Hopkins School of Medicine and specialized in gynecology and urology under Dr. Kelly.

assurances that his soul still lived, and would presently find a place in the purlieus of the heavenly throne. Why his body was not cremated I do not know. He had told me more than once that he wanted it to be.

On Tuesday, the day before the funeral, old W. Edwin Moffett,[1] a member of the Saturday Night Club, called me up in great alarm. He had been to the funeral parlor to pay his respects, and came away convinced that the body was not Max's. "They showed me a man," he said, "with sandy, slicked hair and a reddish moustache. There must be some mistake." I suggested that the dim light and the posture of the dead might have been deceptive—that a man standing erect and full of life looks different from a man lying low, cold and dead. But Moffett would not be reassured, so I called up another member of the club, Israel Dorman,[2] who lives near the funeral parlor, and asked him to slip in and take a look. He reported that the body was undoubtedly Max's. What had deceived Moffett was the way the light was shining on it. Max's moustache had long ago turned gray, but there were still some reddish blond hairs down in the tangle of it, and, with the light coming from an unfamiliar direction, they now showed themselves. As for the hair of his head, he always wore it tousled, but now the undertaker, with characteristic imbecility, had tried to comb it—maybe, in fact, to hide an autopsy cut. Moffett was still convinced at the funeral that there was something wrong. He insisted that Max never had the moustache he had seen on the body. But no one else seemed to be in doubt, so that body went into Max's grave.

The *Sun's* obituary was rather less bad than usual. I had warned the office of Max's probable death four or five days beforehand, and so it was ready. It appeared on a Monday, always a day when morning newspapers have plenty of space, and it was accompanied by an excellent portrait. Hamilton Owens asked me to do the editorial that the *Sun* printed on Tuesday, October 28. The same day there appeared a notice of the funeral in which Max was spoken of, both in the heading and in the text, as *Dr.* Brödel, though the obituary of Monday had made it plain that he had no medical degree. This blunder somewhat

1 W. Edwin Moffett (1871–1957), an old friend of Mencken's, was one of the few professional musicians in the Saturday Night Club. He played in the Baltimore Symphony Orchestra.

2 Israel Dorman (1891–1970) was also a professional musician and was on the faculty of Baltimore's Peabody Conservatory of Music.

upset Paul Patterson and me, but there was nothing to be done about it. On the way to the cemetery Cullen, who is a clergyman's son and inclined to be a shade prissy, let fall a hint that Max was really not the all-out agnostic that all of us had assumed him to be. "The last time I saw him," said Cullen, "he said 'Tom, pray for me.' " A discreet cross-examination showed that Max had said this smiling: he was, in all probability, indulging himself in some sly *Galgenhumor* at Cullen's expense. On returning from the funeral this afternoon I found the following from Cullen's wife, who is at their place on the Eastern Shore of Maryland:

> I am wondering if you wrote the editorial in today's *Sun* about Max Brödel. If so, will you accept my sincere appreciation of it?
>
> I loved Max. The cruelty these last two Summers of depriving him of the joys of his camp in Canada, with its aid to his oppressed lungs, has been a bitter sadness to me.
>
> It may be poor taste of me to express myself thus, but the funeral arrangements for him seem perfectly horrible. However, if they assuaged anyone's grief I suppose Max wouldn't care. Perhaps he would have, with one of his short laughs, likened himself to Lenin. About the pro-Cathedral "incident" he might add: "Dr. Kelly got the better of me, after all."

BALTIMORE, MD.

NOVEMBER 3, 1941.

To the Johns Hopkins Hospital this afternoon to visit Marcia Heath, the widow of my old friend, Eugene B. (Percy) Heath.[1] I was best man at their wedding in Baltimore back in 1904 or thereabout, and godfather at the baptism of their only child, a son who is now 28. I well recall the baptismal ceremony. Both Percy and I were slightly the worse for drink. At the last moment the officiating clergyman, an Episcopalian, turned to me and demanded sharply: "Young man, are you a Christian?" When I answered that I was—officially—he asked me who had baptized me. At a venture I said "Father Chipchase"—the

---

1 Percy Heath figures in one of Mencken's best-known tales, "A Girl from Red Lion, P.A.," in *Newspaper Days*, pp. 227–38.

name of a rummy old Episcopal rector who had been one of the drinking companions of my grandfather Mencken. This satisfied the clergyman, and he went on with the ceremony. Percy and I had also been
more or less tight at the wedding, and I recall that he dropped the
ring and I had some difficulty recovering it. He died nine years ago in
Hollywood, where he had prospered as a writer of movies.

Marcia, who must be nearly 55, still shows some traces of her former blonde beauty. She is, unhappily, on the stupid side, and I marvel
that a man as intelligent as Percy should have stood her silly chatter
for so many years. He probably lived and died without ever discov-
ering that there were such things on earth as intelligent women—that
is to say, he assumed that Marcia was a normal female and so lived
with her contentedly. Despite the fact that his days were spent in
Hollywood, he put in most of his spare time at home and so had no
part in the gaudy sexual society of the place.

Marcia came to the Johns Hopkins seeking treatment for arthritis
in both her hands. Her knuckles were considerably swollen and had
begun to be painful. She was not sent to the hospital by any doctor,
but came in on her own and demanded treatment by the staff. When
it turned out that she needed a really serious investigation she was sent
to Dr. Charles W. Wainwright, and he put her to bed. He found that
her arthritis was not serious and advised her to do nothing about it. It
will persist, but it is of the sort that does not become disabling. Wainwright and his assistants made a thorough examination of her and
found various disabilities. Among other things, she had a severe cystitis. This was cured in a week by one of the sulphanol compounds.
She also turned out to have adenoids. Instead of operating, Wainwright ordered a brief treatment with radium.

Marcia is well-to-do, but somewhat mean. Instead of entering the
Marburg, she took half a cubicle in the Thayer at $4.50 a day. As a
Thayer patient she paid a maximum of but $35 for all the x-rays that
were made of her. In the Marburg she would have paid for them by
the piece, and the cost might have run to $150. She is a well meaning
creature, but rather hard to bear, for her conversation is almost exclusively silly. Like most chatterboxes, she makes a great deal of noise—
indeed, she had the Thayer in an uproar while she was a patient there.
When I got to the hospital this afternoon I found her preparing to
leave. She is to come back in a week to make sure that her cystitis is
really cleared up, and I suppose I'll have to see her again. It is not a
prospect that allures.

Marcia and Percy had only one child—the one for whom I stood as godfather. He is now living in Hollywood. When he was a student in college in California he fell into the hands of a kept lady who got smashed on him, left her keeper and took the boy to live with her. This naturally scandalized Marcia, and after the pair had been living together for three years she insisted that they be married. The bride was seven years older than the bridegroom. To Marcia's immense surprise she made an excellent wife. Unhappily, the boy has lately developed a kidney infection accompanied by a very high blood pressure, and is now virtually an invalid. Before he became disabled he was doing very well in the movies and making a good living. Now Marcia must look after him and his wife. She is now fully reconciled to her daughter-in-law and, in fact, speaks of her cordially and even almost affectionately.

BALTIMORE, NOVEMBER 8, 1941.

August and I went to the Home for Incurables this morning to see our uncle, Charles H. Abhau, my mother's youngest brother. We took him a bottle of whiskey, and found him very lively and comfortable, though he is 72 years old and has been a cripple since the age of three. It was infantile paralysis that made him lame, but in the 69 years of his affliction he had been beset by various other disabilities. Until he was 65 or thereabout he was able to walk with the aid of crutches, but since then he has been confined to a wheel-chair. He married late in life and his wife—Bertha Hennighausen—died soon afterward, so that he has been a widower for nearly twenty years. Until two years ago he lived with a widowed sister and a niece, but as his disabilities increased he concluded that he was a burden to them, and when the new private wing of the Home for Incurables was opened he moved into it. He has a bright and charming corner room on the ground floor, and outside there is a lovely oak grove, alive with busy squirrels. He pays $18 a week for his room, and is apparently well cared for. He has a little money, and in addition he receives a pension of $1,200 a year from the U.S. Customs Service, in which he served as a clerk for many years. He took a degree in law from the University of Maryland in 1904, but never practised.

He looked to be in excellent health this morning and was certainly in lively spirits, but he told August and me that he was incommoded by eczema in his toes and that of late he had noted some symptoms of bronchial asthma, a family failing. But he has been so handicapped all his life that a few more afflictions do not incommode him. He got out his diploma from the University of Maryland and his license to practise, and asked us to advise him about disposing of them, for he has no children. I suggested that the best place for them was a scrap-book in which I have pasted various souvenirs of my mother, his sister. This scrapbook is to go, at my death, to the Pratt Library in Baltimore, which is to receive also all my other family papers. He seemed pleased with this proposal, and gave me both documents.

He is somewhat garrulous, and entertained August and me with anecdotes of days long past. The time of one of them was the day after my birth, which was on September 12, 1880. Uncle Charles was then a boy of eleven. September 12 was always a public holiday in Balti-more—the anniversary of the Battle of North Point—, but in 1880 it fell on a Sunday and the holiday was celebrated the next day. Uncle Charlie always looked for a treat on such occasions, and this time my father had promised to take him and his father, my grandfather Ab-hau, on a buggy-ride to Druid Hill Park. He was to pick them up in the morning, but when the hour arrived he did not appear, and an hour later he was still missing. When he came at last it was with the news that I had been born the night before: there were no telephones in those days, and even important news had to wait. Thus the buggy-ride was not to Druid Hill Park, but to the house in West Lexington street where I was getting my first look at the world. Uncle Charlie said that he was taken upstairs to see me, but was not interested. His mind was fully occupied with his lost trip to Druid Hill Park.

From this we fell to talking of the sharp realism of children, and their innocent callousness to the feelings of others. Uncle Charlie said that in his days on crutches it was an almost every-day experience for children to stop him on the street and say, "Say, mister, why do you walk that way?" He always explained to them, he said, that he was lame, and sometimes they cross-examined him at great length about the nature and causes of lameness. Apparently, he never resented their curiosity. He has always, in fact, taken his afflictions philosophically, though sometimes they have put him to great inconvenience and in-volved severe pain. He seems to be happily settled at last, tranquilly awaiting death. Judging by his appearance, he may well last for years. In fact, he may outlast all the rest of us. For the first time in his life, he is not a burden to others. The nurses and others who wait on him are professionals, and take it as part of their day's work. While we sat with him the head nurse on his floor came in—a rather good-looking young woman named Jorgenson. They were plainly on excellent terms, and she seemed to be very fond of him.

NOVEMBER 10, 1941.

At 11.25 this morning I finished reading the last of the page-proofs of my dictionary of quotations. The last of the galley-proofs reached me on November 3, and was returned to the Plimpton Press the same day. In the book, by my count, there are about 42,260 quotations, and it runs to between 850,000 and 900,000 words. The proofs have occupied me since July, and before that I put in three months reading the fair copy made by Mrs. Lohrfinck from the original cards. At one time or another I must have put at least 60,000 cards into the file. In the final revision I destroyed many thousands.

Thus ends a work that began about twenty-five years ago. At the start I filed quotations only for my own use: a great many good ones were not in the existing quotation books, and seemed worth preserving. I seldom, in fact, used them, for my writing is not allusive, but they kept on piling up, and so it inevitably occurred to me that they would make a book. When I began serious work upon it, in 1932, it appeared at once that a great deal of spade work remained to be done: it would be necessary to make a systematic investigation of all the standard authors. This was too much for me to undertake alone, so I took in Charles Angoff, then my assistant on the *American Mercury*, as an equal partner. Angoff tackled the job diligently, and produced some good cards, but he also turned in a great many useless ones, and toward the end of 1934, after I had left the *American Mercury*, he showed signs of failing interest. By an agreement dated March 4, 1935, I took back his half of the book, but gave him, in compensation for his labor, a half interest in the first year's royalties.

A year or so ago, after I had begun work on the final revision, the Oxford University Press announced that it was bringing out a new dictionary of quotations, and both Knopf and I became somewhat uneasy, for it would appear before we could bring out ours, and it might blanket us. But when the Oxford book finally came out, a month or so ago, I was reassured, for it turned out to be a very poor piece of work, published anonymously and apparently produced by the University Press proof-room. Mine is enormously better, but whether it will sell better remains to be seen. The Knopf office has had no experience in marketing such a book, which must be sold, in the main, direct to the reader. It is now engaged upon the preparation of circulars, the compiling of a mailing list, and other such devices. The printer's bill for setting up the book and making the plates will run beyond $10,000, and the printing, paper and binding bills for the first edition will be even larger. But Knopf is not dismayed, for he has made extraordinary profits this year, and is eager to reduce his Federal taxes by plowing some of them into a book that should have a more or less profitable sale for years to come.

If it does well I plan to bring out a shorter edition, omitting some of the apparatus of the original and reducing the number of quotations to 8,000 or 10,000.[1]

BALTIMORE, NOVEMBER 17, 1941.

Joe Hergesheimer came to Baltimore on November 15 to consult his doctor, Benjamin M. Baker, Jr. I met him at Maxim's in Howard street, and we had dinner there. Later we went to Schellhases's, where we sat with Judge Eugene O'Dunne,[2] Drs. Alan and Manfred Guttmacher,[3] and two young men who were guests of the Guttmachers. They and O'Dunne and I have fallen into the habit of meeting at Schellhase's at 10 o'clock every Monday evening. Hulbert Footner joins us whenever he is in town, and there are often guests. My brother August was a member of the little club until his work with the consulting engineers at the Edgewood Arsenal made it necessary for him to get up every morning at 6 o'clock. Inasmuch as the club usually sits until midnight he had to withdraw.

Joe looked wretched. He has lost weight and his face is white and

1 No abridged edition of *A New Dictionary of Quotations* ever appeared.

2 Eugene O'Dunne (1875–1959) was a judge on the Supreme Bench of Baltimore City. He is discussed further in the entries for November 22, 1944 (pp. 338–342), and June 26, 1945 (pp. 371–373).

3 Drs. Alan Guttmacher (1898–1974) and Manfred Guttmacher (1898–1966)—identical twins—were prominent in the Baltimore medical circles of the time. Alan was an obstetrician and gynecologist who dared to advocate various methods of birth control at a time when the subject was not publicly discussed. Manfred was a psychiatrist specializing in criminal psychology and served as chief medical adviser to the Supreme Bench of Baltimore.

drawn. Maxim had terrapin on his bill of fare, and I tried a plate at his urging, but Joe refused. He drank nothing save water at Maxim's, nor at Schellhase's afterward. He went to see Baker the next morning. Baker tells me today that, despite his haggard appearance, his diabetes showed some improvement. He could be cured by insulin, but he fights off taking it on the ground that doing so would make him a slave to a hypodermic. Baker said that Joe has been keeping to his diet very faithfully—in fact, so faithfully that a certain amount of relaxation was ordered. He is to remain at West Chester until December 15 and then return to Baltimore for further investigation. He agrees that if Baker then advises insulin he will submit. In addition to his blood sugar he shows symptoms of arterio-sclerosis. In fact, Baker believes that his inability to work is due to the sclerosis, not to the diabetes. It is, of course, incurable. Joe told me that he had a 35,000-word serial under way, and that it was going fairly well, but he was very vague about it. It is unhappily plain that his writing days are nearly over. He will never write another book of any pretensions. He may manage to do some trade goods for the magazines, but that is all.

He came to Baltimore expecting that Baker would order him to the Johns Hopkins, and had $500 in cash with him to pay his bills there. While we were at dinner he suddenly recalled that he had left the money in an envelope in his hotel-room. He rushed back to the hotel in a taxi and returned in a few minutes with the news that it was safe. In fact, he had it with him, and counted it with immense relief. His financial situation is precarious. He told me that his wife Dorothy had lately sold some American antique furniture that had been stored in their West Chester cellar. Included was a set of six small Windsor chairs. He said that Dorothy got $4,000 for the lot, but in such matters he usually exaggerates. He lately spent a week in New York at the Algonquin Hotel, as the guest of Frank Case, the proprietor. While he was there he had a meeting with Joan Crawford, the movie star, who is ambitious to do his *Cytherea* as a talkie. It has been done as a movie but not as a talkie.[1] Joe said that he had sold only the movie rights, and that under a recent Supreme Court decision he is free to sell the talkie rights. How much Crawford offered for them he didn't say, but he hinted that it was not more than $10,000.

---

[1] The silent film version of Hergesheimer's *Cytherea* was produced by Samuel Goldwyn in 1924. It was never made into a talking picture.

BALTIMORE, NOVEMBER 22, 1941.

To New York yesterday to attend a twice-adjourned meeting of the board of Alfred A. Knopf, Inc. The business in hand was a proposal to raise the salaries of Alfred A. Knopf as president, his wife Blanche as vice-president, and Joseph C. Lesser as treasurer. This proposal was opposed bitterly by Knopf's cousin, Samuel Knox. The great success of the Shirer book, *Berlin Diary*,[1] which will lift the company's gross receipts for the fiscal year to nearly $1,500,000, has filled Knox with the delusion that it will be possible, soon or late, to wipe out the accumulation of unpaid dividends on the preferred stock—now amounting to nearly $180,000—and so restore the value of the preferred and common stock for which he paid $57,500. Knox is a stubborn and stupid fellow, and so he is not moved by the plain facts (*a*) that there is small probability of another Shirer book turning up, and (*b*) that even if it does turn up it will not earn enough, above taxes, to pay off the accumulations. During the present fiscal year the net income, before taxes, will be at least $75,000, but after taxes it may be no more than $35,000. The excess profits tax, of course, is to blame. The Knopf Company showed very small earnings during the past few years, and so it is heavily soaked this year. The most rational thing to do would be to write off the accumulations on the preferred, but this Knox objects to. Some time in October I had a session on the subject with his lawyer, Samuel Kramer. Kramer told me that he believed it would be impossible to induce Knox to agree to any sensible disposition of the accumulations question, and said that he thought the only feasible way out would be for him to be eliminated altogether by Knopf buying his stock. He and Knopf had a meeting on the subject a week or so ago. Knopf offered $21,000 for his shares of common and preferred and was willing to go a bit higher, but Knox demanded $58,000. The negotiations thus blew up. The board meeting had been twice adjourned in the hope that they might produce a solution, but it was plain to everyone yesterday that none was in sight, so the salary resolution was put through, with Knox voting nay. It provides for a total increase of $7,500 a year. Of this Lesser will get $500. The Knopfs

1 *Berlin Diary* by William L. Shirer (b. 1904) had been published earlier that year by Knopf and speedily became a best-seller. It was an account of the foreign correspondent's experiences in Europe, with particular emphasis on Germany and the rise of Nazism.

will divide the remainder, with Blanche getting about $1,000 more than Alfred. This difference recognizes the fact that she got the Shirer book.

BALTIMORE, DECEMBER 29, 1941.

The year closes upon a gloomy house. August has been racked by a bronchial cough for months, and ten days ago a high wind awoke his old sinus infection. As for me, I have been noticing, for several days past, a faint tingling in my left hand and foot—obviously, the first warning of a cerebral episode like that of July 21, 1939. If it gets worse I'll be floored again, and maybe finished; if it passes off the relief will be only temporary. Thus the days ahead look dark, and I wonder how much I'll be able to do before the inevitable end. Since I finished "Newspaper Days" and the quotation book I have been devoting myself mainly to a detailed record of my days on the *Sun*. It already runs to nearly 200,000 words, and I have got no further than the year 1935. Moreover, there are considerable gaps in what is already on paper. I'd like to finish it, and then do a similar record of my adventures on and with magazines. There are great numbers of documents in my files, but if I don't reduce them to order myself no one else will ever be able to do it. During the past 40 years I have seen both American newspapers and American magazines from the inside. If history is worth anything at all, then maybe this history that I have had a hand in will be worth setting down. But whether it is or it isn't, I get some fun in my closing years out of running it down and recording it. Up to this time, so far as I know, no really honest history of a newspaper, or of a magazine, has ever been written.

I had planned to devote 1942 to putting together a supplement to "The American Language." The amount of new material in hand is enough to make a volume as large as the fourth edition. But now I rather incline to give all my time to the records aforesaid. If I live into 1943 it will be time enough to do the supplement. The Knopfs want me to do a third volume in the manner of "Happy Days" and "Newspaper Days," but it can wait. I have already done 11 pieces for the *New Yorker* that may eventually make chapters for it, and I have given Harold W. Ross, the editor thereof, the refusal of any others that I may do in 1942. He is free to print not more than 12 altogether, and may make his own choices, but he must complete the printing by the end of the year. I'd like very much to do a book to be called "Thoughts in War Time" or something of the sort, to be printed after the war ends, but it is hardly likely that I'll get to it.[1] Despite my physical deterioration my mind remains perfectly clear and I find writing pleasant enough, but I tire easily and so have to take frequent rests. If I work all morning I am played out in the afternoon, and if I resume work at night I can seldom go beyond 9 o'clock. There was a time when I could work steadily, save for the time out for meals and maybe a brief snooze in the late afternoon, from 10 a.m. to 10 p.m., but that is no longer possible.

I went out to Loudon Park Cemetery on Christmas morning with August, and we laid a wreath on the family tombstone. It was the forty-first Christmas since my father's death, the seventeenth since my mother's, the seventh since Sara's, and the second since my sister-in-law Mary's. My mother has begun to recede into the shadows, but Sara is still clearly before me, and I think of her constantly. Nevertheless, I am half glad that she is dead, for the future looks dismal, and 1942 is certain to be the worst year I have ever seen. In a little while the professional patriots will be down on me with demands that I do this or that, and my peace will be gone. Meanwhile, excessive taxes will greatly diminish my income, and I'll have to give up many comforts that I have long enjoyed. My life, on the whole, has been an easy one. I have never lacked anything that I really wanted. In money, I have always had a dollar more than I needed. But the going will be harder hereafter. August and I have decided to go on in Hollins street as long as possible, keeping our servants and trying to be comfortable. How long we'll be able to do so remains to be seen—maybe not long.

1 No such book was ever written.

1942

Mrs. Bertha Bradford Carter, widow of my old chief, Robert I. Carter,[1] was in Baltimore today, and I took her to lunch at the Marconi. She turned out to be a well preserved and not bad looking woman. She has a hawkish nose and a good figure. When she came into the restaurant I naturally assumed that she was the Widow Carter whom I had known back in 1902, and so I spoke to her about her golf playing. It turned out at once that the wife Carter had during his Baltimore days had been divorced, and that this one was his third. His first I never met. He had got rid of her during his early days in Cincinnati.

Mrs. Carter, I gathered, was a young actress at the time Carter met her. After they were married they lived at the Brevoort Hotel in New York. They had no children, and Mrs. Carter has never remarried since Carter's death. She told me that just before the beginning of his last illness he seemed to be in perfectly good health. One night they went out to dinner, and he was in his usually pleasant spirits, though he had protested against going. In the middle of the night he began to rant and roar, and it was obvious that his mind was affected. He was sent to Bellevue Hospital for observation, and in a little while his case was diagnosed as incurable. This was sometime during 1911. He was thereupon transferred to Bloomingdale, and there he died in May, 1914. Mrs. Carter said that he was one of the heirs of the Carter

---

1 An account of Carter appears in chapter nine of *Newspaper Days*, "Three Managing Editors," pp. 154–59.

ink fortune. He was an only child and his mother had a considerable income. She outlived him, however, and so Mrs. Carter apparently got very little of the money, if any. She appears, nevertheless, to be in comfortable circumstances. She told me that she comes to Baltimore off and on to visit a Miss Helen Goldsborough, an old friend. This Miss Goldsborough has a farm near Shepherdstown, W. Va., and the two go there now and then to spend a couple of weeks together.

Mrs. Carter said that Carter had left the New York *Herald* when she married him and was associated with Harrison Grey Fiske, husband of Mrs. Fiske, in the theatrical business. Mrs. Carter appeared to be an intelligent woman. It turned out, on cross-examination, that she knew really little about her husband. He had naturally told her next to nothing about his two previous marriages, and inasmuch as he had no relatives except his old mother, there was no source of information readily available. She knew nothing whatever about his Cincinnati days, and had only the vaguest notion of his doings in Baltimore. I gathered from her talk that she had been in the habit of addressing him as Bob I. This seemed to me to be terrible, but I wasn't called upon to pronounce judgment on it. She told me that Carter was very careful about the care of his red torpedo beard. At night he put it up in an appliance designed to protect it. In particular, he was eager to preserve the bristling, upward flow of his moustache.

Mrs. Carter told me that she was on friendly terms with Ida M. Tarbell, author of the once famous history of the Standard Oil Company, and Viola Roseboro', once managing editor of *McClure's Magazine*. Both are now very old, and Miss Tarbell has become feeble. They are intimate friends, but they live so far apart that they seldom see each other. Miss Tarbell has a small place in Connecticut, and Miss Roseboro' lives in an apartment on Staten Island. The trip from one place to the other is almost as difficult as the trip by train from Baltimore to Pittsburgh.

I arranged with Mrs. Carter to see her again the next time she is in Baltimore.

BALTIMORE, JANUARY 21, 1942.

Blanche Knopf, who had been in Washington, dropped off in Baltimore today to consult her oculist, Dr. Alan C. Woods. She was in a considerable state of alarm, for the vision of her left eye has been failing. Six or seven years ago, being frantically eager to keep her weight down, she allowed a quack in New York, Wolf by name, to give her injections of dinitrophenol, then all the rage for reducing. It actually worked, but it had extremely serious side effects, not at first noticed. One of them was the production of cataracts in the eyes. When this effect was observed the American Medical Association sent out an alarm, and the use of dinitrophenol was abandoned, but it was too late to save many of the women who had received shots of it. Some developed cataracts at once, some showed impairment of the vision without really serious clouding, and some appeared to be escaping altogether. Apparently Blanche was one of the last-named. When I heard of her adventure I induced her to come to Baltimore to see Woods, and he found very little impairment. For several years she visited him off and on, but there was no development. Woods was of the opinion that if she was to have cataracts they would have shown themselves soon after the injections, and so she began to have hope. But a few months ago she noticed that her left eye was impaired, and since then it has been clouding rapidly.

She asked me to go with her to Woods' office at the Johns Hopkins, and I sat in the room while he examined her. He is famous for his forthright manner with patients, and he did not spare her. "The last time I saw you," he said, "you had 70% of normal vision in your left eye. Now you have but 40%. Come back in three months. If there is any further impairment nothing can be done save to wait a little and then operate for cataract. Your right eye appears to be unaffected so far. Your glasses need changing, but I see no sign of cataract. Maybe it will escape. I don't know. I used to believe that the only women who would develop cataracts would be those who came in soon after the injections, but now I am beginning to see late cases. No treatment can do you any good. There is no cure save the removal of the clouded lens. When it is out you will be given spectacles that will serve in its place, and there will be a reasonable amount of vision."

Blanche received this appalling news very bravely. She had, of course, been prepared for it, but nevertheless it was a dreadful shock. She asked a few questions, mainly about the kind of glasses she would have to wear, but only a few. Woods was gentle (for him), but made no attempt to give her any false hopes. The fact that the right eye was still unimpaired was reassuring, but it promised nothing certain, for if the cataract in the left eye had lain dormant for three years, one might develop in the right later on. I was immensely sorry for Blanche, but it was as impossible for me to offer her consolation as it was for Woods. She is too intelligent to be put off with hollow words. After we left Woods I took her to the Belvedere for lunch. She declared that she would never submit to an operation for cataract—that she'd be dead before the time came. I tried to argue that, after the operation, she'd soon get used to the glasses, but it was a feeble effort, for I well knew that she would be blind without them, and that her dependence on them would be an almost intolerable nuisance. Old E. W. Howe, who had both lenses removed by Woods in 1935, told me in 1936 that his glasses gave him no more than 50% of normal vision. Blanche pledged me to keep the news from her husband. They are both extreme neurotics, and given to hysterics. She faced Woods very coolly and courageously, but there must inevitably come a day when, with plenty of time to think of what is ahead, she will go to pieces. Her work in life requires constant reading, and with her vision impaired it will be impossible for her to do it. I am thus very uneasy about her. In parting I urged her to come to Baltimore sooner than Woods suggested. It will be harder to wait than to hear news that is almost certain to be bad.

Woods's habit of telling patients the truth probably works well in the long run, but it makes for excessive unpleasantness immediately. I'll never forget the afternoon when Sara came staggering up the long stairway to our apartment in Cathedral street, after having been told by Woods that she had a tuberculous infection in one of her eyes. It was the only time in all her cruel illness when I ever saw her near collapse. She was so terrified that she was almost out of her mind, and I had a hard time quieting her. Woods, of course, was right in his diagnosis, but in a little while the lesion cleared up without treatment, and though tuberculosis caused her death in the end it never reappeared in her eyes. Nor in her lungs, though twice she had pleurisy. Nor in her remaining kidney, though the other one had got infected and been removed.

When Blanche discovered what the quack had done to her she warned a number of other women against him and the news somehow reached him. He thereupon sent her a letter threatening her with a suit for slander if she talked any more. He had advised her, he said, against taking dinitrophenol, but she had insisted on it. The effrontery of the fellow was really amazing: he must have been well aware that his responsibility was not lessened by the fact that he had allowed a patient to dictate the treatment. Indeed, his very letter was enough to convict him of the most reckless sort of quackery, but Blanche resolved to do nothing, for she was then full of hope that no cataracts would develop. She naturally feared any public ventilation of the matter, for the same vanity that had induced her to take the treatment now prompted her to keep its results secret. Thus her life has been ruined by her frantic desire to avoid putting on weight—a desire that has not only brought her to Woods with cataracts, but also given a great deal of concern to her other Baltimore doctor, Benjamin M. Baker, who has been trying for three or four years to induce her to abandon her starvation diet and eat normally. But even with the lesson of the cataracts before her she resists Baker's advice as much as possible. At lunch after our visit to Woods she had a plate of clear soup and a cracker—nothing more.

BALTIMORE, JANUARY 23, 1942.

I have felt so wretched during the past few days that it has been impossible for me to do any sensible work. My head feels heavy and there is a really severe malaise. It seems hard to believe that this malaise is the effect of arterio-sclerosis; it feels exactly like the kind produced by an infection. But I have no apparent infection. My sinuses seem to be clear and there is no sign of a cold. All last week and the two weeks before I had discomfort in the stomach, but that has now passed off. Despite all this, I manage to get about, and I assume that persons who meet me notice nothing amiss. Yesterday, after two naps during the day, I put in the evening reading and loafing, and then went to sleep at 11 p.m. Today I awoke feeling very sick, but spent an hour or so in the morning trying to get some work done on my income tax return. After lunch I went to the office, and sat briefly with Patterson and Swanson.[1] On my return I took a nap, and woke up full of aches and discomforts. What these symptoms indicate I do not know. Last Spring they got so bad that I could not work at all, and Wainwright sent me to the Johns Hopkins for investigation. He apparently found nothing that medicine could relieve, for he gave me no treat-

1 Neil H. Swanson (1896–1983) served as executive editor of the *Sunpapers*—the only person ever to hold the position—from 1941 to 1954. He was also the author of a number of highly regarded historical novels of which *The Judas Tree* and *The Silent Drum* are probably the best known.

ment, and at the end of the two weeks he advised me to take a holiday. I went to Havana—and returned home still feeling wretched. But soon afterward I began to feel better, and within a few weeks I had finished "Newspaper Days," which had been held up by my illness. When it was off my hands I tackled the galleys and page proofs of the dictionary of quotations—a really formidable job. Meanwhile, I began a narrative of my years on the *Sun*. It now runs to 667 pages of typescript, not counting appendices, and I am still in the year 1936. If I ever finish it, it will probably reach 900 pages of typescript—at least 350,000 words—, for several busy years, notably 1938 and 1940, remain.[1]

BALTIMORE, JANUARY 26, 1942.

The widow of Max Brödel called up. She has sold her house in Guilford for $12,000, got rid of all her household goods save a few souvenirs at auction, and is going to Spuyten Duyvil, N.Y., to live with her unmarried sister, who keeps an inn there, largely patronized by artists. The elder Brödel daughter, Elizabeth, is an anatomical artist like her father, and is now living in New York. The younger daughter, Elsa, is married and living in Norristown, Pa. The son, Carl, is a geologist, now employed by the government in Idaho. Thus a pleasant family life ends. The Brödels were married in 1902, and Mrs. Brödel must be beyond sixty. She had a very serious illness three years ago, but seems to be completely restored. She is sending the Saturday Night Club several volumes of Max's four-hand piano music. He brought in many such volumes when he joined the club in 1911 or thereabout, and they are still in its library. Some time ago I wrote to her, asking whether she wanted them back. She replied that they are to remain the property of the club. There is a Brödel Summer camp at Magnetawan, in upper Canada, not occupied since 1939 on account of the war. It is to be sold like the house in Guilford.

1 Three volumes entitled "Thirty-five Years of Newspaper Work," along with four volumes of "My Life as Author and Editor" referred to frequently in later entries, were bequeathed by Mencken to the Enoch Pratt Free Library with the stipulation that they were to remain sealed until the thirty-fifth anniversary of his death, January 29, 1991.

BALTIMORE, JANUARY 30, 1942.

My gross income in 1941 was $24,450.28, out of which I had to pay $5,048.01 in taxes of various sorts and $4,649.01 in expenses, leaving $14,753.26. On this, during the present year, I must pay $5,050.14 in State and Federal income taxes, which is 34.2% of my net revenue for the year to which it is charged.

BALTIMORE, FEBRUARY 1, 1942.

Paul Patterson's second son, Donald Hamilton, was married in Annapolis yesterday to the youngest daughter of Judge Ridgely P. Melvin. The bridegroom is a graduate of Princeton and was designed by his father for the law, but developed no taste for it and went to sea instead. When, in preparation for the present war, the United States began training reserve officers for the Navy, he went to Annapolis, took the three months' course, and was commissioned an ensign. For four months past he has been serving on a destroyer in southern Atlantic waters. (It was in active service, aiding the English, for at least two months before the United States was officially at war.) It is now repairing at Charleston, S.C., and so the opportunity offered for his marriage. He and his bride left for Charleston last night. They will remain there together until his ship puts to sea, when she will return to Annapolis.

Paul gave a family dinner at his home in Guilford night before last, and asked me to come to it to give him aid and support. He and I and the judge were the only male elders present. I had to take a cocktail before dinner, and after drinking one went on to three—stiff Martinis. At dinner there was white wine, followed by red wine, followed by champagne, and after dinner we drank beer. As a result I slept badly and awoke yesterday morning with a severe gastritis. For lunch I had four soft-boiled eggs, a few pieces of toast and a large glass of milk, and for dinner I had the same. I did not go to the Saturday Night Club, and turned in at 11 p.m. without a drink. I slept well, but the gastritis was still in progress this morning. For breakfast I had the eggs, toast and milk of yesterday, and at lunch I ate a small piece of roast duck with rice: no vegetables, salad or dessert. This afternoon my stomach begins to return to normalcy.

Cocktails always play such tricks on me. I should avoid them at all times. But now and then it is almost impossible to pass them up. I was asked to the wedding at Annapolis, but declined.

BALTIMORE, FEBRUARY 1, 1942.

Joe Hergesheimer came to Baltimore January 27 and entered the Johns Hopkins Hospital as the patient of Dr. Benjamin M. Baker, who has been looking after him for some years past. I was not aware of his coming, but he had a nurse call me up as soon as he got in. When I got to the hospital I found him in a very low and miserable condition. His face was so swollen that his eyes were almost shut, and his body was covered with great patches of eczema. He said these patches itched constantly and kept him from sleeping. He looked to be completely used up, and might have passed for 75. He said that his state was due to the fact that he had followed the diabetic diet prescribed by Baker too rigorously. The result of complete abstention from alcohol, and of almost complete abstention from all starches, was, he said, acidosis, and the acidosis produced the dermatitis. This seemed unlikely to me, but I made no comment. Joe has been showing blood sugar for several years, and Baker has often urged him to go on insulin. But he always refused on the ground that it would make him a slave to a hypodermic needle, and expose him to the risk of violent reactions from either too much or too little insulin. Now he is taking it at last, and when I saw him again, on his third day in hospital, he looked much better. Yesterday, his fifth day, I saw him once more, and there was more improvement. The puffiness in his face is subsiding, and the eczema seems to be slowly clearing up. When I visited him yesterday his nurse had him stripped and was rubbing his patches with an ointment. He told me that it relieved the itching somewhat, but that it was still impossible for him to sleep without drugs. The sleeping powder prescribed by Baker, he said, knocks him off in a few minutes.

When he came to Baltimore Baker was preparing to leave for Miami on a holiday and so he was turned over to Dr. Louis Hamman. He dislikes Hamman, who is a very quiet fellow, and at the opposite pole from Baker, who is exuberant and full of talk. I had to listen to Hergy's objections to Hamman, and did so politely, but they seemed to me to be foolish, for Hamman is unquestionably a competent medical man, and his manner can neither help nor hinder the cure. Obviously, Baker believes that there may be a psychic element in the case, for he asked Dr. Esther Richards, the psychiatrist, to see the patient. She called day before yesterday, and plainly made a good impression. Indeed, Joe was full of her praises, and seemed to think that her call was mainly if not altogether social. When he came in he was in a sad state of mind, and talked despairingly of suicide. He has, he said, lived long enough, and his writing days are over. For four or five years past he has found work increasingly difficult, and about a year ago there was a period of a couple of months when he could not work at all. He told me then that he would sit at his desk for hours, unable to write more than a few words. Baker told me at the time that this disability was not caused by diabetes, but by arterio-sclerosis. He said that there were areas in Joe's brain in which the blood supply was occasionally impeded, and that when this happened it was quite impossible for him to write. Meanwhile, poor Joe struggled on, trying to boil the pot. All the money he made in his days of prosperity was spent as fast as it came in, and today he has nothing save a shrinking equity in his house at West Chester, Pa. He told me yesterday that his expenses at the hospital were being paid with the money of Dorothy, his wife. I assume that he meant by dipping into her capital, for her income is not sufficient. Before he came to this last resort he had raised money by mortgaging his house, and selling some of his antique furniture. His income for several years past has been very small. He has written a good many short stories and novelettes for the popular magazines, but so far as I know has sold but one short story. It seems to be simply impossible for him to undertake any better writing, and he may be right in saying that his days are over. His last book, "The Foolscap Rose," was printed so long ago as 1934. Since then he has sent Knopf nothing fit to publish.

Seeing him was immensely depressing, especially since he came in on the heels of poor Blanche Knopf. There was a time when all of my friends laid up in Baltimore hospitals made quick progress and were soon well, but that time seems to be no more. As they grow older the death-rate among them rises sharply, and every few weeks I go to a funeral. Joe complains bitterly of the cost of staying in hospital, and, characteristically, exaggerates it. On his first day here he told me that his room and nursing were costing him $94 a week, but yesterday he said the amount was $25 a day. He is occupying one of the most expensive rooms at the Marburg, with a private bath. To be sure, it is a great comfort, but many patients get along with less luxurious quarters. He came in with an elegant leather bag full of large and expensive tomes on history. This is now his steady reading. He told me that one of the books—in two volumes, published by the Oxford University Press—cost $30. Thus his old habit of extravagance continues, though he is now almost bankrupt. On my second visit I took him a file of old *Police Gazettes*, sent to me by Joe Katz.[1] He told me yesterday that he had read every line in them, and enjoyed them very much. Yesterday I took him a copy of my quotation book: the first copies had reached me from the Knopf office during the morning. Its 1,340 pages should give him some entertainment while he is laid up. He is in a chair all day, and the hours pass very slowly. He has asked me to say nothing about his presence in town, for fear of bothersome visitors.

His poor wife is lame from an old hip infection and suffers a good deal of pain. He talked yesterday of returning home today or tomorrow, to save expense, but his nurse told me that he should remain a week more, at least. Curing eczema is a slow business, with many setbacks. The insulin will probably do him more good than the ointment.

BALTIMORE, FEBRUARY 3, 1942.

William Lyon Phelps[2] was here for lunch today. He came to Baltimore to lecture at the Peabody last night on Sidney Lanier, as a star of the current Peabody–Johns Hopkins celebration of the Lanier centenary. I dropped in to hear his lecture, and found the hall crowded. Louis Azrael[3] and I stood up together. He spoke extemporaneously and kept to a light tone. In fact, he confined himself mainly to anecdotes, many of which had nothing to do with Lanier. He cited me as the author of the phrase "one-building university"; it is not actually mine, but where I picked it up I don't know. The proceedings began and ended with music. The first number was a group of three Lanier songs, set to music by Howard R. Thatcher, sung by a baritone named Jeffrey Gould, and accompanied by the Peabody orchestra under Stanley Chapple. Thatcher's music was above his average—in places there were actually bursts of cantabile—but it was certainly not good. There

1 Joseph Katz (1888–1958), Baltimore advertising executive. He and Mencken were good friends, and Katz amassed a considerable collection of Menckeniana.
2 William Lyon Phelps (1865–1943), professor of English literature at Yale and author of many critical works.
3 Louis Azrael (1904–1981), columnist for the Baltimore *News-Post* (later *News-American*). After Mencken, he was probably the city's best-known newspaperman.

followed a composition by Lanier himself, for flute and orchestra, with an uncomfortable looking student named John Burgess playing the flute. It was called "Danse des Moucherons" and was almost incredibly bad. Indeed, it sounded like a first-year harmony student's attempt to imitate Chaminade. Happily, it was short. There followed two more Lanier songs, one set by Henry Hadley and the other by George W. Chadwick. Both were bad. They were sung by a contralto named Thelma Viol, a lady wholly devoid of beauty. Phelps's address came next. He was introduced by Dr. Isaiah Bowman, president of the Johns Hopkins. When he shut down I went down to his place in the hall and greeted him and Bowman. They asked me to stay for a Lanier-Dudley Buck cantata which closed the programme, but I pleaded a pressing engagement and went to Schellhase's, where Manfred S. Guttmacher and I put in a more or less dismal hour. I drank two *Seidel* of beer— my first since the Patterson dinner of January 30.

Bowman brought Phelps to the house for lunch today, but could not join us, for the Lanier centenary is keeping him jumping. Phelps complains of asthma and begins to look old, but is still very lively in mind and even in body, despite his 77 years. Our first contact was in 1910, when I reviewed his "Essays on Modern Novelists" in the *Smart Set*, and hailed him as the first university bigwig to treat Mark Twain, not as a clown, but as a great artist. We have been on more or less friendly terms ever since, and at his request are Billy and Henry to each other. He says he likes "Newspaper Days" better than anything else I have done, but I can't make out precisely why. He has printed two very favorable reviews of it, and says he will now proceed to whoop it up in his lectures. Since his retirement from his professorship at Yale he has devoted most of his time to speaking. He was one of the speakers at the recent dinner at New Haven in honor of A. G. Keller's seventieth birthday.[1] I was invited to it, but declined, for I suspected that, like nearly all such affairs, it would be very depressing. Phelps says that it was. The speakers were supposed to keep within 15 minutes, but the first up went to 45, and the second to more than half an hour. Phelps says that he tried to save the evening by telling some anecdotes of Keller's adventures as a tennis player, but that all the other speakers were solemn, and the dinner dragged on until after midnight.

Phelps was very gay at lunch, and professed to be greatly taken

1 Albert G. Keller (1874–1956), sociologist, professor of science of society at Yale.

with Hester's victuals—a mock turtle soup, eggs Benedictine, peas, carrots and fruit. He said it was a perfect lunch, and went back to its merits three or four times. There was, of course, some talk of books. We agreed that Boswell's "Tour of the Hebrides" was grand stuff, and that "Don Quixote" was almost unreadable. Then we fell to talking of Paul Armstrong,[1] the dramatist, whom Phelps knew, but not as well as I. I told him something about Armstrong's three marriages, and about his last illness. We also talked of other Broadway figures of the last generation—among them, A. Toxen Worm.[2] Phelps, in those days, was a steady theatre-goer, as I was, but now both of us find the theatre hard to bear. I took him to the Pennsylvania Station after lunch, and he left at 1.41 for New Haven. Since his wife's death he is looked after by a niece who is a public school-teacher in New Haven. The Phelps house is a roomy one, and Phelps says he is very comfortable. His wife, a pleasant woman, died with great suddenness; in fact, it was all over in a few moments. They had no children. Phelps is rather abstemious, but he told me that after a lecture he needs a big drink in a hurry.

BALTIMORE, FEBRUARY 5, 1942.

William Lyon Phelps's talk, when he was here on February 2, of Paul Armstrong revived in my mind an old project—to do somewhat elaborate sketches of some of the more interesting men I have known. Many likely subjects suggest themselves, for example, Armstrong, Max Brödel, Raymond Pearl, Theodore Dreiser and Edgar Lee Masters. Unluckily, the time remaining to me is not likely to be long, and so I'll probably never get to the business. I hope to include a realistic account of several men—for example, Nathan, John Adams Thayer,[3] Willard Huntington Wright and the two Knopfs, father and son—in a memoir of my magazine days, to be undertaken after my notes of my days on the *Sun* are finished, but even that may never get itself written. Such writing is not easy. It involves a great deal of consulta-

1 Paul Armstrong (1869–1915), playwright and Broadway theatrical figure. Among his better-known plays were *Alias Jimmy Valentine* and *The Deep Purple*. There is an account of Mencken's relationship with him in chapter seven of *Newspaper Days*, "Scent of the Theatre," pp. 115–18.
2 There is an account of A. Toxen Worm, a "theatrical press-agent," in chapter six of *Heathen Days*, "Notes on Palaeozoic Publicists," pp. 71–76.
3 John Adams Thayer (1861–1936) was owner and publisher of the *Smart Set* from 1911 to 1914.

tion of letters and other records, and tedious checking of names and dates, and when it is going smoothly it tends to become tiresome. I have been at work on my *Sun* notes since July, 1941, but I have got only as far as the beginning of 1937, and a number of very busy years lie ahead, for example, 1938. The whole record, if it is ever finished, will probably run to nearly 350,000 words. My recollections of my magazine days will be shorter, if only because there are fewer documents available, but even so they will go beyond 150,000. Once these notes are on paper I'll have a pretty complete and accurate record of my professional life, and if I ever decide to write and print a volume of serious reminiscences the material will be readily at hand, and I'll be saved the interruptions for investigation that often held up "Happy Days" and "Newspaper Days." There will be very little about my private life, and next to nothing about women. Such things, it seems to me, are nobody's business—and I must always remember that what I write may be read by others after I am gone. They are, in fact, not even the author's business. The women a man sleeps with make charming episodes in his life, but it is seldom that they influence the main course of it. Marriage, of course, is quite another story, but my own marriage was too short to have much effect on me. I was within a few days of 50 when it began, and so my ways were set. Moreover, it was unhappily over before I was 55, and so there was still enough resilience in me to enable me to get back on my old track. Since it ended in 1935 I have rewritten and greatly expanded "The American Language," published two books of reminiscences, edited "De Charlataneria Eruditorum," completed my dictionary of quotations, and done a great deal of other writing, beside making two trips abroad and taking an active hand in many *Sun* enterprises.

It is hardly likely that there will be an official Johns Hopkins life of Brödel, though he would make a very good one. I know of no one likely to do it competently; moreover, all the more recent Johns Hopkins biographies have been so bad that the market for such things is spoiled. Tom Cullen, who was probably Brödel's most intimate friend, is too old (74) to undertake it, and is, besides, a very bad writer. Brödel's son, Carl, naturally comes to mind, but Carl is a strange fellow who shows little enterprise, and some years ago, after returning from South Africa, he suffered a mental upset. He is now apparently recovered, but he is so far removed from his father temperamentally that it would be hard to imagine him doing a biography worth reading. I know of no other even remotely plausible candidate. Thus Max, like many another man of high capacities, will quickly recede into the shadows, and if he is remembered at all it will be because of brief and inadequate footnotes in the medical works of men who, in many cases, were much his inferiors. He was the only man I have ever known intimately who was indisputably at the head of his profession. There were other good anatomical artists, but he was clearly the best, and most of the others had learned from him. He was not only an artist, but also an extremely competent anatomist. In his last days he was at work on an atlas of the ear which would have made many valuable contributions to knowledge of the subject. Now and then he would allow himself to be led into discussing this *Arbeit* at the Saturday Night Club—usually by Louis Cheslock,[1] who was interested in it as a musicologist. It was plain that he was doing the ear on a scale never before attempted, and that he was constantly unearthing facts that were new to anatomy. How far this work got I do not know—probably not very far. I suppose it will go to waste, for only a few of the drawings were completed. The rest existed only in rough sketches, unintelligible to anyone else.

I first met Max in 1910, when the Florestan Club was organized. He had been living in Baltimore for at least 15 years, but somehow I had never encountered him. The Florestan Club was an organization of musicians and music-lovers with a clubhouse in Charles street near Center, and I was one of the charter members. One of its enterprises was a series of weekly concerts for members only, and now and then a lecture on some musical theme was included. Max joined the club in its first days, and was put up one night to describe Max Klinger's polychrome statue of Beethoven in Leipzig, then but eight years old. He made a poor impression, not only on me but also on everyone else present. He had really finished his job when he exhibited a colored photograph of the statue and described its materials, but he proceeded to a long and horribly detailed account of the work, and of the life and aesthetic ideas of Klinger. The pedantry that was part of his Saxon heritage was unpleasantly to the fore: he was a *Schulmeister* lecturing to schoolboys. The members were all glad when his discourse was

1 Louis Cheslock (1899–1981), composer, a member of the faculty of Baltimore's Peabody Conservatory of Music, and for many years a member of the Saturday Night Club. He was the editor of *H. L. Mencken on Music* (New York: Alfred A. Knopf, 1961).

over, and we had adjourned to the *Biertisch* in the dining-room downstairs, with Charlie Wettig, the club steward (an old North German Lloyd steward), hauling in the beer. Max turned out to be a quite different man in this friendly environment. His pedantry vanished, and he was presently taking the lead in a beer bout embellished with song. His curly hair, in those days, was still yellow, and so was his straggling moustache. His curls and his big spectacles gave him an owlish, Schubertian appearance. It turned out that he was a master beer-drinker and a very hearty eater. The victims of his lecture all decided that there was good in him, after all.

For some time before this George Boyle, a member of the faculty of the Peabody Conservatory, had been playing with the Saturday Night Club as first pianist. He was an Australian and an extremely competent performer. We tackled anything and everything. Boyle and I would play a four-hand piano arrangement of a symphony, a suite, an overture, or what not, and the rest of the members would join in with their instruments. Many instruments, of course, were always lacking, and those represented were usually represented too feebly, but the piano took care of all the missing parts. Boyle, of course, was an infinitely better pianist than I was, but he was an amiable fellow and so tolerated my clumsy *secondo*. We always played in the violin store of our cellist, Albert Hildebrandt,[1] first in Saratoga street and then in Charles street. Al always had plenty of stringed instruments in his cases, and usually there were half a dozen pianos on his floor. When Boyle left the Peabody and Baltimore, which must have been soon after the Florestan Club was founded, he was succeeded by Brödel. Whose invitation it was that brought him into the Saturday Night Club I forget—probably Hildebrandt's. He could not touch Boyle as a pianist, for he was only an amateur, whereas Boyle was a first-rate professional, but for the purposes of the club he was even better than Boyle, for he was a really marvellous sight-reader and his amateur status made him fall in readily with the fundamental principle of the club—that it met because the members liked to play, and not because they aspired to edify an audience. Brödel's delight in music was immense. He would glow and chuckle when something that he admired

---

1 Albert Hildebrandt (1868–1932), violin-maker and the proprietor of a musical instrument store in Baltimore. He was one of the original members of the Saturday Night Club.

was put on—say, something by Beethoven or Brahms, his favorites—
and he always played accurately and brilliantly, though seldom with
much expression and almost always too loud. He had had long experience at four-hand playing, and soon began to enrich the club library
with books of arrangements from his own large collection. Inasmuch
as Hildebrandt had plenty of pianos we sometimes used two of them
instead of one. Our favorite composition throughout one Winter was
Beethoven's Emperor concerto. Max played the solo part, I played
the accompaniment on another piano, and the rest of the members
chimed in.

There was a constant ebb and flow of members, and at one time .
or another virtually all the principal teachers of the Peabody violin
faculty sat in. Max was a valuable acquisition, not only as a solid,
reliable, all-purposes performer, but also as a grand companion at the
beer-table. So long as Pilsner was procurable, he drank it copiously—
six or eight *Seidel* of an evening. In those days we went to the Rennert
Hotel after playing, and had a private room in the basement, with a
waiter of our own. Max gave the waiter large orders for all the old-
time Rennert delicacies—for example, turkey wings with oyster
sauce—and downed them with a hearty smacking of his lips. When,
following the outbreak of World War I, Pilsner vanished, we switched
to Michelob. Max brought in many visiting performers, chiefly medical
men working temporarily at the Johns Hopkins, and also a number of
more or less permanent members, for example, Raymond Pearl. Pearl
came to the Johns Hopkins in 1918 and Max met him at once, and, on
learning that he played the basset-horn, brought him to the club. Pearl
later transferred to the French horn, and remained a member until his
death in 1940.

Between the two there lay a mutual professional respect and also
a community of tastes, but hidden under it was a certain antagonism,
probably mainly racial, for Brödel was wholly German, and Pearl,
despite his antinomianism, was still a true Yankee. Each, at one time
or another, complained to me of the manners of the other. Both were
heavy trenchermen, but when Pearl went on a diet in 1937 or thereabout and began to cut down on his own intake, it began to be plain
that he was upset by the continued gorging of Brödel. After Prohibition blew up we began to meet after the music at Schellhase's in Howard street, and the two sat opposite each other at the table, with my
place beside Pearl's. More than once I watched Pearl writhe as Max
smeared a huge slice of rye-bread with butter, and then proceeded to

bite half-circles out of it. He also objected, though never vocally, to Max's habit of belching, developed early in 1940. Indeed, I objected to it myself, and upbraided Max for it. His defense was that he could not help it. It turned out in the end that this was unfortunately true. The intestinal disease that finally killed him in 1941 was to blame, though neither he nor we knew it at the time. Pearl's death was a tremendous blow to him, as it was to all of us. He was already ill, and by the end of 1940 it became obvious that something serious was afoot. By the Spring of 1941 I began to notice, sitting beside him at the piano, that his playing was deteriorating. Before that it had been almost unheard of for him to lose his place or to make a mistake of any consequence, but now he began to play raggedly, and after the end of June he ceased to come to the club. But no one, as yet, suspected that he was fatally ill, not even his doctors. They detected some blood sugar but ascribed it to a mild diabetes, and prepared to treat it with insulin. Then came the explosion, and in a few weeks poor Max was dead—of intestinal cancers that may have started in the stomach or pancreas, but were soon all over his abdomen.

His love of music was profound, but he had his preferences and prejudices like the rest of us. In general, he leaned toward absolute music and German music. For most French music he had only contempt, but, like Nietzsche, he excepted that of Bizet. Not much Italian music was ever played in the club, but for the little we did he showed toleration rather than liking. He regarded Tschaikovsky as a maker of sugar-teats, but he had a hearty and even extravagant admiration for Dvořák. He put Beethoven at the head of all composers, even above Bach, but the place of Brahms was but little below. He was also very fond of Mozart and Haydn, and Schubert was one of his enthusiasms. Schumann he liked better than Mendelssohn. For popular music he had no taste, though he got a lot of pleasure out of Vienna waltzes, especially those of Johann Strauss II. It was the rule of the club to close every evening with a waltz, and Max always played them with delight. He would say "They make me feel beerish." I often tried to interest him in this or that piece of American popular music, but always in vain. He could see nothing save trash in the work of such men as Victor Herbert and Reginald De Koven. He had a curious leaning toward the minor mode. Beethoven's C minor symphony, Mozart's G minor and Schubert's Tragic gave him a special and peculiar thrill, and when we put them on he always glowed with delight.

Max's range of information, outside music and his professional interests, was very narrow. Even in medicine he knew very little physiology, and even less chemistry. This ignorance sometimes provoked the polite scorn of Pearl, whose knowledge was really enormous in scope. One night at the beer-table, as I recall, there was some mention of sexual intercourse in human beings, and Max ventured the view that it was a trivial business, and not half as thrilling as was commonly assumed. "After all," he said, "it seldom lasts more than a minute, and never more than two." This astonished Pearl, as it astonished me, and we both had at him. The more we cross-examined him the plainer it became that he actually believed what he had said. When Pearl argued that any man who entertained a lady for so little as two minutes was guilty of a gross offense, not only against her person but also against the peace and dignity of the human race, it was Max's turn to be astonished. He had simply never heard that copulation could be prolonged at will—at all events, far beyond the limits he had set. The question came up at the club on various subsequent occasions, but Max simply could not be shaken. On the heels of this grotesque discussion Pearl announced the founding of an organization to be called the Society for More and Better Fucking in the Home. He said that most of the quacks at the Johns Hopkins—he always spoke of the medical brethren as quacks—needed to be taken into it, and taught some of the elementary Facts of Life. There was some point in this sneer. The students in the medical school are taught a great deal about the pathology of sex, but next to nothing about its normal technic. The subject, indeed, is nowhere mentioned to them save in the Phipps Clinic, where they are taught psychiatry! This I discovered when I made my investigation of the Johns Hopkins Hospital in 1939.

Max had a very unpleasant time of it in World War I, and would have suffered almost as much in World War II if he had lived. In 1915 he had to give up his usual Summer vacations at his camp at Magnetawan, in upper Canada, and this happened again in 1940. His wife stuck to him heroically in the first World War, but I don't know what her attitude was when the second one started. He was much grieved in 1914 when his most intimate friend, Dr. Thomas S. Cullen, a Canadian, began denouncing Germany, but despite this fact they remained on good terms. His position at the Johns Hopkins was very uncomfortable, for some of the principal men in the place were violent Hun-eaters, including his old patron and mentor, Dr. Howard A. Kelly, and his idol, Dr. William H. Welch. He got a lot of consolation in those days from Dr. William S. Halsted, who was too civilized a man to have any faith in the war to save democracy. In the first days of Hitler Max was suspicious of him, but the march of events made him change his mind. Rather curiously, I don't recall ever discussing the second war with him after it began. This was mainly because we seldom met alone. I saw him at the Saturday Night Club every Saturday night, but almost never anywhere else. In the club the war was taboo, for the difference of opinion was too sharp. We had two Jews among the members, a Czech, and Americans of widely varying views. We got along very amicably, as we had got along during the first war, when we played through the four years without a rift.

Max was an excellent cook, and loved to concoct pleasant messes for his friends. During the thirteen years of Prohibition, with all public houses of refreshment either closed or dubious, the club met at the homes of its members, and whenever it was Max's turn to entertain us at his house in Guilford he entertained us royally. One of his specialties was pickled shrimp, a perfect dish for a late supper. Now and then he would lay in a barrel of oysters, and invite us to work our will upon it. He always shucked them himself—and actually enjoyed it. At the beginning of Prohibition I taught him how to brew beer, and in a little while he was the best brewer in the club. Once, coming home in his car from his place in Canada, he got a couple of empty bottles of Labatt's famous ale across the border, and when he reached Baltimore cultivated yeast from the sludge still in them. From this yeast he made an ale that was identical with Labatt's. Whenever he entertained the club he invited a few other guests, usually colleagues at the Johns Hopkins. More than once I have seen medical men of the highest eminence far gone at his table, for he believed that malt liquor that was too weak was not worth drinking.

His death, following so soon after Pearl's, was a devastating loss to the Saturday Night Club. Until his last illness there was a vast energy in him, and he played as he worked—in Nietzsche's phrase, with arms and legs. The club is now in a low state, though it still goes on. I am ordinarily at the piano alone, which greatly limits our repertoire. One Saturday night a few weeks ago we spent the whole evening playing overtures. When four hands are necessary Louis Cheslock plays the *primo*, but Cheslock is a violinist, not a pianist. He is the only member left in the club whose conversation is worth hearing.

BALTIMORE, FEBRUARY 10, 1942.

Lunch today at the Maryland Club with Samuel E. Morison,[1] professor of history at Harvard. He has come down to Baltimore to give a special course in American history at the Johns Hopkins. The same course was given last year by Dr. Charles Beard.[2] In its early days the Johns Hopkins history department specialized in the history of Maryland, and made very effective use of the rich records of the State. Of late it has departed for other fields, and so the working of the records has ceased. Kent R. Greenfield,[3] the head of the department, is a Marylander, but his chief interest is in the Italian Risorgimento. The rest of the members of the staff seem to be nonentities. Some time ago the trustees invited Dr. Merle E. Curti[4] of Columbia University to join the faculty, but the academic counsel vetoed him. This embarrassed Curti very considerably, for he assumed that his appointment was certain, and therefore notified Columbia that he was leaving. Morison says that he is a really competent man, and would have been a valuable acquisition to the Johns Hopkins.

It is plain to see that Morison's opinion of its history department is low, though he is naturally cautious about saying so. I asked him what sort of students he was encountering. He said that they were mainly Jews, and that few of them showed any capacity. The only graduate student who has applied to him so far has been an old woman so preposterous that he turned her out at once.

He is giving a course of lectures on the American Revolution, and will follow it with another on some other American theme. Morison is an extremely pleasant fellow, and somehow recalls George Cutler,[5] a fellow-Bostonian. He wants me to take him on a tour some day of the

1 Samuel Eliot Morison (1887–1976), distinguished American historian. Among his many works are *Admiral of the Ocean Sea* (a biography of Christopher Columbus), *The Oxford History of the American People*, *The European Discovery of America*, and the 15-volume *History of U.S. Naval Operations in World War II*.
2 Charles A. Beard (1874–1948), American historian and educator. His best-known work, written in collaboration with his wife, Mary, was *The Rise of American Civilization*.
3 Kent R. Greenfield (1893–1967), historian, chairman of the department of history at Johns Hopkins University from 1930 to 1947.
4 Merle E. Curti (b. 1897), historian and author of many works on history and political science. His *The Growth of American Thought* (1944) won the Pulitzer Prize for history.
5 George C. Cutler (1891–1956), Baltimore banker and member of the board of directors of the A. S. Abell Company from 1935 to 1945.

older parts of Baltimore, and I'll probably do it. We fell to discussing the differences between the various large cities of the Eastern Seaboard. He called my attention to the rather curious fact that in Boston alone the old families continue to live in the old town. In Philadelphia, Baltimore and elsewhere they move into the suburbs. In Boston, however, they cling to their old houses, and maintain a scheme of life that differs very little from that of 50 or even 75 years ago.

Morison is a sound historian, and an excellent writer. From 1922 to 1925 he served as Exchange Professor of American History at Oxford. Despite this experience, which is commonly ruinous to American pedagogues, he retains a sense of humor and an American point of view.

BALTIMORE, MARCH 8, 1942.

The following is from the leading editorial in this morning's *Sun*:

> The *Sun* is attempting to print every bit of material information about the war, in its military and its civil aspects, that can be printed with safety. At the same time, every attention is paid not only to the censorship rules, but to the responsibilities in wartime which every newspaper and every citizen must bear in guarding against disclosure of information to the enemy. Out of regard for these responsibilities, the *Sunpapers* have voluntarily imposed upon themselves a code of censorship more rigid than the one required or requested by the Federal Government.

In other words, To hell with the news! No matter how onerous the censorship imposed by the wizards at Washington, the *Sunpapers* will accept it without protest and try to go it one better.

BALTIMORE, MARCH 14, 1942.

The end of a dismal week. It began with Theodore Scherer's funeral on Tuesday, and ended with J. Fred Essary's yesterday. Theodore was fetched by heart disease and Fred by a cerebral hemorrhage. The last time I saw Theodore, about a year ago, he was already so far gone that he could barely hobble about: he told me that he could not walk so much as a city block. Fred had been going downhill steadily since 1940. When he retired as chief Washington correspondent of the *Sun* last November—against his frantic opposition—he was given a small office of his own in the National Press Building, close to the *Sun* bureau but not adjacent. He went downtown on March 11, attended a business meeting of the Gridiron Club, had lunch with Baumgartner, former press-agent of the Baltimore & Ohio Railroad, and then returned alone to his office. When, at 4 p.m., he had not got home, his wife went to the office in alarm. She found him lying on the floor in convulsions. He died in a few minutes.

I heard of his death after midnight on March 11. I had been at dinner with George Jean Nathan, and on returning to the Algonquin found telegrams from Patterson and Dewey L. Fleming.[1] Fleming's said that Helen Essary wanted me to be a pallbearer at the funeral on March 13. This put me to some trouble, for a meeting of the board of directors of Alfred A. Knopf, Inc., was scheduled for the afternoon of March 13, and I was booked to attend the dinner in honor of Oswald Garrison Villard's[2] 70th birthday in the evening, and make a speech. I got rid of the Knopf board meeting, but feared that Villard would be offended if I missed his dinner. I accordingly returned to Baltimore on March 12, slept here, went to Washington for the funeral on March 13, and started back for New York from there at 4 p.m. My train reached the Pennsylvania Station in New York exactly on time, but when it was within 100 yards of the platform it got stuck, and remained stuck for 35 minutes. When I got to the Roosevelt Hotel it was 8.45, and the dinner was almost over. The speeches, of course, were still ahead, and I made mine in my turn.

The Essary funeral was very imposing. There was no service at the house in Newark street, but I went there as one of the active pallbearers and had a brief talk with Helen. She had been through a dreadful two years, poor girl, and seemed completely crushed. Fred's death, of course, was a happy release, but it didn't seem so with his body still lying in the parlor. She is a Catholic and Fred was a Baptist, but the funeral was held at the Protestant Episcopal Cathedral. The chapel was full of newspaper men, and there were many standing. The service was in charge of the chaplain of the Senate, a tall, massive and very theatrical looking cleric. He recited the whole service. From end to end his prayer book was kept invisible.

1 Dewey L. Fleming (1898–1955) had been on the staff of the *Sun* since 1923 and succeeded J. Fred Essary as head of the paper's Washington bureau in 1941.
2 Oswald Garrison Villard (1872–1949), author and editor, for many years editor of *The Nation*.

Fred was buried in Rock Creek cemetery, closed in an enormously heavy metal casket and sunk into one of the deepest graves I have ever seen. As I looked down into it it seemed to be at least nine feet to the bottom. The coffin was so heavy that the eight pallbearers and two undertakers really had difficulty handling it.

The Villard dinner was dull, but not quite so dull as such things usually are. The toastmaster, John Haynes Holmes,[1] actually succeeded in holding most of the speakers down to ten minutes. There were nine of them altogether, not counting Villard himself. The best speech was that of Carl Van Doren.[2] He devoted it to reminiscences of his days on the *Nation*, and let fall the fact that the rest of the staff had a hard time dissuading Villard from supporting both Prohibition and the New York book censors.

When I met him in Princeton last week, I made a bet with Van Doren that his speech would run more than five minutes. The stakes were as much beer as either of us could drink. He lost by three minutes, and paid off the bet at the Ritz bar after the dinner. On our way out we picked up S. K. Ratcliffe, the English journalist, now 73 years old. We took him along, but he confined himself to orange juice. Poor Ratcliffe seemed to be in a dreadful state of mind. He told me, as if it were news, that the situation of the English was bad, and that Churchill had informed Roosevelt in Washington that the United States would have to take over the whole war in the Pacific. Van Doren and I pretended to be surprised and shocked.

The dinner was over at 11:15. As I sat at the guest table, which was elevated above the floor, and looked down over the house I was impressed once more with the dreadful effect of moral endeavor upon the female form divine. Most of the women visible were uplifters of one sort or another, and four-fifths of them were hideous—in fact, there were several who seemed almost inhuman. When Villard began to speak I went down to the main floor to hear him better, and sat there with Arthur Garfield Hays and B. W. Huebsch.[3] As I listened,

1 John Haynes Holmes (1879–1964), Unitarian minister, author, pacifist, at one time chairman of the American Civil Liberties Union.

2 Carl Van Doren (1885–1950), critic and biographer, served as literary editor of *The Nation* from 1919 to 1922 and did much to encourage and support the young writers of the time. His life of Benjamin Franklin (1938) was awarded a Pulitzer Prize.

3 Arthur Garfield Hays (1881–1954), lawyer, counsel for the American Civil Liberties Union. He was part of the defense counsel at the Scopes trial in 1925 and the following year defended Mencken when Boston's Watch and Ward Society sought to

my eye roved about and presently it fell upon a really beautiful woman. She was dark and slim, and appeared to be a Latin. I asked who she was, but nobody near me recognized her. When the dinner was over I made efforts to identify her, but the whole audience, by that time, had begun to crowd up to the speakers' table to shake hands with Villard, and she was lost in the shuffle. What she was doing at a festival of liberals I couldn't discover. Perhaps she had got into the place by mistake.

Villard's speech was very silly. It was mainly devoted to arguing that, despite the current military disasters, democracy is bound to win in the long run, if only because it is virtuous. In the course of his talk Villard praised the newspapers for their handling of the war. He mentioned a number of correspondents by name, among them some of the worst now in practice. I recall, for example, Harsch, of the *Christian Science Monitor,* who lately sent a dispatch from Australia so dreadful that its appearance in the *Sun* caused a scandal in the office. He also praised such quacks as Walter Duranty and Dorothy Thompson.

Van Doren told me at the Ritz that the dinner had actually been arranged by Villard himself. The young woman, Mary Hillyer, who was ostensibly in charge of it, was simply his agent. This did not surprise me. As a matter of fact, such dinners are usually promoted by the guests of honor.

My own speech was very brief and light in tone. Others were made by George McAneny, Robert E. MacAlarney, Lewis Gannett, Walter White, Elinore M. Herrick, Carl Van Doren, Joseph Schlossberg and Norman Thomas.[1] Thomas, as usual, did well, and so did White. Gan-

---

ban *The American Mercury* because of the famous "Hatrack" article. His role in the latter case is fully described in the long and detailed history which Mencken wrote some years later but which has only recently been published; see *The Editor, the Bluenose, and the Prostitute,* ed. Carl Bode (Denver, Col.: Roberts Rinehart, 1988); Benjamin W. Huebsch (1876–1964) began his career as a music critic for the New York *Sun* but later became a highly successful publisher. His firm was merged with Viking Press in 1925.

1 George McAneny (1869–1953), banker, publicist, prominent in New York City political and cultural affairs; Robert E. MacAlarney (1873–1945), editor, writer, professor of journalism at Columbia University; Lewis Gannett (1891–1966), newspaperman and author, contributor of a daily book column to the New York *Herald Tribune* from 1930 to 1956; Walter White (1893–1955), prominent journalist and leading figure for four decades in the National Association for the Advancement of Colored People (NAACP); Elinore M. Herrick (1895–1964), consultant on labor relations and member of many arbitration panels; Joseph Schlossberg (1875–1971),

nett, who is an extremely offensive fellow to me, talked too long and was a flop. But the worst failure was scored by Schlossberg, an old time labor leader with a message. The two Irishmen, McAneny and MacAlarney, made sentimental speeches that were very effective. I was greatly surprised when La Herrick arose. For some reason or other, I had always thought of her as a thin, sharp-faced woman. She turned out to be a vast, billowy biddy with bosoms like toy balloons and a backside like a taxicab. She talked of Villard's early service to the cause of woman suffrage, and did very well indeed. I was presented to her after the dinner, and found her a really amusing old gal. She is the chief agent of the National Labor Relations Board in the New York region.

BALTIMORE, MARCH 31, 1942.

On March 29, Palm Sunday, there were 22 inches of snow in Baltimore. The *Sun* of yesterday, of course, had to mention the storm, but it did not give the snowfall—something that every reader was speculating about. I complained at the office today that this was an absurd excess of compliance with the war-time order against giving weather information that could be of use to the public enemy. I argued that if there were actually any rule against giving snowfalls or rainfalls it ought to be resisted as senseless. So far as I could make out, no such rule has been issued: the omission of the snowfall was a mere effort to bend backward. This seems to me to be a ridiculous and even a dangerous attitude for a newspaper to take. In war, as in peace, it should try to ascertain the truth about all public matters, and save when the danger to the national security is clear and real it should tell that truth, Dogberrys or no Dogberrys. But that is a doctrine that seems to have been abandoned in the *Sun* office. It was made official by the White Paper of 1920,[1] but the White Paper of 1920 is as dead as the Constitution of the United States.

---

labor executive, secretary-treasurer of the Amalgamated Clothing Workers of America from 1914 to 1940; Norman Thomas (1884–1968), American socialist leader and six times the Socialist party's (unsuccessful) candidate for president of the United States, and for a brief time (1921–22) an editor of *The Nation*.

1 The "White Paper of 1920" was a twenty-three-page statement drawn up to provide firm editorial and newsroom policy for the *Sunpapers*. There is an account of it in Johnson et al., *The Sunpapers of Baltimore* (New York: Alfred A. Knopf, 1937), pp. 368–72, and another in Harold A. Williams, *The Baltimore Sun 1837–1987* (Balti-

BALTIMORE, JUNE 1, 1942.

On April 15 or thereabout, after a Winter free from colds, I developed a sore spot in my naso-pharynx and consulted Dr. LeRoy M. Polvogt. He painted it with silver nitrate and gave me a 2% solution of sulfadiazine to use as a spray. The silver nitrate produced some relief, but the sulfadiazine only irritated my throat, and after a few days I stopped using it. On April 24 I went to my sister's farm in Carroll county to spend the weekend. I remained until April 26, but grew steadily more uncomfortable, and on April 29 I consulted Polvogt again. He found that my whole naso-pharynx was inflamed, and ordered me to hospital. I entered the Johns Hopkins the same day. It was found there that I was running a temperature of nearly 103 degrees. Polvogt called Dr. Charles W. Wainwright, and I was put on sulfadiazine by mouth, with codeine to make me comfortable. My temperature was down almost to normal in two days, but after that it rose again, and I was kept on the sulfadiazine for about a week. I remained in hospital until May 12. On my return home I was still pretty rocky, but managed to resume work in a few days, and have since finished the long index to my *Sun* record, cleared out the typescripts, proofsheets and other remains of "A New Dictionary of Quotations," and got through various other minor jobs.

While I was in hospital Wainwright and the staff investigated my general condition, and found it far from reassuring. My blood pressure, I gather, has gone up, and there are signs of further damage to my coronary arteries. On my discharge Wainwright told me I could expect to avoid disaster only by leading a quiet life, taking as much rest as possible, and avoiding all severe labor, whether physical or mental. He suggested a long holiday, but inasmuch as it is now impossible to take to the sea and I'd be bored unendurably anywhere on land, I resolved to stay at home. My plans for work are naturally blown up, for I am tired out after a few hours at my desk, and writing is very difficult. I had to ask for more time on the sketches promised

---

more: Johns Hopkins University Press, 1987), pp. 165–68. In several places in the diary (see, for example, the entry for April 29, 1943, p. 250), Mencken claims to have been its author. Williams, however, after admitting that "all three [i.e., Harry C. Black, Paul Patterson, and Mencken] contributed their thoughts, aspirations, and particular points of view," concludes that "credit for the structure, content, tone, and writing belongs to Harry Black."

to Harold W. Ross, editor of the *New Yorker,* and also on my proposed
contribution to the *Festschrift* in honor of Harry M. Lydenberg,[1] the
retiring librarian of the New York Public Library. I had planned to
begin work this Summer on a supplement to "The American Language," and had been sorting out and arranging the immense mass of
new material, but it is now improbable that I'll ever get to it. I had
also planned to do a private record of my magazine days, with notes
about my books, analogous to my *Sun* record, now completed, but it
begins to seem unlikely that I'll ever be fit again for so severe a labor.
It is possible that I may finish a third volume of the "Happy Days"
series, but it is not certain. Eleven of the necessary twenty chapters are finished, but I am in no state to tackle the remainder at the
moment.

Wainwright's warning when I left the hospital was plain enough.
I may have a stroke at any minute, or the coronary occlusion may
fetch me. I am thus giving what energy I can muster up to a final
arrangement of my books and papers. I have begun today to sort out
autographed books and other association items for presentation to the
Pratt Library, and if it were not for my lingering hope of being able
to undertake the magazine record just mentioned I'd give the library
all my copies of my own books and also my collection of books by
other Menckens. If I make any progress with the magazine record I'll
send in the books needed for it as I finish with them. Meanwhile, I
am revising my instructions to August, who will be executor of my
estate, and taking such other measures as the situation suggests. Unhappily, I can work only in brief spells, and there are days when I
can't work at all.

On May 18 I told Paul Patterson of my condition, and proposed
that my work for the *Sunpapers,* reduced in January, 1940, by relieving me of all editorial responsibility, be further lessened, and that my
salary be reduced to what it was before January 1, 1936, to wit $5,000
a year. He objected on the ground that I was still useful to the papers,
and worth more. For one thing, I can still concern myself with labor
matters, which are still in an unhappy state. On May 15, at Patterson's
request, I was present in the pressroom when one Knadler, a young

---

1 Mencken's contribution to *Bookman's Holiday,* the *Festschrift* in honor of Harry M.
Lydenberg, was entitled "Notes on American Given Names" and is on pp. 70–80.
The volume appeared in 1943.

man representing the Baltimore office of the National Labor Relations Board, came in to investigate a charge of unfair labor practices lodged by the pressmen's union. And on May 22 I was in charge of a hearing in the board room when Knadler appeared again to investigate similar allegations by two discharged photographers. Patterson told me that, in addition, I was useful for advice in the news department, as opposed to the editorial department. It seemed silly to force a decision about my compensation for a period that may be very short, so I let the matter drop.

I eat well and usually sleep well, though several times I have been awakened by heart distress. Ordinarily, there are no overt symptoms. My pulse is strong, slow and regular, and I have no shortness of breath. But I tire so quickly that anything approaching sustained work is almost impossible. If I go downtown in the afternoon, say to the *Sun* office, I return completely used up, and have to stretch out for a nap. Wainwright advises me that this nap is necessary. In my better days I worked every night until 10 p.m., but I shortened this to 9 p.m. a couple of years ago, mainly because my brother August, since he went to work at Edgewood, has to turn out at 6 a.m., and thus can't sit late. Two evenings out of three he and I take a couple of drinks together at 9 p.m. I am usually in bed by 10.30, but I seldom turn out my light until midnight. Wainwright tells me that a reasonable amount of alcohol will do me no appreciable damage. I seldom take a drink until 9 p.m. The cellar is full of good wine, but I can't drink it.

Polvogt reports that there is a growth of lingual tonsil tissue at the base of my tongue on the left side. A growth of the same sort developed in 1934. It was so vascular that Polvogt hesitated to remove it by surgery, for the operation would have involved a considerable hemorrhage and might have left scars that were worse than the disease. At his advice I consulted Dr. Curtis F. Burnam, who tackled the growth with radium emanation. This treatment produced such a shrinking that the discomfort disappeared, and for six years I was at ease. But about six months ago I noticed fresh symptoms, and now Polvogt says that there is another growth. It is benign.

Considering my outlook I find myself in a reasonably calm state of mind. After all, I am nearly 62 years old, which is considerably beyond the life-span of the Menckens during the past 200 years. I have had, on the whole, an extremely happy life, despite some staggering shocks. I have done the work that I wanted to do, and have managed to make a good living at it. The value of my property today it would be hard to estimate, but certainly it can't be much less than $100,000. My unearned income in 1941 was nearly $8,000. But nearly all of this went for taxes in one form or another, and it will shrink hereafter. On the ultimate fate of my writings I sometimes speculate idly. At the moment, with the Roosevelt crusade to save humanity in full blast, my ideas are so unpopular that it is impossible, as it was from 1915 to 1920, for me to print them. But when the New Deal imposture blows up at last, as it is sure to do soon or late, they may have a kind of revival. In 1920 I was able to press that revival myself. That will be impossible this time, but the fact does not bother me, for in the long run every man has to shut down, and if he is remembered thereafter it is by the effort of others. Not many American authors will ever leave a more complete record. It took me a couple of years to arrange my papers, and the cost of binding them was very high, but now they are in the Pratt Library, and if anyone ever wants to investigate them they will be easily accessible. It is likely, of course, that no one will ever want to do so, but nothing can be done to change that implacable fact. In the end every man of my limited capacities must be forgotten utterly. The best he can hope for is a transient and temporary postponement of the inevitable.

BALTIMORE, JUNE 8, 1942.

When I got to Patterson's office this afternoon Miss Brennan told me that John Owens wanted to see me. When I dropped in on him a bit later I discovered that he desired to discuss an editorial problem— the first that he has mentioned to me for a long while. It had to do with the situation of the Negroes in Baltimore. Some time ago the *Evening Sun* printed a series of articles on their troubles by Lee McCardell.[1] It showed that they were enormously overcrowded, and that the two sections in which they live were surrounded by firm walls of white neighborhoods. John asked me if I thought it would be a good idea to ask the Legislature to give the city authority to set up a sort of housing commission empowered to seize a whole white neighborhood on the periphery of one of the Negro districts and turn Negroes into

1 Lee McCardell (1901–1963), reporter and later war correspondent for the *Evening Sun.* His battlefield dispatches during World War II earned him considerable fame.

it. He mentioned, as an example, the region west of Fulton avenue, running from Lexington street to Edmondson. The scheme sounded so fantastic to me that I could scarcely believe that he was offering it seriously. I asked him at once what would become of the white people in the neighborhood seized. Also, on what theory could they be asked to give up their homes and then go on a laborious and probably vain search for quarters elsewhere. The neighborhood he mentioned is largely made up of relatively new row houses, and most of them are owned by their occupants. Apparently, Owens had not thought of any of these difficulties, nor had he considered the probable psychological effect of trying to force Negroes on a white section. Obviously, there would be loud protests from the whites along the new borderline.

I listened in amazement, and then suggested that a more rational scheme would be to try to limit the present excessive emigration of Southern Negroes to Baltimore. They are coming in, according to McCardell, at a heavy rate, and are mainly responsible for the increasing overcrowding. Moreover, they are also responsible for the disorders in the Negro neighborhoods. Owens admitted that those disorders were growing serious—in fact, he said that Stanton, the police commissioner, was convinced that serious riots were not far off. The cops are preparing for trouble by laying in machine guns and tear gas. If the outbreak ever comes it will cost white lives as well as black. I told Owens that the decent colored people of Baltimore were even more injured by the emigration than the white people. The overcrowding of houses was producing filthy living conditions, and all sorts of serious crime was increasing rapidly. Owens finally said that he would abandon his scheme to ask the Legislature to authorize the seizure of another white neighborhood. How a man presumably sane could concoct any such nonsense I simply can't make out.

BALTIMORE, JUNE 18, 1942.

In New York this week I discussed with Alfred Knopf the title of my proposed Volume III in the "Happy Days"—"Newspaper Days" series. Knopf suggested "Days Pleasant and Unpleasant," but it seems to me to be bad. I incline toward "Heathen Days," but have also thought of "Random Days," "Gaudy Days," "Busy Days," "Lively Days" and "Gay Days." Knopf is announcing the book under the title of "Heathen Days," but this is only provisional: it is my studio name.

I suggested to Knopf that I might be able to make a small book of very short essays *à la* Bacon and Montaigne, to be called "Studies for Unwritten Books." I have a great deal of material in hand. But he did not appear to fancy the idea. My "Advice to Young Men," so long in mind, is now definitely shelved. It would be impossible to print, in war time, the sort of stuff that I have in mind for the section on a young man's relations to his country.

BALTIMORE, JULY 10, 1942.

Swanson's scheme to build up a staff of *Sun* correspondents in the war areas, mentioned in these notes on February 17,[1] has been put into effect, and with great success. He has got some excellent stuff out of Bradish in Australia—stuff that the American correspondents there have not been able to get past the censor. Bradish, for all I know, may be the censor himself. Swanson has found competent correspondents in other places—for example, Egypt, South Africa and India. In most cases they are Associated Press string correspondents who are glad to have additional work. Some of their stuff comes in over the Associated Press cables via London, by arrangement with Kent Cooper. Meanwhile, Swanson has got rid of the New York *Times* and *Herald Tribune* services, and proposes to bring the teletype operator who filed for the *Sun* in the *Herald Tribune* office down to Baltimore, for service on the copy desk, which is short of good men. The draft has taken a large number of reporters, some of them excellent ones, and Swanson is finding it hard to replace them. He is trying the experiment of substituting women wherever possible, and with some success. He has already developed at least one woman reporter who seems capable of handling general news.

BALTIMORE, JULY 30, 1942.

To Washington today to discuss the situation in Michigan with Senator Arthur H. Vandenberg. The great rabble-rouser, Gerald L. K. Smith, is a candidate for the Republican nomination for the United States Senate there, and I wanted to find out to what extent he was to be taken seriously. If he has any chance of getting the nomination I

1 Not included in the present selection.

think the *Sun* should send a man to cover his campaign, for it is sure to be full of melodrama and grotesque humor. Paul Patterson wants me to undertake the job—that is, if anyone is sent—but I am against it, for my withdrawal from the *Sun* in January, 1941, was a protest against the imbecility of its whole editorial course, and I want that protest to stand.

Vandenberg understood that I was writing about our interview, and so talked pretty freely. He said that there will be three candidates in the Republican primary—Smith, a local judge named Homer Ferguson,[1] and a small-town editor whose name I forget. The editor, he said, is of no consequence, whether political or otherwise, but Ferguson is a really competent man. He has been a State circuit judge in Detroit since 1929, and has made a good record. In 1939 he constituted himself a one-man grand jury, and brought in indictments against scores of local politicians, charging them with various corruptions: the whole pack eventually landed in jail. Unhappily, there is a provision in the constitution of Michigan prohibiting a judge from running for any other office save another judgeship within a year after he leaves the bench. Vandenberg said that seven eminent Michigan lawyers have assured him that this prohibition does not apply to Federal offices, but there is yet some doubt that a senatorship is a Federal office, and that doubt gives Gerald Smith some excellent campaign material.

Vandenberg said that he hopes to see Gerald beaten, but is not too sure of it. He said: "You recall what Huey Long did in Louisiana— and Gerald is smarter than Huey. Moreover, there is nothing against him on moral grounds: he is a very careful fellow. I have to be polite to him: I simply can't help myself. If he beats Ferguson in the primaries he may also beat (Prentiss M.) Brown in the general election, and then I'll have him on my hands. Brown (the sitting junior Senator) is a New Dealer, but many of the other New Dealers don't like him. Gerald has sent in word that if we do not hit him below the belt in the primary campaign, and he is defeated, he will support Ferguson. This, of course, involves a tacit understanding that if he wins we Ferguson people will support *him*. I am on a hot spot, and have to proceed warily."

There is no contest among the Democrats, and under the Michigan

---

1 Homer Ferguson (1888–1982) served as U.S. senator from Michigan from 1943 to 1955, and as ambassador to the Philippines from 1955 to 1956.

law they may vote in the Republican primaries. Gerald is well aware of this fact, and proposes to make a loud appeal to the Catholics among them, all of whom are sore over the suppression of Father Coughlin. Gerald also has the support of the Ku Klux Klan, which has been growing in strength in Michigan, of what remains of the Townsend following, and of all the other groups of crack-pots and malcontents. The C.I.O. is strongly against him, for he has been belaboring it as the agent of the automobile manufacturers, but no one knows how many votes it will muster. Vandenberg won the last time despite its opposition, but he then had the support of the A.F. of L. Today the C.I.O. and the A.F. of L. are on better terms than they were at that time.

Altogether, I gathered from Vandenberg the impression that it would [be] well worth while to cover Gerald's campaign. The primaries are on September 15, and if he wins the Republican nomination he will probably begin a canvass of the State at once. Patterson professed to be interested, but I doubt that he will do anything. His old bold enterprise is gone, and he prefers to let things drift. Moreover, there has arisen in him a disinclination to do anything to embarrass Roosevelt. He is hardly aware of it, and would deny it stoutly if taxed with it, but there it is. The war, in brief, has pretty well wrecked him, and the *Sun* with him.

BALTIMORE, AUGUST 19, 1942.

I went to New York on Saturday, August 15, proceeded to Purchase to spend Saturday night and Sunday with Alfred Knopf, returned to New York Sunday night, and came back to Baltimore yesterday. It rained nearly all the while I was at Knopf's place and also after I got back to New York. Ben Stern came to dinner Saturday night, but there were no guests on Sunday, and Knopf and I put in the time gabbling. Among other things, we went over his early history in the publishing business.

He was graduated from Columbia University at the mid-year commencement in February, 1912, but received his degree *in absentia*, for he had already gone abroad. He remained abroad until August, 1912, and went to work for Doubleday, Page & Company during the following October. It was difficult in those days for a young man, and especially for a young Jew, to break into the publishing business, but his way was prepared by Ralph Peters, president of the Long Island Railroad and a friend of his father. Doubleday wanted the railroad to establish a station at the new publishing plant at Garden City, and Peters' consent seems to have been coupled with a promise that young Knopf would be given a job. His first was in the accounting department, operating an adding-machine at $8 a week. Later he was transferred to the promotion department and raised to $12. That was the most he ever got from Doubleday. In those days F. N. Doubleday was still in charge of the firm.

It had lately brought out an expensive edition of Kipling, and Knopf was sent out on the road to make propaganda for it. Eugene F. Saxton,[1] who was then on the staff, suggested that he see me when he got to Baltimore. He called on me in my old Free Lance office at the head of the grand stairway in the *Sun* Building, and we quickly came to terms. But it was Joseph Conrad, not Kipling, who was the bond of interest between us, for by that time I had begun to tire of Kipling, the great idol of my late teens and early 20's. This must have been during the early part of 1913. I had been writing about Conrad in the *Smart Set* since 1908. Knopf had first heard of him from a clerk named Simpson in Scribner's old downtown bookstore. When he went to England in 1912 he heard a great deal more from John Galsworthy. His introduction to Galsworthy flowed out of the fact that as an undergraduate at Columbia he had done a paper on the early Galsworthy books. He was already full of a scheme to assemble all of the Conrad books for a collected edition to be published by Doubleday, and I promised to give him whatever aid and counsel I could. This edition was duly brought out, but by that time Knopf had left Doubleday and gone to work for Mitchell Kennerley.[2] This move was made in March, 1914. His salary with Kennerley was $25 a week. Incidentally, Saxton, on sending him to see me, had suggested that I might be good for a printable book of my own.

Knopf remained with Kennerley only until May, 1915. Kennerley,

1 Eugene F. Saxton (1884–1943) began his career with Doubleday, Page & Co., but in 1925 transferred to Harper & Brothers, where he remained until his death. He was considered one of the great book editors of his time.
2 Mitchell Kennerley (1878–1950), publisher and editor. At one time he was manager of the New York office of John Lane Company, which brought out Mencken's early books on Shaw and Nietzsche. He also served briefly as business manager of *The Smart Set*.

in those days, was making some noise as a publisher, but he was always hard up for money, and the salaries of his staff were never paid on time. Among the new authors on his list was Joseph Hergesheimer, whose "The Lay Anthony" he had published in 1914 (I reviewed it in the *Smart Set* for December) and whose "Mountain Blood" he was to do in 1915 (I reviewed it in the *Smart Set* for August). Knopf and Hergesheimer met and became friendly, and when Knopf let it be known that he was thinking of going into business on his own account, Hergesheimer agreed to go with him and in fact promised him his next book, which was to be "The Three Black Pennys." Kennerley got wind of this through the fact that his secretary and office spy, a woman with whom he was on intimate terms, found a letter from Hergesheimer on Knopf's desk. He thereupon fired Knopf forthwith in a letter full of moral indignation. Knopf replied hotly, and the two did not speak for twenty years afterward.

Knopf proceeded at once to set up a publishing house of his own. On April 4, 1916 he married Blanche Wolf, and thereafter the two were partners. They invited me to transfer to their flag, but I was tied up by contracts with other publishers, and it was not until 1917 that my first book under the Knopf imprint, "A Book of Prefaces," came out. The American branch of the John Lane Company of London, which had done my "Book of Burlesques" and "A Little Book in C Major" in 1916, had a claim on my next book. I got rid of it by inserting a denunciation of William J. Locke,[1] then Lane's main standby, into "A Book of Prefaces." J. Jefferson Jones, Jr., Lane's American manager, protested that he simply could not print any attack on Locke, and I stood on my rights as author. He thereupon released the book, and, after expunging the sneers at Locke, I handed it over to Knopf. Soon afterward he brought out a new edition of "In Defense of Women," first published by Philip Goodman. Goodman had been a failure as a publisher, and was glad to get rid of it and clear out.

The Knopfs took a house at Hartsdale, near New York, in May, 1916, and I often visited them there. Their son, Alfred A., Jr. (Pat) was born there in June, 1918. In September of the same year they left Hartsdale and leased a house in west 95th street, and there they remained until 1924. I saw them very frequently during those years, and directed their attention to many books and authors. Unfortunately,

1 William J. Locke (1863–1930), popular English novelist.

our correspondence before 1921, save for a few letters, has vanished from Knopf's files, and I never kept any carbons of my own share of it. The first big success of the house was "Green Mansions," by William Hudson. "The Three Black Pennys" followed in 1917. Knopf's early books made something of a sensation. They were full of typographical novelties and niceties, mainly borrowed from Germany, and showed a gay coloring that was in sharp contrast to the sombreness usual in the books of the older publishers. Among the important authors who were attracted by his innovations was Willa Cather, who came in spontaneously, offering to transfer from Houghton Mifflin. But it was not until 1920 that she actually appeared on Knopf's list— with "Youth and the Bright Medusa."

Blanche was not at Purchase. She had returned from an air tour of South America only a few days before, but had dashed off to Washington to make a somewhat mysterious report to the State Department. I saw her on her return yesterday, and gathered that a statesman's complex had seized her: she was full of dark hints about important (and mainly, I gathered, depressing) developments among the Latin Americans. I did not ask for any details. She said that she had got no concrete books of any noticeable merit in South America, but that she had met a great many authors who promised to produce something printable hereafter. On this point I have my doubts. In my *American Mercury* days I tried hard to unearth interesting stuff from Latin America, but always without success. The best I could ever find was almost childish.

BALTIMORE, AUGUST 27, 1942.

Today is the twelfth anniversary of my marriage to Sara. She is now dead for more than seven years, and she begins inevitably to recede into the shadows. Never a day passes that I do not think of her, but my life has been reorganized to do without her, and so it will continue to the end. Despite her frequent illnesses, and the cruel anxieties that went with them, my scant five years with her were completely happy, and I look back upon them with the utmost satisfaction. But sometimes I wonder if her death wasn't for the best. If she had lived longer it would have been as an invalid, uncomfortable and unhappy. When she died I was still in full vigor, but a year later I began to break up, and the spectacle would have given her dreadful distress.

Then came the war and all its difficulties, and now I face some hard years, even supposing that I live at all. As things stand, I have no major worry. Gertie is reasonably well provided for, and it seems likely that I'll be able to go on in reasonable comfort to the end. If taxes reduce me to hard shrift, then I won't have to endure it long, and no one else will suffer with me. Of one thing I am immensely glad—that I have no child. Sara always wanted one, but her illness, of course, forced her to put the thought away. If I had one today, and especially a young one, I'd be in constant agony of mind. In a few years the Mencken family will be at an end in America, for Virginia[1] was never much of a Mencken and is now a Morrison and the progeny of my cousins I do not count. I am rather glad of it. My grandfather, I believe, made a mistake when he came to this country. He was an unhappy man himself and his descendants have had many troubles. I believe, in truth, that immigration is always unwise—that is, when it is not enforced. I believe my chances in Germany would have been at least as good as they have been in America, and maybe a great deal better. I was born here and so were my father and mother, and I have spent all of my 62 years here, but I still find it impossible to fit myself into the accepted patterns of American life and thought. After all these years, I remain a foreigner.

BALTIMORE, SEPTEMBER 10, 1942.

Twice during the night I was awakened by distress in the region of the stomach, and it continues today. It is not severe, but it is enough to bother me. Superficially, it seems to be no more than heartburn, but I know by experience that bicarbonate of soda will not stop it. In all probability it comes from the coronary arteries, and is the beginning of serious heart trouble. There is no cure for it. I can only endure it as patiently as possible.

I have been uncomfortable all Summer, but nevertheless have got a reasonable amount of work done, though "Heathen Days" still lags, and I'll not be able to deliver the MS. in October, as I have promised the Knopfs. Rather curiously, there has been little of the malaise that

---

1 Virginia Mencken Morrison (1915–1980) was the daughter of Mencken's younger brother Charles and thus his niece. She reappears in the entries for March 10, 1943 (p. 240), and August 8, 1945 (p. 377).

afflicted me last year and the several years before. I suspect that it was caused by the infected tonsil tag that Polvogt took out during the Spring. I have also got some comfort in the hot weather by taking frequent doses of table salt, to replace the sodium lost by perspiration. This simple device prevented the disabling fatigue that used to beset me in Summer. The heat was uncomfortable, but in the intervals of it I could at least work.

I have been taking no treatment for hay-fever this season save daily doses of calcium gluconate and vitamins A and D, which probably do no good. I have also used Estivin on my eyes, but that is only a local palliative. On the whole, I have been less badgered than last year, when I was still taking vaccines. For four or five years the vaccines gave me considerable relief, but then they began to fail.

BALTIMORE, SEPTEMBER 11, 1942.

The seat of my office chair, in use for 25 years, is wearing out, my office rug is wearing out, and I am wearing out. As the Chinese say, "it is later than you think."

BALTIMORE, SEPTEMBER 20, 1942.

Going to New York by train on September 15 I noticed a man in my car whose face seemed somewhat familiar. As the train left Newark for the brief run into the Pennsylvania Station he came up to me and introduced himself. He said he was Angermann, a reporter on the Baltimore *Morning Herald* in my own early days. He said he had left the paper while Col. A. B. Cunningham was still managing editor, which must have been before the end of 1900. I had not seen him since—a span of 42 years. He told me that after leaving the *Herald* he got an interest in a woman's dress shop, along with another man, and that the two were so successful that by the late 1920's they owned a chain of 100 such shops through the United States. The Depression reduced their chain to 50, but they escaped bankruptcy and were soon making good profits again. Several years ago Angermann retired, built himself a house at Coral Gables, and has since lived a life of ease. He has an office in Miami and devotes his mornings to looking after his property. From lunch onward he is free. When he asked me about my health I mentioned the hay fever that was bothering me, and he said that he had once had it in a severe form, but had been cured. "By what?" I asked. He replied: "By my wife's treatments. She is a Christian Scientist." I got no details, for by that time the train was running into the station, and we parted. Angermann did not say that he was a Christian Scientist himself, but he somehow looked it. He had the calm, complacent air peculiar to the brethren, and the pale, somewhat pasty complexion.

BALTIMORE, OCTOBER 8, 1942.

I wrote the last word of "Heathen Days" last night, and sent the typescript to Mrs. Lohrfinck for copying. All day today I have been engaged in putting the book together and revising it. It turns out that it needs, in fact, very little revision, and so I'll probably send the manuscript to Blanche Knopf tomorrow. Like "Happy Days" and "Newspaper Days," it runs to about 80,000 words and consists of twenty chapters. The frontispiece will be a photograph of me made by Aschaffenburg last Spring. It shows me at my office desk, with the window behind me looking into Union Square. It was made the day after a heavy snow storm and the trees and lawn in the Square are all white.

I promised Blanche Knopf to get the manuscript into her hands before the end of October, but I began to fear a month or so ago that it would be impossible. Now, as usual, I have made good on my promise, and have even beaten my own original schedule. The Knopfs are planning to bring out the book about March 1, 1943.

BALTIMORE, OCTOBER 9, 1942.

Patterson is in New York this week, attending a meeting of the Associated Press board. I went to the office yesterday and had lunch alone with Swanson. He doesn't, of course, know the condition of John Owens, but he is bound, soon or late, to hear of it. He told me that the draft had almost wrecked the local staffs of the two *Sunpapers*— indeed, some of the men he engaged to take the places of drafted men have now been drafted themselves. He has put no less than fourteen women to work within the last six months. Some of them are doing very well, but so far not one of them has shown any signs of making a competent copy-reader. It is on the copy desk that the chief shortage of man-power shows itself.

Swanson has been trying to reform the woman's page of the evening paper, and with considerable success. His fundamental idea is that it should appeal, not to women with endless money to spend, but to those who must, even with war wages flowing in, do a large part of their own work. He has three young women at work on it, and he says that all of them are doing well. They are at their worst when it comes to make-up. Very frequently after they have made up a page he has to pull it to pieces himself. But Swanson likes that sort of thing, and in all probability it is a job that no managing editor will ever really escape. He is convinced, and so am I, that it should be possible to get out better local pages with much smaller staffs than have been customary in the past. This means, of course, that the average man must be more competent than in the past. I see no reason why that reform should not be achieved. Certainly it was silly to fill the city room with ex-office boys and other fifth raters who could not be trusted even to cover police courts competently. Swanson believes, as I have long argued, that one or two good reporters could cover all the police courts of the town much better than a dozen fifth raters. He told me that he thinks the standard reporter's salary on the *Sun* should be $100 a week, and I agreed with him. I'd certainly rather try to get out a paper with five or six $100 men than with fifteen or twenty $35 men. Salaries have been steadily increasing for the past two or three years, and there are many men who are now at the $100 mark, or close to it.

Swanson is disturbed about such men as Mac Patterson. They will be drafted soon or late, and he is trying to figure out whether he should apply for exemptions for them. Under the current rules a newspaper executive is classed as a worker in an essential industry, and the draft boards are instructed to let him go if his superiors certify that his services are essential. Swanson says that young Mac is doing very well and that he considers him essential, but he naturally hesitates to give any such certificate to the boss's son. If, indeed, he gave it, he would be obliged to give others to a long line of men, some of them not actually essential. I told him that it seemed to me safest to sign no such certificates at all. After all, Mac may escape the draft on some other ground and, meanwhile, it is necessary to avoid the slightest show of favoritism. To all this Swanson agreed.

BALTIMORE, OCTOBER 12, 1942.

While I was with Patterson and Harry Black today Kavanaugh[1] came up to discuss the dreadful calamity that has befallen Paul Brent, an employe in the mailing-room. On October 10, while Brent was at work and his wife had gone to a store, a fire broke out in his house in West Lombard street, and all of his five children, ranging from a girl of 16 to a boy of less than two years, were burned to death. Brent is a poor ignoramus, but a competent man within his limitations, and a very diligent worker. One of his jobs is to stuff *This Week* and the comic sections into the *Sunday Sun*. He can stuff 3,000 papers an hour, which is the office record: the official stint is but 2,000. He is paid $32.50 a week, and sometimes makes a little overtime, but this has been barely sufficient to feed his large family. Now he has five funerals to pay for, and must also replace his furniture, nearly all of which was wrecked in the fire. In addition, his wife is pregnant, and must soon go to hospital. To meet all these expenses he has precisely $50, apparently from an insurance policy on his oldest girl. Kavanaugh suggested that the *Sun* should offer him some aid, and Patterson, Black and I agreed. We decided to send him $750 at once, and to add $250 later on, or even more, if he needs it. We acted as members of the board, which alone can authorize such gifts, but did not constitute a quorum. Kavanaugh, as secretary, was accordingly instructed to get the consent of Edwin F. A. Morgan, which will make a quorum. The board does not meet until October 26. The improvidence of such poor fish as Brent is really almost incredible. A faithful Catholic, he produced children at God's will, and is now, as I have said, about to produce another—that is, if his wife's cruel distress does not cause her to miscarry. He is an honest and industrious man, but it is simply impossible for him to earn enough to support so large a family. What he does is done well, but it is work that any bright child of ten could do. He has been at it for years, and is unfit for anything better.

---

1 Emmett P. Kavanaugh (1894–1956), at that time circulation manager of the *Sun-papers*, became business manager in 1948 and was made a vice president shortly before his death.

BALTIMORE, OCTOBER 13, 1942.

I had to write letters of congratulations today to two venerable acquaintances who have lately brought out books. The first was Bishop Francis Clement Kelley, whose contribution to literature takes the form of an elaborate and complicated allegory called "Pack Rat." The other was Dr. A. G. Keller of Yale. He calls his book "Net Impressions." Both of these tomes are really dreadful, and I got through them only by main force. Nevertheless, I had to write to the authors saying that they were swell. I am only glad that my book reviewing days are over, for it would be difficult indeed to tell the truth about the two books without gravely offending the two men.

"Pack Rat" would have been ten times as effective if Kelley had forgotten his allegory and confined it to straight argument. As for "Net Impressions" it really astonished me to discover how conventional Keller's ideas are. After a lifetime spent in the study of anthropology, he comes to conclusions that differ only occasionally, and then not materially, from those of any average Rotarian. He is, like Kelley, a charming fellow, but it would certainly be a gross exaggeration to say that he has contributed anything really profound or original to human thought, even within the bounds of his specialty. As William Graham Sumner's[1] successor at Yale, he got a very good professional start and he has maintained his position with some skill and diligence, but the anthropology that Sumner left him is the anthropology that he still subscribes to today.

BALTIMORE, OCTOBER 20, 1942.

Oswald Garrison Villard dropped off in Baltimore last night on his way from New York to Washington, and I met him at the Pennsylvania Station and took him to the Maryland Club for dinner. He is becoming deaf, and at his suggestion we proceeded after dinner to his room at the Stafford Hotel, where we could talk more freely than in the club. He is preparing to do a new version of his book, "Some Newspapers and Newspaper-Men," first published by Knopf in 1923,

1 William Graham Sumner (1840–1910), sociologist and economist. He was the author of many books, of which *Folkways* (1907) is probably the best known, and his thought had a considerable influence on the young Mencken.

and wanted me to advise him about changes and additions. When we came to the chapter on the Baltimore *Sunpapers* I was somewhat embarrassed, for it seems to me that most of the hopes Villard had for them in 1923 have failed to be realized. I got rid of the difficulty by advising him to drop the *Sunpapers* chapter altogether. I argued that, inasmuch as it was mainly a forecast, it would have to be rewritten in toto, and that the job would be onerous. He finally agreed, and we turned to other matters.[1]

Villard is enormously irritated by the course of the *Nation* and the New York *Evening Post* since he ceased to edit them. The *Nation* is now a frantic pro-war and New Deal sheet operated by Freda Kirchwey,[2] and the *Evening Post* has fallen into the hands of another wild woman, Dorothy Backer,[3] a daughter to the late Jacob H. Schiff. Every time he sees either one or the other poor Villard has a spell. He is still talking of starting a new weekly of opinion after the war, but inasmuch as he is now more than 70 years old and the war may last for years, it is not likely that he'll ever come to it. We talked at great length of newspapers and newspaper men. I told him that the *Sun* might be able (in case of John Owens's death) to use a good editorial man, and he suggested Irving Dilliard of the St. Louis *Post-Dispatch*. I relayed this suggestion to Patterson today. I know nothing of Dilliard save what is in "Who's Who in America," where he says that he is a member of the Newspaper Guild. He is 38 years old, has an A.B. from the University of Illinois, once worked for the *Christian Science Monitor*, had a year at Harvard as a Nieman fellow, and has been an editorial writer on the *Post-Dispatch* since 1930. I have read but one of his articles—a political piece printed in either the *Nation* or the *New Republic*, discussing Republican prospects in this year's congressional elections. I recall that it seemed well-informed and sensible, though somewhat New Dealish in tone. Villard volunteered to get some

---

1 Villard's book, *The Disappearing Daily* (New York: Alfred A. Knopf, 1944), contained numerous references to the Baltimore *Sunpapers*, most of them laudatory in tone, but there was no chapter devoted specifically to them.

2 Freda Kirchwey (1893–1976), author and editor, held various posts on *The Nation* from 1918 to 1955, becoming finally its editor and publisher.

3 Dorothy Backer (b. 1903), more generally known by her maiden name, Dorothy Schiff, was the first woman newspaper publisher in the country. In 1942 she took over the management of the New York *Post* from her ailing husband, George Backer; they were divorced the following year and she married Ted Thackrey, her managing editor.

specimens of Dilliard's editorials, and to send them to me for Patterson's information.[1]

BALTIMORE, OCTOBER 20, 1942.

Patterson told me today that he had made a brief visit, a few days ago, to John Owens. He was warned to stay no more than ten minutes. He found poor John in a pretty dilapidated state. The muscles of his eyes are out of control, and there is also some difficulty at one side of his mouth. Patterson gathered the idea that he is aware that his illness is probably incurable. He said that he could not hope to get back to work, at best, until after the first of the year. Patterson told him that arrangements had been made to give him a furlough until April, and that he would be free to take more time afterward if he wanted it. Patterson said that the visit was very depressing, and I can well believe it.

When the effort to rehabilitate the *Sunpapers* was under way during the 20's there were eleven men principally concerned—Van Lear Black, Patterson, Adams, Harry Black, Joe Blondell,[2] Murphy, Hamilton Owens, John Owens (as aide to Adams), Stanley Reynolds, William E. Moore (as aide to Reynolds), and myself. Of these, Van Lear Black, Blondell, Moore, Reynolds and Adams are now dead, and Murphy and John Owens are permanently disabled. This leaves only four still in service—Patterson, Harry Black, Hamilton Owens and myself.

BALTIMORE, OCTOBER 23, 1942.

Edward Weeks, Jr.,[3] editor of the *Atlantic Monthly,* stopped off in Baltimore today and I took him to lunch at the Maryland Club. He professed to be eager to get me into his magazine, but I told him that he couldn't print anything I'd be willing to sign, especially on politics. He then said that he'd like to do a few chapters out of "Heathen Days," but I explained that Ross of the *New Yorker* had the refusal of them. But what, he persisted, of something of the same general sort, but dealing with my magazine adventures? I told him that it would be difficult to go into that field without offending men still living—for

1 Nothing ever came of the proposal to hire Irving Dilliard for the *Sun.*
2 Joseph A. Blondell (1889–1934) was secretary-treasurer of the A. S. Abell Company from 1924 until his death.
3 Edward A. Weeks (1898–1989) served as editor of the *Atlantic Monthly* from 1938 to 1966.

example, Nathan and Warner[1]—but he said he thought I could do it, and tried to make me promise to make the attempt. I did not do so, but shall think it over. Ross can't use more than a few of the "Heathen Days" chapters, and I may be able to induce him to surrender his option on the rest. Or I may try one of the magazine sketches that Weeks suggested.

Weeks is 44 years old and has been with the *Atlantic* since 1924. On the retirement of Ellery Sedgwick in 1938 he became the editor. He told me that he bought Sedgwick out at that time, and that Sedgwick now owns no stock in the magazine. Weeks was backed by R. E. Danielson,[2] a man of large means who was formerly editor of the *Sportsman*. Danielson, who is not a Jew, now appears as associate editor of the *Atlantic* and as president of the publishing company. Weeks, if he ever finishes paying for it, will own about a fourth of the stock. He said that Danielson paid Sedgwick for the magazine partly in stock of the Rumford Printing Company—600 shares. Sedgwick now owns about a third of the Rumford stock. Who owns the rest Weeks did not say. He said that Sedgwick, who is now nearly 71 years old, is very comfortable and happy with his second wife, an Englishwoman. He is an ardent Anglomaniac and he is so much upset by the continuing troubles of the Motherland that he walks the floor when bad news comes in. But his wife, who is more philosophical, assures him that virtue will triumph in the end. He returned to the office last Summer to lend a hand when the war depleted the staff, but only as *amicus curiae*. Various publishers are urging him to write his reminiscences, but he hates writing, and so refuses.

Weeks said that his own job drives him frantic—especially the visitors it brings in. I advised him to keep away from the office, and he said he thought it was a good idea. He appeared to be greatly surprised when I told him that I lived in Baltimore all the while I edited the *Smart Set* and the *American Mercury*. It also amazed him to hear that Nathan and I, in our *Smart Set* days, never discussed MSS.—that whenever one of us voted No the other yielded without argument. He told me that the operating costs of the *Atlantic* have been rising, and that its profits are no longer what they used to be. Its best year, he said, was 1928, when it cleared $90,000. He said a good deal of money

1 Eltinge F. Warner (1880–1965), publisher of *The Smart Set*, chose Mencken and George Jean Nathan to be its co-editors in 1914.
2 Richard E. Danielson (1885–1957) became president of the Atlantic Monthly Company and associate editor of the magazine in 1940.

had been wasted, before he called a halt, on circulation promotion—the very thing that wrecked the *American Mercury*. He said that his editorial expenditures—that is, for MSS. alone—run beyond $3,000 a month, and that there have been months when they reached $4,400. I told him that I always got out the *Mercury*, after Nathan left, for $2,500 or less. But I printed a good many more young authors than he prints, and the men of established position have to be well paid.

Weeks, it seems to me, is only an indifferent editor. Despite his 44 years, he still looks, acts and talks young. He told me that Sedgwick's four children are all married. The boy, after leaving Harvard, was at loose ends, and showed no interest in the *Atlantic*. Sedgwick took him to a vocational guide in New York who analyzed his mind by word association, and advised that he be sent to a business school. This was done, and he made a good record, and is now happily and successfully working for a bank in Cleveland.

BALTIMORE, NOVEMBER 7, 1942.

In New York yesterday I called on two of the widows of Paul Armstrong—Rella and Catherine. I found Catherine in an apartment at 315 east 68th street, near the East river, and Rella at the apartment of her brother-in-law Jack at 1 west 67th street. Neither knew that I was seeing the other. They gave me a lot of material for the memoir of Armstrong that I am writing for my "Forty-five Years as Author and Editor." I began work on it on August 27, and the first thing I did was the appendix on Percival Pollard.[1] Then followed that on Armstrong. When the rough drafts of these were finished I went back to the beginning of the record, and have since made very fair progress. It promises to be quite as long as my "Thirty-five Years of Newspaper Work," which, with the appendices and index, runs to 1,687 typewritten pages. If I ever finish it the whole record of my professional life will be on paper, and I'll be free to devote the rest of my days to new books. My first job will be the Supplement to "The American Language." An enormous mass of material for it has accumulated, and

1 Percival Pollard (1869–1911), born in Germany and educated in England, came to the United States while still a young man and established a reputation as a literary critic. His *Their Day in Court* (1909) and *Masks and Minstrels of New Germany* (1911) had a considerable influence on the development of Mencken's own critical ideas.

LEFT: George Jean Nathan and
H. L. Mencken (*Alfred A. Knopf*).
BELOW: Announcing the Hatrack
decision in Boston, 1926
(*UPI/Bettmann Newsphotos*)

Mencken and his wife, Sara Powell Haardt, 1933 (*A. Aubrey Bodine Collection, The Peale Museum, Baltimore*)

In the backyard garden at 1524 Hollins Street, 1939 *(August Mencken)*.
INSET: Formal portrait, 1939 *(Ben Pinchot)*

OPPOSITE ABOVE: Mencken in his second-floor study at Hollins Street, 1939
(*Robert F. Kniesche*). OPPOSITE BELOW: Visiting the home of Alfred A. Knopf,
1940 (*Alfred A. Knopf*). ABOVE: Working on the galley proofs of *The American
Language* (*A. Aubrey Bodine Collection, The Peale Museum, Baltimore*)

Covering the 1948 Republican Convention in Philadelphia *(The Bettmann Archive)*.
OPPOSITE: A page from the diary in Mencken's typing: the beginning of the entry for May 31, 1940 *(Gaither Scott)*. INSET: The Diary of H. L. Mencken, in the five solander boxes in which it lay sealed in a Pratt Library vault for twenty-five years *(Gaither Scott)*

Baltimore, May 31, 1940

Sara is dead five years today -- a longer time than the time of our
marriage, which lasted but four years and nine months.   It is amazing
what a deep mark she left upon my life -- and yet, after all, it is not
amazing at all, for a happy marriage throws out numerous and powerful tentacles.
They may loosen with years and habit, but when a marriage ends at the height of
its success they endure.   It is a literal fact that I still think of Sara
every day of my life, and almost every hour of the day.   Whenevr I see
anything that she would have liked I find myself saying that I'll buy it and
take it to her, and I am always thinking of things to tell her.   There was
a tremendous variety in her, and yet she was always steadfast.   I can recall
no single moment during our years together when I ever had the slightest
doubt of our marriage, or wished that it had never been.   I believe that
she was equally content.   We had our troubles, especially her illnesses,
but they never set up any difference between us: they always drew us
closer and closer together.   Indeed, it was only the last year or so
that was darkened by them, for before that she always recovered quickly,
and seemed to be making a steady gain in health.   I knew all the
while that her chances of life were not too good, but nevertheless
the overt situation was usually reassuring, and so I put fears out of my
mind.   What I wrote of her courage in the preface to "Southern Album" was

all true.   It w
I remember once --
always forthright,
home from his offi
quieting her.   B
and soon afterward
vulnerability to t
throwing it off.
yet she recovered

        Perhaps our

(*Alfred A. Knopf*)

it will take me at least a year to do the book. My plan is to make it exactly uniform with the fourth edition of "The American Language." Every item will be keyed to some passage in "The American Language," and the successive chapters will run in the same order. But I hope to make the book readable even to readers who do not have "The American Language" by them. Like the latter, it will be so done that it can be taken up at any point.

If I had the time I'd like to rewrite some of my earlier books, for example, "In Defense of Women" and "Notes on Democracy." But I doubt that it will ever be possible, for my days are growing short. I'd like also to do a book to be called "Notes in Wartime," or something of the sort, but it is unlikely that I'll ever come to it.

BALTIMORE, NOVEMBER 29, 1942.

I went to Princeton, New Jersey, yesterday to spend the week-end with Julian P. Boyd, the librarian of the University. He is engaged upon a volume of my letters.[1] Joe Hergesheimer joined me at Wilmington, and we traveled the rest of the way together. I put up at the Princeton Inn, a very comfortable little place, and had dinner with Boyd and his wife yesterday evening, and breakfast this morning. They have a charming house in a part of Princeton called Broadmead, and Mrs. Boyd is a very pleasant woman.

The other guests at dinner last night were F. F. Hopper, librarian of the New York Public Library, and George A. Brakeley, treasurer of Princeton. Brakeley, it turned out, is an old newspaper reporter, and after we had had a couple of drinks he and I began to swap reminiscences.

This morning after breakfast H. H. Bender, professor of Indo-German philology at Princeton, and etymological editor of the Webster Dictionaries, dropped in. We had been in communication about the origin of various American phrases—in fact, we have been acquaintances at long distance for many years, though I had not met Bender before. He turned out to be a somewhat savage looking man, with an entirely incredible toupée. He was full of instructive talk about

---

1 Julian Boyd's volume of Mencken's letters had eventually to be abandoned because of the demands made upon him by the multivolume edition of the papers of Thomas Jefferson, of which he was the editor. But the Mencken correspondence which he assembled at Princeton remains an indispensable source for researchers.

Gothic. He told me among other things that the publishers of the Webster Dictionaries have accumulated a file of 6,000,000 cards showing examples of usage. If these cards were edited and published they would make a work on American English quite as large as the New English Dictionary. Bender said that there was no immediate intention of publishing them, but that the possibility of doing it was floating about and that it might be done soon or late.

Hergesheimer looked really wretched. He has lost fifteen or twenty pounds since I last saw him, and has begun to look gray and old. He told me that his diabetes lately sent him to hospital in West Chester. A few days on insulin restored him, but he simply refuses to take it regularly. He and Dorothy are living in Mary Rogers's house at West Chester. The Dower House is leased, and so is the smaller house in Biddle street. Mary Rogers herself appears to be dying. She has some sort of mysterious paralysis, and it has already gone so far that she can't use her hands. Joe said that she is still in reasonably good spirits, but that she realizes her state.

Mrs. Boyd put on a good dinner, and Boyd himself supplied very excellent drinks. Hopper told me that a collection of books and documents relating to Theodore Roosevelt the elder was lately offered to the New York Public Library. It has been assembled by the Roosevelt Association headed by Hermann Hagedorn.[1] Unhappily, the rise of Roosevelt II has so greatly diminished interest in Roosevelt I that it is now impossible to raise money for the operation of the association. It is therefore seeking to dispose of the library. Hopper said that the books were offered to him on condition that they be kept together. Inasmuch as nine-tenths of them were already duplicated in his library, he refused to take them on those terms. He said that they are now being offered to other libraries.

I came home this afternoon through a Winter rain storm. The landscape on the way down was immensely depressing. We'd run along for miles without seeing a human being. There were not even lights in the houses. All their inhabitants, I suppose, having eaten heavy Sunday dinners, were resting in the hay.

Boyd seems to be making reasonable progress with his projected volume of my letters. Unfortunately, he find it difficult to get adequate secretarial help at Princeton, and so he has been forced to do a lot of

---

1 Hermann Hagedorn (1882–1964), novelist, poet, and biographer. The volumes on Theodore Roosevelt mentioned here eventually went to Harvard.

copying himself. Inasmuch as his duties as librarian are anything but easy, he has very little time to spare for the book. Nevertheless, he is in hopes, he told me, of finishing it well before the end of 1943. He said that he has already accumulated and copied 6,000 of my letters.

I don't care much whether he finishes the book or not. He is sending me carbons of all the letters that are copied, and I am thus accumulating a fine collection for my own files. They will be extremely useful as I proceed with my record of my magazine days.

BALTIMORE, DECEMBER 27, 1942.

The Christmas just past was the gloomiest of all the gloomy ones that I can recall. On the Saturday before it, December 19, August and I went out to the Home for Incurables to see my mother's younger brother, Charles H. Abhau. We had not visited him since last Christmas. He is now approaching 74 and is plainly breaking up. His usual garrulity, always hard to bear, has been made worse by incoherence. His talk wanders, and he is constantly stopping to recall some inconsequential name or date, nearly always in vain. Last Spring he had a hemorrhage in his left eye, and is still more or less blind in it. The hemorrhage was caused by hypertension. His blood pressure, he said, is "190 plus," but I suspect that it is actually much higher. He shows mental confusion and looks like a corpse. This poor man has been disabled by infantile paralysis since the age of three, and for a long while past has been steadily deteriorating. He now complains bitterly about the neglect of his doctors, who, plainly enough, have found that nothing can be done for him. In particular, he complains that they have not paid any attention to his eye. I tried to tell him that the hemorrhage would eventually clear up, but in all probability I didn't make it sound very convincing. I think he fears becoming completely helpless like his brother William, who has now been in bed eight years, suffering stroke after stroke but never dying. It is really dreadful to peg out in that lingering way, but it seems to be an Abhau family trait. Only my mother, who was the luckiest of the family, died quickly, and even my mother was full of increasing discomforts for more than a year.

August and I went to Loudon Park Cemetery Christmas morning and found the family gravestone, which is of white marble, lying flat upon the ground, dingy with greasy grime. Every year there are more factories in the Loudon Park region and it is more difficult to keep the stone clean. From the cemetery we went to Gertrude's apartment at 5110 Gwynn Oak avenue, and had Christmas dinner with her. Downstairs was our Uncle William, lying helpless upon his bed and unable to speak. He recognized us, but that was all. In the evening we went to Gerald W. Johnson's house at 1310 Bolton street, and on our way stopped at the Edmund Duffys'. The Duffy daughter, who is named after Sara, is now eight years old. She is a very lively child, and had pretty well worn out her parents by the time we dropped in. As a Christmas present they gave her the privilege of staying up until she wanted to go to bed, but toward 11 o'clock Anne Duffy began suggesting to her that the time had come. She went unwillingly and a few minutes later had bounced back in her pajamas, and was ready for another inning. She gave us an exhibition of her reading, and did very well. She also has a considerable talent for drawing.

At the Johnsons' the usual Christmas night party was much smaller than usual, and a good deal quieter. The Woollcotts were kept away by the serious illness of Marie Woollcott's mother, Mrs. Bloede, and the rest all seemed to be in a low mood. The day after Christmas I went to the annual luncheon at the Maryland Club, and found it almost unbearably dull. There was none of the traditional singing and yowling, and I saw only one drunk. The gayest persons present were two of the sons of Dr. Howard A. Kelly. They got up a crap game after lunch and played furiously, though their father and mother are both in hospital and may die very soon. I sat at table with Paul Patterson, Schmick and Jim Fenhagen, and we had as guests Captain Leland P. Lovette, U.S.N., and W. R. Haley, business manager of the Manchester *Guardian*. The usual Christmas bill-of-fare was put on— pigs' tails, sauerkraut and hominy. Poor Haley made heavy weather of it, for I gathered from him that it is not considered decent in England to eat pigs' tails, and both the sauerkraut and the hominy were novelties to him, and it was plain that he did not like them. It is usual to have wine at these luncheons, but the atmosphere was so depressing that Patterson suggested that we forego it. Instead we drank Scotch highballs. I drank one, and had had two small Manhattan cocktails before. By 2.30 most of the members began to depart, and by 3 I was back home myself. A very gloomy party. Next year, in all probability, there will be none at all. The effects of the war are beginning to show themselves. The American people realize at last that they are in for what may be a long, bloody and immensely costly struggle.

1943

I went to bed at 11 o'clock last night, fell asleep almost at once, and so heard nothing of the usual whistle-tooting and pistol-firing. August reported this morning that there was much less of it than in the past. We were invited to see the old year out at Hamilton Owens's house at Riderwood, but had to decline, for August was disinclined to use gasoline and tires and risk his car on a long and difficult run, and moreover, he had to go to Edgewood early this morning and so wanted to get to bed reasonably early. The Owenses have been giving these New Year's Eve parties for a dozen years past, and I have gone to most of them. In all probability last night's was the last, for getting to and from any place in the country becomes more and more onerous.

I begin the new year in a state of physical discomfort, and it is seldom that I can put in a real day's work. Nevertheless, I have made some progress with my projected record of my magazine days, and have in fact got beyond page 300 of the fair copy. This brings me down to the year 1916. In addition, I have written more than 250 pages of appendices on various authors, among them, Paul Armstrong, Percival Pollard, Frank Harris,[1] James Huneker and Harry Kemp,[2] and am now at work on Harry Leon Wilson[3] and

---

1 Frank Harris (1856–1931), Irish-born American journalist, biographer, and novelist. He is chiefly known for his rather scandalous "autobiography," *My Life and Loves* (1923–1927), which was banned in both America and England for many years.

2 Harry H. Kemp (1883–1960), known as the "tramp poet" because of his nomadic life, was also a novelist and playwright.

3 Harry Leon Wilson (1867–1939), novelist and playwright. A prolific contributor to *The Saturday Evening Post*, he is remembered chiefly for *Ruggles of Red Gap* (1915) and *Merton of the Movies* (1922).

W. L. George.[1] My plan is to keep the main narrative flowing as freely as possible. Whenever a man pops up who needs detailed treatment I put him into an appendix. Other appendices are devoted to important documents—for example, the agreement by which George Jean Nathan and I took over the editorship of the *Smart Set* in 1914. If the narrative goes on at its present rate I'll not finish it until the end of 1943, if then. It will probably be even longer than my "Thirty-Five Years of Newspaper Work, 1906–41." I am trying to document it as carefully as possible. It can't be printed during my lifetime, or the lifetimes of the persons principally dealt with, but it may be useful as a record later on.

BALTIMORE, JANUARY 4, 1943.

The worst part of the Winter may still be ahead of us, but there are already signs of Spring. The severe cold before Christmas was followed by a week of warm rains, and today some of the bulbs in the backyard are putting out shoots. On New Year's day, under the old pear tree, a few of these shoots were two inches high. On the pear tree itself the blossoms are beginning to swell and to show touches of red. The Spring of this latitude is full of false starts. By February 1, if the weather is mild, it seems to be coming on with a rush, but two weeks later Winter may return. This oscillation goes on for a long while, and when real Spring bursts upon us at last it is followed almost immediately by Summer. In March of 1934, when Sara and I returned from the Mediterranean, we found the temperature 80 degrees in New York, though it had been below zero when we sailed early in February. Contrariwise, on March 2 of 1942 there was a heavy snowstorm. It shows in the frontispiece to "Heathen Days."

BALTIMORE, JANUARY 8, 1943.

This afternoon I went out to see John Owens, who lives in Homeland, about six miles from the *Sun* office. I found him sitting up in his room, and in very good spirits. The lesion in his medulla oblongata, or wherever it is, seems to be clearing up. His two eyes are still out of

---

1 Walter L. George (1882–1926), novelist, journalist, and critic, who lived in Paris, London, and America. He was a confirmed feminist.

coördination, and so he wears a patch over one of them, but otherwise he seems to be fast recovering. He can walk a little and his doctors have advised him to try getting up and down stairs. He told me that his illness came on very suddenly. First he felt a tingling in the finger-tips of his left hand, then there was a numbness in the whole hand, then it progressed to the arm, and finally his whole side was disabled. This sounded like a cerebral hemorrhage to me; on what ground the doctors locate the lesion in the medulla I do not know. John's mind is perfectly clear; his voice sounds natural. He said that he was fast re-covering his taste for tobacco, and that he was having sherry with his meals, and only the other day got an overdose and felt tipsy. I took him a box of Cabañas cigars. He is still unable to read, but his sight is much better than it was, and he hopes to resume very soon. He told me that he was fully convinced, a month ago, that he was dying. One day he had a severe attack of vertigo and decided that the end had come. He accordingly sent for his brother-in-law, Mark S. Watson, to give him a few final instructions. When Watson failed to appear John lay in bed, patiently awaiting death. He said that he felt no fear of it: his whole thought was about Watson, who would forever regret, he figured, failing to get to the house before he died. John's charming daughter, the wife of John E. Semmes's son, who is a Marine officer, introduced me to a Miss Dashiell, a slim, graying and rather attractive woman. This, I suppose, is the lady John was planning to marry when he fell ill. She is a relative of his late wife. The obvious relief of Mrs. Semmes was really touching. She had been watching by her father's bedside for months, pretty well convinced that he would die inevita-bly, and now he was recovering. She took me in to see her baby, a very pretty little girl, now just old enough to notice a visitor. Her husband is somewhere in the South Seas, and so is her brother.

BALTIMORE, JANUARY 10, 1943.

The sidewalk in front of the *Sun* office has been leaking for some time past, and of late the incoming rain-water has done some damage in the pressroom which extends under it. A few weeks ago Schmick engaged a contractor to tear it up and relay it, with suitable water-proofing. The contractor reported that he could not proceed without priority orders for material from the dunderheads in charge of such things. When the proper dunderhead was found he refused to issue them. "Very well," said Paul Patterson. "We can put up with it a little longer—but I am wondering what I am going to say to the union." "What union?" demanded the dunderhead, pricking up his ears. "The pressmen's union," replied Patterson. "It has been raising hell." At once the dunderhead began to hem and haw, and in half an hour the priority orders were in the hands of the contractor. He is now hard at work digging up the old sidewalk. The joke lies in the fact that the pressmen had actually made no complaint at all, either as individuals or through their union, which is a small company union. The leakage damaged paper and menaced certain auxiliary machinery, but did not affect the operation of the presses or the comfort of the men.

BALTIMORE, JANUARY 13, 1943.

At the office today Schmick showed Harry Black and me the petition he is sending to the coördinators at Washington for an extra allowance of paper for the *Sunpapers,* on the ground that the growth of the war industry in the Baltimore region has greatly increased their natural circulation. Under the rules lately promulgated every daily paper is to be limited in 1943 to the amount of the paper it used for its actual paid circulation in 1941, plus 3% for wastage. Schmick is asking for an extra allowance of 15% and believes that he will get 10%. He is making plans to reduce the office consumption of newsprint by various devices. The maximum allowance for returns is already cut down to $2\frac{1}{2}\%$, all save a few of the rural delivery routes have been abolished, and the street vending-boxes in the city and suburbs have been abandoned. There will probably be further squeezes before the end of the year. If, when and as they come Schmick proposes to suspend the noon edition of the evening paper and the night-before edition of the morning, and cut down on street sales as much as possible. In the end, he believes, he may have to stop street sales altogether. He is also in favor (as I am) of abandoning the Saturday evening edition of the *Evening Sun.* There is no advertising in it, and it represents a heavy dead loss. But in order to do that he will have to induce the Hearst paper to join him, and that may be difficult. My belief is that if the Saturday evening paper is ever suspended it will never be revived.[1] Many papers in other cities have already abandoned it.

---

1 The management of the *Sun* must have given this matter long and careful consid-

Schmick is optimistic about the issue of the negotiation with the Typographical Union, which has been going on for months. He says he has assurances from both Brannock, the president of the Baltimore union, and Wilson, the leader of the radical faction therein, that there will be no strike like that of last year. Nevertheless, he reports that the Baltimore union has asked the International to authorize a strike vote, and that Baker, president of the International, says he will have to do it.

BALTIMORE, JANUARY 14, 1943.

Judge Eugene O'Dunne, the two Guttmacher brothers—Alan and Manfred—, Hulbert Footner and I have fallen into the habit of meeting in Schellhase's back room every Tuesday evening, beginning at ten o'clock. Manfred Guttmacher, who is a psychiatrist, is now a major in the Army Medical Corps, stationed at a large Army lunatic asylum near Williamsburg, Va., and so he can seldom join us, but the others are pretty regular in attendance. We drink a few beers and discuss the sorrows of the world. Now and then there is a guest. On Tuesday of this week there were two—Robert C. Cook, editor of the *Journal of Heredity*, and Dr. L. B. Tuckerman,[1] of the Bureau of Standards. Both live in Washington. Cook had joined us more than once before, but Tuckerman was a newcomer. He turned out to be a very interesting man, though hardly of prepossessing exterior. He is squattish in figure, with a noticeable paunch, a misshapen nose and a straggling mustache and Van Dyke beard. His specialty is the physics of aeronautics, and he was full of curious stuff about parachutes, high altitude flying, airplane accidents, and so on. Many such accidents, he said, are completely inexplicable. Whenever the engineers on the spot cannot determine the cause, what is left of the fallen plane is sent to him in Washington, and he studies the fragments in his laboratory. Not infrequently he is quite baffled. In the case of planes that fall at sea it is impossible to do more than guess, for usually no wreckage is recovered. I asked him what caused the accident which killed Captain Musick of the Pan-American Airlines, and he said frankly that no one

eration, for the Saturday edition of the *Evening Sun* was finally suspended in March 1984.

1 Louis B. Tuckerman (1879–1962) had served with the National Bureau of Standards since 1919. He contributed many technical and scientific articles to various journals and was the inventor of several aeronautical devices.

knew.[1] He explained at length how parachute troops are trained, and especially how they are taught to land safely. As they reach the earth they are usually moving with the speed of a man who has jumped twenty feet, and if they didn't know the tricks of landing they would be badly hurt. As it is, they come down without injury nine times out of ten.

Cook is a layman, but he edits the *Journal of Heredity* successfully, and apparently knows a great deal about the subject. Alan Guttmacher and I can follow his talk comfortably, but I can see that it is largely unintelligible to O'Dunne and Footner, who know nothing about biology.

BALTIMORE, JANUARY 15, 1943.

Hester the cook has a daughter, Elsie, who is the wife of a colored letter-carrier and the mother of two children. Some time ago I endorsed her application for a job at the Edgewood Arsenal, and she got it. She was graded as an unskilled laborer, and paid $3.60 a day. This morning Hester told me that she had been promoted to the rank of spray painter, and her pay lifted to $5.76 a day. It is amazing, with such opportunities open to colored women, that any of them go on working as domestic servants. Hester herself is probably too old for a government job; moreover, she is lame. But Emma Ball, the maid, could get one easily, and be sure of rapid promotion, for she writes a good hand and is pretty intelligent. I am paying her $17 a week, which is considerably above the scale for housemaids in Baltimore. In addition, I give her a bonus of $150 a year, a present of $20 at Christmas and another of $20 when she begins her annual vacation of two weeks. Hester is paid $22 a week, with the same bonus and presents. Thus Emma receives $1,074 a year, besides her meals, and Hester $1,334. They have Thursday and Sunday afternoons and evenings off, and do not come to work until noon on Saturday. When I am out of town August often lets them off all day. They eat precisely what he and I eat.

1 The reference is to the crash of Pan-American Airways' *Samoan Clipper* in January 1938. The plane was coming in for a landing at the airport of Pago Pago, in Samoa, when it burst into flames and disappeared into the Pacific Ocean. Captain Edwin C. Musick, its pilot, and his six crew members all perished.

BALTIMORE, JANUARY 17, 1943.

My old friend Maxwell Cathcart died the other day and is to be buried tomorrow. At the Saturday Night Club last night the members tried to guess his age. Their guesses ranged from 72 to 81. He was actually 68. But he had always seemed oldish, and in late years he looked positively ancient. There was never a more amiable fellow, or a more futile one. He came of a family that included some rich members, and was himself plainly a gentleman, but he spent all his life as a bank teller and never showed the slightest sign of a capacity for anything better. He had a resonant bass voice and was an ardent and sincere music lover, but he was too timid to become a performer. More than once, when I was out of service, he was pressed to take the second piano in the Saturday Night Club, but he always shrank from it. When he was in his cups he liked to sing, but only informally. He was at his best doing old musical comedy songs, with himself at the piano.

I met him for the first time when the Florestan Club was organized in 1910. A bachelor, he became one of the regular frequenters of the clubhouse in Charles street near Center. He and W. Edwin Moffett, then also a bachelor, played interminable games of pool. Both were clumsy players, and Moffett, every time he missed a shot, would exclaim, "Oh, shit!" Max was quite as bad a player, but more patient. There was some real gaiety in him, and at the bi-weekly dinners of the Sunday Dinner Club, a club within the Florestan, he was always a leader in the merriment. Many's the time that all of us were boiled together. Max also had some wit, and was the author of some of the best stanzas of Willie Woollcott's burlesque patriotic song, "I Am a One Hundred Percent. American, Goddamn!" But all this was for the privacy of the club. Outside, he was very shy.

He read a great deal in his early days and was a constant patron of the old Mercantile Library in Charles street near Saratoga. He followed it when it moved to Center street near Charles. But his reading was so dispersed that he never acquired a sound grip on any subject: he knew a little of everything, but only a little. He joined the Saturday Night Club many years ago, and seldom missed a meeting. Unhappily, the club became so overcrowded during the later days of Prohibition that the houses of those members who entertained it in rotation were jammed to suffocation. It thus became necessary to reduce the membership, and a committee consisting of H. E. Buchholz and Dr. Franklin Hazlehurst[1] was appointed to devise a scheme of relief. The committee brought in a report proposing that those members who did not entertain themselves keep away from the meetings unless specifically invited, for though some of the entertaining members had room for them others did not. This let out poor Max, for he lived in cramped quarters with a widowed sister who was a Prohibitionist, and thus could not entertain the club himself. We were sorry to lose him, but it could not be helped. No other member, so far as I know, was ever invited to his house. We knew, in fact, but little about him. He apparently took no interest in his bank job, and seldom mentioned it.

Back in 1912 or thereabout he was beset by a tic that caused him to wag his bald head in a grotesque manner. All the doctors in the Florestan Club tried to cure him, but in vain. The tic remained to his dying day. The doctors, unable to discover its cause, concluded that it was of psychic origin, but that was plainly only an evasion. Max bore his affliction with equanimity, but it must have interfered seriously with his duties as a bank teller. In his later days he was a pathetic figure. He had aged dreadfully, and as he walked along the street with his head bobbing he looked like Father Time without the whiskers. He saw Moffett oftener than he saw anyone else. Moffett says that, for the past year or two, he complained of pains in his left arm—obviously, a sign of heart impairment. But he seems to have died in the end of a respiratory infection.

There is something tragic to me about the life of so charming and yet so futile a fellow. Everyone who knew him liked him, and yet everyone was conscious of something feeble about him. His days were spent in dull drudgery and he got only transient satisfactions out of his leisure. He never had any projects or ambitions. The only women he appeared to know were old ones. If he ever traveled I never heard of it. Now he is dead, and in a little while nearly all of his old associates will be dead too, and nothing whatsoever will remain of him, not even a name.

BALTIMORE, JANUARY 19, 1943.

I gave a dinner at the Maryland Club last night to Julian P. Boyd— a sort of return for his entertainment of me at Princeton. Present:

1 Dr. Franklin Hazlehurst (1882–1946), physician and long-time member of the Saturday Night Club. See the entry for June 24, 1946 (p. 417).

Boyd, Joe Hergesheimer, John E. Semmes, Franklin F. Hopper (librarian of the New York Public Library), Joseph L. Wheeler (librarian of the Enoch Pratt Free Library), George A. Brakeley (vice-president and treasurer of Princeton University), my brother August and me. The dinner passed off pleasantly enough. We had oysters, terrapin, steamed turkey with rice and a dessert. Before dinner: sherry and old-fashioned cocktails. With it: Jesuiten Garten. Afterward: brandy, Scotch highballs and beer. I dropped into the club at noon to see how the preparations were coming on, and found that the steward was having a hard time getting enough butter for the terrapin, which takes a lot. But he got it somehow. I took my own cigars—Cabañas that I bought in Havana in the Spring of 1941.

I had made reservations at the Belvedere for Brakeley, Boyd, Hergesheimer and Hopper, but at the last minute Hergy decided to spend the night at the home of Mrs. Spaulding L. Jenkins, a block from the club, and Hopper decided to take a sleeper back to New York. Hergy showed up looking very pale and weazened, and at 10.30 or thereabout he said that he was all in and left the club. He told August, who sat beside him, that if it were not for his wife Dorothy, he would kill himself. He said that he was sick beyond remedy and would never be able to write again, and that life had thus lost all purpose and meaning. I incline to believe that there was more in all this than mere talk. He has been in a depressed state for several years past, and though he occasionally steps out of it, as he did when I visited him in West Chester on January 5, such breaks begin to become few and far between.

BALTIMORE, FEBRUARY 1, 1943.

It becomes more and more difficult for me to do any effective work. After a couple of hours at my desk I am beset by discomforts in the heart region, and have to lie down. A year or so ago I would recover from such a spell in half an hour, but now it takes a couple of hours. Meanwhile, there are shooting pains in my left arm, and I have occasional attacks of mild dizziness. Outwardly, I look quite well, and so everyone assumes that I am in prime condition. Yesterday I tackled my income-tax return as trustee of my mother's estate, and after four hours' hard work found that I had made a serious error, and had to do the whole work over again. My own return will keep me busy for two or three days.

BALTIMORE, FEBRUARY 4, 1943.

My gross income in 1942 was $23,499.93, but I am paying taxes upon but $14,701.66. My claim for expenses is $5,374.08, and I paid $829.78 in deductible taxes. The rest of the deduction consists of a claim of $2,594.41 for contributions. I began, during 1942, to send my collection of autographed presentation books and other association items to the Pratt Library. They went in three lots, running down to the letter N. After they had gone in, during the Summer, an income-tax auditor who came in to audit my 1941 return told me, to my surprise, that I could claim their full market value, though most of them, of course, cost me nothing. I thereupon asked Major Drake, of James F. Drake, Inc., New York, to appraise them, but he was going off to the war, and recommended G. A. Baker & Company, publishers of "American Book Prices Current." The head of the firm, Edward Lazard, made the appraisal for $40. He reported that the three lots were worth $6,170. This, of course, was far more than my 15% allowance for contributions, but I took as much as I could. I shall send in the remaining books during 1943, and have already had them appraised. They are worth $1,734, which will probably be under my allowance.

Paul Patterson told me today that his income in 1942 was $112,000 and that he is paying more than $68,000 in Federal income tax alone. Counting in State income and property taxes, he will pay taxes on the year to the amount of about 80% of his income.

BALTIMORE, FEBRUARY 18, 1943.

I went to New York on Sunday, February 14, and the next day I proceeded to Alfred Knopf's place at Purchase to spend the night with him. He is living there alone, and he confided to me on the way out that he is becoming very lonely. Blanche seldom goes to the place, and then only when there are guests. Unhappily, it is now becoming almost impossible to round up any guests, for the place is somewhat isolated and getting to it involves the use of a motor car. Knopf told me that most of the houses in the neighborhood had been vacated by their owners and that the nearest neighbor he was on good terms with lived six miles away. Nevertheless, he goes out every evening and has no company after dinner save his dog.

The weather was extremely cold, and when I awoke Tuesday

morning the temperature at the front door was 6 below zero. I slept under double blankets and was reasonably comfortable. Knopf himself has an electric blanket. He says it keeps him warm, but obviously it doesn't throw much heat into the room, for during the night his dog left his room and came to mine. Apparently, mine was somewhat warmer.

Despite his loneliness, Knopf lives comfortably enough. He has a new cook—a Swedish woman, who seems to be excellent. She turned out a dinner of which the principal dish was a fine sauerbraten. Knopf and I made a heavy meal of it. Before dinner we ate a marinated herring apiece, washed down with Aquavit. At dinner we had an excellent Rhine wine, and afterward I drank beer.

I slept very well, and the intense cold was really not very uncomfortable. However, when I got to New York and started to walk from the Grand Central Station to the Algonquin Hotel I came near freezing. The temperature in town must have been as low as in the country, and in addition there was a violent wind from the West. When I got to the hotel my ears felt as if they were about to fall off. On my return to Baltimore I found the temperature nearly 30 degrees. It seemed almost Spring-like.

BALTIMORE, MARCH 4, 1943.

We had another inquiry at the *Sun* office last night into an accident in the press room. Once more, a plate flew off while the press was running at full speed, and came very close to injuring a number of the pressmen. The investigation made by Kavanaugh indicates that no one was to blame. The plate that broke was properly fastened, and there was no other evidence of carelessness in the operation of the press. All of the men concerned were members of the International Union. This was a fortunate circumstance, for the union has been trying to convince the National Labor Relations Board that the *Sun* fires its members when there are accidents, but does not fire members of the office union.

The inquiry was carried on by William D. Macmillan, attorney for the *Sunpapers* in labor matters, and E. P. Kavanaugh. I was present, but took no part in the proceedings. The inquiry was taken down stenographically by Mrs. Lohrfinck. Among the witnesses was John Hopkins, an ignoramus who performed some notable feats of perjury during the proceedings before the National Labor Relations Board in 1938. He said that the flying fragments of the plate came near hitting him, and he confessed that he was tremendously scared. All the witnesses, including Alfred C. Miller, superintendent of the press room, agreed that no one was to blame for the accident—that is, all save Fred Hofsass, a machinist in charge of the presses. Hofsass, who turned out to be enormously more intelligent than any of the other witnesses, insisted that some one must have been to blame, and hazarded the guess that the plate had been insecurely fastened. Inasmuch as he stood alone, Kavanaugh decided to accept the opinion of Miller and the others.

BALTIMORE, MARCH 10, 1943.

My niece Virginia, after long delays and frequent alarms, has at last produced a baby. It is a boy and is to be named David Mencken Morrison.[1] Like any other primipara, Virginia calculated inaccurately, and so she began to announce the imminent birth of the baby at least six weeks before it actually appeared. During her last month her doctor detected a sudden rise in blood pressure. Fearing eclampsia, he sent her to hospital at once. After two or three days there she was completely recovered, and the actual delivery was accomplished without accident, though it seems to have been a rather difficult one. Her husband reported immediately afterward that the baby was somewhat damaged, but it has now recovered completely and seems to be a lively and vigorous youngster. Virginia herself is doing very well. She is nursing the baby and reports that he has a magnificent appetite.

He is the first child born in our family since Virginia was born herself, now nearly twenty-seven years ago.

BALTIMORE, MARCH 15, 1943.

August's temperature is down to normal, and he seems likely to make a good recovery. I am still intensely uncomfortable myself, and my plan to go to New York this week for a round of engagements has had to be abandoned. I was booked to take Edgar Masters and his girl Alice Davis to Lüchow's for dinner, and to bring . . . along. Alice

1 David Mencken Morrison, Mencken's grandnephew, was killed in a plane crash in 1974.

insisted on arranging a cocktail party for before dinner—greatly to my alarm and distaste, but I couldn't do anything about it. I also had a dinner engagement with Ralph Colin, one of the Knopf directors, and another with Channing Pollock.[1] I was booked to proceed to Princeton at the end of the week for a session with Julian P. Boyd, who had invited Edwin G. Conklin, the biologist, now a man of nearly 80. My head infection made me feel so miserable that this trip to New York was a sheer impossibility, and I was rather glad of the chance to send telegrams begging off all these engagements. The dinner with Masters and . . . would have been pleasant enough, but the cocktail party preceding promised to be a horror. I was not at all eager to see Colin or Pollock, and I had begun to fear that the trip to Princeton would not be as pleasant as my last one.

BALTIMORE, MARCH 25, 1943.

Alfred Knopf dropped off in Baltimore yesterday evening, and we had dinner together at the Belvedere Hotel. He came down from New York on the Congressional Limited, the prize train of the Pennsylvania Railroad, and should have arrived in Baltimore at 7:23. When I got to the station I was told that the Congressional had actually left New York thirty-five minutes late, and when it finally reached Baltimore its lateness had increased to an hour and ten minutes. The war traffic has begun to disorganize even the Pennsylvania. I found that the Belvedere has suspended its ordinary dinner on Wednesday nights and substituted a buffet meal. This buffet meal was excellent, and Knopf and I enjoyed it very much. Rather to my surprise, he drank a Bourbon highball with it, and told me that he had drunk another one on his way down on the train. So far as I can recall, this is the first time I have ever seen him drink whiskey, though I have often seen him drink such things as Aquavit.

BALTIMORE, MARCH 30, 1943.

Joe Hergesheimer was here yesterday and I had him to dinner at the Maryland Club last night. After dinner we went to Schellhase's for a few beers. He looked rather better physically than the last time I

1 Channing Pollock (1880–1946), author and playwright. His most successful play, *The Fool* (1922), was inspired by the life of St. Francis of Assisi.

saw him, though he is still thin. He told me that he is at work upon a history of Chester county, Pennsylvania, and that he believes the job will take him all year. Some anonymous donor has given the Chester County Historical Society $100 a month for a year to pay him, with an allowance in addition for secretarial and research aid. He said that he expected to knock off the book in a few months, but that he is now just finishing the introduction. It is to be a history with few names: there will be more about the geology and economic history of the county than about its notables. It sounded pretty dismal to me, but Joe professed to be greatly interested.

He came to Baltimore from Washington, where he had been a guest for several days of Mrs. Evalyn McLean,[1] who has an enormous house and entertains on a lavish scale. Night before last he was the guest at dinner of Huntington Cairns,[2] a Baltimorean who, until lately, was solicitor to the Treasury. Cairns has now got a well-paid life job in the Mellon Art Gallery. Regarding his duties Hergesheimer was somewhat vague. One of the other dinner guests was Robert Williams Wood, formerly professor of experimental physics at the Johns Hopkins and one of the worst bores ever seen on earth. Hergy said that he ruined the dinner. Now and then Wood calls me up, usually on Sunday nights, and I have a dreadful time getting rid of him. He is always looking for publicity of one sort or another, and I never get any for him, but he continues in hope. As in the last war, he now pretends that he has a hand in the design of all the new guns, bombs, etc., that the Army and Navy are using. This is buncombe: his inventions, in fact, never pan out. Cairns is a smart fellow and writes very well, but he wastes too much time on philosophy. He is now engaged upon a book on Plato. I'd as lief do one on Harding.

I urged Hergy to do a Washington novel. The town presents a really astounding picture, and no one, so far, has attempted to do it. Hergy promised to fall upon the job at once, but he will never tackle it. His days as a novelist, I believe, are definitely over. It seems to be

1 Evalyn Walsh McLean (1886–1947), prominent Washington social figure.
2 Huntington Cairns (1905–1985) was for many years secretary of the National Gallery of Art in Washington and the author or editor of numerous books, including *The Limits of Art* (1948) and *Legal Philosophy from Plato to Hegel* (1949). He and Mencken became good friends, and he edited *H. L. Mencken: The American Scene* (New York: Alfred A. Knopf, 1965), the largest and most representative of all the posthumous Mencken anthologies.

downright impossible for him to plan and execute an imaginative book. In part this is due to his poor health, which revolves around an excess of blood sugar, but there is also a mental collapse—a sort of playing out. If he went on insulin he'd probably feel much better, but he refuses to do so. He even refuses to follow the diet prescribed by Ben Baker. It excludes, of course, all starches and sugars, and both beer and wine are on the forbidden list. Yet Joe insisted on drinking a couple of *Seidel* of beer at Schellhase's.

He complains bitterly of his lack of money, but he is always moving about and usually puts up at private houses where the tips must run to much more than hotel bills. In Baltimore, last night, he was the guest of Mrs. Spaulding L. Jenkins. She is a pleasant woman, but I simply can't imagine staying at her house. Hergy is still hopeful of getting a government job in Washington, apparently in one of the innumerable propaganda departments, but his prospects certainly do not look good. He begins to be full of whims and crochets. He has now discovered, for example, that Julian P. Boyd is a dubious fellow, though they were the best of friends only a few months ago. He has also discovered that Marcella du Pont is a neurotic, and that her statements of fact are not to be relied on. Poor Dorothy, I suspect, is having a stormy time with him.

BALTIMORE, MARCH 31, 1943.

My health deteriorates steadily, and anything resembling sustained work is now impossible. After my struggle with my mail in the morning I begin to feel exhausted, and by noon I am beset by discomforts in the region of the heart. At any other time of the day or evening two hours of work are enough to floor me, and I have to lie down. I take a nap every afternoon before dinner, but it restores me very little, and I always awaken feeling wretched, as I do every morning on arising. Of late I have been sleeping fairly well at night, and have been aroused only seldom by heart discomforts—always following long, vexatious, more or less idiotic dreams. Up to a few weeks ago such attacks were frequent, and more than once, awaking in the middle of the night, I began to believe that my end had come. At all times there is a dreadful malaise, suggesting that of influenza. I feel unutterably miserable.

Perhaps I should see Wainwright, but the last time I did so he gave me no relief, and offered none. Very often there are vague pains in the region of the pit of the stomach, whether from the stomach itself or from the heart I do not know. Last Sunday night I was aroused four times by severe heartburn. It yielded each time to bicarbonate of soda, but every time save the last it came back.

I have been making very slow progress with my record of my magazine days, and have barely reached the years 1916 and 1917. If I could put in four or five hours a day upon it, I'd move quickly, but so much sustained work is now impossible. After an hour at my desk I begin to tire, and after two hours I am useless.

BALTIMORE, APRIL 8, 1943.

We hauled Eddie Murphy to the crematory this morning. He died in Orlando, Florida on April 4th. He had been ill for years, and was retired by the *Sun* four years ago. His principal affliction for a long while was heart trouble, but just before his retirement he developed active tuberculosis. After some months at Asheville he returned to Baltimore, but Maxson, the staff surgeon, decided that he was unfit for service, and so the board retired him. He died at Orlando after only a few days of active illness.

His wife, Julia Austin, whom I have known since she was a little girl, prepared to bring the body home, but found that it was impossible to get any train accommodations except an upper berth. Finally the railroad people advised her to come home by car, and this she did with a colored boy of Orlando driving her. She arrived in fairly good shape, and was able to attend the funeral at Jenkins's funeral parlor this morning. I called her up at Orlando as soon as I heard of Eddie's death and she asked me to arrange the funeral. He had been born a Catholic, but had quarreled with the Church and had requested her to see that he was turned off by an Episcopal clergyman and that his body be cremated. She told me that he had been greatly impressed by Sara's simple funeral in 1935 and wanted his own to be similar. I tried to recruit the Rev. Richard Baker, Ben Baker's brother, for the ceremony but it turned out that he had a war engagement that he couldn't break. I then began shopping around among the other Episcopal clergymen of the town but found them all engaged. I finally called the Rev. Hugh Powers, rector of the parish of the Holy Innocents, to which my sister Gertrude ostensibly belongs. Powers read the service in a very dignified manner, but Paul Patterson told me later that he thought it had been a little too long. It ran 18 minutes. After it was over Kavanaugh, two other men and I accompanied the body to the crematory. We simply deposited it in the place and then left.

Eddie and I had been friends since the year 1900. We often differed on matters of *Sun* policy, but nevertheless we kept on good terms. In the days when he was managing editor of the *Evening Sun* and had authority over the editorial page, he often chopped my articles, and sometimes he held them out altogether. I never complained of this, for it has always been my theory that an editor should have absolute authority.

Murphy had been greatly upset in late years by the activities of the Newspaper Guild. When, in 1938, the Guild won an election in the office he was tremendously surprised. He had been predicting that it would be beaten by a vote of at least two to one.

He leaves Julia well provided for. He owns a good house in Guilford and has left a considerable amount of insurance. One of his policies for $75,000 was taken out by the *Sun* many years ago and the *Sun* has always paid the premiums. In addition, Murphy owns 350 shares of stock in the A. S. Abell Company. This is recapturable, but under the formula established it will probably bring Julia at least $13,000. She has no immediate relatives in Maryland. Her brother, who took to evil courses, died in prison some years ago, and one of her three sisters is also dead. The other two are living in California. Murphy's brother, who lives in Hanover, Penna., refused to come to the funeral because an Episcopalian was reading the service. Julia told me a long story about the reasons for Eddie's desertion of the Church, but I must say that it seemed rather improbable. My own guess is that the battle with the Archbishop was largely responsible. Murphy took the Archbishop's blasts very badly and was full of a yearning for revenge. In general, his attitude toward the Catholic Church was rather respectful. I well recall times when he objected to things that I had written about it in articles for the *Evening Sun*. It was, in fact, generally understood in the office that he was tender on the subject.

BALTIMORE, APRIL 9, 1943.

Paul Patterson gave a dinner at the Maryland Club last night to Haley of the Manchester *Guardian*. The guests were principally the younger executives of the *Sun*. Captain Leland P. Lovette, U.S.N., came over from Washington and with him he brought one of his associates, Commander Barry. I did not go to the dinner, but dropped in afterward. As I entered Barry was finishing a speech. It seemed rather boastful and hollow to me, and I was not surprised to discover afterward that Barry was somewhat in liquor.

Haley had made a speech before I got in, but he was called on for another later on. This second one was very brief and was mainly devoted to describing a press conference at Navy headquarters in Hawaii. A number of newspaper correspondents were present and the chief hero on exhibition was the commander of an American submarine squadron on the Japanese front. This commander reported that he had sunk three or four small transports and probably disposed of several thousand Japanese soldiers. One of the reporters asked him what he had done when those soldiers were thrown into the water. His answer was: "I machine-gunned the sons of bitches." The officer in charge of the conference thereupon said to the reporters: "Please remember, gentlemen, this is off the record."

BALTIMORE, APRIL 14, 1943.

Blanche Knopf was here yesterday to consult Dr. Alan C. Woods. I could not ask her to lunch, for I had a lunch engagement at the Merchants Club with Spaulding Albert, advertising manager of the *Sunpapers*, to meet Don Tobin, the new manager of the O'Neill department store. But I met Blanche at the Belvedere at 2.30 and we palavered until she left for Washington at 4.30. We discussed at some length the future of the business. Her son, Alfred, Jr., shows no sign of wanting to enter it after the war, even if he survives, which is not too probable, for he is an aviator.

BALTIMORE, APRIL 15, 1943.

I had lunch yesterday at the Merchants Club as the guest of Spalding Albert, advertising manager of the *Sunpapers*. Don Tobin, the new manager of the O'Neill department store, was also a guest. He is an extremely charming young man, and greatly resembles F. Scott Fitzgerald. He is a Dartmouth college graduate and felt an inclination toward store-keeping even in his college days. He has been extremely successful, and came to Baltimore from Hartford.

He told me that the life of a department store manager is now one grand series of headaches. He said that in the O'Neill store there was little difficulty about counter help, for most of the saleswomen are oldsters who have been on the staff for years, but he said that in the office there was a constant overturn of labor. Girls came in knowing nothing. They were taught laboriously, and after a while reached pay of as much as $40 a week. Thereupon they quit to go to work in a war plant at even more money and the whole grind had to be repeated.

Tobin said that there was absolutely no stock of silk in the Baltimore stores. He said that Bonwit Lennon some time ago advertised ready-made silk dresses at $99 and that all of the other department store people are still wondering where they got them. Tobin said that the new rayons are not only as good as silk but even better. I complained that those I had tried for pajamas washed badly, but he said that in the new ones that difficulty has been overcome. He said that rayon dyes better than silk and is more durable. I'll bear this in mind whenever the time comes to renew my stock of pajamas. I used to buy lengths of silk at Hutzler's annual silk sale and then have pajamas made up by McPherson, but for two years past there have been no silk sales.

BALTIMORE, APRIL 23, 1943.

Emma, the maid, reports that Prudence, the laundress, had a fire in her house yesterday and that a large basket of my laundry was destroyed. It included 11 shirts, 4 suits of underwear, 2 suits of pajamas, 5 handkerchiefs, 13 pairs of socks, and numerous bath towels, wash cloths, bathroom mats, and other such things, not to mention 5 table doilies, 8 curtains, 5 aprons, and one of Emma's uniforms.

I discover on inquiry of Irving Rolker, the insurance man, that these losses are not covered by my insurance policies.

BALTIMORE, APRIL 26, 1943.

In New York last week I had a brief palaver with Alfred Knopf about my own books. I begin to tire of the record of my magazine days that I have been preparing, and feel like laying it aside for six months or so in favor of some other work. Various enterprises suggest themselves—first of all, my projected supplement to "The American

Language." Another is "Advice to Young Men," so often and so long postponed. Another is a sort of Mencken Encyclopedia, made up of extracts from my writings over many years, arranged by subject and probably with additions. A fourth is a smaller book of aphorisms, partly reprinted but mainly new.[1] I have materials in hand for all these books, not to mention "Homo Sapiens," which has been in my mind, off and on, for years. Knopf said he was in favor of the supplement to "The American Language." Unhappily, I have gathered so many notes for it that putting them in order and writing the text would be a really formidable job, and I fear that my strength would not be sufficient for it. The doctors urge me, in fact, to tackle nothing involving hard and sustained work. But I am inclined to make the attempt nevertheless, for even if I break down before the job is done the part completed may make a saleable book. Knopf pointed out that I might also start one of the smaller books and put in licks on it in the intervals of my work on the supplement. I have often carried on two books at one time in the past. But the past is not the present, and my old capacity for heavy work is gone. It is only on very fortunate days that I can sit squarely at my desk for more than a few hours.

BALTIMORE, APRIL 26, 1943.

Joe Hergesheimer is in New York this week as the guest of Frank Case at the Algonquin Hotel. He spent a week there last year on the same terms, and told me later that he was uncomfortable and would never do it again. He said that for part of the time he was unendurably lonely in his apartment, and that for the rest of the time he was oppressed by the need of being polite to Frank and Bertha Case. They were very kind, and he is fond of them, but he was bound more or less by their engagements. But now he is trying it all over. This irresolution is one of the most marked symptoms of his general deterioration. He is always making plans and resolves and then abandoning them. Every time I meet him he promises to settle down to a serious novel, but so far as I know he has never actually written a line. The last time he was in Baltimore we talked of a novel about Washington

---

1 The projected Mencken Encyclopedia eventually became *A Mencken Chrestomathy*, published in 1949, and the "smaller book of aphorisms" became *Minority Report*, the manuscript of which was lost after his 1948 stroke and which appeared only posthumously in 1956.

in wartime. He has plenty of material for it, and if he were in a normal state of mind and body he would make a good job of it. He promised faithfully to tackle it, but I know very well that he has not done so.

It is now more than eight years since Joe has done anything worth serious attention. I well recall that he had begun to turn to trash in Sara's time, for she was much upset by it. And Sara will be dead eight years on May 31.

BALTIMORE, APRIL 29, 1943.

Paul Patterson returned to Baltimore from New York last Friday with a severe laryngitis, and was put to bed by Dr. Maxson. He had been played out by the round of publishers' meetings in New York, including the annual meeting of the Associated Press. They went on for ten days and were very fatiguing. Two weeks ago Col. Robert R. McCormick, publisher of the Chicago *Tribune*, tried to induce Patterson to run for president of the Associated Press against the incumbent, Robert McLean of the Philadelphia *Bulletin*, a blundering and incompetent man, often at odds with Kent Cooper, the general manager. It has always been Patterson's ambition to be president of the A.P. and he was thus sorely tempted, but he saw that it would be unwise to encourage a split among the A.P. directors in the face of the government's current suit, so he refused to meet McCormick for a discussion of the business. Harry Black and I both advised him that this decision was a sound one. Soon or late McLean is bound to go, for he is irritating to directors and staff alike, and shows very little competence, despite his constant industry. When that time comes Patterson will be the logical candidate for his post. To take it now, on the motion and with the help of McCormick, would be very unwise, for many of the other members of the board dislike McCormick intensely, chiefly because he has opposed Roosevelt in the *Tribune* on the war issue, and are, in fact, more violently against him than they are against Roosevelt.

On Sunday morning, April 25, lying in bed at his house, Patterson was amazed to find on the last page of the *Sunday Sun* a flaming interview with Mayor Howard W. Jackson, now a candidate for reëlection. In it Jackson was permitted to state his claims to votes on his own grounds; it was, in fact, an immensely effective campaign document. Inasmuch as it has been the stated policy of the *Sunpapers*, ever since the White Paper of 1919, to keep political *Tendenz* out of the news columns, this interview aroused Patterson's dudgeon, and despite his illness he started an investigation at once. From his son, Maclean, managing editor of the *Sun*, he found that the interview had originated in the office of Hamilton Owens, acting editor-in-chief of the *Sunpapers*, though it was actually written by Harry S. Sherwood, borrowed from the *Evening Sun* local staff for the purpose. Hamilton Owens, in fact, had not only recruited Sherwood to write it, but had laid out its plan in some detail. He was therefore brought to the mat, and made the defense that the whole enterprise had been ordered by his superior, John W. Owens. John Owens is still on sick leave, but he has begun to telephone suggestions to his editorial staff, and sometimes sends in evangelistic editorials of his own. Jackson, it appeared, called him up last week, said that the campaign was going badly, and asked for help. Disregarding the White Paper, and Patterson's years-long effort to keep political propaganda out of the news columns, he had thereupon ordered the interview. Now that it had been printed there was nothing to do save to print one with Jackson's Republican opponent, Theodore R. McKeldin,[1] in precisely the same place and covering the same space. This was done, with Sherwood dug out on Sunday to do the job.

When Patterson told me all this yesterday I could hardly keep from laughing in his face. Once more the chickens are coming home to roost. John Owens is an old-time *Sun* man, trained under Frank Kent, and it is simply impossible for him to see any unwisdom in using the news columns to support candidates. The news columns and the editorial columns are all one to him, and in both he runs to an extravagant and unintelligent partisanship. Once, I recall, he told me flatly that he thought the doctrines set forth in the White Paper were false and pernicious, though he knew that I had written it. Since the beginning of the war his editorials have been screams instead of arguments, and it was mainly because of his insane evangelistic whooping that I stopped writing for the editorial page of the *Sunday Sun* in January, 1941. Before that time I had frequently remonstrated to Patterson against what was being printed, but since then I have kept silent,

1 Theodore R. McKeldin (1900–1974) served two terms as mayor of Baltimore, from 1943 to 1947 and again from 1963 to 1967, and two as governor of Maryland, from 1951 to 1958.

content to watch maliciously his reduction of the *Sunpapers* to their old level. Thus I got a certain amount of joy out of Patterson's ire, and if he noticed it he had only himself to blame for it. When John Owens melodramatically resigned in the face of the enemy at the time of the battle with Archbishop Curley, Patterson should have let him go. I argued for it very earnestly, but he was solicited to come back, and ever since then he has kept Patterson in a kind of terror. It will be impossible, of course, to do anything about the Jackson interview. John is still ill and must be handled tenderly. Moreover, Patterson is intimidated by him and will not venture to tackle him. The blame, if any, will be heaped on Hamilton Owens, though everyone knows that he has no policy or principles of his own, but simply sings loudly whatever hymn is currently lined out.

BALTIMORE, MAY 13, 1943.

I went to Washington today for lunch at the Army and Navy Club with General James K. Parsons, formerly commander of the Third Corps Area, with headquarters in Baltimore, and now retired and living in San Antonio, Texas. The old boy has come north in the hope of getting some employment in the war, but though he looks to be in perfect health he is sixty-six years old, and there is no room in the Army for men past sixty. There are some exceptions—for example, George C. Marshall, the present Chief of Staff, who is sixty-two—but they are not many. All the field commanders are much younger. D. D. Eisenhower, in command in North Africa, is but fifty-three, and there are plenty of generals who are younger. Parsons told me that there is hardly a West Pointer in the Army, with more than five years of experience since leaving the Academy, who is not at least a lieutenant-colonel. He said that virtually all the company officers in the service, and nearly all the majors, are youngsters who have been taken in from civil life since conscription began.

The general is not too optimistic about the future, despite the successes in Africa. He believes that Hitler will abandon Mussolini, and that Italy will thus fall readily, but he thinks that getting over the Alps to tackle Hitler at home will be a formidable job. He says that the victories in Africa were almost wholly due to superior air power. Why Hitler withdrew his air he does not know. Its present state, in fact, is a mystery to the Army chiefs at Washington. The most common belief is that he has run short of air officers, and is trying to train more. There is no evidence that his production of airships has fallen off.

The general is an Alabaman, and when I last saw him was planning to buy a small daily newspaper in Talladega and have some fun. He told me that he had made a tentative arrangement to take it over at a very moderate price. But before the deal could be put through a number of war industries were established in the vicinity, thousands of yokels swarmed in, business began to boom, the paper doubled and tripled its receipts and the price became prohibitive. I asked the general why he had chosen to live in San Antonio. He said that it was because the town has a balmy climate and is full of retired Army officers, just as Annapolis is full of retired Navy officers. They constitute a pleasant society, and he has plenty of golfing partners. He himself once commanded the Army post in the town, and thus knows a great many of the local bigwigs. He invited me to come down for a visit, but I had to reply that the state of my health made it unlikely that I'd ever be able to undertake so long a journey. The train service to and from the South is now so bad that travel is a genuine affliction.

BALTIMORE, JUNE 2, 1943.

Dr. F. E. Townsend, the old age pension man, dropped off in Baltimore yesterday and I took him to lunch at the Belvedere. He had with him a mysterious stranger whose name I did not catch. The stranger was a short, squatty fellow with a goatish beard, but seemed to be quite young. I somehow gathered the impression that he was some sort of pedagogue. Obviously, he is the latest wizard to fasten himself upon the poor doctor. I asked Townsend what had become of those who buzzed around him four or five years ago. He replied, with a sad smile, that they had all departed, and that all of them had turned out to be rogues. One got the Townsend weekly into debt to the amount of $25,000, and the doctor had to take up a special collection among the old folks to restore it to solvency.

He stopped off in Baltimore to consult me about an autobiography that he has just finished. I asked him how long it was, and he said about 2,000 words. It turned out on cross-examination that there were 160 typewritten pages, which indicates a manuscript of at least 40,000 words. The doctor asked me if I thought he should submit it to a commercial publisher or publish it himself. I advised him to publish it himself.[1] He said that he thought he could sell at least 5,000 copies to the old folks at $1.50 apiece. My own belief is that he'll be able to sell more. He has concocted a plausible plan for giving his local leaders a commission of 50¢ a copy. This will inspire them to force the book, not only on the old folks, but also on everyone else they can reach.

The doctor, who is now 76 years old, looked to be in good health, but he is somewhat thin. He told me that he spends a large part of his time traveling about the country by air, visiting and haranguing his customers. He said that there are now more members on his rolls than ever before, but when I pressed him for precise figures he evaded the subject. My guess is that his movement has bogged down to the irreducible minimum of incurable come-ons. He has abandoned his old demand for a $200 pension, and the amount promised is now somewhat vague. But he has stuck to all his other ideas, including his insistence that every pensioner be forced to spend his pension within thirty days after receiving it.

The doctor told me a long tale about his cousin, a man of his own age, who lately came down with cancer of the prostate. He said that at his advice the cousin submitted to castration and that the effects were magnificent. The cancer vanished and the patient put on 40 pounds of flesh. This seems plausible enough. Castration for cancer of the prostate is now widely practised. Apparently the testicular hormones encourage the development of the cancer and when the supply of them is cut off it tends to wither. Townsend told me that his cousin is now strong enough to operate a three-acre chicken farm and is otherwise in prime condition. He said that he was thinking seriously of getting castrated himself. His prostate is normal, but he believes that he is underweight and that adding 30 or 40 pounds would improve his general health. He said somewhat primly: "My reproductive stage is now over, and I see no reason why I shouldn't sacrifice a couple of useless glands."

Meanwhile, he is giving himself regular injections of some sort of testosterone preparation. He told me that it is the most effective stimulant he has ever discovered. When, after a long trip across the country, he finds himself in a low state of mind and body a couple of shots fill him with vim and vigor. He didn't mention any specific effect upon his gonads and I didn't ask him.

---

1 Dr. Townsend's autobiography, *New Horizons*, appeared later that year under the imprint of the J. L. Stewart Publishing Company of Chicago.

He added some interesting reminiscences of his days as a doctor practising among poor people. Once, he said, he was called on to deliver a moron girl who was having an illegitimate child. It turned out when the child was born that it was stone blind. A gonococcal infection in the mother had worked its way into the uterus and had destroyed the child's eyes before any measures could be taken against it. Townsend said he looked at the poor creature, which was a girl, and said to himself: "What a dreadful life lies ahead of you. Here you are—a girl, stone blind and illegitimate, with a half-idiotic mother. What chance have you in this world?" His answer to his own question, he said, was to load a syringe with a lethal dose of morphine and inject it into the poor baby's arm. An hour later it was an angel.

BALTIMORE, JUNE 2, 1943.

Today I handed the following to Edgar Ellis, librarian of the *Sunpapers,* and asked him to put it in the envelope bearing my name in the morgue:

Baltimore, June 1, 1943.

Save in the event that the circumstances of my death make necessary a news story it is my earnest request to my old colleagues of the *Sunpapers* that they print only a brief announcement of it, with no attempt at a biographical sketch, no portrait, and no editorial.

H. L. Mencken[1]

NEW YORK, JUNE 14, 1943.

On Saturday afternoon, June 12, I went to Princeton to visit Dr. Julian P. Boyd, who has under way a volume of my letters. I got off the train at Trenton and then proceeded by a local train to Princeton Junction, where Boyd met me with his car. There was dinner at his house in the evening. . . . Another guest from New York was Thom-

1 Mencken's wishes in this matter were disregarded. Two big stories dominated the front page of the *Sun* for Monday, January 30, 1956: a fire at a church festival had killed ten people and injured 230 more, and the local transit company had gone out on strike. The account of Mencken's death had to be squeezed in between these two things. Nevertheless, there was a news story, a long biographical account by Hamilton Owens, several shorter pieces, a full page of pictures, and an editorial.

as W. Streeter, a rich lawyer and promoter who is a member of the advisory council of the Princeton University Library, of which Boyd is the librarian. Streeter . . . and I put up at the Princeton Inn. Once I was registered Boyd took me to the library and introduced me to two women of the staff who have undertaken to do an enormous bibliography of my writings. If they ever actually carry out the scheme they have outlined, it will run to at least 15,000 items. It will include not only everything I have ever written myself, but also everything that has been written about me. Most of this, of course, I will have to furnish myself, for the only record of it is in my scrap-books. The ladies are still at work on such obvious things as my contributions to the *Smart Set* and the *American Mercury*. I warned them that they have taken on a really herculean job, but they insisted that they were ready to go through with it. Once they have finished the more accessible stuff I'll give them some help, and then wait to see what happens. In any case their labors, even if not completed, will be of some use to me in preparing my record of my magazine days. But it is hard to imagine anyone else wanting a Mencken bibliography on so vast a scale. Nothing even remotely comparable to it has ever been attempted before in America. E. H. O'Neill, of the English department of the University of Pennsylvania, also has a Mencken bibliography under way, but it falls far short in scope of that planned by the two women. O'Neill came to Baltimore to see me on February 18, 1943, and I heard him at length. He made only an indifferent impression on me, and I have no hope that he will ever complete the work, but the two women may conceivably stick to it. When I told Boyd that it seemed cruel to me to let them undertake so dreadful a labor, he replied that they regarded it as a welcome relief from their regular duties at the library, which are even worse.[1]

After my session with them Boyd took Streeter . . . and me to call on President Harold W. Dodds[2] at his house. Dodds had set out what he called a grog-table, but I drank iced tea, and so did he, and so did Streeter . . . and Boyd. I opened the subject of a master's degree for

---

1 Neither the O'Neill nor the Princeton bibliography ever appeared. The standard (and exhaustively complete) work is *H.L.M.: The Mencken Bibliography*, compiled by Betty Adler with the assistance of Jane Wilhelm and published by the Johns Hopkins Press in 1961. She updated it with *A Ten-Year Supplement* in 1971. *A Second Ten-Year Supplement*, compiled by Vincent Fitzpatrick, was published in 1986.

2 Harold W. Dodds (1889–1980) was president of Princeton from 1933 to 1957.

Paul Patterson, and had a chance to discuss it with Dodds without the others hearing. He was very cagey but seemed inclined toward it—mainly, it appeared, on the ground that it would please Harry C. Black and thus encourage him to make some fresh donations to his *alma mater*. I told him that Black would undoubtedly be pleased, but that Patterson really deserved it. It would be easy for him, I said, to get a couple of LL.D.'s, but he prefers the M.A. of Princeton. Dodds then asked me why I had never accepted an LL.D. myself, and I replied that the only degree I craved was that of D.D., which would enable me to perform marriage ceremonies in Maryland. He is a very amiable and even effusive fellow, and seems to be a quite typical American college president. His wife came in and invited us to see the gardens of the presidential palace, which turned out to be lovely. The wet Spring has greatly prospered the lawns of Princeton, and the whole place looks peaceful and restful. It is easy to understand the charm of life in a college town—at all events, for the man who likes quiet. As for me, I am a cockney, and could not be contented save in a large city.

At dinner at the Boyds' the other guests were Dr. E. G. Conklin and a woman named Marquand, the widow of one of the benefactors of Princeton. La Marquand turned out to be a handsome and charming woman, but I was chiefly interested in Conklin, who was professor of zoölogy at Princeton from 1908 to 1933 and is now professor emeritus. He is nearly 80 years old but seems to be in very good health. He is a mousy old fellow with a white moustache, and somehow suggests a retired bookkeeper, but he is actually a biologist of the first chop, and I was delighted to sit down with him. Our mutual friendship for Raymond Pearl started us off, and we were soon on very good terms. In the course of the evening Streeter let fall something in favor of so-called psychical research, and at once Conklin fell upon him with vigor. He sought to retreat behind the authority of Joseph B. Rhine, of Duke University, and there I had him, for I spent an afternoon with Rhine on the Fred M. Hanes lawn at Durham three or four years ago, and came away convinced that he was a complete jackass. I like Conklin very much and hope to see him again. He is not only a scientifico of genuine attainments; he is also a very pleasant old fellow, despite his very conventional exterior. We had old-fashioned cocktails before dinner, and at the meal drank some Alsatian wine . . . and some Château Clemens that I had brought from Baltimore. After dinner I got down a few beers. I turned in at midnight and slept very well. The Princeton class of 1903 was holding a reunion at the inn, and during the late afternoon its members got down a great many mint-juleps on the lawn. But by the time I turned in they were all asleep, and most of them were still asleep when I turned out Sunday morning.

Mrs. Boyd invited me to breakfast at the Boyd house in Broadmoor . . . but I had heard of her servant troubles and so declined. When I tried to get breakfast at the inn I found that it was too late, for the dining-room had closed, and I could find no other eating-place in the neighborhood. We were booked to go to the house of Willard Thorpe, one of the young professors of English, at one o'clock and I assumed that we would have lunch there, but though Thorpe set out some drinks there was no mention of lunch, and I actually got nothing to eat until nearly 4 o'clock, when . . . I lunched in the Pennsylvania Station in New York. Thorpe is at work on a large-scale history of American literature, and has collected a large number of early American novels. He has them stacked in shelves which completely cover the walls of the largest room in his house. This room, which is done in pine, looks out upon a fine lawn, with trees beyond. Altogether, the place is very attractive. Thorpe had brought some piano duets from the Princeton library, and he and I shut the door on the others and tackled Schubert and Mozart. We played for half an hour or so, but Thorpe's technic was hardly equal to the music, and I was glad when the performance was over. Streeter had left for New York early in the morning. Boyd had too little gas to take . . . me to Princeton Junction, so I had to go from Princeton there in a little jerk-water train. In the station I met Gilbert Chinard,[1] professor of French at Princeton and an old acquaintance of mine, and he joined me for the trip to New York. . . .

In the evening I had dinner at Lüchow's with . . . George Nathan, who has been laid up for eight weeks by neuralgia, and suffering very severe pain. He looked somewhat dilapidated and had little to say. Eckstein, the *Wirt* at Lüchow's, told us of his troubles. He is allowed one meat point a month for every meal he served in December, 1942. This gives him 47,000 points a month, which is far too little. The idiots

---

1 Gilbert Chinard (1881–1972) had taught French and comparative literature at the Johns Hopkins from 1919 to 1936, and it was there that Mencken came to know him. He transferred to Princeton in 1937.

in charge of such things have made the rule apply to all eating-houses alike, which works greatly in favor of the cheaper places, for many of the meals they served in December consisted of nothing more than a glass of milk and a slab of pie, whereas those served by Eckstein were nearly all of full size. He had but two meat-dishes on his bill of fare— roast beef and the sausage he makes in the house. I had a plate of jellied soup and an order of cold whitefish in aspic, both very good. I drank a *Seidel* each of six of the beers on draught, and found them all bad. The best was Schaefer's, which used to be the worst in New York before Prohibition. The worst was Prior's, made somewhere in Pennsylvania.

From Lüchow's Nathan and I went to the Stork Club and there met Walter Winchell.[1] His thoughts seemed to be concentrated on war propaganda, and I was glad when he left us. I was in bed at the Algonquin by midnight. There was a stiff wind blowing through my room all night, and I slept very well.

NEW YORK, JUNE 15, 1943.

Blanche Knopf handed me a slip today showing the following sales of my three *Days* books to yesterday:

Happy Days	10,953
Newspaper Days	8,763
Heathen Days	8,492

A third edition of "Heathen Days" is now on the press. The first edition was 7,500 copies, the second was 1,500 and the third is 1,500. The jump in the sales is due to an order for 800 copies for the Navy, received on June 10. These copies will go to the libraries of ships and shore stations. In addition the Council of Books in Wartime has sent in a request for permission to print 50,000 paper-bound copies on thin paper for the use of American forces abroad. This council, I believe, consists mainly of publishers, but the Army, Navy, Marine Corps and Coast Guard are represented. It borrows the plates and pays for the printing. One of the conditions is that none of the books shall be distributed in the United States: they are all to go to the forces overseas. I am to receive one cent a copy royalty—little enough, but there seems

1 Walter Winchell (1897–1972), widely known newspaper gossip columnist of the time.

to be no way to decline. It will cost the government 12½ cents a copy
to print the books. Large numbers of them, of course, will be brought
home after the war, but by that time the sales of the regular edition
will be over.

BALTIMORE, JUNE 20, 1943.

Rachel Hawks called up this morning to remind me that it is just
42 years since I was best man at her wedding to Arthur.[1] This was my
first service as best man. I was then less than 22 years old; Arthur
himself was about 25, and I think that Rachel was 23. At all events,
she told me this morning that she is older than I am. Arthur is a rather
stolid and uninspiring fellow, but nevertheless I believe that their marriage has been happy. Rachel, who is a sculptor, has occupied herself
with her work, and though her success has not been brilliant, it has at
least been satisfying.

She and Arthur had been married nearly fifteen years before they
had a child. That child was a son, Marshall. He is now a lieutenant
in the army, and was lately married himself. Rachel told me that he
seems to have got a good wife. He is stationed in Mississippi, and his
bride is a native. When he sent me the announcement of his engagement he half apologized for picking her from the Worst American
State, but I assured him that my low opinion of its people was confined
to the males. I called his attention to the fact that my own wife came
from the neighboring State of Alabama. Young Marshall is an earnest
and decent but apparently rather futile fellow. He is greatly interested
in the stage, and has told me that when he escapes from the army he'll
very likely devote himself to it, probably in the capacity of stage manager and producer.

Rachel is a little woman, and very energetic. The success of the
Hawks household has been due to her almost entirely, not to Arthur.
He is a lethargic and lazy fellow and never undertakes any exertion
without prodding. He has a job with the Consolidated Gas and Electric Company as a sort of superior press agent, and is as beautifully
content with it as if it were the office of Pope.

---

1 Arthur Hawks had been one of Mencken's closest friends when they were in school
 together and was later instrumental in helping him secure his first newspaper job
 on the Baltimore *Morning Herald.*

BALTIMORE, JULY 4, 1943.

I have about finished my notes to the three "Days" books, begun six or eight weeks ago. They include all sorts of additions and corrections. When I undertook them I thought that I'd be able to get all of them into one box, but they have now gone to at least 100,000 words, and there will have to be a box for each of the three books.[1] I have had Mrs. Lohrfinck make two fair copies. One will go to the Pratt Library at my death, with the provision that it be kept sealed until twenty-five years after my death or the year 1970, whichever is the more remote. The other will go to some other library on the same conditions. There is a lot of stuff in the notes that could not be printed now—for example, the real names of people who appear under invented names in the books. I have also dug a lot of stuff out of the *Sun* morgue, about such figures in old-time Baltimore as Eugene Grannan, John Weyler, Major Richard M. Venable, Al Herford, Fred Gottlieb and Max Ways.[2] Many of the clippings in the morgue were so yellow and brittle with age that it was hard to handle them. They are now copied on all-rag paper and so a little of the history of Baltimore is saved from oblivion. I have added many glosses and commentaries of my own.

At the urging of Harold W. Ross I have also begun a new series for the *New Yorker*, but it remains to be seen how far it will go, and I am determined that it shall not make another book. Three volumes of reminiscences in the same mood are enough: if I ever set down any more of my memories the job will be done more seriously. I hope, soon

1 The three boxes of "Additions and Corrections" to the *Days* books were opened at the Enoch Pratt Free Library on January 29, 1981, the twenty-fifth anniversary of Mencken's death. They were something of a surprise. Everyone present for that occasion knew of the five-volume "Diary" and the four boxes of "Letters and Documents Relating to the Baltimore *Sunpapers*," but the existence of the "Additions and Corrections" had not been suspected.

2 Eugene Grannan was a Baltimore District Court judge; there are anecdotes about him in *Newspaper Days*, pp. 22–23 and 29–30. John Weyler, warden of the Maryland Penitentiary, appears in the same work, p. 31. Major Richard M. Venable, "a member of the City Council and one of the stars of the Maryland bar," is described in that book, pp. 43–48. Abraham Lincoln ("Al") Herford, a boxing promoter and manager, has a whole chapter (chapter eight, "A Master of Gladiators," pp. 96–106) devoted to him in *Heathen Days*. Fred Gottlieb, "a rich brewer who was also an amateur flautist," is mentioned in *Newspaper Days*, p. 142. Max Ways, city editor of the Baltimore *Morning Herald*, gave Mencken his first job as a reporter and is a major figure throughout *Newspaper Days*.

or late, to resume my record of my magazine days, now stalled at the end of 1918. It can't be printed while some of the persons dealt with are still alive, but I see no objection to depositing it with public libraries, to be held confidential for at least twenty-five years like "Thirty-five Years of Newspaper Work" and my notes and additions to the three "Days" books. In these days, even setting aside the question of private feelings, it is impossible to write and print freely. We are hobbled by a censorship that, at best, will last a long while.

BALTIMORE, JULY 8, 1943.

Marcella du Pont came to Baltimore from Washington yesterday, and I took her to lunch at the Belvedere. I met her at the hotel at 1 p.m, and had to start her back at 2.41, for the labor hearings mentioned in these notes yesterday were in progress.[1] She had little to say, and was, in fact, rather tiresome. She told me that Joe Hergesheimer had invited her to visit him and Dorothy at Stone Harbor, N.J., and she proposed that I go along. I refused, and advised her to refuse herself. Joe, according to her account, is working on his projected history of Chester county, Penna., and apparently making heavy weather of it. One day last week he called her up in Washington, told her that he was greatly in need of an out-of-print book that he named, and calmly suggested that she get it for him from a bookseller she patronizes. She said that Joe has fallen into the habit of accepting and expecting such favors, and begins to take them as a matter of course. The last time he was in Washington he allowed her to buy him a box of cigars. She said that he reports that he and Dorothy are living without a servant, and that they share the cooking between them. The cottage is small, and when Joe is at work Dorothy goes to the beach. There is one guest-room, and when two guests are present the male one apparently has to bunk with Joe. I told Marcella that I simply could not imagine putting up in such a household. I'd be ashamed to lay such burdens on Dorothy, who is lame and in pain. Obviously, Joe's talk of cooking is mere talk. Dorothy undoubtedly does it all, and also the dish-washing and parlor-maid work. I told Marcella that if I ever visited them I'd insist on putting up at a hotel—if there is one at

---

1 Not included in this selection.

Stone Harbor—and that I'd greatly prefer not visiting them at all. The trip to Stone Harbor is apparently long and onerous.

Marcella said that Thurman Arnold[1] had told her that he (Arnold) had got Joe a job in the government service a year or so ago at the request of Evalyn McLean, but that when he reported the fact to McLean she told him that Joe refused it. This sounded extremely improbable. Either Arnold or McLean was lying, and maybe both. Joe, as a matter of fact, would have taken anything that offered him as much as $4,000 a year: he told me so himself at the time. The job that he tried so hard to get from Dexter M. Keezer was no better. I begin to suspect that he is completely done for. He is not only ill and quite unable to do any decent work: he has also begun to lose all his old dignity, and even his self-respect. Marcella told me, on the authority of Dorothy, that when he was engaged, a year or so ago, in packing books and destroying papers preparatory to leaving the Dower House, he accidentally discharged a pistol. He was alone in the house at the time. When Dorothy got back she found the marks of the bullet in the baseboard of his bedroom. This tale has an unpleasant smack. He is actually very much afraid of firearms.

His deterioration has been in progress for nearly ten years. Sara is now dead more than eight years, and before her death she warned me against reading the stuff that he was writing at the time, saying that it would grieve me to see him doing such miserable work. To the best of my knowledge, he has made no serious effort, for five years, to write anything better. The Chester county history is a hack job, and he will make a mess of it, as he did of his Sheridan, for he lacks altogether the capacity to write sober history. His state worries me, but there is nothing that I can do about it. Of all the writing men I know he has fallen the farthest. Even such psychopaths as Sinclair Lewis at least make some effort to work, but Joe has simply given up.

BALTIMORE, JULY 10, 1943.

Schmick is chuckling over the discomfiture of Harry J. Grant, chairman of the board of the Milwaukee *Journal*. Some time ago he

---

1 Thurman W. Arnold (1891–1969) held various government posts before and during World War II and was the author of a number of books on jurisprudence and political science.

set up a scheme whereby virtually all the employes of the paper might acquire stock in it on easy terms, with representation on the board of directors. Now the editorial employes have elected a director who is one of the most violent supporters of the American Newspaper Guild in the office. More and more I am becoming convinced that all efforts to buy good-will are in vain. The working people of the United States have been persuaded by political and union demagogues, whether rightly or wrongly, that the boss is inherently and incurably evil, and any overture from him is resented as "paternalism." This paternalism has become a vague and all-inclusive bad word on the order of Nazism, capitalism, isolationism, etc. It covers a great range of hatreds, some of them rational enough but the rest purely gratuitous. Nothing that the boss does can be right. The fulminations of the Newspaper Guild are all based upon that sorry theory. I have been giving an attentive reading to its organ, the *Guild Reporter*, for several years past, but I can't recall a single article in it, or even sentence, that admitted any sort of honesty or decency in newspaper publishers. One and all, they are assumed to be scoundrels, and denounced as such incessantly. Even those who have yielded most readily to the guild's demands, and praised its purposes and its programme, have not escaped, for example, Joseph Pulitzer of the St. Louis *Post-Dispatch* and J. David Stern of the Philadelphia *Record*.

BALTIMORE, JULY 12, 1943.

The war is now nearly four years old and the United States has been an active belligerent for nineteen months, but so far its effects upon my own life have been curiously slight. To be sure, I am debarred from printing anything about its issues, but that is no great deprivation, for I am anything but a propagandist and even if I had the utmost freedom to write and print I'd probably make no effort to dissuade the American people from their follies. My belief is that they are incurable—that is, by anything resembling argument. They may be brought to their senses, in the long run, by catastrophe, but that will probably not come for a long while. Meanwhile, I go on comfortably and peacefully, and, despite ill health, have done a great deal of writing. No one, so far, has molested me, though my opposition to the theory on which the United States is carrying on the war is well known to everyone who knows me at all. I am too old to be thought of for military service, and it is easy for me to throw off the occasional suggestions that I join in the production of official propaganda. No one has so much as suggested that I buy war bonds, and in point of fact I have bought none. All four of the books that I have published since the war began have had a generally good press; in fact, they have been treated more politely than any of my books preceding them. I am sometimes denounced in the newspapers, especially in the South, but these denunciations have been milder than they used to be. My mail continues large, and I am frequently urged by strangers, including men in the service, to attack the quacks who now run the country into bankruptcy.

My situation with respect to the *Sunpapers* amuses me without irritating me. I am paid a liberal salary for very easy work, and remain on good terms with my old colleagues, though all of them know that I believe the course they are pursuing is almost insane. My relations with Paul Patterson continue friendly, though we are no longer on our old footing of intimacy, for I have told him more than once, and in very plain words, what I think of his conduct of the paper. Nevertheless, he needs me outside the area of editorial policy, and calls on me often for advice and support. Apparently he still cherishes his old notion that I am a good business man. At all events, he never undertakes a major enterprise without consulting me, and more than once he has let me persuade him against something that he had set his heart on. He needs this steadying, and he knows it. For half a dozen years past he has shown a progressive falling off in both professional skill and common sense, and of late his progress in that direction has been greatly hastened. He is no longer the smart fellow that he once was, which bears out my old theory that it is impossible to be a fool in one direction and a wise man in others. When he began to let the English take him into camp he began to lose his wits all over, and today, compared to what he was in 1920, he is a really pitiable object. The mere advance of the years, of course, has had something to do with this. He has lost a good deal of his energy and enterprise, and is now definitely an old man, though it would amaze him to hear it. But much more importantly he suffers from the fact that there was no body of sound and coherent ideas in him when the pressure began. He had really given no serious thought to the questions that the war threw up, and so he was an easy mark for propagandists. Moreover, he was dragged along by his intense yearning to be well regarded outside the office—one of the chief symptoms of his lamentable inferiority complex. I am more than ever convinced that the way up from slavery is an onerous and stormy route. In times of stress and storm the man who follows it is apt to go to pieces. This, I think, has happened to Patterson.

It is possible that when he gets back from England he will have gone so far that he is unendurable, and in that case I'll clear out of the *Sun*. If so, there will be no moaning of farewell. The fact that I have to leave the paper will be far more discreditable to it than to me. Its historians of the future, in truth, already have something in that direction to explain away, to wit, my refusal, in the early part of 1941, to continue writing for it. I am in grave doubt that there will be any such historians of the future. It is, at present, passing over a peak, and unless all signs fail it will go downhill hereafter. Newspapers, like men, have their youth, their maturity and their old age. If anything is plain it is that there will be radical changes in American journalism during the next fifty years. The plan of newspapers will be revised, and they may lose many of their present functions. The *Sunpapers* are not as well prepared as they should be to meet such revolutions. The group of men that rehabilitated them after the last war is fast playing out, and very few youngsters of any force and originality are in sight. Of the men now active in their management only Schmick and Swanson show any genuine capacity, and Schmick is sixty and beginning to slacken. His son is a worthy young man, but like Patterson's son he does not rise to the level of his pa.

The general slowing down is probably to my advantage, for if steam were hissing in all the boilers, as in the 1920–30 period, I'd be tempted to work far beyond my declining strength. As it is, I am in an almost ideal situation for an aging man. I do precisely what I want to do. On most weekdays save Saturdays I drop in at the *Sun* office to gossip with Patterson, Black, Swanson and Schmick, but if I fail to show up there is no harm done. I write what I please, and even the impossibility of discussing the war does not incommode me, for I have no desire to discuss it. The chickens are coming home to roost, and I content myself by watching them. If I awaken feeling badly there is no pressure on me to do any writing: everything may be put off until tomorrow. I am at great pains to avoid jobs with a time limit. They are offered constantly, but I almost always decline them. My domestic situation is very comfortable, despite the lack of a woman in the house. August and I have two good servants, and they take care of us admirably. The best lunches I ever get in Baltimore are in my own house. I like them so well, in fact, that I never lunch out if I can help it. I hear vaguely of food rationing, but only vaguely, for nearly everything I like is still on the house bill-of-fare. My cellar is full of excellent wines and liquors, and there is an ample reserve of canned goods—enough to see me through any probable shortage. Finally, I have pretty well got rid of social obligations. I go out relatively seldom, and have guests even seldomer. Two evenings out of three August and I have a few quiet drinks together in our living-room, and they are always first-rate drinks.

My health continues to deteriorate, but some of the discomforts mentioned in these notes for January and February have passed off, at least for the moment. The discomforts around the heart that bothered me in February have disappeared, and I sleep pretty well despite the current heat, and have few disturbing dreams. My heart, of course, is still impaired, and I suspect that my blood pressure is rising, but if so neither has yet put me to any really serious inconvenience. After abandoning cold showers for three or four years I resumed them at the beginning of the present Summer, and they appear to produce no bad effects. My appetite is excellent, and I can still drink all the alcohol I want, which is less and less as year chases year. My present limit is three bottles of beer of an evening, or two stiff highballs. But on occasion I can go further without any damage save a certain amount of languor the next day. My throat is still uncomfortable, but not unendurably so. The other day I had LeRoy Polvogt examine it. He told me that there was no sign of infection: what bothered me was simply the mass of scar tissue in my old tonsil crypt on the left side. There have been three operations there. I suggested to Polvogt that he try to cut out all the scar tissue, but he protested that that would only make an unpleasant situation worse. Some fine nerve ends appear to be caught in it. The result is discomfort, but not actual pain. I smoke a great deal less than I used to. On most days I do not go beyond three cigars, and sometimes I fall short of three. I haven't smoked a pipe for three or four years.

That I'll ever be able to do my projected supplement to "The American Language" I begin to doubt. The material is all in hand, but it would take at least a year of very hard work to reduce it to copy. I am so constituted that it would be impossible for me to undertake such a job without overdoing it. However warily I started out I'd soon be working eight or ten hours a day. The doctors tell me that such a pace would soon wreck me, though once it was normal to me. I am approaching sixty-three, and can't escape that fact. If I could get a holiday at sea it would do me a lot of good, but holidays at sea are now unknown in the world. I go to New York very seldom, and never enjoy my visits, for they always involve going out to Purchase with Alfred Knopf, listening to the complaining of his wife, or doing something else that I don't want to do. Railway travel is becoming more and more uncomfortable. Going to New York, I get seats readily enough by ordering them by mail four or five days in advance, but the return trips present hazards, and more than once I have been forced to use an inconvenient train, simply because no seats were available on a more convenient one.

BALTIMORE, JULY 14, 1943.

Last night, after various false starts, I wrote the preface to a new book. As I have planned it, it will consist of a series of brief paragraphs—and sometimes mere sentences—worked up from the notes that I have been accumulating for years. Additional matter may come out of my magazine and newspaper stuff, especially my shorter contributions to the *Smart Set* and the *American Mercury* and my Baltimore *Evening Sun* articles, but most of the material will be new. The dominant theme will be the validity and value of common sense. I am still fishing for the title. It may be something vague, such as "This and That," or it may include some specific mention of common sense. Unhappily, the book starts out with a hex riding it, and so I am not too sure that it will ever be finished. I had done the preface before I noticed that the day was the 13th.[1]

BALTIMORE, JULY 28, 1943.

When I finished filing my accumulated correspondence last week I planned to get to work on my book, but the weather was so uncomfortable that I could not settle down to it, so I resolved to put in a

1 This must refer to *Minority Report*, the manuscript of which, as has already been explained, was lost and forgotten after his 1948 stroke. Mrs. Lohrfinck came across it almost by accident some years later, and it was published posthumously in 1956. What is surprising here is that one would not have thought he had begun it this far back.

little more time on organizing my records. First I gave a couple of days to the Mencken family papers, then I cleaned up various small jobs, and then I tackled the Tyson notes on language. These notes were made by F. H. Tyson, a lawyer employed by the Standard Vacuum Oil Company at Hongkong. He was a faithful reader of "The American Language" and began sending me memoranda about usage in the Far East while the fourth edition was in progress. He is mentioned in it in a footnote to p. 277. He died in Hongkong about two years ago, just in time to escape the onslaught of the Japanese, and his wife returned to America with his papers. Some time ago she asked me if I'd like to have his notes, and I naturally said yes. When she sent them to me they turned out to be very large in number; in fact, the little envelopes in which they were filed filled a box a foot and a half long by almost as wide and high. A few dips into it indicated that it contained a good deal of matter that would be useful to me, but there was also much that would not, so it needed a careful going over. That going over I have just finished.

The business took me three and a half days, for there must have been at least 2,500 envelopes, and some of them contained a dozen newspaper clippings and other notes. Most of the stuff turned out to be useless for my purposes, for it consisted of observations that are more accessible in other places, but I dug out at least 1,000 clippings that can be plowed into my projected supplement to "The American Language." Going through the lot was a tedious task, but nevertheless very interesting, for Tyson was an intelligent man, with a sharp eye for the picturesque and humorous. I could not help thinking, as I went through his notes, of this rather curious end to all his long labors. He must have put in hundreds of hours, out there in Hongkong, reading and clipping. He apparently made a regular search, not only of the China Coast papers, but also of the papers of Australia, South Africa and the Malay States, and of the London *Times, Telegraph, Morning Post, Express, Mirror, Sunday Times, Observer* and *News of the World*, not to mention a large miscellany of magazines. Well, here was a stranger, 10,000 miles away, passing final judgment on his work. What interested me I put into my own files; what didn't went into my waste-basket, and from my waste-basket moved to the trash-burner in the backyard. I'll give him credit in my supplement for all of his material that I use, but the rest has now vanished from the earth.[1] In the

---

1 In the preface to Supplement I of *The American Language* (p. vii), Mencken ac-

long run my own enormous accumulations will go the same way. Even if I make a large hole in them for the supplement there will be plenty left, and that plenty, after my death, will fall into the hands of someone whose interests are not precisely mine. Thus some trash-burner will get it as my trash-burner has got Tyson's.

BALTIMORE, AUGUST 11, 1943.

Home from New York this afternoon. On Monday (August 9) I took Blanche Knopf to lunch at No. 21, and last night I went out to Purchase with Alfred. The heat in New York during the day was really infernal, but the temperature dropped at the end of the afternoon, and after a change of clothes at Purchase I felt enormously refreshed. We had the usual heavy dinner, and put in the evening gabbling and playing phonograph records. We also tackled Schubert's "Rosamunde" ballet as a piano duet. Knopf turned out to be a bad reader, but after some effort he managed to make shift with the *secondo*. The next time I go to Purchase I'll take along some easier duets. I begin to believe that he really likes his lonely life at Purchase. The care of the place interests him enormously, and he is content to put in his evenings reading manuscripts, playing phonograph records and romping with his dog. He told me that he had lately turned away what appeared to be a good offer for the place. It is assessed at $45,000, but cost almost twice as much. A year or two ago he was eager to sell it, but now, so he said, he looks forward to spending his old age on it.

Book publishing, at the moment, is prosperous, and the company is making money and accumulating a surplus. Unfortunately, that surplus can never become large enough to take up the accumulation of unpaid dividends on the preferred stock: the current rates of Federal taxation are far too high for that.

Knopf and I spent some time discussing my own plans. He believes I should tackle the proposed supplement to "The American Language" at once. It may be the last thing I do, but that will be better than leaving the accumulated material in chaos. We also talked of various other projects. One is for a sort of omnibus of my own writings—partly from books now out of print, but mainly from newspapers and

---

knowledged his indebtedness to F. H. Tyson, "whose widow," he said, "after his lamented death in 1942, made me a present of his extraordinarily rich collection."

magazines.¹ Knopf asked me to prepare a schedule of the contents. Another scheme that we discussed was for an anthology of prose and verse made up of my own favorites. He suggested the title of "The Mencken Reader."² Such books have been brought out by Alexander Woollcott, W. Somerset Maugham and others, and all of them have sold well. The American people like predigested reading. In this case, also, Knopf asked me to prepare a schedule. A third plan we talked of was for a reprint of the three "Days" books in one volume, with maybe a few added chapters.³ This we put on the shelf for future reference. I asked Knopf if he was willing to sell "A New Dictionary of Quotations" to the World Publishing Company, of Cleveland, which is eager to take it on, and is famous for its immense sales. He said no. Later on, he added, he hoped to induce Harry Scherman of the Book-of-the-Month Club to make the dictionary one of his dividend books. This would mean a distribution of something on the order of 100,000 copies. There are, however, several disadvantages. One is that Scherman pays the author but 5 cents a copy royalty on his reprints. Another is that he would not stand the expense of a resetting, which the book badly needs, for it is full of errors as it stands and I have accumulated a lot of excellent new material.

BALTIMORE, AUGUST 25, 1943.

I went to Washington today to see Col. Livingston Watrous of the Army, deputy director of the Special Service Division. This division is in charge of all indoctrination work, and publishes a great variety of bulletins, papers, pamphlets and books for the soldiers. I was interested especially in its series of pamphlets on the countries that American troops are now quartered in, most of them containing sections on the local languages. Those for Australia, New Zealand, Northern Ireland and Great Britain contain vocabularies of words differing in American and English. Watrous received me very politely, showed me many of the documents his men are preparing, and introduced me to some of his subordinates. He has very large quarters and a staff run-

---

1 *A Mencken Chrestomathy*, containing a large collection of his out-of-print writings, appeared in 1949.
2 No such "Mencken Reader" was ever published.
3 A one-volume edition of the *Days* books, entitled *The Days of H. L. Mencken*, was published in 1947, but it contained no new material.

ning to hundreds of officers and civilians. On his desk was a copy of "Heliogabalus." He told me that he often re-read it, and asked me to autograph it, which I did.

His office is in the famous Pentagon Building at Arlington, which I saw for the first time. After the taxicab comes into sight of it there is a good mile of weaving through the maze of roads which surround it. The track doubles back on itself several times. Once inside, the visitor has to present himself at a reception desk, where very polite girls hear his business. Mine telephoned to Watrous, and then informed me that a guide would be sent down to show me to his office. She warned me that it might take the guide 15 minutes to get to the reception desk. Within ten minutes a young colored girl showed up, and I followed her along half a mile of corridors. I had been given a badge at the reception desk and had to show it when I entered the building proper. On my return I had to show it again, and also a pass that Watrous had given me, covering the pamphlets his secretary had wrapped up for me.

The Pentagon Building is so huge that it is downright comic. Also, it is extraordinarily ugly. It cost, so I have heard, more than $100,000,000, and houses nearly 100,000 jobholders. The surrounding grounds, broken up by the winding roads, are even more hideous than the building.

BALTIMORE, AUGUST 26, 1943.

I have been hard at work for three weeks past sorting out the materials for my projected supplement to "The American Language." They consist of letters, pamphlets, newspaper and magazine clippings, and notes of my own, and must run to at least 30,000 items. They now fill 27 transfer cases, and I am ready to begin work. I have arranged them by chapters in "The American Language," with some of the chapters divided into sections. The supplement will be hooked to my fourth edition page by page, but I shall add enough explanation to make it comprehensible to a reader who hasn't a copy of the book by him. I shall probably add a few new appendices. One will be devoted to things appearing in my earlier editions that I omitted from the fourth—for example, my translation of the Declaration of Independence into American. Another will be given over to inarticulate languages—for example, the sign-language of the Indians, that of deaf-mutes, cattle brands, gestures, and so on. It will take me, even with the best of luck, all of a year to finish this job.[1] Meanwhile, my record of my magazine days, now brought down to the end of 1918, will have to wait. I'd like, from time to time, to put in some licks on my proposed small book of notes, but in all probability it will be impossible.

BALTIMORE, AUGUST 30, 1943.

Yesterday (Sunday) I began work in earnest on the supplement to "The American Language." Between 11 a.m. and 9 p.m. I managed to get about 2,000 words on paper. This writing is mainly drudgery: it involves a tedious examination of almost endless notes. That drudgery falls into my present mood, for I am severely beset by hay-fever, and with it has come the usual depression.

BALTIMORE, SEPTEMBER 15, 1943.

The severity of hay-fever this year has somewhat interfered with the writing of the supplement to "The American Language"; nevertheless, I have got about 23,000 words on paper so far. In addition, I have put in a great deal of time sorting and arranging the material. It is so vast in amount that it must be divided and sub-divided with care, else I'll get lost in it. It is now gradually taking such shape that more rapid progress with the actual writing should be possible as soon as I am restored to normalcy.

BALTIMORE, SEPTEMBER 23, 1943.

While I was at work this morning there was a clatter down in the hall, and when I got there a deliveryman was picking up Emma Ball, the colored maid, who had slipped on the waxed hardwood floor and struck her head on the staircase. I gave him a hand, and in a little while she had recovered, though the blow had dazed her. I have warned her over and over again against giving the floors too high a polish. More than once I have fallen on them myself, and one night I

---

1 At this point Mencken apparently thought of the supplement to *The American Language* as being in one volume, and had no idea that there would eventually be a "Supplement II." Even so, the proposed appendices that he mentions here were never written.

came down on the back of my head. But it is impossible to talk anything resembling discretion or judgment into a colored woman. They
are all essentially child-like, and even hard experience does not teach
them anything. Emma, it appeared, was bruised only slightly, but the
episode gave me a turn, for if she had been badly hurt it would have
thrown the house into chaos, for Hester Denby, the cook, is too old to
do all the work alone and getting another maid—at all events, one as
good as Emma—would probably be impossible. She came to work in
Cathedral street during the Summer of 1935, when I had to get rid of
the sassy and inefficient maid that Sara had left me. This inefficient
maid came to work during Sara's last illness, and hence ran wild.
Hester objected to her violently, so I turned her away. I found Emma
at an employment agency in Mulberry street near Paca, and she has
been in service ever since. She is extraordinarily good. She keeps the
house as clean as an operating-room, and is also an excellent waitress.
I pay her $17 a week, with a bonus of $200 a year added, and she has
Thursday and Sunday afternoons and evenings and Saturday mornings
off. In addition she gets a vacation with pay every Summer, and this
year I gave her three weeks instead of the usual two. A year ago, on
setting off for her old home in Virginia by bus, she lost her baggage.
It contained her whole wardrobe, and she produced a memorandum
showing that it had cost her, new, about $130. The Greyhound Bus
Company delayed reimbursing her for a year, and then, taking refuge
behind some Interstate Commerce Commission regulation, refused to
pay her more than $25. I gave her $100 and let her keep the $25 when
it came in. Today I was told by Hester that she (Emma) had lately
laid out $5.50 for the replacement of a lost oyster-fork, apparently
dropped into the garbage-can. I issued strict orders prohibiting anything of the sort in future. All damage to house property, I told Emma
and Hester, is my risk, and their only duty about it is to report it
at once.

The accident this morning set me to thinking about my dependence
on these two colored women. If they quit tomorrow August and I
would be in a really desperate state, and it would probably be impossible for us to go on keeping house, for servants of their fidelity and
capacity are now virtually unprocurable. They are, to be sure, expensive—Hester is paid $22 a week, along with all of Emma's other priv-
ileges and perquisites—, but there is no reason why I should attempt
to save any money, and so far I can afford them. If they left the house

would soon be in a frightful mess, and victualling would become very difficult, for the last decent restaurant in West Baltimore—Knoop's in Baltimore street near Stricker—has been shut down by the proprietor's illness. As it is, I eat lunch in the house at least five times a week, and dinner almost every evening. On Thursday nights, when the servants are off, August and I usually patch up a meal out of cans. For Sunday evenings Hester leaves us a plate of excellent sandwiches, and I get down my half with a few bottles of ale or beer.

I am even more dependent upon Rosalind Lohrfinck, my secretary. She knows my business inside and out, and saves me an enormous amount of work. In fact, it would be impossible, without her aid, for me to undertake anything as complicated and onerous as the supplement to "The American Language," now in progress. She is an extremely rapid stenographer, and knows all my regular correspondents. In copying typescripts she is so accurate as to be almost miraculous: in fact, she sometimes goes a whole week without making a single mistake. If she left me I'd be almost helpless, and if the two colored women left also my life would be changed almost as much as if I lost an arm.

BALTIMORE, OCTOBER 10, 1943.

On my trip to Purchase, N.Y. on October 2 I missed a train for the second time in my life. I left Baltimore on a Pennsylvania train due at New York at 4.45 p.m. and planned to leave for White Plains from the Grand Central at 5.19. Inasmuch as it was a Saturday afternoon, with the street traffic light, that left me plenty of time to go from station to station. But the Pennsylvania train was late, and when I got into a taxicab I had just twelve minutes to reach the Grand Central. The driver, a colored man, made very good progress, but at Madison avenue he was held up by traffic lights, and so I reached the gate three minutes late. Fortunately, there was another train within fifteen minutes, and though it was a slow one I reached Alfred Knopf's house at Purchase in plenty of time for dinner. The first time I missed a train was in my schooldays, when I traveled home to Mt. Washington by the Northern Central every day in Spring and Autumn. I always go to a railroad station at least fifteen minutes before my train is scheduled to leave, and sometimes I am there half an hour before. It has always been my boast that I never miss trains, but on October 2 the effects of the war on all the American railroads fetched me at last. The Pennsylvania trains, in normal times, are almost invariably on time. But now the road is demoralized, there are delays and accidents, and a few weeks ago the Congressional Limited had a bad wreck at Philadelphia, and killed more than fifty people. I have used it scores and scores of times during the past thirty years.

BALTIMORE, OCTOBER 18, 1943.

Grove Patterson, editor of the Toledo *Blade*, called up this morning and I asked him to lunch at the Maryland Club. He is leaving for England in a day or two by one of the English air-liners that depart from Baltimore. He is going as the guest of the British Ministry of Information. Grove is a pleasant fellow and I was glad to see him. He is an excellent speaker and has a hand in Republican politics in Ohio. He told me he thought it would be a complete impossibility to beat Roosevelt in 1944, but that he hoped for a Republican House, with a good show to follow when the inquest on the war begins. He said that Governor John W. Bricker of Ohio, who has been one of the leading Republican aspirants, has decided to keep out of the fight and run instead for a fourth term as Governor. Grove seemed to believe that Willkie[1] would get the Republican nomination—probably by a sort of default. Tom Dewey is most likely too smart to seek it, or to take it if it is offered to him, and the rest are virtually out of the running. We talked of some of them, especially Vandenberg and Taft. Grove said that Taft is actually a very intelligent and able man, but that his unimpressive exterior is a fatal impediment to his hopes. The boobs simply do not rise to him. As for Vandenberg, he is a sharp fellow too, but looks and acts the smart aleck, and so repels the plain people.

I told Grove that I had resolved not to cover next year's conventions for the *Sun*. He urged me to reconsider my decision, and predicted that, when the time comes, I'll do so. It will be impossible, he said, for me to resist the show. We shall see.

1 Wendell L. Willkie (1892–1944) had appeared as a dark horse at the Republican National Convention in Philadelphia in 1940 and had succeeded in winning the nomination but was roundly defeated by Franklin D. Roosevelt in the election that followed. He made an effort to secure the nomination again in 1944 but was unsuccessful—it went to Thomas E. Dewey, who was also defeated by FDR.

BALTIMORE, OCTOBER 24, 1943.

Another crazy woman has taken to badgering me, recalling the one who gave me so much trouble in 1931, when Sara was ill in Cathedral street. Her name is Mae Osborne and she hails from Conowingo, Md. She began writing to me several years ago, saying that she had written a novel about Maryland and asking me to read it and advise her about its disposition. After putting her off as long as possible, I saw her one day at the *Sun* office. She brought her MS. with her, and I read it soon afterward. It turned out to have a certain slender interest, but it was badly designed, and a few months later I took her to lunch at the Marconi to discuss it with her. Both of our meetings were thus very formal, with other persons present. Some time ago she went to University, Va., to live, and since then she has been bombarding me with letters declaring that she is mashed on me, that her heart is breaking, and that I must relieve her by marrying her. It is only too obvious that the poor woman is insane. I have tried to put her off with letters, but now she threatens to come to Baltimore. This nuisance afflicts me at a time when I am up to my ears in the supplement to "The American Language" and am feeling extremely rocky physically. What can be done about it God knows. I have certainly not made love to her; on the contrary, I have been at pains to treat her very formally, for she does not interest me. Next, I suppose, she'll be making threats, and I'll have to ask her family to take care of her. The country is swarming with such poor lunatics. I receive letters from them constantly, and now and then one pops up in Baltimore, and I have a dreadful time getting rid of him—or her, for they are often women.

BALTIMORE, OCTOBER 29, 1943.

On Wednesday morning, before setting off for West Chester, I had a palaver with Kavanaugh at the *Sun* office. This was at Patterson's request, and the object was to find out the real reason for Kavanaugh's insistence that he be relieved of labor negotiations. I came away from him convinced that his ill health is actually at the bottom of it. His stomach ulcers still afflict him, and he continues on an unappetizing and dispiriting diet. After a long labor meeting he sleeps badly, and his physical discomforts are exacerbated. He told me that he'd be glad to continue if he could be relieved of the early stages of the negotiations, which tend to be long-drawn-out and irritating. The labor spokesmen like to gabble, and always offer a series of proposals that they know will not be considered. Sometimes it takes weeks and months to get through this mummery. I asked Kavanaugh if he had any substitute to offer—that is, in the *Sun* organization—and he said no. Young Schmick[1] is too young and unseasoned to take over, and Bertsch, the circulation manager, has his hands full. After a somewhat long discussion Kavanaugh proposed that Bertsch be relieved of some of his present duties and put in charge of labor preliminaries, and that a man named Woodward be employed to help him in the circulation department. This Woodward, it appears, is a man of 45 or thereabout, and a circulation manager of long experience. He worked for the Philadelphia *Inquirer* for years, but quit in the end because he couldn't get along with the Annenbergs, who are low-grade Jews. Since then he has done some work for the Philadelphia *Bulletin*, and is at present attached to the paper-rationing office in Washington. Kavanaugh said that Woodward could relieve Bertsch of the circulation department routine sufficiently to enable him (Bertsch) to give some time to labor matters. He argued that Bertsch is in the line of promotion for his own job, and ought to get some experience in this field. He (Kavanaugh) is willing to enter all negotiations in their final stages, and to keep an eye on Bertsch.

I took all this to Patterson and Harry Black and they seemed to think it offered a way out. In fact, they professed to be delighted with it. Whether or not Woodward can be hired remains to be seen. Kavanaugh is plainly much worried about his health. He is in constant discomfort, must stick to a mushy diet, is forbidden alcohol, and can have only a few cigarettes a day. He looks haggard, and his normal gloom is greatly accentuated. He said that his threat to resign if he were not relieved of labor negotiations was not intended to be taken seriously. His whole career, he said, has been made on the *Sun*, and he looks forward to spending the rest of his life in its service. But he is obviously in doubt that his state of health will ever permit him to succeed Schmick as head of all business departments. He told me that Schmick's gradual retirement from activity has greatly increased his

---

1 William F. Schmick, Jr., succeeded his father as president of the A. S. Abell Company when Schmick, Sr., retired in 1960 and continued in the post until his own retirement in 1978.

own burdens, and that the prospect of beginning a struggle with the press-room, mail-room and composing-room unions, with the garage, the stereotype foundry and possibly the engraving department to follow, really alarms him. His doctor has cautioned him to take things easy, but with so many irons in the fire he simply can't.

BALTIMORE, OCTOBER 30, 1943.

I went to Washington yesterday to testify for *Esquire* in the proceedings before the Postoffice. The solicitor thereof has threatened it with an order taking away its second-class privilege on the ground that it prints obscene pictures and articles, and it is up for a hearing before a department committee consisting of Walter Myers, the fourth assistant postmaster-general and two other jobholders. This committee is something new. In 1926, when the then solicitor, Horace J. Donnelly, barred the April issue of the *American Mercury* from the mails, the only hearing I could get was before Donnelly himself, and it was naturally farcical. But under the existing procedure a magazine may appeal to a committee of three officials, none of them directly concerned with the business. They then make a recommendation to the postmaster-general, who ordinarily acts upon their advice. If they decide against the magazine it can appeal to a Federal district court. This is what I did in 1926, but without the intermediate hearing.

I got to Washington at 1 p.m. and went into session with Arnold Gingrich, the editor of *Esquire*. He had an elaborate portfolio containing all the pictures and articles complained of, and we went through it page by page. I was genuinely astonished by the puerility of most of the charges. The postoffice wowsers had listed a number of completely harmless words, for example, *backside, behind, bawdy-house* and *son-of-a-bitch*, all of which have appeared in unchallenged books and magazines thousands of times. I had expected that they would have some reasonable evidence against *Esquire*, for it is actually rather rowdy, but there was none whatever. I was called to the stand at 2 p.m. and testified for about an hour. It was plain from the start that Walter Myers, the chairman of the committee, was a relatively civilized man. He not only let me say whatever I pleased, including a round denunciation of the postoffice for its course in the *American Mercury* case; he also fed me admirably. The other two members of the committee looked more dubious; one of them, according to Gingrich, is a Southern Methodist. But Myers did all the questioning, and they said nothing. They looked at me hostilely at the start, but before it was over I had them laughing.

The cross-examination by the postoffice lawyer, one Hassell, was very feeble. He was prompted from time to time by a man sitting behind him, but these promptings nearly always led him into traps— for example, when he mentioned the *American Mercury* case, when I got a chance to say that I was acquitted, that three different Federal judges had denounced the postoffice, and that I thought its course was dishonest, ignoble and ignominious. After the hearing the prompter approached me in the corridor and introduced himself as an assistant solicitor named O'Brien. Then I recalled him. At the time of the *American Mercury* hearing he had taken me aside and told me that he thought Donnelly, his superior, had a very feeble case, and should drop it. Now, Irish-like, he was still playing the traitor. I did not pause to parley with him. If he thinks the *Esquire* charges are also silly, as he said plainly (and proved by his disingenuous prompting of Hassell), he should say so. But he values his job above common decency. Of such sort are the swine now running the United States.

Gingrich thanked me for coming to his aid, and offered to pay my expenses, but I refused. It was a genuine pleasure to testify for him. It at least gave me a chance to state under oath my opinion of the postoffice wowsers. The more I denounced them, the more Myers chuckled. He is an Indianan. Gingrich told me that he has hopes of getting a verdict. He says that the Southern Methodist is plainly against him, but that Myers will probably have influence enough to swing the committee.[1]

BALTIMORE, NOVEMBER 5, 1943.

I went to dinner at the Hamilton Street Club last night with Willie and Marie Woollcott. The only other guest was Samuel Hopkins

---

1 Despite Mencken's testimony, *Esquire* lost—the postmaster-general ordered the withdrawal of its second-class mailing privilege on the ground of the morally objectionable nature of its contents. The magazine appealed, and after a long and complex series of legal maneuvers, the case eventually reached the Supreme Court. On February 4, 1946, in a unanimous decision, the Court overturned the ruling. Justice William Douglas, who wrote the opinion, declared that existing law gave the postmaster general "no discretion to withhold the second-class privilege from a mailable newspaper or periodical because it failed to meet some standard of worth or value or propriety." Such a power, he said, "would be a power of censorship . . . abhorrent to our traditions."

Adams,[1] who is writing a life of Willie's late brother, Alec. Why a man with such serious writing behind him should devote himself to the career of so shallow a fellow it is hard to make out. I gathered from his talk that he and Alec were hardly on intimate terms while Alec lived; indeed, the only bond between them seemed to be the fact that both were graduates of Hamilton College. Nevertheless, he is proceeding with the biography, and had come to Baltimore to get material from Willie and Marie. Willie professed to have very little: he said that he saw Alec but seldom, and knew next to nothing about his doings. Marie showed an obvious hostility to him—something that surprised me, for there was a time when she admired Alec extravagantly. It soon turned out that her change of view had been produced by Alec's will, which left precisely nothing to her four daughters. His actual last will left his whole property to an Irishman named Hennessey, who had been acting as his "secretary" for some years, but this will, made in Vermont, had one less witness than the state law required, and was thus set aside. This revived his penultimate will, which divided all his property between Hennessey and a quack doctor in New York. I was always under the impression that Alec was not really a homo, but now I begin to doubt. Certainly his relations to Hennessey were extremely suspicious. Why he should have cut off his four nieces I don't know. He appeared to be on good terms with them, and at one time showed them a great deal of attention. I well recall the time when he promised to induce the Lunts to put the eldest of them, Nancy, on the stage. Alas, the Lunts went back on this arrangement, if it was ever actually made, and Nancy is now married to a young college instructor named Smith, and the mother of twin boys. Smith lately lost his job in one of the Vermont colleges and is now working in a war plant in Baltimore. Of the other girls, Joan and Barbara are also married. Polly, the youngest and prettiest, is still single. Joan, who is in newspaper work, has taken to radicalism, and is somewhat noisy and unpleasant. She was in the forefront of American Newspaper Guild politics in Philadelphia, where she worked on the *Bulletin.* Barbara proposed to follow her into newspaper work, and was given a trial on the *Sun,* but she failed to make good, and Neil Swanson fired her.

1 Samuel Hopkins Adams (1871–1958), newspaperman, novelist, and historian. His *Alexander Woollcott: His Life and His World* appeared in 1945.

Willie had a couple of heart attacks six months ago, and has done no work since. He is still, in theory, superintendent of the ink and paste factory of his late father-in-law, Victor G. Bloede, but I doubt that he ever returns to activity. How much money Bloede left I do not know, but it must have been a considerable amount. The share of Marie, I assume, is enough to keep her and Willie, now that their daughters are clearing off. The dinner at the Hamilton Street Club was very pleasant. Gino, the steward, provided an excellent beefsteak and some very good California wines, and the four of us had the club-house to ourselves. Despite his heart attacks and the stomach ulcers that came near killing him ten or twelve years ago, Willie ate and drank very heartily. After dinner, he, Marie, Adams and I sat at the fire until midnight. Once, when I mentioned Dr. Thomas S. Cullen, the Johns Hopkins surgeon, Adams exclaimed: "Good God, is *he* still alive?" I replied that Cullen, though seventy-four years old, is not only alive, but operating. Only a few weeks ago I met him in the Maryland Club with Abraham Flexner,[1] and he seemed to be full of life. Adams, who begins to look old, is but three years younger.

BALTIMORE, NOVEMBER 8, 1943.

I had two guests to lunch at the Maryland Club today—R. J. Baumann, of Erie, Pa., who collects my books, and a Virginian named Davis Ratcliffe, now a lieutenant in the Army. Ratcliffe was an insurance adjuster in peace times, and is now engaged upon Army insurance work, with an office in Baltimore. He turned out to be a dull fellow, and Baumann was but little better. Baumann, as we parted, told me that his wife was expecting, and asked me for permission to name the baby after me, if it turns out a boy. I protested that this would only bring the poor child bad luck. I always avoid, when it is possible, having babies named after me. It sets up connections and obligations that are apt to be nuisances.

---

1 Abraham Flexner (1886–1959), educator who wrote many books on education and was on the staff of the Carnegie Foundation for the Advancement of Teaching.

BALTIMORE, NOVEMBER 13, 1943.

When he was here on November 4 Stewart Holbrook[1] told me that H. L. Davis,[2] the author of the excellent novel, "Honey in the Horn," has gone to pieces, and appears to be half insane. Four or five years ago Davis sent me some chapters from a new novel he was engaged upon, and I liked them very much. But since then he has made no progress with it, and I seldom hear from him. Holbrook says that his wife has left him, and that he is living in squalor in a small California town. He gets drunk at parties when he visits San Francisco, and pukes at the table. Resorting to the toilet, he misses the bowl and urinates on the floor. Altogether, Holbrook reports him to be in a sorry state. It is a pity, for he has great talent.

BALTIMORE, NOVEMBER 15, 1943.

At a board meeting at the *Sun* office this afternoon. Despite the enormous increase in Federal taxes and in operating expenses, 1943 promises to be the best year that the *Sunpapers* have had for a long while. Their net income for its first ten months, before taxes, was $1,860,000. Taxes for the period ran to $1,086,000, which left about $775,000 for what may be called the net net. Schmick reported that the net before taxes, for the whole year, promises to run to $2,250,000. Out of this will have to come taxes to the amount of more than $1,250,000, leaving nearly $1,000,000 for the stockholders. With this net income it will be possible to lift the dividend to $6, but doing so, of course, will be extremely inadvisable, and no one seems to favor it. These results greatly surprised me, and also all the other directors. It seemed certain, at the beginning of the year, that we could not maintain the $5 dividend without dipping into the surplus even more than last year, but the avalanche of so-called "institutional" advertising saved us. That advertising is nine-tenths buncombe. It represents only an effort by large corporations to get rid of enough of their income to keep them out of the excess-profits bracket—and at the same time purchase official good-will by whooping up the government's bond

1 Stewart H. Holbrook (1893–1964), journalist and historian.
2 H[arold] L. Davis (1896–1960), novelist and poet. Mencken had encouraged Davis to pursue a writing career and published some of his pieces in *The American Mercury*. *Honey in the Horn* won both the Harper and the Pulitzer Prizes in 1936.

issues. Nearby all this bogus advertising is devoted mainly to the bond issues: the corporations paying for it have little to say about themselves, and that little is said in small type. The whole business is but one more evidence of the fact that the war is being carried on in an atmosphere of false pretenses. The quacks at Washington set the tune for the entire country, and especially for Big Business.

BALTIMORE, NOVEMBER 19, 1943.

Home from New York after two busy and fatiguing days. After the *Sun* board meeting on November 15 the throat and nose infection that began to afflict me on November 14 became acute and I was very uncomfortable. I went to the Johns Hopkins on Tuesday morning, November 16, to consult Dr. LeRoy M. Polvogt. He made an application of silver nitrate to one especially inflamed spot, but told me that the mucosa were infected throughout the region. He prescribed a solution of sulfadiazine 25% and ordered me to spray my nose and throat with it every two hours. I used it for the first time at noon, and lay low all afternoon. Twice there were flashes of nausea, but they were very brief. By dark I was beginning to feel comfortable, and by the time I went to bed the roof of my mouth was healed and the soreness further down was passing. On Wednesday morning I seemed to be greatly improved, but I was still in doubt whether it would be possible for me to make my projected trip to New York. I went to see Polvogt again a little before noon, and he found that I was so much better that travel would not be dangerous. I left at 2:43, had a comfortable train trip, and got to the Algonquin feeling almost well.

I had an engagement for dinner with Mrs. Fred M. Hanes, who was at the Pierre, but she telephoned that she was laid up by what seemed to be influenza. Thus the dinner was called off, and I went to bed before 9 p.m. and slept until 10 the next morning. I then saw Betty Hanes at the Pierre and found her in a very miserable state, with a racking cough and great prostration. She looked, in fact, wretched. Her husband had gone home, but with her was a young woman from Winston-Salem named Brevard and also a trained nurse. Betty, who is 62 or 63 years old, has chronic bronchitis, and has suffered from it a great deal during the past few years. She was in a gloomy mood, and told me that she thought her days were numbered. I tried to cheer her, but there was not much to say, for I believe she is really pretty ill, and she knows it. A charming woman, intelligent and civilized. She had a husband before Fred, but he has been forgotten. She told me that Fred's mother, now about 85, is in reasonably good health, but needs a great deal of attention and is thus something of a nuisance. Betty had planned to go home tomorrow, but she must now wait until next week. When I called up Thursday morning La Brevard was hard at work trying to get railroad reservations for next Wednesday—a most difficult business. When I reached New York myself I tried to get a Pullman seat for the return trip today, but there were none left on any afternoon train. I went aboard the 2:30 for Baltimore without any, but the Pullman conductor dug up a seat for me. It was No. 13 in the last car—a very bad spot—, but I got home safely, and in fact dozed most of the way. My throat infection is now quite gone. The sulfadiazine disposed of it in less than 48 hours.

I spent six hours yesterday with the Knopfs. When I got to the office at 12:15 to go to lunch with Alfred, Blanche was not there and had not been heard from. He suggested taking Joseph C. Lesser with us, and when we got to the St. Regis Blanche breezed in. I was genuinely shocked by her appearance, for I had not seen her since her return from London. She insisted that she had got enough to eat there, but what she got must have been deficient in vitamins, for she looked thin and haggard.

Blanche's trip to London was apparently as fruitless as her trip to South America. She came home with precisely nothing in the way of a good book. She told me that she had commissioned several, but did not say who is to write them. She stayed at the Ritz in London and probably got rid of $2,000 or more entertaining Englishmen, who are always eager to eat and drink at the expense of visiting Americans. While she was abroad the book of Sumner Welles,[1] late Under Secretary of State, went to some other publisher. For two or three years past she has been pouring into my ears the tale of her intimacy with Welles. She even said that her South American trip was made at his request, and that she devoted it mainly to secret work for the State Department. Time and again she went to Washington to see him, and when she set off for London she told me that he had arranged for her

---

1 Sumner Welles (1892–1961), diplomat, undersecretary of state in the administration of Franklin D. Roosevelt, and an intimate of the president. The book referred to was probably *The Time for Decision*, published in 1944 by Harper & Brothers.

passage by air. And then he sold his book to another publisher while she was away! I had often warned her that Welles was not to be trusted.

I had an engagement to meet Paul Palmer at his apartment in the Volney at 6:30. Palmer and I were to dine with Albert Jay Nock, and when I got to the Palmer apartment he was already there. I had not seen him for at least three years. He is now beyond eighty and begins to look it. His hair and moustache are snow white and he is very thin, but his face still shows a good color. We put in a quiet and pleasant evening. Palmer had proposed that Nock and I do a book together, setting forth at length our views of the war. To that end Palmer wrote an introductory letter to Nock and sent it to me. Unhappily, it seemed to set us off on the wrong foot, for it plainly contemplated a sort of debate, and Nock and I are too close together in our ideas to debate effectively. I suggested that Palmer try again, and he agreed to do so. The book, of course, can't be published until after the war. Even then there will probably have to be a long wait, for my experience in the last war convinces me that the worst interferences with free speech come after hostilities are over, not while they are going on. In all probability the book will never be written, for Nock is now too old to tackle it to any effect, and I have too many other irons in the fire. Palmer, Nock and I dined together: Palmer's wife went to the theatre. The dinner was very good, and we got down a bottle of excellent claret. I dropped Nock at the Prince George Hotel afterward, and was in bed at the Algonquin a little after midnight.

This morning I slept until 10:30 and then went down to 165 Broadway to see Allen Walker Read.[1] He and I and two of his colleagues had lunch at a fish restaurant at the foot of Fulton street. After lunch I leaped for the Pennsylvania Station and my train.

BALTIMORE, DECEMBER 2, 1943.

My old friend, David Newbold, who lived at Hollins and Gilmor streets when I was a boy, came down to Baltimore from Philadelphia today and I took him to lunch at the Maryland Club, along with his

1 Allen Walker Read, philologist. He was on the staff of the *Dictionary of American English*, and Mencken drew heavily on his writings for the fourth edition of *The American Language* and the two Supplements. See the entry for January 29, 1944 (p. 298).

brother-in-law and my other old friend, Roscoe Peacock. David begins to look positively antique, but he is still lively in mind and remains a faithful Episcopalian and a high tariff Republican of the first chop. It is always amusing to me to meet such men in these days. On the one hand they are convinced that Roosevelt is next door to a maniac, and on the other hand they have succumbed to the English propaganda and are thus forced to support him in the matter of the war. Those who are relatively intelligent—and one of them is David—see clearly that Roosevelt is working his wicked will upon them under cover of the war, but so far they have not devised any scheme to circumvent him. All this makes them intensely unhappy and hence converts them into amusing spectacles, for nothing is more comical than a man suffering from his own follies.

Newbold called for a drink consisting of half Dubonnet and half French vermouth. I tried one myself and found it not unpalatable. Peacock drank old-fashioned cocktails. We thereupon fell upon a mess of terrapin, and both guests pronounced it perfect. Unhappily, it was not. The terrapin itself was excellent, but there was an obvious shortage of butter in the kitchen and so the sauce that came on with it was 90 per cent. terrapin juice and only 10 per cent. butter. It should be at least half melted butter, and so it is normally at the Maryland Club. The next time I put it on I'll make sure that a sufficiency of butter is at hand.

On my way up to the club I met S. Blount Mason, Jr., its secretary, on the street. We walked along together and he told me the following curious story: some time ago two members of the club nominated for membership a man named Winter, who had recently come to Baltimore as a high official in one of the shipbuilding plants. This Winter seemed to be a presentable fellow, and he was promptly elected. Immediately afterward he took a room in the club and spent all of his leisure hanging about the place. One day he was seen entertaining an elderly and palpably Jewish gentleman in the dining-room, and some one asked who his guest was. It turned out that the guest was his father. When this news was brought to Mason he started an investigation, and presently found that Winter's actual name was Winternitz. He was, in fact, a brother to the Dr. Milton C. Winternitz who went from the Johns Hopkins to Yale thirty years ago and there became professor of pathology and dean of the medical school. Mason laid the matter before the board of governors and it was decided that nothing could be done about it, but when his sponsors were notified they proceeded to action at once. It appeared that they had not suspected that he was a Jew and knew nothing about his change of name, as he had not informed them of the fact in his preliminary talks with them. One of them went to him and told him that the discovery of the facts had greatly embarrassed him (the sponsor) and Winter-Winternitz resigned at once.

Mason told me that there was no objection in the board of governors to bringing an occasional Jew to a meal in the club, but that this applied only to out of town Jews, not to local ones. There was a time when the club always had one Jewish member, but the last was Jacob Ulman. Ulman was married to a Christian woman, a great-granddaughter of Thomas Jefferson, and had little to do with the other Jews of Baltimore. When he died the board of governors decided that he should be the last of the Chosen on the club roll. There is no other Jew in Baltimore who seems suitable.

Mason told me that the house committee is having a dreadful time with the club's servants. A large number of them have quit for war jobs, and the newcomers are decidedly inferior. A new waiter put to work last week quit in a few days because he was forbidden to accept tips. To be sure, the members contribute to an enormous tip fund at Christmas, but this brother refused to wait so long.

BALTIMORE, DECEMBER 16, 1943.

Morris Fishbein,[1] editor of the *Journal of the American Medical Association*, was here today to harangue the Kiwanis Club, and after he had delivered his Message I had a little session with him at the Emerson Hotel. Fishbein is probably more than 50 per cent. quack, but nevertheless there is a shrewd Jew in him at bottom, and I am inclined to believe that his services to American medicine have been extremely valuable.

He tells me that the recent Supreme Court decision declaring medical men subject to the Sherman Anti-Trust Act has produced very little actual damage. The hospitals are still able to determine the qual-

---

1 Morris Fishbein (1889–1976) was assistant editor and then editor of the *Journal of the American Medical Association* from 1913 to 1949 and the author of many books and articles on medical subjects.

ifications of their visiting staffs, and specialists are still free to refuse
to have anything to do with practitioners who seem to them to be
quacks. The only thing that is forbidden is joint action, and that prohibition, of course, can be evaded very readily.

Fishbein told me that the American Medical Association's war on
irregular practitioners is making good progress, despite the fact that
most States now have laws licensing osteopaths, chiropractors, optom-
etrists and other such frauds. He said that no effort is being made to
have those laws repealed. Instead, States are being induced one by one
to pass what are called basic medical training laws. These provide, in
brief, that no man may be licensed to practise any sort of medicine
without first completing an adequate training in chemistry, bacteriology, anatomy and physiology. Fishbein said that these basic medical
training laws have pretty well ruined the chiropractors in many States,
and that they are driving the osteopaths into efforts to qualify as regular practitioners. Some time ago the osteopaths got a bill through
Congress permitting the Surgeon General of the Navy to appoint members of their order to posts in the Navy's medical staff. McIntyre, the
Surgeon General, simply refused to make any appointments. When a
committee of Congressmen sent for him and asked him why he was
not doing so he told the members frankly that he considered osteopaths
quacks; that none would ever be appointed while he was in office. He
followed this with his reasons, and they seemed to be so rational to
the Congressmen that nothing more was heard of the matter.

Fishbein said that a large number of the principal labor leaders of
the United States are diligent customers of osteopaths, chiropractors
and so on. He said that some time ago the labor unions got control of
a radio station in Chicago and proceeded to give time on it to a notorious quack. When Fishbein protested to the labor leader in charge
the latter replied primly that the quack was his family doctor. The
matter was disposed of eventually by the arrest of the quack on the
charge of homosexuality.

Fishbein told me that he believes all the higher officers of the American Army should be examined by psychiatrists. He says he sees plain
evidence that some of them are not altogether normal, and that in a
few cases he is sure that they are not. He said that General Patton,
who was lately hauled up for an assault upon a wounded soldier, was
plainly more or less cuckoo. He is an extremely excitable and noisy
fellow, and always bursts into tears when his emotions are stirred. His

infirmity is well known in the Army, but nevertheless Roosevelt insisted upon giving him a high commission.

Fishbein promised to let me have his whole file of materials relating to medical terminology. It should be useful to me in the preparation of the supplement to "The American Language."

Fishbein spends over half his time touring the country and making speeches. He is an extremely busy fellow, and gets through a really appalling amount of work every week. He writes a daily medical column, contributes a monthly article to one of the women's magazines, writes a great many editorials for the *Journal of the American Medical Association*, and also does a lot of other literary work. He told me that his output runs to 15,000 words a week, and that he keeps three secretaries busy. He said that he often dictates a 3,000-word article in less than an hour.

The *Journal of the American Medical Association* is suffering from a paper shortage, like the newspapers. The average size of a number has been greatly reduced, and a lot of good advertising has been declined.

BALTIMORE, DECEMBER 31, 1943.

I close the year rather more comfortable than I started it. The old distress about the heart, which began back in 1938, now bothers me very seldom, and I have had few spells of quick breathing at night. Now and then there are days when I have a full feeling in the head and other signs of rising blood pressure, but they are not many. Despite the unusual severity of hay-fever this year, I have managed to do a fair amount of work during its second half. I now have more than 500 pages of the supplement to "The American Language" in fair copy, on paper, which must amount to about 150,000 words. In all probability, I'll run far over the limit that must be set for the book; if so, I'll proceed at once to a second supplement. There is enough material in hand to make half a dozen. The work is often tedious, but I rather like it, and on days when I am feeling reasonably well I knock out a good deal. The horrible malaise that beset me a year ago is now much less marked, and I begin to suspect that I may have beaten it with cold baths in the morning, begun during the Summer. They are probably bad for my heart, but they at least make me feel better. Taking one night with another, I sleep very well. August and I usually close the day together, sitting by the fire and taking a few drinks. I seldom go out in the evening. My customary ration is either three bottles of beer or two Scotch highballs. August drinks one bottle of ale, or, rarely, a rye highball. This moderate alcoholization helps me to sleep, and I never notice any bad effects from it. But whenever I drink more I feel somewhat rocky the next day, and usually have a touch of gastritis.

When Paul Patterson is in town I commonly drop in on him at the *Sun* office in the afternoon, and there put in an hour more or less in gabbling with him, with Harry C. Black, with William F. Schmick, and with any other office dignitary who happens in. I like to hear the office gossip, and do not mind offering advice when it is asked for, but I seldom volunteer it, and on the whole the *Sunpapers'* problems do not greatly interest me. Their editorial course is now so far from anything that seems rational to me that I have virtually washed my hands of them. Patterson knows this, but insists that I stay on, and I see no reason why I should give up $9,000 a year for the sake of escaping a little boredom. I am still a director in the corporation and seldom miss a board meeting, and Patterson often consults me on Associated Press business. The affairs of the A.P. have been badly manhandled, and he is as much responsible for it as any other, but there is still some possibility of straightening him out, and I rather enjoy the effort.

Without August I'd be lost indeed. He and I read much the same books, are interested in many of the same things, and think alike about all matters of any importance. I thus enjoy sitting with him in the evenings. He has a very pungent humor, and his comments on the mountebanks now running the world are often excellent. Now and then I miss writing for the *Sun,* but not often. That episode in my life is now definitely over, and I don't want to revive it. Patterson always talks on the assumption that I'll help to cover the two national conventions next Summer, but I [am] not inclined to do it. It would be simply impossible for me to write about them without playing down all my real opinion—and I am too old, and too set in my ways, for any such pussy-footing. The *Sunpapers,* as John Owens has debauched them, are in no need of my help, and I have long outlived my need of them. They degenerate rapidly to the estate of third-rate provincial journals. No one quotes them. No one attends to their ideas. No one gives them any thought. There was a time when all the more ambitious young newspaper men of the country sought jobs on them, but that time is no more. It amuses me to reflect that they may be remembered hereafter—that is, in their Patterson epoch—largely and perhaps even mainly because I worked for them. The only other man they have produced who has ever got the slightest amount of national attention is Gerald W. Johnson, and now Johnson has quit his job—to the relief of everyone, for he has been deteriorating for ten years past.

Reckoning up, I find that my contributions to this Diary in 1943 have run to more than 65,000 words, the equivalent of a good-sized book.

1944

The usual New Year luncheon at the Maryland Club today was the dullest that I have seen since I joined the club. The crowd was small and extremely quiet. The heavy boozing of past years was simply not visible. I noted in particular how few young men were present. There was indeed an almost complete absence of uniforms. In the whole place I noticed no more than a dozen.

Paul Patterson, John Semmes, Schmick and I had a table in the main dining-room. Our guests were Frank Knox,[1] Secretary of the Navy; Captain Leland P. Lovette, head of the Navy's press section; a major of Marines, who is aide to Knox; a naval captain (a newspaper man in civilian life, who is also one of his aides), and Mark S. Watson of the *Sun*, who had recently returned from six months as a war correspondent in North Africa and Italy. I forget the names of the Marine major and the naval captain. I sat beside Lovette and we had a very pleasant session. Knox was in excellent humor, and seemed to enjoy the party very much. The day was his 70th birthday, and we celebrated it by having the waiters bring in a small birthday cake with three candles. Despite his age, Knox looked to be in excellent condition and was certainly in good humor. When the colored musicians, who always serve New Year's luncheon at the Maryland Club, came up to play "Happy Birthday to You" it was the one touch of merriment that I noticed during the whole meal. The wine list offered by the club was

---

1 Frank Knox (1874–1944), newspaperman, Republican vice-presidential candidate in 1936, secretary of the navy under Franklin D. Roosevelt. He was to die less than four months later; see the entry for April 29, 1944 (p. 317).

so meagre that we decided not to order anything from it. Instead, we stuck to highballs and beer. I had one highball and one bottle of beer. Knox and his two aides left for Washington at about 3 o'clock, but Lovette lingered on. At 4:15 I took him to Mt. Royal Station, where he boarded a train for home.

Toward the end of the luncheon Charlie Baetjer, who is the treasurer of the club, came up and suggested that Knox be asked to say a few words to the assembled members. I vetoed that at once. Knox had been invited to Baltimore on the promise that he would not be asked to make a speech. He was in a happy mood, and it was plain that calling on him suddenly would upset him. Baetjer agreed quickly, and so no more was said of the matter.

Lovette told me that he is now near the head of the list of Navy captains. He must make a captain's cruise, however, before he can be advanced to the rank of rear admiral. He said that in all probability he'd be assigned to the command of a task force in the Pacific, and hinted that his tour of duty there would be short. When it is completed he'll return to Washington with the rank of rear-admiral, to resume charge of the Navy's press office. He has conducted its affairs with great skill, and is enormously popular among newspaper men. He was in command of a destroyer squadron at Pearl Harbor, and his flagship was destroyed. He lost not only all of his clothes, but also a considerable library that he had aboard. In that library were several books of mine. He told me that when he returns to the Pacific he will take along only a few books, for he doesn't want to suffer another such destruction of his library.

Knox I have known ever since the negotiations with the Hearst papers regarding the granting of an Associated Press franchise to the *Evening Sun.* That was nearly twenty years ago. He is an extremely amiable and friendly fellow, and while he served as general manager of the Hearst newspapers he showed a very considerable professional skill. However, I see no evidence that he is a man of any great intellectual capacity in general. His mind is that of a small town newspaper proprietor of some shrewdness. He is, however, smart enough to let better men solve most of his problems for him. He has apparently got together a really competent general staff for the Navy and he lets it have its way.

Lovette told me that the term *leatherteat* is his own invention. He suggested it at a conference when a brief name for the Marine Corps' women auxiliary, analogous to *wave* and *waac*,[1] was under discussion. He and the marine major said that it was not in general use. The marines' chosen name for their female aides is *bams*, from *big-assed* marines, or *broad-assed*. The marine major said that the Washington philologians are now wrestling with the embarrassing problem of inventing an abbreviation for Columbia University Nurses Training-school. The initial letters, of course, would not do at all.

BALTIMORE, JANUARY 12, 1944.

I went to New York Sunday afternoon, January 9th, to round up a lot of more or less vexatious business. On the train I met Leonard Weinberg, the Baltimore lawyer. He and I have been on good terms for many years. When I first knew him he was a stenographer in the courts. He studied law in the University of Maryland evening school and began to prosper from the moment he set up practice. He now represents a great many of the richer Jewish firms in Baltimore, including L. Greif & Brother, one of the largest clothing manufacturers in America. He has been chiefly concerned in late years, of course, with labor cases. Rather curiously for a lawyer of rich employers, he has maintained a level head, and on occasion has actually represented unions. He is a highly intelligent fellow, and his observations are always sharp and sound. He told me a great deal of interesting stuff about the clothing business in the United States. He said that some of the largest and best known manufacturers are not far from bankruptcy. The industry is still afflicted by sweat-shop competition. Any Jewish cutter who saves a few hundred dollars can start a little factory. He does his own cutting and farms out the fabrication of the clothes to home workers. His brand, of course, is worth nothing, but the cheaper clothing retailers offer him a ready market, for he can undersell the big manufacturers.

In New York on Sunday night I had dinner with Paul Palmer. Some time ago he proposed to me that Albert Jay Nock and I engage in a correspondence on the issues of the hour, with a view to making an eventual book. Palmer himself launched this project with a letter to

1 During World War II, WAVE was an acronym for Women Accepted for Volunteer Emergency Service (in the U.S. Navy), and WAAC (eventually shortened to WAC) meant Women's Army Auxiliary Corps.

Nock, and last week he sent me Nock's reply. I had to tell him, unhappily, that the project seemed to me to be unfeasible. The truth is that Nock and I are so close together in our main ideas that it would be impossible to get up much interest in the correspondence between us. There would be no conflict whatsoever, but only an incessant ratification and acquiescence. I convinced Palmer that the book was impossible, and he said he would drop it. He is working for DeWitt Wallace on the staff of the *Reader's Digest*. He is getting a large salary, and his work is not uninteresting, but he told me that he is very eager to get rid of it. As soon as the war is over he proposes to move abroad and stay there. I argued with him that this was foolish—that no native American is ever actually happy in Europe. He admitted that this was true in normal times, but argued that after the war life in the United States will be virtually unendurable. He believes, as I do, that Roosevelt will probably go down into American history as a great hero. It is one of our Heavenly Father's characteristic jokes upon the American people, and in the usual bad taste.

On Monday night I had dinner with George Nathan at the Colony, and later we went to No. 21. There we met Howard Cullman and his wife, and put in a rather pleasant evening. Cullman, who is a rich tobacco man, has enormously increased his wealth by backing theatrical shows. He put up the money for "Life With Father," and has since been getting dividends at the rate of 100 per cent. a month. He is not an uninteresting man, and his wife is a charming though far from intellectual woman. They have a country place in Westchester near Alfred Knopf and I have visited them there. Cullman proposed that he and I meet sometime during the Spring and engage in a cigar-making match. He promised to get the tobacco and the tools. He gave me a cigar that seemed excellent to me, and when I praised it, went out to the cigar counter and returned with 50. It is put out by Benson & Hedges in Fifth avenue. He and his brother are in control of the firm. They also have heavy interests in other tobacco factories and operate an investment trust devoted wholly to tobacco stocks.

On Tuesday I had lunch with Blanche Knopf at Voisin's in Park avenue. I used to lunch there often with Sam Knopf, but had not been in the place more than once since his death eleven years ago. It is still a good restaurant, and we had a very fair lunch at a reasonable price. Blanche looked to be in much better condition physically than she was the last time I saw her.

In the afternoon there was a Knopf board meeting. When the minutes were read by Lesser, Sam Knox objected to their approval on the ground that he wanted to consult his lawyer, Kramer, before voting. This statement, of course, brought down upon him the wrath of Alfred, and for a few minutes the atmosphere was full of electricity. I intervened by explaining to Sam that his proposal involved a violation of orderly procedure. A director in a corporation has no right to consult lawyers in determining his vote. He must take the responsibility himself. After the meeting I left the place with Sam and he insisted on me stopping at his apartment in Park avenue. As on so many other occasions in the past, we there went over the whole situation at length. I think I convinced him that he made a mistake at the board meeting. I told him that his remedy, if Kramer advised him to object to the minutes as they stand, was to make a motion for their reconsideration at the next meeting. Why he objected to them I couldn't make out. They had been drawn by Ben Stern, the lawyer, and seemed to me to deal with the events of the long meeting of last November very discreetly. I argued with Sam that it is always unsafe for a corporation board to fill its minutes with minute accounts of transactions either incompleted or abandoned. It would certainly be preposterous in the present case to record the fact that the board agreed to buy Sam's stock from the treasury and then found that it was unable to do so because of a shortage of funds in the surplus. Such inconclusive business had better not be mentioned at all.

Alfred's report of operations during the second half of the company's fiscal year, ending October 31st, was very satisfactory. There was a net profit of $40,000 for the six months, after Federal taxes of $63,000. The sales were $665,000. The gross profit on them was 46.82% and the net profit, after taxes, $6\frac{1}{8}$%. The current assets of the company are now $501,000 and the current liabilities $245,000. The surplus is now $59,000, just about enough to buy Sam Knox's stock. It would be imprudent, however, to wipe out the surplus for that purpose, as it might be difficult to renew it. Thus the Knox transaction seems to be on the shelf. The accumulated arrears on the preferred stock now run to $185,000, or between $65 and $66 a share.

The rest of my time in New York was spent visiting the sick. I went down to the Chelsea on Monday and took Edgar Lee Masters' girl, Alice Davis, to lunch and then proceeded with her to the hospital where he is incarcerated. It is a sort of convalescent home in the remotest reaches of the Bronx. The address is 750 east 232nd street. Alice

had been there before and volunteered to steer me. We went by subway to 205th street, and then, after walking around for twenty minutes, proceeded to take the elevated line to 230th street. Unhappily,
no elevated train came along, and it was so cold on the platform that
we couldn't stand it, so we returned to the street level and took a
trolley car instead. Altogether, we were more than an hour and a half
on the way. The so-called sanitarium in which Masters is staying is an
old-time private house in a large yard. It lies in a sparsely settled
neighborhood, and is altogether rather bleak looking. We found him
in his room and had a pleasant enough visit with him. It had to be
short, for Alice was in fear that his second wife, Ellen, might show up
at any minute. Ellen has now moved down to the Chelsea in his old
quarters. She has taken full charge of him and given Alice to understand that no intervention by friends is wanted. Alice has made inquiries about the old boy's bank account and found that he has more
than $1,000 on deposit. Two weeks ago when his hotel bill became
due and there was no money in hand to pay it and the hotel threatened
to put his books, clothing and other traps into storage, I sent Alice
$100 and with it she staved off the hotel management. Masters doesn't
know where this money came from—in fact, he probably doesn't know
that the bill has been paid. My visit with him was short, for it was
only too evident that he was in an extremely enfeebled state. He talked
rationally enough, but in the manner of an extremely tired man. Physically, he looked thin and peaked. He is 75 years old and I begin to
have some doubt that he'll ever recover fully. Coming home Alice and
I were fortunate enough to pick up a taxicab within a block of the
sanitarium, and so we returned in some comfort. She is a devoted
slave, but not too discreet. I suspect that her violent antagonism to
Mrs. Masters has caused some trouble.

The next morning Joe Hergesheimer dropped in on me at the Algonquin. I was unaware that he was in town. He explained that he
was there to look into a proposal that he do some radio crooning. He
seemed vague about the subject of his speech or speeches, and I didn't
press him for details. Apparently, Frank Case's daughter, Margaret
Harriman, is involved in the business, for Joe had spent the previous
night at Margaret's apartment discussing it with her. He told me that
he was also hopeful of getting a commission to make radio talks for
the National Art Gallery at Washington, of which Huntington Cairns
is now a high official. He said that he and Dorothy, having got rid of
the Dower House and sold virtually all their furniture and silverware,

are now preparing to settle down in their cottage at Stone Harbor. Dorothy's lameness is such that she must cut down her activities. They have therefore concocted a scheme whereby she will look after the house every day until 5 or 6 p.m., after which he will take over. He told me that he proposes to do all the cooking. How long this arrangement will last remains to be seen. I am certain that he'll tire of cooking in a little while. Moreover, his own physical state is anything but reassuring. He looked peaked and old, and needs a great deal of rest. He told me that his history of Chester county is still unfinished. The monthly payments for it stopped on January 1st, but he has yet a good deal of work to do. He told me once more, and for the hundredth time, that he was firmly resolved to write no more fiction. He and Dorothy propose to live the rest of their lives on the money obtained from the Dower House and its furnishings. The income from that money will not be sufficient to keep them, but they are apparently planning to make regular dips into the principal. Joe told me that the whole would last for ten years at least, and that he had no expectation of living so long. Dorothy has a little property of her own, and so she'll be able to go on if she survives him. I begin to suspect that it will be a miracle if she lives ten years herself.

Tuesday night, after the Knopf board meeting and my visit to Sam Knox, I went down to Second avenue in the lower East Side to see my old friend A. H. McDannald.[1] He is laid up at the New York Eye and Ear Infirmary with pneumonia, his second attack in a year. When he became ill it was impossible to get a room for him in any regular hospital, but his brother, who is the chief surgeon of the Eye and Ear place, found a small one for him there. He seemed to be very comfortable and was, in fact, plainly recovering. He told me that his illness was so severe that he couldn't sit up in bed, but that after a couple of days the sulfanol drugs began to restore him. He is, however, very weak and will probably have to take a long rest after he is discharged.

BALTIMORE, JANUARY 29, 1944.

M. M. Mathews[2] of the University of Chicago, one of the subeditors of the *Dictionary of American English*, was in Baltimore today,

1 A. H. McDannald, a former *Sun* man, was Mencken's traveling companion on two voyages, both described in *Heathen Days*—chapter nine, "A Dip into Statecraft," pp. 115–17, and chapter eleven, "Roman Holiday," pp. 128–49.
2 Mitford M. Mathews (1891–1985), philologian. He was the editor of *Dictionary of*

and I took him to dinner this evening at the Maryland Club. He turned out to be a very curious fellow—in appearance and manner not unlike a country preacher. Nevertheless, he knows a good deal and he told me a lot of interesting stuff about the editing of the DAE.

The job, which was begun in 1925, took nineteen years. The first nine of them were devoted to collecting material. Sir William Craigie, the chief editor, kept a firm hand upon the whole process, and the dictionary as it stands shows not only his prejudices, but also the gaps in his knowledge. He knows, as a matter of fact, very little about American speech and what little he knows seems to be distasteful to him. It was his established policy to exclude every word possible. There was also a good deal of Scotch prudery in him, and so he frowned upon Americanisms that seemed to him to be vulgar. As a result, the dictionary is sorely deficient in that department.

The fact that Craigie was Sir William made him a great social figure in Chicago, and his wife was one of the queens of academic society. Mathews said that some of the youngsters on the staff of the dictionary devoted themselves to cultivating her. One of them was Allen Walker Read. As a result of his high standing with her, he was permitted to devote a large part of his time to his own enterprises, and was able to produce some really excellent papers on the history of American English. But the other members of the staff, forced to grind away at their dull jobs for eight hours a day, resented his neglect of his official duties, and in the end Craigie had to bring him to book.

Mathews is planning to do a one volume shorter version of the DAE. It will not be confined to material in the larger work, but will also include a lot of stuff that Craigie excluded. In this material are many interesting things. Mathews is a dull fellow, but he unquestionably knows his stuff, and I am convinced that he'll make a useful work of the shorter dictionary. He proposed that I join him in editing it and offered to bracket my name with his own on the title page, but I declined. I told him that I had too many other irons in the fire. I promised, however, to give him whatever help I can, and it is possible that there may be some material useful to him in my files.

Mathews, back in 1931, brought out a book called "The Beginnings of American English" that I have found extremely useful. It is a report of some of the earlier discussions of Americanisms, and having it at

---

Americanisms (1951), a shorter but more complete version of the *Dictionary of American English*.

hand saves me many trips to the library. There is enough material in the early literature to make another volume of the same sort. I proposed to Mathews that he do it at once, but he showed little interest in the enterprise.

He told me that the printing bill for the DAE ran to $68,000, though the print order was for but 2,500 sets. The editorial costs were between three and four hundred thousand dollars. The staff at its maximum consisted of nine men and women. At various times a large number of students and W.P.A. clients were also put to work, but their help was of little value.

There was terrapin on the bill at the Maryland Club and Mathews, who had never tasted it before, decided that he wanted to try it. I joined him in eating it, and it turned out to be excellent. He said that he liked it very much, and offered evidence thereof by eating a large portion. Not many novices like terrapin at the first trial.

BALTIMORE, FEBRUARY 5, 1944.

I had lunch at the Marconi today with my old friend, Junius B. Wood, perhaps the greatest traveler since Marco Polo. He was on the foreign staff of the Chicago *Daily News* for many years, and as its correspondent visited the most remote parts of the world. He not only visited them; he also settled in some of them. Such places as Moscow, Bombay, Buenos Aires and Cape Town are as familiar to him as Chicago. Unfortunately, there is little in Junius's conversation to bear out the old belief that travel broadens the mind. His observations have left him what he was at the start—a second-rate newspaper reporter. At lunch today he gave over half an hour to telling me about his difficulties in getting six corncob pipes through the Russian customs. He was at that time Moscow correspondent of the *Daily News*, and wrote to me asking me to send him some pipes. I did so, but when they reached Moscow he had a hard time getting possession of them. The Russian customs' dogberries, never having seen corncob pipes before, couldn't make out what they were, and so decided to levy upon them as toys. The duty, according to Junius, amounted to something on the order of $15. With the aid of his interpreter, he entered a bitter protest, but the customs authorities refused to be moved. He then appealed to higher-ups and in the end got the pipes through without paying any duty at all.

Junius said that General Brehon B. Somervell,[1] who is now a Class 1 figure in Washington, is the protégé of Harry Hopkins, and, as might be expected, a considerable jackass. He said that Somervell built an oil pipe line into Alaska 1,500 miles long and then found when he turned oil into it that the temperatures up there were too low for pipe lines. The oil congealed and the pumps simply could not force it through the pipe. Junius said that Somervell's 2,500-mile road to Alaska is almost as laughable. It is laid over swampy land that freezes hard in Winter, but becomes a kind of soup in Summer. The road is thus usuable in Winter only. The minute the Spring thaws begin it becomes impassable. It cost many millions, and more millions are now being spent in an effort to give it a solid bottom. Meanwhile, the newspapers describe it as a great triumph of human genius.

Junius's wife, who is childless, is a dog fancier, and he and she were in Baltimore today for the current dog show. She is exhibiting a couple of dachshunds, imported from Germany before the war.

BALTIMORE, FEBRUARY 11, 1944.

Coming out of the Pratt Library in a snow storm this afternoon, I encountered Vincent dePaul Fitzpatrick, managing editor of the *Catholic Review*.[2] He backed me up against the iron railing of the Cathedral across the street and told me some of his troubles. Some years ago, it appears, he employed a Jesuit priest as an editorial writer. The priest, he said, produced a large supply of interesting and effective editorials but, unfortunately, they showed a progressive tendency toward heterodoxy. In the end, Fitzpatrick became alarmed and consulted one of the older priests of the diocese. The old priest at the start refused to listen to him—on the ground that a layman had no right to question a priest's theology. But when Fitzpatrick insisted on him reading one of the editorials, so far unprinted, he became alarmed also, and the Jesuit was brought upon the carpet. But instead of contrition and repentance, he exhibited only defiance, and the net result was that he pulled off his Roman collar and threw up his commission to save souls. According to Fitzpatrick, he is now at work as a bar-

1 General Brehon B. Somervell (1892–1955) was commanding general of the Army Service Forces in World War II.
2 Vincent dePaul Fitzpatrick (1885–1953) had been managing editor of the Baltimore *Catholic Review* since 1920.

tender at a saloon in Charles street between Read and Eager. I had heard nothing of this episode. The other Jesuits in Baltimore kept it very quiet.

One day last week Monsignor Nelligan, secretary to Archbishop Curley, called up the *Sun* office and made a bitter protest against a full-page ad advertising the 5-cent books of E. Haldeman-Julius.[1] In view of our difficulties with the Archbishop in 1934 every one in the office was disinclined to pay any attention to him, but Patterson advised Schmick to call me up and I advised him to kill the Haldeman-Julius ad forthwith. The Archbishop's objection is to the fact that the 5-cent books include a number by an ex-priest named Joseph McCabe, in which the popes and the Church are violently attacked. My own objection to Haldeman-Julius is that he is a highly dubious Jew. Twelve or fifteen years ago Samuel Knopf and I decided to bar his advertising from the *American Mercury*. His 5-cent books are mainly trash, and he sells them by all kinds of high pressure scheming. One of his devices is to give old books new and inflammatory titles. He has done this with many of the stories of de Maupassant. He makes one of them suffice for a whole 5-cent book, and on the cover he gives it a title that de Maupassant never heard of. Some of his titles, though they are not obscene in themselves, plainly promise obscenity within. His books are printed very badly, and are not worth even five cents. They have a large circulation among schoolboys. Haldeman-Julius's real name is Emanuel Julius. He went out to Kansas many years ago, married a girl named Haldeman, a niece of Jane Addams, and hyphenated her surname with his own. She had some money, and with it he acquired control of the old *Appeal to Reason*, one of [the] early Communist papers. When it blew up he began to devote its printing plant to the production of cheap books, and his 5-cent series is one of the results. He has launched at different times at least a dozen magazines, but not one of them has succeeded. Nor has he ever succeeded in selling books at higher prices.

Fitzpatrick told me that the call to the *Sun* office was probably not actually inspired by the Archbishop. He said that Nelligan most likely

---

1 Emanuel Haldeman-Julius (1889–1951), author, editor and publisher. He was sometimes called the "Henry Ford of publishing." His *Little Blue Books*, which started out selling for a quarter but later (because of mass production methods) were reduced to 5 cents, were in many ways the forerunner of today's paperbacks and reached an enormous audience in the period between the two world wars.

made it on his own motion. Nelligan is a son of the late John Nelligan, for many years a director in the A. S. Abell Company. The old man was a pious Catholic, but nevertheless not abject. At the time of our battle with the Archbishop he advised John Owens and me to stand up against him. He made no specific recommendation regarding our conduct of the battle, but he said plainly that he thought we were entitled to state our case in our own words. If it had not been for this support I incline to believe that Paul Patterson would have knuckled down to the Archbishop. He was badly alarmed.

Fitzpatrick told me that the Archbishop apparently seldom reads the editorials in the *Catholic Review*, and that when they depart from his own position and his attention is called to them, he seldom makes any uproar. He is plainly convinced that the editorial page of a Catholic paper, like that of a daily paper, may be safely disregarded. His own roaring is done on the first page.

Fitzpatrick assured me that it grieved him sorely to have to write so much abuse of the *Sun* at the time of our battle with the Archbishop. I am inclined to believe that this is only an afterthought. He was at that time sore at the *Sun* because certain assignments that he craved while he was on its reportorial staff had been given to others. He is now getting along into middle age, and has settled into a job that fits his talents precisely. He is not good enough for a daily paper, but he runs the *Catholic Review* with some skill.

BALTIMORE, FEBRUARY 18, 1944.

The annual dinner of the *Sun* Route-Owners' Association last night was the usual dull affair. It was held at the Lord Baltimore Hotel, and there was a large turnout—in fact, the largest in the history of the organization. Nearly all the *Sunpaper* functionaries, from Patterson, Black and Schmick down, were on hand, and each had paid $5 for his ticket, for the route-owners have the pleasant custom of sending bills to their guests a couple of weeks in advance. I sat at a table with Patterson, Yardley[1] the cartoonist, and several of the older carriers and retired carriers—among the latter an ancient named Utermohle, now 86 years old. He was a cigarmaker at one time in his remote youth, so

---

1 Richard Q. Yardley (1903–1979) was editorial cartoonist for the *Sun* from 1949 to 1972.

we always have plenty to talk of. When one of the recurring depressions flabbergasted the cigar trade he went to work as a letter-carrier. This was in the early 80's. The beginning wages of a letter-carrier, he told me, were then $11 a week, and the highest pay he could hope for after long service was $1,000 a year. Utermohle was supposed to be protected by civil service rules, but when a new postmaster came into office he was got rid of by assigning him to a one-horse collecting cart. After one day of it he quit, and soon afterward became a carrier for the *Sun*.

The old boy drank eight or ten glasses of the beer served at the dinner—a horrible brew of unknown name—and I had to go along with him. Patterson, who arrived at the hotel somewhat tight, demanded a bottle of Scotch, but the waitresses reported that there was none to be had. He then called for the banquet manager, and presently the manager brought in a bottle and slipped it to Patterson with a great show of secrecy. It was, he said, his own private stock. What it cost I don't know, but when I saw the label I had to laugh, for it showed that the "Scotch" had been made in the Virgin Islands. I took a sip to try it: it tasted like bad rum that had been used to preserve anatomical specimens. Patterson got down a highball of it, but Yardley refused to drink it, and instead proposed to slip out and get a bottle of actual whiskey. Patterson protested but Yardley made off, and in ten minutes returned with a fifth of Vat 69. I stuck to beer, but Patterson, Yardley and a few of the others at the table got down the bottle before the evening was over.

The show was the usual rowdy combination of lodge-party acts. The last turn was by a Spanish dancer. As she bounced on the lights were dimmed and a small spot was aimed at her back, which was bare to the waist. She did a very voluptuous dance, and soon proceeded to highly indecent contortions. She would grab a man from the row of chairs fronting the dance floor, pull him to his feet, clasp him tightly, and then engage in a realistic imitation of copulation. Some of the victims took it lightly, but others appeared to be vastly embarrassed. Old Utermohle crowded to the front expectantly, but the dancer had apparently been warned to let him alone. The climax was a long and lascivious struggle with James W. Sennett, the president of the Route Owners' Association. When this was over the dancer dropped her dress, pulled off a pair of false breasts, and let it be known in a bass voice that she was actually a man. It was an amusing act, and I was completely deceived. Sennett, of course, knew the truth, but most of the others had no suspicion of it. The dancer asked all the guests to keep it quiet, for, as he explained, he hoped to fool many other gangs of Baltimore banqueters before the end of the Winter.

I got home early, and was in bed by midnight. The evening had been long and somewhat weary.

BALTIMORE, MARCH 17, 1944.

Paul Patterson dropped in last night for our long-delayed palaver about the national conventions. When it was decided that both would be held in Chicago this year he made arrangements at once for accommodations for the *Sunpapers'* staffs at the Blackstone Hotel. This was in January and he told me at the time that he was counting on me to go along as in the past. I replied then that I was disinclined to do so and suggested that we have a session some evening to discuss the matter. He had been putting off that session ever since. About three weeks ago I reminded him that the time was growing short, and we had better fall on the business. He made various excuses thereafter, but yesterday afternoon he called me up and proposed that we meet last night. I was willing, and so he came in.

I told him without preliminaries that it would be impossible for me to help cover the conventions for the *Sun*. He had known all the while, of course, that that was what I would say, but he professed to be surprised and asked me my reasons. I replied that the principal one was that the *Sunpapers*, in their manner of supporting the war, had departed so far from my notions of sound journalism that I simply could not write for them. I had quit doing so early in 1941, and I was determined to keep my name out of them unless and until they returned to what seemed to me to be honest and reasonable courses. Inasmuch as I saw no indication of any such change, and believed that it would be impossible so long as he (Patterson) remained in charge of them and John W. Owens continued as their chief editor, I had concluded, I said, that I was out for life. Patterson protested against this position as too rigid and too scrupulous, and said that he was willing to give me his personal guarantee that anything I wrote would be printed, no matter how far it departed from the paper's policy. He argued that the thing I have been in the habit of doing, the running story from the press-stand, did not necessarily involve any consideration of issues, and that I would be quite free to depict the participants in the two conventions precisely as they appeared to me, without any regard to the validity or non-validity of their ideas. I replied that this freedom would be only apparent. I'd be conscious all the while that I was writing for a newspaper with which I had no sympathy, and that fact would incommode me at every turn and inevitably set me to trying to figure out, maybe in moments of severe stress, what I could decently write and what I couldn't. Moreover, I said, experience had taught me that Owens and some of the others could not be trusted to acquiesce in any agreement that I made with Patterson himself. I recalled to him what happened in 1920, when I covered my first national convention for the *Sun*. At that time, writing from Chicago, I expressed some doubt that Woodrow Wilson's word was worth anything, and on my return to Baltimore via San Francisco I found that J. Haslup Adams had demanded, with a threat to resign as editor unless his demand were granted, that I be fired from the staff, and that John Owens and Frank Kent had supported him. Patterson said that nothing of the sort was likely in 1944, but I replied that it remained a possibility, and that I did not propose to submit myself to any such attack by my inferiors, or to make any use of their unwilling tolerance. It was this episode of 1920 that really launched the long effort to reorganize and rehabilitate the *Sunpapers*, and in that effort I had a principal hand. But now, I said, they had gone back to where they were before, and I had become too old and had become too disheartened by their deterioration to undertake anything of the sort again.

Patterson then proposed that I go to the conventions anyhow, if not as an active correspondent, then as a sort of correspondent emeritus, or even as a mere guest. He said he would miss me sorely if I didn't. I replied that I would miss the show just as sorely, for it would be the first time since 1920 that I had not seen it (I actually covered my first pair of conventions for the Baltimore *Morning Herald* in 1904), but that I was determined to stay home. Emergencies, I said, are bound to arise at such times, and it would be psychologically impossible for an old reporter to stand idly by if help were needed. Within twenty-four hours I'd probably be at work. If not, then all the other correspondents would notice the fact, and it would produce a great many embarrassing inquiries and a lot of gossip. Not a few correspondents would record my idleness in their dispatches, and if they did not hint that there was trouble in the *Sunpapers'* outfit, then they could be trusted to hint that I was disabled by age. In either case the talk would be unpleasant, and it would be much easier and more logical to stay away altogether. My absence would not interest the correspondents half so much as my presence doing nothing. They would conclude that I had some other more interesting enterprise in hand, and let it go at that.

All this discussion was in the frankest terms. I told Patterson that I resented the decay of the *Sunpapers* during the past ten years, and that I held him responsible for it. It was his business to find a competent editor for them, and at that business he had failed, either by incapacity or by neglect. He replied that he realized he was temperamentally unfit for it. He was, he said, a news man first and last, and editorial questions always bored him. He was thus disposed to leave the editorial pages in charge of whoever seemed able to run them without bothering him, however bad that running might be. He interfered only as a last resort, and hence very seldom. He then asked me why I had not made more suggestions myself. I replied that I had not done so because it seemed to me to be useless—that only a complete cleaning out could ever have solved the problem, and that I was convinced after the battle with the Archbishop, in 1934, that no such cleaning out was possible. In that battle John Owens got the upper hand of Patterson, and the history of the papers since is largely the history of Patterson's fear of him. Patterson did not attempt to deny this. He argued that he had to endure Owens' treason in the face of the enemy in 1934 for the good of the paper. If he (Owens) had been permitted to go he would have spread the story that he had resigned because the *Sun* refused to stand up to the Archbishop, and that this might have been ruinous. I replied that the plain facts were there to refute any such fable. The *Sun's* long-delayed statement, prepared by me and revised by Patterson, certainly did not knuckle down to the Archbishop. On the contrary, it refused all of his demands, and that it so refused them was understood by the priests of the archdiocese at the time, and is still understood today, as Vincent deP. Fitzpatrick, editor of the *Catholic Review*, was telling me only a few weeks ago.

We soon got on the subject of the war, and I said flatly that I thought the *Sun's* course was not only ignorant and absurd, but also not a little disingenuous. It had gone over to the English in an abject and ignominious fashion, against all reason and all the obvious facts. Worse, it had yielded supinely to the most outrageous fiats of the Roosevelt censorship, and had even exceeded them. This shook Patterson somewhat, for he likes to think of himself as a news editor, and he insisted that in handling the war news the *Sun* had done good work. In particular, he said, he was proud of the work of its foreign correspondents. I told him that they were actually feature writers, not news correspondents, and that he himself, in his handling of them, acted as a mere feature editor. They sent in a great deal of gossipy, cheerful and so-called "human interest" stuff, but there was no evidence that any of them had ever tried to deal with the war realistically. Any reader dependent upon the *Sun*, I said, must believe that the Italian campaign had been a brilliant success, and that Admiral Nimitz had already sunk half the Japanese ship tonnage. Mark Watson, in his military reviews, made some effort at the start to tell the truth, but since Patterson took him to England to be indoctrinated he has kept pretty well to the party line, though with occasional cautious bulges into frankness. Watson, as everyone knows, is a timorous fellow, and would be the last man on earth to buck the paper's policy. But what then, asked Patterson, of the Associated Press stuff? Hadn't I myself once praised one of its young correspondents? True, but that was early in the war. Today the A.P. copy is almost as puerile as that of the *Sun*'s own correspondents. Kent Cooper, the general manager, is another feature man disguised as a news editor. He has made the A.P. report "bright" at the cost of its old dogged accuracy. Half the stuff it sends out is so preposterous that no sane man credits it. Here I hit a tender spot, for Patterson, as a director in the A.P., has been one of Cooper's sturdiest supporters, and he knows very well that I think Cooper has made a mess of his job. I have, in fact, often told him that I think Cooper was primarily to blame for the proceedings against the A.P. by the Department of Justice, and that I believe it would be improved immensely by a thoroughgoing reorganization and the appointment of a new general manager.

The talk drifted back to John Owens and I spoke of his enormous ignorance of foreign affairs. All he knows is what he reads in the Manchester *Guardian*, and his chief hero in Washington is the unspeakable Cordell Hull, one of the most shameless politicoes ever seen there. Patterson defended Owens by saying that he himself is responsible for the paper's attitude toward the war—that he was urging the support of England at a time when Owens was still in doubt. This I am inclined to believe, but certainly it is nothing for the head of a presumably intelligent newspaper to boast of. I told Patterson that, in my judgment, the English had found him an easy mark, and had made a monkey of him. He made a long and rambling defense, but did not attempt to dispute the main fact. In the course of his talk I gathered *(a)* that he believes that the English captured 300,000 Germans in North Africa, and *(b)* that he is entertained while in London by an Englishwoman who is at the head of one of the women's auxiliary organizations—perhaps characteristically, he did not know its name. He also let fall the proud fact that she is a countess. He ended by saying that he wished he could return to London with Watson in April, to stay another three or four months, but that he feared the national conventions would make it impossible. I replied that there was really no need for him to go to the national conventions. There will be too little white paper to cover them in the *Sunpapers'* usual manner, or even in any approximation of it. Why not leave the job to Dewey Fleming and Paul Ward, with such help as they may need supplied by the home office? Unless Roosevelt decides to retire, they will hardly be exciting. The A.P. reports will be quite good enough for the *Sun* as it stands today.

The conversation then widened, and I made the rather surprising discovery that Patterson was densely ignorant of the Constitution of the United States, and had not looked into it for years, if indeed he had ever looked into it at all. He asked me quite innocently why the Bill of Rights was spoken of as a separate document, and seemed amazed when I told him that it was embodied in amendments. He asked me to tell him briefly how that came about, and I did so. I also sketched the history of the Constitution itself, and he seemed to be hearing something quite new to him. In the end he asked me to recommend some short book on the Constitution that would make him understand precisely what was in it. I told him that many such books existed, but that it would be much quicker and more satisfactory to read the Constitution itself. It could be done, I explained, in fifteen minutes, which surprised him all over again. If I didn't know him so well I'd have suspected that he was trying to spoof me. But it was plain from his talk that his ignorance was not feigned. He never reads anything save newspapers, and even among newspapers he confines himself pretty strictly to the *Sunpapers*. The only magazines he looks into are *Time, Life* and the *Editor and Publisher*. He even dislikes to read the documents necessary to his daily work. Time after time he has pushed a mass of papers relating to the A.P. across his desk and asked me to read them and give him my verdict. Every time I have offered such a verdict he has adopted it as his own. His gloomy evenings at home, policing his troublesome family, are spent to the tune of the radio. He listens to speeches, and to all the worst of the so-called comic programmes. I have never gone into his house, with the radio on, without begging him to shut it off. So far as I know, he has never once tried the experiment of tuning in on a programme of decent music.

I told him that I believed my salary ought to be again revised downward, as it was in the early part of 1941. I said that I was essentially an editorial man, and that I had become immovably convinced that it would never be possible, save in the unlikely event that I survived him, to serve the *Sunpapers* again in that capacity. They had removed so far from what I thought intelligent newspapers ought to be that I refused to have anything to do with them. They were back in the wallow that we had tried to pull them out of in 1920; they were, in fact, back to the dull orthodoxy that marked them in the last days of the Abells. When they made a show of independence it was hardly more than false pretenses—perhaps ameliorated by a childish sort of self delusion. They would oppose a fourth term for Roosevelt, but all the while they would support him in the war-mongering that made it virtually inevitable. Some time ago Patterson offered to bet me a dinner for six men that they would *not* support Roosevelt in 1944. I accepted the bet gladly—and explained that I hoped to lose. Patterson mentioned this bet and I reiterated my hope. He then went on to say that he was determined that they should support whomever the Republicans nominate, even Bricker.[1] I couldn't help laughing. "You will *think* they are supporting him," I said, "but John Owens will whoop up Cordell Hull ten times for Bricker once, and Ham Owens will carry on his usual covert rooting for the New Deal."

We fell to talking about editorial writers, and I told him that, in my judgment, there wasn't a single first-rate man, or even a second-rate man, on the present staff. Of all that have been in the service since 1920 only Gerald W. Johnson has ever made any noise outside

---

1 John W. Bricker (1893–1986), governor of Ohio from 1939 to 1945. At the time of this entry he was seeking the Republican presidential nomination, but lost to Thomas E. Dewey.

the office—and Gerald, inside, began to deteriorate ten years ago, and during his last five years was hardly more than a problem child. The rest are nonentities. During the years following 1920 some men of ability came on the paper, for example, James M. Cain and Paul Palmer, but they all cleared out quickly. After 1930 I never made any recommendations, for the best men were becoming wary of the *Sun* and I hesitated to advise any good one to take a job under the two Owenses. From time to time Patterson would urge me to find him some capable youngsters, and once he offered, if I could unearth a really first-rate editor, to put him over the two Owenses. At various other times he offered me the job myself, and once he proposed to make me vice-president in charge of all editorial matters. But I had begun to suspect by then that the situation was intrinsically hopeless, and that it would be a cruel disservice to a really good man to introduce him into it. I said so frankly last night. Patterson took it quietly. The truth is that he is not interested in editorial matters. The third-raters of the present staff meet his requirements sufficiently. They have no ideas, and most of them can't write, but they are at least willing to sing whatever hymn is lined out by the two Owenses.

At eleven o'clock, one of the *Sun* drivers, Bender, brought a car to take Patterson home. We had each got down three stiff Scotch highballs by that time, and Patterson, in addition, had drunk two before dinner at home. He was thus in an expansive mood, and invited Bender in to have a drink. Bender took a cigar but refused the drink, on the ground that he never touches alcohol when he is at work driving a car. He sat by the fire for half an hour, listening to the innocuous tail-end of our conversation, and then started home with his passenger. The evening left me somewhat melancholy. It is depressing to see the *Sunpapers* come to such a pass, and it is even more depressing to see Patterson content and complacent. He had a superb opportunity in Baltimore, but he has muffed it. There was a chance to build up a paper that would show its heels to the country, but all he has produced is a highly prosperous but incurably dull and stupid party organ. The English, in the end, will laugh at him; in fact, I suspect that they are doing so now. They have a magnificent talent for nabbing such ambitious but ill-informed men, but it is perhaps to their credit that they never have any respect for their victims.

This afternoon, at the office, Patterson said that he refused to believe that I would actually keep away from the national conventions.

"That question," he said, "is still open." "There was never a question," I replied, "that was more tightly closed." I then brought up again the matter of my salary, which we had discussed inconclusively last night. He protested that it was not too high—that I was earning it easily by my services in labor and other such matters. All the other principal functionaries in the office, both upstairs and down, he said, were being paid more. We got nowhere, and ended by agreeing to discuss the business at some future time. I think I'd be more comfortable if there were at least a token reduction. I want to feel free to decline to take any hand in editorial affairs. I said that I believed that my coming to the office five times a week was a bad idea—that we were often reduced, in the absence of business, to idle gossip. I proposed that instead of doing so I stand on call at all times, but come in regularly only for lunch once or twice a week. To this he agreed.

BALTIMORE, APRIL 19, 1944.

Harry Black called me up somewhat mysteriously this morning and said that he wanted to see me at the *Sun* office this afternoon. I suggested 2.30 and he agreed. We met in the office of Paul Patterson, who is in New York on Associated Press business. He plunged into business at once. He has come to harbor doubts, it appeared, about young Maclean Patterson,[1] who has been managing editor of the morning edition for a year or more. I gathered that he had been talking to Neil Swanson. Maclean, said Black, is an excellent man for routine matters and may be trusted to keep the paper out of trouble; moreover, he gets on very well with the men. But he has no ideas, and is letting the paper bog down. I began to smell a nigger in the woodpile. Some time ago Paul told me that Black has taken to calling up Maclean at night and afflicting him with numerous suggestions. At least half the time these suggestions are incoherent, for Black is usually well loaded by the time he finishes dinner. There was a time when I was his victim, but I managed to shake him off, and he has since practised on various others, with poor Mac doing current service. He was full of a plan to take Mac from the managing editor's desk and put him to some sort of writing. It was a scheme, he recalled, that worked in the case of

1 W. Maclean Patterson (1912–1976), son of Paul Patterson, served as managing editor—later general managing editor—of the *Sunpapers* from 1942 to 1952.

Frank R. Kent, Sr., and it might work again. But it seemed to me to be baloney and I said so. Mac has been tried at writing, and without success. His talents, such as they are, lie in the direction of management, and he'd never do as well as a columnist or a Washington correspondent as he is doing as managing editor. Moreover, the present is no time for experimenting, and the fact that Mac has few ideas is perhaps fortunate. I argued along this line at some length, and, seeing Black shaken, seized the chance to rub it in. The *Sunpapers*, I said, are in a state of suspended animation. The intellectual independence and love of novelty that marked them fifteen years ago are no more. They have settled into a conventional rut, and I, for one, am too old and too discouraged to make any attempt to drag them out of it. "Don't forget," I said, "that the men who tried to make something of them are now all past sixty. Also, don't forget that no real reorganization and rehabilitation would be possible in war time. As for me, I am content to let them peg along. It is a far from glorious course, and it offers nothing interesting to men of active mind, but it is at least safe. The best you and I can do is to hand over the property, undamaged, to our successors. The job of pulling the papers out of their present wallow is one for younger men. Swanson is still young enough to take a hand in it—that is, if the war ends in a reasonable time—, and he can be trusted to find even younger fellows to help him. He is the only really first-rate man on the staff at the moment, but one is enough."

It was plain to see that all this daunted Black, but he took it without challenge. After all, he said resignedly, Swanson is responsible for Mac and has promised to handle the situation if he turns out to be hopeless, and we may as well let him do so. I agreed, but Black continued with complaints. The *Evening Sun*, he said, has lately developed a number of good men, but the morning edition has none. This is not true, and if it were true it would not be discreditable to Mac, for Swanson handles all hiring and firing on both papers himself, and is the man responsible if the morning paper shows no youngsters of real competence. He is, at best, working under severe handicaps. All the best young men are being pulled into the war, and if he catches an older one of any merit it is a sort of accident, even a miracle. In any case, nothing can be done at the moment. It would be useless to attempt any general reorganization of the news department so long as the editorial pages remain at their present low level, and there is not much hope of improving them while John W. Owens has any voice in them. As for Hamilton Owens, he is a mere weather-cock. He was a smart and competent editor in the palmy days of the *Evening Sun*, but now, with John riding him, he is a bad one.

Thus Black and I parted, with him suggesting that we resume the discussion at some time in the future. I agreed, but am certainly not eager to go on with it. Mac, it seems to me, has done pretty well—considering his difficulties. It is no easy thing for the boss's son to make his way without arousing jealousy and envy. I reminded Black that he and I were both in that unhappy position in our early days, and should sympathize with Mac. He is, to be sure, very far from brilliant, but he is quite good enough for the sort of paper the *Sun* has become. If he really had ideas, and tried to execute them, he'd meet with very formidable resistance from everyone save Swanson. As for Swanson, I believe he is too smart to undertake anything on a large scale until John Owens is disposed of, and there is something resembling a renaissance of intelligence. He, too, I believe, though he has not said so, is waiting patiently for the dawn of a better day. I am quite convinced that it will never come until both John Owens and Paul Patterson are out.

BALTIMORE, APRIL 21, 1944.

Hester Denby, our colored cook and housekeeper, had an accident last Sunday, April 16th, that has put her left arm in a cast and taken her out of service. I spent the morning cleaning the wine-vault in the cellar, and went in to the kitchen to borrow a dust-brush. Hester started for the pantry to get it for me, slipped on the floor, and came down heavily, with her arm under her. I lifted her up and applied ice to her wrist, but the pain was severe, and I urged her to have an x-ray. I offered to take her to the Johns Hopkins, but she said she had a doctor she trusted, and made off to consult him. The next day the x-ray was made, and it was found that her thumb had been dislocated and a small bone in the wrist broken. This examination was made at the University of Maryland Hospital, and the doctors there put on the cast. Hester comes in every morning, does the marketing, and keeps an eye on the house, but is unable to cook. She says that all pain has disappeared. How long she will be disabled I do not know. I have already paid her x-ray bills and I'll pay her doctor's bill also. The accident was caused by her own inadvertence. She bustled toward the pantry without watching her step. Emma has been cooking in her absence, and doing it very well.

BALTIMORE, APRIL 22, 1944.

I had lunch at the Belvedere today with Dr. Ola E. Winslow, professor of English at Goucher College and Sara's old and faithful friend. I was to meet her in the lobby at 12:30, but at that moment I was still at my desk at home. I had forgotten the engagement completely. When Emma the maid came in at 12:30 and asked me if I was having lunch in the house I said yes, but then remembered, and began a frantic telephoning to the Belvedere. After five minutes' delay I had Miss Winslow on the line, and she very politely waited. I finally arrived at 12:55.

She told me that she is leaving Goucher for a year. Wellesley has offered her more than her Goucher salary to take over for the head of its English department, who is on leave, and she will begin work in August. She is to teach what she described as "advanced Shakespeare" and also American literature. Her work will be concentrated into three days a week, and she will have every week-end off, including Monday. This will enable her to make frequent visits to her farm in Maine, her great pride and delight. She will have five weeks' holiday at Christmas, and proposes to spend them in Baltimore. She will keep her apartment here. At Wellesley she will have a room in a dormitory for unmarried members of the faculty.

She is obviously hopeful that Wellesley will ask her to remain after her year is up, but somewhat doubtful about it, for she is near the age of retirement. She said that she has no claim on Goucher for a pension. She might have joined its pension fund by contributing $2\frac{1}{2}\%$ of her salary over the years, with the college contributing another $2\frac{1}{2}\%$, but she has not done so. She told me that Goucher, under David A. Robertson, is now in the last stages of disintegration. The student body has declined to 600 girls, and the revenues are much depleted. When a teacher leaves or dies, which happens frequently, no substitute is employed, but there is a closing of ranks. As a result all the members of the faculty are overworked. In addition to their heavy teaching loads they have to sit upon innumerable committees, for Robertson, an utter ass, is incompetent to run the place, and shoulders all decisions upon the faculty. Miss Winslow said that she sometimes had as many as three meetings a day, most of them long and vexatious.

I'll be sorry to see her leave Baltimore, for I have enjoyed our meetings at lunch—perhaps four or five times a year. She is an intelligent woman, and knows how to write. Unfortunately, it has been impossible at Goucher, at least during the past few years, for her to do any work on her books. At Wellesley she will have plenty of leisure, and the Harvard library will be less than an hour away. She told me that the library of Wellesley itself is rich, and has offered to get for her any book she wants. The college has a roll of 2,000 students.

Robertson, whose first wife, a huge grenadier of a woman, was killed in an automobile accident a couple of years ago, is now married to a rich widow. Miss Winslow believes that he will retire at 65, and devote himself to enjoying his new prosperity. He is probably the worst college president ever heard of. Ever since he took charge of it Goucher has declined steadily.

BALTIMORE, APRIL 27, 1944.

I went to New York on Sunday, April 23 for the A.P. orgies, and had dinner with Blanche Knopf at Voisin's Sunday night. After dinner, for which we had to wait at least an hour, we went to her apartment at 24 west 55th street, for a gabble. The house is a new building in the ultra-modernist manner, and her apartment is done in white and pale shades of gray, with here and there a touch of metallic copper. The effect is appalling, and she says that it is almost impossible to keep the place clean. It is smaller than her last apartment in 54th street, but costs $2,500 a year. Its only attraction is a roof-garden about as big as a dining-room table. Living in it must be enormously uncomfortable. It is, in fact, almost as bad as the arty quarters that Paul Palmer has in the Hampshire House in 59th street, also predominantly white, with ghastly modernist prints on the walls and furniture fit only for a boudoir. The talk in 55th street got nowhere and I left early, considerably saddened. I told her I believed the little book of prayers for soldiers,[1] just brought out by the house, disgraced its list and damaged its trade-mark. There are actually prayers by Generals Eisenhower and Patton—the latter the hero who lately got into the

---

1 The volume, entitled *Soldiers' and Sailors' Prayer Book*, was edited by Gerald Mygatt and Chaplain (Lt. Col.) Henry Darlington, D.D. It sold for $1.

newspaper by cuffing a wounded soldier. I said that such trash undid the work of years, and left the house imprint ridiculous. I added that I believed the preposterous books by war correspondents and other fakers were almost as bad. Blanche undertook to defend them, on the ground that they sold well. Yes, I said, they sold the firm down the river. She said that there would be fewer of them hereafter, and that she was making hard efforts to unearth better books. I doubt it. She and Alfred have both lost most of their old skill and intelligence in that direction. They actually admire some of the worst books they are printing.

The idea for the book of prayers, she said, came from Bernard Smith, the sales manager. What his name was before he changed it I do not know. He, too, is a Jew, and moreover, a jackass.

BALTIMORE, APRIL 29, 1944.

Frank Knox, Secretary of the Navy, who fell ill in New York last Monday and was thus unable to attend the annual luncheon of the Associated Press, died yesterday in Washington. My relations with him, such as they were, are described at length in "Thirty-Five Years of Newspaper Work, 1906–1941." I encountered him off and on, and he was always very friendly. The *Sun* of this morning prints a highly laudatory editorial on him: the truth about him is told in Oswald Garrison Villard's "The Disappearing Daily," just out. This book is a reworking of Villard's "Newspaper and Newspaper Men," first published in 1923. In the latter there was a very complimentary chapter on the Baltimore *Sunpapers*, largely based upon materials that I supplied. When the new version of the book was projected Villard dropped off in Baltimore to see me about the revision. After a somewhat long argument I induced him to omit the chapter on the *Sunpapers* altogether. The story of their deterioration would have caused an uproar in the office, and I'd have been blamed for it. Villard agreed to omit them from his record, I believe, mainly because he is an ever-hopeful liberal, and hates to admit that any good cause has gone to pot.

BALTIMORE, MAY 10, 1944.

At the Associated Press meeting in New York last week I fell in with a general in the Army whose name I don't recall. He was in the air arm and appeared to be a Southern cracker—a tall, slim, somewhat evil-looking fellow with pale blue eyes, set too close together. When I let fall the fact that I have yet to make my first trip in an airship he almost fainted: it was simply impossible for him to imagine anyone falling so far behind the march of Christian enlightenment. I thereupon added that I own no automobile, never listen to the radio, see a movie no more than once a year, object to air-cooling, and am just getting used to a horse and buggy. By this time he was almost in collapse. If I had added that I buy no war bonds, and never contribute to either the Red Cross or the Community Fund I suppose that he'd have needed medical attention.

BALTIMORE, JUNE 10, 1944.

If I had been able to keep up the pace I set when the Supplement to "The American Language" was begun last October, I'd be near the end of it by now. As it is, I am very far from the end, and begin to doubt that I'll be able to finish it by Christmas—if, indeed, I ever finish it at all. The progress of my physical deterioration is alone to blame. I am in excellent shape mentally, and the book interests me, and I want to complete it. But the number of days on which I am incapacitated increases steadily, and there have been, of late, whole weeks during which I could do little work. Last night and today I have been in wretched discomfort. I was kept wakeful a good part of the night by a mild but persistent pain in the solar plexus region, no doubt related to my heart condition, and all day I have felt full in the head, with occasional touches of faintness—equally without doubt a symptom of my rising blood pressure. As I was shaving yesterday morning and cold water from the washstand spigot doused my right hand, it went numb, and the same thing happened again this morning. I have no downright headache and never feel dizzy, but there is often a sense of engorgement and pressure in my head, with mild stinging about the ears and jaws. With such things going on it is very difficult to work. I begin a section of the book with my ideas flowing freely and plenty of notes in hand, but in a little while I am forced to suspend, for it is almost impossible, at least for me, to write in physical discomfort. I have had to do it often enough in my time, but it took a great deal of outside pressure to keep me at it. Now that pressure is off, and so I give up.

My relations to the *Sunpapers* continue to worsen. It took Patterson

months to be convinced that I was really resolved to keep away from
the national conventions, but he seems to believe it at last. I avoid as
much as possible any discussion of editorial matters, but sometimes it
can't be avoided. Of late he has given most of his attention to a plan
to buy a radio station. I hate to see it done, but begin to believe that
it is necessary and inevitable. For six or eight years past there has been
a steady movement of national advertising from the newspapers to the
radio, and after the war it may take on the proportions of a flight.
Nine people out of ten, I believe, now get their first news of everything
from the radio, and have begun to think of it as they used to think of
the newspapers. Newspaper sales are still good, but that is chiefly due,
in Baltimore, to the war-time increase in population. Advertising holds
up, but a large part of it is bogus, representing only an effort by large
industries to bury their war profits and escape taxation. When real
competition is resumed I suspect that most of it will go to the radio.

All this does not distress me too greatly, though I have given my
whole life to newspapers. I am convinced that they have abandoned
their functions, and in an abject and ignominious manner, in the present war. Nine-tenths of them, and even more than nine-tenths, print
the official blather without any attempt to scrutinize it. No matter how
preposterous it may be they never challenge it. Those that have correspondents of their own, including the *Sunpapers*, are just as bad as
those that depend on the press associations. It is a disgraceful spectacle, but I do not believe that anything can be done about it. Roosevelt
has taken the press into camp as certainly as he has taken the Supreme
Court. It has ceased altogether to be independent and has become
docilely official. If there is ever any revolt it is much more likely to be
led by the radio than by the newspapers.

BALTIMORE, JUNE 16, 1944.

Patterson shoved off for Chicago at 4 o'clock this afternoon. I
dropped in on him at the *Sun* office at 2:30 and we had a little farewell
session. He seemed to be hopeful up to the last that I'd change my
mind and go with him. However, I stuck to my resolution and we
finally parted amicably enough.

He told me that the reports from Chicago are to the effect that
covering the two conventions this year will be extraordinarily uncomfortable. The *Sun* bureau has been able to get only one room with two

single beds. In all the other rooms the men will have to sleep two in a bed. This is bad enough in normal times, but in the heat that usually settles down on Chicago in July it will be almost unbearable.

Patterson told me that he had half made up his mind to pass up the Democratic convention. I am sorry that I am missing the two shows, but I simply couldn't accept his invitation to see them as a sort of guest. At such affairs emergencies are always arising, and within two hours after I got to town I'd be volunteering for work. Moreover, I always think of national conventions as assignments to be covered, not as mere shows to be gaped at. I simply can't imagine myself sitting in the press-stand doing nothing.

BALTIMORE, JULY 17, 1944.

I returned this morning from Roaring Gap, N.C., where I spent a pleasant holiday with Dr. and Mrs. Fred M. Hanes at their Summer place on top of the mountain. I left Baltimore last Monday evening, July 10, for Winston-Salem, where I was met Tuesday morning by the Haneses' colored factotum, William Bibby, who took me to the Robert E. Lee Hotel, where I joined Fred's brother, Ralph, for breakfast. William then hauled me the sixty miles to Roaring Gap. In the past I have always enjoyed such trips with him, for he is a very talkative fellow and what he has to say well indicates what the thriftier and smarter colored folk of North Carolina are thinking. But this time, because of the gas shortage, he had to take another passenger—a Winston lady whose name I forget—and in her presence he was shy and silent. Moreover, she did a great deal of talking herself. We dropped her at the Whitestone Inn on the mountain, and I found Fred and Betty Hanes waiting for me at their house. My trip to and from Winston was very comfortable. I made my booking a month in advance, and got compartments both ways. The trains were air-cooled and I slept very well. Going down we reached Greensboro, the junction-point, precisely on time, but there we were detained waiting for a connecting mail train, and at Winston we were about 40 minutes late. Coming home, the train was on time at Washington, but there the Pennsylvania train for New York was a little late starting. I had breakfast on it, and reached home by 9.15 A.M. Despite the war, the trains were not overcrowded.

The Haneses, as always, were immensely amiable, and I greatly enjoyed my six days on the mountain, the top of which is 3,000 feet above sea-level. Their house is not directly on the summit, but very near it, and the view from the terrace is magnificent. The house is built of native stone and native chestnut and is very well arranged. The main room, perhaps fifty feet long, is decorated with souvenirs of Fred and Betty's big-game hunting in East Africa fifteen years ago. It has a huge fireplace and plenty of comfortable chairs and makes an excellent lounging place on cool evenings. At one end is the dinner-table. It seats 12 or 14 people, but is hardly noticed in so large a room. Beyond it are the pantry and kitchen, and adjoining it at the other end is Betty's bedroom. This end is two stories high, and upstairs are Fred's quarters. When I go to Roaring Gap I do not sleep in this main house, but in another building near-by, called the playhouse. It has a big room quite as large as the one I have just described, and also a kitchen, a game-room, and three bedrooms, each with a bath. I commonly use the far bedroom, which is as quiet at night as a sailing-ship at sea.

I first met the Haneses at Chapel Hill in 1926, when Paul Patterson and I were making a tour of the South. This was at the home of Dr. Archibald Henderson, professor of mathematics at the University of North Carolina. We became friendly at once, and I have since visited them very often, not only at Roaring Gap but also at Winston-Salem, where they were living up to twelve years ago, and afterward at Durham, where Fred is professor of medicine in the Medical School of Duke University. They are an extremely intelligent and pleasant couple and I always enjoy seeing them. Sara, in her time, went with me, and she and Betty were very friendly. Betty, in late years, has been beset by chronic bronchitis, and at times she has been very ill, but some time ago one of Fred's colleagues in the medical school took her in hand, and she now seems to be much better, though she still shows some shortness of breath. She told me confidentially that Fred has lately developed a high blood-pressure, and is considerably worried by it. He did not speak of it directly himself, but seemed to assume that I knew of it. I noted that he took only a mild and single drink before dinner, and next to nothing in the evenings, and that he had cut down on his golf. Both he and Betty are now beyond sixty. We spent the days lazily and had many a long gabble. We went out to dinner once and to lunch once, and also visited Fred's old mother, now 86 years old, but most of the time we were about the place. Betty is a perfect hostess. Her guests feel at ease and are not bothered.

I probably got some benefit from the rest and the high altitude, but my sleep for the first three nights was broken by the spells that so often beset me at home. I'd wake out of a sound sleep feeling faint and uncomfortable, and for half an hour I'd lie awake, with my pulse strong and unhurried but a somewhat rapid respiration. Then I'd fall asleep again and sleep soundly until morning. I said nothing to Fred of this. After three days I slept better. I took a nap in my room every afternoon, sometimes of two hours. Altogether, I must have slept at least ten hours in every twenty-four. Betty's catering, as always, was excellent, and I ate heartily. I drank nothing until just before dinner in the evening, when I commonly got down a Scotch highball. I had brought a flask of Bourbon with me, but after taking a drink from it on the train going down, did not touch it more than once or twice at bedtime. I took the galley-proofs of the first (or sample) part of the American Language Supplement with me, but did not correct them until the day before I started home. I had no reading matter save a few magazines in my bag, but depended upon the house library. In my bedroom I discovered H. Kyd Douglas's "I Rode With Stonewall"[1] and read it with great pleasure. It is a vivid and excellent narrative. Douglas was still alive when I was a young reporter, and I often heard him make speeches at Confederate potlatches. He was a tall, thin, smooth-shaven, white-haired old fellow, and was much esteemed as an orator. I had always assumed that, like most other Civil War heroes, he was largely fake, but his book showed that he had had a really gaudy career in the Confederate Army.

Ralph Hanes came up from Winston on Friday and we had dinner with him and his wife DeWitt. There were plenty of drinks, and I got down three Scotch highballs. One of the guests was a Mrs. Windsor or Winsor, a former wife of Elliott Roosevelt. She turned out to be a far from beautiful young woman. I saw little of her, for after dinner she and several others went to a room to play gin-rummy. The next day, Saturday, I sat beside her at lunch at the house of Tino Lenfranchi, an Italian married to an American woman. She gave me to understand that she packs a hate for the whole Roosevelt family, but is unhappily convinced that Franklin will be reëlected in November. She is staying at the Whitestone Inn and has three children with her—one boy by Elliott and two by her subsequent husband. Betty told me that

1 Henry Kyd Douglas (1840–1903), youngest member on the staff of General Thomas J. ("Stonewall") Jackson. The book that Mencken speaks of was published by the University of North Carolina Press in 1940.

feeling against Roosevelt is so bitter on the mountain that some of the children refuse to play with the Roosevelt boy. La Winsor had little conversation, but the lunch staged by Lenfranchi and his wife was excellent. They have a charming cottage overlooking a sweep of superb scenery, and serve meals at a long table at the edge of the terrace outside. Thus a given guest sees only those to his two sides, and while he eats the whole panorama is before him. Lenfranchi's principal dish was a very fine spaghetti, and with it he served red wine. Before lunch he gave me my choice of an appetizer, and I chose Italian vermouth with a shot of Fernet-Branca. It was excellent.

Fred Hanes's old mother has a cottage of her own, probably half a mile from his. Her face is distorted by paralysis and she is forced to remain in her room until the afternoon, but mentally she seems to be in full vigor. Certainly there is no sign of weakness in her talk. DeWitt Hanes has a scheme to get her a stenographer and set her to dictating her reminiscences. It seems to me to be an excellent idea, and I urged Fred to support it. The old lady was born in Winston, and has seen it develop from a small village to a rich industrial town. Her late husband was one of the founders of its now enormous tobacco business, and all of her six sons are men of distinction in their several lines. One of them, John, has made a fortune in Wall Street and was for a time under-secretary of the Treasury. When the Hearst organization faced bankruptcy he was retained to rehabilitate it. He soon found that $20,000,000 would be needed to effect the business, and applied for the money to his banker friends. They laughed at him, but he dug it up in some way or other, and after several years of hard work and great anxiety accomplished the seemingly impossible. Hearst is now solvent again and John is a hero in Wall Street. I know him only slightly, but am very well acquainted with Fred, Ralph, Jim and Rob. All of them have charming wives, and these wives seem to get on together very well. No less than four of the six sons of Mother Hanes— Fred, Jim, John and Rob—are listed in "Who's Who in America." I think the old lady's story would make a very interesting narrative, and that dictating it would relieve her from the cruel boredom of her illness. She is a faithful Methodist and favors Prohibition, but she seems to make no objection to the decidedly contrary views of her sons and daughters, sons-in-law and daughters-in-law. Some of them go to church occasionally as a sort of solatium to her, but not one of them is actually pious.

The Whitestone Inn, which used to show heavy deficits, is now a big success, thanks to the skillful management of Walter Bovard, who is helped greatly by his busy and clever wife. In Winter he operates a hotel at Palm Beach. The inn is crowded to the doors this Summer, with a long waiting list. The only Jew on the guest list is Milton J. Rosenau, the sanitarian. He got in on the score of his acquaintance with Fred Hanes—and immediately proposed to bring in other Jews. But Bovard, by various devices, has managed to keep them out. In the days when I first knew it the guests of the inn came mainly from the South, but now they also come from the North. Getting to and from it is not easy, but they seem to like it. There is a golf links adjoining, and not far away is a lake used for swimming, boating and picnics. The Haneses seldom see anyone save members of their own large family and a few Winston intimates. There are enough people in this relatively small circle to make it very pleasant.

One of the newcomers to the mountain is Mrs. Hendricks, the wife of a member of the Duke faculty. She is a pianist and a good one. One afternoon Betty invited her to the playhouse, and we had some music. She played Bach, Chopin and Debussy beautifully, and I joined her in a couple of duets—Mozart's "Kleine Nachtmusik" and the Mottl arrangement of Gluck, both often played by the Saturday Night Club. She played the primo parts very well at sight, but was not satisfied with her performance, and insisted on doing the Gluck over and over. That afternoon and the next day we must have done it six times. The Hanes piano, an upright, was in very bad condition, and Betty set out to get another. As incredible as it may seem, it had come up from Winston within three hours. It had been a wedding present from Mother Hanes to a young couple forced to store it because of the husband's war service, and Ralph Hanes, who was still in Winston, dug it out of the storehouse and started it on its way in response to a telephone call. It turned out to be a first-rate Steinway grand, and I greatly enjoyed playing on it. The Mozart and Gluck were the only duets in hand, but on her second appearance Mrs. Hendricks brought a four-hand piano arrangement of the Beethoven symphonies, and we played the first movement of the Eroica. If I ever make another trip to Roaring Gap and Mrs. Hendricks is still there I'll send a package of the club's music ahead of me.

I returned to Winston with Ralph Sunday afternoon, and he and I had dinner with Kenneth Mountcastle and his wife. May Mountcastle is the chief promoter of music in Winston, and this week is staging a

Piedmont Festival of four days, a very ambitious enterprise. The conductor is George K. Raudenbush, and he and his wife were present at dinner. It was a very pleasant evening. I cleared out at 9 o'clock to make my train, and was asleep by the time it got to Greensboro.

JULY 19, 1944.

The Hanes place at Roaring Gap, N.C., is in the midst of one of those mountain areas that are supposed to be inhabited by "the only pure Anglo-Saxons left in the United States." They turn out, on acquaintance, to be a wretchedly dirty, shiftless, stupid and rascally people. Every Winter, while the cottages on the mountain are vacant and the hotel is closed, the gallant hillmen swarm in to loot and destroy. Last year they broke into Fred Hanes's house, forced every cupboard door with ax or crowbar, and made off with several truck-loads of clothes, linen and tableware. Also, they smashed into his boathouse, and took everything removable from his electric launch, including all its lights. Many of the things stolen were useless to mountain people and unsalable in the mountains, but they were taken nevertheless. At the same time many other houses were similarly entered and robbed, and the same thing goes on every Winter. The cottage-owners believe that the thieves come mainly from the direction of Sparta, the county-town, and the identity of some of them is said to be known. But it would be useless to attempt a prosecution, for the country juries hate the rich people of Roaring Gap and would turn loose anyone accused of robbing them, even if he were taken in the act. Moreover, the thieves would immediately seek revenge by burning down houses. Even as it is, there is grave danger that they will set off a big fire some Winter night. Last Spring Betty Hanes found large gobs of candle grease on her furniture and floors, and also marks of oil lamps. In fact, the damage that the thieves did was almost as bad as their stealing. Such are "the only pure Anglo-Saxons left in the United States." Physically as well as morally they are a poor lot. The women are dumpy, puffy and pale, and the men are tall, thin and cadaverous. The war industries have brought thousands of these anthropoids to Baltimore, and the neighborhood of Hollins street is full of them. Along with the lint-heads from the Carolina mill-towns they live in old and decrepit houses, a whole family to a room. They are so filthy and destructive that the Jews who own the houses have begun to turn them out and put in blackamoors.

One of their curious characteristics is their apparent hostility to all growing things. The backyard of any house they occupy is soon reduced to a desert of sand and trash: they even stamp out the weeds. Not one of them has ever been known to cultivate a flower. The Negroes are much more civilized. All save the poorest and most wretched of them try to grow flowers in pots, cans and window-boxes, and some of them have very pretty gardens, though their taste naturally runs to the more gaudy colors. In the alley behind Hollins street there is a colored couple that has three window-boxes of beautiful petunias. August and I, for several years past, have been unable to make petunias grow in our backyard, but these darkies succeed with them beautifully. The same little house is kept well painted—obviously at the cost of the tenants, for the Jew who owns it never spends a cent on decorations. The colors used are garish, but they are at least characteristically niggerish, and the occupants plainly take some pride in the appearance of their house. No linthead or mountaineer ever shows any feeling for beauty. They all live like animals, and are next door to animals in their habits and ideas.

BALTIMORE, JULY 23, 1944.

Mrs. Lohrfinck, my secretary, is laid up at the Union Memorial Hospital, I am disabled by a lame back and feel wretched, and as a result I have done no work on the American Language Supplement since I got back from North Carolina. Mrs. Lohrfinck appeared to be in good health when she came in to take dictation Tuesday morning, and the two of us got through a huge pile of accumulated mail. She returned for more on Wednesday, and still showed no sign of illness. But on her return home to transcribe my dictation she began to feel rocky, and soon after noon she called me up to say that she had a temperature of 102 degrees. Her doctor, called in the afternoon, at first suspected influenza, but the next day he found signs of pyelitis and ordered her to hospital. I saw her yesterday and found her pretty ill. Her temperature is normal in the mornings, but it leaps up in the afternoons, and has got as high as 104. In all probability she will be ill for weeks. Doing my own mail, I begin to realize what a heavy burden it is, and how much she helps me in handling it. It pours in from strangers all over the world, including soldiers in such remote places as Burma, Attu, New Guinea and Persia. I have always made it a point to reply politely to any letter from a correspondent not obviously insane, but doing so without help is a heavy burden. This burden seems to be one of the penalties of writing books. There are days when I receive 25 or 30 letters, mainly from persons I don't know, and some of them call for information that it takes precious time to assemble. The mere reading of my mail sometimes takes two hours, for many of these volunteer correspondents write at length, and by hand.

Last Tuesday afternoon, coming down the third-story steps with a big bag of laundry in my hands, I slipped and fell heavily. It was the third time I had come down at the same place since my return to Hollins street in 1936. I skinned my left arm but got the chief blow in the small of my back. I was very uncomfortable at the dinner to Jim Fenhagen on Tuesday night, but managed to get through it. The next morning I was so stiff and sore that I could barely lace my shoes. This morning I dropped in on Dr. Charles W. Wainwright and he gave me a looking over. He found that there was no apparent damage to bones or kidneys, but that I had a huge black bruise to the left of the backbone, just under the ribs. He advised me to apply heat if the pain became unendurable. It seems to be passing off, so I have done nothing, but I am still lame, and every movement causes a twinge.

Meanwhile, I have been full of other malaises, some of them crippling. When I get up in the morning I feel faint and miserable, and before noon I am usually forced to suspend work and lie down. Judging by my sensations I suspect that there is an occasional acute enlargement of the heart. I feel stuffed and smothered on the left side, and have to rest until the discomfort passes off, which usually takes an hour. Yesterday I had three such spells, and had to suspend work on this diary every time. Serious writing, of course, is next to impossible, and I have not done a stroke on my book for three or four weeks. I must tackle it in earnest this week, or it will never be done at all. I have a good appetite, and usually sleep well enough—save for an occasional sudden awakening with a faint feeling—but I feel miserable all the time, and there are days when even routine work is almost impossible.

BALTIMORE, JULY 27, 1944.

Despite the revolt of John Owens, Patterson is determined that the *Sunpapers* must support Dewey, and at the office today he showed me a proof of the first editorial to that end, written by Hamilton Owens. It is a long and somewhat windy piece that will fill nearly three columns on the *Sun* editorial page, but it seems to me to be good enough for its purpose. After all, the whole matter is more or less moot. Dewey may be whooped up on the editorial pages, but Roosevelt will have the front pages all to himself, and he may be trusted to fill them with war news certain to convince the booboisie that he is a great moral hero and virtually indispensable. The *Sunpapers* themselves will confect and pay for a large part of this rubbish, for little else is coming from their correspondents at the front. Moreover, they are firmly committed to the doctrine that Roosevelt was inspired when he horned into the war, and in consequence their objections to him on other grounds will be hollow and futile. I do not envy Owens the job of writing the campaign editorials. He is, however, well fitted for the job, for his own principles are highly elastic, and he excels at the however style of writing. The main argument against Roosevelt is that he manoeuvred the country into the war, and will bankrupt it in consequence, but that will never be mentioned.

Hamilton told me that he will do all the writing himself, with occasional assistance from Ives.[1] Wagner, editor of the morning *Sun*, professes to have lost faith in the New Deal, but he is by no means for Dewey. Aiken, editor of the *Evening Sun*, still inclines toward Roosevelt. He is a Tennessean, and will never get over it. I advised Hamilton to let both of them devote themselves to other themes. It would do no good to put them to writing against Roosevelt, for they would produce very feeble and unconvincing stuff. Moreover, the morale of the office will be furthered by excusing them from violating their so-called convictions. In any case, their aid will not be needed, for Hamilton and Ives will be able to turn out all the copy necessary. The *Sunpapers'* support of Dewey, at best, will be only formal, and after the first few weeks Hamilton will avoid the subject as much as possible. It seems to me that Dewey is an even weaker reed than Landon

---

1 Charles P. Ives (1903–1982) was a columnist and editorial writer for the *Sun* from 1939 to his retirement in 1973.

and Willkie. He is not quite as nefarious as Willkie, but he is certainly less honest than Landon. He is already howling for the war with the best of them.

BALTIMORE, AUGUST 2, 1944.

Mrs. Lohrfinck continues very ill at the Union Memorial Hospital, but there seems to be a turn for the better, and when I saw her this afternoon she was beginning to be cheerful. Typhoid, pyelitis and all the other things suspected have now been excluded, and it is definitely established that she has virus pneumonia. She has not been so told, but is assured that she has only bronchitis, but I am sure she suspects the truth. Despite the infernal heat of the last ten days—she went to hospital July 21—she appears to be reasonably comfortable, but as yet she can't sit up, for every time she does so there is violent coughing. The boredom is beginning to afflict her. She'd like to read, but can't. Virus pneumonia is seldom fatal, but it is resistant to the new drugs, so convalescence is usually slow, with the patient much prostrated. I suspect that she'll not be fit to resume work until the end of August. Meanwhile, I am struggling with my mail, and making heavy weather of it. Yesterday it took me from 9 a.m. until noon to read my incoming letters and write replies. It is onerous work, and three hours of it leave me played out.

I have done no work on the Supplement to "The American Language" for five or six weeks. In part this is due to my wretched physical state, but there is also the fact that I had begun to go stale. The job is extraordinarily tedious and fatiguing. Sometimes it takes me all day to do two pages of the typescript. On a single page I may have to stop twenty times to look up references. But I hope to resume the writing as soon as the weather becomes bearable. It has been really infernal for two weeks, with high temperatures and even higher humidity. Hay-fever is due August 25, but it seldom disables me until the second week in September, and even then I can usually do a fair day's work. I had hoped to finish the Supplement by October 1, just one year after I began it, but it is now plain that that will be impossible. Unless I am floored again I may be able to complete the job by the end of the year. During the hot weather I have felt sleepy all the time. There was a time when I really enjoyed work in the Summer heat of Baltimore, but that time seems to be past.

At the Maryland Club last night Paul Patterson gave a small dinner to two Canadians and an Englishman who sailed from Baltimore by the British air-line later in the evening. The Canadians, Coleman and McPherson, are government officials, and the Englishman, whose name I forget, is connected with the British Treasury. They turned out to be agreeable fellows, and the dinner was very pleasant. We started with mint juleps, and drank Rhine wine with the meal. Later came beer. The others present were John E. Semmes and Hamilton Owens. McPherson said he was an old customer of mine, and Coleman also seemed to be familiar with some of my books.

BALTIMORE, AUGUST 12, 1944.

Mrs. Lohrfinck is ill indeed. There is evidence that a secondary infection has followed the virus infection, and that endocarditis has set up. She had had a vigorous round of the sulpha drugs, but they had to be discontinued, for they caused almost continuous nausea. Penicillin then followed, but it apparently had no effect. Her temperature continues high, she is unable to eat, and signs of exhaustion begin to show themselves. She is in reasonably good spirits, but is very weak.

BALTIMORE, AUGUST 16, 1944.

It seems to be plain that Mrs. Lohrfinck has endocarditis, and her outlook is not good. There is already evidence that emboli have broken loose from the infected heart valves and lodged in the brain. Her mind seems to be perfectly clear, but her speech is affected. She has difficulty finding words, and it is hard to understand her. Dr. Walter A. Baetjer, who has been called in consultation, ordered all drugs discontinued, but is now planning to make another trial of penicillin, this time by the continuous drip method.

BALTIMORE, AUGUST 18, 1944.

Dr. Baetjer told me at the hospital today that it is now certain that Mrs. Lohrfinck has endocarditis. He said he believes that the organism is the streptococcus viridans, but that it had been impossible, so far, to find it in the blood stream. He said that the outlook is anything but good, but that some encouraging reports had been coming in about the efficacy of penicillin, and he thus has some hope. The patient bears the treatment very well. The drug goes into a vein drop by drop, day and night, along with glucose. She has to lie in one position for hours on end, but does not complain. It is too early to look for any great improvement, but she is certainly no worse. Her temperature is gradually falling, and she is beginning to take solid food. She remains in excellent spirits, despite her long confinement to bed.

Meanwhile, I am doing all my own mail. Fortunately, it is mid-Summer, for the burden of it is always lightest then. Mrs. Lohrfinck's sister, Mrs. Clare Crump, has offered to give me some help with it, and also to copy the accumulated typescript of the American Language Supplement. She will be the third Redding sister to work for me.¹ She is married and has a daughter twelve years old, but insists that she can spare enough time from her household to do my work. I have been making good progress with the book, despite the infernal heat. Today hay-fever began to afflict me, a week ahead of its usual time.

BALTIMORE, AUGUST 29, 1944.

Mrs. Lohrfinck seems to be considerably improved, and there is now some hope of her recovery. After nearly two weeks of penicillin treatment by continuous drip it was discontinued last night, and she was given a whole-blood transfusion. Her temperature has been down almost to normal for a week past: it has never been above 99 and a fraction. She is in excellent spirits, and has begun to eat heartily. The doctors now have some hope that the heart-valve infection has been arrested, and that there will be no more emboli. But they will keep her in bed for another week at least.

Mrs. Crump has done some letters for me, and very well. She has also copied more than 70 pages of typescript, and has another 70 or

---

1 In 1921 Mencken, no longer able to handle his increasing correspondence and the typing of his manuscripts himself, hired as secretary a young woman named Margaret Redding. She worked for him for about seven years, but then married and moved away from Baltimore. As a replacement she recommended her own sister, Mrs. Rosalind C. Lohrfinck, the subject of these current entries. Mrs. Lohrfinck remained Mencken's secretary for the rest of his life and handled all of his mail after his 1948 stroke.

80 in hand. She is, of course, not as familiar with my work as her sister, but she shows the same quiet competence. I begin to realize, with Mrs. Lohrfinck ill for six weeks, how much I have been depending on her for fourteen years past. She is an almost perfect stenographer, and she does all my other work quickly and beautifully. I shudder to think of my difficulties if she is still ill when the time comes to do the List of Words and Phrases for the American Language Supplement.

BALTIMORE, SEPTEMBER 6, 1944.

As of this day, I own stock in 58 different corporations. All of it is paying dividends.

BALTIMORE, SEPTEMBER 26, 1944.

Tonight at 8.30 I finished the first volume of the Supplement to "The American Language." It was begun early in August, 1943, but I did not settle down to steady writing until the end of the month. This was in the midst of a severe attack of hay fever, and I have just got through an even worse. In addition, I have been ill off and on in other ways, and during the early Summer there was a period of six or seven weeks when I couldn't work at all. Following this almost immediately came Mrs. Lohrfinck's serious illness, still in progress, though she seems to be recovering. Thus I have done pretty well. The first volume runs to more than 350,000 words, and I have got at least 100,000 more on paper for Volume II, which will be ready, if all goes well, by the end of 1945.[1] Knopf proposes to bring out the first volume as soon as possible. The final revision remains to be done, but it should not take more than a few weeks. I'll probably deliver half of the MS. as soon as it is done, and let the printers begin on it. The first 33 pages are already set up, and I have made the List of Words and Phrases and the Index for them. Completing the two will offer me a formidable job when the page-proofs come in, for it is by no means certain that Mrs. Lohrfinck will be able to give me any considerable assistance. The two Supplements will be identical in format to "The American

1 Supplement II was not published until 1948.

Language," but on account of the paper shortage Knopf will have to print them on thinner paper, and cut more off their margins. I am in hopes that when the war is over it will be possible to reissue them exactly uniform with the trade edition of "The American Language."

BALTIMORE, OCTOBER 11, 1944.

I finished the typescript of Vol. I of the Supplement to "The American Language" last night, and all that remains is for Mrs. Crump to copy a dozen or so pages and folio them to the end. The Index and the List of Words and Phrases, of course, are yet to be done, and with Mrs. Lohrfinck still disabled the whole burden of the job may fall on me. Hay-fever is now definitely over, but some of its sequelae continue. I have, at intervals, a dry cough, there is a sore spot on my lower lip that refuses to heal, and my sleep is still more or less disturbed. The temperature on the roof outside my bathroom, when I arose this morning, was 45. Fallen leaves fill the backyard and the street before my office window. Darkness comes down soon after 6 p.m. and there is a sad, sickly feeling in the air. The year is drawing to its close, and I look forward to 1945 without too much hope. I am definitely aging, and throwing off a 700-page book is no longer the easy task it used to be. I plan to devote the next six months to some miscellaneous writing, including a few articles for the *New Yorker* and other magazines, and maybe a short book setting forth my conclusions about human life on this ball. In all probability it will be impossible to print it, if I do it, until after the war—and the uproars bound to follow the war. I also hope to get my remaining papers in order. The time has come to see to my shutters.

BALTIMORE, OCTOBER 15, 1944.

Today is the one hundredth anniversary of the birth of Friedrich Wilhelm Nietzsche. If it is noted anywhere in America it will be on the ground that Nietzsche was a wicked fellow and the inventor of all the deviltries of Hitler. I can see little hope for this great Christian country. It has been going downhill steadily throughout my time, and its pace of late has been fast accelerating.

BALTIMORE, OCTOBER 30, 1944.

Mrs. Lohrfinck returned to work this morning—her first attempt since July. She looked pitifully thin and pale, and I suggested that she had better wait a few weeks before resuming, but she protested that she was tired of idleness and eager for occupation. For the first time since her first days with me, now more than 14 years ago, she had to interrupt me. Ordinarily, she can take dictation as fast as I can dictate, which is fast indeed, and it is very rare for her to make an error, even the most trivial. But the letters that she returned this evening showed a good many, and in several cases she misunderstood me altogether, and I had to rewrite the letters myself. She has a lingering difficulty with speech, much less than it was but still noticeable, and she is greatly concerned about her eyes. In her right eye the field of vision has been narrowed, apparently by emboli, and the ophthalmologist she consulted yesterday told her that this narrowing may be permanent. She will forget it when she gets used to it, but for the present it worries her greatly. Her actual vision is not impaired. I called her up tonight to reassure her. I told her her letters were perfect, but she knew better. The intelligent suffer much more when they are ill than the stupid.

BALTIMORE, NOVEMBER 2, 1944.

It is astonishing how little the war impinges upon me. I am, of course, rooked like everyone else by excessive taxes, and now and then some eatable that I like is unprocurable (or procurable only by giving up an enormous number of ration points); but in general I am hardly affected by the great effort to save humanity and ruin the United States. So far, no one that I know has been killed in the war, or even injured, and I find it hard to pump up any interest in the tall talk in the newspapers every day. It is no wonder that those who take it seriously are convinced that the war will be over in a few months, or even a few weeks. There are occasional complaints in the *Editor and Publisher,* from correspondents returned from the field, against the boastful nonsense given out by Army and Navy headquarters, but the newspapers print it without questioning it. The *Sunpapers* lead in this patriotic work. Their correspondence from the various fronts seldom undertakes to tell precisely what is going on: it is simply rooting for the home team. I long ago gave up protesting against it. Paul Patterson not only believes that it is what the readers of the *Sunpapers* want; he also swallows most of it himself. I have some doubt myself that anything better would be feasible. If any effort were made to report the war objectively and truthfully there would be a public sensation, and a great deal more denunciation than approval. The American people are now wholly at the mercy of demagogues, and it would take a revolution to liberate and disillusion them. I see no sign of any such revolution, either in the immediate future or within the next generation. When the soldiers come home it will become infamous to doubt— and dangerous to life and limb.

BALTIMORE, NOVEMBER 13, 1944.

I went to the Johns Hopkins (Homewood) on November 10 to address the Stuart and Tudor Club, founded by Dr. William Osler, who left it his collection of books by his will, and enough money to keep it going. It consists, in theory, of persons interested in English literature of the Golden Age, but it also includes a miscellany of Anglomaniacs. I had been invited to harangue it often in the past, but always put it off. Some time ago I decided to take a look.

The club meets in a sizable room in Gilman Hall, apparently its permanent quarters. Bookcases line the walls and there are tables and chairs in the center. There were perhaps 60 men present, some of them soldier-students in uniform. I knew only a few of them—John C. French, the retired librarian of the Johns Hopkins; Dr. J.H. Mason Knox, Jr.[1] (an ass); J. Louis Kuethe,[2] and one or two others. Kemp Malone[3] came in late, in the belief that the proceedings were to start at 9 p.m., not 8.30. I gave the brethren their choice between a reading of the section on American profanity in Supplement I of "The American Language" and an impromptu discourse on journalism. They chose journalism, and I tried to tell them about the profound changes

1 Dr. J. H. Mason Knox, Jr. (1892–1951) was a specialist in child hygiene and clinical pediatrics and was associated with the Johns Hopkins Hospital and School of Hygiene and Public Health throughout most of his career.
2 J. Louis Kuethe (d. 1973) was director of the Johns Hopkins University Library.
3 Kemp Malone (1889–1971) was professor of English literature at the Johns Hopkins. His specialty was Old and Middle English, and he was an authority on Chaucer.

that technological advances—especially the invention of the lino-type—have made in American newspapers.

I spoke for about half an hour, and then called for questions. Very few of them showed any sense: indeed, they were all much less intelligent than those propounded to me every Spring by the boys of the Current Events Club at the City College. It was obvious that most of the questioners were radicals, and it appeared to me, in the rather dim light, that many of them were Jews. One asked: "What do you think of *P.M.*?"[1] My reply was: "It can't be thought of in terms of American journalism. It is simply a Yiddish paper printed in English." There was a keg of bad beer, and after the main meeting was over and most of the men had gone home I sat for a while with the lingerers. One was Bryllion Fagin,[2] whom I had never met. The room was very hot and uncomfortable. Kuethe and another man (whose name I forget) motored me home toward midnight.

This Stuart and Tudor Club is supposed to include the intellectual élite of the Johns Hopkins academic department, and poor Osler hoped that his legacy would make it a center of the enlightenment. I can see nothing in it save a gang of third-rate pedagogues. There was not a man present, save Malone, who really knew anything beyond the common, and I could discover no sharp and interesting mind among the younger members. The Johns Hopkins, under Isaiah Bowman,[3] seems to be going downhill steadily. All the language departments are distressingly weak, and so are the history and economic departments. The main energies of the university are now devoted to training soldiers in various technical skills needed in the war. The old enthusiasm for pure learning is gone. In the whole faculty there are not six men of any genuine distinction.

I was told at the meeting that I have been elected an honorary member of the club, but I have heard nothing of this since. I sincerely hope that the news was false.

---

1 *PM*, a New York-based daily tabloid published from 1940 to 1948. The paper was noted for its liberal and pro-labor policies, reflecting the views of its editor, Ralph Ingersoll.

2 N. Bryllion Fagin (1892–1972) was professor of English and drama at the Johns Hopkins and director of the university's Playshop.

3 Isaiah Bowman (1878–1950) was president of Johns Hopkins University from 1935 to 1948.

BALTIMORE, NOVEMBER 16, 1944.

I had lunch today with Joseph L. Wheeler,[1] the retiring librarian of the Enoch Pratt Free Library. He has a bad heart, and was out of service for four months in the Spring and Summer. He has done an excellent job at the library, and I have always regarded him as a reasonably contented man, but he told me a long tale of woe, most of it having to do with the imbecility of his board of directors, which is self-perpetuating. There are two or three intelligent men on it, but the rest are Prominent Baltimoreans of the stupidest sort. . . . Wheeler is in fear that when he clears out the library will turn downhill, and I incline to believe that his forebodings are well justified.

He is eager to start a library school in Baltimore, better than the training school he already maintains at the library. He told me that the libraries of Maryland now consume about 40 graduates of such schools every year, and that most of them are not natives of the State, and do not stay long. He believes that a local school would train enough local young men and women to supply the demand. When I last heard of this scheme he was talking of asking the Johns Hopkins to take charge of the school. I told him today that this seemed to me to be a bad plan, for the Johns Hopkins is in a state of advanced deterioration, and is hardly likely to recover hereafter. I suggested that it would be much more sensible to ask Curly Byrd,[2] the go-getting president of the University of Maryland, to take the school into his organization. Wheeler's eye lighted up, and he replied that this was his own notion too. But he fears that one of his directors, who is also a director of the Johns Hopkins, will insist that the Johns Hopkins have it. I advised him to wait until he was formally retired, and then go to Byrd. I offered, in fact, to go with him. The scheme is his, not the directors'.

Wheeler asked me if I thought he should make a public statement when he clears out, setting forth the future needs of the library and handling the present directors realistically. I advised him to do it, but I suspect that he will lack the resolution when the time comes. It is a pity to see a competent and diligent man closing his career amid such harassments. Today he had another woe: he had just received news

[1] Joseph L. Wheeler (1884–1970) was director of the Enoch Pratt Free Library from 1926 to 1944.

[2] Harry C. ("Curly") Byrd (1889–1970), president of the University of Maryland from 1936 to 1953 and a colorful figure in the state politics of the time.

that one of his three sons was missing in Italy. I tried to console him by arguing that the missing usually turn up, if only as prisoners of war, but he is too intelligent to be deceived by such talk.

I described to him at length the books and MSS. I propose to leave to the library at my death, and asked him if he thought his successors could be trusted to keep some of them secret for fifteen years afterward, as I shall require. He said yes, but I am not too sure of it. If the man appointed in his place turns out to be an idiot I'll probably give the whole lot to the New York Public Library—and at once.

BALTIMORE, NOVEMBER 18, 1944.

Joe Hergesheimer was here a couple of weeks ago. He told me that the most violent of all the Nazis in Washington is an old woman named Lee, the widow of a grandson of the General. She has a fine house and plenty of money, and has now reached such an age that she can safely speak her mind freely. Joe said that she insists at dinner parties on arguing that the greatest man living in the world today is Hitler.

BALTIMORE, NOVEMBER 22, 1944.

For some years past I have been sitting of an evening, at more or less regular intervals, with Judge Eugene O'Dunne of the Supreme Bench of Baltimore, a friend of forty years. I became acquainted with him in 1904 or thereabout, when he was a young deputy State's attorney of Baltimore, and I was an even younger city editor. We began to meet in the back room of Schellhase's restaurant at 412 north Howard street in 1938 or thereabout, not for any serious purpose, but simply to drink a few beers together and pass the time of day. We were joined presently by the two Guttmacher brothers—Manfred, a psychiatrist and then medical adviser to the Supreme Bench, and Alan, an obstetrician. Later my brother August and Hulbert Footner began to sit in, and from time to time one or another of us brought a guest or two. We met every Wednesday evening at 10 o'clock and continued until midnight. Unhappily, the advance of the New Deal brought Schellhase labor troubles, and he had to close his place earlier and earlier. We moved up our meeting time to 9 p.m., but in the end had to clear out, for Schellhase, at the demand of his waitresses and kitchen help, was soon closing at that hour, save only on Saturday nights. About the same time Manfred Guttmacher entered the Army Medical Corps, and Footner was floored by a series of heart attacks. For a while O'Dunne and I were homeless and couldn't meet at all. Then we experimented with the Park Plaza restaurant (formerly the Longfellow) at Madison and Charles streets, but didn't like it. Of late we have been meeting intermittently, but with increasing frequency, at the Maryland Club, of which we are both members. We can't invite Alan Guttmacher there, for he is not a member, and as a Jew can't become one. Usually we find quiet at a table just outside the bar, but sometimes the club drunks invade us and drive us out. That happened two weeks ago. But when we met again last night we were undisturbed.

O'Dunne told me of a curious brush he is having with Monsignor Joseph M. Nelligan, rector of the Cathedral and chancellor of the Archdiocese of Baltimore. O'Dunne, who is a Catholic, is a member of the Cathedral parish, and last Sunday dropped in for Mass. Nelligan was the celebrant, and in the course of the service made the usual parish announcements. One was to the effect that one of the women's sodalities of the parish was trying to raise money for the renovations of the stations of the cross, and had projected a lottery to that end. He asked all members of the congregation to send in money for tickets, but warned them that they should not use the mails, for mailing anything relating to a lottery was forbidden by Federal law. This announcement naturally surprised O'Dunne, for he knew that lotteries were also forbidden by the State law of Maryland, and the same day he dispatched a letter to Nelligan, protesting against a priest in high place encouraging his parishioners to do an unlawful act, and describing to them a plan that would presumably save them from punishment. Nelligan returned an evasive answer by mail, and O'Dunne, who is a somewhat fiery fellow, became so hot that he showed the correspondence to the *Evening Sun*'s court reporter, Miller. Miller brought it to the office, and Miles H. Wolff, managing editor of the *Evening Sun*, sent another reporter to Nelligan's office to ask what he had to say about it.

Nelligan's reply was typical: he denied that O'Dunne had been present at Mass Sunday morning. Reliable agents, he said, reported that the judge had actually been at St. Ignatius's church in Calvert street, which is operated by the Jesuits, and is a formidable and much disliked rival to the Cathedral. I did not tell O'Dunne about this reply, for I knew it would provoke him to some violent action, and it was plain that he was sufficiently wrathy as it was. He said that he had showed the correspondence to Hamilton R. Atkinson, the police commissioner, who is himself a Catholic, and to Bernard Wells, the State's attorney, who is another, and that Wells had called up Nelligan and told him that he (Wells) fully supported the protest. Wells is interested because he is constantly embarrassed, when lottery agents of one sort or another are brought in by the police, by their protests that they have been doing nothing worse than the Catholic Church is constantly doing with its raffles, bingo games, etc.

The *Sun* can't print the story unless and until it comes out into the open, for O'Dunne showed the correspondence to Miller only in confidence, and it is improbable that Wells will ask the grand jury to indict Nelligan, though the lottery has been carried through as announced. At the last session of the Legislature an act was passed making bingo games lawful, provided their proceeds go to charity, but how this has been reconciled with Article III, Section 36 of the Constitution of 1867, which ordains that "no lottery grant shall ever hereafter be authorized by the General Assembly," I do not know. Under cover of the act bingo games are a principal feature of all the street carnivals that beset Baltimore in Summer, and all of them are operated for profit. The police seldom make any effort to enforce the State laws against lotteries, save in the single case of the numbers game, but the Postoffice smellers are vigilant for violations of the Federal act forbidding the use of the mails to promote them. O'Dunne told me that Nelligan's letter to him, admitting categorically that the Cathedral lottery was to be held, was itself probably a violation of this act.

The whole episode is very amusing, and if it gives some trouble to the Archbishop, Michael J. Curley, I shall not repine, for he is a bombastic and bellicose fellow, and a little hard sweating will do him good. O'Dunne told me that the Hearst paper has got wind of his exchange with Nelligan, and is trying to induce him to give it copies of the letters. I doubt, however, that it will print the story, for Curley would roar and rage against it, and dealing with a scandal that has not got into the courts is always difficult and dangerous. I advised Paul Patterson that, in my judgment, the *Sunpapers* had better avoid it unless Wells acts, but that all possible information should be collected meanwhile. That information includes Nelligan's denial that O'Dunne was present at the Mass whereat the announcement was made. If this denial is ever printed, O'Dunne will break into an uproar worthy of the Archbishop himself, and the town will have a circus. But such things seldom actually get into print. The significant thing in the present case, it seems to me, is Nelligan's refusal to admit to O'Dunne that his advice to his customers was immoral. Obviously, his reply was dictated by the Archbishop. The story is bound to get about town, and Wells will be embarrassed more than ever by the numbers operators who try to hide behind Holy Church.

O'Dunne told me that his old colleague, Robert F. Leach, Jr., one of the champion money-borrowers of Baltimore for many years, lately made a narrow escape from arrest for embezzlement. He was called on in O'Dunne's court to file an accounting of an estate of which he is trustee, and swore that the $1,300 in cash included among its assets was in the Calvert Bank. On being ordered to produce a certificate of deposit from the bank, he hemmed and hawed painfully, and finally said that he had made a mistake—that $600 of the money was in cash in his office safe. He was then ordered to produce it, but came back next day saying that he had made another mistake—that it was in the bank along with the rest of the money. O'Dunne then sent a bailiff to the bank with orders to get a transcript from the ledger, and the bailiff returned with the news that the balance credited to the estate amounted to but $3.50. O'Dunne then brought Leach into court again and ordered him to produce the remainder within 24 hours. He did so the next day. He got the money, so O'Dunne told me, by borrowing it from William Curran,[1] a rich criminal lawyer and the Democratic boss of Baltimore.

Leach is himself a competent criminal lawyer, and might have a good practice if he were not so lazy. He served a term as State's attorney and made a very creditable record. But he prefers to live by borrowing, and O'Dunne says that he owes many thousands of dollars to hundreds of Baltimoreans, including some of the judges and most of the better heeled lawyers. It is not recorded that he has ever repaid a loan. In his days as State's attorney he was called upon to prosecute disbarment proceedings against the late Harry B. Wolf.[2] He carried

1 William ("Willie") Curran (1885–1951) was a powerful Democratic party boss in Baltimore for many years.

2 Harry B. Wolf (1880–1944), a prominent Baltimore attorney, was charged with obstruction of justice in connection with a sensational murder case in the city in 1920. He was convicted, disbarred, and fined $100. After numerous attempts over the years, he was readmitted to the bar in 1940.

them on with vigor and Wolf was duly disbarred, but all the while Leach's note for $1,000 was in Wolf's safe. Wolf never mentioned it— and Leach never paid it. He is a pleasant fellow, and I have known him for 30 years, but I'll avoid him hereafter. His runner-up as the champion borrower of Baltimore is Jerome P. Fleishman, formerly an advertising agent but now a professional dead beat. Fleishman came to me four or five years ago with a sad tale of illness at home and I lent him $100. It has gone with the wind. I found out afterward that he had got $100 loans from scores of other men, including many newspaper men. I occasionally meet him on the street. He always pretends not to see me. Why he should have taken to this petty swindling I don't know. There was a time when he had an apparently prosperous advertising business. Maybe he lost it by borrowing from his clients.

BALTIMORE, NOVEMBER 23, 1944.

I went out to the Home For Incurables at Keswick road and 40th street yesterday afternoon to see my old uncle, Charles H. Abhau, who has been a patient there for four or five years. He will be 76 years old on December 22. He was crippled by infantile paralysis at the age of three, but all through his youth and manhood he managed to get about on crutches. In his late teens he entered my father's cigar-factory as an apprentice cigarmaker, and soon became one of the best workmen in the place. Inasmuch as he could not carry molds to and from his bench he specialized in hand-made goods, and for years was assigned to the Marguerite and La Princessa brands, the best on the firm's list. He made them perfectly. He was slow but he was extremely painstaking, and during my three years in the factory in the late 90's I never heard of a single complaint against his work. My father was very fond of him, but always believed that he was not long for this world, for in addition to the lameness left by his infantile paralysis, he had a number of other uncomfortable malaises, including very severe eczema. Once I heard my father say to my mother: "Charlie will never see thirty." But now my father is dead for 45 years, and Charlie is still alive. He is, however, visibly deteriorating, and listening to him is something of a toil, for he has a high blood pressure, has suffered a mild stroke or two, and becomes somewhat vague in his speech. For three years he has been bothered by a mysterious ulcer on one of his fingers. Good surgeons have seen it, but apparently they can't cure it.

It is painful only intermittently, and meanwhile it gives him something to talk about. He took off the bandage yesterday and showed it to me. It looked to be unimproved, but he seemed to believe that it was getting well.

Not long after my father's death in 1899 Charlie took a civil service examination and was appointed to a post in the Baltimore Customs House. A few years later he decided to study law and was graduated LL.B from the law-school of the University of Maryland. In those days its lectures began at 5 p.m. and it was thus possible for him to attend them. He played for some time with the idea of setting up practise, but his disability got in the way, and he finally decided to stick to the Customs service. He remained at his job for more than 30 years and was finally retired on a pension. Meanwhile, when he was approaching 50 he astounded the family by getting married. His bride was Bertha Hennighausen, the daughter of an old-time German pastor of Baltimore. He had known her since her childhood. Their marriage was very happy, but after a few years she died. He then took to boarding with his sisters, and finally with his niece, Eva Abhau Hampe, but when Eva acquired two children he realized that he was a burden to her, and decided to go to the Home For Incurables.

Despite its depressing name, this institution is very comfortable and even charming. It occupies a group of well-designed brick buildings set in the midst of an old wood. Uncle Charlie has a room on the ground floor of one of them, in a corner. There are two windows, and he can look out into the wood and watch the squirrels at play. He pays $21 a week for his room. When he entered the place the price was $18, but it was raised at the beginning of 1944. I visited him in April and found him in some distress. A very methodical man, he had made a budget that precisely exhausted his pension, and he feared that the increase in his board would make it impossible for him to continue sending flowers and holiday presents to his nieces, grand-nieces and grand-nephews, as he had been doing for years. I offered to make good the deficiency, and sent him a check for $156 on April 5. He is now comfortable again, but he told me this afternoon that he is very lonely. When a man is ill and housebound for years on end, his old friends either die off or grow tired of him. Thus he receives fewer and fewer visitors. Charlie fell out of the habit of reading several years ago, when a sclerotic hemorrhage in one of his eyes half blinded him. It has passed off, but apparently his sight is still somewhat affected. He spends his time looking after the trivial business of his life and gabbing with other patients. He told me that one of them, an old man, drops in on him every evening to smoke and talk. But most of the other patients are confined to their rooms, and the ambulant ones seldom last long. In consequence he has to be making new friends all the time—a difficult business at 76.

His lifelong miseries have not broken his spirit, and he is still good-humored and even, in a sad way, merry. Today I found him much distressed by the news that Eva Hampe's oldest child, a boy of seven, has developed asthma. The asthma-eczema diathesis runs in the Abhau family, and has been its curse for years. My mother had what was apparently a severe attack of asthma in the early 80's, though it was diagnosed by the quacks of the time as tuberculosis, and there are signs of it in my brother August. My mother's sister, Louisa Caskey, suffered horribly for years. I well recall how I rushed news of the discovery of adrenalin to her, immediately it was announced. Her doctor, a neighborhood looker at tongues, had not yet heard of it. But though adrenalin gave her temporary relief, its effects did not last, and she was presently suffering again. My own hay-fever comes out of the same pot, and so does my sister's. Aunt Louisa lasted a long, long time, and indeed died only a few years ago. Such terminal agonies are characteristic of the family. Her brother, William C. Abhau, was in bed for seven years, and it took a multitude of strokes to kill him. Her sister, Minnie Werner, was crippled by arthritis for fifteen or twenty years. My mother, the luckiest member of the family, developed sclerosis obliterans in 1923, and I lived in terror that there would have to be amputations, but she died quickly and easily of an intercurrent infection on December 13, 1925. In these days the new drugs would cure that infection, but to what end? They would simply leave her with the sclerosis, which was painful and incurable. On some near tomorrow it may be cured too, as so many other once-fatal conditions are being cured, but not yet.

I only hope that I escape the Abhau curse when my own time comes to die. Every rational man must want the quick death that my mother had—and my father before her. My brother August and I, sitting by the fire in the evening, often congratulate ourselves on the fact that we have no children, and that there is only one child in our whole immediate family. This is my niece Virginia Mencken Morrison, the daughter of my brother Charlie. She now has a boy nearly two years old, but he belongs to his father's family, not ours, and he seems so remote (I have seen him but once) that we do not speculate or worry about his fate. I can imagine nothing more distressing today than the thoughts of a man with a family growing up. The boys stand a good chance of being butchered in their young manhood, and boys and girls together face a world that will be enormously more uncomfortable than the one my generation has known. There will be wars off and on for years to come, and in the intervals of peace every American will be burdened and afflicted by the national debt. I read yesterday that it amounts even now to $6,800 a family—far more than the average American family accumulates as capital by a lifetime of work. By the time Roosevelt is got rid of at last it may be two or three times as much.

DECEMBER 25, 1944.

The last of the page proofs of Supplement I, "The American Language," came in from the Plimpton Press yesterday. The book, it appears, runs to 683 pages, which is fourteen pages shorter than "The American Language," fourth edition. This for the main text. But there is more front matter than in the fourth edition, and the Index and the List of Words and Phrases will be longer, so I made a pretty close guess.

August and I spent Christmas Eve quietly at home, with no callers and no telephone calls. I slept badly and have been feeling wretched all day. I had hoped to spend the whole day at work upon the Index, but I had to stop and lie down this morning, upset by heart pains and a general feeling of malaise. August and I had lunch with Gertie, and were home again by 3.30 p.m. I had a nap of more than an hour, and then resumed work on the Index. I am hopeful of finishing it by the end of the week, and also the List of Words and Phrases, but the latter is mainly Mrs. Lohrfinck's job, and when I last saw her, on December 23, she looked wretched.

It has been a dismal Christmas. The temperature is about 35 degrees, and rain has been falling intermittently all day. There was snow four or five days ago, but it was light and the rain has washed it away. On the long trip to Gertie's house in Gwynn Oak avenue I saw but two Christmas trees in houses. There were no tree ornaments in the stores this year, and the effects of the war are beginning to be felt in

a thousand ways. The Christmas news from the front must be extraordinarily depressing to persons who have relatives in Eisenhower's
army.[1] The Army press-agents are making desperate efforts to turn the
German break-through into a German rout, but I suspect that even
the generality of Americans, as stupid as they are, are beginning to
doubt this official optimism.

1 In mid-December the German army, which had been in retreat for weeks, suddenly
launched a surprise counteroffensive through the Forest of Ardennes in southeastern
Belgium, northern France, and northern Luxembourg, with the objective of split-
ting the Allied army groups. The American forces, quite unprepared for this onslaught, had to yield much ground. In what came to be known as the "Battle of the
Bulge," the German offensive was turned back and the original lines were restored,
but American casualties were heavy.

1945

Captain Leland P. Lovette dropped off in Baltimore yesterday to see Paul Patterson and me, and we had a pleasant couple of hours. I met him at Pennsylvania Station as he came in from Washington and took him to Paul's house in Guilford. Later I took him to the station on his departure for Philadelphia. His ship, the battle cruiser *Guam*, is lying at the Navy Yard there. It has just come in from a practise cruise. Lovette says that its performance was excellent, and he seemed to be very optimistic about its usefulness.

On its way from the West Indies to Norfolk it ran into a tremendous storm 300 miles from Hatteras. All the life-rafts were swept away, one of the boats was lost, and at times the ship showed a 30% roll. Inasmuch as the crew consisted largely of men who are novices to the sea, they suffered severely and at one time 60% of them were disabled. Nevertheless, they snapped to work just as it reached Hampton Roads, and when an admiral came aboard to inspect the ship he was surprised to find everything in first-class order. Lovette is naturally very proud of it, and was full of interesting stuff about its performance. It is now refitting at Philadelphia, and in about ten days it will start for the Far East through the Panama Canal.

Lovette told me that he met Doris Fleeson's[1] fiancé, Judge Clark, in London, and was not favorably impressed. He says that Clark is a very sour fellow, and he predicts frankly that Fleeson will find him dull. He has, however, plenty of money, and that may help.

---

1 Doris Fleeson (d. 1970), newspaperwoman, Washington correspondent for the New York *Daily News* and United Features Syndicate. There is no record that she married the Judge Clark referred to in the entry.

Lovette also encountered Mark S. Watson in London. One day Mark induced him to go to a Presbyterian tabernacle to hear a Scotch minister. Lovette went through curiosity, and was rather surprised to find that Mark was a very pious fellow. He says that he prayed earnestly and showed all the signs of a devotee.

BALTIMORE, JANUARY 22, 1945.

For the first time since her return to work Mrs. Lohrfinck turned in a batch of letters this evening in which there were no gross errors. She has been recovering steadily, but only slowly. For the first month I had to greatly reduce my rate of dictation, and after that she still showed difficulty in reading her notes. But of late she has been doing better and better, and today her work was almost up to its old-time form. She was so good before her illness that she spoiled me. I could dictate to her at high speed for an hour or more, giving her 50 or 60 letters and a lot of notes and other stuff, and she would bring it in without an error.

She has finished copying the long List of Words and Phrases for [the] "American Language" Supplement, and is half way through the Index.

BALTIMORE, JANUARY 23, 1945.

C. Braxton Dallam, head of the Home For Incurables, called me up last night to say that my old uncle, Charles H. Abhau, who has been a patient there for five years, is showing definite mental symptoms, and may become troublesome. I went out to the home this morning to look into this. At Dallam's suggestion I first saw the superintendent, a pleasant elderly nurse named, I think, Bechtel. She showed me a report on Uncle Charlie by the house doctor, T. C. Wolff. It was to the general effect that his senile deterioration was producing paranoid symptoms, with delusions of persecution, and that there were suicidal and even homicidal overtones. Inasmuch as Uncle Charlie is confined to a wheel-chair and can't stand on his legs, the chances of him doing harm to anyone else seemed to me to be very slight, and I said so. The nurse agreed, but suggested that he might try to kill himself—say, by getting out of his room at night and pitching down a stairway in his chair.

She told me, and Dallam had told me, that the Home was inclined to keep him as long as possible, and that he would not be turned out unless it became necessary to put him under restraint. She said that such cases were not infrequent, and that the patients were usually sent to Spring Grove State Hospital. I told her I could imagine more pleasant places, and she replied that some of the private mental hospitals nearer Baltimore were comfortable and well run. "The matter of cost," she said, "is usually the main thing." I told her that it could be disregarded. She said that so far Uncle Charlie had not been troublesome, but that in senile dementia the condition of the patient usually worsens. I left her with the understanding that nothing will be done without giving me ample notice. She suggested that it might be well, soon or late, to employ a man to watch Uncle Charlie at night, and said that she thought she could get one. I told her that I would see to the cost.

I then visited Uncle Charlie in his room, and found him in a much better state than I had expected. For the most part he talked quite rationally. His only visible delusion was to the effect that two other patients on his hall were spreading scandal about him, and talking against him in loud tones, by night as well as by day. He said he could hear them. One of their tales, he said, was to the effect that he had lately become the father of twins. They also accused him of having "a Jew boy" in his room. He showed annoyance at this, but did not say anything about revenge. I tried to reassure him by saying that these men, because of their long illnesses, had lost their minds, and urged him to dismiss their gabble as only an unhappy infirmity. He seemed to be impressed by this, and in fact grasped at it. He then talked of other things, including my own adventures with slanderers, as recorded in "Menckeniana: a Schimpflexikon."[1] He said he had read the book, and remembered it clearly. He volunteered the remark that what these sick men were allegedly saying about him was a good deal less vicious than what apparently sane men had said about me. Altogether, he appeared to me to be at least nine-tenths sane, and his ordinary talk, if anything, was more coherent than usual.

I remained about an hour, and left him in what seemed to be a

1 *Menckeniana: A Schimpflexikon* was a representative selection of the critical abuse hurled at Mencken over the years by many writers. It was compiled from his clipping books by Sara Haardt before their marriage and published by Knopf in 1928.

tranquil mood. He agreed that the rules of the Home against cluttering up rooms with books, pictures and other such things were reasonable, and even said that he saw no objection to doling out whiskey to the patients by the drink, with the doctor deciding how much is to be allowed each day. He told me that some time ago the head nurse on his hall had asked him how much money he had on him, and that when he said $17 she told him that it was too much for his small needs, and proposed to take away $10 and deposit it with the cashier. To this, he said, he agreed readily. He explained that he deposits his monthly pension check with the cashier, that she deducts his board for the month, and that the rest is at his disposal. He had no complaint to offer against the Home, save in the case of one nurse. This nurse, he said, made off with a copy of the *Saturday Evening Post* that he had been keeping for the night watchman. But he admitted that she had done so openly and without any protest from him.

My hope (and belief) is that he will not become violent, and that it will thus be possible for him to remain at the Home. He is beginning to be hospital weary, and would like to return to one of his nieces, but he knows very well (and admits) that they could not give him the attention he needs. The poor old man is in a really pitiable situation, but nothing can be done about it. He'd have been fortunate if he had died eight or ten years ago, when his total disability began. Unhappily, all the members of his family (save only my mother) have made long and dreadful jobs of dying, and so I fear he may last a long while. He has enough income to pay his way at the Home, but if he were transferred to a mental hospital he would need help. Dallam and the superintendent seem to be very friendly, and both have assured me that he will not be sent away save as a last resort.

He told me that he thinks he had a mild stroke six or eight months ago, and I suspect that he may be right. He said that the symptoms could be best described as an all-over feeling of wretched discomfort. Knowing that little or nothing could be done to relieve him, he said nothing to the doctor, and after a while he began to feel better. He looks pretty well now, though he is very thin. He told me he eats and sleeps well, and is comfortable in his room. He seems to have got over the belief that the administration of the Home was determined to get rid of him. This was the form of his beginning delusion at Christmas, when I last saw him. Now his suspicions are concentrated on the two unnamed fellow-patients down the hall. He has been visited of late by his niece, Lulu Ireland; by his nephew, Wilmer Caskey; and by his brother's widow, Gertrude Abhau. All are fools, and their silly alarms certainly did not improve his condition. But now he seems to be relatively quiet again, and I am hopeful that he will continue so. He is the first member of either the Abhau or the Mencken family to show mental disturbance, and his, of course, is only a function of his senility. He has arterio-sclerosis, and apparently his blood pressure has been rising. If he could die quickly it would be a mercy, but the Abhaus have an almost incredible tenacity of life. Thus he may last for years. He is 76 years old.

BALTIMORE, JANUARY 29, 1945.

My heart symptoms continue and tend to grow worse. Night before last I had the worst spell so far. I awoke from a disturbed and idiotic dream with a sense of smothering, and lay awake the better part of an hour. My pulse was but 72 and my heart was beating strongly, but there was a general feeling of considerable discomfort, with a sense of impending collapse. It interests me to note how little the fear of death is present at such times. It ought to be there, but it simply isn't. I lie in bed trying to figure out whether I should call to August for help and go to hospital, but I always decide against it, and gradually fall asleep. My last thoughts are of my business affairs, now in pretty good shape. Supplement I to "The American Language" is finished; my instructions to my executor are up to date; I have no affairs in progress that could not be wound up quickly. I am sorry that I'll probably not be able to finish some of the projects I have long had in mind, for example, the little book to be called "Advice to Young Men," the second volume of "The American Language" Supplement, and a book recording my thoughts about the war and about life in general, to be published after I am dead. But I do not mourn over these things, and my days are fairly placid and contented, though it irks me to be unable to work and for the first time in my life I am experiencing boredom. Maybe there will be some improvement later on, and I may be able to return to my desk, but it seems unlikely. Looking back over a life of hard work, I find that my only regret is that I didn't work even harder. But this is somewhat absurd: I have actually worked hard enough. There is very little to show for it, but considering my bad start and rather meagre opportunities, I have at least accomplished something. I am only sorry that I'll probably not live long enough to take advantage of the reaction from the present war—if, indeed, there is ever any reaction. Sometimes I doubt it. The American people seem to be committed to mountebanks for ever more.

BALTIMORE, FEBRUARY 25, 1945.

I have felt so wretched for weeks past that work has been almost impossible, though I have managed to finish a short buffoonery for the *New Yorker* and a chapter for the Spiller "Literary History of the United States,"[1] both begun last Autumn. My right eye shows sclerotic changes, and the new glasses prescribed by Alan Woods are still uncomfortable. Also, there is a sore spot in the crevice between the base of my tongue on the left side and the wall of my throat, and two treatments by Polvogt have failed to heal it. But these are only minor troubles. My mind seems to be working badly, and when I sit up to the typewriter I quickly grow nervous and fuddled. It is thus very difficult to do any continuous writing. I have been trying to revise and expand the enormous stock of notes on all subjects that has accumulated in my files, and to rewrite some of my old *Smart Set* and *American Mercury* stuff, but have made only the smallest progress. If I could get all of this matter into printable shape I might be able to make a book or two of it, despite the war censorship, but so far I have been unable to do so. It is perfectly possible that my writing days are over, though I believe I am still good enough to do the second supplement to "The American Language." I have had such periods of doldrums in the past and got through them, but this time I seem to be worse hobbled than ever before.

BALTIMORE, FEBRUARY 28, 1945.

Another *dies non*. I tried to work this morning, but after half an hour had to stop. I suspect that there was some heart enlargement. I felt very uncomfortable and vaguely faint. I lay reading until lunchtime, and after lunch went downtown. It was unpleasant getting

1 The piece constitutes Chapter 40 of *Literary History of the United States*, ed. Robert E. Spiller et al. (New York: Macmillan, 1946; 4th ed. 1974). It is entitled "The American Language" but runs to only thirteen pages and has only a remote relationship to its immense namesake.

about, for sleet was falling and walking was insecure. After dropping into the *Sun* office and doing various errands—including a visit to Dr. Leslie Gay, the hay-fever man, who gave me an injection—I returned home and stretched out again. Such dismal, fruitless days have been common of late. It seems to be impossible for me to settle down to steady work. I make frequent attempts, but they come to nothing.

Paul Patterson wants me to go to San Francisco with him in April. Some sort of international conference is to be held there, with all the chief politicoes on the Allied side in attendance.[1] Patterson proposes that he and I go as what he calls "observers." I certainly don't want to play any such footling part, either there or anywhere else. When I see such a show I want to write about it—and it is obviously impossible, in these days, for me to do any writing for publication about public affairs. My point of view is wholly hostile to that of the *Sunpapers*, and my very vocabulary is under interdict. I could not write five lines without getting beyond the bounds of the permitted.

Patterson plans the San Francisco junket simply because his job bores him beyond endurance. He reaches out eagerly at every excuse to get away from the office. If he could get a passport he'd set off for London tomorrow. Unfortunately, there seems to be opposition in Washington to letting newspaper publishers go abroad. I have heard much speculation as to the reasons for this, but none of it is convincing. The most plausible theory is to the effect that Roosevelt fears an application from Joseph M. Patterson, and maybe even Colonel Robert R. McCormick.[2] In order to bar out these enemies, it is said, he has shut down on the whole fraternity. Patterson believes this. I remain in doubt.

BALTIMORE, MARCH 5, 1945.

I awoke yesterday (Sunday) morning feeling utterly miserable. My head felt full (though there was no headache or dizziness) and the left side of my face was faintly numb. I made various efforts to work during the day, but found it impossible. I was not only in great discomfort

1 The occasion was the founding conference of the United Nations, at which the UN charter was drawn up and signed by representatives of some fifty countries.
2 Joseph M. Patterson (1879–1946) was the founder and publisher of the New York *Daily News;* Colonel Robert R. McCormick (1880–1955) was editor and publisher of the Chicago *Tribune.*

physically; there was also some mental confusion. This continued until this morning, when, in dictating to Mrs. Lohrfinck, I actually forgot the name of Julian Boyd. I put in a restless night, with irrational dreams, all of them involving some sort of futile effort. In brief, I go on deteriorating, and seem to be the scene of a race between my arteries and my heart. It has become almost impossible for me to remember anything. If an idea occurs to me I must make a note of it instantly, or it is gone forever. This morning I thought of a good idea for a *New Yorker* piece, but tonight I haven't the slightest recollection of it.

Fortunately, I manage to keep up a good front, and no one appears to notice that I am ill. I get through my daily session with Paul Patterson very well, and also see various other people. Today I had lunch with Joseph L. Wheeler, the retiring librarian of the Enoch Pratt Library. He brought with him a long memorandum of the agreement between us about my books, his idea being to bind his successors. He is planning to leave Baltimore April 2, and will settle on a small farm near Rutland, Vt. He told me that a man has been selected for his job, with his advice and approval, but refused to tell me the man's name, for he has not yet accepted.[1] Wheeler said that he is highly competent, and sufficiently young to be good for a long term in office. Three of the ancients on the library's board of trustees are threatening to retire, and Wheeler is in hopes that better men will be chosen to succeed them. But inasmuch as the board is a self-perpetuating body this is by no means certain.

BALTIMORE, MARCH 28, 1945.

I am a subscriber, at the moment, to the following periodicals: the *Editor and Publisher*, the *Guild Reporter*, the *London Times Literary Supplement*, *American Speech*, *Language*, *Publications of the American Language Association*, the *New Yorker*, *American Notes and Queries*, *Consumers' Research*, *Your Investments*, the *Nation*, the *American German Review*, the *International Journal of American Linguistics*, the *Negro Digest*, *Newspaperman*, *Studies in Linguistics*, *Der Pennsylvaanisch Deitsch Eileschpiggel*, the *Monthly Supplement*

1 Dr. Wheeler's successor as director of the Pratt Library was Emerson Greenaway (b. 1906), who served in the post until 1951.

to "Who's Who in America," and maybe three or four more. In addition I receive the following gratis: the *Congressional Record,* the *William Feather Magazine,* the *Taxpayer* (Melbourne, Australia), the *Quarterly* of the Library of Congress, the *Saturday Review of Books,* the *New Leader,* the *Federal Union World,* the *Mexico News, Columbus,* the *Journal of the American Medical Association,* the *Virginia Quarterly,* the *Prairie Schooner, Adobe y Mesquite* (Tucson, Ariz.), the *American Mercury, Esquire, Gardens Houses and People* (Baltimore), the *Household Magazine,* the *Column Digest,* the *Thinkers' Digest,* the *Etude, Retort,* the *Freethinker,* the *Bulletin of the New York Public Library,* the *Virginian* (published by the inmates of the Virginia Penitentiary, Richmond), the *Bulletin of the Teachers' Alliance* (New York), and several others. Finally, I receive a great many odd numbers of other periodicals, sent in from time to time by various customers. They include perhaps half a dozen Army and Navy papers, issued by the soldiers and sailors. Marked copies of newspapers and magazines reach me almost daily, and I also get a large number of clippings, some of them in foreign languages.

I marvel constantly at the amount of printed matter that thus passes over my desk. I look through nearly all of it, but mainly only in search of items for my collection of material about the American language. The rest of it goes into my big waste-basket unread. That waste-basket holds about a bushel, and is filled every two or three days. It is also the repository of some of the innumerable propaganda circulars, pamphlets and broadcasts that come in regularly. The rest of them go into a carton which I ship, when it is filled, to the New York Public Library. During the past five or six years I have probably sent the library at least 25,000 such items. They range from the announcements of new messiahs to the appeals of charity racketeers, and from the annual reports of corporations to paper-bound volumes of amateur poets. The waste of paper in this great Republic is really appalling. If all the useless printing were cut off there would be an ample supply for all necessary purposes, and no need to ration newspapers and book publishers. But it is precisely the useless printing that is *not* cut off.

BALTIMORE, APRIL 1 (EASTER SUNDAY), 1945.

I put in an hour and a half this morning cleaning the pony-stable in the yard and rearranging its constantly accumulating contents—an annual job. I burned a lot of rubbish and filled an ash-can with the rest. The yard is gay with flowers and new leaves, though the dogwood has not yet blossomed and there is still no new growth on the ivy. I shall give over next Sunday morning to raking up and burning the surviving Autumn leaves, and to ridding the vines of dead shoots. This Spring renovation is always a laborious business, but I like it, for it takes me into the sun, and gives me some exercise. It was warm enough this morning to be pleasant, but not warm enough to set me to sweating. At 12.30 August and I went to Gertie's for lunch. She is preparing to move to the country in about two weeks. She made a trip there the other day and found the farmers full of alarms. The early Spring has made everything flourish prematurely and they fear that a killing frost may follow. They are also concerned by the heavy drafting of farm-boys. Some of them are left with no help whatever, and it will be impossible for them to grow their usual crops. Four or five years ago, when I was on a visit to her, Gertie pointed out a sturdy farm-boy tramping up the road. He was courting a girl in Westminster, she said, and three evenings a week, after a hard day's work in the fields, tramped five miles there from his home toward Uniontown, and then five miles back. He duly married the girl, and they presently had a baby, now three years old. A few days ago news came that he had been killed in the war. Such is the price that poor people pay for Roosevelt's itch to glitter in history.

BALTIMORE, APRIL 1, 1945.

Under date of March 26 I had a curious letter from Charles Honce of the Associated Press, proposing that I do some articles for the A.P. on the coming international conference at San Francisco. "The running spot story," he said, "will be handled by a large spot staff, so that you will be able to write your own ticket as to when, how often and on what subjects you will write." I had to decline, of course, as I had already declined to cover the conference for the *Sun*. It would be simply impossible for me to cover it, or even to mention it, without making plain my opinion of it, and of the war with it, and no American newspaper would dare to print what I wrote. I was wise to quit writing for the *Sun* back in January, 1941, for it was obvious by then that Roosevelt would horn into the war soon or late, and I knew by bitter experience in the last war that I'd be throttled at once. Since then I have thought out many likely articles, but not one of them has been printable. In these days, indeed, my very vocabulary is prohibited. I couldn't so much as mention Roosevelt, or Churchill or any of the other frauds without having to face a savage official onslaught, with all blows directed below the belt.

The common notion that free speech prevails in the United States always makes me laugh. It is actually hedged in enormously both in peace and in war. All the ideas with which my name is associated had to be launched during the interval between 1925 and 1940, and even in that interval there were several attempts to silence me—for example, the "Hatrack" episode. Twice in one lifetime I have been forced to shut down altogether—first in 1916 and then in 1941. Even during the interval I have mentioned I was constantly menaced by censorships of a dozen different varieties, and they greatly incommoded me while I was editing the *American Mercury*. The American people, I am convinced, really detest free speech. At the slightest alarm they are ready and eager to put it down. Looking back, I sometimes marvel that I managed, despite this implacable hostility, to launch some of my notions. War, in this country, wipes out all the rules of fair play, even those prevailing among wild animals. Even the dissenters from the prevailing balderdash seek to escape the penalties of dissent by whooping up the official doctrine. From that ignominy, at all events, I have managed to escape. I have not written a line in this war, and I wrote none in the last, that I am not prepared to ratify today. There has been no acquiescence in my enforced silence.

It is highly improbable that even the rudiments of free speech will be restored in my time, as they began to be restored in 1925. There will be a state of war so long as Roosevelt is in office, for if he made peace he would lose all his war powers, and his disintegration would follow quickly. Thus I'll never see any freedom again. It is hardly a prospect to fill me with patriotic frenzy. The government I live under has been my enemy all my active life. When it has not been engaged in silencing me it has been engaged in robbing me. So far as I can recall I have never had any contact with it that was not an outrage on my dignity and an attack upon my security.

BALTIMORE, APRIL 13, 1945.

The *Sun* editorial on Roosevelt this morning begins: "Franklin D. Roosevelt was a great man."[1] There are heavy black dashes above and below it. The argument, in brief, is that all his skullduggeries and imbecilities were wiped out when "he took an inert and profoundly isolationist people and brought them to support a necessary war on a scale never before imagined." In other words, his greatest fraud was his greatest glory, and his sufficient excuse for all his other frauds. It is astonishing how far the *Sun* has gone in this nonsense. When the English fetched Patterson and John Owens they certainly did an all-out job. I know of no paper in the United States, not even the New York *Herald Tribune,* that croons for them more assiduously.

Roosevelt's unparallelled luck held out to the end. He died an easy death, and he did so just in time to escape burying his own dead horse. This business now falls to Truman, a third-rate Middle Western politician on the order of Harding. He is fundamentally against the New Deal wizards, and he will probably make an earnest effort to turn them out of power, but I have some doubt that he will succeed. They have dug in deeply and they may be expected to fight to the bitter end, for once they are out they will be nothing and they know it. The case of La Eleanor is not without its humors. Only yesterday she was the most influential female ever recorded in American history, but tomorrow she will begin to fade, and by this time next year she may be wholly out of the picture. I wonder how many newspapers will go on printing her "My Day."[2] Probably not many.

It seems to me to be very likely that Roosevelt will take a high place in American popular history—maybe even alongside Washington and Lincoln. It will be to the interest of all his heirs and assigns to whoop him up, and they will probably succeed in swamping his critics. If the war drags on it is possible, of course, that there may be a reaction against him, and there may be another and worse after the war is over at last, but the chances, I think, run the other way. He had every quality that morons esteem in their heroes. Thus a demigod seems to be in the making, and in a little while we may see a

1 Roosevelt had died very suddenly at Warm Springs, Georgia, of a cerebral hemorrhage the day before.
2 "My Day" was the title of a syndicated daily column which Eleanor Roosevelt began writing in 1935 and continued for many years.

grandiose memorial under way in Washington, comparable to those to Washington, Jefferson and Lincoln. In it, I suppose, Eleanor will have a niche, but probably not a conspicuous one. The majority of Americans, I believe, distrust and dislike her, and all her glories have been only reflections from Franklin. It may be true that it was she, not he, who really invented the New Deal, but if so Franklin hogged all the credit, and was rewarded with nine-tenths of the popular faith and admiration. I believe she got most of the blame for the raffishness of her children. The average Americano believes that she should have stayed home and policed them. Her husband was on the battlements, saving humanity, and it was her duty to watch the home fires. Her state today is not without its pathetic touches. She is alarmingly homely, she has lost her job, and she is growing old.

The Baltimore Hearst paper, the *News-Post*, handled the great news with typical cynicism. Hearst is one of the most violent enemies of Roosevelt, and all his papers have been reviling the New Deal, and even propagating doubts about the war. But the whole first page of the *News-Post* is given over this afternoon to a large portrait of Roosevelt flanked by two flags in color and headed "Nation Mourns." The editorial page is filled with an editorial saying, among other things, "The work and name of Franklin Delano Roosevelt will live on, not only today or tomorrow, but in all the annals of recorded time." This, as I have noted, is probably a fact, but it is certainly not a fact that tickles Hearst. He is, however, an expert in mob psychology, and does not expect much. The *Sun* is in far less rational position. It certifies to Roosevelt's greatness in all seriousness.

BALTIMORE, APRIL 15, 1945.

All the saloons and major restaurants of Baltimore were closed last night as a mark of respect to the dead Roosevelt, whose body passed through the city at midnight. It was silly, but it gave a lot of Dogberries a chance to annoy their betters, and so it was ordained. As a result, the Saturday Night Club missed its usual post-music beer-party for the first time in forty years. All during Prohibition the club found accommodations in the homes of its members, but last night no member was prepared, so the usual programme had to be abandoned. August and I came home, had a couple of high-balls, and then went to bed.

Roosevelt, if he had lived, would probably have been unbeatable, despite the inevitable reaction against the war. He was so expert a demagogue that it would have been easy for him to divert the popular discontent to some other object. He could have been beaten only by a demagogue even worse than he was himself, and his opponents showed no sign of being able to flush such a marvel. The best they could produce was such timorous compromisers as Willkie and Dewey, who were as impotent before Roosevelt as sheep before Behemoth. When the call was for a headlong attack they backed and filled. It thus became impossible, at the close of their campaigns, to distinguish them from mild New Dealers—in other words, inferior Roosevelts. He was always a mile ahead of them, finding new victims to loot and new followers to reward, flouting common sense and boldly denying its existence, demonstrating by his anti-logic that two and two made five, promising larger and larger slices of the moon. His career will greatly engage historians, if any good ones ever appear in America, but it will be of even more interest to psychologists. He was the first American to penetrate to the real depths of vulgar stupidity. He never made the mistake of overestimating the intelligence of the American mob. He was its unparallelled professor.

BALTIMORE, APRIL 25, 1945.

After a couple of weeks of relative comfort I was awakened at 1.30 this morning by the worst heart upset so far. There was the usual discomfort under the sternum, and for a while my heart, though its beat was strong, missed every fourth beat altogether. I lay still, and this soon passed off. As I waited to see what would turn up I noted the curious psychological effect before recorded in these notes. That is to say, I was quite unaware of any fear of death. What really occupied me was speculating whether I'd be awake a long time, or soon fall asleep. As it happened, I was awake perhaps twenty minutes. When I arose this morning I felt very wretched. In fact, I have never felt worse. But after shaving and bathing I began to feel better. A certain amount of malaise, however, has continued.

I begin to suspect that Scotch whiskey may be bad for me. About 8 o'clock last night my nephew-in-law, David Morrison, called up to say that he was in town with a colleague from Lancaster, Pa., Carl Graham. I invited them to come to the house, and they arrived at about 8.30. David called for Scotch and I drank two high-balls with him. August drank ale, and Graham asked for sherry. I have noted in the past that my heart spells usually follow Scotch. When I drink rye or bourbon or beer I seldom have them. Why there should be this difference—if it actually *is* a difference, and not only a coincidence— I can't make out. The amount of alcohol I get down is about the same in all cases.

BALTIMORE, APRIL 30, 1945.

Old Lillie Fortenbaugh, our next-door neighbor for nearly fifty years, died last Thursday afternoon, April 26, and was buried today. As incredible as it may seem, I did not learn of her death until Saturday, forty-eight hours afterward. The news then reached me from my sister Gertrude, who called up from the country, and reported that she had encountered the death notice in the *Sun*. August was laid up with bronchitis on Thursday, Friday and Saturday, and I was indoors Thursday evening and all day Saturday until after Gertie's call. I was in and out of the house on Friday, but, as usual, used the back gate, and thus did not notice the flowers on the Fortenbaugh push-button. It turned out that Emma and Hester, the colored servants, knew of the poor old girl's death all the while, but, in the secretive manner of colored people, they did not mention it.

Lillie must have been close to seventy. She was a complete moron and led a life of utter vacuity. August went to the funeral this afternoon and came back reporting that the officiating clergyman spoke of her church work, and that her brother Charlie, also enormously stupid, mentioned her "civic work" (his own phrase), but all this was probably only funeral politeness. Lillie, in fact, spent most of her time by day roving about the shopping district, looking in windows and pricing things that she didn't buy. When she grew tired she took a seat in a department-store rest-room, and there watched the flow of shoppers. Toward the end of the afternoon she went to a movie. Her evenings were devoted to the radio. We could hear it faintly through our wall, but it was not disturbing. To the best of my recollection she seldom turned on music, and never any good music. Her preference seemed to be for speeches, and for the yowling of so-called news commentators.

In her earlier years Lillie banged the piano every evening, and had a good many visitors, but of late years strange voices have come through the wall only seldom. There were servants in the house in those days, including a low-comedy colored butler, but of late most of the housework has apparently been done by Lillie's younger half-sister, Ethel. Ethel was married years ago and had a son, but soon her husband left her, taking the son along, and of late she has been at home most of the time, with occasional ventures into practical nursing. When her husband sued her for divorce, his main allegation was that she was sub-normal mentally. I was summoned by the family to deny this, and did so as in duty bound, but the judge was not deceived, for he had her before him. When I returned to Hollins street in 1936 I had a clash with Lillie about the barking of her dog. Her reply to my complaint was to accuse me of shooting at it! The dog barked less after that, but of late it has been resuming its old uproar, and only last week I planned to complain to the police. Now, I suppose, it will disappear.

The lives of such poor simpletons always fascinate me. It is hard to imagine them being endurable. So far as I know, Lillie never did anything in all her years that was worth doing, or said anything worth hearing. Yet she showed a considerable complacency, and I have no doubt that she was well satisfied with herself. The conversations that went on between her and her brother and sister must have been marvellous indeed. I seldom did more than pass the time of day with her myself, and when I called at the door on learning of her death it was the first time I had crossed her threshold for years. The house, in so far as I could see it, turned out to be a museum of archaisms. There was even a crayon portrait of her father hanging over the parlor mantelpiece. The wallpaper and carpets, not to mention the furniture, looked to be at least fifty years old, and it was only too apparent that they were hideous even when young. Thus Lillie lived out her days. She got along, somehow, without intelligence, information or taste. She had no desire to learn anything, and in fact learned nothing. Her ideas at seventy were her ideas at fifteen. It is hard to think of a more placid life, and she apparently enjoyed it, but it is likewise hard to think of one more hollow. It was as insignificant, almost, as the life of her dog.

BALTIMORE, MAY 3, 1945.

It is a curious fact, but nevertheless a fact, that my piano technic seems to improve with age. I never practise, and seldom touch a piano save at the Saturday Night Club; in fact, the one in the house has not been opened for years. Nevertheless, I find it possible to play things today that would have stumped me a dozen years ago. Even my left hand is gaining more or less facility. In theory, the reverse should be the case, for my sight is naturally not quite as quick as it used to be, and my congenital incapacity for manual operations grows worse instead of better in other directions. But when it comes to playing second piano I am definitely better than I used to be.

BALTIMORE, MAY 5, 1945.

Last night I finished reading the two volumes of the Diaries, Reminiscences and Correspondence of Henry Crabb Robinson,[1] brought out in London in 1869, with Thomas Sadler as editor, and reprinted "from advance sheets," by Fields, Osgood & Company of Boston the year following. So far as I know, it has never been reprinted since. I had heard of it for many years, but never came to looking into it until a few weeks ago, when I asked George Pfeffer, the old book dealer, if he had it, and he dug up a copy from his cellar. This copy was inscribed "Margaret J. Preston, 1870," and had probably been in stock since before I was born, for Pfeffer's predecessor, Smith, set up business in the 70's. It turned out to be immensely interesting stuff. Robinson was a nonentity, but he had the faculty of scraping acquaintance with famous men, and with some of them he became very intimate. His recollections of Goethe, Schiller, the Schellings, Wordsworth, Coleridge, Lamb and other eminentissimos of the early Nineteenth Century tell little about them that is unobtainable from other sources, but there are human touches that are very charming. Robinson was one of the first, if not actually the first Englishman to be educated in Germany, and his pictures of life at Jena, Weimar and Frankfurt in 1800 and thereafter are illuminating and instructive. He remained a violent Germanophile until his death at 92 in 1867. I am very fond of such books. They make capital reading for the hour or so between going to bed and falling asleep. I can't recall ever falling asleep in fifty

1 Henry Crabb Robinson (1775–1867), English journalist and barrister, traveled widely in Germany as a young man. The posthumous work that Mencken refers to here was edited, says the *Dictionary of National Biography*, from "thirty-five closely written volumes of 'Diary,' thirty volumes of 'Journals' of tours, thirty-two volumes of 'letters' (with index), four volumes of 'Reminiscences,' and one of 'Anecdotes.' "

years, save on a few occasions when I was ill or much in my cups, without reading at least half an hour. The theory that the practise is damaging to the eyes seems to me to be buncombe. My eyes, despite some sclerotic changes, are perfectly good at 65. I not only read in bed every night; I also do nearly all my daylight reading lying down. I believe fully in the Chinese maxim that it is foolish to do anything standing up that can be done sitting, or anything sitting that can be done stretched out.

BALTIMORE, MAY 11, 1945.

A woman named Le Clare Peach, living at 1505 west Lombard street, called me up yesterday to ask my aid in her efforts to police Union Square. She is given to good works, and usually takes the lead when there is any reform movement in the neighborhood. I told her that I'd be glad to sign any protest or petition that she prepared, for my own attempts to clear nuisances out of the square have had very little success. Several years ago the cops made some melodramatic raids upon the smoke-eaters who used to sit on the benches, but that was hardly more than an idle show, for the smoke-eaters were actually harmless. I saw them sitting there of a morning, drowsing off their day's ration of paint-store wood-alcohol, but they made no noise, and I never saw one of them molesting a child or anyone else. The dogs that roared in the square by day and the oakie and linthead youngsters who howled in it by night were not challenged by the cops save when some resident complained. My brother August, who sleeps in the front of the house, had to complain a number of times. The linthead drabs, many of them hardly more than fourteen years old, would bring their beaux into the square at 11 p.m. or thereabout, and for an hour or more afterward there would be an uproar, with love-making by capture. The cops came rushing up on August's demand and chased them out, and after a while they sought some other arena.

But the dogs remained, and my complaints to the S.P.C.A. were in vain. One afternoon a bitch in heat appeared on the Hollins street side of the square, and presently half a dozen dogs were after her. The one she finally favored operated on her in full view of a gang of children, while all the other bucks howled dismally. When I called up the S.P.C.A. I was told that it was too late in the day to send its dog-wagon. While this performance was going on—it lasted more than an hour—the noise was so loud that I had to suspend work. No cop appeared. Miss Peach tells me that at least a dozen dogs appear on her side of the square every afternoon, not one of them licensed or on leash. The alleys of the neighborhood swarm with them, but despite the Health Department's warning that hydrophobia is afoot no effort is made to dispose of them. Every linthead family has a dog, and so has every Negro family in Fairmount avenue, just north of Baltimore street. Not long ago, as I passed the corner of Fairmount avenue and Gilmor street, six dogs rushed out in a pack.

Miss Peach says that, on her complaint, the cops recently investigated the public toilet in the square. They found it was a favorite resort of homosexuals. She says that they arrested and jailed forty-four, including three clergymen. What the evidence was against the prisoners I do not know, and I am inclined to be suspicious of it, for linthead children are not above making charges for purposes of blackmail. Miss Peach says that linthead girls of twelve or thereabout come into the square at night to pick up men and boys. If this is true I have not noticed it. Moreover, I do not object to it, so long as it is not accompanied by shrieks and shouts, for one of the prime purposes of any public park is to provide a place of assignation for the young. There is no room in the crowded living quarters of these poor creatures for receiving and enjoying their beaux. As for the damage to their virtue, it is purely imaginary, for only a rare linthead girl remains a virgin after the age of twelve. Her deflowering, in fact, is usually performed by her brothers, and if not by her brothers, then by her father. Incest is almost as common as fornication among these vermin, and no doubt it is largely responsible for their physical and mental deterioration. Everyone who knows the Southern poor whites knows this, but it is not mentioned in official reports.

The other day, walking down Baltimore street, I happened to fall in behind two linthead girls further along in years—perhaps sixteen or seventeen. They were talking loudly and I could not help overhearing. Their gabble was almost incredibly obscene—an endless stream of dirty words, repeated over and over again. They must have heard me walking behind them, but they showed no sign of it. Save from an occasional drunken soldier, I have never had the honor of hearing so gorgeous a display of indecency.

BALTIMORE, MAY 14, 1945.

I have written a letter to Will Durant, whose "Caesar and Christ" I have just finished reading, and another to his publisher, Max Schuster, congratulating them on the excellence of the book.[1] It is a thing of really extraordinary merit—beautifully designed, full of sound learning and sound sense, and wholly free of platitude and sentimentality. There is probably no better conspectus of Roman history or of early Christian history in English. It came out last year, but I let it lie on my table for months without looking into it, for my opinion of Durant was not too high. He seemed to me to be only a popularizer, and full of unwarranted pretensions. But now he has done a serious historical work of genuine value, and I have read it with great pleasure. My letter to him, praising it, is the first I have written to an author for four or five years. The last was a note to John Gunther, on "Inside Asia,"[2] which I read by chance at the home of Fred and Betty Hanes at Roaring Gap, N.C. Gunther, in general, is a third-rater, but in that book, at least, he did a really good job.

BALTIMORE, MAY 26, 1945.

I have been engaged for six weeks past in trying to get some order into my almost interminable notes, which have been accumulating for years. I have dipped into them from time to time for materials for books or articles, but the surplus has always mounted steadily. In large part it consists of pencilled notes that record only fragments of ideas and would be unintelligible to anyone else; indeed, some of them are already unintelligible to me. I am thus undertaking to reduce them to some sort of coherence, in the hope that I may make use of many of them hereafter. The rest I shall leave for the edification (or derision) of posterity. When, as and if I ever finish the job I shall go through my old *Smart Set* and *American Mercury* stuff, much of it never used in books, and try to rescue such parts of it as seem worth preserving. It would be madness to proceed from it to my newspaper stuff, which I could hardly hope even to read in less than a couple of months. What

1 *Caesar and Christ* (1944) was the third volume in what would eventually become Will and Ariel Durant's eleven-volume "Story of Civilization."
2 John Gunther (1901–1970), American journalist, wrote a series of "Inside" books: *Inside Europe* (1936), *Inside Asia* (1939), *Inside Latin America* (1941), *Inside U.S.A.* (1947), *Inside Africa* (1955), and *Inside Russia Today* (1958).

my total writings for print amount to I do not know, but they must run to 10,000,000 words at least. Large parts of them have dealt with transient and forgotten themes, and are now dead, but whenever I dip into them I am struck by the number of ideas that still seem more or less valid and significant today. I have thrown off, in my time, an enormous number of such ideas—possibly more than any other American writer of my time. But not many of them have ever been adopted (or even seriously considered) by MM. my countrymen.

BALTIMORE, MAY 30, 1945.

Sara will be dead ten years tomorrow. It seems a long, long while, yet she still remains living to me, and seldom a waking hour passes that I do not think of her. My marriage, so long delayed, was very happy, despite the anxieties caused by her frequent illnesses, and the plain fact that her chances of life were not too good. She was enormously considerate, and she had good humor—a quality as rare in women as it is charming. We were nearly five years together, and in all that time we never had a serious quarrel. Our differences were always trivial, and they never left any bitterness. I believe that she was as contented as I was, but I sometimes wonder how we'd have got on after ten years of marriage, or fifteen. There is, of course, no telling, but the experience of others seems to indicate that marriage inevitably wears out, if not altogether, then at least around the edges. I incline to believe that we'd have survived this letting down without real damage. Marriage is nine-tenths talk, and up to her last illness we were still amusing each other. We had decided from the start that occasional separations would be good for us, and it turned out to be true. There were plenty of chances for them in my routine of life, and we might have made them longer. It is possible that World War II might have set us at loggerheads, but I doubt it. Another imaginable source of serious difference was her desire for children, or at least for a child. I was implacably against it. Her bad health, of course, made motherhood impossible for her, but if she had recovered there might have been another story to tell.

I went out to Loudon Park Cemetery this morning to visit her grave—my first trip there since Christmas. I laid some white carnations over the place where her ashes are buried. They were bought from an Italian roadside vendor in Frederick avenue, opposite the cemetery gate. They were very charming, and they seemed to me to be somehow more fitting than anything formal. I go to the cemetery so seldom because I can't get rid of the feeling that it is a banality. I need no such reminder to make me remember her. I shall not forget her. My days with her made a beautiful episode in my life, perhaps the only one that deserves to be called romantic. It seems to me to be vain and even a bit silly to resist the irremediable, but I think of her with tenderness and a kind of longing. I can well understand why the more naïve sort of people cling to the hope of a reunion after death. But I do not share it. I said goodbye to her forever at the Johns Hopkins Hospital on May 28, 1935. She was then unconscious, and dying. I never saw her afterward, and I did not look upon her in death. It was too dreadful a thing to face. When I think of her, it is as she was in her days of relative good health, when she was gay, and amusing, and infinitely charming.

I found the Mencken cemetery lot in reasonably good order, despite the fact that the cemetery managers have posted a notice at the entrance, saying that they are unable, because of the war, to give the place their usual care. Some weeds were growing amid the ivy. I pulled them out, and threw them on a nearby trash pile. The rain of the past few days has made a puddle in the carving of the family coat-of-arms on the flat tombstone, and dirt from the air—how foul Baltimore has become!—has turned it into mud. But this is inevitable, and perhaps as it should be. The mud will dry, leaving dark shadows in the carving. The names carved on the stone already show darkly, but the white surface is still clean and bright. I had the stone made and erected in 1926, following the death of my mother. My father's tombstone was a hideous thing of granite, bearing the Masonic G and compass. I had it removed and broken up. The present stone is of marble, with a plain border and the coat-of-arms at its head. Beneath the arms are the names and dates of the dead. There is room left for all the rest of us. My own name will be there soon enough.

BALTIMORE, JUNE 1, 1945.

I had James T. Farrell,[1] the novelist, to lunch at the Maryland Club yesterday, along with his brother, Dr. John A. Farrell, a psychiatrist on the staff of St. Elizabeth's Hospital, Washington. Farrell

---

1 James T. Farrell (1904–1979), Chicago-born author of the *Studs Lonigan* trilogy and many other novels laid in the South Side slum section of his native city.

is 41 and his brother looks to be considerably younger. Farrell has done some novels of excellent merit, all of them dealing with the poor Irish among whom he was brought up in Chicago, but he is not very good company, and I see him very seldom. There was a time when he was a Communist, but he seems to have recanted, for the Reds now denounce him violently. He told me that he has finished the first volume of a tetralogy and also a book of short stories. He is a hard worker, especially at rewriting. He said that he was in communication with Dreiser, and that Dreiser had lately sent him part of the MS. of "The Bulwark," which has been under way, off and on, for nearly 30 years. I have written to Dreiser twice of late, but have got no reply. Apparently I am in his bad graces once more—maybe because I did not applaud his deposit of all his papers, including my letters to him, in the University of Pennsylvania Library. They should have gone to the New York Public Library, but Dreiser always handles his affairs badly. What he has been living on of late I do not know. The Jews of Hollywood have certainly not given him much money.

The medical Farrell turned out to be a believer in the mental cause of mental diseases. He was full of tales of sailors and marines in his care, driven crazy by the horrors of service in the South Seas. One of them, he said, came home with such an advanced case of jitters that he leaped upon a table and began to cry every time he heard an airplane. Such evidence, to me at least, proves only that this poor fellow was crazy before he was drafted. The examining psychiatrists, if they were even half competent, would have screened him out. Thousands of men who have gone through precisely the same experiences remain completely sane. But it is hard to find a psychiatrist intelligent enough to think of this elemental fact. My guess is that most recruits to psychiatry are young medicoes who crave quick and easy jobs, and realize that they are unfit for anything better. An asylum doctor has a good livelihood assured for life, no matter how little he may know and learn. I asked Farrell what treatment was prescribed for such patients as the one mentioned, but he was very vague in his answer. Apparently they are left to themselves. If they get well, psychiatry has achieved another triumph; if not, it is God's will.

BALTIMORE, JUNE 2, 1945.

For several years past I have been receiving letters from a woman named Mae Osborne, whose present address is R. D. #2, Bel Air, Md.

She first wrote to me several years ago, saying that she had written a novel and asking me to advise her about finding a publisher for it. I saw her one day at the *Sun* office, and at her request looked through her MS. A bit later I took her to lunch at the Marconi, and gave her the names and addresses of some likely publishers. On both occasions my meetings with her were in the presence of other persons. I have not seen her since, and have answered her numerous letters only briefly. Many of them are to be found in a file marked "H.L.M. Private Correspondence," on a shelf in the cupboard in my office in Hollins street. Some time ago she began to afflict me with amorous suggestions, but I refused to see her further, and have informed her more than once that I am not interested in such doings. Yesterday, June 1, she called me up at home, and demanded to see me. She was in an hysterical state, and said that her business was "a matter of life and death." I refused, however, to see her. She then became much excited, and gave every evidence of being insane. I have been in doubts about her sanity, in fact, for a long while, and have kept her letters because I feared she would develop into a nuisance. She now threatens to do so, and I make this memorandum in order to show precisely what my relations to her have been. I have never, whether directly or indirectly, made any suggestion to her that justified her present delusions, which apparently take sexual forms. Her novel had some slight merit, but needed extensive reworking. Since advising her about it I had seen none of her writings save a couple of brief sketches, too slight to be published. Such maniacs constitute one of the chief afflictions of an author's life. In Sara's time one of them made such an uproar in Cathedral street that I had to ask the police to take her away. She turned out, on examination, to be a paranoiac with homicidal tendencies.

BALTIMORE, JUNE 3, 1945.

I have in bank or in hand at the moment more than $48,000 in cash. I may need it. My own health is deteriorating steadily, and I may be floored at any moment by a cerebral hemorrhage. If I have inherited—which God forbid—the tremendous capacity to survive which runs in my mother's family, I may be in for a long and very expensive period of disability. There is also August to think of: his chronic bronchitis may put him on his back soon or late, and keep him there for years. My sister Gertrude seems to be in excellent health, but she will be 59 years old in November, and her last illness, too, may be prolonged and costly. The one obligation I recognize in this world is my duty to my immediate family. We should be, taken together, completely self-sustaining. We should go out of the world at the end having paid our way in it in full.

BALTIMORE, JUNE 26, 1945.

My old friend, Judge Eugene O'Dunne, who retired from the Supreme Bench of Baltimore City the other day on reaching the age limit of seventy years, was given a complimentary dinner at the Emerson Hotel last night. It was a hot and sticky night, and such affairs are always bores, but about 400 men and women turned out. The ladies were members of the Women's Bar Association of Baltimore City, and they had their own large table. At the conclusion of the speeches one of them arose and announced that the guest of honor had been elected an honorary member of their association. At this all the assembled lawyers laughed, which somewhat disconcerted the girls.

The dinner was arranged by Simon E. Sobeloff,[1] a smart Jew who is now City Solicitor, and is reputed to harbor judicial ambitions. The toastmaster was Judge Morris A. Soper,[2] formerly chief judge of the Baltimore Supreme Bench, then Federal district judge in Baltimore, and now a judge of the Fourth Circuit Court of Appeals. Soper, in the days when I first knew him, *c.* 1912, was a pious Methodist, and he still describes himself as a Methodist in "Who's Who in America," but service on the bench has worn off his old austerities, and before dinner last night he got down a number of cocktails, and was pleasantly jingled when he arose to start the proceedings. He is an amiable and amusing fellow, and a good judge. Before the scheduled speaking began he introduced Governor Herbert R. O'Conor and former Governor Phillips Lee Goldsborough,[3] and both made brief and graceful

1 Simon E. Sobeloff (1893–1973), after serving as city solicitor, went on to become chief judge of the Maryland Court of Appeals and solicitor general of the United States.

2 Morris A. Soper (1873–1963) was to go on serving as a judge of the Fourth Circuit Court of Appeals until 1955, when he took "qualified retirement" at the age of eighty-two.

3 Herbert R. O'Conor (1896–1960) served as governor of Maryland from 1939 to 1946

speeches. A great many other Baltimore notables were present, including Dr. Hugh H. Young, Dr. William A. Fischer (president of the Maryland Club), a dozen or more judges, Mayor Theodore R. McKeldin of Baltimore, and two ex-Mayors, Jackson and Broening.[1]

The first listed speaker was William Curran, for many years Democratic boss of Baltimore and lately appointed Attorney-General of Maryland. Curran is very sensitive to newspaper criticism, and sweats heavily under the gibes of Hamilton Owens of the *Sun*. He devoted two-thirds of his speech to a clumsy effort at satire against Owens, embodying the proposal that Owens be made his successor as Boss. It failed to come off, and was in grossly bad taste, for the party was in honor of O'Dunne, and no one was interested in Curran's grievances. When he sat down I followed. I had prepared a short speech, but began with an extemporaneous answer to Curran, predominantly clownish. I omitted the last two paragraphs of my speech, and so managed to finish in less than ten minutes—the record for the evening. Soboloff followed with a very clever burlesque opinion, supposed to be by O'Dunne, and Judge Emory H. Niles[2] followed with a burlesque commencement address to the graduates of the Supreme Bench, class of 1945. Soboloff's buffoonery was very well done, but it was too long, and before he got to the end of it he had lost the audience. Niles was much less amusing, but he shut down quickly. O'Dunne's reply was very brief. The party assembled at 6.45, and the show was over at 10.20.

The dinner was bad, but not half so bad as most of the public dinners of these famine days. The chief dish was cold-storage turkey. There were cocktails unlimited before the diners sat down, but nothing to drink afterward. This seems to be the prevailing American programme. It is very hard to bear. Before the dinner was half over I was famished for a drink, but I had to put up with ice-water. In view of the bad state of my throat I was in fear that I might make a mess of my speech, but I managed to get through it without any hacking. For part of the evening I sat beside old Goldsborough. He complained that

and as U.S. senator from 1947 to 1953; Phillips Lee Goldsborough (1865–1946) had been governor from 1912 to 1916 and U.S. senator from 1929 to 1935.

1 William F. Broening (1870–1953), mayor of Baltimore from 1919 to 1923 and again from 1927 to 1931.

2 Emory H. Niles (1892–1976), chief judge of the Baltimore Supreme Bench from 1954 to 1962.

I had used him roughly during the early days of Prohibition, and assured me solemnly that he had never been in favor of it. The word of honor of a politician is worth exactly nothing. He actually pulled hard for the drys, and I never denounced him without very good reason.

If anyone ever proposes to give me a complimentary dinner I shall leave town at once. There is nothing more dreadful. O'Dunne had asked all the speakers to spare him flattery, but every one, of course, had to anoint him more or less. He really enjoyed this eulogy, but nevertheless he must have had some uncomfortable moments. I sat at his right hand. As usual, I met a great many men whose faces I recalled, but whose names I could not remember. I have suffered all my life from this sort of forgetfulness, but it grows steadily worse as I grow older. Among the guests were a number of minor politicians, apparently rounded up by Willie Curran. Only one man got so drunk that he had to be thrown out. I was told he was one of the court stenographers.

After the dinner George Newcomer[1] introduced me to a lawyer who had come from Washington, and the three of us went to a place called the Cavalier, in St. Paul street, for a few beers. The only malt liquor available was Gunther's, which is very bad, but we were so thirsty that we managed to get it down. I had never been in the Cavalier before. It turned out to be a very filthy bar, with [a] dismal-looking eating-room attached. While we sat at a table a drunk tried to horn in, but we brushed him off.

BALTIMORE, JULY 11, 1945.

I lost a tooth today—my third to go. Like the two before it, it was in the lower register of the right side. The three of them leave a considerable gap, and it remains to be seen whether I can get on without them. If not, my dentist, Thomas Jackson Bland, will attempt to supply their places with a bridge. But I shall not let him put in a bridge if I can help it.

This tooth had an inlay on top of it that almost amounted to a cap. Some time last Autumn I began to have vague pains in it. At the end of March, while Bland was on holiday, it took to downright hurting,

1 George Newcomer (1897–1982), lawyer, played second violin in the Saturday Night Club.

and his substitute, Dr. William L. Meyer, made an x-ray examination of it. He found that the root was healthy, but that there was trouble in the pulp and nerve. When Bland returned he examined it also, and advised me to undertake no treatment. It might go on, he said, quietly enough; if not, he would then deal with it. While I was in North Carolina last week it bothered me a little, and on my return it became painful. Bland took off the cap this morning, and considered the question of removing the nerve. But that would have left me with a dead tooth, and he advised against it. It would be better, he said, to have it out at once. So I went to the office of my old friend, Dr. B. Lucien Brun, in Park avenue, and he extracted it.

It had stout roots, and Brun had to pull hard, but there was no pain, and I felt well enough less than an hour afterward to eat lunch with Patterson, Swanson and Wolff at the *Sun* office. Brun recalled that the first tooth I lost, more than twenty-five years ago, was a sacrifice to an error in diagnosis by the late Lewellys F. Barker. In that day teeth were being removed wholesale, and Barker, always a faddist, ordered mine out, thinking it responsible for the tongue pains that then badgered me. But when Brun extracted it the roots turned out to be perfectly healthy. Brun specializes in extractions, and has a magnificent technic. After the gum is anesthetized he approaches his patient with his forceps held *behind* him, and then suddenly falls upon the doomed tooth. He is an amusing fellow, and I always enjoy encountering him, but not professionally.

I have no complaint against the behavior of my teeth. Those in front are sound, and though the molars all have inlays they do their work well, and with no discomfort. This is certainly not a bad state of affairs for a man approaching 65. I only hope the rest of my teeth last until I am shoveled away at last. My mother, dying at 67, had all of hers save two or three. She went to her dentist, the late Julius Smith, every three months, and I go to Bland on the same schedule. When anything needing remedy shows up he tackles it at once.

BALTIMORE, JULY 12, 1945.

My only formal exercise takes the form of walking, and I probably average a couple of miles a day. Even when I have no shopping to do and do not leave the downtown area I commonly walk up Charles street to Lexington with Harry C. Black after our afternoon palaver at the *Sun* office, and then strike westward toward Lexington market. Sometimes I board a trolley-car for home at Fayette and Paca streets, but more often I walk further out Baltimore street, and sometimes I get beyond Fremont street. This must be a walk of at least a mile. On other days I sometimes walk as far north as the Richmond market area and then return to Fayette or Baltimore street afoot. But this is not all the exercise I get, for I often do more or less active work in the back-yard, and even on bad days I run up and down the house stairways not less than a dozen times a day. There is a lot to be done in my office, and sometimes it involves considerable activity—for example, getting down my heavy record books from the top shelf of the bookcase on the west wall. While I was at work on Supplement I to "The American Language" I often had to consult the heavy volumes of the *New English Dictionary* so often that I became really tired. My belief is that a man of my age, especially one in my physical state, gets all the exercise he needs from such activities. When I go beyond them, say on long walks or at heavy work in the yard or cellar, I begin to feel exhausted, and have to take a rest. I never play any game, and am glad that I have not learned to do so, for all of them waste a great deal of time. The job of playing the piano with the Saturday Night Club, usually for nearly two hours on end, is itself a brisk form of exercise.

BALTIMORE, JULY 15, 1945.

My accumulation of unpublished records begins to grow formida-ble. I have three large volumes, running to 1,643 pages, of my "Thirty-Five Years of Newspaper Work, July 30, 1906 to the end of 1941," and in addition two even larger boxes of *Sun* documents. Also, I have got down to the end of 1918 in my record of my adventures on magazines and as an author of books. Finally, I have four letter files filled with miscellaneous notes in duplicate, four boxes filled with a diary begun in 1930, and a box of "Autobiographical Notes, 1941–." These things are all to go to the Enoch Pratt and other libraries at my death, always on the condition that they are not to be opened until some years af-terward. With them will go a detailed record of the "Hatrack" case, prepared some years ago. I often wonder how many of these papers, if any, will survive for any length of time. They are bound to be neglected as I pass out of memory, and some of them, in all probability, will be forgotten altogether. Beside, there is the risk that some or all of them may be destroyed in some future war or in a revolution. The United States has got through two World Wars without suffering a scratch at home, but this is not likely to happen the next time. If there is ever any raid on American libraries by radicals my papers will be among the first destroyed. I have sought to get 'round this possibility by sending duplicates to different libraries, but it may not work. In all these records I have tried to tell the plain truth, regardless of tender feelings. Whenever possible I have supplied documentation, and in most cases I have been able to do so. Thus my papers offer useful materials for a history of American literature and American journalism in my time—that is, if anyone ever thinks to write it, or wants to learn the truth. I don't care greatly. I have done my best to record that truth as I have observed and experienced it, and that is as far as I can go.

BALTIMORE, JULY 26, 1945.

The first copies of Supplement I to "The American Language" reached me today. The book weighs 2 lbs. 7½ ozs., which is precisely 1 lb. less than the fourth edition of 1936. Nevertheless, the two volumes look almost of a size. Knopf did well to wait for the paper for the Supplement. It is smooth and excellent, and the printing, as usual, is perfect.

Last week I went through a set of the unbound sheets, and unearthed forty or fifty errors. Since then Knopf has found a few himself, and one of his men, Weinstock,[1] has found more. The first run of the Supplement is from plates, but the type is still standing, and so it will be possible to make corrections for the first reprint. The first run is 7,500 copies. Knopf tells me that he is planning to go back on the press immediately with a second run of 5,000. All this means that my royalties during the next year will run high, and that the thieves at Washington will get more of my hard-earned money.

---

1 Herbert Weinstock (1905–1971) was executive editor at Alfred A. Knopf, Inc., from 1943 to 1959 and served as a consultant thereafter. He was also the author of numerous books on music, including studies of Handel, Rossini, Chopin, and Tchaikovsky.

BALTIMORE, AUGUST 6, 1945.[1]

I begin to fear that my plan to push through my memoirs of my magazine days and then tackle Supplement II to "The American Language" will have to go the way of my plans for "Advice to Young Men" and "Homo Sapiens." I have been sleeping badly for two or three weeks past—something new for me—and feel wretched all day long. Vague discomforts in the region of the heart make it hard to get to sleep, and I am awakened every night by crazy dreams of struggle. I lie awake afterward for half an hour or more. In the morning there is a soreness over my breast-bone, on the left side. It seems to be superficial, but sometimes there is also an unpleasant sensation underneath. I suppose I should go to Dr. Wainwright, but if I did so he would probably order me to bed, or at least forbid all work, so I hesitate to do so. Since the cerebral episode of the Summer of 1939 I have been deteriorating steadily, though with a few remissions. There have been periods of as much as four or five weeks when I couldn't do any writing, and got through my day's routine only with difficulty. I get as much rest as possible, and always stretch out at least once during the day, but I nevertheless feel tired all the time. It is an unpleasant way to peg out, but there seems to be no help for it. Nothing can be done to reduce my blood-pressure, and there is no cure for my coronary condition. If my sleeplessness continues I'll be floored before long. I can imagine nothing worse. So long as I can get about more or less I can stand my discomforts, but if I were put to bed I think I'd collapse in short order.

BALTIMORE, AUGUST 8, 1945.

My niece Virginia and her husband and baby were here all day, and we had them to lunch and dinner. The boy is now two years and five months old, and is a very bright and active little fellow. He speaks quite clearly, and can make all of his wants known. Virginia has trained him to be polite, and reminds him every time he forgets to say "please" or "thank you." I like a polite child, so I got along with him

1 This was the date on which the United States dropped the atomic bomb on Hiroshima in Japan, but there is no mention of the event here or in any subsequent entries.

very well. I had laid in an armful of toys for him, including a wheel-barrow, but most of them were poor stuff, for the toy manufacturers have taken advantage of the war to palm off a lot of sleazy materials and workmanship. The boy's name is David Mencken Morrison. Like any other healthy youngster, he preferred toys of his own contriving to those I had bought for him. He had a lot of fun with a couple of cardboard cartons, and showed a good deal of ingenuity in putting them to use. During the day I took him to a neighborhood ten-cent store, as I used to take his mother, but he saw nothing that he wanted. Hester the cook had prepared two enormous meals, rations or no rations, including some special dishes for the boy, but at lunch he ate next to nothing. At dinner, however, he made up for it by getting down an enormous amount of food.

It was something of a chore to face such a visitor for more than eight hours on end, but I managed to endure it. During the afternoon I got a short holiday by taking Virginia to Loudon Park Cemetery to see her mother's grave. The tombstone was half covered with ivy, and there were some weeds beside it, but I had it clean in five minutes. The cemetery company no longer has a sufficient staff to attend to such things: there is a notice to that effect at the entrance. Virginia and I tried to buy some flowers, but we could find only one florist in the cemetery vicinity, and he was out, though his greenhouse was wide open. Virginia's husband, David M. Morrison, has been drafted, and is due to report in camp August 16. He is a mechanical engineer, and has been excused from service so far because he has been engaged in producing war materials. But now the fools in charge of the press-gang propose to take him. There is, however, small likelihood that he will ever get to the front, for the war is plainly in its last gasps.

Virginia has no conversation and it is thus hard to entertain her. When she was a small girl I enjoyed her visits very much, for she was bright and talkative, but after adolescence she dried up and now she can talk of nothing save trivialities. So far as I can make out, she reads nothing. Her husband is a little better, but not much. They are un-happily typical of the Republic in these later years. They are both college graduates, they are bringing up a boy for the next war, and they seem to have a wide circle of friends, but their range of interest is apparently limited by cards, shopping and idle gossip. Virginia at-tends to her household duties and palavers with other young wives; David, when he has a holiday, goes hunting. He brought August and me some venison chops, kept in cold storage since his last hunting trip. They were frozen hard. I gave him a bottle of Scotch and Virginia a bottle of wine. It was plain that she and her husband were not much interested in August and me, and for all our effort we could pump up little interest in their ideas and doings.

They had hardly set off in their car for Lancaster, Pa., where they live, when I had a telephone call from Washington from Adolph Torovsky's[1] daughter-in-law, Vivienne. Her news was that the old boy had just dropped dead in Annapolis. It was a shock indeed, for Adolph and I had been friends for at least forty years. He had played with the Saturday Night Club for a long while, and has been making the long and uncomfortable trip from and back to Annapolis every Saturday night, in all weathers. He was a Czech and a charming fellow— indeed, I have known no more charming fellow in this life. He will be sorely missed.

BALTIMORE, AUGUST 15, 1945.

When the end of the war was announced last night I was in my office, working on my record of my magazine days. My first news of it came with the blowing of factory whistles and ringing of church bells. Even the nuns of the House of [the] Good Shepherd clanged their bell, though only briefly. This was at 7.05 p.m. The uproar went on intermittently for two hours, with morons dashing by in their automobiles, blowing their horns. At 8.50 I went to Baltimore and Gilmor streets to mail letters. A few dozen of the neighborhood oakies, lintheads and other such vermin were gathered there in ragged groups, but they were making no noise. At 9.10 the celebration in West Baltimore ceased abruptly, and after that there was only an occasional toot of an automobile horn. I heard a couple of shots about midnight: they seemed to come from the linthead barracks in the 1500 block of Baltimore street.

The *Sun* of this morning reports that the crowd in Baltimore street, from Eutaw to the Fallsway, ran to 200,000. For 200,000 read 50,000: such estimates are always grossly exaggerated, especially when made

1 Adolph Torovsky (1878?-1945), long a member of the Saturday Night Club, had also been conductor of the U.S. Naval Academy Band for many years and was retired with the rank of lieutenant.

by the police. In my reportorial days I often counted a crowd, and then asked the cops to estimate it. They always at least doubled it, and usually tripled or quadrupled it. Any number above 1,000 staggers a policeman.

The American people will now begin paying for their folly. The bills will keep on coming in for 50 years.

AUGUST 19, 1945.

The servants are on holiday, but August and I are getting on very well. Yesterday I made a mess of lentils and sausages, and it turned out that there was enough for two meals. The refrigerator is full of fruit, carrots, turnips and hard-boiled eggs, and with the aid of rye-bread I can make a lunch very easily. For dinner we dig up stuff from the store of canned goods in the wine-vault, with bread, fruit, cookies and milk to help it. Day before yesterday our dinner consisted of an excellent canned clam-chowder heated with an equal amount of cream: it was really very good.

With the servants away life in the house is much calmer than usual. We eat our meals in the kitchen, and the dish washing takes only a few minutes. To be sure, the place is gradually growing dirty, as are the two bathrooms, but I'll put in an hour cleaning up all three before the servants return. They are very useful, and they look after me splendidly, but I begin to realize how much I am a slave to them. They decide when I am to eat and what I am to eat. Now I am quite free, and it is very pleasant. August commonly has lunch downtown, and I do also about half the time, but we eat dinner together, and enjoy preparing it. We eat in our shirtsleeves and take a turn in the yard afterward. It is a kind of camping-out, but without the heavy labor.

BALTIMORE, SEPTEMBER 12, 1945.

My sixty-fifth birthday, and I am, as usual, in the midst of severe hay-fever. I began taking vaccines from Dr. Leslie N. Gay last Winter, but they have failed completely, and I have been very uncomfortable. Nevertheless, I have managed to keep at my desk, and my record of my magazine days has made some progress since I resumed it in the early Summer. The fair copy has now reached p. 856, and the 28 indices[1] so far finished and copied run to 552 more. I have reached the year 1921 in the narrative, and shall presently tackle three long and important indices—on Sinclair Lewis, James Branch Cabell and Ernest Boyd. It is my present plan to continue work on the record until the end of the year. By that time I'll be tired of it, and ready for some diversion. What I'll tackle I don't know, but maybe it will be Supplement II to "The American Language," or a volume of notes, or a new "Prejudices" book. I began the magazine record in 1942, but laid it aside a year later to do Supplement I to "The American Language."

When I was 40 I had no expectation whatever of reaching 65, and in fact assumed as a matter of course that I'd be dead by then. My father died at 44 and my grandfather Mencken at 63. Perhaps I have lasted so long because my health has always been shaky: my constant aches and malaises have forced me to give some heed to my carcass. To be sure, I have always worked too hard, and taken too little exercise; moreover, I have eaten too much and maybe also drunk too much; but on the whole I have been careful. If I live long enough I hope to add an appendix to my magazine chronicle giving my medical history. So far as I know, no one has ever set down such a record of himself, though all books by literati are full of complaints of illness. To this end I have got memoranda from the various hospitals where I have been a patient. I was ill all through my later teens and early twenties, and it was not until I was 30 that I ever felt really brisk and lively. At the moment my blood pressure is above 160 and I have a coronary heart condition. As these notes show they have frequently incapacitated me during the past five years, but I have managed all the same to do a lot of work. Since my sixtieth birthday I have published five books—"Happy Days," "Newspaper Days," "Heathen Days," "A New Dictionary of Quotations" and Supplement I to "The American Language" —and two of them have been of formidable size. All have got good notices and sold well. No other lustrum of my life has ever been so productive.

I often wonder, looking back over my years, whether I have got out of myself all that was there. In all probability I have. I got a bad start and have vacillated more than once between two careers. Even now, though I have lost interest in daily newspapers, I give a part of my time to the Baltimore *Sunpapers*. It seems to me that they are in

1 Here, and in the sentence following, he undoubtedly meant to say "appendices."

a sad state of deterioration, and I begin to fear that there is no hope of ever rehabilitating them; nevertheless, I hang on, looking, at least subconsciously, for a miracle. When I resigned the editorship of the *American Mercury* at the end of 1933 I cleared out of magazines to stay, and I have had nothing to do with them since. What I'll be able to do hereafter remains to be seen. I have had to scrap two book projects that entertained me for years—for "Advice to Young [Men]" and "Homo Sapiens"—but others remain, and it may be that I'll be able to execute one or two of them. Meanwhile, I am getting my records in order, and even if I die tomorrow they will be in pretty fair shape. There is, indeed, probably no trace in history of a writer who left more careful accounts of himself and his contemporaries. I have tried hard to tell the truth. At bottom, this is probably subjectively impossible, but I have at least made the effort.

BALTIMORE, SEPTEMBER 24, 1945.

George S. Schuyler,[1] the Negro journalist, was here last night, and August and I put in a couple of hours palavering with him in Hollins street. He is now in charge of the New York office of the Pittsburgh *Courier*, and has quarters at Seventh avenue and 125th street, with a staff of nine. He writes editorials for the *Courier*, does his weekly column, and copy-reads news copy, though he does not write any of the latter himself. He said that the *Courier* now has six or eight regional editions, and sells 280,000 copies a week. Its gross intake last year was nearly $2,000,000. This indicates a net profit of more than $100,000 a year, and maybe close to $150,000. The chief proprietor is Mrs. Robert S. Vann, widow of the Pittsburgh lawyer who guided it to success. Schuyler says that she is so light in color that she could pass as white anywhere. Another stockholder is Lewis, formerly business manager and now president of the publishing company. This Lewis is somewhat timorous, and on the entrance of the United States into the war he took Schuyler's column from its old place on the editorial page, and buried it on a more obscure page. Every now and then he kills a

1 George S. Schuyler (1895–1977), American journalist. In addition to the encomium here, Mencken wrote in Supplement I, *The American Language* (p. 619n): "Mr. Schuyler is the most competent journalist that his race has produced in America. There are few white columnists, in fact, who can match him for information, intelligence, independence and courage."

column that alarms him—for example, one sent in lately, arguing that Roosevelt had tricked the Japs into the war. Schuyler is a cynic and does not object. He has a good job, and doesn't fume against the censorship.

His view of World War II and of the events likely to flow out of it is substantially mine, so our confab was free from argument. He has a white wife, but is very dark himself, with plainly negroid features. I have been following his doings for nearly twenty years, and have made various attempts to interest white newspapers and magazines in him, but without success. He is unquestionably the most competent Negro journalist ever heard of. Unlike nearly all the rest, he has no itch for public office, and is completely devoid of the usual cant. When I compare him to any of the dunderheads now roaring on the *Sun*, I am sharply conscious of his enormous superiority. He is not only much more intelligent than they are; he is vastly more honest.

BALTIMORE, OCTOBER 11, 1945.

I returned this afternoon from Joe Hergesheimer's place at Stone Harbor, N.J. I went there on Monday afternoon, October 9, and so spent two nights with Joe and Dorothy. Marcella du Pont, who is still living in Washington, met me on the train going up and I squired her down to Stone Harbor. We killed the wait of an hour or more in Philadelphia by going to Wanamaker's store and buying two copies of Sinclair Lewis's new novel, "Cass Timberlane." Bennett Cerf (Random House) has brought it out in a volume of 390 pages, $4\frac{5}{8} \times 7\frac{1}{4}$ inches in size, weighing only 14 ounces. The price is $2.75, which seems enormous for so small a book. Today I brought Marcella homeward as far as Baltimore and she continued alone to Washington. The wait in Philadelphia was of but 15 minutes. I was somewhat irked when I heard that she had been invited, for she is very talkative and energetic, and I wanted a rest, but she turned out to be in a quiet mood. I slept Tuesday night from 11 p.m. to 9 a.m. and then had a two hours' nap in the afternoon. Last night, after so much sleep, I was a bit restless, but probably got in at least seven hours more. Beside the Hergesheimers I saw no one save John and Noma Hemphill, who came to dinner last night. Both are very fat. Joe drinks nothing but beer. He prepared cocktails before dinner both evenings, but I was abstemious.

Joe has been suffering from an eye infection, and it impedes his vision. He has been seeing an oculist in Philadelphia, and went there with Marcella and me today. In theory, he has been at work on his autobiography, but in fact he has done nothing. He showed me a single page of much interlined and wholly unintelligible manuscript, and told me that it represented seven hard days of effort. This sounded incredible, but it is plain that he can't write. He is full of complaints against Knopf for letting most of his books go out of print and melting the plates, but they went out of print simply because they had ceased to sell, and the plates were melted under a government order that those of all books that had sold less than so many copies for a year past must be turned in for the metal in them. Knopf is preparing to bring out a new edition of "The Three Black Pennies," but it is delayed by the paper shortage, greatly to Joe's discontent. He blames Knopf, but is quite irrational. He thinks that Knopf should keep *all* of his books in print, despite the fact that some of them had no sales for years. I proposed that he pick out four or five that he really cherishes, and prepare them for reprinting. Then, if Knopf refuses to reset them, he can turn to some other publisher. I suggested Scribner.

Joe looks very badly, what with his sallow complexion and sore eye. He told me that he is in constant discomfort, and can do little reading, his one permanent consolation. He reads only very serious books, mainly in history. He showed me a new one by A. L. Kroeber, dealing with the rise and fall of cultural configurations—music, the drama, the sciences, etc.—and recommended it as a masterpiece, but I could find little in it save the obvious. How he manages to put in his days I can't imagine. He gets up at 6 a.m. and busies himself with domestic chores, including cooking, but they are over in a few hours. He also pretends to cook lunch and dinner, but I suspect that Dorothy really does most of the work. A colored woman comes in a few times a week to help them. Joe turns in at 9 p.m. and gives over three hours or more to reading. But with his eyes in trouble this is almost impossible. He is a sad object, and there seems to be no help for him. Sometimes I find myself toying with the idea that he is entertaining what the Freudian quacks call a death wish. That is, he is tired of life, sees nothing ahead, and covertly hopes for death. John Hemphill told me that he is convinced that the poor fellow will not last long. He has written nothing fit to print for more than ten years. It is a dreadful finish, indeed.

I always enjoy palavering with Joe, even when, as now, he is un-comfortable and intermittently peppery. He and I have been close friends since 1914, and have never had a serious difference. Despite his inability to write, he still talks amusingly, and shows no other sign of mental decay. His case is most distressing, and more than a little mys-terious. I am his age precisely, and I am full of ills, but I have written and published five books since I was sixty, and all of them have been well enough done to sell well and get preponderantly favorable no-tices. I am in hopes that when Dr. Benjamin M. Baker gets home from the war, about Christmas, I'll be able to induce Joe to see him. The quacks he has consulted have done him no good. Though his blood count is about 200, they tell him that he needs no treatment save a mild diet—and then let him drink beer. Certainly it would be easy to imagine a more salubrious drink for a diabetic. But Joe insists that he is *not* a diabetic.

Dorothy, as always, is kind and charming. She is now past 60 and begins to look it, though there is still very little gray in her hair. Her limp grows more marked, and seems to give her some pain. I noted that she had to ask Joe to tie her shoe-laces. She has been a good wife to Joe—indeed, one of the best ever heard of. Life must be difficult for her in that remote cottage on the beach, with no one to talk to, day in and day out, save a sick man. The place is very comfortable, but it is only ten feet above sea level and less than 100 yards from the breakers. They lulled me to sleep night before last—a very soothing sound. But I hate to look at the ocean from the shore. When it is not menacing it is banal.

BALTIMORE, OCTOBER 15, 1945.

There was a regular meeting of the *Sun* board today—the fourth meeting of the board in two weeks. In the absence of Harry Black, who is still at Sea Island, I presided. Only routine business was trans-acted. The radio project, greatly to my relief, seems to be dead. Schmick reported a new cut in the *Sunpapers'* news-print ratio—not by the bureaucrats in Washington but by the paper company. Despite repeated categorical promises to do so, it now alleges that it is unable to deliver the *Sunpapers'* needs for October, and that there may be further cuts in November and December. Inasmuch as Schmick has just promised the Baltimore department-stores to give them an increase of 10% in their existing allotment of 60% of their 1942 lineage, this leaves him in a very uncomfortable position. He believes that the paper company has taken on some new customers—a foul attentat against the *Sunpapers*, which have been its largest customers for some years past, and were its first of any size in the United States. My own guess is that it has been increasing its shipments to England. All government rationing of paper will cease January 1. Some time ago the company promised to give Schmick 35,000 tons in 1946. It remains to be seen whether this promise will be carried out. Belknap, the head man of the company, is coming to Baltimore on Thursday to discuss the situation.

BALTIMORE, OCTOBER 16, 1945.

Dr. Leslie has decided that Mrs. Lohrfinck is suffering from pyelitis, and that it promises to be mild. He is putting her on the sulphonamides. She is in bed, but has no pain and is eager to get up. She hopes to return home in four or five days and to resume work next Monday, but about that I am doubtful. I took her Sinclair Lewis's "Cass Timberlane" and George Nathan's new book to read. This morning her brother-in-law, Arnold Lohrfinck, delivered at the house a large section of the appendix on Lewis in my record of my magazine days. She had finished it, but fell ill before she could bring it to me. I am planning to shelve this record long enough to revise and rewrite "Treatise on the Gods."[1] If Mrs. Lohrfinck returns to service I should be able to finish this job by the end of November.

BALTIMORE, OCTOBER 20, 1945.

An almost perfect Indian Summer day. It is warm, but not hot; bright, but not glaring. The rays of the setting sun, shining horizontally through the trees in Union Square this afternoon, made a really magnificent blaze of light and color. The backyard is fast fading, but

---

1 The revised edition of *Treatise on the Gods* appeared in 1946. In the preface Mencken wrote: "In the first four sections [of the first edition] I found no need of more than a few small changes, so they remain substantially as originally written. But Section V had to be reworked rather elaborately, for in its first form it was full of contemporary references that had become stale and irrelevant, and in some cases almost unintelligible."

there is still some life in it. One petunia was blooming this morning, and there were half a dozen morning glories in flower on the pony-stable and along the upper fence. The scarlet sage was still brilliant, though its flowers begin to fall. Nearly all the pears have tumbled from the pear-tree, but a few remain, and the starlings are hard at work on them. Back and front, I can now see clear through the trees. A month ago they shut me in with impenetrable walls of green.

Last night I slept very badly. There was a feeling of fullness in the head and vague pains all over the body. At 2 a.m. I turned on my light and picked up a book. Fifteen minutes later I was drowsy and put it down, and soon afterward I was asleep at last. But I felt very rocky this morning, and this afternoon took a nap. I could do no work all day.

BALTIMORE, OCTOBER 24, 1945.

This afternoon I found Paul Patterson in his office alone, and got my long-sought chance to discuss my own relations to the *Sun* with him. I told him that I was thinking seriously of clearing out as of January 1. I am now 65 and it is too late for me to hope to have a hand in any possible rehabilitation of the *Sunpapers*. I said that I believed that they had been falling away from the White Paper of 1920, which I wrote and still believed in, since the *Evening Sun* under Hamilton Owens, supported by Harry C. Black, began supporting Roosevelt in 1933, and that the business was completed by the row with Archbishop Curley in 1934. I told him once more that I believed he had made a fatal mistake when he did not let John W. Owens resign at the conclusion of this row, that he had thereby allowed Owens to get the upper hand of him, and that giving Owens a free hand with the editorial pages was mainly responsible for their deterioration. I said that he also (Patterson) was directly responsible for this deterioration, if only by his easy yielding to his English friends. The course of the United States in World War II, I said, was dishonest, dishonorable and ignominious, and the *Sunpapers*, by supporting Roosevelt's foreign policy, shared in this disgrace. I added that I believed there was no chance to get them back on the right track—that is, the track of ascertaining the news and telling it honestly—so long as the two Owenses were in positions of authority, and that I did not think he (Patterson) would ever get rid of them. I said that there were two good men in the office—Neil Swanson, who had tried to hold up the news department, and Mark S. Watson, who had tried to tell the truth at the beginning of the war—but that they would be helpless so long as they were surrounded by fools.

Patterson tried to make me admit that the *Sunpapers* had covered the war adequately, but I refused to do so. They printed, I said, mainly drivel, and developed no correspondent fit for anything better save Watson. Watson is a competent man, but somewhat timorous, and when Patterson took him to London he saw the handwriting on the wall, and made little further effort to get at the truth behind the official Army propaganda. It was this propaganda that the *Sunpapers* printed, not the actual news. They made no effort whatsoever to get beneath the glittering surface, and they gave no support to other papers that did so, for example, the Chicago *Tribune*. From first to last they were official organs and nothing more, and taking one day with another they were official organs of England rather than of the United States. I said that I could not imagine myself ever writing for them again—that is, so long as the Owenses ran their editorial pages. If I ever undertook any further newspaper writing it would have to be for some other paper.

I told Patterson that I was beginning to be heartily sick of my daily meetings with him in his office. At these meetings I heard of nothing but business office problems. Schmick and Kavanaugh were usually present, but Swanson was called in but seldom, and the Owenses never. I said that I was an editorial man, and that while I was interested more or less in paper and labor problems, my real interest was in collecting and interpreting the news. I said that John Owens was a country evangelist and nothing more, and that his rhetorical fulminations were a disgrace to decent journalism. I added that Hamilton Owens was a time-server with no more principle in him than a privy rat, and that it was inconceivable that he would, or could, ever get together an editorial staff worth hell-room. I suggested that the one way out, if there were any actual intent to restore the papers to common sense and common decency, would be to put Swanson and Watson in charge of them, with full powers.

Patterson attempted some defense, but it was feeble, and I refused to grant the soundness of any part of it. I told him that the only sort of newspaper I was interested in was the sort we tried to set up in 1920—a paper doubtful of politicians of all sorts, and devoted mainly to unearthing the facts underneath their pretensions. I said that the *Sunpapers* had failed miserably here, not only in the nation and in international affairs, but also in State and city affairs. They took every quack's pretensions at his own valuation, and even now were swinging to the support of the preposterous Truman, perhaps the cheapest and least honest man ever to sit in the White House. I said I believed that this was a violation of their plain duty to their readers—if they had any. But instead of discharging it courageously and intelligently, they were following the radio down the road to complete imbecility. For years past, I said, the *Sunday Sun* had been catering to morons exclusively. There was not a line in it aimed at educated and enlightened readers. Its editor was Cooling, the worst jackass in the office. It was rich in comics and other such trash, but devoid of sense. John Owens had gradually chased away all the foreign correspondents who once gave it some dignity, and our news from abroad was now coming from ex-police reporters too stupid to see through official propaganda.

I went on to the recent attempts to barge into the radio business, and said that I regarded them as excessively unwise. The radio, I said, was plainly aiming at the stupidest people of the country, and made no effort whatsoever to interest their betters. I said I believed that we should let it have them, and devote ourself to enterprises that it was too cowardly and too unintelligent to undertake—above all, the effort to turn up the facts beneath the surface of official news. If we went into the radio we'd soon be devoting all of our time and energies to it, and the *Sunpapers* would cease to exist as organs of anything save public imbecility. Soon or late there is bound to be a demand for something better, and the *Sunpapers*, rich and successful, are in a prime position to supply it. But as they are going today they are headed squarely in the other direction, and in a short time they will be wallowing at the bottom. Such journalism, I said, was not the sort that interested me. I believed that it was time for me to clear out.

Patterson looked distressed by all this, but listened politely. He said that he wanted to think over what I had had to say, and promised to give me a reply within a reasonable time. He said that he would resign himself if I quit the *Sun* board, but this was probably only talk, for he needs the money that he gets as president and stockholder. His family, always expensive, promises to be even more expensive hereafter, for only one of his six children is self-sustaining. I sympathize with him in these difficulties, and have tried more than once to help him, but I see no reason why they should excuse the mess he has made of his job. His fear of John Owens is at the bottom of most of his errors. Why he should fear so hollow and incompetent a fellow I don't know, but there is the fact. As I left him he was talking vaguely of setting up an editorial council, but I told him that, while I believed the two Owenses ought to be members of it, I did not think I could work in harmony with them. My opinion of their capacities is far too low, and in the case of Hamilton Owens I also doubt his bona fides. Moreover, there is Harry Black to consider. If he has a seat at any editorial council its sessions will be largely devoted to listening to his idiotic giggling. He has got down to such a point, intellectually, that it is hard to either talk to him or listen to him.

My own position is very uncomfortable. I naturally hesitate to break ties that have endured, off and on, since 1906, but I find that going to the office, in these later years, simply irritates me. No enterprise that I am really interested in is ever discussed. I have to listen to Schmick's troubles with the paper men and the bureaucrats, and to Kavanaugh's tales of his bouts with the labor unions, but I hear next to nothing of matters bearing on my tastes and training. My sessions with Patterson alone have deteriorated into rounds of gossip, boring to me and I suppose to him also. The money that I get for attending them is useful, but I could exist without it. Unhappily, my health is such that it is unlikely that, writing for other papers and magazines, I could earn any substantial income. Nevertheless, I could get along, for between royalties from books and income from investments I have enough to keep me.

BALTIMORE, OCTOBER 25, 1945.

On October 21, a Sunday, the Fortenbaugh dog (see this Diary for July 4, 1942)[1] made such an uproar in the late afternoon that I had to abandon work on my revision of "Treatise on the Gods" and was unable to take my usual nap. The next day I sent the following note to Charlie Fortenbaugh:

Dear Charlie:

Your dog barked yesterday from about 5.30 p.m. to 7 or thereabout. I called up your house but got no answer; appar-

---

1 This entry is not included in the present selection.

ently there was no one home. As a result of this uproar I had
to abandon some important work on which I was engaged. Such
interruptions to my work cost me money, and disturbances of
my rest, at my age, are dangerous to my health. I have been
aroused from sleep as early as 6.45 a.m. and as late as 12.30
midnight.

I must ask you once more to stop this nuisance. So long as
your sister was living I remembered her plea that she felt insecure in the house without the dog. But that reason is now gone.
I am therefore trusting you either to teach your dog to stop
disturbing the neighborhood or to get a dog less noisy.

There was no answer to this, but since October 23 the dog has
barked very little, and then not at unseemly hours or very loudly. This
morning Charlie's sister, Ethel Oertel, who lives with him at 1526
Hollins street, came in to ask permission to enter her house by our
back roof: she had forgotten her key. I did not see her, but August
helped her. She told him that the dog is as much of a nuisance to her
as it is to us, and that ever since the death of her old sister Lillie she
has been trying to induce her brother to get rid of it. She has friends
at Catonsville who are willing to take it. She said that after my complaint in 1942 she silenced it for a while by throwing water on it when
it barked, but that her brother objected. He is a complete moron, and
reasoning with him is difficult. When a month or two ago, the police
undertook a search for unlicensed dogs in Southwest Baltimore, Ethel
became alarmed, for their dog has no license. But Charlie insisted that
none was needed, and finally Ethel had to go downtown and buy one
herself. August told her that we were joined in our complaint by other
neighbors, that we were losing patience, and that if the nuisance were
not soon abated we would seek a legal remedy. Poor Ethel is herself
very stupid, but not as stupid as her brother. She told August that
taking care of the dog is a heavy burden to her. It barks not only in
the yard but also in the house. It is a large and ferocious animal, and
has a bark that is really ear-splitting. If it is not soon disposed of I
shall ask Captain John Harris, of 1522, and Leon Asner, of 1520 and
1528, to join me in a complaint to the police. If that fails I shall sue
Charlie for damages. I think I can prove them.

BALTIMORE, NOVEMBER 3, 1945.

August calls my attention to something that I have hitherto over-looked: that there are few, if any, bobby-soxers among colored girls. The white ones are now among the conspicuous fauna of the country, and get a great deal of pained consideration from the national moralists. They run in age from eleven to fifteen or so, and get their name from the fact that they go barelegged and wear short socks that roll over their low shoes. Their clothing is usually of the sports variety, and they look frowsy and often dirty. When they are in groups they talk loudly and make other attempts to attract attention. In Baltimore, and I suppose elsewhere, they are accused by viewers with alarm of giving boys access to their persons, and it is alleged that not a few of them, during the war, engaged in venery, either as a patriotic service or for pay, with the soldiers swarming into town from the nearby camps. This last I have always doubted, for it would be hard for an adult to find a safe place for operating on them. That some of them, and perhaps many of them, are loose may be true, but it was also true of their grandmothers in my youth. I was seduced at fourteen by a girl of my own age, and she had thrown off the pall of virginity before I tackled her. This girl renounced fornication soon afterward, settled down to rectitude, married well, and at last accounts was a much respected grandmother. Such experiences in early youth probably do no harm: indeed, Havelock Ellis[1] once argued that they were most likely beneficial. The Baltimore bobby-soxers, taking one with another, are far from appetizing. They have thick legs, imitate a boyish burliness, and are quite unfeminine both in appearance and manner. It is seldom that one encounters a really charming maiden among them. Why they are so few among the colored people I don't know, but August suggests that it may be because the colored school-teachers are strict policewomen and discourage rowdiness among their pupils. A colored youngster who appears in school clad as some of the white bobby-soxers are clad would probably be sent home.

---

1 Havelock Ellis (1859–1939), British scientist and author. His most famous work is the multivolume *Studies in the Psychology of Sex.*

BALTIMORE, NOVEMBER 11, 1945.

This morning I pulled down the morning-glory vines from the pony stable. They have been dried out for weeks, though they continued to produce a few blossoms until about ten days ago. The white morning-glories on the dooryard fence are still blooming. I spaded about half of the lower flower plot, and scattered lime and powdered cow manure. The leaves of the trees are nearly all down, and save for the white morning-glories the yard has taken on its bleak and dismal Winter aspect.

BALTIMORE, NOVEMBER 18, 1945.

I pulled down the last of the morning-glories this morning. They came in late this year, but they bloomed beautifully and prodigiously. We have never had a better show. August and I dug up and raked the yard, and put in lime and dried cow manure, and it is now asleep for the Winter. But the scarlet sage at the kitchen door is still blooming.

There are diapers fluttering from the wash-line in the yard next door, at 1522. They are the first on display in this house or the two adjoining for fifty years. The baby belongs to Captain and Mrs. John Harris, the latter formerly Margaret Stricker. It has been christened Margaret Constance, and I have already sent it my usual silver rattle— my regular gift to new babies for more than thirty years. One of the first to get one was Maclean Patterson, who now has two children of his own. This time I could not have the rattle engraved. There is not a single engraver of silver at work in Baltimore. Even Kirk[1] has none.

BALTIMORE, NOVEMBER 21, 1945.

I had an appointment today to take a naval officer named Price to lunch at the Maryland Club, but he called up during the morning from Washington to say that he couldn't come, so I suggested to Paul Patterson that he and I lunch together instead. It was a fortunate accident, for when he and I left the club for his office no one else was there and for half an hour, miraculously, there were no telephone

1 Samuel Kirk & Son, Inc., Baltimore jewelers and silversmiths. The firm is no longer in business.

calls. I seized the chance to tell him that I thought we should return to our conversation of October 24, recorded in these notes, and try to settle the issues between us. He seemed to be reluctant but I pressed him, and we were quickly hard at it. I said, first, that I was determined to do no more writing for the *Sunpapers*, now or hereafter, save in the highly improbable event that their present editorial pages are completely reformed. I said further that I wanted to reserve the right to write for any other periodical, including any other newspaper, at my discretion. Thirdly, I said that I was tired of coming to the office every weekday save Saturday—that most of the matters that came up did not interest me, and that I had nothing to contribute to them. Fourthly, I said that I'd be willing and glad to continue in an advisory capacity, and to be on call for service whenever I was really needed and could be useful, but that I must insist upon a reduction of my compensation.

We went into all these things at some length, but I stuck to my ultimatum. In the end Patterson agreed to all of its specifications. My pay is to be reduced from $9,000 a year to $5,000 as of January 1, which seems to me to be a reasonable retainer. "I'll agree," said Patterson, "provided you are willing to take a bonus whenever any considerable load of work is thrown on you." "I agree to take it," I replied, "and promise further to send you a bill if you ever forget it." I told him that I did not want to have any more hand than necessary in any present or future radio business, for I was convinced that the *Sun's* entry into radio would mean its final collapse as a newspaper of any dignity. I told him also that I was not interested in the rotogravure Sunday supplement which he, Swanson and Schmick were now concocting—he described it in the course of our palaver, perhaps inadvertently, as a kind of *Look*—and believed that what we really needed was a section for relatively intelligent readers. He admitted frankly that the furiously moral and mainly unintelligible articles that John W. Owens is now writing for the editorial page of the morning paper are very silly stuff, but told me that he saw no way to get rid of them. I suggested retiring Owens altogether, if necessary at full salary, but it was plain that he feared to undertake it. We then went back to Owens's treason at the time of the row with the Archbishop, and he tried to justify it on the ground that John's resignation would have bucked up the Archbishop and maybe done grave damage to the *Sun*, but I insisted that this was only the more reason for getting rid of John when the row was over. But this was an old discussion, and we got nowhere. The fact has long been plain that Patterson is afraid of Owens, and that Owens knows it, and is capitalizing it. Like any other intensely moral man, he is quite devoid of the sense of honor.

Patterson told me that he wanted me to stick around as long as he did himself. He said: "I have no one else to talk to, and I hate to see so old a relation ended." So do I, but I must get clear of duties that keep me unhappy, and interfere with my other work. I hung on for year after year, hoping against hope that Patterson would pull himself together, and clean up the mess on the two editorial pages, but it is now manifest that he will never attempt it. "I have," he said, "a good deal less energy than I used to have." The same is true of me, and I am eager to devote my few remaining years to really productive work, and to rid my mind of concern about the *Sunpapers*. I can give them useful service in more than one field—for example, labor relations—but I have lost all hope that they'll ever return to a sane and honest editorial course. They have ceased to be papers of importance, and I once more called Patterson's attention to various evidences of it. He had nothing to say in reply: the fact is only too plainly apparent. It is a pity that they have come to their present low estate, but it is now too late to do anything about it. No one in the office, save only Swanson, has any ideas worth hearing. Harry Black has been useless since he took to the bottle, and Patterson himself is so bedevilled and bewildered by his children that there are whole days on which he scarcely gives any attention to *Sun* business.

BALTIMORE, NOVEMBER 25, 1945.

The Fortenbaugh dog, after a long, long reign as the neighborhood nuisance, seems to be on its way out at last. This morning Captain Harris and Leon Asner came to the house, and after discussing the business we called in Charlie Fortenbaugh. I told him, with the support of Harris, Asner and August, that we had all come to the end of our endurance, and that the noise would have to cease. He is an extremely stupid fellow, and made only the feeblest resistance. In fact, he admitted that the dog was a nuisance to him also. He protested that he couldn't get rid of it today (a Sunday), but we told him that we'd give him a reasonable time. In the name of the others, I warned him that if he delayed we'd go to the police, and in addition I notified

him that I'd sue him in the civil courts. The whole unpleasant business
was over in twenty minutes, and after that we discussed other neighborhood matters, especially the plan to sand-blast the front of all our
houses, and the attempt to restore good order in Union Square. Harris
and Asner, who came in at 11 a.m., remained until nearly one, and
the party broke up in amiable spirits.

BALTIMORE, DECEMBER 3, 1945.

I began work today on Supplement II to "The American Language," but made very little progress. It is the chapter dealing with
American pronunciation and will be the hardest in the book, for I have
very little interest in phonology and do not know much about it. Unhappily, I have collected a really enormous mass of notes, and putting
them together will be a heavy labor. Once I have finished the first
three sections of the chapter, the rest of the book will be relatively
easy sailing, though it, also, will involve some tedious drudgery. I feel
like anything but work, but I must step into the job if it is to be
finished by the end of 1946.

BALTIMORE, DECEMBER 14, 1945.

The oakies, lintheads, hill-billies and other anthropoids who
swarmed into Baltimore in search of war jobs have now begun to go
home, and in Southwest Baltimore there is a marked decrease in their
number. Two years ago the Hollins street neighborhood swarmed with
them, and August and I encountered a great many fantastic specimens
on the street. But now they are departing, and a whole day sometimes
passes without me seeing one. It was never difficult to recognize them.
No such shabby, ill-fed men and filthy, slatternly women and children
had ever been seen in Baltimore before. They were numerous in the
shopping areas, and it was not uncommon for the natives, encountering a grotesque specimen, to stop and stare. The women, as a rule,
were heavier than the men. They were all shapeless, and their dirty
hair was pushed back in a kind of waterfall, cut off straight at the
level of the shoulder. The men, save in the coldest weather, wore no
coats, and even then they lacked overcoats, but used sweaters or mack-
inaws instead. The children all looked starved. These poor creatures
brought their native eating habits with them, and in Baltimore, as

in the Appalachian uplands and the Carolina mill-towns, subsisted mainly on fat-back and corn-meal. They kept the Baltimore hospitals busy, especially the obstetrical wards. Indeed, I don't recall ever seeing one of the younger women without a child or two dragging at her heels or in her arms. They also gave the police plenty of business. Many of the women locked up their children for days at a time, and went on drunks, and the men did a good deal of fighting. I only hope Baltimore remembers them, for they provided dramatic ocular evidence as to the true nature of the "only true Anglo-Saxons," so much whooped up in the South. It was plain that all of the European immigrants in Baltimore, including even those from the Mediterranean and Balkan lands, were much superior to them. This was also true of the Negroes. Unhappily, the low-class blacks who formed part of the war-time immigration show no sign of returning home. They find life in Baltimore much pleasanter than it was in their native wilds, and when hard times come again they will all go on the dole. The city jail is already full of them, and four or five are in the death-house. One of the latter raped a respectable white woman in an extraordinarily barbarous manner, beating her into insensibility, breaking her nose, and covering her with blood. Also, he gave her syphilis. He is now awaiting hanging.

BALTIMORE, DECEMBER 15, 1945.

I begin to enter the world of the aged, and find it rather curious. My memory is gradually fading, and I sometimes waste a lot of time trying to recall a name or a word that should be at the tip of my tongue. The other day I put in the better part of an hour searching for *capon*, which I wanted to use in a note dealing with Maryland cookery. Very often, in these later days, I forget the name of a man I have known for years. Another symptom of encroaching senility that is unpleasant is the multiplication of minor aches and pains. I used to turn out of bed in the morning feeling wide-awake, brisk and full of energy, but now I am sore and used up. Apparently I have no actual arthritis, but my joints do not work as freely as they used to, and it is not until I have had a shave and a shower-bath that I begin to feel limber and alive. Meanwhile, the steam pressure in my tubes is declining, and I grow tired after a spell of work that would have seemed trivial ten years ago. When I get home from the *Sun* office in the late afternoon I am so near to exhaustion that I stretch out at once, and am usually soon asleep. I used to work every evening until 10 o'clock, but now I am done for at 9, and sometimes at 8. Let me overeat ever so little, or take one drink too many, and I feel as if I have been on a substantial jag. All this is very unpleasant, but it is nevertheless not unendurable, and I am learning to bear it. I can't do more than half as much work as I used to do, but so far I have noticed no deterioration in its quality. To be sure, I do not have as many good ideas as I had in my prime, but those that pop up continue to be pretty good ones. If I had the energy to write down everything I think of I could produce 2,000 or 3,000 words of printable matter every day.

BALTIMORE, DECEMBER 20, 1945.

I got home this afternoon after two days in New York. I went there on Tuesday morning, December 18, for the Knopf board meeting in the afternoon. In the evening I had dinner at Lüchow's with George Nathan and George C. Cutler of Boston, formerly president of the Safe Deposit and Trust Company in Baltimore, and a member of the *Sun* board. Cutler is a charming fellow and I was delighted to see him. We had roast goose for dinner, and dined under the immense Christmas tree that Lüchow always sets up. After dinner the three of us went to the Stork Club for a night-cap, and there we met William R. Hearst, Jr. As usual, he was very cordial. He brought up once more the proposal that I do some articles for the Hearst papers. I told him that the Hearst emissaries always tackled me on the wrong ground. They talked of money, whereas what interested me was the question whether I could really write what I wanted to write.

The Knopf board meeting in the afternoon was a long one. Sam Knox, as usual, was absent: he reported that he was ill. He has not attended a meeting since September, 1944. Alfred had asked a member of the firm of accountants which examines the books of the house to come to the meeting. He has a large practice among publishers, and Alfred wanted him to tell the members about the salary scales prevailing among them. He reported that most of them pay their minor executives more than Knopf pays, so we ordered some substantial raises. Lesser was in favor of giving the run-of-mine employés large Christmas bonuses, but the rest of us voted him down. They belong to a C.I.O. union and the union goons make frequent demands, many of them extravagant and not a few preposterous. I am in favor of giving such enemies of the house as much as they can get, but not a cent more. But what of the employés who do not belong to the union? They are the best workers in the office, and do not come and go like the unionists. I argued for giving them larger bonuses than the latter, on the plain ground that they are worth more. Lesser protested that this would give the union leaders something to complain of. I then suggested that one or two union members of unusual diligence and usefulness be chosen for larger bonuses also. This plan was adopted. It will not shut off the union leaders altogether, but it will at least weaken their argument. Most of them are Jewish communists. Nearly a majority of the employés do not belong to the union. It has never been able to rope them in, and has not, as yet, demanded a closed shop. As employment slackens it will be easier to deal with.

The board meeting was placid. Lesser's base pay was raised from $13,500 a year to $17,500. In addition he will get a bonus of $4,000 or more. He is worth the money, for he is the backbone of the office. Bernard Smith, the sales manager, was raised to $12,500, and Jacobs, the manufacturing man, to $10,000. Both will also receive substantial bonuses. After all this business was finished Alfred suggested that the directors of the corporation, who now receive $20 a meeting, had been overlooked. He proposed something between $100 and $250. I objected to this, and Ralph Colin, the only other director who is not on the staff payroll, joined me. We agreed that it was better for us to retain our status of disinterest, especially in view of the fact that there will be more rows with Sam Knox and the Josephys hereafter. The company has done a business of $2,000,000 in 1945, and earned enough to pay off some of the accumulated arrears on the preferred stock. We will consider this at a special meeting in January. With the excess profits tax removed, we may be able to make another such payment in 1946. This is not very good news to me, for I'll receive a heavy royalty check in January, and these additions will throw me into a high income-tax bracket, so most of my money will go to the job-holders.

I had lunch with Anita Loos[1] on Wednesday. It was snowing and

---

1 Anita Loos (1893–1981), novelist and playwright. Her most famous work is *Gentlemen Prefer Blondes* (1925), which, according to legend, was inspired when Mencken and George Jean Nathan passed over her—an attractive and intelligent brunette—in order to focus their attention on a vapid and empty-headed blonde girl.

there was a heavy wind, so we ate at the Plaza, where she is staying. She is returning to California today. Anita is a cynical and amusing woman, and I always enjoy seeing her. In the old days she and her husband and Nathan and I had many amusing sessions. Her husband, unhappily, is now incurably insane. At 5 p.m. I met Abel Green,[1] editor of *Variety*, at No. 21, and we had a few drinks. I had no engagement for the evening, so I dined alone at a fish-house in 47th street. The weather was wild, and I was in bed before 10 o'clock. This morning I went to the Knopf office to try to settle the dispute between Alfred on the one hand, and Joe Hergesheimer and his lawyer, John Hemphill, on the other. It appeared, as I half expected, that Joe's account of the matter was grossly in error. It is not true, as he told me, that Alfred has let all his books go out of print, and melted the plates. The plates for all save one are still intact, and many are still in print and in stock. Of "The Bright Shawl," for example, 800 copies remain in hand, and the sales have dropped to 40 or 50 a year. Of "Quiet Cities," 139 are in stock, with sales of but 9 copies in five months. Other books still in stock are "Balisant," 256 copies; "Java Head," 1,300; "San Cristóbal de la Habana," 600; "From an Old House," 72; "The Foolscap Rose," 10. Among those out of print are "Berlin," "Cytherea," "The Limestone Tree," "The Party Dress," "Tampico," "Swords and Roses" and "Tropical Winter." There is no demand for any of them. Grosset and Dunlap are bringing out a new cheap edition of "The Three Black Pennys" in the near future. Alfred told me that Joe's royalties average $1,500 a year. They come mainly from "Java Head." It is never prudent to accept his own account of his affairs. He led me to believe that Knopf was trying to close him out, but there is no evidence for it. The unpleasant correspondence between Hemphill and Knopf, to be found in my Knopf file for November and December, 1945, was quite unnecessary.

BALTIMORE, DECEMBER 29, 1945.

When I got to the breakfast table this morning August handed me a telegram received during the night, reading as follows:

---

1 Abel Green (1900–1973) was, in addition to being editor of *Variety*, an author and theatrical producer.

Teddy was taken ill 3 a.m. and rallied for a while, but passed away 6.50 p.m. today. He loved you.

Helen Dreiser.

At once I recalled that I had sent Dreiser a somewhat ribald letter two days ago, in response to a jocose Christmas greeting from him. I told August of it, and said: "It will hardly make consoling reading for the widow." He was sorting the morning mail, which had just come in. "Here is your letter," he said, and threw it to me. I had overlooked stamping it, and it was returned for want of postage!

I had seen little of Dreiser during recent years, but we exchanged letters off and on, and continued on amicable terms. He was an enormous figure in my life in my earlier writing days. I first met him in 1907, and for years afterward we were very intimate. It was probably my eager defense of him against Comstocks and other fools that first established me as a critic of books. But despite our intimacy and the hand I had in many of his affairs we were never really close friends, for I was a congenital skeptic and he was of the believing type of mind. When, a little while back, he wrote to me that he had joined the Communist party I could only smile a bit sadly, for I had seen him succumb to too many other gangs of quacks to be surprised. This afternoon the New York *Times* asked me by wire for a 1,000-word "estimate" of him. I declined politely.

1946

On this New Years day, as on many others in the past, the daffodils in the backyard are beginning to show signs of life. Their thin, dark-green shoots, in fact, were visible several weeks ago, and they apparently got through the snow and sleet of Christmas without damage. They will probably not grow much during January, but by the beginning of February they should be showing signs of blossoming. By that time there will also be plenty of signs of new life in the trees and shrubs. The Baltimore Winter is not long, though when it is cloudy it seems long to human beings. The town gets 50% of all the possible sunshine in the course of the year, but most of it comes in Summer. January and February are commonly dismal, and sometimes they bring severe snow and sleet storms. There is a common saying in Maryland that though February is the shortest month of the year it always seems the longest. By its end everyone is tired of dark days, and eager for the March winds which blow the clouds away. But March can be stormy too, and some of the worst blizzards I can recall came in its first days. Their virtue is that they do not last long. Even a heavy snow is disposed of by the reviving sun in a few days.

The check I received from the Knopf office this morning, covering royalties for the half year ending November 1, 1945, was for $14,547.68—the largest check, and by far, that I have ever got for my books. Of this amount, $10,650.89 was earned by Supplement I to "The American Language," which came out late in August. The sales to November 1 were 14,829 copies. I was especially delighted to notice how much the new book had pulled up the sales of "The American Language," fourth edition, first issued in 1936. The latter, for some years, had been selling less than 800 a half year, but during the six months ending April 30, 1945, with Supplement I already talked of, it sold 1,185, and brought me $861.08, and during the April 30–November 1 period, with the Supplement reviving interest in it, it sold 3,260 and brought me $2,424.47. My royalties from both "The American Language" and Supplement I for the November 1, 1945–April 30, 1946 period will again be large. Many people, as I discovered by the requests for autographs that came in, bought the two together as a Christmas present. Unhappily, most of the $14,547.68 that came in today will have to go for income tax, for so heavy an addition to my usual income will throw me into a much higher bracket. Thus I'll get very little for my hard work. But it is pleasant to think that a book of mine has done so well after my sixty-fifth birthday—better, indeed, than any book of mine in the past.

BALTIMORE, JANUARY 7, 1946.

I dropped in on Dr. Wainwright this afternoon, and he reported on the examination he made three or four weeks ago. My blood pressure, he said, is still considerably short of alarming. It shows a general tendency upward, but it is not much higher today than it was four or five years ago. The diastolic pressure, which has gone several times above 100, is now below it. Wainwright said that I show some albuminuria, but that it is not serious. My liver, lungs, prostate and stomach appear to be normal, though my stomach exhibits an abnormal activity. Wainwright suggested that the sub-sternal discomfort which often forces me to stop work in the late morning or impedes my sleep at night may be relieved by eating a cracker and swallowing half a glass of milk. I shall try it. He said that the nightmarish dreams which not infrequently awake me with a start at night, and leave me intensely uncomfortable and sleepless for half an hour or more may be prevented by taking one of the milder barbiturates, and he gave me a prescription for Seconal. I shall not take it unless I really need it. I forgot to tell him that my right eye, which shows sclerotic changes, has been deteriorating of late. My palaver with him, on the whole, was reassuring, though he said he could do nothing for the malaise which besets me nearly all the time. He said that he did not advise me to reduce my mild rations of alcohol, and he said nothing about tobacco. He said a long rest might do me good, but agreed that idleness, to a man as active as I have been, would be an unendurable affliction. If Sara were living I might take a holiday with her, but I simply can't imagine doing it alone. After the first week I'd be frantic for occupation.

BALTIMORE, JANUARY 9, 1946.

In Baltimore, at the moment, there is not a single decent beerhouse. The last was Schellhase's in Howard street, which still survives as a restaurant but began to close at 9 p.m. when the war razzle-dazzle began. On Saturday nights it keeps open its backroom to accommodate the Saturday Night Club, but we are expected to clear out before 12 o'clock, and usually do so by 11.30. The Negro kitchen help and the white waitresses refuse to work at night, and Schellhase is making so much money out of his eating business that he is disinclined to put on two shifts. His place, both before and immediately after Repeal, was a very pleasant place, and I went there many an evening at 10 o'clock and sat until midnight. He served the best beer obtainable, both imported and domestic, and offered very good light lunches at moderate prices. But now he has only the Anheuser-Busch beers on tap. Budweiser I can't drink, for it is so hoppy that it gives me heartburn, and Michelob sells at 25 cents a seidel. Whether or not he will ever have German beer again remains to be seen; probably not, for most of the German and Bohemian breweries seem to have been destroyed in the war, and the imbeciles at Washington may be trusted to lay prohibitive duties on the beer of those that survive. The tax on domestic beer is now at the point of diminishing returns, and very few of the brews available are good. The best I know of is National Premium, made in Baltimore, but it comes only in bottles. Piel's beer, which was excellent just after Repeal, is now very inferior, though the brewery lately made a batch of the excellent Kapuziner. But this batch was for friends only, and none was put on sale. I got three cases.

There is nothing more comfortable and pleasant than a good beerhouse, but I suspect that it has gone to stay. I know of only a few in New York. Lüchow's offers very good food, but the best beer it has on tap is Prior's, of Allentown, Pa., which is surely no great shakes. Moreover, the place now closes at 11 p.m., and is closed all day and evening every Monday. Baltimore has no beerhouse of even the second grade. One can only choose between gaudy and uncomfortable night clubs and dirty saloons. Not one of them offers decent draft beer. The hotels have also stopped serving it, and so has the Maryland Club. *Sic transit.* The decent pleasures of life have diminished enormously in my time.

BALTIMORE, [JANUARY] 13, 1946.[1]

My father died 47 years ago today. It is a long, long while ago; indeed, he is now dead nearly three years longer than he lived. But I was 18 when his end came so early and so suddenly, and I therefore remember him quite clearly. Taken ill on New Year's night, 1899, while sitting at home quietly with my mother, he was done for in less than two weeks. What fetched him was acute nephritis: it must have originated in an infection, but what that infection was will never be known. The first symptom was a convulsion, and when the end came he was in another convulsion, with hypostatic pneumonia to help it.

If he were alive today he would be a member of that class of reactionaries which is execrated by all right-thinking Americans. He worked diligently at his business, kept his family in comfort, and laid a little by. When he came to die, still a young man, he had accumulated enough to maintain his wife and children indefinitely. I was already 18, as I have said, and in a little while I was self-sustaining, but Charlie was but 16, Gertie was but 13, and August was but 10. The yield from his estate enabled my mother to bring them all up, and her life was secure and comfortable until she died in 1925. What remains of that estate still provides about half the income of Gertie, with a little over for the others. The old family home at 1524 Hollins street, which he bought in 1883, is still in good condition, and August and I live in it. Such men are not much esteemed in these days, but I remain of the conviction that they were good citizens, just as they were good husbands and fathers.

1 This entry is actually dated June 13, 1946, but Mrs. Lohrfinck obviously made an error in typing it. Its position in the sheets, plus the fact that August Mencken, Sr., died on January 13, 1899, establish beyond any doubt that January 13 is the correct date.

BALTIMORE, JANUARY 25, 1946.

I returned this afternoon from a brief trip to Wilmington, Del., and New York. I left on Tuesday morning, January 22, and got to the house of Alfred and Marcella du Pont in time for lunch. Joe and Dorothy Hergesheimer were there, both of them looking somewhat peaked. In the evening Judge John Biggs, Jr. and his wife came in for dinner. Alfred du Pont's state is really shocking. He has lost a lot of weight and looks very haggard. His doctors have advised him that he has a stomach ulcer, and have urged him to go on a bland diet, with no smoking and no alcohol, but he insists on drinking two old-fashioned cocktails before dinner each evening. Joe, who is diabetic, similarly insists on drinking beer. Both want to see Dr. Benjamin M. Baker when he returns to practise in Baltimore, but it is hardly likely that they will show any improvement so long as they break training so grossly. Biggs has grown fat and now has a massive neck. He is a New Deal Federal judge, and my opinion of him is very low, but he was polite enough during the evening. Hergy proposed to take him on for a full-length debate, but I vetoed this. Mrs. Biggs is a pleasant woman.

I proceeded to New York on Wednesday. On the train I met Walter Myers, the fourth assistant postmaster general, and we had dinner together in the evening at Lüchow's. Both of us ate roast goose. Myers told me a lot of interesting stuff about the inner workings of the Post-office. He is confident that the Supreme Court will decide for *Esquire* in the case lately argued.[1] He is tired of Washington and is planning to return to Indianapolis to practise law. His two sons, lately released from the service, are now keeping up his office there. He is an agreeable fellow, but somewhat given to long anecdotes.

On Thursday I went to a lunch arranged by Fred Melcher, of the *Publishers' Weekly*. His paper gives an annual prize to the best book of the year—that is, the best book physically—, and this time it went to Supplement I to "The American Language." The contents of the book do not concern the judges: they confine themselves to format. The party was at the Roosevelt Hotel, and only about 20 persons were present. I was called on for a brief speech. I confined myself to whooping up the printers, designers and so on who had a hand in the Supplement. After lunch Alfred, Blanche and I returned to the Knopf

1 See the entry for October 30, 1943 (p. 278).

office, and there I had a palaver with Sidney Jacobs, the manufacturing man, lately home from the war. We discussed the new edition of "Treatise on the Gods," and the format of my projected Christmas book.[1] It now takes six or seven months to make a book.

In the morning I saw Barnhart and Linscott, of Random House, at the Algonquin. They are planning a new dictionary,[2] and wanted me to sit on an advisory committee. I refused on the ground (plainly stated to them) that I disliked Bennett Cerf, the racketeering head of Random House, but offered to give them some aid on the side. They will probably make a bad dictionary. In the evening Nathan took me to dinner at the Colony. A swell dinner, but not quite to my taste. We met Walter Wanger,[3] and had a pleasant palaver with him. I hadn't encountered him for some years.

BALTIMORE, FEBRUARY 13, 1946.

There was a special meeting of the *Sun* board at 2 p.m. today. Present: Morgan,[4] Patterson and myself. This was less than a quorum, but Fenhagen, who is disabled by a broken arm, consented to be counted as present. Semmes, Black and Schmick are in the South. The object of the meeting was to pass a resolution authorizing the management to apply for a television license. I thought that this had been done long ago, but it must have been neglected. The radio engineers and lawyers at Washington, who are fertile in alarms, sent in a demand at the last moment, saying that the application would have to be filed immediately.

Patterson and I had lunch together, and discussed the business at length. In the course of our palaver he handed me the papers filed by the Washington *Star* in a similar case. Glancing through them, I was

1 *Christmas Story*, originally published in *The New Yorker* for December 30, 1944, as *Stare Decisis*, appeared in book form in 1946. More about the story appears in the entry for August 29, 1946 (p. 421).

2 Possibly this refers to the *Random House Dictionary of the English Language, Unabridged Edition*, which did not actually appear until 1966, twenty years after this entry was made. The *American College Dictionary*, also bearing the Random House imprint, came out in 1947, but one would suppose that at this point it was too close to completion for the editors to be asking Mencken, or anyone else, to serve on an advisory committee for it.

3 Walter Wanger (1894–1968), Hollywood film producer.

4 Edwin F. A. Morgan (1892–1965), lawyer, senior partner in the firm of Semmes, Bowen & Semmes, and a director of the A. S. Abell Company.

amazed to discover that the *Star* had been compelled to file a complete balance sheet—not of its radio subsidiary, but of the parent company. I pointed out that if the *Sun* presented an application it would have to do the same, and that this would lay open the most private business of the company to hostile labor leaders and other such buzzards, for all such applications are public documents and copies may be obtained by anyone on the payment of small fees. I was again amazed, and doubly, when Patterson told me that the *Sun*, in its previous applications for AM and FM licenses, had already filed such statements. Later Flaherty told me that it had been done three separate times. Along with the balance sheet must go a statement of earnings for four years past.

Why I was never informed of this rule I do not know. If I had heard of it I'd have protested violently. For more than a hundred years the *Sun* has been going to great pains to keep its business to itself, and all efforts by outsiders to get access to its balance sheets have been resisted. But now it has opened its books to any comer, and the next time the Newspaper Guild tackles the office the figures will no doubt be produced, for the Federal Communications Commission office, like every other office in Washington, is full of Communists, and they will tip the Guild.

I told Patterson once more, and for the hundredth time, that I believe it was folly to try to get into the radio business. Everything that might be accomplished by owning a station would be obtained by buying a substantial minority interest in one of the existing companies. No one in the office understands the radio business, and if Schmick and Kavanaugh undertake to learn it the job will take them off their regular and proper work. Moreover, the investment will be enormous. The rebuilding now about to be begun at the *Sun* office will cost more than $1,000,000 and new equipment will cost $2,000,000 more. These are bottom estimates. The final cost will no doubt be much more. The radio engineers, all of whom seem to me to be quacks, differ widely in their guesses as to what operating a radio station will cost. One of them says that television alone will cost $100,000 a year, with no substantial revenues in sight, but another estimates $400,000.

The *Sun* has already got options on the top floor of the Baltimore Trust Building and on a site for a radio tower in the Pimlico region. These options cost something. In addition, the radio engineers, lawyers, etc., constantly send in heavy bills. The total cost to date has probably been $50,000, with nothing whatever to show for it. The chances that the *Sun* will get an AM or ordinary radio license are apparently nil, and there is little likelihood that it will get FM and television licenses. This madness irritates me extremely. I am completely against it. I urged Patterson today to abandon the whole project and give some attention to editorial matters. I told him that the *Evening Sun* editorial page of yesterday was a disgrace to journalism. He stared at me dumbly. He is afraid to tackle the editorial pages, and is not really interested. Twenty years ago the two *Sunpapers* were making a noise in the world, and showing their heels to the other American newspapers. But now they have been brought down to the level of the Washington *Star*, the Philadelphia *Bulletin*, and the Cowles papers. Their prestige has vanished altogether. No one pays any heed to them, in or out of newspaper offices.

The rebuilding scheme and the radio venture will cost an enormous amount of money. To undertake them in the face of the fact that heavy increases in labor costs are certain within the next two years will be to imperil the paper's surplus, and open the way to all sorts of serious difficulties. In brief, the situation is very bad, and it seems impossible to awaken Patterson to its dangers. As for Morgan, all he had to say was that, as a general principle, he was opposed to owning minority interests. But even Patterson admits that a substantial interest in one of the local stations would give the *Sun* everything it hopes to gain by venturing into the radio business, and at enormously less cost. Indeed, he is again trying to negotiate with one of the local stations. But his mind, of late, shows a great vacillation, and he is meanwhile pushing the idiotic effort to get AM, FM and television licenses.

BALTIMORE, MARCH 29, 1946.

I have been ill all week and unable to work. When Wainwright examined me on Monday morning he found that my head infection, as usual, had moved down into the trachea. It inflamed my larynx on the way, and for two days I was scarcely able to speak. He advised spraying the upper nose and throat with sulphadiazine, but it did no good and I abandoned it. Instead I resorted to benzoin vapors, generated by a little electric heater beside my desk, and they gave me considerable relief. There was not much cough or discharge, but the malaise was severe, and I have spent most of my time reading and snoozing. On Monday afternoon, March 25, came a telegram from Betty Hanes, saying that her husband had died at 1 p.m. It was, of course, not unexpected, for he had been desperately ill since Christmas, but it was nevertheless a shock. Ordinarily, I'd have gone down to Winston-Salem for the funeral, but I had to call up Betty and tell her that I was unfit to travel. The Hanes have been good friends for twenty years, and I have visited them at their Summer place at Roaring Gap, N.C., almost every Summer. Now that is done for, as so many other pleasant things are done for. Betty herself has been ill more or less for four or five years.

BALTIMORE, APRIL 14, 1946.

To Washington yesterday for the Spring dinner of the Gridiron Club. Paul Patterson and I made the trip in one of the office cars, and he took my bag to the Hotel Statler and registered me. I got off somewhere in the outskirts and went by taxi to St. Elizabeth's Hospital, where Ezra Pound[1] is locked up. The superintendent, Dr. Winfred Overholser, received me politely and took me to the building in which Pound is confined. Inasmuch as he is charged with treason he is in the strictest confinement, and all visitors must see him in a barred room in the presence of a guard. St. Elizabeth's, which is in far Southeastern Washington near the Navy Yard, covers 350 acres, and I had some difficult finding even the central office. The grounds were full of lunatics, mainly colored, but they were apparently harmless and even disinclined to escape, for between them and the main gate there was only a single guard.

Overholser had written to me that Pound liked candy, so I took him four pounds and also some books. He came in looking well and even somewhat jaunty. He still wears his beard and was well dressed. I asked him if he were short of money, and he said no. His English wife, who is still in Rapallo, Italy, has lately come into her patrimony. How she gets money to him he didn't say. Overholser told me he could

---

1 Ezra Pound (1885–1972), expatriate American poet with an enormous influence on the development of modern verse. After World War II Pound was arrested and charged with treason on the ground that he had broadcast Axis propaganda from Rome to U.S. fighting forces. At his trial he was judged to be insane and committed to St. Elizabeth's Hospital, where he remained from 1946 to 1958. Upon his release he returned to Italy.

use a small sum for minor needs, and I shall send him a check. Overholser said that he is suffering from paranoia, and that his recovery is unlikely. He talked rationally, and we had a pleasant chat of half an hour or so. He insisted that he had never categorically advocated Fascism in his broadcasts, but inasmuch as he whooped up Mussolini that fact is irrelevant. I assured him that all the heat against him would be gone in a year or two, and that it would probably be possible by then to obtain his liberation. This seemed to console him. He said that he is sleepy all the time and is thus unable to do any writing. "I'll not tackle poetry again," he said, "for three years." He said that he was uncomfortable when he was first confined, but that he now has good quarters and decent meals. He objects only to the exercise period, which keeps him on his feet for three hours daily. Obviously, he is in a low state of vitality. We talked of various things—with the guard listening. When I told him that Edgar Lee Masters had lately received a $5,000 poetry prize he seemed pleased. He said that he had included Masters in an anthology years ago, but did not know him. I did not mention Bennett Cerf's unsuccessful attempt to bar him (Pound) from an anthology lately published.

Bill Crawford, a Newark newspaper artist, showed up at the Statler with his sketches for "Christmas Story." They seemed to me to be excellent, and I told him to go ahead with the drawings. With him was Henry Suydam, editor of his paper, a dull fellow. The Gridiron dinner was the stupidest I can recall. There was absolutely no humor in the sketches presented, and most of the songs were tuneless. The speaker of the evening was Harold E. Stassen, of Minnesota. His speech and President Truman's reply were mainly devoted to joshing about Stassen's candidacy for the Republican nomination in 1948. Truman also paid his satirical respects to three newspaper columnists who frequently criticize him—Walter Lippmann,[1] David Lawrence[2] and Frank R. Kent. It was good-humored stuff, but I think Kent did not enjoy being bracketed with two Jews. Stassen, when I encountered him before the dinner, fell on my neck as if we were old friends,

1 Walter Lippmann (1889–1974), influential American newspaperman and political commentator. It was Lippmann who, reviewing Mencken's *Notes on Democracy* in 1926, called him "the most powerful personal influence on this whole generation of educated people."
2 David Lawrence (1888–1973), editor, columnist, author of numerous books on journalism and politics.

though I recall meeting him previously only once. This is the way of politicians.

I sat next to George Radcliffe[1] and near Frank Kent. Opposite me was Tony Muto,[2] a news-reel man who is an old acquaintance. Muto, who is an Italian, managed to collar a large supply of drinks. He got two bottles of sherry, four of Beaulieu red wine and three or four of champagne. But I drank very little—two Scotch highballs before the dinner, some sherry and wine at table, and a bottle of beer afterward. The usual booze-parties went on before and after, and I met many old friends. I was in bed by midnight, with a Seconal capsule aboard, and slept very well. When I awoke this morning I felt better than for five or six weeks past. I caught the 10.30 a.m. B.& O. train and was home before noon. This afternoon August and I put in more than two hours in the yard—our first chance this year. I cleaned out the stable—a dirty and heavy job—and got through various other chores. Next Sunday we will be spending Easter with Gertie at Frizzellburg, so it will be April 28 before we can do any planting. By that time the ground should be warm.

BALTIMORE, APRIL 16, 1946.

John Dos Passos[3] called me up the other day to say that he was in Baltimore and hoped to see me. His wife is a patient at the Johns Hopkins Hospital, and he has come here to look after her. He is the guest of Dr. W. Horsley Gantt,[4] the son-in-law of Dr. Edward H. Richardson, Jr., the surgeon. This Gantt has some sort of piddling job at the Johns Hopkins, and devotes himself chiefly to animal experiments. He went to Russia after the last war to study under Pavlov, the Russian physiologist, and has been repeating Pavlov's work ever since. He is a dreadful bore, and I always try to avoid meeting him. I therefore suggested to Dos Passos that he and I have lunch together at the Maryland Club today. We had a pleasant enough session, but it was

1 George L. Radcliffe (1877–1974), U.S. senator from Maryland.
2 Anthony ("Tony") Muto (1903–1964), motion picture producer specializing in newsreel coverage of international events.
3 John Dos Passos (1896–1970), American novelist. His best-known works are *Three Soldiers* (1921) and the trilogy *U.S.A.* (1937).
4 W. Horsley Gantt (d. 1980) was an expert in Pavlovian psychology and founded the Pavlovian Society of America in 1956.

certainly not exhilarating. Dos Passos is an extremely amiable fellow, but seldom has anything to say. The result is that the other party must bear the whole burden of the conversation. I have never heard Dos Passos venture upon an argument, or even advance an idea. Altogether, my brief session with him was amicable, but somewhat fatiguing, and I left him as soon as possible.

What he is up to at the moment he didn't say, and I didn't ask him. His first book, "Three Soldiers," was an extremely important event, if only because it was the first volume by an American veteran of World War I that attempted to tell the truth about the war. His later books have all seemed to me to be dull, and I don't recall getting to the end of more than one or two of them.

BALTIMORE, APRIL 29, 1946.

I am getting a little work done on Supplement II, but only under great difficulties. My head infection has been kept going by the continued cold, damp and windy weather, and I am seeing Dr. Polvogt tomorrow. For some weeks past there have also been uncomfortable heart symptoms, chiefly dull aches and a feeling of oppression in the sub-sternal region. When Joe Hergesheimer was here on April 23 I felt so rocky that I could hardly sit up, and when lunch was over I returned home and stretched out for a rest. Save for one night, I have slept pretty well and have had no need to take Seconal. But I always feel wretched in the morning, and getting through shaving is an unpleasant business. I usually buck up a bit after my shower, but by 11 a.m. I am unfit to go on with my work. My best time comes after dinner in the evening. Usually, though not always, I am able to put in a couple of hours on my book. In the race between my deteriorating coronary arteries and my general arterio-sclerosis, the arteries seem likely to win. Thus I'll probably have only a brief struggle when my time comes, which is a consolation, though only a sorry one. Within the past two weeks two old friends, both of them Johns Hopkins doctors, Walter E. Dandy and Louis Hamman, have died quickly of coronary attacks. I should see Benjamin M. Baker, who has returned to practise, but there is really nothing that he can do for me. If I manage to finish Supplement II I'll be lucky. My plan to carry my record of my adventures as author and editor from 1922, where it now stops, to the present time will probably go glimmering. It is a pity, for there is a large amount of interesting stuff in my files for the later years, and if I die before I finish much of it will be unintelligible. I knew so many American and English authors during the 1914–1930 period that my account of them should be of interest and use to future historians of the national literature.

BALTIMORE, MAY 5, 1946.

After two weeks of rain, cold and high winds, today (a Sunday) opened gloomily, but by 10 a.m. the sun was shining and in the afternoon the temperature was up to 70 degrees. August and I spent the morning in the backyard. We planted morning-glory seeds, prepared the ground for the petunias that should come in from Cook the florist this week, banked the ferns with peat moss, trimmed the vines, and did a lot of other chores. I became so warm at work that I took off my coat, but in a few minutes a chilly west wind came up, and I had to put it on again. The yard never looked more lovely. The trees, the vines along the fences, and the ivy on the ground all show the bright greens of Spring, and the coleus that I have been setting out (bought in Lexington market) are flourishing. But in a little while this first blush will fade, all the greens will grow darker, and the yard will settle down for the struggle with the heat of a Baltimore Summer.

BALTIMORE, JUNE 17, 1946.

Gilbert Chinard, professor of French at Princeton, and his wife were in Baltimore yesterday, and I took them for dinner last night to Maria's restaurant at Albemarle and Fawn streets. This place is in the heart of the Italian quarter, and but a block from the waterfront. Maria is a bosomy Italian woman who has attracted uptown people to her tables by offering food in the best Italian style. It is very heavy stuff, and can be got down only with the aid of red wine. Chinard, who is from Bordeaux, and his wife, who comes from the Rabelais country, were apparently delighted; at all events, they ate heartily, and were full of praises of Maria. Chinard told me that the Institute for Advanced Study, now at Princeton, was first offered to the Johns Hopkins. It was declined at the urging of Daniel Willard, then president of the board of trustees—first, because he objected to independent institutes in the university establishment, and second, because the do-

nors were Jews. Chinard said that full members of the Institute are
paid from $15,000 to $20,000 a year, and hold their appointments for
life, but that young associates, whose posts are only temporary, get
much less—some of them as little as $1,800. The Chinards live across
the street from Albert Einstein in Princeton, and Mrs. Chinard said
that the old man is a very innocent and charming person. When his
wife died he brought an old-maid sister from Germany to keep house
for him. She spoke good French, but no English, and the faculty ladies
found it hard to make up to her. One day several of them, feeling that
she was neglected and lonely, called on her and proposed to come in
now and then to play chess with her and her brother. Her reply was:
"Out of this house! My brother would never allow jazz!"

BALTIMORE, JUNE 20, 1946.

I got in this afternoon after two days in New York. I reached there
on Tuesday, June 18 just in time for the annual meeting of the Knopf
stockholders. Sam Knox, as usual, was not present, nor did he turn up
for the directors' meeting which followed. There was very little business. Alfred Knopf, who is leaving for England today, said that he was
planning to go to Los Angeles in the Autumn to tackle his sister, Sophia
Josephy, and her husband. They own a substantial block of 7% preferred stock, and he hopes to induce them to waive the accumulated
unpaid dividends on it, and to consent to its conversion into either 4%
stock or common. My guess is that he will find this a difficult business,
but I offered no suggestions. There is now an unpaid accumulation of
about $154,000 on the 7% preferred, or $55 a share. The company has
been doing well of late, but it seems to me to be highly unlikely that
the present boom will continue. The sales for the fiscal year ending
June 30 were $2,047,000—the largest in the company's history. The
net profit was $102,000, as against $87,000 for the year before. But
most of this went toward repairing the damaged state of the corporation's finances, and the earned surplus at this minute is but $7,000.
Out of this will have to come a quarterly dividend of $1.75 on the
preferred. This will be for the current year, and will not diminish the
accumulated deficit. The imbecile financing of old Samuel Knopf is
still burdening the company, though he is dead nearly 12 years. I own
150 shares of preferred and 50 of common. Lesser estimates that the
book value of the preferred is $154 and of the common about $120,

which makes my equity worth nearly $30,000. But this is a purely theoretical value. In the open market it would probably not bring $10,000, and everyone knows that I'd not offer it in the open market.

On Tuesday evening I picked up Marcella du Pont, who was at the Ambassador, and took her down to Lüchow's, where we found Edgar Lee Masters and his wife, just in from Charlotte, N.C. Masters was a sad spectacle. He can walk only with assistance, slowly and with a shuffling gait, and he told me that he still finds work impossible. Ellen Masters was in high spirits, and drank wine and beer with considerable zest, but the old boy ate and drank very little, and had next to nothing to say. I believe he is convinced that he is not long for this world, and I incline to agree. The two women ate very hearty dinners. At 10 p.m. Masters began to suggest going home, and soon afterward we broke up. I dropped Marcella at her hotel, went back to the Algonquin, and was in bed at 11 o'clock. I slept until 10 a.m. yesterday.

I had lunch at the Stork Club yesterday with Roger Butterfield, a young man on the staff of *Life*. He had been assigned by Daniel Longwell, the managing editor, to prepare an interview with me. He had sent in some written questions, but they were not very helpful. I'll have to concoct both questions and answers myself. After lunch we went to Butterfield's apartment, and there talked a while. He looks to me to be a second-rate reporter, and my guess is that the interview will never be printed.[1]

George Nathan and I had dinner at the Colony, and then went to No. 21, where a television set had been installed in a corner, with chairs for about 30 people. We were given front seats. The television set was supposed to show us the Louis-Conn fight going on at the baseball grounds, but its small images danced in a way that hurt our eyes, and often faded out. We nevertheless saw the fight, and the last round was pretty clear. It is amusing to think of fools paying nearly $2,000,000 to see so sorry an exhibition. Conn danced away from Louis from the first bell, and seldom struck a real blow. It was, in fact, a dancing performance rather than a prize fight, and I am full of suspicion that it was phoney. When the time came Louis simply walked in and knocked out Conn in ten seconds. There was never anything even remotely resembling a contest.

After this burlesque was over Nathan and I walked downtown and

---

1 Roger Butterfield's interview, entitled "Mr. Mencken Sounds Off," appeared in the August 5, 1946 issue of *Life*.

dropped in at the Algonquin for a farewell drink. He told me that Eugene O'Neill, the dramatist, was advocating me for the Nobel Prize, and predicting confidently that I would get it. This seemed sheer imbecility, but Nathan insisted that O'Neill is serious. The Swedes want to give it to an American, and can't agree on a candidate. They will get plenty of nominees once the news gets about, and my guess is that it will go to Louis Bromfield or some other such mucker. Willa Cather probably deserves it more than any other, but she has been out of sight and mind so long that the Swedes seem to have forgotten her. O'Neill himself received the prize in 1936, Sinclair Lewis in 1930 and Pearl Buck in 1938. Dreiser, who deserved it more than any of them or than all of them put together, never got it. If any feelers ever reach me from the Swedes I shall say nay instantly.[1] But they will never come: O'Neill is simply dreaming. He probably still remembers the fact that it was I who discovered him. I haven't seen him or heard from him for years. He told Nathan that the value of the prize, which was $42,000 when he got it, is now $60,000.

BALTIMORE, JUNE 22, 1946.

When I lie down my heart thumps in a way that makes it hard to get to sleep. First it bangs along for ten or twelve beats, then it misses a beat, and then there is a thump that actually shakes my body. No pain goes with this, and no shortness of breath. What it signifies I don't know, but certainly it can't be a good sign. I am able to work more or less, but I tire quickly, and have to take it in short sessions. Today I have been making notes for an interview with me that Roger Butterfield proposes to print in *Life*. It is not an easy job, for the best stuff is unprintable in any such magazine. I have been writing and tearing up—and so wasting time. Once this nuisance is cleared off I hope to resume work on Supplement II, but I begin to doubt that I'll ever finish it.

BALTIMORE, JUNE 24, 1946.

My old friend Frank Hazlehurst died yesterday morning at 4 o'clock. He had been suffering from heart disease for four or five years, and it had become increasingly evident of late that his days were short.

1 The 1946 Nobel Prize for literature was awarded to Hermann Hesse of Germany.

He stuck it out very bravely and refused to go to bed. He played with the Saturday Night Club on Saturday night, and we parted hardly more than four hours before his death. He looked very badly and was in obvious distress, but he insisted on playing to the end. August drove his car to Schellhase's, for it was plain that he was not fit to drive it himself. There his wife met him and drove him home. She got him into bed and he fell asleep, but just at dawn he awoke her and in a few minutes he was dead.

Frank grew up in Hollins street and I had known him since boyhood. He was an almost exact contemporary of my brother Charlie. He was the last person on earth, aside from the members of my family, who called me Harry, my stable name in boyhood. All of my other friends have called me Henry, and Sara used it likewise.

Frank was an amiable fellow, but somewhat lazy. He got an excellent medical education at the Johns Hopkins and in Germany, and there was a time when he seemed likely to develop into an extremely prosperous nose and throat surgeon, but he quickly deteriorated into a general practitioner, and for many years he ran a small clinic in East Baltimore. Of late he was confining his practice to the Catonsville area. He lived for years a mile or so beyond Catonsville, and devoted a great deal of his time to his vegetable garden. In his earlier days he was a very active athlete, and until four or five years ago he played tennis constantly. He married a German girl thirty-five years ago, and she survives him, along with a daughter and two granddaughters.

By a curious coincidence, the *Sun* of this morning reports that Joseph L. Wickes[1] also died yesterday. Wickes was cellist of the Saturday Night Club about twenty-five years ago. He was a bad one, just as Frank was, but nevertheless he was an amiable fellow and everyone liked him. His age at death was 84.

August and I went out to Catonsville yesterday afternoon to call on the widow. She said nothing about serving as pallbearers at Frank's funeral, which will take place on Wednesday, June 26. Rather curiously for a medical man, he wanted to be buried not cremated, and this will be done. His wife told me that he had refused for a year or two to take medical advice. He was probably wise in this. He knew precisely what the brethren would tell him and he also knew that it

1 Joseph Lee Wickes (1862–1946) had been a traffic engineer for Baltimore's Public Service Commission for many years.

would do him no good. In brief, he was reconciled to death and awaited it with serenity.

BALTIMORE, JULY 8, 1946.

A strange tenant moved into the Fortenbaugh house last week, and August suspects that she is Charlie's wife. Apparently she has her mother with her. She and Charlie had been separated for years, but according to the neighborhood gossip he had been seeing her regularly. The furniture that she brought in indicated a taste considerably higher than that of the Fortenbaugh family. Some of the furniture was really quite charming. Also she lugged in some large piles of back number magazines. Perhaps she is literary.

Two or three weeks ago a woman named Lees, who operates the Century Hotel at Charles and Mt. Royal avenues, called me up to say that Charlie's sister Ethel, Mrs. Oertel, was holed in there in a state of extreme intoxication. She had been in the place for four or five days and Mrs. Lees was beginning to be uneasy about her. All efforts to reach Charlie by telephone had failed, so I was called up. At the same time a policeman telephoned me asking for information about poor Ethel. All I could tell him and Mrs. Lees was that she was a periodical alcoholic and quite harmless. For several days Mrs. Lees kept calling me. Finally she reported that Ethel had disappeared. I advised her to communicate with Ethel's former husband, Oertel, once a druggist and now a dentist. A little while later Oertel himself called up and said that he was willing to take care of her, though they had been separated for years. What happened after that I don't know. Ethel is not in the house next door, and I suspect that either Charlie or the police may have sent her to an insane asylum. The poor woman is obviously upset mentally. She has been in the habit for some years past of going on a big drunk after completing a case as a practical nurse. Once she called me up from the Joyce Hotel, and it was obvious that she was very far gone. Until this last time, however, she always managed to conceal her infirmity. Mrs. Lees now says that her talk is quite irrational.

This is another chapter in the melancholy saga of the Fortenbaugh family. The old man was a periodical drunkard, and the mother of Charlie and Ethel was also more or less given to the bottle. There was a step-sister Lillie who died a year or so ago, who went the same way.

Once I encountered her sitting on the front steps of their house in an advanced state of liquor. I have heard that Charlie himself goes on occasional drunks.

If the new tenant is actually his wife there will probably be quarreling in the house in the very near future. This will be nothing new. It has been under a curse ever since it was built. The first tenants, the Eckhardts, rowed very frequently. Their successors, the Hancocks, were worse. The Fortenbaughs in the old man's time had frequent battles in the grand manner, and in the days before Charlie definitely left his wife she often came to the house demanding justice and set up dreadful uproars on the front steps. We shall see.

BALTIMORE, JULY 10, 1946.

The first morning-glory bloom showed this morning, in one of the window-boxes in the side-yard. It is a Heavenly Blue. Within a week or two there will be dozens in blossom, and the Scarlett O'Hara will quickly follow. The first petunia appeared on June 1. Day before yesterday August counted more than 200. It has been the best year for the yard that I can recall. The wet weather in the Spring gave everything a good start. Signs of dryness began to appear a few days ago and August and I put on the hose. After it had drenched the yard a brief but heavy rain came up. We begin to be superstitious about this. As soon as we get out the hose it begins to rain.

BALTIMORE, AUGUST 17, 1946.

Sara and I were married sixteen years ago today. Certainly there has not been a day since her death that I have not thought of her, and in all probability there have been very few waking hours. It would hardly be accurate to say that I go on mourning her: I hope I am too much of a philosopher to agonize over the irremediable. But surely I think of her. She left an ineradicable mark upon my life. She is not forgotten.

BALTIMORE, AUGUST 24, 1946.

I got home today from the Johns Hopkins Hospital, where I spent ten days taking a penicillin cure for my old head infection. I felt perfectly well save for the local irritation, but inasmuch as the injections were given every three hours, day and night, I had to stay in the hospital. This infection has bothered me off and on for years, and I believe that it was exacerbated when Dr. Curtis F. Burnham gave me a somewhat heavy x-ray treatment for some excess lingual tissue at the base of my tongue. The lingual tissue was disposed of, but the treatment left my whole throat somewhat dry, and it has usually given me some trouble during the late Winters. This Winter I began to be afflicted in February, and the disturbance continued through the Spring and into the Summer, though in the past it had always yielded to the first really hot sunshine. Polvogt, the nose and throat man, tackled it with various local applications from February onward, but they gave me only temporary relief. Some time ago Ben Baker suggested that it might be a good idea to try a stiff course of penicillin. After he went on his vacation early in August the glands in the left side of my neck began to be sore, and his associate, Wainwright, decided to try penicillin at once.

I entered the hospital on August 14. It was a somewhat tedious siege, but I could go and come as I pleased during the intervals between injections, and so had a more or less comfortable time of it. The injections were given at 3, 6, 9 and 12 o'clock, a.m. and p.m. On August 17 I left the hospital after the 9 p.m. injection and spent the rest of the evening with the Saturday Night Club. The next day I went home for lunch, and the day following attended the monthly meeting of the *Sun* board. In the intervals I managed to get through a file of the *Congressional Record* running back to April. I had no visitors in hospital save August, and managed to stave off flowers. One night I attended a meeting of Arnold Rich's[1] pathology staff, and was entertained by the gloating of its members over a false diagnosis in the Harriet Lane Hospital. The injections were not painful and left no soreness. When the nurse came in at 3 a.m. to give me one I was sometimes asleep again before she got out of the room.

BALTIMORE, AUGUST 29, 1946.

The first copies of "Christmas Story" reached me from the Knopf office this morning. If this little book sells well the functionaries of the staff will probably take all the credit. The truth is that I had a hard

---

1 Dr. Arnold Rich (1893–1968), professor of pathology at the Johns Hopkins, was a member of the Saturday Night Club.

time persuading them to print it, and that even after they were converted they made a mess of their job. The first pictures they proposed to use would have ruined the book off-hand, and even after Bill Crawford was discovered and his excellent illustrations were in hand, I had a dreadful time persuading Jacobs to make the coloring bright enough. The first proofs were so dull that they looked almost funereal. I am very far from satisfied with Jacobs's design of the book, but I suppose that it will do. Certainly Crawford's pictures are excellent.

BALTIMORE, SEPTEMBER 19, 1946.

I got back to Baltimore this afternoon after two days in New York. I went there on September 17 to attend a Knopf board meeting. The business before it was a proposal to buy a house near Hartsdale, New York, and move the office there. This house was formerly the country home of Paul Warburg.[1] Of late it has been occupied by an apartment house. The price asked is $80,000. I am full of doubts about the move, but inasmuch as Alfred Knopf is hot for it, I voted for it. After all, in a business so personal as his I think his desires should be followed whenever possible. He needs more space in New York, but rents are so high that if he finds it it will increase his operating costs by $25,000 a year. It will probably cost him $20,000 to move into the new place and make it fit for his business, but in the long run his expenses will be less than they are now in New York. He says that all of his principal executives are willing to follow him into the country. Many of his clerks, of course, will probably quit, but that will be an advantage. He realizes himself that there are now too many Jews in his office. Once he gets to Westchester county he should be able to find supplies of labor of a more desirable sort. The Warburg building, a stone house of twenty-five or thirty rooms, is not actually in Hartsdale, but about two miles in the country. It is surrounded by five acres of ground. Getting to it from Knopf's house at Purchase will be quite easy. Blanche, of course, is bitterly opposed to the move, and I don't blame her, for if she maintains her office she'll have to go out to Westchester every day.[2]

1 Paul Warburg (1868–1932), German-born banker, noted for warning of disaster by wild stock-market speculation seven months before the October 1929 panic.
2 Nothing ever came of this idea, and the company continued to operate from its offices in New York City.

Samuel Knox has resigned from the Knopf board. He is really very ill, and probably won't last much longer. Alfred is going to California in October to try to induce his sister Sophia and her husband to consent to a reorganization plan that will wipe out the accumulated deficit on the preferred stock and convert the stock to one class common. I am not too sure that he can get their consent to this. If he does, then he will have three-fourths of the stockholders with him, and under the New York law that will be sufficient to put the plan through. Under that law Knox, who is sure to dissent, will have two recourses. On the one hand, he can silence his objections and come in. On the other hand, he can demand that the company buy his stock at a price to be fixed by appraisers. These appraisers will be appointed by the court, and may be trusted to deal with him realistically.

BALTIMORE, OCTOBER 30, 1946.

Today I retired my old Bible, bought in 1904. During the writing of the two Treatise books I put it to very heavy use, and it is now in tatters, with the binding and many of the leaves loose and some of the leaves torn. It has served me for more than forty years, and I retire it with some regret. Its original cost, I believe, was 50¢. Today I dropped into the Methodist bookstore in Charles street and bought another Bible of substantially the same print and binding. The price was $1.50. Even God, it appears, begins to profiteer.

BALTIMORE, NOVEMBER 3, 1946.

August and I put in the morning cleaning up the yard. There was very little to do. Most of the leaves have now come down and are disposed of. The morning glories on the stable are still blooming. A few of the flowers are of full size, but most have shrunk to that of the petunias. Despite their smallness, they are extraordinarily beautiful, for the colors seem to improve as they shrink.

The petunias have long since given up the fight, though the leaves of most of them are still green. The coleus have faded in color and grown tall and rangy. All of the beautiful lower leaves are gone, and those that remain are small and dull. These coleus were beautiful all Summer and even into October—in fact, it was one of the most successful seasons in the yard that we have ever had. The petunias, while they lasted, were really magnificent, and the morning glories were gorgeous. I planted some scarlet sage and it appeared to be growing well, but so far there has been only one flower. It is a bright orange red in color, and is directly outside the kitchen door.

BALTIMORE, NOVEMBER 4, 1946.

Today I turned over to Mrs. Lohrfinck nearly 6,000 words of Supplement II. It comes to the end of the verb section of Chapter IX. The book has been going badly, but of late I have done better with it and my hopes of finishing it by next Spring are reviving. I started out planning to include in it revisions and extensions of Chapters VII to XI of "The American Language" and also Appendix I, but begin to fear that so much manuscript will be accumulated by the time I get to the end of Chapter XI that I'll have to leave out the Appendix altogether. I had in mind, in a second appendix, to devote sections on the sign language, children's language and other such things, but they will probably have to be abandoned altogether.[1]

BALTIMORE, NOVEMBER 10, 1946.

The weather has been warm for the past week, and as a result the yard is still more or less green, though most of the leaves have fallen. The daffodils under the pear-tree have begun to come up. They usually do at this season. They do not seem to be damaged by frost, and by New Year they begin to flourish in earnest. August and I have gathered a double handful of morning-glory seeds, and more are ripening. There were plenty of blossoms on the vines during the past week—one day, about twenty. They were small but they were lovely, with colors not seen during the Summer.

Last night the Saturday Night Club played the Brahms Sextette in B flat, Opus 18, Schubert's Unfinished Symphony, and the first move-

---

1 In the preface to Supplement II (p. v), Mencken wrote: "I had hoped also to give a little space to the subject of Chapter XII, to wit, the future of American English, and to present some new matter about the non-English languages dealt with in the Appendix. Yet more, I had hoped to take up in a second Appendix certain themes not discussed at all in the fourth edition—for example, the language of gesture, that of children, the names of political parties, cattle brands, animal calls, and so on. But my notes turn out to be so enormous that I have been forced to close the present volume with Chapter XI, lest it grow to an impossible bulk."

ment of Beethoven's Third—nothing else, not even a waltz. What an evening! Present: Hemberger,[1] Cheslock, Moffett, Newcomer, Waite (the new cellist), Strube,[2] Dorman and me, with August as the only listener. Arnold Rich, who has had virus pneumonia, is still laid up. Moffett, who is beyond seventy, looked a bit tired. He had had an orchestra rehearsal in [the] morning, a concert in the afternoon, and the club at night. Today he has another orchestra rehearsal in the morning and a concert of the Baltimore Symphony tonight.

BALTIMORE, NOVEMBER 13, 1946.

I had a note from Gertie this morning saying that she has been ill for three days with vertigo and nausea. She is still in the country and I called her up at once. It took half an hour to get her by telephone. She then told me that she was feeling much better. Her trouble is that she works too hard on her little farm. She tries to carry on operations that would burden two or three people, and so she is in a state of chronic exhaustion. She forgets constantly that she'll be 60 years old on November 17th.

August and I are planning to bring her back to Baltimore as soon as possible. She'll be much safer in her apartment, and I'll be able to get Ben Baker to give her a looking over. My guess is that her blood pressure is rising, and that heavy physical work with it floors her. She turns out early in the morning and is busy all day. To be sure, she takes a nap in the afternoon and goes to bed early, but the amount of energy she expends is too much. Moreover, she has been worrying about the state of her old dog, Anastasia. Anastasia is now more than twelve years old, and has become sorely crippled by asthma, tumors and other afflictions. I am in hopes that Gertie will take her to a veterinarian and have her put to death.

---

1 Theodore Hemberger (1871–1956) was the first professional musician to become a member of the Saturday Night Club. He had previously been conductor of the Scranton (Pa.) Symphony Orchestra but came to Baltimore to assume the leadership of the Germania Männerchor. He was also a violin instructor at the Peabody Conservatory of Music.
2 Gustav Strube (1867–1953) also taught at the Peabody Conservatory and was the first conductor of the Baltimore Symphony Orchestra.

BALTIMORE, NOVEMBER 19, 1946.

Nine-tenths of the people who call me by telephone I don't want to talk to, and three-fourths of the people I have to take to lunch I don't want to see.

BALTIMORE, DECEMBER 15, 1946.

With Paul Patterson I went to Washington yesterday afternoon for the dinner of the Gridiron Club. As usual, it was very tiresome. Some of the sketches were long, and very few of them were amusing. Paul and I began touring the suites where preliminary refreshments were on tap at 6 p.m., and visited them again after the dinner was over. I had a drink either in my hand or in front of me from 6 o'clock until 3.15, but I managed somehow to keep sober, and turned out at the Statler Hotel at 11.15 this morning feeling reasonably lively. The Statler is probably the worst hotel on earth, though one of the most pretentious. It is full of gadgets marked "For Your Protection"—bags to hold drinking-glasses, paper tapes over the toilet bowls, etc.—but its comforts are very meagre. I had a small room with a couch bed, and the maid forgot to make it. I disliked fetching her at 3.30 a.m., so I made it myself—a very crude job. But the drinks I had aboard made me sleep very well.

When I saw the diagram of the banquet-hall I was considerably upset, for my place was at the elevated guest-table two places from Truman on the one side and three from the Duke of Windsor on the other. At first glance I thought the boys were out to have some fun with me, but when I protested they said they were not. Pete Brandt, the president of the club, thus explained it: "We always have justices of the Supreme Court, Senators, Governors, ambassadors and so on at the high table: this time we thought we ought to have one of our own people, and we chose you." At my left was the British ambassador and at my right the Philippine ambassador, Joaquin Miguel Elizalde. Beyond the former was some other ambassador, and then came Truman. Beyond the Filipino came Charlie Ross, Truman's confidential secretary, and beyond Charlie, the Duke, with Alf Landon at the Duke's right. I got on well enough with the British ambassador, but spent most of the evening palavering with the Filipino, who used to be the Philippine delegate in Congress and turned out to be an old customer of mine. The British ambassador asked me to explain the skits, but I advised him to sit through them without trying to understand them. Some of them were difficult even to me. But the music was very good, and during one of the intermissions W. F. H. Santelmann, leader of the Marine Band, played an arrangement of the Missouri Waltz, apparently his own, that was ingenious and excellent.

There is a sort of seventh-inning stretch at about 10 o'clock, and the guests all rush for the pissoirs. When I got to the nearest I found dignitaries lined up before each stall, with the Duke at the end of one line. Patterson, who was with me, was enchanted by this spectacle, and whooped it up as a proof of the Duke's democratic spirit. But what else could he do? The brethren ahead of him had full bladders and could not give him place. I was disinclined to get into line myself, so I started out to find another pissoir. At the door I met Felix Frankfurter, who suggested that we try the cubicles opposite the stalls. It cost five cents to get into one, but the money was well spent. When I left mine I held the door open and let some other guest in on my nickel. Frankfurter, as usual, was very attentive. In the middle of the dinner he came down the line from his place, put one arm about the neck of the British ambassador and the other about mine, and urged us to become friends. When he departed the ambassador told me that Frankfurter was the first man he met on his first visit to the United States, years ago. The ambassador also told me he had been warned that I was anti-English. I replied that this was a gross calumny, circulated by Japs. We got on very well, and I invited him to come to Baltimore some day for lunch at the Maryland Club.

The Gridiron dinners in themselves are horrible bores, but I like to go to them to meet old friends. At the booze parties before and afterward I met scores this time, ranging from Jack Knight[1] to Gene Buck[2] and from Vandenberg to Dutch Schultz.[3] All these brethren were more

1 John S. Knight (1894–1981), newspaper publisher, owner of various papers throughout his long career.
2 Eugene Buck (1885–1957), producer, song writer, librettist for many musical comedies.
3 It is uncertain whom Mencken is referring to here. "Dutch Schultz" was the *nom de guerre* of Arthur Flegenheimer (1902–1935), a notorious gangster of the Prohibition era, but, even leaving all other considerations aside, the fact that he was slain by a rival mob in 1935 rules him out here. There is in the Mencken correspondence at the New York Public Library an envelope bearing the name of Arthur L. Schultz, apparently on the staff of the Topeka (Kansas) *State Journal*, but its contents—a

or less in liquor, and hence very amiable. My neighbor, Elizalde, told me that his brother had been beheaded by the Japs, but he did not seem to be much perturbed by it.

The speech was made by Bricker of Ohio, Tom Dewey's running-mate in 1940. It began well enough, but soon deteriorated to platitudes. Truman's reply was even worse.

1955 New Year's greeting card and a typewritten note of thanks from Mrs. Lohr-finck—can hardly be said to establish beyond all doubt that he is the person of whom Mencken is speaking.

1947

Last Tuesday, January 14, I went to Wilmington, Del., to spend the night with Alfred and Marcella du Pont. Joe Hergesheimer and his wife Dorothy were there, and also Huntington Cairns. I met Cairns on the train going up to Wilmington and had a chance to discuss poor Joe's affairs. Cairns is one of the members of a committee managing a fund set up by one of the Mellon ladies, lately deceased. This fund is very rich. Mrs. Mellon, during her lifetime, devoted it to publishing books by Jung and other Freudian followers. She was interested in such subjects, and her surviving husband is still carrying out her wishes. Cairns, however, is full of hopes that he'll be able to divert Mellon to more useful publications. The fund does not actually publish; it simply stakes books that might not be published otherwise.[1]

I made some propaganda at once for Allen Walker Read's "Dictionary of Briticisms." Cairns professed to be greatly interested and promised to tackle Mellon. The Read book certainly should be published, but equally certainly no commercial publisher could afford to undertake it. It will probably run to three volumes folio. I have seen specimens of it and have a high opinion of it.[2]

---

1 The "fund" to which Mencken refers here is the Bollingen Foundation. It was established by Mary Mellon (1904–1946), and its original purpose was indeed to publish an English translation of the collected works of the Swiss psychologist Carl Gustav Jung. After her tragically early death as the result of a riding accident, her husband, Paul Mellon, carried on the work of the foundation and greatly expanded its scope. There is a detailed account of its founding and operations in William McGuire, *Bollingen: An Adventure in Collecting the Past* (Princeton, N. J.: Princeton University Press, 1982).

2 Read's "Dictionary of Briticisms" was apparently never published.

Cairns also told me that the Mellon he works with has been known to pay pensions to worthy artists who have got into difficulties. I suggested at once that Joe Hergesheimer would be a suitable candidate and Cairns agreed. Whether or not anything will come of it remains to be seen.[1] Joe told me Wednesday morning, when a chance offered for a confidential talk, that his financial situation was very distressing. Sometime ago he actually had to dip into Dorothy's heritage to keep the house at Stone Harbor going. He said that he has since repaid this loan, but that he fears he may have to make another. If Mellon could be induced to pay him a few thousand dollars a year it would relieve his anxieties and ease his last years. He looked wretched, and I am thoroughly convinced that he hasn't a long while to live. He told me that his heart often gives out as he is walking along the street and that he loses consciousness. This I doubt. He often exaggerates his physical state. Ben Baker has lately told me that his heart is in fair condition, but that his arterio-sclerosis has played the devil with his brain. This explains the fact that he is quite unable to work. I tried to encourage him by proposing that he adopt a new plan—that is, to write out his own ideas casually as if talking them, and then return to them later and polish them. I am pretty sure that he can't do this, but nevertheless it may entertain him and convince him that he is recovering.

I returned to Baltimore on Wednesday. On Thursday, January 16, I spent the whole afternoon at the *Sun* office in consultation with the lawyers preparing the *Sun's* defense in its trial for contempt of court.[2] The next day (Friday) I had to be in Court at 10 o'clock, but it was

1 McGuire, in the work cited above, says (p. 207): "In 1947, H. L. Mencken appealed to Cairns for aid to the novelist Joseph Hergesheimer, who was living in poverty in Stone Harbor, N.J. The Foundation awarded Hergesheimer a fellowship (nominally, for writing his autobiography) that supported him until his death in 1954."

2 On June 9, 1947, Mencken wrote to his old friend, Supreme Court Justice Felix Frankfurter: "In January of this year, the *Sun* was cited for contempt because it had printed a statement by the police that a boy accused of a crime was technically not guilty, and that they would not press his prosecution. This was a fact, and the opinion of the police was confirmed by the State's Attorney's office. Nevertheless, the outraged judge, Conwell Smith, cited the *Sun* and there was a trial. Fortunately, it was before Judge Emory H. Niles, who promptly acquitted the *Sun*, and also the police, who were likewise charged. I was a witness in the case, and testified regarding the history of the rule. Judge Niles's acquittal rather disappointed me, for I was eager to get the question involved before the Court of Appeals, and to go from there, if necessary, to your own court. I still believe that my contention that a newspaper should not be punished for an act of an officer of the court is a sound one." See *The New Mencken Letters*, ed. Carl Bode (New York: Dial Press, 1977), p. 576.

nearly 2 o'clock when my own turn came to testify. By that time I was in a state of collapse, for I had developed an acute infection on my return from Wilmington and it was making rapid progress. I left the court-room before the lawyers presented their arguments and went to Ben Baker's office. He found that I was running a small temperature and ordered me to go home and go to bed. He prescribed the new penicillin for oral administration. It is given with calcium gluconate and is not digested in the stomach. He also gave me codeine to relieve my cough. The next morning I was still pretty sick, but in the course of the day the penicillin got in its work and by nightfall I was beginning to feel very much better. Yesterday (Sunday) I continued to make progress and this morning I am almost normal. This was certainly a remarkably quick cure of a really violent infection. Baker told me that the penicillin would have no efficacy against the short-lived virus infection that apparently lay underneath, but that he believed it would prevent the usual secondary infections. Apparently it has done so. It is now Monday morning and I feel reasonably well—in fact, I am planning to go to the *Sun* board meeting at noon today. I have no cough, there is no discharge from the nose, and my voice is recovering its resonance. On Saturday I was flowing from the eyes, nose and mouth, there was a racking and very painful cough, and I could hardly speak.

It always distresses me to meet Joe Hergesheimer. There was a time when a session with him was an enormous stimulant, but his troubles have become so hopeless that seeing him fills me with despair. His poor wife is in a dreadful state of distress. She not only sees him deteriorating steadily; she is also alarmed by their financial position. Joe told me that if he became convinced that he could never recover he would commit suicide, and so save Dorothy from an unnecessary and perhaps ruinous expense. This, however, is probably mere talk. He has been threatening suicide for a long while. Dorothy herself is anything but well. She holds up bravely, but her hip infection is obviously painful and taking care of the house is a heavy burden. They are forced to ask visitors to Stone Harbor in sheer desperation. The loneliness of life there would be unendurable without an occasional break.

BALTIMORE, FEBRUARY 17, 1947.

The other day I dropped into the *Sun* office and found Paul Patterson engaged in the board room with at least sixteen or eighteen men. I gathered instantly that radio was the theme, and so departed. The next day he told me that the meeting was a sort of congress of radio operators in Philadelphia, Baltimore and Washington, and that its object was to pool their manifold interests and iron out their various differences. Apparently the session was long and vexatious, for he was in bad humor and presently told me that he wished he had courage enough to scrap all the radio enterprises of the *Sun*. I offered at once to introduce a resolution in the board instructing him to do so, but as usual he hesitated. Some of these days I may do it without his permission, and see what happens. My guess is that the resolution will be defeated, with only one vote in its favor, but I am sure that in the long run something of the sort will prevail.

I am thoroughly convinced that monkeying with the radio is dangerous to the *Sun*, and certain to do heavy damage. There is absolutely no reason why the paper should take any interest in such enterprises. It has plenty to do as a newspaper, and is making an enormous amount of money. Entering the radio business will simply mean that the attention of all the principal executives will be diverted from their proper work and the paper will suffer.

I have been making various attempts to put down this radio craze and I have had some success, but so far there has been no overt action. When, in January, I proposed to the board that the new building be built in sections, one of my chief arguments was that we face an indefinite and probably large expenditure for radio, and might easily exhaust our surplus and become short of money. Everybody agreed to this last, but the remedy suggested was simply to borrow. I am against borrowing if it is at all possible to avoid it, and shall oppose vigorously every movement in that direction. Under cover of the discussion, I managed to get through a resolution limiting the administration's expenditures on radio to $500,000. Patterson and Schmick are instructed, in case it appears likely that any expenditure beyond that amount will be necessary, to go to the board for specific instructions. This will give me a chance to fight the fight all over again.

The enormous profits built up last year were, of course, almost accidental. They came, first, from the great advertising boom that followed the easing of the paper supply, and, secondly, from the even greater reduction in Federal taxes. This year will probably also see heavy profits, but I am not at all sure about next year. As things stand, the surplus and these new profits taken together will probably suffice to pay for the new building and its equipment. But I'd certainly tremble to go into paying for them with a vague and probably enormous contingent expense for radio hanging overhead. My belief is that radio does harm to newspapers, and that its reputed benefits are all imaginary. The possible profits are always greatly overestimated by those who itch to take to the air.

In the case of the *Sun* I believe that the enthusiasm of Schmick, and to some extent even that of Patterson, is due to the fact that the kind of newspaper Babbitts they ordinarily associate with are all in radio and all disposed to boast of it. It pleases such nonentities to have intimate relations with crooners and other such swine.

What is needed in the *Sun* is not a widening of interests, but a concentration of energy on the problems in hand. Patterson told me only the other day that he thought Schmick was slipping. That he himself is slipping has only been too manifest for five years past. The enormous difficulties of building and equipping the new building will keep both of them jumping for five years to come.[1] They will have no time or energy to monkey with radio. The same goes for Kavanaugh. He has too many jobs as it is, and is certainly not in the best of health. Labor relations alone will keep him jumping.

The persons told off in the office to deal with the projected radio enterprise are all eighth-raters. The chief of them is the reporter who was sent to Japan after the surrender of the Japs and made himself memorable by sending home the worst correspondence received by the *Sun* during the whole war. Swanson is already wasting too much of his time on radio business. I have notified all hands, not once but dozens of times, that I am irrevocably against this folly, and shall oppose it without ceasing.

BALTIMORE, MARCH 12, 1947.

I had an appointment with Alan C. Woods this morning for an examination of my eyes at the Wilmer Clinic, but when I got to the

---

1 The *Sun's* building at Charles and Baltimore streets, erected after the Great Fire of 1904, had long since become overcrowded and inadequate, and in 1946 the board of directors authorized the construction of a new plant. After some delays, a site on North Calvert Street—the present location—was decided upon. It was completed and occupied in 1951. Many of the entries in Mencken's diary at this time, not included in the present selection, deal in the most meticulous detail with the financing and construction of the new building, and with some of the technical problems involved in moving equipment from the old plant to the new one while continuing to get out the papers on a day-to-day basis.

Johns Hopkins his secretary told me that he was laid up with the flu.
My eyes were then examined by his resident, McPherson—a very bright
and pleasant young man. McPherson found that they were in relatively good condition and that there was no need to change my glasses.
He said that he could find no sign of glaucoma, and that the sclerotic
manifestations in my right eye were no worse than when Alan Woods
examined them. This was in January, 1945.

From the Wilmer Clinic I went to the Marburg to pay a visit to
Edward L. Palmer, the architect, who has been laid up for two weeks.
He had a coronary attack while driving down to Gibson Island with
his wife, and she took him to the hospital in an ambulance. The attack
was not very severe and he began to recover at once. I expected to find
him in excellent condition and ready to leave. Unhappily, I found his
nurse looking grave, and she presently took me aside and told me that
he had had a cerebral accident last night. She told me that I could see
him, but warned me that he would be somewhat confused in mind. I
found him looking very well, but plainly not quite aware of what was
going on. He recognized me instantly, but he had practically nothing
to say and I cleared out in a few moments.

I had lunch at the Maryland Club with Paul Patterson, and told
him of all this. He was naturally much distressed, for he and Palmer
are old friends, and moreover Palmer is in charge of the whole design
and building of the new *Sun* building. He has served the *Sun* as architect for many years, and he is familiar with all of its mechanical
problems. Happily, most of them have now been solved, and the actual erection of the new building and the installation of its equipment
may be carried on by others.

The combination of coronary disease and apoplexy is surely not
reassuring. Palmer is over 70 years old, and it is highly improbable
that he'll ever make a full recovery—indeed, the chances seem to me
to be very slight that he'll recover at all.

Patterson's reaction to the bad news was characteristic. He drank
two rather stiff whiskey-sours at lunch. He and I encountered Jim
Fenhagen in the Club and the three of us lunched together. When the
meal was over Patterson was already fuddled and I did not go to the
office with him.

BALTIMORE, MARCH 31, 1947.

I am so superstitious that I hesitate to set it down, but it is a fact that my health has been better during the past year than for four or five years preceding. Age, of course, creeps up on me, and my old energy is much diminished. After three hours at my desk I must stop for rest, and it is seldom that I can endure more than two three-hour sessions in a day. Indeed, there are days when even two hours exhaust me, and occasional days when one is enough, or I can't work at all. But these last are not many, and I usually get in a fair amount of work, seven days a week. The gastritis that used to badger me has disappeared altogether, and sometimes I go through a whole month without a single dose of bicarbonate of soda. My old head infection, unhappily, goes on, though only intermittently. Last Summer it got so bad that I went to the Johns Hopkins and took a 10-day course of penicillin. There was no apparent immediate benefit, but when the Autumn came on I was more comfortable than usual. A month or so ago the infection resumed, and I am still somewhat hoarse from the drip into the larynx, but there has been little other discomfort. I have a spell of faintness now and then, but not often. An hour on my office couch always restores me. Discomfort in the heart region is infrequent. Ben Baker believes that it has nothing to do with the heart, but is caused by a distended stomach. He has given me an anti-spasmodic tablet that seems to relieve it.

I have lost three teeth since childhood, and there are indications that I may soon lose a fourth. I am going to Bland, the dentist, tomorrow to have an inlay set into an incisor tooth that has been eroding for years, and several others begin to show the same wear. But the teeth remaining, though all those save the front ones have inlays, hold up pretty well, and there is seldom any pain in them.

BALTIMORE, MAY 13, 1947.

I finished the text of Supplement II to "The American Language" last night. The Preface remains, and also a section on Negro dialect, passed over along the way. Also, I must revise the whole, read the proofs, and make the two long indexes.

BALTIMORE, JULY 27, 1947.

Since finishing the revision of my second supplement to "The American Language," now nearly a month ago, I have been lying fallow. I came out of the job feeling very tired, and have since recovered only partly. There have been frequent symptoms of arterial disturbances—flashes of light before the eyes, a full feeling in the head, a dull ache in the occipital region, a numbness of the lips, and so on. The weather, up to today, has been generally cool and stimulating, and I have slept fairly well and eaten heartily, but the impulse to write has been in abeyance, and I have occupied myself by filing letters, putting together a couple of articles (one of them was already written and needed only editing) for *American Speech*, and tackling other such chores. One Sunday August and I spent most of the day cleaning up the kitchen after the plumbers and painters who had rebuilt it. Hester and Emma went on holiday July 1—Hester for three weeks and Emma for the whole month—and August and I have had the house to ourselves. I have gone out for nearly all my lunches, but we have got most of our dinners and all of our breakfasts for ourselves. Whether or not I'll be able to get back to work before hay-fever comes on remains to be seen. Today is hot and sticky, but if the temperature and humidity drop during the coming week I may be able to resume my typewriter. I have enough projects in mind to keep a healthy man busy for four or five years. I often wonder whether I'll go that long, and when my discomforts are on me I doubt it. My doctor, Benjamin M. Baker, is on holiday, but I hope to see him soon after he returns, August 1. Meanwhile, I have been more or less busy with Richard F. Cleveland and John T. Kenny,[1] planning my resignation of the trusteeship of my mother's estate and the transfer of all its business to the Safe Deposit & Trust Company. I hope this can be effected without delay. What I most fear is that I may become disabled, and that managing the estate may thus present serious difficulties.

1 Richard F. Cleveland (1897–1974), son of President Grover Cleveland, was a member of the Baltimore law firm of Semmes, Bowen & Semmes. John T. Kenny was an officer of the Safe Deposit & Trust Company.

BALTIMORE, JULY 30, 1947.

I awoke this morning in a considerable state of confusion. It was impossible for me to write a line on the typewriter without striking wrong keys and making blunders in spelling, and for [a] while I could scarcely write by hand or sign my name. In talking, too, I found it necessary to grope for words. This has been gradually passing off, but I still find typewriting difficult.[1] It is a warm, humid day.

BALTIMORE, AUGUST 13, 1947.

I saw Dr. Baker on August 6. He told that what probably fetched me was a small embolus. It must have been somewhere near the speech center, for my speech was affected for a week afterward; in fact, it is still slightly affected. I have to frame a sentence somewhat carefully, and now and then I hesitate for a word. For some days it was quite impossible for me to write by hand. The letters simply jumbled, and I could hardly sign my name. Typewriting was just as difficult; in fact, is is still difficult, and I must write very slowly. Baker found that my heart was in pretty good condition. There was no enlargement, and no other disquieting sign. Nor could he find any neurological symptoms. My blood pressure was 160—not any higher than it was a year ago.

I have had a very unpleasant fortnight. The weather has been hot and humid and the first signs of hay fever have been showing. Unable to do any writing, I have put in my time selecting and editing material for the "Mencken Omnibus" that Knopf proposes to get out. It is a somewhat tedious job. I am not reading all my old stuff, but I am trying to look through it. How much there is altogether I don't know, but certainly there are millions of words. Out of this vast mass I am to select about 350,000.

BALTIMORE, AUGUST 23, 1947.

I am gradually recovering my capacity to write, but only gradually. I can now sign my name in something resembling its old form

---

1 He had had a slight stroke—or one perhaps not so slight. The typing of this and the succeeding entries is strewn with errors.

and make fewer errors in other writing by hand. But my typewriting is still slow and pained, and I strike many wrong keys. It is still impossible for me to tackle the pieces that I have promised to the *New Yorker,* but I begin to believe that I may be able to do so by the middle of September. All this has been a dreadful experience. It is hard for a man as active as I am to be disabled.

I have put in my time preparing copy for the Mencken Omnibus that Knopf is planning. I have got out a lot of stuff from the first four *Prejudices* books, and some from my early *Smart Set* book reviews. Most of it has needed a good deal of revision. It was full of references to the affairs of the time, some of them now almost unintelligible. But after cleaning them out, I find myself with [a] good deal of printable stuff. I shall pile it up without plan, and then make my selections. It is probable that a great deal will be left over. If the Omnibus sells well it will not be wasted, for we can make a second volume of it. But I hear that the publishing business is in a dreadful state, and both the "Omnibus" and the second supplement of "The American Language" may run aground.

The proofs of the second supplement have begun to run, and I have finished reading Galley 51. As soon as Galley 100 is reached the Plimpton Press will begin to make up, and I'll be able to begin on the two long indexes.

BALTIMORE, OCTOBER 13, 1947.

I have felt so wretched of late that work has been very difficult. Following on hay-fever came an itching which kept me scratching, and then followed a malaise that was almost disabling. It felt like that of influenza and was accompanied for several days by pains in the legs. Maybe I actually had an infection. If so, it seems to be passing off, though I still feel tired and out of sorts.

I have put in my time arranging my files and other records, reading proof on Supplement II to "The American Language," and getting together material for the proposed omnibus volume of my early writings, now out of print. The latter has been more or less amusing, but also somewhat tedious. Mrs. Lohrfinck has already copied 300,000 or 400,000 words, and I'll probably have 1,000,000 before I settle down to make my selections. I want to call the book "A Mencken Chrestomathy," but Knopf rather bucks at chrestomathy. However, I think it is good, if only because of its strangeness, and I hope to convert him. Most of the stuff will come from the six "Prejudices," "Notes on Democracy," "In Defense of Women," "A Book of Burlesques," etc., but I have also dug out a lot from magazine and newspaper files, never before printed in books. Some of it, not read for years, strikes me as pretty fair.

There is an express strike in New York, and as a result the parcel post is swamped. Packages of proofs shipped to me on September 25 and 26 and October 7 are not yet here. Two of them contain page proofs, so that making the two indexes is greatly impeded. Nevertheless I have received and got through pp. 70–149 of the page proofs. I am doing the index of names myself, but in the case of the words and phrases I am simply marking the extra proofs and letting Mrs. Lohrfinck make the cards. It is a laborious job, and we'll probably be at it until Christmas. When the book will be ready I don't know. It is running longer than I thought, and Knopf will probably have to charge $10 for it. All book prices have nearly doubled since 1940.

BALTIMORE, OCTOBER 23, 1947.

On Tuesday, October 21, I went down to Stone Harbor to visit Joe Hergesheimer and Dorothy. I met Marcella du Pont at Wilmington and we drove down in her car. It was an extremely beautiful day, and I enjoyed the trip very much. Both Joe and Dorothy seemed to be in good spirits and reasonably good health. Joe told me that he has finished 30,000 words of his autobiography, but he did not offer to show me the manuscript. At this rate it will take him something on the order of ten years to complete the 100,000 words that he plans. I gathered from his talk that the book is autobiographical only incidentally. In the main it is a discussion of his fundamental philosophical ideas. Inasmuch as he knows nothing about philosophy, my guess is that the thing will make very dull reading. He told me that writing it by hand had begun to fatigue him, and that he had thought of turning to the typewriter.

On Wednesday Carl McCardell, who is a member of the staff of the Philadelphia *Bulletin*, came down for lunch. He turned out to be an extremely pleasant fellow, and I was delighted to see him. He has lately been in Europe for the *Bulletin*, and among other things called on Max Beerbohm[1] at Rapallo. Ezra Pound told me that Beerbohm lived upstairs a garage and that his apartment is so noisy that life in it is almost unendurable. McCardell said that this is inaccurate. Beerbohm's place, he said, is actually a pleasant villa, with trees around it, and so far from the main highway that automobiles can't be heard at all. Whether Pound's statement was a deliberate lie or simply an evidence of his insanity I don't know.

McCardell appeared at lunch alone, but when it was over his wife suddenly popped up. Why he had not brought her I don't know. She turned out to be a very goodlooking and pleasant woman. The episode recalled a day in December, 1925 when Dreiser came to Hollins street on a bitter cold day, and I had not discovered until he had been sitting an hour that Helen, later his wife, was parked in a Ford up the street. I rushed out and insisted on bringing her to the fire. How Mrs. McCardell occupied herself while her husband was lunching with us I don't know.

BALTIMORE, OCTOBER 30, 1947.

I went out to Paul Patterson's house in Guilford this afternoon to see the first broadcasting of the *Sun*'s television equipment. The subject was two races at Pimlico. It seemed to me to be a very poor show. The pictures danced all over the little screen, there were frequent breaks, the sound was accompanied until near the end by deafening static, and both the photography and the patter were badly managed. Altogether, I'd not give ten cents for an hour of such entertainment, even if it showed a massacre. Patterson, as usual, ran the show in all its details. Every time the pictures began to move more or less smoothly he manipulated the dials and made them dance or fade out. Every few minutes he called up the studio in the O'Sullivan Building with inquiries or orders. When the show was over he called up to offer lavish praises. Apparently he thought it was swell.

The sponsor was the Hecht chain of department stores. It had models wearing new dresses, and three or four announcers, and was on the air at least a fourth of the time. One of the two cameras broke down and we got only long distance views of the two races. It was impossible

---

1 Max Beerbohm (1872–1956), English essayist, critic, and caricaturist, author, among other works, of *Zuleika Dobson* (1911).

to see the numbers on the horses, and in consequence much that went on was vague. The *Sun* announcer, a young man in the sports department, was poor at the job, and there were intervals of complete silence. Meanwhile, the loud-speaker at the track was vaguely audible. The man at its mike seemed to know his business. At all events, he kept up a steady flow of talk.

What this Noble Experiment is costing I can't quite figure out. Certainly the whole battery of radios—A.M., F.M. and television—will set us back nearly $1,000,000 before it is in working order, and producing any revenue. Schmick seems to fear that television can never pay for itself, but he argues that it is fine promotion for the papers. Among whom? I can imagine only very stupid people looking at it, at least in its present form. It is not even as well developed as the movie was in the days of "The Great Train Robbery."

BALTIMORE, DECEMBER 8, 1947.

I have been so hard pressed, of late, by the page-proofs and the two long indexes of Supplement II to "The American Language" that I have had no time or energy left for this diary. I awoke this morning feeling faint and with strange sensations around the heart. I managed to get through my morning dictation, but felt considerably used up afterward. But Sara's sisters, Ida McCulloch and Philippa McClellan, were in town, and I managed to take them to lunch at the Belvedere, along with Ida's son, Wick Stevenson. When I got home I felt wretched and had to stretch out for a little rest. Tomorrow morning I must go to New York for [the] Knopf board meeting tomorrow afternoon.

1948

BALTIMORE, JANUARY 19, 1948.

At noon today, for the first time in more than two years, I found myself in the happy position of having nothing on my desk—that is, nothing exigent. Save for a few galley-proofs of the List of Words and Phrases for my second supplement to "The American Language" no more remains to do on that book—and they will be off my hands in a week or so. Working hard yesterday and the day before, I finished another piece for *The New Yorker*. And I am pretty well up to date on my filing of papers and other such chores. Thus I feel singularly free and at ease, and my psychical state reflects itself in a feeling of physical well-being. This, of course, won't last. In a little while I'll probably be beset by one of the head infections that afflict me periodically, especially toward the end of Winter. Indeed, there is already a forerunner in a tenderness of the glands in the left side of my neck. But even that will be bearable, for the Winter is now half over, and August and I are planning to go to Florida toward the end of February. The anticipation of this holiday—my first in six years—bucks me up considerably. I only hope that I am not floored in the grand manner before we can shove off. Our tickets are bought and our hotel reservation is in hand.

BALTIMORE, JANUARY 25, 1948.

I have spent today, a Sunday, tearing up the notes accumulated for "Homo Sapiens," a book long since abandoned. Most of them were got together in the 1927–28 era, and consisted of my own notes, passages copied out of books, newspaper clippings, and pamphlets. Some of the pamphlets I decided to keep; the rest are going to the New York Public Library. The passages from books were mainly tracked down and copied for me by Sara. It was a somewhat melancholy business, interring the remains of a book on which I once set such high hopes. But I am now too old to tackle anything so laborious—and too many other enterprises remain.

BALTIMORE, FEBRUARY 22, 1948.

August and I are shoving off this evening for St. Petersburg, Fla., where we propose to stay two weeks. It is my first real holiday since I went to Germany before the war. I have been worn out by my heavy work on the second supplement to "The American Language," and need a real rest. I am having no mail forwarded, and hope to get in some undisturbed loafing. Approaching 68, I am no longer capable of the grind that used to delight me. When I get back I hope to write some pieces for the *New Yorker* and maybe a few for other magazines, and to put together the proposed omnibus of selections from my out-of-print books. Mrs. Lohrfinck has already copied about 500,000 words of material. The rest I should be able to get together in a few months. I want to call this book "A Mencken Chrestomathy," but Knopf is dubious about the name. I am not set on it and if he thinks of a better I'll be glad to join him. The *New Yorker* pieces will eventually make a book on the order of my "Days" books. When I'll have enough for it remains to be seen.[1]

BALTIMORE, MARCH 12, 1948.

August and I returned last Saturday morning from our two weeks in St. Petersburg, Florida. We had a pleasant time of it, and the visit was a considerable success. We left Baltimore in a sleet storm, but during all our time at St. Petersburg the weather was perfect. Since our return the weather has been cold, but we have borne the change

1 Several articles, similar in content and treatment to the *Days* books, appeared in *The New Yorker* during 1948, but they were not sufficient to make a book and they have never been reprinted elsewhere. A series of "Postscripts to the American Language" also appeared in the same magazine; Huntington Cairns included two of them, "Hell and Its Outskirts" and "The Vocabulary of the Drinking Chamber," in *H. L. Mencken: The American Scene.*

very well. The maximum temperature we encountered in Florida was 88 degrees. This morning it was 19 degrees at my bedroom window. That is a drop of nearly 70 degrees, but I nevertheless feel comfortable.

For the first four days of our stay in St. Petersburg we were quite alone. We spent our time walking around the streets, taking bus trips to the Keys along the Gulf coast, and loafing beautifully. Then, unhappily, a young reporter on the St. Petersburg *Independent* discovered us, and we began to be beset by callers. The ensuing telephone calls and notes were nuisances, but nevertheless we continued to be physically comfortable, and so we enjoyed ourselves.

At the end of the first week the St. Louis baseball brethren turned up in St. Petersburg for their Spring practice. The stadium where they operated was only a few blocks from our hotel. We went twice a day, and enjoyed the practice immensely. The feats of the brethren, indeed, were more spectacular than one could ever hope to see in an actual game.

On the last day of our stay I discovered that Grantland Rice[1] was also in town but, unfortunately, we missed a meeting.

We found a really good restaurant in St. Petersburg, and another in Tampa, which is only forty-five minutes away. A third, somewhat inferior to the other two, is in Bradenton, across Tampa Bay. This is a trip of 2½ hours. We made it in a converted yacht and enjoyed it very much. The weather was fair, and there was just enough wind blowing to give the yacht a gentle roll.

I did no work whatsoever at St. Petersburg—indeed, I read nothing save the local newspapers and the murder magazines. It was a pleasure to get away from my usual burden of mail. When we got home last Saturday morning I went to the branch Post Office at Pratt and Bentalou streets and fetched my collected mail home. This was before 10 o'clock in the morning. It took me until 8 at night to open, sort it and read it.

BALTIMORE, MARCH 21, 1948.

Edgar Kemler, who is at work on a book on me, has been sending me the final drafts of some of his chapters. They are written well enough, but they are full of small errors. I agreed with Kemler to

1 Grantland Rice (1880–1954), noted sportswriter and commentator.

correct him on points of fact, but made the provision that I should not attempt any criticism of his opinions. He is a young Harvard pink, and thus finds me somewhat mysterious, and even a little horrifying. Nevertheless, he has done an honest job. Unfortunately, he has dragged it out for so long a time that he begins to be weary of it himself. He put in some really heroic work on gathering the materials. I gave him permission to consult my clippings, books, manuscripts and other documents in the Pratt Library, and he spent a whole Summer abstracting them. The result was that he accumulated so much material that it began to confuse him. His book, I fear, will be a dull work, and I am in some doubt that he'll find a publisher for it.[1] Nevertheless, a copy of it will exist somewhere, and it may be useful in future. Kemler's capacity for error in detail really amazed me. He would certainly make a bad newspaper reporter.

BALTIMORE, MARCH 25, 1948.

I went to New York on March 23 to attend a meeting of the Knopf board of directors. Inasmuch as Knopf is still laid up at his home in Purchase with his broken leg, the members had to go to his house for the meeting. I met them at the Knopf office in Madison avenue, and we proceeded to Purchase in two automobiles. It was a rainy, dismal day, and hence the journey was far from exhilarating. Knopf's house in itself is dismal, and when we arrived there it seemed dark and foreboding. Blanche ordered a wood fire made, and after that things were better. The board meeting took only half an hour. When it was over the other directors, including Blanche, returned to New York. I stayed for dinner with Alfred. We dined, as usual, in a remote corner of his sitting-room, with only two candles to light the room. I sat on one of the two backless benches to his refectory table. Due to the fact that he is still on crutches, he had a chair pulled up for himself, but he did not offer one to me. The dinner, as usual, was excellent, though the first bottle of wine that we tackled turned out to be corked.

After dinner we sat gabbling for about three hours. Their son, Alfred Jr. (Pat), who has been living with his father, is about to move to New York. He simply can't stand the commuting, and I don't blame

1 Kemler's book, *The Irreverent Mr. Mencken*, was published in 1950 by Little, Brown.

him. In order to get to his desk at a reasonable hour in the morning, he has to leave at 7 a.m.

The directors' meeting developed the fact that the profits during the first three quarters of the 1947–48 fiscal year were about $32,000. This is not much, considering the fact that the business done was well over a million dollars. I believe that Knopf has cluttered up his office with too many functionaries. He told me that he had begun to think the same thing himself. How to get rid of them is a serious problem. One of his difficulties is that he has enmeshed himself with the Communist members of the Office-Workers Guild. When it was organized he was one of the first publishers to submit to it. In those days he was a New Dealer, and regarded his act as highly virtuous. He was soon disillusioned, and he has been unable so far to rectify his colossal blunder.

On the morning following the board meeting at his house I returned to New York. I took Blanche to lunch. Immediately after lunch we went back to the office in Madison avenue, where there was a press conference called by William Cole, the Knopf press-agent. I expected only a small attendance, but at least eighteen or twenty were present. The thing passed off well enough, but I assume that the pinks among the visitors will plaster me, as usual. This press conference, of course, was called to promote Supplement II. The first printing of the book runs a little short of 12,000. How many will be sold in advance of publication I don't know but the record yesterday, with half the country uncovered, was nearly 5,000. I have made a new contract with Knopf whereby the payments of royalties will be limited to $2,500 in any six months. This is now permitted by the Revenue Act. It will save me from such ruinous windfalls as hit me after Supplement I.

Nathan and I went to dinner at Lüchow's last night, and afterward we went to Number 21. We could find nobody there that we knew, so we proceeded to the Stork Club. There we encountered Bill Curley, one of the higher Hearst functionaries, and young David Hearst. They had their wives with them and we had a pleasant enough hour gabbling with them. I was in bed at the Algonquin by 12 o'clock.

BALTIMORE, APRIL 28, 1948.

I have received word today from Marianne Dieke, medical student in Leipzig, that the Mencken portraits in the law school of the University of Leipzig escaped destruction in the war. Likewise, the Ibsen collection that I sent to the library of the university after World War I is still intact.

This Marianne Dieke is the daughter of the artist[1] who made copies of the Mencken portraits for me sometime in the 20's. He is now dead. The daughter is studying medicine at Leipzig. I hear off and on both from her and her mother.

BALTIMORE, APRIL 30, 1948.

Blanche Knopf came to Baltimore yesterday to consult Dr. Alan C. Woods about her eyes. I took her to dinner last night, and squired her to Woods's office at the Johns Hopkins this morning. He found that her cataracts have so far advanced that the sight of her right eye is practically gone, and that the sight of the left one is about 40% of normal. She can read only with the aid of a large magnifying glass. Nevertheless, she shrinks from having the cataracts removed, and Woods told her that she could go on safely as things stand. The seeing apparatus of the eyes does not seem to be affected: there are only the clouded lenses. He said he believed that it would be wise to have the cataracts removed at once, as he has had done in his own case, but that it would do no damage to wait a while. She is to report to him again in about a year, or whenever her sight so far deteriorates that she can't read at all. Woods, ordinarily a forthright and even brusque fellow, was very gentle with her. He recited his own experience at length, and did not overlook the discomforts of the cataract operation and its sequelae. Blanche left him much relieved. She dreads the thought of being dependent on glasses, even contact lenses. I had her to lunch today and afterward took her to Dr. Benjamin M. Baker's office, for a general looking over. Her health seems to be excellent, and at Maria's restaurant last night she ate the heartiest dinner I have seen her get down in years.

She told me that the sale of Supplement II to date is 8,451. Supplement I, now three years old, has sold so far 25,225.

1 Max Dieke (d. 1935) was the German painter who made the copies of which Mencken speaks here. There is one of Otto Mencken (1644–1707), two of Lüder Mencken (1658–1726), and one of Johann Burkhard Mencken (1674–1732). These copies now hang in the Pratt Library's Mencken Room.

BALTIMORE, MAY 1, 1948.

I gave a dinner at the Maryland Club last night to Justice Felix Frankfurter, of the Supreme Court. Frankfurter is an old acquaintance and I got to know him pretty well at the time of the "Hatrack" affair in Boston in 1926. I suggested that he bring another guest and he nominated Lord Inverchapel, the retiring British ambassador, whom I had already met in Washington. The others present were Philip Perlman, an old *Sun* man, now Solicitor General in Washington; George T. Washington,[1] his chief assistant; Judge Robert France, of the Supreme Bench of Baltimore; Edwin F. A. Morgan, Owen Hitchins, of Cumberland, Hamilton Owens, and my brother August. We had a very pleasant evening and all of the diners got a little jingled, though no one was overcome.

Washington, who is a collateral descendant of the original George, told a curious story. Not long ago he was assigned to represent the Department of Justice at an international conference in Switzerland and asked the State Department to make him a hotel reservation in London, where he was to stop on the way. No answer. On the ship nearing England he wirelessed the same request to the embassy. No answer. When he reached London two representatives of the embassy met his train and told him that he had accommodations at Dorchester House, a very good hotel. He asked why there had been no answer to his wireless. After some hesitation the embassy brethren explained. When his message was received, he was not recognized, and there was doubt as to whether he was white or colored. So two reservations were made—one at Dorchester House in case he turned out to be white, and the other at some much inferior hotel in case he turned out to be a blackamoor.

Inverchapel told me that in his early days, when he was plain Archibald John Kerr Clark, he was a suitor to Lady Elizabeth Bowes-Lyon, who married the Duke of York in 1923 and is now Queen Elizabeth of England.[2] She gave him the air and in 1929 he married a Chilean woman. They were later divorced, but have remarried.

1 George T. Washington (1908–1971) was a judge of the U.S. Circuit Court of Appeals for the District of Columbia, and served on many government boards and commissions.

2 The Queen Elizabeth referred to here was the consort of King George VI and mother of the present Queen Elizabeth II.

The Maryland Club's bill for the dinner mentioned in this diary for May 1 is $161.67. This is more than $16 a head for a quite modest meal, with no more than a moderate amount of drinks. Even so, the club loses money on its dining-room and the profit on the bar barely makes it up. I'll give no more such parties until prices return—if they ever do—to the rule of reason.

At five o'clock yesterday morning August, who sleeps in the front of the house, was awakened by police at the door. I heard the noise vaguely, but assumed that he was leaving early for work out of town, and quickly fell asleep again. At seven there was more noise, and this time August called me. His news was dreadful indeed. Just before the first call Elsie Burley, the daughter of our old housekeeper, Hester Denby, had suddenly gone crazy and attacked her mother and her ten-year-old son with a knife. This was in their house at 1439 west Franklin street, only six blocks from Hollins street. Hester's screams brought the neighbors, and they called for the police, who sent Hester and the boy to the Franklin Square Hospital and started a search for Elsie, who had made off. As she fled, according to the neighbors, she exclaimed "Now for the boss!" This is what brought the police to our door the first time. They told August that they were hunting for Elsie all over West Baltimore, and warned him she would probably come to Hollins street. At seven o'clock she duly appeared on the front steps, barefooted and armed with two bottles, and when August looked out of his window called up that she was in trouble and wanted to see him. He telephoned to the police at once, and in a few minutes they appeared and took her away. Also, they gave him the shocking news that poor Hester had died immediately on reaching the hospital.

August and I put in almost all of yesterday on this appalling business. Elsie's older son and his father, both in the Army, were away at distant posts, and it was hard to find out just where they were. I finally located the son, Thomas, at Denver, Colo., but when I attempted to reach him by telephone the post spokesman told me that he could be summoned home only through the Red Cross in Baltimore (to prevent, I suppose, bogus summonses). The Red Cross ladies here were very polite, and the young man was soon started back to Baltimore by train, but it was not until this morning that his father was found on maneuvers in Tennessee. The father and Elsie, the Red Cross found, had been divorced, but of this I had known nothing. Nor had Hester told Emma Ball, our maid, and her associate in the house since 1935. August and I attended the police court hearing in the afternoon, and the police let me talk to Elsie. She is clearly completely insane. I asked her what had happened to her mother and she stared at me blankly. Apparently, she had no recollection at all of the murder. I finally fetched out of her the news that her ex-husband was stationed at a camp near Norfolk, Va., and it was through this information that the Red Cross found him. The boy is on a train bound East from Denver and should reach here tomorrow. When the father will turn up I don't know.

Elsie apparently had shown some signs of mental aberrations a day or two before she attacked her mother. On May 23rd she summoned firemen to put out a mysterious fire in their house. There was no suspicion at the time that this fire was incendiary, but now it seems that such was the case. One of the firemen was attacked by a dog in the house and the fire department demanded that the dog be isolated for ten days to make sure that he did not have rabies. I went to the house with the police and the dog was fetched out and turned over to the Society for the Prevention of Cruelty to Animals. It will keep the animal for ten days at its dog shelter and then report to the police.

I had not seen Elsie for thirteen years. Immediately after Sara's death, when I had to fire a maid, she came to Cathedral street to help her mother. She was then a slim and goodlooking woman. Today she is immensely fat. She fled the house barefooted and in very sloppy clothes.

The family situation is most unfortunate. Hester leaves a brother of 73, who is dying in Wilmington, Delaware, and another who is a hopeless cripple. There are also two sisters, Rosie, who lives in Baltimore, and Isabel who lives in Atlantic City. I went down to see Rosie this morning. She lives in a little alley, and is obviously very poor. Her crippled brother lives with her. She has taken charge of the boy, wounded by his mother. He is ten years old, and a very bright and handsome youngster. He was cut over the left eye and also in the back of the head, but the wounds are not serious. What caused Elsie's outbreak I simply can't imagine. She was apparently on the best of terms with her mother, and certainly her mother was devoted to her.

I had never been in their house in Franklin street before. It is a small house of two stories, and though very meagrely furnished, is quite neat. The kitchen, which was Hester's laboratory, is worthy of a much finer house. In it, I believe, she frequently made preserves which she sold to the Woman's Exchange. She was an extremely diligent woman, and during her fifteen years' service I had found no complaint against her. Her old mother, now 94 years old, is in Wilmington, along with the dying brother. I was away over the weekend. Elsie called up Saturday morning asking my brother's permission for her mother to go up to Wilmington over Saturday and Sunday. He gave it, but it now turns out that the trip was never made. Probably Elsie began to cut up on Saturday and the poor old woman was afraid to leave her.

BALTIMORE, MAY 29, 1948.

Poor Hester was buried from the Holland funeral parlor this morning. There were two clergymen at the service, and a young soprano sang some hymns very beautifully. Both preachers had to be heard, but nevertheless the ceremony lasted only a little over forty minutes. August and I went to it, but we did not proceed to the cemetery. The young grandson, who was attacked by his mother at the time Hester was killed, was present. He had got rid of his bandages. His aunt Rosie indulged herself in a few shrieks, but otherwise the service was very decorous. The rather small undertaking parlor was filled. I was told that there were no mere curiosity seekers present—that all of the mourners were actually friends. It appeared by the remarks of the clergy that Hester was a member of two churches. This seems incredible, but it is not uncommon among colored people. I had been unaware that she was pious at all.

BALTIMORE, JUNE 2, 1948.

Emma Ball, the maid, is settling down to her new job as housekeeper, and doing very well. Her cooking is already really excellent, and she seems to be determined to improve it. I see her giving hard study to a cook book in the kitchen.

Unfortunately, Emma belongs to the Afro-American race, and shows many of its psychological stigmata. When I handed her Hester's house key, she made various improbable excuses for not carrying it.

Last night she confessed to August and me that she hated to touch it. August therefore gave her his own key and took Hester's. She said that she had been unable to sleep for two whole nights after Hester's death, and managed to sleep on the third only by taking what she described as ammonia.

BALTIMORE, JULY 16, 1948.

I returned yesterday from the Democratic National Convention in Philadelphia.[1] With the air-cooling system cut off in my bedroom, I managed to get through the uproar without damage. Last night, the closing session ran until 3 a.m., but I came out of it not only unharmed but actually feeling fit. After it was over I went to the Ritz, where all of the men of the *Sunpaper* staffs presently gathered, and we had a very pleasant gabfest. Tony Muto, the newsreel man, joined us. I finally got to bed at 6 a.m. I was up at 2 p.m., and got home by 6. I was in bed again at 11.30 and slept until 9 o'clock this morning. In Philadelphia, of course, I lost some sleep and my meals were very irregular. Once I got lunch at 5 p.m. and once I got dinner at 10 p.m.

The flat was comfortable, despite the fact that the maid, who had been on holiday, did not show up until Saturday, after we had been in residence for two days. Patterson insisted on preparing breakfast for me, though I ate nothing but a bit of fruit, a piece of bread and a cup of coffee. After the first day he insisted on bringing me a glass of orange juice while I was shaving in the bathroom. Once he cooked some eggs for himself. They seemed to be edible, though I did not try them.

The convention was a show of almost incredible obscenity. Truman, when he arrived to accept his nomination, looked scared, despite his truculence. I sat only twenty feet from him with a clear view of him. Despite his braggadocio, it was plain that he was not sure of

1 Paul Patterson and his son Maclean had worked hard on Mencken to get him to resume his coverage of the national conventions, interrupted in 1944, and he finally broke down and agreed to go. He covered the Republican convention June 19–22, the Democratic one July 10–15, and that of Henry Wallace's Progressive party July 23–26 (see the following entry for July 26). All were held in Philadelphia.

himself. Old Alben Barkley,[1] a political hack of the most dismal sort, took the Vice-Presidential nomination without any apparent enthusiasm. When he and Truman appeared on the platform to accept, Truman had his wife and daughter with him. Barkley had only one daughter with him, though he has two. He looked sad to me. His wife died last Fall, and it was only too obvious that he was thinking of what she was missing. The Truman women and Barkley's daughter are all homely, and they did not stay on the platform long.

My work from the stand on the last night was very onerous, but I enjoyed it immensely—in fact, I always like to cover such stories. They involve a great deal of hard and rapid writing, but when they are done they are done. I sent in at least four leads during the course of the evening, two of which got into the paper. The other two seem to have got lost in the shuffle.

One day Patterson and I went to a supper party given by Bob McLean, of the *Bulletin*, at his place in the country forty minutes west of Philadelphia. The place turned out to be lovely, and the party was excellent. I met a large number of people whom I knew, including some Philadelphians. Mike Bender, the *Sun* handy man, hauled us out to the place, and then brought me home. I had to come in sooner than Patterson because there was a night session in the hall. As I was leaving Dorothy Thompson, Anne O'Hare McCormick[2] and Rebecca West[3] showed up, and I invited them to ride with me. All of them are somewhat bulky, so I jammed them in the rear seat together and sat with Bender in front.

Paul Patterson, it seems to me, is doing a little too much drinking. He begins putting down a Scotch at noon, and he keeps at it until he goes to bed. On some of the days he must have packed away at least six highballs. He held up very well, but I thought he showed signs of confusion more than once. I remonstrated against this boozing, but in vain. It apparently makes him feel better, and he is determined to keep on with it. My guess is that in view of his liver infection it will floor him soon or late.

The convention was inconceivably idiotic—in fact, I have never seen worse. The Southerners, who were supposed to be its clowns,

1 Alben W. Barkley (1877–1956), U.S. representative and senator from Kentucky, was vice president in the second administration of Harry S. Truman.
2 Anne O'Hare McCormick (1882–1954), journalist for the *New York Times*.
3 Rebecca West (1892–1983), English novelist, critic, and political journalist.

really turned out to be its most dignified participants. They carried themselves in a manner so calm and careful that the gallery applauded them far more than they booed them. Whether they will be able to hold their line sufficiently to do real execution upon Truman in the South remains to be seen.

BALTIMORE, JULY 26, 1948.

I arrived home at noon today from the Wallace Convention. I went to Philadelphia on July 22nd and was quartered, not in the flat that Patterson and I occupied during the Republican and Democratic Conventions, but at the *Sun*'s main headquarters in the Ritz-Carlton Hotel. I shared a room with Yardley, the cartoonist, and was very comfortable. One night he awoke me by his snoring, but a few clouts across his backside cured him. On my second morning at the Ritz I had a brief dizzy spell on arising, but it did not seem to be serious. The weather turned cool yesterday.

I took a hand in the Henry Wallace[1] press conference on the day he got to Philadelphia. Ordinarily, I do not ask questions at such affairs, but this time Wallace nettled me by his reference to what he called Pegler's[2] stooges. I challenged him to say publicly that I was one of them, and he admitted that I was not. Why he did not answer Pegler's questions about the mystical notes more frankly I simply don't know.[3] If he had admitted that he wrote the foolish letters that Pegler

1 Henry A. Wallace (1888–1965), secretary of agriculture under Franklin D. Roosevelt and vice president in Roosevelt's third term. In 1944, Roosevelt dropped him in favor of Harry S. Truman. Wallace formed his own Progressive Party in 1948 in order to run for the presidency, and its convention in Philadelphia—the only one the party ever held—is the one Mencken describes here.

2 Westbrook Pegler (1894–1969), journalist and author, winner of the 1941 Pulitzer Prize for reporting.

3 The reference is to the so-called Guru letters which became an issue in Wallace's campaign. Some years earlier he had fallen under the influence of a Russian philosopher, mystic, and painter named Nicholas Roerich. Roerich's admirers had erected a huge building in New York to house his paintings, and the letters were addressed by Wallace to Frances R. Grant, the vice president of this institution. They are written in a highly mystical vein: Roerich himself is referred to as "the Guru" and "the Blessed One," FDR at first as "the Flaming One" and later as "the Wavering One," and Cordell Hull as "the Sour One." Wallace himself had the code name "Galahad." Westbrook Pegler published some of them in his columns in order to expose Wallace to ridicule, though it is generally admitted that not all the letters were authentic.

frequently publishes the effect would have been next to nothing. As it was, he convinced everybody in the room that he was their author, and what is more he offended all the assembled newspaper people save a few Communists by his evasions.

His convention was a magnificent obscenity. All the worst idiots in the United States were there, and the Communists played on them with great skill and facility. The Maryland delegation bucked at one stage, but was quickly overwhelmed. This same delegation introduced a resolution denouncing me as anti-Semitic and anti-Negro, but the Communist presidium refused to entertain it.

I was very comfortable at the Ritz-Carlton and found the work easy. It delighted me to discover that my old facility for rapid writing in the face of a moving news story had not been lost. I worked, indeed, with such facility that my last word was always written within five minutes after the show ended.

Last night, which was a Sunday, nearly the whole *Sun* staff dined together in our quarters in the Ritz. Bruce Earnest promised confidently that he would get us some beer, though the sale of beer is forbidden in Philadelphia on Sunday. Unfortunately, he found at the last moment that he could not locate the only man in the hotel who could supply it, and so he got some friendly joshing.

I grew very sleepy after dinner and turned in about 10 p.m. I slept until 9 a.m. this morning and came home on the B. & O. alone.

BALTIMORE, AUGUST 12, 1948.

I went to New York day before yesterday to join Grantland Rice and Harold Ross at dinner at Lüchow's. This dinner had been planned by Rice for a long time. The only other guest was Nathan. It was a pleasant party indeed, and we broke up early. I was sound asleep by 12 o'clock.

Yesterday I took Blanche Knopf to lunch at No. 21, and in the evening Nathan and I had dinner together at a French place in the west Forties. The victuals were very bad, and the bottle of wine served to us was so atrocious that we had to send it back. This place is one of Nathan's discoveries. It seems to me to be hopeless. After dinner he and I went to the Stork Club, and there encountered Bill Curley, of the Hearst organization, Walter Winchell and Abel Green, editor of

Variety. All of these men were accompanied by their wives. We had a very pleasant session, and again I got to bed early.

Blanche Knopf's sight seems to be deteriorating steadily. When I dropped in on her at the office before lunch she was trying to read a letter with the aid of a large reading-glass. She seemed to be unable to make out parts of it, so she handed it to her secretary, who read it to her.

I had only a brief visit with Alfred. I hear from his son, via Nathan, that he has now taken to playing tennis. Such imbecilities at his age are really almost incredible. If he breaks his leg again he'll probably be crippled for life. I discussed with him my projected omnibus, and we came to terms. I am to turn in the manuscript as soon as possible, and he will schedule it for next year, probably for the late Summer. It will be impossible to produce it for the Spring, and in any case he believes that the Autumn is better. I told him that I'd also probably give him a small book, made up of my old notes, with the title of "Minority Report." He may schedule it either before or after the omnibus.

Hay fever has begun to toy with me. My eyes smart, my throat is dry and I have sneezed once or twice, but no more. I'll not begin to take Ben Baker's new drug until the symptoms become overt and active.

BALTIMORE, SEPTEMBER 14, 1948.

Today I completed the first draft of "A Mencken Chrestomathy." It runs to 265,000 words. Knopf will probably complain of this as excessive, and he will be supported by the present extravagant cost of printing. I myself feel that there are things in the present text that had better come out, so we should be able to reach an agreement without difficulty. There is an excess of copied material about equal in bulk to the matter now in the book. Thus, if the "Chrestomathy" has an encouraging sale I'll be ready to produce a second volume. My books frequently run in series—for example, the three volumes of "The American Language," the three "Days" books, and the two "Treatises."

BALTIMORE, SEPTEMBER 20, 1948.

There was a *Sun* board meeting this afternoon, and Paul Patterson turned up for it. He seemed clear enough in mind, but his physical state was really distressing. The effort to cure his dropsy has greatly reduced his weight, and he looked haggard. After the meeting he went to New York by air to attend an Associated Press committee meeting.

Our own board meeting was mainly given over to hearing about the extra expenses that are accumulating on the new building. Things overlooked are turning up very often, and some of them will cost a lot of money. I am convinced indeed that the total cost of the new building will run hundreds of thousands of dollars beyond the final estimate, and that, even so, there will remain many things—for instance, an air-cooling system—that will have to be put in soon or late, and probably soon.

Television costs are also mounting and, meanwhile, the net receipts of the company are diminishing. They are already down, in fact, almost 25%. The gross receipts still hold up, but they are impeded and diminished by constantly increasing costs, especially for labor.

BALTIMORE, SEPTEMBER 22, 1948.

I went to New York yesterday afternoon for the quarterly meeting of the Knopf board. The report for the quarter ending July 31st showed a loss of a few thousand dollars. There was also a loss in the preceding quarter. The board meeting was brief and amicable. Blanche was in Europe, and there was thus no provocation for a row.

In the evening I went to Purchase to spend the night with Alfred. He had invited Eugene Meyer and Mrs. Meyer.[1] The dinner was eaten in the dark, on Alfred's backless benches. Mrs. Meyer inclines toward uplifting, and is somewhat alarming. She is now carrying on a campaign against what she describes as a Catholic plot to seize the public schools. I argued with her that if it succeeded the schools would be greatly improved but, like all uplifters, she has no sense of humor. She

---

1 Eugene Meyer (1875–1959), owner and publisher of the Washington *Post*. His wife, Agnes (1887–1970), was associated with him on the paper and was the author of several books.

dragged me into a side room to belabor me. Also, she invited me to dinner in Washington. I simply can't imagine going.

The evening in general was a bad one, but I slept well. When I awoke in the morning the temperature outside was down to 42 degrees. I was home again by 1 p.m.

BALTIMORE, OCTOBER 9, 1948.

One night about a week ago I awoke short of breath. What caused this I do not know, for I had been sleeping peacefully and had taken no exercise of any sort for hours before going to bed. It was about 2 a.m. After trying in vain, for five or ten minutes, to get to sleep again, I turned on my light and took up a book. After reading for half an hour or so I found my wind returning, and so turned the light off and got to sleep again.

For two weeks past I have been having discomfort in the sub-sternal region—not severe but nevertheless annoying. I have taken some of Dr. Baker's stomach pills—they are supposed to relieve pyloric spasm— but apparently this discomfort does not come from the stomach at all, but from the heart. It is a considerable nuisance, for so long as it lasts work is next door to impossible. I have been trying to resume writing my reminiscences of my magazine days, but so far have got nowhere.

The loss of memory that goes with age afflicts me more and more. I often find it impossible to recall a name that is quite familiar to me. The other day, for example, I couldn't remember that of Tom Butler, one of the directors of the *Sun*, though I know him well enough for us to be on first-name terms. A few moments ago I could not recall the word *pylorus* and had to look it up in an encyclopedia under *stomach*.

BALTIMORE, OCTOBER 17, 1948.

I talked to Paul Patterson by telephone this morning and he told me he plans to come to the *Sun* board meeting tomorrow. He is facing his illness bravely and seems to be cheerful, but his condition is very disquieting. He is suffering from cirrhosis of the liver, and there seems to be little prospect of a cure. He has had severe ascites, there is persistent anemia, and he is only too plainly deteriorating. Six days ago he was sent to the Union Memorial Hospital for blood transfusions. The first two went off very well, but the third produced a chill, and he was sent home. Harry Black told me the other day that Dr. Charles W. Maxson, the staff surgeon of the *Sun*, had advised him the day before that recovery seemed to be hopeless. Maxson said, in fact, that Paul might die in five months, though on the other hand he might live for the better part of a year. Black pledged me to say nothing of this to the other members of the board, but they all suspect that the case is hopeless. Fenhagen and Semmes told me that that was their opinion only a few days ago.

To see Paul fading out is to me a really racking experience. We have worked together for 36 years, and though we have often differed seriously we have kept on good personal terms throughout. He was, in his day, a man of high capacities and extraordinary vigor. But in late years he has shown a steady falling off. Black puts the beginning of his deterioration eight years back. My own recollection is that I began to notice it in the early days of 1941, when I quit writing for the *Sun*. For the past three or four years he has been only too plainly under par. The chief symptom of his decline has been his increasing tendency to put off decisions. Nearly every member of the board, at one time or another, has urged him to do something about the two editorial pages, which are now appallingly feeble and banal, but he has refused to do so. I tackled him on the subject little more than a month ago, but he flatly refused to discuss it. This was certainly not his attitude in his good days. He might fight back violently, but he would always listen.

Black is uneasy about the important business now impending—for example, the building of the new plant in Calvert street and the better organization of the television enterprise. I have told him that I think we can afford to let both ride for six months, and he agrees. The new building needs careful and almost daily supervision, but looking after it is passing to others. Some of those others are competent enough, but so long as Paul himself is alive they must carry on under his shadow, and will be cautious and irresolute. Others, in my judgment, are quite unfit to handle business on such a scale . . . .

The television enterprise has got into a hell of a mess, and needs reorganization. It is costing the paper a great deal more than anyone anticipated, and operating it profitably seems to be far off. I have long objected myself that the salaries of many of its important functionaries are still charged to the newspaper—for example, Swanson, Paul Menton (sporting editor), Schmick, Kavanaugh and Patterson himself. Patterson, until he became disabled, was giving at least half his time to television, and Swanson (who says that he has now withdrawn) was giving more than half. But the high salaries of these men have been charged wholly to the newspaper, and not in any part to television. I have wanted to call for a complete and accurate accounting, but with Patterson so ill I hate to do so. Black agrees that we ought to have it, and so do all the other members of the board that I have consulted.[1]

BALTIMORE, OCTOBER 27, 1948.

Last night I harangued the members of the Women's Club of Roland Park and their husbands and other victims—a rare thing for me, for I have long refused to make speeches in Baltimore, and have very seldom lifted my rule. How I came to succumb this time I really don't know: no doubt it was because the president of the club, a lady named Cook, began to pester me more than six months ago, and kept at it mercilessly. The hall of the clubhouse was packed and there were many standees. It was very hot in the place, and my harsh sweating on the platform made it plain that my hearers were having an equally tough time of it below, so I shut off my remarks after 40 minutes. My theme was "How Presidents Are Made," and I gave them some of the same stuff that I gave the lawyers of the Rule Club at the Elkridge Club last Summer. It was hard to wring laughs out of that fuming audience, and when they came they were only snickers. Everyone seemed to be relieved when it was all over. Certainly I was myself. There was nothing to drink afterward save a pale fruit punch, devoid of alcohol. I was so dry that I gulped four or five cups of it. The ladies gave me a pleasant present—a box of Behring cigars in the Corona size that I like. After the show I had to stay awhile to shake hands. I met various old friends, including Arthur Hawks and his wife Rachel. Rachel was as lively as usual, but Arthur seemed only half alive. He has always been a stupid fellow, but since his retirement from the Gas Company he has become stupider than ever. I was best man at his and Rachel's wedding nearly 50 years ago. It was my first service as best man.

Mrs. Marie Bauernschmidt[2] offered to drive me home, but I said it

---

1 At the bottom of the second sheet containing this entry, someone—probably Mrs. Lohrfinck—has written: "HLM's typescript—one of his last!"
2 Mrs. Marie Bauernschmidt (1875–1962) was head of the Public School Association

was too far and we finally compromised on dropping me at Charles street and North avenue. I then walked down to the Pennsylvania Station and got a cab for Hollins street. When I got home it was only a little after 10.30. I had a Scotch and soda with August and was in bed by 12 o'clock. It will probably be a long while before I fall for another such folly.

BALTIMORE, NOVEMBER 5, 1948.

I went to Philadelphia yesterday to harangue the American Philosophical Association last night. My subject was the machinery by which Presidents of the United States are elected, and I undertook to give the assembled scientificoes an accurate account of it. I heard afterward that some of them were shocked; they thought that I was too cynical. These brethren were the younger men. All the young professors of America with few exceptions were brought up under New Deal influences, and seem to be unable to throw them off.

The lecture was given at the old United States Customs House. This building, which includes a fair size hall, is now in the custody of the American-German Society. It was borrowed for the lecture by the American Philosophical Society, which is very ancient and was founded, in fact, by Benjamin Franklin. The hall was nearly full. The audience was rather solemn, and in consequence I got relatively little response, but now and then there was a wave of snickers.

Before the lecture there was a dinner at the Benjamin Franklin Hotel. I sat at the head table next to Dr. Edwin G. Conklin, the president of the association. He is 85 years old, but he was very chipper. He showed me an angry looking scar on his head, and told me that he had got it by being knocked down by a street-car. In the same accident he broke his pelvis in three places. This was about three years ago. Despite his age, he recovered quickly, and now looks to be as good as ever. He is a charming old fellow, and I had met him before at Princeton. He is professor emeritus of biology there. His career in biology has been very remarkable, and he is greatly respected by the other biologists.

At my other side at the head table sat Mrs. Arthur Compton, wife

---

and a self-appointed guardian of Baltimore's public morality. Her attacks could strike terror into the hearts of the city's political bosses.

of a Nobel Prize winner in 1927. She turned out to be a stoutish and chatty woman, who seemed to talk pleasantly and yet to say very little. Her husband sat opposite me at the large, round table, and I got no chance for a palaver with him. But he was under my eye throughout the meal, and for a while I was puzzled by the fact that he looked extremely familiar. Suddenly it occurred to me that he was almost an exact double of a Greek named Lambros who used to keep a drugstore at Baltimore and Gilmor streets.

Conklin had proposed, through Julian Boyd, librarian at Princeton, that the American Philosophical Society give me its gold medal, but I begged off. It is my belief that I should avoid all such things. Every other American author of my years is an LL.D. three or four times over, but I have always ducked honorary degrees, and I should duck other honors as well. I induced Sinclair Lewis to refuse the Pulitzer Prize, and I was in hopes of being able to induce him to refuse the Nobel Prize also. Unhappily, his wife, Dorothy Thompson, was all for taking it, and I failed.

I got to Philadelphia yesterday in time for lunch with Julian Boyd and his wife. We went down to Bookbinders' restaurant on the waterfront, and I ate a noble mess of soft clams. After the lecture last night I returned to Bookbinders' with Boyd and his wife, the Knopfs, who had come down from New York to hear me speak, Marian Godfrey[1] and a man who seemed to be the head of the Philadelphia Museum, and hence her boss. Marian told me that she was trying to raise a million dollars to explore a recently discovered ruin in the Yucatan. She said that it is a find of great richness, but that making the journey and listing its treasures will be very expensive. I told her that I'd pray for her.

We sat at Bookbinders' until about 11 o'clock, and I then returned to the Benjamin Franklin and had a sound sleep. In the morning I had breakfast with Julian and his wife and departed for Baltimore a little after 10 o'clock.

The lecture from my standpoint was not much of a success. It was plain that the assembled scientificoes expected something far more optimistic and reassuring. I met some of them but not many, for the crowd was rather large and getting about in it was almost impossible. The lecture I gave them was sound enough, and I am tempted to try

---

1 Marian Godfrey (later Marian Boyer) was at this time secretary and acting director of the University Museum of the University of Pennsylvania.

it on some more hospitable audience. A shoemaker should stick to his last: I am certainly not fitted for haranguing the learned.

BALTIMORE, NOVEMBER 15, 1948.

Paul Patterson turned up at the meeting of the *Sun* board today looking better than he has looked for months. There seems to be a reasonable hope, indeed, that he may recover. When he returned from the conventions in the Summer he was in a really perilous state. Dr. Charles Maxson, the *Sun* surgeon, told me yesterday that his liver had bulged down to the level of his bladder, that his blood count was alarmingly low, and that he seemed to be fast breaking up. The diet and other treatment prescribed by his doctor, Dr. Ward Allen, seems to be working. It was described at length in the *Journal of the American Medical Association* for October 23, 1948, page 543 *ff.* Maxson says that it works in about 30 per cent. of the cases. A cured patient, of course, is not cured completely. His disease is simply arrested. In order to keep going he must avoid alcohol altogether. Patterson has managed to do this so far, but I am wondering whether he will hold out. It is always possible, of course, that some improvement in the treatment may enable him to drink at least a little. Certainly he misses his Scotch very sorely. Nevertheless, he has stood up to the drill with great courage, and his apparent recovery is largely due to his own resolution. His mind is now perceptibly clearer than it was, and he doesn't look so ghastly. Maxson, who was formerly very pessimistic about him, is now showing some hope. He is still, of course, a sick man, and in all probability he'll never be able to resume all the burdens that he formerly bore, but he may nevertheless manage to carry on his job.

This was the last entry that H. L. Mencken made in his diary. Eight days later, on November 23, the thing that he had feared for so long happened—he was stricken by a massive cerebral thrombosis. Physically he recovered pretty well, but the stroke permanently damaged certain brain areas and left him without the ability to read or write. No further literary work was possible. He lived for another seven years, cared for by his devoted brother August, and died in his sleep at Hollins Street during the night of January 29, 1956.

Index

There is no listing for "Mencken, H[enry] L[ouis]," since of necessity it would have required reference to every entry in the Diary. Books, articles, and other works by him are indexed individually under their titles.

The editor and publishers wish to acknowledge with gratitude the kind permission of the following institutions to quote from materials in which they hold copyright:

The Baltimore Evening Sun: Excerpts from Monday Articles by H. L. Mencken, and other editorials and columns. Reprinted by permission of The Baltimore Evening Sun.

The Johns Hopkins University Press: Excerpts from *The Baltimore Sun 1837–1987* by Harold A. Williams. Copyright © 1987 by The Johns Hopkins University Press. Reprinted by permission of The Johns Hopkins University Press, Baltimore, Maryland.

The Trustees of the University of Pennsylvania and *The Theodore Dreiser Collection, Special Collections, Van Pelt Library, University of Pennsylvania:* Excerpts from letters of Theodore Dreiser to H. L. Mencken. Copyright © by The Trustees of the University of Pennsylvania. Reprinted by permission of The Trustees of the University of Pennsylvania and The Theodore Dreiser Collection, Special Collections, Van Pelt Library, University of Pennsylvania.

The editor is also very grateful to Ms. Mary Markey, of Baltimore City's Peale Museum, for her kind cooperation in making available the pictures from the A. Aubrey Bodine Photographic Collection, and to Mr. Gaither Scott for his expert reproduction of pictures in the photographic archives of the Pratt Library's Mencken Room.

Charles A. Fecher was born in Baltimore in 1917, was educated there, and lives there still. He is the author of *The Philosophy of Jacques Maritain* (1953, 1969) and of *Mencken: A Study of His Thought* (1978), and edits *Menckeniana*, the Enoch Pratt Free Library's quarterly journal of Mencken studies. In addition, he has contributed articles and short stories to *The Critic*, *The Catholic World*, and *The Sign*. He is married and has two daughters.

A NOTE ON THE TYPE

The Diary of H. L. Mencken was set in Caledonia, a face designed by William Addison Dwiggins (1880–1956). It belongs to the family of types referred to by printers as "modern," a term used to mark the change in type styles that occurred around 1800. Caledonia was inspired by the Scotch types cast by the Glasgow typefounders Alexander Wilson & Son circa 1833.

W. A. Dwiggins designed some three hundred and twenty books for Alfred A. Knopf from 1926 to 1956, and he was instrumental in establishing and maintaining the distinctive visual style of the Borzoi Books. Nearly all the books by H. L. Mencken published by Knopf were designed by Dwiggins. Mencken refers to Dwiggins's work in an entry in his diary dated August 22, 1941.

This book was composed by Creative Graphics, Inc., Allentown, Pennsylvania, and was printed and bound by Fairfield Graphics, Fairfield, Pennsylvania. The design and ornamentation were appropriated from W. A. Dwiggins by Peter A. Andersen.